Complete P

Jon Silkin was born in London in ? Jewish immigrants from Lithuania. Following National and a period as a manual labourer, Silkin became Gregory Fellow in Poetry at the University of Leeds. He founded *Stand* magazine in 1952 and the Northern House press in 1965. His publications include eleven volumes of poetry and many critical works and anthologies, notably *Out of Battle*, his study of Isaac Rosenberg, Wilfred Owen and other poets of the First World War. He held writing fellowships and chairs in the USA, Australia and Japan. Jon Silkin died in November 1997.

Jon Glover was born in Sheffield in 1943 and grew up in south London. He studied English and Philosophy at the University of Leeds, where he met Jon Silkin and began a long association with *Stand* magazine, of which he is now Managing Editor. Jon Glover is an Honorary Fellow of the English Association, an Honorary Fellow of the School of English at the University of Leeds and holds an honorary doctorate from the University of Bolton, where he is Professor Emeritus of English and Creative Writing.

Kathryn Jenner graduated with a BA and MA from the University of Leeds before working as an Archivist in the Special Collections unit of Leeds University Library. While there, she catalogued the Jon Silkin archive and worked on the poetry and notebooks of Geoffrey Hill. She compiled the Leeds Poetry 1950–1980 online resource: http://leeds.ac.uk/special-collections/collection/12/leeds_poetry_1950_1980.

Also available by Jon Silkin from Northern House/Carcanet

Making a Republic

Jon Silkin

Complete Poems

Edited by Jon Glover and Kathryn Jenner

NORTHERN HOUSE

CARCANET

First published in Great Britain in 2015 by
Northern House
In association with Carcanet Press Limited
Alliance House
Cross Street
Manchester M2 7AQ

www.carcanet.co.uk

A CIP catalogue record for this book is available from the British Library

ISBN 978 1 84777 240 4

The publisher acknowledges financial assistance from Arts Council England
and from the Stand Magazine Support Trust

Typeset by XL Publishing Services, Exmouth
Printed and bound in England by SRP Ltd, Exeter

This volume of Jon Silkin's *Complete Poems*
is dedicated to his memory and with gratitude to all those who
lived and worked with him to make these poems possible.

The volume is also dedicated to the late Chris Sheppard, Head
of Special Collections and Brotherton Fellow at the University
of Leeds, who worked tirelessly to acquire, and make available
for research and creative thought, the archives of poets.
Publication of Jon Silkin's *Complete Poems* was made possible
through his foresight and love of literature.

Contents

The Portrait and Other Poems (1950)

Unpublished and Uncollected Poems, c. 1950–1954

The Peaceable Kingdom (1954)

Unpublished and Uncollected Poems, c. 1954–1958

The Two Freedoms (1958)

Unpublished and Uncollected Poems, c. 1958–1961

The Re-ordering of the Stones (1961)

Unpublished and Uncollected Poems, c. 1961–1965

Nature with Man (1965)

Unpublished and Uncollected Poems, c. 1965–1971

Amana Grass (1971)

Unpublished and Uncollected Poems, c. 1971–1974

The Principle of Water (1974)

Unpublished and Uncollected Poems, c. 1974–1976

The Little Time-keeper (1976)

Unpublished and Uncollected Poems, c. 1976–1980

The Psalms with their Spoils (1980)

Unpublished and Uncollected Poems, c. 1980–1986

The Ship's Pasture (1986)

Unpublished and Uncollected Poems, c. 1986–1992

The Lens-Breakers (1992)

Testament Without Breath (1998)

Making a Republic (2002)

Unpublished and Uncollected Poems, c. 1992–1997

Appendix

Acknowledgments

Many people have been instrumental in helping to prepare Jon Silkin's poetry for this volume.

I would like to thank Professor Michael Schmidt, founder and director of the Carcanet Press. He was Jon Silkin's editor when Carcanet published *The Principle of Water* and *The Little Time-keeper*. More recently he supported the re-establishment of Northern House as an imprint of Carcanet. Silkin's posthumously published *Making a Republic* was the first book in this list. The production of a volume of this size has involved Schmidt's time, skill and tolerance. Carcanet's managing editor Helen Tookey has supported the project throughout, as have Alice Mullen and Okey Nzelu.

Kathryn Jenner catalogued the Silkin Archive, including manuscripts of all of the poems, while working on the Leeds Poetry 1950–1980 project in Special Collections at Leeds University Library. The then Head of Special Collections, and Brotherton Fellow, the late Chris Sheppard, facilitated the Library's acquisition of Silkin's personal and literary archives as well as those of *Stand*. He was untiring in his help with preparing this volume, as have the current Head of Special Collections, Katy Thornton, and the Leeds University Librarian and Keeper of the Brotherton Collection, Dr Stella Butler. The poetry archives acquired, catalogued and safely stored for research access at the University of Leeds have enabled scholarship, publication and the celebration of recent poetry to flourish. Professors John Barnard, Ed Larrissy and John Whale have all encouraged research on Jon Silkin and this book is, in no small measure, a tribute to their vision.

I started to work with Jon Silkin in Leeds in 1963. Silkin always collaborated with others, whether in producing *Stand* or in seeking help with his own poems. Many of those people who shared poetry with Silkin are, for me, part of a continuing dialogue speaking through his poems; the talk started years ago, and has been an active element of interest and advice till the present. I would like to offer special thanks to Kate Lamb, Lorna Tracy, Toshiko Fujioka,

Rodney and Ella Pybus, and Jeffrey and Judith Wainwright, and to Elaine Glover (who joined the community of writing from New York State in 1964), all of whom have been editors or advisors to *Stand* and/or Northern House. They have advised on the preparation of individual manuscripts for this book, and on the introduction.

We have studied many of Silkin's prose manuscripts as well as his books of criticism. Three poets, connected through Leeds, recur in his letters, lecture notes and published prose from the 1960s till his death. Geoffrey Hill, Tony Harrison and Ken Smith remained for Silkin models of moral and technical engagement in poetry despite personal disagreements. Their spirits, real though silent, have, we hope, guided us in interpreting the manuscripts. Tony Rudolf has celebrated many silent conversations, and we have also been aware of Silkin's dialogues with Jewish poets Emanuel Litvinoff, Dannie Abse, Michael Hamburger, and Rudolf himself, as writers whose language contextualises that of Silkin. Peter Lawson has also helped.

Postgraduate students at the Universities of Leeds and Bolton have given time to looking at Silkin's poems, offering views from the perspective of newcomers both to his work and to the world of poetry in the second half of the twentieth century. I thank especially Lucy Burnett, Jack Butler, Hannah Copley, Phil Isherwood, Owen Lowery, Stella Pye, Amy Ramsey, Emily Timms and Emma Trott. Their interest in poetry has already become manifest in writing for *Stand* – something that Silkin would have encouraged and enjoyed had he lived to see it.

I have been supported during the years spent on research for this book by Mollie Temple and George Holmes, Vice-Chancellors of the University of Bolton, by Pro-Vice-Chancellor Robert Campbell, and Research Leaders Dr Paul Birkett and Professor David Rudd. My Head of Department, Sam Johnson, has provided commitment, funding and space for which I am very grateful. The School of English at the University of Leeds supported Jon Silkin during his lifetime and has supported study of his work since his death. The current Vice-Chancellor, Sir Alan Langlands, has been interested in the research leading to this book and the continuing relationship between *Stand* and the School of English at Leeds.

Kathryn Jenner now has an unrivalled knowledge of Silkin's poems, having transcribed all of his published books and manuscripts, often from complex and semi-legible papers. Given her experience in cataloguing the Geoffrey Hill archive, and part of that belonging to Tony Harrison, all held in Leeds University Library's Special Collections, it has been a pleasure and a privilege to work with her on editing Silkin's *Complete Poems*. Richard Davis, Richard High, Karen Mee, Fiona Gell and many other staff of Special Collections helped me round the Archives in more ways than one. I am grateful for their kindness and professionalism.

My wife Elaine and our daughters, Abigail and Rhiannon, all knew Jon Silkin and his work. They have been generous in their support and interest in this project and I offer them my thanks.

Jon Glover

The process of selecting previously unpublished poems for inclusion in this collected edition of Jon Silkin's poetry would not have been possible without the AHRC-funded Leeds Poetry 1950– 1980 project. Running from 2005 to 2007, the project was undertaken collaboratively by the University of Leeds' School of English and Special Collections at Leeds University Library. I was privileged to work on the project alongside Professor Edward Larrissy, Professor John Whale, the late Christopher Sheppard and Dr Oliver Pickering, and was assisted by Stephanie Nield. The project not only led to the cataloguing of significant archival material relating to poets associated with the University at the time of the Gregory Fellowship scheme, but revealed the significance of Leeds as a centre for creativity and the myriad literary networks in operation. I would especially like to thank Professor Larrissy for the opportunity to discuss the poetry associated with the project.

Jon Glover has a unique knowledge of Jon Silkin and *Stand*, and of poetry at the University of Leeds during the 1950s and 1960s. His insight was invaluable to my work on the Leeds Poetry 1950– 1980 project. The opportunity to work with him on this book has been an immense privilege.

Kathryn Jenner

Acknowledgments are due to the following, where many of the poems included in this volume were first published. Jon Silkin's personal acknowledgments are also reproduced here from his published collections.

Uncollected Poems, c. 1950–1954
Chanticleer, Poetry Manchester and *The Poet.*

The Peaceable Kingdom
Chanticleer, Jewish Quarterly, Olivant, Poetry and Poverty, The Window, First Reading BBC (John Wain) and *New Verse BBC.*

Uncollected Poems, c. 1954–1958
African Affairs: Journal of the Royal African Society, Listen, Poetry (Chicago) and *Truth.*

The Two Freedoms
Bottegha Oscure, BBC Third Programme, *Mavericks, Poetry* (Chicago), *Truth, Encounter, New Statesman, London Magazine, Stand, Jewish Quarterly, Poetry Review,* PEN 1956 and 1957, *Meridian Books* (USA), *Midstream* (USA), *The Poet, New Chapter, Outposts* and the Hebrew Section of the BBC.

Uncollected Poems, c. 1958–1961
Poetry and Audience.

The Re-ordering of the Stones
Encounter, New Left Review, New Poets of English & America (2nd series), *New Statesman, Oxford Opinion,* PEN 1958, *Poetry and Audience* (Anthology 1953–60), *Prospect, Stand, Time & Tide, Times Literary Supplement, Tribune, Universities' Poetry 1961, Writers Against Apartheid, Penguin Contemporary Verse* (ed. Kenneth Allott), *Geste* and *Gryphon.* Also New Sound Productions and the BBC Third Programme.

Uncollected Poems, c. 1961–1965
Poetry and Audience.

Nature with Man
Agenda, Alarum, Avon Books (NY), *Birmingham Bulletin, Clare Market Review, Il Contemporaneo, Encounter, Flash Point* (E.J. Arnold), *Geste, Glasgow Herald, The Glasgow Review, Irish Times, Jazz Poems* (Studio Vista), *Marxist, New Durham, New Opinion, Neue Deutsche Hefte, Of Books and Humankind* (Routledge), *The Observer,* PEN (1963), *Poetry and Audience, Poetry Review, The Review, Scope, Sewanee Review, Shenandoah, Stand, Time and Tide, Times Literary Supplement, Universities' Poetry* (4 and 5). Also *New Poetry BBC* (Terence Tiller), BBC Scottish Television, Granada TV, *The Poet's Voice* (George Macbeth).

The first eight of the 'Flower' poems were broadcast as *The Living Poet* (George Macbeth); a smaller group appeared in *Granta* (then edited by John Barrell), and the first nine were published in pamphlet by Northern House (Leeds).

Amana Grass
BBC *Poet's Voice* and *Poetry Now*, *The Blacksuede Boot*, *Borestone Mountain Poetry* (1972), *Choice*, *Form*, *The Iowa Defender*, Iowa State Liquor Store, *The Iowa Review*, *Journal of Creative Behavior*, *Lines*, *Massachusetts Review*, *Midnag*, *12 x 12* (Camden), *North American Review*, *Northwest Review*, *Poetry and Audience*, *Scratch*, *Stand*, *Sumac*, *Times Literary Supplement*. 'Meetings' was published in *Penguin Modern Poets* 7 and was published together with 'Brought up with Grass' and 'Snow Drop' by Chatto & Windus and Wesleyan University Press. The Pym-Randall Press published the first three of *Six Cemetery Poems* in their pamphlet series as *Three Poems*.

The Principle of Water
Antaeus, *British Poetry 1972* (The Baleen Press, Arizona), *European Judaism*, *Fuse*, *Here Now*, *Iowa Review*, *Jewish Quarterly*, *New Poetry* (Australia), *New Statesman*, *Orbis*, *Outposts*, *PEN* 1973, *Poetry* (USA), *Poetry Book Society Supplement* (1971), *Responses*, *Scotsman*, *The Valley Press* (USA), *Times Literary Supplement*, *Tribune*, *Vanderbilt Poetry Review*. Also the Sceptre Press, the Scolar Press, and George Stephenson and the Mid-Northumberland Arts Group for the entire *Killhope Wheel* sequence. 'The People', produced by John Scotney, was broadcast on the BBC Third Programme, as were other poems in this collection.

'I would like to acknowledge the help and encouragement of Lorna Tracy, Rodney Pybus, Michael Schmidt, Emanuel Litvinoff, Eric Northey and Merle Brown – though this need not be taken to imply an unguarded liking for the poems on their part.'

The Little Time-keeper
The Arts Council (*New Poetry* I and II), *Agenda*, *Europa Litteraria* (Italy), *Four Zoas* (US), *Jewish Chronicle*, *The Milton Celebrations*, *Meanjin* (Australia), *Meridian*, *Minnesota Review*, *New Statesman*, *Poetry and Audience* (Leeds), *Poetry North East*, *The Shakespeare Celebrations*, *Southern Poetry Review* (USA), *Stand*, *Sydney Morning Herald*, *The Age* (Australia), *The Blacksmith* (Australia), *Times Literary Supplement*, *Threshold* (Belfast), *Tribune*, *Canberra Poetry*, and the Keepsake and Sceptre Presses. The author wishes to acknowledge Tyne Tees Television, and the BBC, in particular for the broadcasting of most of the group 'The Little Time-

keeper'. The author gladly acknowledges his debt to Charles P. Mount-
ford for his book *Winbaraky and the Myth of Jaripiri* (1968) and in particular
for 'The Creation of Winbaraku', chapter 2.

Uncollected Poems, c. 1976–1980
New Statesman.

The Psalms with their Spoils
Avon Books, BBC, *Boston University Journal*, *Chonnam Tribune* (Korea),
Contemporary Literature (University of Wisconsin), 'Homage to Osip
Mandelstam', *Iowa Review*, London Broadcasting, *London Magazine*,
Looking Back (Sceptre Press), *Massachusetts Review*, *New Poetry 4* (Arts
Council/Hutchinson), *New Statesman*, *Overland* (Australia), *Parnassus*
(USA), *Poetry Nation Review*, *Pen Broadsheet*, *Poetry Review*, *Screever*,
Sewanee Review, *Short Line* (USA), *Siddha* (India), *Southern Review*, *Stand*,
Sunday Times, *Times Literary Supplement*, *Tribune*, *Wittenberg Review* (USA).
A poem was printed in *Hand and Eye*, a collection privately published as
a tribute to the poet Sacheverell Sitwell. The Ceolfrith Press and the
Sceptre Press each published in their pamphlet series 'Into Praising',
'Jerusalem' and the 'Lapidary Poems'. The BBC broadcast 'Joy, lined with
metal', and the *Tablet* and the *Nantucket Review* published the group.
Bananas published 'I in another place'. 'The Barbarians' was published by
Journal 7 (Birmingham University).

The Ship's Pasture
Agenda, *Al Hamishar* (Israel), *Arab Times Supplement* (Kuwait), *Between
Comets: a festschrift for Norman Nicholson at seventy*, edited by William Scam-
mell, *Critical Quarterly*, *Equivalencias* (Spain), *Graham House Review* (USA),
Hubbub (USA), *Iron Magazine*, *Ironwood* (USA), *Jewish Chronicle*, *London
Review of Books*, *Louisville Review* (USA), *Ma'ariv* (Israel), *Menard Press*,
Minnesota Review (USA), *Moznayim* (Israel), *New Statesman*, *New Poetry 6*,
Ninth Decade, *Not just another pile of bricks*, *Poems for Poetry 84* (Poetry
Society), *Poem of Thanksgiving* (edited by Paul Kavanagh), *Poetry Australia*,
Poetry Ireland Review, *Poetry Review*, *Poetry Now* (BBC), *The Poet's Voice*,
Post Modern Writing (Australia), *Prairie Schooner* (USA), *Prospice*, *Quarto*
(New University of Ulster), *The Reaper* (USA), Schools' Poetry Associ-
ation, Sixth World Congress of poets, *Stand*, *Telescope* (USA), *Thalatta*,
Times Literary Supplement, *Wooster Review* (USA), *Words*. *Footsteps on the
downcast path*, part of which was written at Mishkenot Sha'ananim,
Jerusalem, 1980, was produced on the BBC by Fraser Steel, and published
in the US by *Michigan Quarterly* and in the UK by Mammon Press. The
'Salome' poems were published in the *Poetry Review* when it was edited
by Roger Garfitt. *Autobiographical Stanzas* were published by Taxus Press.

The Ship's Pasture was published from Boston by The Heron Press. 'The achievers' was given a prize at the Cheltenham Poetry Competition, 1985.

Uncollected Poems, c. 1986–1992
Lines Review.

The Lens-Breakers
Agenda, *American Poetry Review* (USA), *Antioch Review* (USA), *Bogg* (USA), *Cencrastus, Encounter, First and Always* (Faber), *Images of Africa* (Wateraid), *The Independent, In forma di parole, Iowa Review* (USA), *Kenyon Review* (USA), *Korean Herald, Lines Review, London Review of Books, Metaphor beyond time* (UPLI Korean Center), *Mississippi Review* (USA), *Morden Tower (High on the Walls), New Letters* (USA), *New Writing* (1991), *Poetry Ireland Review, Poetry Review, Prospice, Skoob Review, Stand, Staple Magazine, Tel-Aviv Review, Tikkun* (USA), *World Poets* 1990. A version of a poem originally published by *The Jewish Chronicle* has 'disappeared' into a section of 'Thirst'. *Staple Magazine* gave prizes to two poems in this collection. Acknowledgment also to the BBC, BBC Radio Solway, 'A Time for Verse', and BBC Radio Three for the broadcast of a group of poems from the collection, and to National Public Radio (USA). Also, for support and generosity in providing residencies: The American University (Washington DC), Dumfries and Galloway Arts Association (in conjunction with the Scottish Arts Council), Hawthornden Castle, the Isle of Wight Education Authority together with Carisbrooke High School, and the Program of Creative Writing at the University of Iowa.

Making a Republic
Agenda, The American Poetry Review, The Bay Press, *The Centennial Review, Closer Links, Comparative Criticism, Cuirt Journal* (Ireland), *Electric Rexroth* (Japan), *European English Messenger, European Judaism, Icarus, The Independent Jewish Chronicle, The Jewish Quarterly, Living Room* (Japan), *London Review of Books, New Letters, New Writing* 5 and 6 (Vintage with the British Council), *New Statesman and Society, Orbis, Ore, Other Poetry, Pigeonhole, Poems for Bosnia, Poems Now* (Mito, Japan), *Poetry and Audience, Poetry Kanto* (Japan), *Poetry Review, The Poet's Voice, Prairie Schooner, Printed Matter* (Japan), *Quarry* (Canada), *Salzburg Poetry, Stand, Staple, Sunday Telegraph, Ulitarra* (Australia). Some of the poems were translated into Japanese by Toshiko Fujioka and published in the following Japanese magazines: *Poems Now* (Mito) and *Choryu Shi Ha* (Tokyo).

'I gratefully acknowledge a generous bursary from The Arts Council of England in 1995 which enabled me to continue working on the poems in this book. I especially wish to thank my colleague, the poet Peter Bennet, for all his work on the poem "Watersmeet", the drafts of which together with the final version were published under the title of "Watersmeet" by David Stephenson of The Bay Press. My gratitude to both. I would like to thank my students and colleagues at the University of Tsukuba, who provided the context in which I learned what it means to start again, and where some of these poems were written or drafted. I am grateful to *The Rialto* for printing "A Woman from Japan", the longest poem in this collection, and for entering it for the Forward Prize. I also had a great deal of help from Rodney Pybus during and after this period and my gratitude is expressed to him and to the poet Richard Kell.'

Chronology

Note: the titles and dates of Jon Silkin's books and other publications are included in the Select Bibliography.

1930	Born 2 December in London. His father, Joseph Silkin, and mother, Dora (Doris) Rubinstein Silkin, were both from families who had left Lithuania to escape the pogroms. His paternal grandfather, Abraham, sold fruit from a barrow, taught Hebrew, and cleaned synagogue toilets. His maternal grandfather, Harris, had a paint and wallpaper business in Swansea. Joseph joined his elder brother Lewis in the family law firm. Lewis, who had started work on the London docks, became a prominent member of the London County Council, Labour MP for Peckham, and the first Baron Silkin of Dulwich. Jon was named after Jon Forsyte in Galsworthy's *Forsyte* novels.
1935–1939	Attended Dulwich Hamlet Preparatory School.
1939–1945	Evacuated first to Paddock Green, Kent, then to his aunt's house in Swansea, then to Dol-au-Cothy House, Pumpsaint, Carmarthen, and then to Wycliffe School, at that time based near Lampeter.
1945–1947	Dulwich College, from age 14 to 16. Left in the summer of 1947 with a School Certificate in a few subjects, though not Latin.
1947–1948	Worked as a filing clerk and a reporter on a local newspaper.
1948–1950	National Service in the Army, which he left as a Sergeant in the Education Corps. Served in garrisons at Brecon, Wales; Bodmin, Cornwall; and Hawthorn Camp, Corsham, Wiltshire.
1950	Publication of *The Portrait*.
1950–1952	Various jobs, including gravedigging and filling at Fortune Green Cemetery, West Hampstead, and bricklayer's labourer. Slept on friends' floors and sometimes lived rough on the streets; at one point was in hospital for three weeks with malnutrition. During this time the Army tried to retain him as a reservist, threatening him with call-up to serve in

Korea and jail if he refused. Eventually he was discharged.

1952   Worked as a janitor for the National Cash Register Company.

Stand magazine founded with £5 redundancy money after Silkin was fired from his toilet-cleaning job for attempting to form a union.

Living with Cynthia Redpath in Swiss Cottage. First son, Adam, born.

At the Ben Uri Gallery he met Emanuel Litvinoff, A.C. Jacobs, Philip Hobsbaum and Louise Golding, and later Alan Brownjohn, Bernard Bergonzi and Cecil Day-Lewis.

1953   Moved to Blackheath where he and Cynthia lived until 1955.

Second son, David Emanuel, born.

1954   Publication of The Peaceable Kingdom.

Friendships with Chatto & Windus staff, including Cecil Day-Lewis. Associated with many figures in the poetry world including members of the Institute of Contemporary Arts (ICA).

Third son, Richard, born.

1955   Moved to Pimlico. Lived with painter Susan Benson. He was an occasional member of The Group, the informal writing workshop that had moved from Cambridge to London.

1956   Teaching at the Town and Country School, London.

Moved to 10 Compayne Gardens, the house of novelist Bernice Rubens and her husband Rudolf Nassauer. He shared the top flat with playwright David Mercer and Malcolm Ross-MacDonald.

1957   Production of Stand ceases owing to lack of funds.

1958   'People in Coffee Houses' broadcast as part of the People Today series on the BBC Home Service (20 January 1958). Silkin would continue to be involved in BBC broadcasts on poetry, including Poetry Now.

1958–1960 Gregory Fellowship in Poetry at the University of Leeds.

1959   Collaboration with University Head of Fine Art Maurice de Sausmarez on an exhibition of the manuscripts and artworks of Isaac Rosenberg at the University of Leeds. Assisted by Rosenberg's sister, Annie Wynick, who visited Leeds for the exhibition opening.

1959   Enrolment as a Special Studies student to study English Literature at the University of Leeds. During his time as student, he also taught courses in poetry at the University's

	Extra-Mural Department.
	Work on *Out of Battle* begins – it is published 13 years later in 1972.
1960	*Stand* relaunched from Silkin's flat in Leeds with financial help from Leeds businesses. Help also came from London writers and friends at Leeds University.
1962	Graduated in two years from the University of Leeds with a First Class BA in English Literature – the first First Class award in English in twenty years.
1963	Northern House founded through the University of Leeds with Andrew Gurr and Ken Smith, later joined by John Barnard.
1964	Publication of the first three Northern House Pamphlets: Silkin's *Flower Poems*, Geoffrey Hill's *Preghiere* and Ken Smith's *Eleven Poems*, followed by Tony (T.W.) Harrison's *Earthworks*.
	First visit to Israel. He soon returned to live for five months in Tel Aviv.
1965	Faber Memorial Prize for *Nature with Man*. Poems reflect on the birth of his daughter Rachel to Wendy Oliver.
	Relocation to Newcastle-upon-Tyne, prompted by an offer of funding for *Stand* from the North-East Association for the Arts.
	Visiting lectureship at Denison University, Ohio.
1968–1969	One-year residency at the Iowa Writers' Workshop, University of Iowa. Returned to England with Lorna Tracy.
1973	Married Lorna Tracy.
	Verse play *The People* broadcast by the BBC; later published in *The Principle of Water* (1974) and in an altered form in *Selected Poems* (1980).
1974	British Council lecture and reading tour of Belgium and Luxembourg.
	Three-month lecture tour of Australia, sponsored by the Australian Council for the Arts' Travelling Fellowship Scheme and the University of Sydney.
1976	C. Day-Lewis Fellowship at Aylestone School, Brent, North London.
1979	British Council tour of Scandinavia.
	Northern Arts Durham Writer in Residence.
1980	Visit to Israel, including Mishkenot Sha'ananim and the University of Tel Aviv.
1981	Bingham Poet in Residence at the University of Louisville.
1983	Elliston Poet in Residence, University of Cincinnati.

Residency at King's College, Taunton. *Gurney* written as a verse drama to be performed by the school's pupils.

1984   *Gurney* first performed by pupils of King's College, Taunton at the Brewhouse Theatre, Taunton (June).

11th Annual University of Surrey Poetry Lecture on the poetry of D.H. Lawrence (22 October).

1984–1985   Inckproductions tour of *Gurney* in the north east of England and at the Oxford Union Arts Festival.

1986   *Gurney* staged by Pentameters Theatre Company in Hampstead, London, under the title *Black Notes*, and with a stage set designed by Kirill Sokolov.

Elected Fellow of the Royal Society of Literature.

1990   Dumfries and Galloway Arts Association Writer in Residence.

Residency at Carisbrooke High School, Isle of Wight.

1991–1993   Teaching English and American Literature at the University of Tsukuba, Japan. During this time he met the Japanese poet Toshiko Fujioka.

1994   Returned to England with Toshiko Fujioka, first living in Beamish, County Durham, and then in Newcastle-upon-Tyne.

Senior Fellow in Poetry at the School of English, University of Leeds.

Continued to tour the UK giving readings, workshops and lectures, and resumed more hands-on editorial work on *Stand*.

1997   Died 25 November in the Freeman Hospital, Newcastle-upon-Tyne. Burial 28 November, Bushey Jewish Cemetery, near London. Orthodox rite. Stone-setting 29 November 1998.

Introduction

Jon Silkin: a life of writing and publishing

During his lifetime, 1930–1997, Jon Silkin became well known as a poet at home in the UK and abroad, from the USA to Japan, and from Australia to Sweden. Some of his poems entered the world of 'favourites' for BBC radio listeners. He influenced many writers and teachers, and his contributions to the discussion of war poetry were eagerly sought after for publication. As a speaker on Isaac Rosenberg and Wilfred Owen, he was always in demand. As an editor, his books such as *The Penguin Book of First World War Poetry* were popular and offered a perspective on Great War writers with the special edge of coming from someone who had known key figures such as Siegfried Sassoon, Herbert Read and David Jones. He had worked with Isaac Rosenberg's sister, Annie Wynick, in promoting the crucial Jewish writer's poems and paintings. He was approachable, always writing new commentaries on contemporary poetry, and regularly broadcasting on BBC radio. He was happy and energetic in promoting others, often through his quarterly journal *Stand*. But, as so often happens, after his death his reputation has waned and his role as a key reference point in post-Second World War poetry has almost vanished from recent textbooks and anthologies.

Almost twenty years after his death it is surely timely to look again at Jon Silkin's poetry. We have been privileged to be able to work through his massive archive, housed in Special Collections at Leeds University Library. As well as giving us a chance to re-read all of his books and pamphlets, it has revealed a large stock of totally unpublished manuscripts as well as poems published in journals but never collected by Silkin himself into individual books. We hope that this new *Complete Poems* will remind readers who have known his work, maybe over many years, what an exceptional poet he is. We also hope that the newly discovered work will offer all readers an exciting and demanding route into the work of a great writer. Having lived with this enormous range of poetry for several years while working on this volume, I find it has changed my sense of what was important in recent poetry, and themes related to his vital book, *Nature with Man*, recur in this introduction. I hope that the words of that book's title, and of the poem that gave the book its title, will stimulate some new and exciting insight as we face ecological change and possible disaster. Silkin lived with poetry as part of our lives and deaths in nature, whether loving or terrifying. The language of poetry, indeed any language, was not applied to or stuck over processes of life and death as a descriptor; it was integral to a whole substance.

The aim of this introduction is threefold: to describe some of the books from which Jon Silkin's poems have been chosen for inclusion in this volume; to indicate the vast range of journals and broadcast media in which the poems collected by Silkin himself for publication first appeared, together with the range of journals in which we have had to seek uncollected poems; and to offer a view of Silkin's life mediated through his lifelong obsession with editing and being published and printed. For the purpose of introducing what we hope is a complete edition of Silkin's work we have resisted the temptation to write a new full biography. There are other easily accessible sources of information on Silkin's life – see, for example, Select Bibliography: Interviews, Biographies, Memoirs and Obituaries, p. 874. The approach of listing the books with some new information about how they came into existence, seems fair and relevant.

While we have scoured all the journals from Jon Silkin's own library, we have found relatively few poems that appeared in journals but were not later collected in volume form. The majority of the previously unpublished poems have been found in Silkin's own papers. He saved meticulously all of the drafts of poems that are well known. He also saved multiple copies and drafts of poems which never found their way into print. We have read as many of these as possible and, in our view, we have found them well worth their first publication here. In many cases, the drafts were saved in order of composition and, despite the movement through pen and/or pencil to typescript, often with hand-written alterations (one may suspect during the typing process), we have been able to choose in each case what is probably the last version he worked on.

One of Silkin's characteristic working methods was to expand a first draft into one or more longer versions, sometimes in several numbered sections. The separate sections themselves became longer and longer. They evolved down new routes containing additional material. Sometimes the language became more complex and full of imagery. Sometimes it is as though the initial range of metaphor has developed into a complex intertwining and multi-layered vision. The multi-layering takes over as the dominant force; the medium becomes the message. Sometimes the sections have individual names which themselves change. Sometimes the sections become identifiable new poems and the original material no longer has a linear thread. For Silkin to try to move from what may have had a simple original intention would, indeed, become fallacious in the new format. The new poems become specific entities in their own right.

We have tried to select the most interesting and challenging of the entities that have emerged. Sometimes it has been impossible to decide on one correct pattern or structure. Silkin famously believed in an organic process of writing in which adherence to pre-existing stanzaic forms or intellectual overviews might induce a betrayal. In making the choices that we have, we hope that the poems on the page are successful in an organic form. In some cases, the increased complexity, line by line, seemed to us to leave behind a simpler, if less overtly 'willed', exploration. Perhaps the shorter, apparently clearer lines would have had more impact now, even if Silkin himself might have felt that such brief simplicity played into the English love of patterned sub- or super-structures. We recognise that some perfectly good material has had to be left aside, since multiple successive pages of one draft would have had to be reproduced *in toto* for the reader to live with, or we would have had to attempt to produce a version that Silkin would have recognised and been prepared to negotiate with. There are some drafts, with enormous variations, which completely defeated us. Some are tens or hundreds of pages long. We felt that it would be best to leave those to another day and a supplementary volume which might include more of the plays that verge on verse-drama.

In selecting poems from the archives we had to make choices from working drafts dating back to the early 1950s up to Silkin's death in 1997. It is often hard to establish why a poem that had gone through many drafts and detailed revisions was abandoned.

One aspect of Silkin's life that has been demonstrated through confronting the sheer size of the archive is that he wrote poetry and prose daily, often throughout the day, and in different circumstances. He didn't need to be at one desk in one chair in one room. As he travelled increasingly widely throughout the UK, the United States, Europe, the Middle East, Australia and the Far East, he wrote everywhere. There are drafts on the backs of envelopes, on the backs of letters and on the reverse side of hundreds of submissions to *Stand*. Submissions sent in without a stamped, self-addressed envelope were saved for drafting, either in pen or typescript. It might seem bizarre or disrespectful to others' creative work. But given the volume of new poems Silkin continually wrote, it must have seemed fair game; it saved a considerable amount in paper.[1] It is worth recalling that he never acclimatised to computers, even in their early days. All the drafts are handwritten or typed on old-fashioned typewriters.

In many cases, we feel that the range of previously unpublished work will give a new insight into the breadth of Silkin's personal, political and literary interests. Given the number of poems from which he had to choose when preparing a new volume, we have discovered that he must have thought hard about the identity and coherence of each collection. The poems left aside were not second-rate; they were not part of the vision for each book. He was writing new work constantly, so there was little hope that the abandoned poems from a given period would find a home in another or later volume.

The way that the poetry publishing business works is that individual poets, unless exceptionally popular, will only be chosen for a new volume every few years, and each book will usually be limited to an extent in the region of 64 to 128 pages. Silkin's own experience with the costing and production of *Stand* meant that he was all too familiar with publishers' budgets. Our suspicion is that he must have become accustomed to choosing a selection per volume on grounds which may now look arbitrary.

Jon Silkin was only 19 when, in June 1950, he arranged for a contract with the small press Arthur H. Stockwell to print his first book of poems. The contract was safely filed, as are most of his other publishing agreements, and is remarkable for many reasons. Firstly, it was signed by his father, Joseph. Was this because, as a 'minor', Jon Silkin could not sign a legally binding document, or because he was still in the army and likely to be on the move? Perhaps it seemed more businesslike to be writing to a publisher from Herne Hill in London, rather than from an army barracks. Silkin's father was a lawyer and, while they were not always on the best of terms, it is probable that entering into a publishing contract seemed to the son a demanding task and one that required proper scrutiny. Hence Joseph Silkin signed. Secondly, it is extraordinary that the short manuscript existed at all. Jon Silkin started National (military) Service aged 18 in late 1948. His education had been interrupted by the war and he was evacuated to Kent in 1939, then to Swansea, and then to the Welsh countryside. After some time at Wycliffe College[2] – located in Lampeter during the war – in 1945 he returned to Dulwich College. Either he was expelled or quietly asked to leave, or his parents thought that his regular truancy and apparent lack of academic commitment meant that a struggle with the school authorities wasn't worth the trouble. Much later in his life he sent a highly personal 'Questionnaire' to his mother asking her to fill in missing facts about his life, such as whether or not he had been 'expelled'. (How strange that he did not know!) By the end of two years at Dulwich he had passed some of the old School Certificate examinations (from autumn 1945 when he was 14 to summer 1947 when he was 16), but not Latin, which he would have needed to enter his father's law firm or university. In approximately 17 months between leaving Dulwich College and entering the army he worked as a filing clerk and as a local newspaper reporter.

During two years of service he became a Sergeant Instructor in the Education Corps. It is now hard to imagine the personal and social contradictions involved. While Jon Silkin came from a highly educated family and read avidly, one cannot believe that he had readily acquired the knowledge and skills to instil basic literacy in older soldiers, some of whom would have seen the horrors of active service. He had to apply twice to be trained for the Education Corps, but was given a chance the second time. He must have seemed sufficiently qualified to those who put him in charge. And despite the normal duties of army life, and his role in the Education Corps, he had the time, skill and dedication to write enough poems by the spring of 1950 to make the publication of a book seem a natural and worthwhile aim. Stockwell's may not have been a prestigious firm. I have not discovered any evidence as to why Silkin and his father did not try London firms, and specifically why they chose Stockwell's in Devon. For those who were part of the poetry world, there would have been access to small magazines and publishing houses in London willing to promote poetry. Presumably, while still in the Education Corps, he could have had little contact with 'real' publishers.[3] His dedication to poetry was very practical (and strangely traditional) in the sense that it was founded in reading the Bible and in reading selected great English poets. But he was not yet part of a community of writers with experience of editing, publishing and networking. However, the Stockwell contract does offer royalties and it outlines the number of volumes to be printed (750), cover price (9*d*) and design.

After agreeing to lose the title 'Sergeant' before his name on the front cover, and on receipt of the third payment from him of £4 15*s* 0*d* to cover the costs, the book was printed. In its small way it reveals many interesting features of the process of a popular or communal inheritance of the business of writing poetry after the war and up to mid-1950. Silkin later revealed that the book sold twenty-three copies. There was a very brief notice in the *South London Observer*.[4]

Poetry volume by Silkin's nephew

Aged 20 […] Jon Silkin, a former pupil of Dulwich College, has just had his first book published – a 16 page volume of poems.

Jon is the nephew of Lord Silkin of Dulwich. He may go into the family law business, but he would like, if possible, to make his living by writing.

Some of the poems were written before he joined the Army for his period of National Service – he served as an Education Corps sergeant in England – and some were written while soldiering.

Jon Silkin has also written a play but that has not been published. He is at present working on a book.

His poems are written in simple, clear and expressive language and a healthy disregard for punctuation is shown. Several are in the first person.

Silkin chose not to reproduce the poems in his later selections and collections. While he did not deny the existence of *The Portrait*, the 1950s brought such immense personal and literary changes for him that perhaps he went on to see these early poems as of minor importance compared with the enormous success of those that appeared in *The Peaceable Kingdom* in 1954. The poems in *The Portrait* and others from the 1950s never published at the time, or printed in journals but not reprinted in books, are included in this new *Complete Poems*.

At the beginning of 1951 Silkin was still only just 20 and needed to earn his keep, to find a social role and personal identity, and to develop his passion for poetry. He was in perpetual conflict with his parents, would not re-sit Latin to allow him to enter legal training, and had no obviously 'fitting' qualifications to prepare him for a job; at least not a job with stability and a future. It seems that he was determined to invent himself as someone in touch with, and shaped by, the same forces that formed ordinary working people. To him, 'fitting' into a convention did not offer an easy choice. During the war he had, in effect, to fend for himself. His parents rarely visited him in Wales, and there was no way that holidays could be allowed in London still under threat of bombs or invasion. Disturbed (in many ways) schooling from the age of 14 to 17 did not confirm a return to a happy academic boyhood, and two years in the army would not prepare anyone for a normal family life. While dropping out and taking 'gap years' may seem psychologically sensible preparations for adulthood now, in 1951, when it could be said that he had become used too early to a detached and disturbed life, Silkin was faced with abnormal options: more detachment, rebellion, and disloyalty. If, in some awful ways, he had grown to see himself as unfamiliar with family life, even as rejected by his parents, if he had gone through more enforced self-discovery by 19 than many go through in a whole lifetime, what cool, calm and reasonable decisions leading to a 'working-class' – and essentially poor – future could he take? Poverty had, for him, to be cultivated; the 'good life' was unacceptable on the basis of political, moral and emotional grounds. By the early 1950s, a sort of dissociation was habitual. For many, then and now, a period at university would have allowed for structured rebellion. So, how might Silkin continue to rebel anew, at the age of 20, without some tacit parental support or without being able to pull the safety cord of access to family money?

Early in 1952, Silkin started the magazine *Stand*. Since the appearance of *The Portrait* he had worked in various unsatisfactory jobs and had met many people in the poetry world. The need to read, write *and* publish was soon established as a natural way of life for him. Essentially, these activities *were* to become his identity, and they distinguished him from someone seeking the more conventional middle-class routes of seeking work in publishing or in a university or through some related charitable or media-friendly calling which would provide a regular income. However strange it might now seem, manual labour, routine office work or teaching English as a foreign language were probably, to him, a sufficient, indeed necessary, source of financial support. To function in the common life was a real and loveable vocation. He could enjoy, though it was often not 'happy', the struggling symbiosis of writing, liaising with other writers, and 'hands-on' publishing. Inevitably, he shared his rough working life with other writers, and his life of writing with other workers.

On the one hand, life might seem something of what John Osborne's 'angry young man' could have had. On the other, it was living out the mutuality of creative writing and communication with ordinary life that informed the vision of T.S. Eliot and Bonamy Dobrée when they set up the Gregory Fellowships at the University of Leeds, of which Jon Silkin was to become a beneficiary.[5] It is surely a strange, and as yet unexamined, aspect of post-war life that there was such a coincidence of thought and practice (in work, creativity and educational theory) between Silkin, *Stand* and his 'community of writers', and Dobrée, Eric Gregory, T.S. Eliot, Herbert Read and Henry Moore and their 'community of writers and artists'.

Silkin was, by the early 1950s, meeting writers of all age groups. Some were in networks through small magazines; some through haunts in Soho, 'Fitzrovia' and Swiss Cottage. Some met in pubs, some in coffee bars such as the Cosmo, where he met Danny Abse, Michael Hamburger and Elias Canetti. Bloomsbury and, across the Tottenham Court Road, Fitzrovia, were to afford links to Dylan Thomas and others whose identities as poets straddled the war.[6] Some ran magazines and organised poetry readings; others would make what would become the crucial break into the north of England. James Kirkup and John Heath-Stubbs, the two first Gregory Fellows in Poetry at the University of Leeds, were among the earliest poets to appear regularly in *Stand*. Kirkup describes his life just off the west side of the Tottenham Court Road before his move to Leeds.[7] Bonamy Dobrée lived in Bloomsbury when he wasn't in Leeds; Eric Gregory lived in Chelsea. While the 'northernness' of emerging poetic identities in the 1950s was important, the north (Gregory, the Bradford printer, and Dobrée, Professor of English at Leeds) had important roots in the south, and in central London in particular. Important new poets were emerging in Oxford, including Geoffrey Hill, whose arrival in Leeds in 1954 was facilitated through Heath-Stubbs and Dobrée. Young writers at this time may not have consciously thought of exploiting 'networks' but, de facto, the late 1940s and early 1950s in London offered friendship, support (including floors to sleep on), and a literary and historical familiarity of aims that was there for anyone confident enough to knock and enter. By the end of 1953 Silkin had met many important writers, and had written the manuscript of what was to be *The Peaceable Kingdom*. He was a very different writer from the sergeant who had produced *The Portrait* only three years before.

The contract for Silkin's next book – one that some think his greatest – was signed on 6 April 1954. This time he didn't have to pay the publishers but received an advance of £10. The document notes:

> Whereas the Author has written a literary work at present entitled THE PEACEABLE KINGDOM consisting of 17 poems or thereabouts it is mutually agreed between the parties as follows…

This time the contract was with Chatto & Windus, and signed by Cecil Day-Lewis and Jon Silkin himself. It was also signed, as a Director, by Ian Parsons, who was to become the editor of Isaac Rosenberg's *Collected Works*. Day-Lewis became a friend, and the link with Rosenberg's poetry, facilitated by Parsons, was important to Silkin from then on, as a Jew, as a scholar of First World War poetry, and as an editor. The book (only 39 numbered pages) appeared later in the year with the 17 poems originally submitted. The acknowledgments page lists the places where some of the poems had first appeared, including *Poetry and Poverty*, *Chanticleer*, *First Reading* (BBC, John Wain), *New Verse* (BBC), *Varsity*, *The Window*, *Olivant* and *Jewish Quarterly*. The journals are exemplary as the sort that brought together post-war editors and poets (and, one hopes, readers), often, like *Stand*, with a mission. Silkin was still only 23 but he was a voice on the BBC. Studying the records of Silkin's growing reputation may now offer a reader insight into how a new star appeared. Such study is worthwhile given the current interest in social media, and the Silkin archives are a treasure trove for discovering how writers found a place in hierarchies of communication. The BBC and the national press, including the *Times Literary Supplement*, might be thought to have been elitist and impenetrable. In practice, writers such as Silkin, and his *Stand* co-editor Gordon Wharton, could find themselves picked out for regular slots as reviewers and broadcasters despite their lack of paper qualifications and personal contacts to the power structures through the ancient universities.

Between 1952 and 1955 Silkin was in a relationship with Cynthia Redpath. She had given birth to their first son, Adam, who was to 'die in a mental hospital aged one', and to their second son, David Emanuel. By a happy chance, while they were living together he had discovered in a secondhand book the world of the American folk artist Edward Hicks, whose *Peaceable Kingdom* offered the moral and visible structure of many of his poems for the rest of his life.[8]

The manuscript for the next book, *The Two Freedoms*, was delivered with 28 poems to Chatto & Windus and the contract signed on 1 July 1957, although it did not appear until 1958 (with 29 poems). The poems had previously appeared in *Botteghe Oscure*, *Mavericks*, *Poetry* (Chicago), *Truth*, *Encounter*, *New Statesman*, *London Magazine*, *Jewish Quarterly*, *Poetry Review*, *PEN Anthology* 1956 & 1957, *Meridian Books* (USA), *Midstream* (USA), *The Poet*, *New Chapter* and *Outposts*, as well as in *Stand*, and broadcast through the BBC Third Programme and the Hebrew Section of the BBC. When comparing this list to the acknowledgments in *The Peaceable Kingdom*, it is clear that there are two 'strategic' changes. Journals that had published Silkin in the UK now include, in addition to the *Jewish Quarterly*, two other major current affairs and political papers in which poetry was an important element but perhaps a 'filler' nonetheless: *Encounter* and *New Statesman*. Further, there are three journals from the USA, including the internationally important *Poetry* (Chicago). *Mavericks*, *Stand* and *Outposts* mark an identified trio opposing the Movement, and reflected a political and aesthetic link between Dannie Abse, Silkin and Howard Sergeant. Some of the *very* small journals (*Chanticleer* and *The Window*) have gone, but there is an important new one: *The Poet*, edited by William Price Turner from Glasgow. *The Poet* was indeed small – normally no more than 16 pages – but it published important poets from Scotland, England and the USA. Silkin appeared in it, and there was a whole issue dedicated to poems by Gordon Wharton. Price Turner was to follow Silkin as Gregory Fellow in Poetry at Leeds University from 1960 to 1962, thus adding to the links between small magazines, Dobrée, Gregory and Leeds. Dobrée mentioned Kirkup and Heath-Stubbs in his Cambridge Clark Lectures (1952–53) and a wider group of young poets from the small magazine network in an article published in the USA.[9] Being chosen as a reference point by one of the most important university-based English critics, and by figures such as Anthony Thwaite ('Mr Silkin's first book of poems is the most hopeful I have read for a long time; it should be bought, and read, and remembered'[10]) labelled Silkin an important figure in both the UK and the USA.

Silkin was earning money washing dishes in a café on Villiers Street near Charing Cross station when, while walking down the Strand, he heard that he was to succeed Thomas Blackburn as Gregory Fellow in Poetry at the University of Leeds.[11] He was living with playwright David Mercer and playwright and novelist Malcolm Ross-MacDonald at 10 Compayne Gardens, London NW6. He rented the rooms from Bernice Rubens (and sub-let a room to Mercer). Ross-MacDonald recalls driving Silkin to Leeds to see what it was like: his first visit to 'the north'.[12]

By the time he delivered his next manuscript to Chatto & Windus at some date (day and month not on the contract) in 1961, Silkin had organised a major exhibition of the paintings and manuscripts of Isaac Rosenberg at the University of Leeds, with help from the poet's sister, Annie Wynick, and the Head of Fine Art at the University, Maurice de Sausmarez. He had encouraged students and staff in becoming writers. He had re-started *Stand*, following its closure due to lack of funds in 1957. Also in 1960, at the end of his two-year Gregory Fellowship, he started to study for a BA in English, which he was to complete with first-class honours in only two years.[13] And, of course, he continued his own writing.

The Re-ordering of the Stones, published in 1961, contained 27 poems. In 1993, in an *Agenda* issue reflecting on the 1960s, Silkin said, 'Most of the poems were written in the (for me) relatively short period of 1959–60.'[14] The list of acknowledgments shows new changes. There are big journals, important anthologies and some small magazines, the latter all from Leeds:

> *Encounter, New Left Review, New Poets of England and America* (2nd Series), *New Statesman, Oxford Opinion, PEN* 1958, *Poetry and Audience (An Anthology 1953–60), Prospect, Stand, Time and Tide, Times Literary Supplement, Tribune, Universities' Poetry 1961, Writers Against Apartheid, Penguin Contemporary Verse* (ed. Kenneth Allott), New Sound Productions, BBC Third Programme.

On one hand, this list reveals the relentless process of submitting, dealing with acceptance and rejection, then revising proofs, and providing such biographical information as each journal required or allowed. On the other, it confirms that Silkin was by then so well established that key poems by him were essential for definitive anthologies. Particularly in the 1950s and 1960s, anthologies provided touchstone poems for the reading public and for current poets to dwell on – so *these* were the trends. Silkin produced his own anthology, *Living Voices*, for Vista Books in 1960.[15] He was in Donald Hall and Robert Pack's *New Poets of England and America*[16] and Kenneth Allott's *Contemporary Verse*,[17] which were often used as source books for students and writers within and outside universities. Allott's book included statements by Silkin and Geoffrey Hill on their own poems. Such published self-reflection on a few of their own best known poems indicated the existence of a new canon, bringing with it associated critical thinking. *The New Poetry*, edited by A. Alvarez, also showed Silkin's role emerging: although he was not included in the first edition in 1962, he was in the second edition which appeared in 1966. *Poetry and Audience (P&A), Geste* and *Gryphon* are all University of Leeds periodicals in which Silkin's poems appeared. *P&A*, founded in 1953 by Ralph Maud, was published weekly, costing 1*d*. It existed informally as a journal funded by the Students' Union, with a tradition that the editor was appointed annually by members of the board (fellow undergraduates). With, or without, help from the current Gregory Fellow in

Poetry, the editor dealt with submissions from outside Leeds, such as poems by Philip Larkin and Ted Hughes, and within Leeds from staff, such as Geoffrey Hill, and students, such as Tony Harrison, as well as from current and former Gregory Fellows, including John Heath-Stubbs, Thomas Blackburn, Jon Silkin, William Price Turner and Peter Redgrove. Ken Smith and Tony Harrison both edited *P&A* and later became editors of *Stand*. The dynamics of this community of writing were extraordinary.

In the late summer of 1965, Silkin, with friends and colleagues including Kate Lamb and Ken Smith, left Leeds to read in the Edinburgh Festival. When he returned, he took up an offer from the North-East Association for the Arts (the north-east England regional branch of the Arts Council, later known as Northern Arts) to edit *Stand* from Newcastle-upon-Tyne. Seven important years in Leeds were over. He later looked back on them as a sort of golden age which acquired a wistful or glorious haze: 'Wordsworth's "Bliss was it in that dawn to be alive" seems about right enough. My only additional comment is that, like so many positive periods in one's life, one isn't fully aware of its value till afterwards.'[18] Much of his poetry from Leeds, including the time of his BA degree studies and the re-forming of *Stand*, was included in *Nature with Man*, also published in 1965.[19] The acknowledgment network of journal and media publications has again changed, although it represents Silkin's habitual ambitious and exploratory use of magazines and broadcast media as a method of extending contact, recognition and readership. This pre-book publication process of individual poems was part of his way of life. While it was time-consuming and arduous, it was, for Silkin, a vital aspect of being a poet, and forming the identity and existence of 'a poem'. In some ways it exemplified Stephen Greenblatt's 'New Historicist' negotiation and exchange: the poem did not exist without the process in which it was formed and used. Silkin often handed or posted drafts to friends with invitations to comment. For him, the hard work was natural and necessary. The list of titles reflects his continued presence in the United States, and now in Europe and in translation:

Agenda, Avon Books (NY), *Birmingham Bulletin, Clare Market Review, Il Contemporaneo, Encounter, Flash Point* (E.J. Arnold), *Geste, Glasgow Herald, The Glasgow Review, Irish Times, Jazz*

Poems (Studio Vista), *Marxist, New Durham, New Opinion, Neue Deutsche Hefte, PEN* (1963), *Poetry and Audience, Poetry Review, The Review, Scope, Sewanee Review, Shenandoah, Stand, Time and Tide, Times Literary Supplement, Universities' Poetry* (4 and 5), *New Poetry BBC* (Terence Tiller), BBC Scottish Television, Granada TV, *The Poet's Voice* (George Macbeth). The first eight of the 'Flower Poems' were broadcast in The Living Poet (George Macbeth); a smaller group appeared in *Granta* (then edited by John Barrell), and the first nine were published in pamphlet by Northern House (Leeds).

Leeds journals are there but so are journals from other universities. He is also appearing in some of the most important, and fashionable, poetry magazines, such as Ian Hamilton's *The Review*. *Sewanee Review* and *Shenandoah* carried weight in the United States. Some poems appeared in books which Silkin had been commissioned to select for and edit, including *Flash Point* and *Jazz Poems*. There were appearances on television and on a range of radio programmes. The 'Flower Poems', characteristically, were published in at least three formats before they appeared in *Nature with Man*. They may have originated in the garden of his house at 144 Otley Road, Leeds,[20] though in many ways they are not poems 'about' visible ordinary plants. They are not external to man for study and conscious simile-making but integral to 'nature *with* man' (my emphasis). Silkin describes briefly in *Agenda* how the impact of Leeds grew on him: '*Nature with Man*, also published out of the Leeds period, in 1965, seems to me to have grown directly, if in a more fleshed way [than *The Re-ordering of the Stones*], from the Leeds Sixties.'[21]

That said, exploration of the relationship, as parts (organs and limbs) of the same body, or self-destructively separate and violently detached, is integral between man and the physical environment in Silkin's work from this point on. It is perhaps hard for the average 'English-educated' reader to think into a founding and fundamental 'nature' as consisting of biblical desert, rock, mountain and sun as opposed to the green worlds of Shakespeare, Wordsworth and Keats. For Silkin, the dynamics of Old Testament conflict and reconciliation in the Middle East offered a perfectly real and relevant (historic or modern) setting for poems of sex and war. 'Nature' was not instinctively the Forest of Arden or

Cumbria. If Milton and Blake were added to the crop of poets and their natural worlds that Silkin worked with, then the reader simply receives an even wider verbal and visionary landscape. The absurd and surrealistically prophetic story of the title poem, 'Nature with Man', is a great work to re-read decades later with our twenty-first-century fear of humanity's profligate exploitation of the environment. While in the '60s and '70s Silkin and many others may have believed in Banning the Bomb, it is a reassuring shock to find that his poems on landscape and flowers may be re-read (re-discovered?) as fundamental orations of the new century's eco-poetry.[22]

In August 1965 a contract was drawn up to publish Silkin's *New and Selected Poems*. The first version of the document outlines a three-way arrangement between Silkin's first American publisher, Wesleyan University Press, Chatto & Windus and the author. Chatto & Windus's version was not signed until 16 November 1965. Despite the book's title there were only four completely new poems: 'Brought Up With Grass', 'My thin, sharp bird's breastbone', 'Snow Drop', and 'Meetings'. The rest were selected from *The Peaceable Kingdom*, *The Two Freedoms*, *The Re-ordering of the Stones* and *Nature with Man*, including most of the 'Flower Poems'. The book appeared at the end of July 1966, and the UK edition, complete with the Chatto & Windus imprint and address, was actually printed in America. It marked another milestone in the establishment of Silkin's status and reputation.

Silkin's landscapes were transformed or reconfigured during and after his first visits to the United States in 1965 (at Denison University, Ohio) and 1968 (at the Iowa Writers' Workshop, University of Iowa). He returned to Newcastle in 1968 with Lorna Tracy, a brilliant short story writer. She was to become his wife and a mainstay of editing *Stand*. The next book with Chatto & Windus, published in 1971, reveals what might now be seen as an intimate and literary revolution in his work. The acting out of writing as an organic process was for him always a bodily exploration and reconciliation. It was also a process in which he was thinking of readers as participants in the art and arguments with and for him.

Amana Grass, although it contained his new poetry from 1965 to 1970, is one of Silkin's shorter books. It consists of 48 pages, 26 poems. The contract with Chatto, reflecting the fact that the manuscript had already been delivered, was signed on 18 May 1970. Another contract was agreed on 9 November 1970 with the

Wesleyan University Press to print and publish an American edition. By this time Silkin's work, particularly through his presence at the University of Iowa, but also through his relentless reading tours, was widely known in the United States. As usual, part of the process of selling, idea-seeding and assimilation involved getting his poems published in a wide range of journals and broadcasting media. Poems in *Amana Grass* appeared prior to book publication in BBC *Poet's Voice* and *Poetry Now*, *The Blacksuede Boot*, *Borestone Mountain Poetry* (1972), *Choice*, *Form*, *The Iowa Defender*, Iowa State Liquor Store, *The Iowa Review*, *Journal of Creative Behavior*, *Lines*, *Massachusetts Review*, *MidNAG*, *12 x 12* (Camden), *North American Review*, *Northwest Review*, *Poetry and Audience*, *Scratch*, *Stand*, *Sumac*, *Times Literary Supplement* and *Penguin Modern Poets* 7. The Pym-Randall Press published the first three of *Six Cemetery Poems* in their pamphlet series as *Three Poems*. It is interesting that the majority of the journals listed are American, and although he was based in the midwestern state of Iowa, poems appeared in Michigan-based *Sumac* and the *Massachusetts Review*, as well as in the UK on the BBC, in the *Times Literary Supplement*, in *Lines* in Scotland, and in Leeds' *Poetry and Audience*.

There were complexities and contradictions. Silkin was profoundly impressed by the space and intellectual vigour of the United States. He was obviously determined to find a wide readership, and to meet and talk with audiences, often university staff and students, in as many settings as possible. His established 'subject matter' absorbed American landscapes. However, *Amana Grass*, with its long title poem and the important 'Six Cemetery Poems', adopted neither an easy-going American tone nor an urban agenda from 'Beat' or 'New York' poetry. Nor did he abandon some of his main psychological or internalised landscapes. The grass of 'Amana Grass' might have seemed relatively exotic and different – but it was still 'grass'. Growing plants were normally a major element of Silkin's natural worlds which grew with him, from the hearing of grass in Isaiah to seeing it in the prairies (and then to stranger historicised nature in Australia, the Middle and Far East, and back to the Bible). Cemeteries, too, had been his place of work[23] and one of his imaginative summations – death and burial are there from *The Peaceable Kingdom* in the early 1950s to his last poems in 1997. Was it inevitable that, despite his relocation in Iowa, thousands of miles from England, two aspects of his biblical and poetic intelligence, grass and graves, were, if not conservatively superimposed on Hicks's world, rediscovered?

Publication of *Amana Grass* marked the end of Silkin's relationship with Chatto & Windus after nearly 20 years. He had to find a new publisher and the innovative Carcanet Press, formed in Oxford and by then based in Manchester, seemed an ideal home. Having started by publishing pamphlets by young poets, and translations, Michael Schmidt, editor and director, had become a lecturer at the University of Manchester, and by 1974 had created a publishing house with an astonishing list of poetry and prose. As an operation based in the north, keen to promote both new and established talent, Carcanet would perhaps have seemed a profitable riposte to the London-based presses. *The Principle of Water* appeared almost exactly 20 years after *The Peaceable Kingdom*.

The Principle of Water, despite its reference points being apparently very different from those in *Amana Grass*, actually followed some similar patterns. It has three major sections, all of which occupy British and European territories. Many poems had been published previously, the acknowledgments citing *Antaeus*, *British Poetry* 1972 (The Baleen Press, Arizona), *European Judaism*, *Fuse*, *Here Now*, *Iowa Review*, *Jewish Quarterly*, *New Poetry* (Australia), *New Statesman*, *Orbis*, *Outposts*, *PEN* 1973, *Poetry* (USA), *Poetry Book Society Supplement* (1971), *Responses*, *Scotsman*, *The Valley Press* (USA), *Times Literary Supplement*, *Tribune*, *Vanderbilt Poetry Review*, the Sceptre Press, the Scolar Press, George Stephenson and the Mid-Northumberland Arts Group, and the BBC Third Programme.

The 'Killhope Wheel' sequence, published as a large-format pamphlet by the Mid-Northumberland Arts Group in 1971, found Silkin exploring his relationship with the past and the historical detail of conflict and violence which attracted him to a location in County Durham where lead had been mined. Through his own voice and his dramatisation of the striking miners' voices, he enacts the unity between working landscape and working human. 'Landscape' might seem to be easy to sentimentalise. Indeed, the European places of this book were not 'nice' historical or tourist sites; they were the positions of what Geoffrey Hill has recently called 'fields of force', where language is aligned with an uncontrollable but controlling electricity.[24] The poems' voices act out the sense of being drawn in to life and death. Silkin cannot stand back and meditate; the seething legacy of rock, metal and violence takes over the poems and their structure. They might have the awful self-involvement of anti-prayers:

> The spade digging in the sunlight illuminates the face of
> my God.
>   Blind him.
>
> ('Spade')

'The People' is a long verse play. Silkin wrote several plays which were performed, both on radio and on stage. 'The People' was broadcast on BBC Radio in 1974,[25] and is the only play we have included in this volume, despite the others also being poems in essence. Characteristically, 'The People' dramatises individuals as they explore relationships and the possibilities of love while bringing a child into life in a world of death – the Shoah. Each poem has a named speaker; indeed, one can imagine listening to many of Silkin's poems and inserting notes indicating who or what is speaking. Conflicts of voices, against and over each other, are the essential mode of Silkin's poetry.

The last main group in the book responds to places new to him – the Shetlands – and places already explored in *The Re-ordering of the Stones*: Yorkshire's continued persecution of the Jews after 1190 when, in Clifford's Tower in York,

> [...] eight hundred Jews
> Took each other's lives
> To escape christian death
> By christian hand; and the last
> Took his own.
>
> ('The Coldness')

In 'The Malabestia', three women who had escaped the fate of Clifford's Tower by becoming Christians are put to death by Richard of Acaster, a baron who thought he could avoid his debts to the Jews by killing them. It is a fascinating sequence which works in Silkin's ceremonial evocation, and a celebration of the body's leaking, or draining, into the land, with earth and water becoming part of the human. Nature with man is not prettified. Three women died and their commemoration, if it is such, is in their transformation:

A blank quietness shading foliage
circling itself; a circular morass
of pond-without. Mud adheres the flesh.
The principle of water stirs through it.

('The Malabestia', I, 2)

We should note that the biblical is still integral to Silkin's voicing
of experience. One might have expected America to have substi-
tuted a new list of the important; but returning to the Shetlands
and Acaster Malbis renewed what were the nearer demands of
history in the present – so, not directly the racial politics of Black
experience, Vietnam and feminism in America. However, the
influence of biblical and Miltonic tones has given way to something
freer. The book ends with a truly paradoxical poem, 'Isaiah's
Thread'. The words of Isaiah make active commands to Silkin. But
his responses are informal, up-to-date, though complex, since he
always knows he has to think and re-think. In Part 1 of the poem
he responds to natural and spiritual demands in the negative:

Go, go, go it said. I flew into the earth's rim.

And grew cautious. No indeed, I answered.

But in Part 2, the act of making an expression changes everything:

What shall I cry? Cry. Why must people by people
be torn?

Yes, I said.

I undid my hand, and fastening to it
a stone dilapidating from a house, crouched
in the grass's time.

('Isaiah's Thread')

In 1974 Silkin provided an introduction to Robert Shaw's
anthology *Flash Point*.[26] The book included twentieth-century
poems from Thomas Hardy to Geoffrey Hill, Sylvia Plath and
James Simmons. While *Flash Point* may be of no direct relevance

to *The Principle of Water* or to Silkin's next book, *The Little Time-keeper*, the introduction focuses on an issue which always concerns him in his own writing and his responses to that of others:

> The first decision is whether or not the poet has finely and powerfully drawn his particular experience or act of feelings into a responsive language. But the moment this has been done – while it is being done – the experience itself is being tested. Is it genuinely felt? Has that feeling, if it is honestly felt, been conveyed with literary honesty (these two are not synonymous)? And then, and this in our present society becomes increasingly important, do I dissent from the conveyed experience so strongly that I reject the poem? And if I reject it, can I distinguish between what I reject, and the way it has been written? Can a distinction between these two be drawn at all?[27]

Of the 67 poets he only refers to Hill, Tomlinson and Eliot, with the majority of his discussion being on Eliot and the sort of distinction outlined above. There is a substantial diversion on the religious background and meanings of a medieval poem which is set out in Middle English spelling and typography. The role of introductions as an orientating device for Silkin's own poetry and his attitude to it may emerge as an important subject from this point on. The book was probably aimed at schools as a classroom text. The introduction concludes in a combative way which may not have increased sales:

> 'What have I to do with poetry?' is sometimes also the attitude of a few teachers; as if poetry were a sort of pill, small enough, but something to be got out of the way; or a 'free' period in which no 'real' work need be done (unless it be sixth-form work, and then the respectable examination, the adolescent's hurdle, needs to be faced).[28]

The Little Time-keeper was published in 1976, organised jointly by Carcanet, the Mid-Northumberland Arts Group, and Wild and Woolley, Sydney, Australia. It also appeared in the same year from W.W. Norton in New York and George J. McLeod in Toronto. As usual, many of the poems had appeared in journals, including *Agenda*, *Europa Litteraria* (Italy), *Four Zoas* (US), *Jewish Chronicle*,

The Milton Celebrations, Meanjin (Australia), *Meridian, Minnesota Review, New Statesman, Poetry & Audience* (Leeds), *Poetry North East, The Shakespeare Celebrations, Southern Poetry Review* (US), *Stand, Sydney Morning Herald, The Age* (Australia), *The Blacksmith* (Australia), *Times Literary Supplement, Threshold* (Belfast), *Tribune* and *Canberra Poetry.* Poems had been published in pamphlet form by the Keepsake and Sceptre Presses, most of 'The Little Time-keeper' had been broadcast on BBC radio, and Tyne Tees Television is also acknowledged.

The book continues Silkin's archaeology and geology of human love, and violence, in ignored or forgotten places. It is perhaps strange, now almost paradoxical, that he spent so much energy on spreading knowledge of his poetry, reaching audiences through national TV and radio, but the substance of so many of the poems was rooted in the local. By 'local' I do not mean 'small' or 'ephemeral'. The ceremony, or drama, in which he experimented with new components of nature with man was perpetually redis-covered in particular places. Thus, in 'Entropy at Hartburn', the whole business of the universe occurs in one small place:

> Hartburn divides night on itself
> with a shutter. 'Mildred clamp out the dark.' Cream lace
> embroiders its holes.
>
> The huge energies untwine, and stars
> slither away on the braids.
>
> ('Entropy at Hartburn')

It might be tempting to think of the place in which the universe runs out of steam as being necessarily anonymous, inconsequential, irrelevant. Yet, of course, the process here dramatised in Hartburn is anything but nameless. And however one might be mystified, or annoyed, by the sudden appearance of a woman, 'Mildred', it is precisely that shock which engages the reader. The engagement is with a stunning mix of the scientific and ma~~ with Silkin's religion – or the command for M curtains', pro and contra the universe, with la Church: it is getting short of breath. But we s commands in the 'morass'.

In the late 1970s Jon Silkin and Michael

disagree on a number of matters concerning poetry, culture, religion, politics and history – a fairly large battlefield. Silkin had to find another publisher and his next books were hosted from London with Routledge & Kegan Paul. 1980 saw a volume of new poems, *The Psalms with their Spoils*, and *Selected Poems*, a generous choice from *The Peaceable Kingdom* through to *The Little Time-keeper*. There is an interesting note to the *Selected Poems* indicating Silkin's reasons for making changes to some earlier published poems, particularly 'Amana Grass' and 'The People', both of which had whole parts removed. In this *Complete Poems* we have kept the original versions.

The Psalms with their Spoils was compiled from the normal range of journals, including some from America but also from Australia, Korea and India: *Bananas*, *Boston University Journal*, *Chonnam Tribune* (Korea), *Contemporary Literature* (University of Wisconsin), 'Homage to Osip Mandelstam', *Iowa Review*, *Journal 7* (Birmingham University), London Broadcasting, *London Magazine*, *Looking Back* (Sceptre Press), *Massachusetts Review*, *Nantucket Review*, *New Poetry 4*, *New Statesman*, *Overland* (Australia), *Parnassus* (USA), *Poetry Nation Review*, *PEN Broadsheet*, *Poetry Review*, *Screever*, *Sewanee Review*, *Short Line* (USA), *Siddha* (India), *Southern Review*, *Stand*, *Sunday Times*, *Tablet*, *Times Literary Supplement*, *Tribune*, *Wittenberg Review* (USA). A poem was printed in *Hand and Eye*, a collection privately published as a tribute to the poet Sacheverell Sitwell; groups of poems appeared in pamphlets from the Ceolfrith and Sceptre Presses, and the BBC broadcast 'Joy, lined with metal'. It is an astonishing list. The American journals alone include some of the most prestigious poetry and critical magazines in the world. In the UK, there are major national newspapers, and the British journals range from Michael Schmidt's *Poetry Nation Review* to the Poetry Society's *Poetry Review*. For once, *Poetry and Audience* is not there. It is interesting, too, that some of the major groups following *The Little Time-keeper* were printed in full (in journals or as pamphlets) or broadcast in full on the radio. The years of spreading the word had paid off; editors and readers wanted the new poems, and that special relationship that can be felt when a poet's most recent work is seen for the first time in the journal to which you, or your library, subscribe was fulfilled.

Perhaps Jon Silkin's reputation in the decade from 1980 on was at its highest. As well as the individual volumes of poetry, he had already published what is still regarded as a key critical text on writers of the First World War, *Out of Battle* (Oxford University Press, 1972), *Poetry of the Committed Individual: A Stand Anthology of Poetry* (Gollancz and Penguin, 1973) and the *Penguin Book of First World War Poetry* (1979). As well as bringing out *Stand*, with meticulous regularity, the two new books from Routledge must have impressed many with his stamina, energy and creative intellect. Anyone appearing in the bookshops (heaps of his books, and himself amongst the shelves, reading poems aloud in an astonishingly dramatic voice, and promoting *Stand*), or being reviewed that often must have been, indeed *was*, a vital figure in the poetry world. Yet in all this time he was not paid a salary from a university post, although he often gave readings, ran workshops and gave lectures in libraries, universities, colleges and schools. When he visited the USA and Australia he was paid for a period of 'residency'. A personal income derived through *Stand*, resulting from profitable use of Arts Council funding, advertising and sales (through bookshops, but often personally, as described so lovingly by Ag Jones in the 200th issue of the magazine[29]) was his living. Writing poems was the fundamental process of making the bricks that would make their homes in, or as, books. Writing and publishing were not an adjunct to a 'normal' life; they were life.

Given its breadth of distribution and potential sales, *The Psalms with their Spoils* was written firmly within the focused problems and explorations that had been confirmed and heightened by work in America, not slackened. The very title is curious. One thinks of the 'spoils of war' – goods, property and sex taken illicitly, and through violence, by warriors in or after battle (as a sort of 'just' payment for their efforts?). How can psalms give or take such warlike payments? How could psalms be spoken, or sung, at the moment of taking or giving violence? Is this an ultimate hypocrisy? The first poem, 'The Cathedral Chair', perhaps makes one expect a Larkin-like homage to the holy. But the chair is a broken office swivel-seat thrown in a skip. Silkin chooses in his head, or in reality, to strip the decayed upholstery, 'and sit cupped, / in its thinking the idea sepalled / of the most dear absences'. The third poem is 'Resting Place', which returns again to York and to the sale in 1230 of land to the Jews for a burial plot. The plot is now a tarmac-covered car park. The fourth poem is 'Jerusalem'. The fifth, 'Into Praising', also starts in Jerusalem, with the Romans mauling the Jews. In effect, Silkin works through these landscapes into arguments and consequences. They form yet more ceremonial anti-prayers:

> These three conditions, in which
> we are human; to love
> and be loved past
> what is reasonable. So we do and would
> be done by.
>
> The second is to be tortured,
> and not to love's the third,
> the half-lie half-loved,
>
> where to be born we risk
> for sure one of these. The thigh caught up
> with heavenly nakedness.
>
> ('Into Praising')

The next book of poems was published in 1986, also by Routledge. *The Ship's Pasture* again offered a challenging title. Do ships graze? Do they sail through fields? As a title for readers who did not know Silkin's work it might have had an attractive, surreal feeling. For those who knew his work it may have hinted at the even greater praise of water – not 'nature' with man, as a combining of the human and earthly above the tide mark, but now 'the sea' with man. Water, bearing ships, leads to other lands and lives. But England, surrounded by water, is where the vessels of our journeys stop, rest and feed.

> I rose from England much refreshed, but returned
> at evening; much undone that was once good
> prior to this mean juncture. It was joy,
> beside myself, to see the new fields. Whose
> is this land that, like waiting flesh, turns
> with a kiss, domestic, but yet is
> a local habitation with no substance or name
> sustaining it? It is the ship's pasture,
> its interlinking husk of submarine,

COMPLETE POEMS

sea-spike, the sleeted fields of destruction:
for payment, for emolument. I am
a part of this...

('The Ship's Pasture')

Here is a quite open appearance of Silkin the pilgrim, the visionary, the travelling anti-priest. The tone could be from *Piers Ploughman* or *The Pilgrim's Progress*. He returns to the north and finds himself and his place:

...This is what it is. Northwards,
a new Jerusalem with the lamb lies separate
its shade dense and lovely.

('The Ship's Pasture')

In the six years since *The Psalms with their Spoils*, poems had been published in an even more varied and international range of journals: *Agenda*, *Al Hamishar* (Israel), *Arab Times Supplement* (Kuwait), *Critical Quarterly*, *Equivalencias* (Spain), *Graham House Review* (USA), *Hubbub* (USA), *Iron Magazine*, *Ironwood* (USA), *Jewish Chronicle*, *London Review of Books*, *Louisville Review* (USA), *Ma'ariv* (Israel), *Michigan Quarterly, Minnesota Review, Moznayim* (Israel), *New Statesman, New Poetry 6, Ninth Decade, Not just another pile of bricks, Poems for Poetry 84* (Poetry Society), *Poetry Australia, Poetry Ireland Review, Poetry Review, The Poet's Voice, Post Modern Writing* (Australia), *Prairie Schooner* (USA), *Prospice, Quarto* (New University of Ulster), *The Reaper* (USA), *Stand, Telescope* (USA), *Thalatta, Times Literary Supplement, Wooster Review* (USA) and *Words*. Anthologies also feature in the acknowledgments alongside *Between Comets: A festschrift for Norman Nicholson at seventy* (edited by William Scammell), as do the BBC, Mammon, Menard and Taxus Presses, the Schools' Poetry Association, the Sixth World Congress of Poets and Mishkenot Sha'ananim (Jerusalem). Many aspects of Silkin's interests, both their range and their often intense focus, are revealed in this list. There is the deeply 'felt' process of travel and discovery; the two-way pressure of noting the new (and being visible there) while requiring contact with culture from the old – England (the north) *and* his historic, Jewish identity. Australia *and* Israel, radio *and* printing, universities, schools *and* informal community groups. There are Arab and Israeli journals; celebrations of the international and cross-cultural, and part of a festschrift for Norman Nicholson, a poet who stayed in one town in the Lake District throughout his life. And Silkin's poetry is, in this volume, if anything, speaking even more confidently from this international language and experience, while 'feeling' the historical present. The poems are dramatic, verbalisations of the extraordinary; they are not simple descriptions.

While some of the historical poems are consciously based in exploring a language both torn and compressed between times and cultures, some in *The Ship's Pasture* overtly bring original figures and their speech into the modern. 'Poems concerning Salome and Herod' uses a seedy setting for what is often portrayed as luxurious, and the words are offhand and urban. But note how the mode switches into the dazed or hazy multi-layering of vision almost immediately:

Look, she said then, made thin and small. I'm still
a damsel. Look, have a cigarette.
Ah, I say, no thanks. The mutant air weeps.

Go on, she tells me. 'I think I feel afraid.'
Well if you are, then don't. The bed-shaped room
contains a primus and a fire. Chased limbs,

thin face, her buttocks fondled to thin moons.
– But kiss me, please. Or see here, a different prize.
She kneels, and, from a chest under her bed

she lifts the Baptist's head up to the light.

('Salome's life')

To move from 'no thanks' so quickly to 'The mutant air weeps' is a surprise. One might almost hear a precedent in these lines for overheard or imagined conversations in *The Waste Land*. Despite his horror at Eliot's anti-Semitism, Silkin admired his work immensely. And the characteristic interplay in Eliot between the rendering of facts and overt speech from player-participants, and tacit, unheard comments of the main observer-narrator, is here in Silkin. Perhaps such techniques, involving a balance between the observable (realistic?) and the lightning, but silent, internal manipulation and response has always been part of his poetry; although in many poems, from the earliest publications to the last, it is the internal drama only which reaches the page.[30] I suspect that the internal switches in 'ownership of the voice' have been thought of as uncertainty of tone, and have led to some readers reacting with concern about what they perceive as over-dense, 'clotted' or 'gnarled' language.[31] Pausing (as one has to do when reading Eliot or Virginia Woolf) to get used to voices enacting the 'mutant', the changes of lens, or swapping vocal cords, one needs time to acclimatise to Silkin's drama. Perhaps with this *Complete Poems* it will seem more natural and involving to follow the 'voice plays'. There has been a significant interval since his death and one might hope for a new hearing of his language games; indeed, reflecting on Wittgenstein's understanding of language freed from scientistic or realistic one-to-one limitations, Silkin's 'shifts' may now come more easily to the reader.

There was a six-year gap before the next book. *The Lens-Breakers* was published in 1992 by Sinclair-Stevenson. In the interval Silkin had been producing substantial pamphlets of poem-sequences and working on *The Penguin Book of First World War Prose* (co-edited with Jon Glover, and published by Viking in 1989 and Penguin in 1990). He continued to edit *Stand*, as well as teaching, running workshops and giving readings. Between 1991 and 1994, he was mostly based in Japan, where he lived with Toshiko Fujioka, and taught English and American literature at the University of Tsukuba. As one might expect, the poems in *The Lens-Breakers* had been published widely, with acknowledgments including *Agenda*, *American Poetry Review* (USA), *Antioch Review* (USA), *Bogg* (USA), *Cencrastus*, *Encounter*, *First and Always* (Faber), *Images of Africa* (Wateraid), *The Independent*, *In forma di parole*, *Iowa Review* (USA), *The Jewish Chronicle*, *Kenyon Review* (USA), *Korean Herald*, *Lines Review*, *London Review of Books*, *Metaphor beyond time* (UPLI Korean Center), *Mississippi Review* (USA), *Morden Tower (High on the Walls)*, *New Letters* (USA), *New Writing* (1991), *Poetry Ireland Review*, *Poetry Review*, *Prospice*, *Skoob Review*, *Stand*, *Staple Magazine*, *Tel-Aviv Review*, *Tikkun* (USA) and *World Poets* 1990. Poems were broadcast by BBC radio in the UK and by National Public Radio in the USA. Looking at this list, prestigious American journals occur most frequently. If you remove the Scottish, Irish and Asian titles, English magazines are in the minority. This may have been Silkin's choice; perhaps he preferred to send poems abroad. It may have been influenced by the decisions of non-UK editors – they liked his work and hoped to receive submissions. It may have been that he was becoming less popular in England. Certainly, some of the poems in *The Lens-Breakers* suggest that his relationship with England and the English had become, in the recent usage, conflicted. Whether or not the speaker of 'To a lighthouse' is Silkin himself, it is symptomatic:

> After years I turned home, self-hatred
> shredding my leaves, my feet huge
> as a horse-chestnut's leaf, dray, Clydesdale
> useless for loads. How I forfeited self
> with hatred, how I stabbed it over
> and planned death.
>
> ('To a lighthouse')

And he returns to the theme of *The Ship's Pasture*. The traveller is brought back for nourishment, however ambivalent:

> This resort of ships, my home.
> Between the privacies of break-water I fed
> self-hatred, as I was fed
> madness and seaweed…
>
> ('To a lighthouse')

However, although the poems are related to the present and to events in his personal life, there is the recurring schema of connections leading outwards to the wider world and other links feeding inwards. Graves, burial and water strain, stain and strain (the other meaning) through the religious earth. The first poem in the volume seems to make a clear pitch at his established readers' knowledge of him; and to present something comprehensible to a new reader:

> With a sickle, I tended the dead in London
> shortening the grass that had flowered
> on their bodies, as it had in my child's.
> And I piled the soil over the paupers' flesh
> in their flimsy coffins which split. What else

was I to do? It became
my trade, my living.

('Urban grasses')

There again is that sense that nature with man is not just an aesthetic trope; it is a real and active merging: 'as it had in my child's'. It is not a pretty compensation; the grass is 'in' for a reason.

The whole of the second section is worth quoting in full since it involves a dialogue with himself, with the dead, and with himself as the future dead person. Questing and questioning are still there, and it is a poem of ruthless self-exposure. But is it a poem of anger and rebellion, as it might have been in previous books? The poem structures its own answer:

> Earth, I shall be unhappy to not know
> how you go on, when I'm like those
> I tended, shearing the grasses
> above their foreheads. I felt tenderness
> yet I did not know them – and how should I re-assure
> because you are nothing now. Yet you are nothing.
> Could I have dared tell them?
> and therefore I remained silent.

('Urban grasses')

The book ends with 'Fathers', a poem reflecting on his father's ashes. That said, 'reflecting' is hardly accurate or adequate. As usual, it is a poem of dialogue – between him and his mother, between him and his father, and between them all and our merging, again, with nature. It would appear from the poem that he scattered his father's ashes on his mother's grave. Somehow, it seems as though this 'reintegration' of person with person and flesh with the soil has been written with his finger:

> …leaving
> the father's spiny fibres, by her
> chewed to gossamer,
>
> his consubstantial self in her dry diligence
>
> the father my ignorant
> finger made dust of.

('Fathers')

Several friends of Jon Silkin have told me that they heard him describing poetry as 'sculptural'. I may have heard the same, though none of us can give a date or a precise interpretation. It is not clear whether he meant 'sculptural' to explain the process of writing (putting it together or chipping it out) or to help the reader to see or feel the components of a poem as though they were tactile. I have often thought of relating the 'sculptural' to Wilfred Owen's 'Strange Meeting'. Silkin had an enormous familiarity with the poem and had studied the manuscript drafts.[32] In some ways it parallels a lot of the structures of Silkin's own poems. Owen imagines escaping from battle 'Down some profound dull tunnel'. It is a journey into the rocks, underneath a battlefield, and eventually the speaker realises it has been an escape of sorts but an escape into hell. He meets the soldier he had himself killed, who reflects on their experience of war and proposes 'Let us sleep now'. The 'sullen hall' is full of the dead, 'the encumbered sleepers'. In a way, the escaping soldier has to feel his way into a mortuary, or an awful gallery in which the living have been turned into still, dead sculptures. The gallery itself has been 'scooped' and 'groined' as though it were a primitive mine, or itself a chiselled work of memorial art. And while Owen 'seems' to have escaped, Silkin is often going through the same process as he merges with the earth. Penetrating the underworld, as the dead do, is something which fascinated Owen; and for Silkin grass, roots and water engage him on a similar journey. As he follows the language of 'merging with death' he produces not a two-dimensional, flat experience, but one that is three-dimensional, with tangible, if slippery, forms.

'Lens-breakers' is a remarkable poem mixing the sculptural with a very personal understanding. Try not to think of this as reportage or, as Keith Douglas thought of seeing the outside world, 'extrospection'. Imagine that what is being seen is also seeing. Imagine Silkin's mind projecting outwards and inwards as the lenses from a disused lighthouse lantern are being broken up. Imagine, as in some early theory of light and eyesight, that the lighthouse lens works both ways: it illuminates the world for ships to navigate and without it they are 'lost'; imagine, too, that it is like the human eye, a source of information and intelligence. Now imagine that, as men so often have done,

They wedge at a sledgeable angle, and splinter

the eyes, like a peacock's feathers' eyes, their alert
serene mercury heating to a chlorophyll
in a leafy beam of fifteen miles,
that cannot see. The light flutters
like a butterfly, I'm sure.

On hammers, blistering glass.
The ostrich digests iron; the loch's
wary salt shunts glass under it. The lighthouse
wears no eyes.

('Lens-breakers')

They destroy their own means of perception and sight. As a poem,
'Lens-breakers' engages with the banality of such behaviour: it is
not a planned act with the hauteur or superiority of poetry, it is in
with the muck:

The men of divine darkness spattered with drunk vomit
after their work. Tools
lean in the corners of housing.

('Lens-breakers')

After returning to England from Japan in 1994, Silkin and his
partner, Toshiko Fujioka, lived first at Beamish Hall in County
Durham, and then in Jesmond, Newcastle-upon-Tyne. As well as
continuing to edit *Stand*, he wrote poems with the same energy as
ever. He also worked hard on a new critical book that was, in
effect, a study of what poetry is, its sounds, rhythms and methods
of organisation. It used enormously impressive close reading of
major twentieth-century poets, including some on whom he had
previously written critical studies or whose work he had edited.
As so often, it was also in part a collaborative work for which he
asked friends and colleagues to add an appendix. It provides an
important insight into recent poetry in general, and his own work
in particular. *The Life of Metrical and Free Verse in Twentieth-Century
Poetry* appeared from Macmillan in the UK and St Martin's in the
USA. He also became involved in proposals with Sheffield
Academic Press, which had an important background in publishing
Jewish and biblical studies but no experience in publishing poetry
(although they had published a study by Neil Roberts of Peter

Redgrove's poetry[33]). He negotiated a contract to produce his next book, *Making a Republic*, and, with Jon Glover, was working on a project with the Sheffield press to write himself, or commission, a number of study guides on contemporary poets. He also agreed with the Cargo Press, Cornwall, to produce a small collection of his poetry with Jewish connections. This appeared in 1998 as *Testament Without Breath*. Of these projects, only *The Life of Metrical and Free Verse in Twentieth-Century Poetry* appeared before he died in November 1997. *Making a Republic* appeared in 2002 from Carcanet/Northern House.

The sources for poems in *Making a Republic* include *Agenda*, *The American Poetry Review*, The Bay Press, *The Centennial Review*, *Choryu Shi Ha* (Tokyo), *Closer Links*, *Comparative Criticism*, *Cúirt Journal* (Ireland), *Electric Rexroth* (Japan), *European English Messenger*, *European Judaism*, *Icarus*, *The Independent*, *Jewish Chronicle*, *The Jewish Quarterly*, *Living Room* (Japan), *London Review of Books*, *New Letters*, *New Writing* 5 and 6 (Vintage with the British Council), *New Statesman and Society*, *Orbis*, *Ore*, *Other Poetry*, *Pigeonhole*, *Poems for Bosnia*, *Poems Now* (Mito, Japan), *Poetry and Audience*, *Poetry Kanto* (Japan), *Poetry Review*, *The Poet's Voice*, *Prairie Schooner*, *Printed Matter* (Japan), *Quarry* (Canada), *The Rialto*, *Salzburg Poetry*, *Stand*, *Staple*, *Sunday Telegraph* and *Ulitarra* (Australia). To sustain such a list of journal publication was a remarkable testament to Silkin's energy. Between finishing the poems for *The Lens-Breakers* and almost completing those to appear in *Making a Republic*, Silkin had left his lecturing post in Tsukuba, received an Arts Council England award to support his writing, and had further developed his collaborative writing methods. He also became a Visiting Fellow in the School of English at the University of Leeds, and began the lengthy process of negotiation leading to the relocation of *Stand* there. He imagined that he would be able to put some distance between himself and the day-to-day running of the magazine, so lightening some of the burden on him given his increasingly worrying state of health. The reader may imagine the difficulty this strategy would pose for someone whose very living had been dedicated to writing, sharing *and* editing.

Many of the journals listed in his previous books were acknowledged again; most from the UK and the USA but five from Japan. *European Judaism* and *The Jewish Quarterly* are there, and *Poetry and Audience* from Leeds is back. The group of poems to appear first as a group was in a substantial pamphlet, *Watersmeet*, published with facsimiles of the drafts by The Bay Press. Silkin worked on this sequence in collaboration with Peter Bennet. Again, the poem as a process of dialogue was celebrated.

There are various forms in which poets might collaborate. When Silkin worked creatively with another person, was it a response to uncertainty or a feeling of enjoyment from prompting a complementary insight? The drafts of 'Watersmeet' were passed to and fro. Some other poems were translated into Japanese by Toshiko Fujioka, and I can only surmise that this might have provided a useful sounding board for seeing and hearing key aspects of his work through a language that provided almost a different medium. Doubtless, he advised and commented. But there are two other relationships indicated in the poems which almost acknowledge a sort of collaboration. 'Two Poems Concerning Jews in England' is dedicated to Emanuel Litvinoff. Perhaps it was Litvinoff, through his advice on 'The Coldness', who helped Silkin to speak both of and for the Jews. 'The Jews of England' explicitly links his own lineage through to the deaths of his parents and his son in London:

> We cannot fight for each other
> who fight each other. It is death that's flowered
> our common hatred, and unshared sorrow.
> Sometimes in my weeping, I taste their salt.
>
> ('The Jews of England')

And in the second poem, 'The Jews in England', he associates this bodily lineage with the birth of his language, his form of 'English'.

> I had no voice, and borrowing one I made English harsh
> which is your tender complex English.
> It is your language, and I must look for mine.
>
> ('The Jews in England')

It is possible that this is a 'persona' poem giving voice to his Japanese partner, but as so often in his work, the process of merging and exchange is paramount. Litvinoff, who had spoken Yiddish and fought with the Allies against Germany in the desert, had helped Silkin to see his own self as a form of translation; and here was

Silkin remaking himself in England, having had (or chosen) to remake himself in Japan. The transformations of language as a personal 'identifier' are multiple and complex, and they reopen the notion of delayed collaboration with Wilfred Owen in forms of escape into a sculptured tunnel of words, conflict and identity – and, ultimately, death. In a sense, for Silkin, the sculpture of language was as much an 'escape' into battle as out of it. All of the participants in this dialogue are war-experienced, if not war-weary.

The next poem re-enacts similar parallels. 'The Life of a Poet: i.m. Isaac Rosenberg, in the First War' is dedicated to Denis Silk. Silk was born in London in 1929, like Silkin, did National Service, and then went to Israel where he worked as a journalist for many years. He was also a major poet and editor. Silkin worked with him and they were talking in their last years of producing a new edition of Rosenberg's poems.

> Rosenberg, you do not talk easily. You write
> and life springs up poems like warriors
> in the war which killed you.
>
> ('The Life of a Poet')

In part, it is a poem 'of address', speaking to and with people whose implicit replies and demands determine Silkin's interventions. Rosenberg's refusal, as Silkin saw it, of the formal organisations of tone in English poetry, offered a means of collaboration over the years and beyond death; active, organic language spoke upwards and downwards, as it were, through burial. But like many poems in *Making a Republic*, 'The Life of a Poet' is intimately personal. That intimacy includes a shared political breadth of language and speech – who owns, oppresses or frees up what I say?

The more one re-examines the poems in *Making a Republic*, and keeps in mind his work on the Cargo Press pamphlet compiled at the same time, the more one is encouraged to see Silkin's work as a whole. This whole included a repeated self-examination and self-dramatisation in relation to events and surroundings with which he had lived since childhood and early adulthood. If this offers a new coherence, some of it might seem to be at odds with aspects of how he was perceived and how he projected himself, on at least some occasions.

A test case might be based on how he used to introduce 'Death of a Son' in public readings compared with how that poem might now be read as part of a life-long exploration of death, burial, and nature merging with man. He used to read the poem as an implicit or explicit protest against the inhumanity of the State and its agencies towards the vulnerable. These words are from his introduction on the 1967 Argo (vinyl) record including his reading of 'Death of a Son':

> This is a poem called 'Death of a Son (who died in a mental hospital aged one)'. When this book was first reviewed on the BBC the critic then said that he thought this poem was a poem of acceptance. Well, that may be, although acceptance and resignation – I think that was the word he used actually – is not really part of the vocabulary of this poem and I'd like to explain precisely why. Adam – that was the child's name – when he was nearly one year old, was summoned by County Hall, together with his mother, to come in order that he might be Certified. And what happened was that the mother and the child were kept waiting in a draughty corridor for about four hours and Adam caught pneumonia and died shortly afterwards. Now I know that defective children are subject and very vulnerable to illness, and it seems probable, perhaps even likely, that Adam would have died very early on. My own feeling, looking back on the whole thing, is that he didn't need the LCC to help him on his way.[34]

It is worth recalling that 'County Hall' was the massive headquarters building of the London County Council, set immediately across the River Thames from the Houses of Parliament. 'Certified' is a word hardly used today, though it was commonly understood to mean officially judged as mentally insane or incapable of normal, rational behaviour. Silkin's description seems to come from another world now, especially when applied to a baby. Particularly difficult seem the mismatch of a formal, legal and constitutional setting for what amounted to 'abuse'. Oddly, though Silkin excludes himself from being present, he would have had a very clear sense of the geographical authority of the location, given his family background in law, and the fact that by 1952 his uncle, Lewis, had been Deputy Leader of that same LCC, was the first Baron Silkin of Dulwich, and had held ministerial roles in the Labour government.[35]

With this certification, Adam would be cared for in the mental hospital of the poem's title. I have listened to Silkin introduce this poem many times in public readings, as well as having transcribed his words from the record. Usually his live account would be factually similar, and it contained a similar mix of calm anger, sorrow and disbelief (at the 'authorities'). But perhaps there were also two levels of dissociation. He did not explain his own apparent absence from County Hall, or his family's association with the building. He also did not record or prepare readers for the substance of the poem on the page or his reading of it. The words in the poem itself, and his son Adam's death, are in another world; not the world of law, medicine, institutions or cruel misunderstandings, but one of a visionary 'counter-reality', in which the awesome solidity of the massive stonework of County Hall have become the crazy bricks and mortar of Adam's body.

It might be worth exploring this duality further in the published poems and in the poems included in this volume for the first time. It might be tempting to suggest that the 'dissociation' noted here indicated something ill thought through. Perhaps he was not aware that his public face of angry campaigning, and overt political commitment, might seem at odds with the mysterious, even religious, core of so many of the actual poems. However, I would like to suggest that in practice the vision of 'nature with man' was not separate from the hurt, politically active person, but was fundamental to it.

Silkin's unpublished and uncollected poems

Each of Silkin's books had its own organisation and rationale. Of course, there were also restrictions of costs and the publisher's own feeling for the appropriate size of a poet's next slim volume. This *Complete Poems* offers a chance to make new overviews, and to raise many queries. The obvious questions regarding the poems left out by Silkin himself from books published in his lifetime might be: Are they any good? Are there many poems which, by Silkin's own standards, were obvious failures? Might many, or any, have fitted within the ethos, themes and techniques of his books from each relevant period? What, if anything, do the 'new' poems add to our understanding of Silkin and his work? Are there poems which are outstandingly interesting and make one ask why on earth they have not been published before now? We must bear in mind that some of the poems that we have included were published in journals, but never chosen for inclusion in the books. Readers will, we hope, be as puzzled as we have been by Silkin's choices.

We have found nine uncollected poems written during the period up to around 1954 and *The Peaceable Kingdom*. They are varied in technique and theme. But one astonishing fact is the extent to which they fit within the patterns of thought and feeling that seem to have been unifying factors throughout his life. 'Gentile, Mohhamedan' (sic) affirms that we all die

> the same death
> Man is provided for.
> There's not a crouched-up breath
> That is not joined in death's
> Perplexity.
>
> ('Gentile, Mohhamedan')

And, bearing in mind the role played by Isaiah, and Edward Hicks's *Peaceable Kingdom*, in Silkin's poetry from the 1950s till his death, it is fascinating to find in the same poem:

> … Now, upon the earth
> The lion and the lamb
> Never shall be at one.

Several poems speak from within gardens, flowers, flames. Some involve the sea and ships (and submarines) in ways which prefigure components of *The Ship's Pasture* nearly 40 years later. Two stand out as radically different, and add something new. 'Manley's Hands' is unusual as a poem of personal experience and observation.

> When I needed advice
> I would find Manley in his shop
> standing, shortly, master over his tools;
> as he explained, construed, and defined
> the arts of his calling
> for my working…

>   From fifty-nine years'
>   feeling out the seams
>   of sanded planks rendered flush,
>   Manley's hands were wood-worn smooth…
>
>   ('Manley's Hands')

'For a mad child among mad children (The Fountain Hospital, 1953)' has an awkward beginning, but partway through changes into a moving evocation of the non-contact, which is contact nonetheless, between himself and the disturbed children from their own other worlds:

>   So I must care for them rather than bear
>   The charity of the mad, who like ghosts can leave
>
>   Me when they choose, though I cannot embrace or kiss them.
>   Beyond the ordered communication of words
>   (I include charity, sentiment here, affection)
>
>   You cannot reach them by desiring this;
>   But as they smile and touch you, you may go –
>   No-one can touch till the other desires it so.
>
>   Though the mad go trampling through our kingdom still
>   These children eat when hungry, when they are dead lie still.
>
>   ('For a mad child among mad children…')

It is an astonishing product of form (long rhyming lines) and a philosophical querying of the meanings of words, with his self-reflection on being with those called mad.[36]

Between 1954 and 1958 there are 21 unpublished poems ranging from 'To My Son', again on life and death, 'And on the ground rests like…', again on our closeness to the earth, 'She is milk-tender beauty…', again linking the flow of liquids from the body to the merging processes of nature with man, to a poem in which Kierkegaard addresses his God, and a poem celebrating Albert Schweitzer's visit to England. This last was published in *Africa Today*, an early example of Silkin's going out of his way to find unexpected places for his poems. It is now hard to read – is it a hymn to Schweitzer or does it suggest something patronising? It concludes thus:

Command us, for our actions, this atonement;
Let us see the clearing in your tiger shade.

Example.

We have your actions; we have these words; cut down the dark
Glades. Cut down, you say. We might follow.

> ('The Forests: On the occasion of
> Dr. Schweitzer's visit to England')

The declamatory tone ('Command us, for our actions…'), seems
alien now. But perhaps we have to recognise and allow such a tone
for the young Silkin, since he, like many others, positioned himself
within possible languages after the war. Circumstances
'commanded' actions with accompanying orations; should not
poets fall in?

Silkin experimented with a rugged 'the-landscape-can-take-it'
tone in 'War Song to an Ocean Headland', rueful anger in a poem
of failed love, 'By that house where we met…', and more explo-
rations of flowers, gardens, roots and parks. It is sometimes difficult
to feel positive about the 'thinking poems' when the tone actually
distances both writer and reader from what might be happening:

Hostile to the age? But if the garden change
The qualities of its growth, be one of these
Who struggles with new complexities,
Though you fight casually. Look to this ground…

> ('Park: to G.S.F in his anger and bitterness')

The last two lines seem to sum up something more interesting
poetically than what was prepared in the long poem that precedes
them:

Walk through the park, against time's plunging stream
Though walking the new, enriched ground is dread.

> ('Park')

From 1958 to 1965 Silkin was based in Leeds although, towards
the end, he was increasingly exploring other places in the UK and
other countries. He was writing more poems than could appear in

The Re-ordering of the Stones in 1961, and we include 25 here – enough for another book. Some are long and illustrate the scope of his interests, with some of the tensions. 'A Walk in the Sun' is as much a struggle in 'the ferocious dark … walking in the atrocious dark' as a reflection on the pleasures of sunlight. It is in 27 diamond-shaped stanzas. Many of his recurring images, or nightmares, are there, and the dialogues are with animals as well as with someone holding a knife.

> Never before was I so
> Unwilling
>
> To pass my earthly
> Heritage which is a small walk in the sun
> But the knife blade
> Sings so
>
> Sweetly in the hot night
> I am afraid with all my heart to die.
>
> ('A Walk in the Sun')

Birds are singing but the dogs are around. On one hand, it could be read as a 'confessional' poem (appropriate for the date) which paints personal pain into a mythologised setting. On the other, it might be seen as overfull of diversions; the heart-wrenching events are never revealed. Although one might suggest that in some ways it parallels the awful conclusion of Kafka's *The Trial*, it perhaps does not justify its conclusion with such terrible logic. 'Palinurus', derived from Virgil's *Aeneid*, mixes the business of voyaging, navigating, betrayal and social loyalties with the sea and its underworlds. This is a vital poem in preparation for reading *The Ship's Pasture* more than twenty years later. 'The Making Act' is about Haydn and music. 'For the disestablishing of Authority (Poem to be laid reverently on the gown of every University when it dies)' is opposed, as it were, by 'For the Poor: Poem on the City of Leeds Rubbish Tip'. The former is an overworked satire; the latter is an interesting amalgam of many of Silkin's reference points: fire, water, the rejected. It is in long lines, and is here followed by 'Tip' which, with short lines, is a slimmed down and altered version. 'For the Poor' and 'Tip' give a good example of the way in which

Silkin either expanded or reduced his drafts. 'Europe' is an example of his main components working at full throttle:

> The stream is, the roaring stones are
> Full of God. The tree hides him
> Like sap. He openly smiles…

('Europe')

Whereas 'A Space Together' shows them working more quietly and effectively:

> Then soft as thoughts within
> Love's companioning, she nears,
>
> And bares silently
> The feet she came on.
>
> And like a fawn moon
>
> Subdued in its brilliance
> Of lustred fawn snow
>
> She bares all herself.

('A Space Together')

At their best, these poems would add new topics and techniques to *The Re-ordering of the Stones*. They certainly help to develop one's sense of the overall patterns and concerns of Silkin's thinking. Often the threats and horrors are self-imposed within the poems' structures; he exposes, and experiments, with his own responses and metaphoric refuges. At best, the metaphors shiver into a real sense of naturally creative merging, attack or death's decay.

There are 35 uncollected or unpublished poems between 1961 and 1965, again enough for a whole volume that could have appeared before, or along with, *Nature with Man*. One extraordinary poem, 'Much did you think', seems to have been prompted by an interview, 'No Politics, No Poetry', between Silkin and Anthony Thwaite which was published in *Stand*:[37]

> Much did you think
> Of the mutilated creatures

That move in my poems:
The fly that is torn, and the sharp
Fox who is followed…

('Much did you think')

It is partly a re-imagined dialogue with Thwaite, partly a conver-
sation with England and the English, in which Silkin argues for a
pact whereby his critics will admit that Jews have been killed, and
that he, then, will cease engaging with his tortured and slaughtered
animals. The interview was celebrated when published, whether
or not it recorded a fair impression on either side. However, the
poem was just in encapsulating what were probably Silkin's
emotions, and makes a singular mark in dramatising the various
attitudes without being abstract and distant:

What do you think to this?
Come; make a pact.

('Much did you think')

There are poems which might seem overtly political or
programmatic, at least from their titles: 'Why We Are All Socialists'
and 'What Each Person Wants'. Both explore political conscious-
ness in friends or colleagues and, of course, in the speaker as he
narrates the vision (bearing in mind that the vision includes the
apparent reality of drinking too much). Both poems end with
extraordinary assumptions about how the world will work; it is
surreal, or caught up in some post-apocalyptic self-consumption.
This is the first conclusion:

By working in the world
Where, like a plant-owner, greed fingers
Its seated swollen belly,
Fobbed with a hunter-chain.
The flesh bears itself on.

('Why We Are All Socialists')

In some senses these are very personal poems, despite their political
frameworks. In virtually all in this group, the personal is political;
person, body and social interaction are inseparable. Even what
might seem an ordinary conversation between lovers is manifest in
verbal self-analysis:

Speaking of love, you said,
'Not morals, but passion entails
Forms from the shifting splinters
Of processes – from which
We say love is stable,
Permanent.' 'Love' I said
'Is...' You completely
Leaned forward, and kissed me
As if you were naked.

('Choosing')

Many of the prompting conversations or conflicts – whether between man and woman, or person and stone – fall into similar structures; the speaker is prompted by some act of love, or perceived indifference, so that the 'other' is out there, but plays no active part in the debate. It would be wrong to say that the prompt comes from some perverse muse, but the notion that Silkin is literally and metaphorically 'the author' of his own perplexed self-analyses in these poems is not far from the case. In some ways, the long, thought-based and thought-provoking poems in this group are a profound and moving success. Some, one might suspect, are the result of deeply intimate mental wounds. However, this whole section of uncollected work from 1961 to 1965 is very well developed and is worthy of attention as an important achievement in Silkin's overall body of work; a hitherto unknown component of poetry in English from the 1960s.

There are only nine unpublished poems filed from 1965 to 1971. They seem well thought through. As so often, Silkin explores the anatomy of qualities and beings that one would not have thought possible. Who would have conceived of a reaction to the water-dispute between Israel and Jordan depending on the scent of eucalyptus:

From fierce
Syria, Arab smells irrigate our glands,
dilate and secrete, conflict with an
intelligence of what a plant is that is Arab.

[...]

The Jordan brims us
with a fertility that's a
contagion
of them in us

the mortality
of water;
the dear
in it.

('Water Dispute')

The poem fits well into his sensuous causality of relations between
the environment and the human. Nevertheless, the oppositions
might seem too schematic.

The physical intrusion of words into living things is a frequent
surprise, and an engaging, if perplexing, theme. Words, gender and
nature interplay, and many aspects are personalised. 'Kevin, can
you remember' is a remarkable fusing of processes – mixing
concrete, planting trees, and 'rooting' a man. 'Sea Anemone', in a
similar way, tries to draw together, and also to extract physically,
opposing perceptions – the sea anemone as fixed, 'grown /
Through rock' and yet actively sexual, aggressively ambivalent in
its identity:

... it is a plant animalising
Its members, an animal
Cautioned to the rock, stuck there
For food.

('Sea Anemone')

Surely Silkin will have been thinking of Lawrence's poem when
he wrote 'Snake'. Lawrence's novels and poetry were important
to him, and perhaps both men shared something of the same fasci-
nation with the earth's movements:

The bodies of the dead linger
In the earth's fertile skin, where substance is molten,
And rests, coiled like a slack whole spring,
Waiting to be tempered.

('Snake')

There are nine poems from 1971 to 1974 that did not appear in *The Principle of Water*. They include a fairly long poem, 'The Clay Image', which typically embeds Silkin's active process of feeling his way into the natural as it felt its way into him. There is an epigraph from the Proverbs of the Digger Indian: 'In the beginning God gave to every people a cup of clay and from this cup they drank their life'. There is an initial speaker, then a dialogue between Man and Clay, followed by a concluding speaker. In some ways it re-enacts the underworld interpenetrations of Dylan Thomas's 'A Refusal to Mourn the Death, by Fire, of a Child in London'. Strangely, the speaker is already dead:

And so, Love, if this is the flesh which wraps
These fulfilled dead in vessel of clay flesh
I, being dead, one of those dead who glide
Through the city like angel fire-torn with
The burning multitudes of shrapnel...

('The Clay Image')

Here, the clay is very much the clay as it appears in the Bible, and Silkin offers an interesting mix of being the product of God's hands, and his (Silkin's) being the maker.[38] He often writes as though performing a religious ceremony, and it is as though a biblical prompt will produce such a lengthy 'act' or ritual:

MAN
I have been given hands that I may know
The gentleness of plants, the moisture which
Clings to each leaf and clips within its bowl
Light, and all raying elements of air
Which congregates inside that glistening O.

('The Clay Image')

Sometimes in this group of poems, as in others, it is as though the energy of prayer-like language takes hold of him and, willy-nilly, he finds himself praying, or giving the words of prayer to another dramatised speaker:

'I can't. Cloisonné, the blessed
shape in jadeite

et al. My breath's white
shape over glass survives me. Have

I no life but yours
in the next world, all
that spring away?
Lord, answer me.' I ask

('All-eying moon, fury')

From the two years between *The Principle of Water* and *The Little Time-keeper* we have included only two unpublished poems. 'Where much grass drinks from its side' uses two locations – Shap in Cumbria, and the River Tawe, flowing from the Welsh hills to Swansea. Both have long lines (twenty to twenty-five syllables in some), and both work hard on the ways that man and nature exploit and injure each other. It could be said that they show another way in which Silkin's language sometimes gets into a flow which might be self-destructive:

As I moved to
the road again, it [a sheep] was sufficient, turning its head
once more, watching; trod uphill then;
white, territorial; inside a ringed oiliness, a wool coiled like
hoops of muscled electrodes, a strength.
Belongs here, dies, here. Then's pecked, torn, chewed in balls
of woollen meat in a bird's crop stocks.
Out, shat.

('Where much grass drinks from its side')

The other poem is, by contrast, short, sharp and mysterious. It ends with these stunning lines:

Bluebells silence the woods
from which children spill
mauve hair.

('The map hovers open')

These two poems highlight the tension that Silkin himself iden-tified between what he saw as the opposing opportunities of imagism versus narrative. He was tempted to exploit both.[39] He saw that even in lengthy poems with a background (or foreground) story he couldn't resist letting language 'just happen'. The temptation to 'slow down', to let interpenetrating metaphors and similes do what they want, was something he either enjoyed successfully or (depending on the reader's point of view) failed to control. Perhaps he did not appreciate that intense image-making could itself tell stories and explore action. In the quotation above, the long line 'white, territorial; inside a ringed oiliness, a wool coiled like hoops of muscled electrodes, a strength' implies so much action that one wants to stop and, as it were, muscle in; similarly, the bright image of children who 'spill / mauve hair' draws one into immense possible narratives. Did he fear losing control? If so, such fear was perhaps counterproductive, since in the long poems many extraordinary, energetic images may be weighed down by explicit psychological and moral drivers.

The next group of unpublished poems dates from around 1976 to 1980. They share themes of betrayal, including self-betrayal. They explore how place of residence may give people an identity which leads to belief, conflict and death. The first poem, 'In Mary's reign Justice Barton convicts George Marsh of Protestantism at Smithills', uses a local legend from Bolton, Lancashire, that, after his conviction, the Reverend George Marsh in 1555 'stamped his foot on the stone outside the withdrawing room saying, that if his faith was true he would leave his footprint on the stone for all time. This stone […] bears a dark stain roughly the shape of a man's foot'.[40] The story should have made a perfect poem for Silkin – a man is persecuted for his belief and, because of that belief, has the power to write himself into stone. He wrote it the night of his visit to Smithills Hall, but afterwards felt it not good enough to appear in a book.[41] One might wonder whether the reason was that George Marsh's transforming power was provided by 'local history' rather than by the 'field of force'[42] of language.

'Samson's Hair' is also a poem of transformation through adversity and betrayal, although here the fates of Samson and Absolom (Silkin's spelling, although in the Bible it is Absalom), resulting from their long hair, are part of a different power of language. Indeed, the fact that Absolom was killed after he was caught by his beautiful long hair in a tree is something which allows Silkin to share the dynamics of revenge with, or through, Isaac Rosenberg's eyes:

On the other hand, I can understand Absolom's hair.
It is beautiful, clearly, like the sun in its fullness, the moon red
with vengeance.

('Samson's Hair')

Rosenberg uses the setting for an incredible evocation of a sort of
spiritual or aesthetic suspension:

> Caught still as Absalom,
> Surely the air hangs
> From the swayless cloud-boughs
> Like hair of Absalom

('Chagrin')

It might almost be a moment of 'negative capability' before, or at
a time of, battle.[43] That said, it is perplexing that, out of the still
air, Silkin derives a validation of battle, at least in someone's voice:

> This is the most beautiful hair
> in the kingdom, the justifiable
> cause for all revolt,
> and then, the oak.

('Samson's Hair')

In poems from this group Silkin seems to have been allowed (by
himself?) to say without complication or query that some events
or places are just 'beautiful':

> No ancient
> glory, not Jerusalem. But very
> beautiful, very
>
> beautiful. Here a bird treads air
> with a smaller bird, her daughter perhaps.

('Six Poems from Metoula', 1)

Metoula is a small Israeli town near the Lebanese border. To
suggest that the 'Six Poems' are relaxed would be to give the wrong
impression. But their short lines offer up moments of perception
that are doing enormous work without having to strain. Perhaps
the very setting, so close to historical and present conflict, was

enough to perform, by implication, his usual self-conscious self-undermining. It is as though he had come to accept that multi-dimensional border territory was home to him; no need to excuse or justify – here, in all its complexity, was his life.

Was this carried on into the seven unpublished poems between 1980 and 1986? Some use particular places to great effect, and usually with a sense of confident acceptance. That said, there is often a wild sparkle from sites and their history. For example:

> … and fear and gentleness trot like paired cats
> aching for home. Earth holes down three spaces,
> three pools of Solomon's, crusher to filament
> a sensual wilderness. They crush, with an idea
> of God, like fiery skulls.
>
> ('Filaments of the plain')

'The broad Ohio' is another poem of place and river-water; at least that is where it starts. But it metamorphoses into a love poem in which hair is a magical stream:

> Preponderance of hair, that blond thought
> streams the pillow…
>
> ('The broad Ohio', 2)

The six years from 1986 to 1992 produce twenty-one more unpublished poems. *The Ship's Pasture* and *The Lens-Breakers* were Silkin's two longest books of poems (96 pages each) but there were plenty left over. Some are major and complex works. 'A woman from Giannedes' is a dramatic monologue spoken by a woman who was supposed to have been a servant to T.S. Eliot. It is followed by a note about Eliot's anti-Semitism as expressed in *After Strange Gods*. It is a worrying poem and I have not been able to find a source for the particular link with a small Greek town. 'A box of seeds' adds to the complex world of lenses in *The Lens-Breakers* and links it with burial and grass, particularly in 'Urban grasses'. Perhaps 'A box of seeds' is an original longer poem from which others published in the book were cut out and saved. 'The life that is marriage', 'Thief' and 'Veining' are all troubled and troubling; they veer between his reactions to lovers and to his parents. 'Words from below the level of speech' is philosophically rooted in discovering language while emerging from the turmoil of relationships:

> Love, we're in the thick of things, yet not
> blown away by secrets, or the screw's words,
> the whitened roses spattered pink, this summer's night
> where I stood without you.
>
> ('Words from below the level of speech')

'Hospital' is an important sequence of five poems. Hospitals played important roles in Silkin's life, from the birth and death of Adam, the birth of David, and on till his parents' illnesses and deaths, and finally to his own death. Hospitals were the living and dying sites of much nature with man, and these poems are vital to understanding Silkin's poetry as a whole. Some of the poems seem to be set in London in a hospital by the Thames (possibly St Thomas's). The water-traffic, the machinery of hospital treatments, the inner mechanisms of the body all link together:

> On this water, three
> linked barges with demi-johns of chemical
> which, if it spills, the brickwork will lip
> with stalactite-like stains.
> These drive within clear sight
> of the hospital, where nothing heals
> today but as the body can.
>
> ('The sick themselves')

He also uses an overt rhetorical trick of double meanings with the linguistic and medical meanings of 'prolepsis'. In 'Prolepsis' he must have been conscious of the word's use as a device to bring forward an event from the future (e.g. 'the walking dead'), and its use for the increasing rapidity of paroxysms:

> If he breathes and if he builds
> atoms in a crux pathogens will release
> and be eaten by, give the wrists
> in their supple activity, use the needles
> saintly against pain, devoted
> to prolepsis and hope.
>
> ('Prolepsis')

The last poem of the group, 'Hatred and generosity', brings together many of Silkin's most visionary religious impulses. Facing the deaths of others, and chewing on his own, his world is filled with 'noiseless platonists / for whom essence palely imitates / the Messiah's splendour', and, with more philosophical double-takes, he returns to the outside world where death treads on to meet him/us while he himself is (enacts or embodies) death:

> The shaded forms at dawn, pattering the curbs
> of granite half-resolve, the tread over
> white bristling moors, footprints patching intent
> to frost. Why is so much breath here
> and no more? Where are
> there sufficient beds? Snow is filling them.
>
> ('Hatred and generosity')

These lines seem to me to reveal a poet all too conscious of the contradictions in his language, and in himself. On the one hand, one asks why on earth such a moving poem was not published before. On the other hand, the very title of this concluding poem in the group reveals something in his world that he found hard to cope with in public.

As described above, in relation to *The Lens-Breakers*, 1992 to 1997 were momentous years for Silkin and those who lived and worked with him. He seems to have been writing with his usual unstoppable qualities, and so the major collection that he himself prepared, *Making a Republic*, was accompanied by work on other new poems sufficient for another whole book. Some are long, and some are sequences. These may have been difficult to place in journals. But often, the subject matter is frightening and difficult – not only for the potential reader but, one feels, for Silkin himself. The poems in this section are not in any conventional sense 'confessional'; he is unlikely to have felt better as a result of the act of writing or publishing. Despite being involved on the page in entangled and protesting debates with his parents, and with the physical world, one does not find atonement, forgiveness or relief. Perhaps he found some creative or experimental pleasure in having got so far, and a determination to continue to confront, and fight with, the difficult forces. But there is little, if any, appeal for help from others or from 'nature'.

'Two Women' (1 and 2) are unusual in naming individuals and building their speech into the poems. But these are not simple poems 'of record'. Each woman speaks about, or is part of, an apparently natural process, one with which she may be familiar but the writer is not. The first seems 'about' silk spinning; the second 'about' death in a natural (Norwegian) environment:

> You spoke of Earth's spontaneous cruelty.
> And she retaliates. 'I dislike' she says
> 'your writer's fictions, underpinning me.'
>
> ('Two Women, 1. The silk-machine')

> Judy, modest Quaker, you have died. The fledgling, too,
> that lifts a downy menacing under-coat. To retrieve
> nothing from grass's spears. In Norwegian's
> icy experiment, you died. The face
> is blameless.
>
> ('Two Women, 2. A Quaker's death')

Does the dialogue only happen to reveal the invincibility of the other side? In many poems, making love with a human 'other' or, in effect, with air and earth, is an act of self-confirming desperation:

> As the plane slowed, my chest
> as if the Rockies' huge brown lit spine
> we cleared – my sense of you
> as one your land still feasted, opened.

>   … Is it that we
> are too much for each other, hill
> of bone too much, like earth's breaking open
> pain that spurs grass, the lilac cereal?

> Who ever you are, yet who
> but you, your sullen widths of heat…
> … Or amongst
> no child, but three cats pissing
> in urban soil plums
> are flowering. Where will

we be? O, jubilate.

('Jubilate')

I hope that these quoted excerpts from such a long poem will show the complexity of what Silkin is doing. In part, it is a poem of dialogue in which he is thinking about another person. But he is also thinking, inevitably, as their aeroplane descends after crossing the Rocky Mountains, of himself as part of the wider world. And (as so many do when coming in to land) he thinks his mortality and that of others. What is he celebrating as he tries to 'account for' his relationships? What does being a 'wife' (he doesn't mention 'husband') mean? As so often, his responses to such ceremonies are blurred through the force of poetry into links between the powers of language and the powers of the earth. The final words, 'O, jubilate', are profoundly ambiguous. The quotation from Psalm 100 (which is used in the Anglican Canticles) is perhaps there as an intimate and sad irony.[44] It is interesting that 'Make a joyful noise' is addressed to 'all ye lands'. 'Lands' probably means 'countries' or 'peoples'. But for Silkin, in this poem, the physical earth is there implied as well.

What we have called 'Three Poems' is clearly a numbered group but has no definite overall title. Each poem, however, does have a title: '1. Opening the voice of the hungry', '2. Travel by night-train', and '3. Moon snow'. The poems are very long, and hard to summarise, but probably respond to memories of the atom bombs in Japan, and meld with the Shoah and more personal events in England and Scotland. One evocation of a post-bomb city brings out all of Silkin's extraordinary metaphors:

> In the city, charred fatty clothing
> with merged globules of hair, the body's shade
> fixed to a broken wall. I'm dust and light.
> The dead in the bomb's brain, like burned
> out midges, flit in a follicle of uprooted dust.
> Ghosts offer their old-style
> beery smiles like a twisted bottle-opener –
> Japanese beer, a flowery taste: spills
> over the flat Inn flotsams of dried liquid
> its bulge dried in the bomb's hovering fist.

('Moon snow')

The figures of speech are deft, ingenious and shocking; yet they put on the page what one assumes is the extraordinary emotional complexity of Silkin's own brain. One feels that 'The dead in the bomb's brain, like burned / out midges' must record his own skull's inner workings at their terrible worst.

'The soul is ghosted from its flesh' is a poem of great anger and pity. The images of the soul, the flesh and the ghost are played on and related in Silkin's increasingly involved and tortured ways. It is a poem emerging from his consciousness of the killings and cremations of Maidanek in Poland and Buchenwald in Germany. Coats appear as souls which surround the bodies as they, the souls, leave them:

> The soul is ghosted from its flesh
> and the coat comforts the body as if
> it were its soul sifting in cold, on lumpen beautiful stone,
> you don't see this much nowadays.
>
> ('The soul is ghosted from its flesh')

Coats cover doomed bodies as if they were heavy, woven, filthy and now cold auras. The bodies they had once protected are now gassed and dead, so the coats are cast aside as the 'soul's earthly / substance and version'. They are then gassed again to fumigate them, presumably for some form of re-use:

> These rags were more docile than those
> who wore them, less weeping, these twice gassed,
> in their nondescript beauty, in his ragged eyes,
> rack on rack of gassed–drab coats.
>
> ('The soul is ghosted from its flesh')

The poem develops into a visionary cry of fear, despair and torment: 'Jew-woman, my immortal / sexual hatred has you at death's remove'. Having convinced himself of the real presence of the Camps' revelation (enactment?) of man's untrustworthy causal relationships with the Hebrew Adonai, or the Christian God, he has no answers or atonement. This is one of the most self-critical, yet frightened, poems in the whole collection.

'Sally sally' may be one of many poems which refer to real people by name. But it is typical in combining reality with Silkin's compassionate feeling and involvement in the language and grammar of being. Sally has grown in the ten years since, presumably, the poet last saw her:

> She stares at me, such ten years
> like moisture, drop away. People say
> evanescence, but I say death of a form,
> her first dying. The essential irrevocable child-sense
> >> passion, re-woven.
> >> ('Sally sally')

It is a strange mixture of wonder at the child's growth with an inevitable reflection on the philosophy of his own mode of perception. It is a half-amusing, half-rueful digestion of what may have been a jovial chat with the parents: 'People say / … but I say…'. The philosophy ('death of a form') seems Plato come home, forms as the ideal models of life cast aside as a chrysalis. And 'home' is in the outside world where Sally lives – it is her body – but it is also the progressing and speeding machine inside the poet's brain.

Poem after poem reflects on the impending end of Silkin's life. I may be completely misreading 'God said, "in this lifting rim of your life…"', but it seems to plead with his elders to flush him down the toilet with the 'excrement of goodness' to meet God. There is an instant reply: 'fuck you, you're not the angel we thought you were. / Go.' Later he continues his simultaneous emotional and analytical responses to what he sees:

> >> … I see a man, split
> in rags hit by a bus onto a
> pedestrian island, quite still; I am safe,
> essence of my disorder,
> horror nulling itself, some charge in me
> betrayed and ceasing, as this traffic
> hubbed to its spidery riving of mercy
> from its soul, motion vanishes.
> >> ('God said "in this lifting rim of your life"')

This might be an awful parody of the well-known 'I-might-fall-under-a-bus…' (comic?) prediction. In practice, it is partly a complex, shocked and shocking re-working of Rosenberg's 'Break of Day in the Trenches'.

The remaining unpublished or uncollected poems from Silkin's last years include some of his most personal and revealing work. 'Relations', concerning his dying father, opens with one of his recurring images, that of ships at sea or in port:

> Now you're dead father isn't it time we ceased
> speaking, alive silence also held,
> like a wall of wave over
> us two ships, to disintegrate
> its stone?
>
> ('Relations')

Unusually, he and his father speak and touch, though their languages are confused. God is part of the dialogue, and the poet maintains his activity (rather than abstract belief) as a participant in the speaking flux between the living and the dead which combines in the disintegration of the body:

> blessings, father, upon your head
> when I last saw your skull, the day before,
> now way past the grave, what do I know, but still
> air becomes the wind deposing its touch over the earth,
> earth's fatuous kiss. God has not forsaken me.
>
> ('Relations')

There are poems stemming from his Welsh maternal grandparents and his Welsh grandfather's work with stocks of wallpaper ('The line'). And what might be seen as an informal sequence exploring fire may possibly concern his father's cremation, which he may have seen as cheating the more 'normal' kiss of the earth. But, as ever, words such as 'about' or 'concerning' miss the essentially exploratory or ceremonial quality of each poem. The fire group includes 'The basics of fire', 'How fire may find its gentleness', 'Fireball' and 'The sub-text of sadness'. The last of these is one of the major poems of this period. It opens with a characteristic invocation of some catastrophic, explosive event in which Silkin the poet has to search for a response and to join in what dialogue is possible – with himself (himselves?), between others, and

between the heated flux of elements around. The dialogue – nego-
tiation, rather – is perhaps hard to follow. He and his parents and
family, living and dead, chew over possession of their house and
its rooms. As so often, rooms in Silkin's poems are where possession
and sex (possibly love) take place. Rooms are owned, possessed,
and allow for discovery. In a sense, rooms are an extension of the
body, and Silkin continues to merge the owned rooms and furni-
ture of his family house with the new, but recurring, ownership
of and by hospitals:

> I said, the house I now live in
> where you lived, fills with girls, and their men.
>   You said, 'take me to father's and my bedroom.'
> in which brocade hung, colour of rezina.
>   You leaned at the head of this motored hospital bed,
> Me at its foot, much befriending space between…
>
> ('The sub-text of sadness')

There is an unstoppable impulse to speak as though a dead person
is more alive and demanding than the living:

> That's her. But God,
> I am permitted to speak with you, who alive
> am able to speak to you, who dead cannot.
> As I am alive, won't
> you speak with me? For which, thanks.
>
> ('The sub-text of sadness')

It is not an easy poem, though it has an extraordinary trick. Silkin
becomes a London bus-driver or conductor. It is as though passen-
gers become the poet's paying guests. It is shift work, and he is
paid by his 'gentle Maker'. But the passengers also pay, and get
tickets (poems?) in return. And just as he has to help his parents on
their onward journeys, so he feels that he may be about to clock
off:

> I have one further shift, then I accept
> I will switch my lights, these paying guests
> their blessed onward tickets. Forgive me
> for the faint-hearted religious patter.

> Go on, buddy, speak a few words
> won't you, spare a word, immensity wreathed in silence?

> I pass my hand through you.

('The sub-text of sadness')

Some late poems come from time spent in Spain, and a re-discovery of Spanish language and poetry, and the history of the Jews in Spain. At one point Silkin even thought of moving to northern Spain, where the scholarship, philosophy and historic civilisation of the Moors fascinated him, as did the fate of the Cathars in Languedoc. In this group are 'Dark', 'Cathars', 'A room in the Moorish kingdom' and 'Los Barrachos'.

'Motherland' is a long and vital poem in Silkin's work. While it may not be the last or greatest, it certainly sums up a lot of the ideas, emotions and personal projections into his writing process that had become familiar. Starting with his mother's breaking her hip, he pays a tribute to her elderly beauty and her courage:

> Your open face beautiful,
> as mine is not, forms with age. You smile
> and move with a frame. A step, and then another,
> as Hebrew multiplies its basic forms.

('Motherland')

Quickly he has moved into manipulating grammatical, philosoph-ical and religious 'forms'. Then the poem instantly moves to his true, visionary landscape, merging the 'angel born to avenge' with what he admits is his own 'unwillingness for pain'. The angel 'has his job' (as did the bus-driver-poet Silkin) and 'He electrifies me, this / sophisticated being, until that energy / flings me to burn…'.

It may still be possible to come to Silkin's poems from a political context, either through his anger at the treatment of Jews, or from his known sympathy with left-wing political action. But the central thinking of 'Motherland' offers to include the reader in passions more personal – although one may broaden the 'personal' to include all the history of torture, sex, conflict and love which has grown with and into his poems. 'Ashes' might contain verbally, and in reality, all this history: camp victims, ashes of warfare and industry, ashes of our loved ones. But for many readers, the overtly religious here and in other late poems may come as a surprise:

> Is the next world ashes? The stars, mother
> laugh excitedly? Against grief's solid calm
> is reconciliation,
> like a little dancing movement
> in a neutron bulb, possible where giant angels
> fledge and practise wings
> in the webs scabbed with our dead lives?
> Earth's people install
> the plucky angels to rule, and the
> mouth-water on our bodies, crunching deaths,
> only deaths, or we'd disband
> their clapping philohuman wings, barbules
> and hook. We'll have no tyrant goodness
> purse its flashy wings on us. Look, you.
> It's our bones they suck. So we absolve
> us in their punishment, composing
> hosannas, 'Lord, save us'
> or 'Lord, we praise you.'
> Either will do.

('Motherland')

It is tempting to continue quoting till the end, since it is a poem which shows Silkin talking himself into reconciliation, and the reader, if at all sympathetic, will have to follow the movement along, rather than asking to locate a translatable truth or a nice description. 'Motherland' is not a poem 'about' something; it does something. In these lines from near the end, Silkin joins with his mother to sum up history, general and individual:

> Dare we mother, in
> this world's ash and filth
> with kin in the blood,
> in reconciliation mix with the angels, aspiring our
> goodness, who like us
> double-form a dark-and-white grace?
> This is imagined and unnamed.

('Motherland')

We include two late poems in this section that had a restricted circulation in *Testament Without Breath*: 'Arum Lily' and 'The Mimulus Showing Itself'. This handsomely produced booklet, which included some of Silkin's most important poems with Jewish concerns, was arranged in the summer of 1997, before his death in November of that year. It was published by Derek Hines with the Cargo Press in 1998. Seen in the context of the other late unpublished poems, Silkin's desire to offer a clear and relatively brief summation of his poems from his Jewish life and understanding is perhaps more significant than many of his readers might have thought at the time. And the two late 'flower poems' are doubly interesting as a result. They are less tonally aggressive than some from this period but, perhaps as a testament to reconciliation, they are quasi-persona poems in which flowers, at least partly, do the speaking:

> I, arum lily, by this dry water,
> Who am filled with witnessing, unable to die.
> Josephus, apostate, touch me with your darkness.
> One summer's evening fills with history's long spokes.
> Mary, in the recall of all, hurtles like a message from God
>   through my rooted being,
> God of limits.

('Arum Lily')

Re-ordering Jon Silkin

Re-reading the published poems, and studying seriously the unpublished and uncollected work, over a number of years has been exhilarating, frightening and perplexing. One of my major reactions has concerned the fact that I, and perhaps many others, knew only part of such a public figure. The preoccupations of so much of the unknown work add to what we knew, but also query and change it. There are at least three new factors to consider. First, Silkin's immediate family – by which I mean his parents, relatives and children – were troubling figures in his life and poetry until his death. Second, these troubles were imaginatively, religiously and politically integrated with what was, for him, an unavoidable and physical obsession with bodies from conception and birth, through to illness, death and burial. Third, while Silkin was well known as a reader, lecturer, editor and 'sharer' of his own creative processes, and was often thought of as a subversive, politically left-wing and active campaigner, the newly available work forces confrontation with a person more seriously troubled psychologically than one might have believed. He was known as an articulate, argumentative, stimulating, affectionate member of any group; and yet we find someone increasingly worried by and engaged with his Jewish identity and with a religious construction of reality – from his own body and mind to nature, Nature, earth, Earth and the world in general.

Does what I suggest provoke a de-politicising of Silkin and his work? Obviously, in my discussion of the publishing and discovery of his known and unknown poems, I have not had the time and space to link what I have written to all of his published critical and theoretical work; for example, to his 'living' with the Great War poets, including Isaac Rosenberg, as though they were his contemporaries. He was an indefatigable and long-term supporter of the poetry of others, including Ken Smith and Geoffrey Hill. He was one of the later twentieth century's most careful and illuminating 'close readers' of poetry, and a tactful and encouraging helper of others beginning the business of writing poetry – in schools, universities or adult writing and reading groups. Until his death, he had engagements throughout the UK. For many people, he was the most publicly accessible voice of contemporary poetry. The paradox now emerges that this voice was articulating a more anguished and, dare one say, unusual inner life than many might have foreseen.

I am not suggesting that we should now discount Silkin's interest in left-wing, Communist or even Trotskyist thinking, his support for CND, or Trades Union activism, or for Israel, or against any activity likely to foster anti-Semitism or inhumane, violent behaviour by individuals or societies. Silkin was known for his active sympathies and they added to many people's complex politicising of reading and writing poetry. However, this well-known spreading of a political context now needs to be recontextualised in what seems an even more complex mind than we might have thought.

Many will have read 'Death of a Son' and 'The Coldness' in ways which at least saw such poems as exposing man's inhumanity to man, and the proximity of guilty involvement and self-justification in the most shocking treatment of others. What will need some further thought is Silkin's burial theology. That flowers grow and blossom is gratifying if also part of an all-consuming, even aggressive Nature; that the underworld yields minerals for industry, war and exploitation is part of history. That soldiers and miners dig for victory or profit may be true, but in Silkin's poetry it would perhaps be too obvious; Rosenberg's rat had a sense of the lie of the land closer to Silkin's own than that of many.

It has been tempting to try to explain the persistence of Silkin's interpenetrating, 'flowing' nature with man through some eco-theological overview. While there are now Jewish theologies of man's misuse of nature, I suspect that Silkin was not conscious of such thinking as an external psychological or theoretical driver for his poetry. What emerges from the extent and timeless quality, in both the published and unpublished work, of themes of burial and divine re-ordering of flesh suggests that these concepts were largely self-discovered. From *The Portrait* and *The Peaceable Kingdom* to the last poems, he seems to have engaged with a theology that emerged through his own writing, and more from his own reading of the Bible and Milton, Rosenberg and Hill, than through academia.

There are several threads that weave together. Wales, wartime evacuation, isolation from family, discovery of community, his mother's Welsh background, all recur repeatedly; the psychology of parental domination together with being a parent, and finally (very late in his life) seeing his mother and father through illness to old age and death; sex and the sexualised landscape; the Shoah, English, European and American 'normalisation' of Jewish persecution; his discovery of totally different cultures, landscapes, language and personal qualities in Japan. These threads all offer broad settings through which to re-read individual poems.

Was it through the accidents of the commercial publishing process that more of the poems included here are only just being made available? Obviously, Silkin was very prolific as a poet, and the time needed to see new volumes into press more often would have been difficult for anyone. As I have outlined, writing poetry and seeing it published was only one part of his life. Did he consciously leave some of the more challenging poems on one side? Or did he prioritise what he thought were the 'best' poems and leave the others for posterity and the chances of finding publication after his death? Could he have thought some of them were more like private diary entries, records of his most challenging, self-loathing or frightened feelings? I suspect that, from the most practical to the most deeply psychological, most of these questions will have some application to the unpublished work and, by reflection, to the well-known poems also. Whatever the answers might be, readers now have the opportunity to engage with the full range of Silkin's work, from poems written in his teens all the way to those, such as 'Motherland' and 'Will', written towards the end of his life in the late 1990s. We therefore hope that readers of this book will share our gratitude for the fact that Jon Silkin believed it worthwhile to save all of his poems.

Notes

1 To make a list of the writers, famous or unknown, and their letters with Silkin's poem drafts on the reverse, would be an intriguing task, even if it induced rueful or wry smiles.

2 In the 1990s Jon Silkin returned to Wycliffe to read his poetry.

3 Slim volumes of poetry sold well during the war itself, when the printing of long novels was adversely affected by paper rationing. However, after 1945 production of poetry books fell.

4 *South London Observer* (20 December 1950).

5 The Gregory Fellowships in the Creative Arts were instituted at the University of Leeds in 1950. Over the course of 30 years, a number of (largely) young poets, painters, sculptors and composers took up the fellowships, their remit being to contribute to and influence creativity at the University, while developing their own work.

6 Michael Bakewell, *Fitzrovia: London's Bohemia* (London: National Portrait Gallery, 1999) provides useful maps and background, and lists the pubs.

7 James Kirkup, *I of All People: An Autobiography of Youth* (London: Weidenfeld and Nicolson, 1988). See especially p. 146 onwards, where pubs, clubs, addresses and people are discussed.

8 A detail from a Hicks picture forms the cover of this volume. Visionary 'acquisition' and adaptation of biblical material informed much post-war poetry by Silkin, Dannie Abse, Emanuel Litvinoff and others. Silkin wrote a revealing article on Hicks in *Stand*, vol. 19 no. 2 (1978).

9 Bonamy Dobrée, *The Broken Cistern* (London: Cohen and West, 1954); 'English Poets Today: The Younger Generation', *Sewanee Review*, LXII (1954), pp. 598–620. The article refers to John Heath-Stubbs, James Kirkup, David Wright, Jon Silkin, Vernon Scannell and Geoffrey Hill, amongst others.

10 Jacket quotation on *The Two Freedoms*, first edition, following a quotation from Emanuel Litvinoff: 'An authentic new voice in poetry [...] with something to say and a determination to say it his own way'.

11 'Silkin on Silkin: Jon Silkin talks about his life and reads a selection of his

poems', video recorded by Adrian Mitchell in Sheffield, 1992. Leeds University Library, BC MS 20c Silkin/9/2.

12 Malcolm Ross-MacDonald, 'Jon Silkin between 1957 and 1989: A brief memoir' (2003); personal memoir in possession of Jon Glover and Leeds University Library BC MS 1909.

13 Although Dobrée would have been involved in Silkin's appointment as a Gregory Fellow, he had retired by the time Silkin actually took up the fellowship in 1958. His tutors included G. Wilson Knight and Norman Jeffares. Geoffrey Hill knew him and *Stand* published some of Hill's greatest poems from the 1960s, including 'September Song' and 'Funeral Music', but Hill did not act as Silkin's tutor.

14 Jon Silkin, 'Living through the Sixties', *Agenda*, vol. 31 no. 2 (1993), p. 59.

15 *Living Voices*, ed. Jon Silkin (London: Vista Books, 1960). The anthology comprises only 48 printed pages and most of the poets are represented by just one poem. Many had, by the year it was published, appeared in *Stand*, although only John Heath-Stubbs and Geoffrey Hill had links with Leeds.

16 *New Poets of England and America*, ed. Donald Hall and Robert Pack, Second Selection (Cleveland, Ohio: Meridian Books, 1962). Poets had to be under 40 to be included in this anthology. Of the 62 poets, a significant number – including Gene Baro, Donald Hall, Michael Hamburger, Geoffrey Hill, Peter Redgrove, Jon Silkin, Adrienne Rich and Anthony Thwaite – were linked through Oxford and /or Harvard Universities, and/or through the Group, and/or through *Stand* and Leeds University.

17 *The Penguin Book of Contemporary Verse*, ed. Kenneth Allot, 2nd edn (Harmondsworth: Penguin, 1962).

18 Jon Silkin, 'Living through the Sixties', *Agenda*, vol. 31 no. 2 (1993), p. 59.

19 1965 also saw the publication of *Penguin Modern Poets 7: Richard Murphy, Jon Silkin, Nathaniel Tarn*. Interestingly, Silkin's fifteen poems are not presented in chronological order, the first being 'Astringencies: The Coldness'. The Penguin Modern Poets series, three poets per volume, sold widely and represented a version of a modern 'canon'. Silkin's inclusion was a happy event; the availability in bookshops made his poems more visible than in the individual volumes from Chatto & Windus. Few people will now recall that an agreement between Penguin and UK bookshops, including WH Smith, meant that to stock one Penguin meant they had to stock them all, Penguin Modern Poets included.

20 The community of writing at 144 Otley Road seemed both natural and extraordinary. At various times Kate Lamb, student and jazz bass player Danny Padmore, Kevin and Trish Fitzpatrick, and Jon and Elaine Glover lived there. They all helped to produce, edit and sell *Stand*. There seemed to be a perpetual dialogue about poetry in general and Silkin's in particular. The talk was infectious and early work by students was discussed seriously.

21 Jon Silkin, 'Living through the Sixties', *Agenda*, vol. 31 no. 2 (1993), p. 59.

22 I consider briefly in section 3 of this introduction, 'Re-ordering Jon Silkin', the potential links with ecotheology.

23 He had worked as a gravedigger.

24 Geoffrey Hill, Oxford Poetry lecture, 'Poetry and "the Democracy of the Dead"', 3 December 2013; podcast available at media.podcasts.ox.ac.uk/engfac/general/mt13-hill-lecture.mp3. See also Ludwig Wittgenstein, *Philosophical Investigations*, translated by G.E.M. Anscombe, 2nd edn (Oxford: Blackwell, 1958): 'That first judgement is *not* the end of the matter, for it is

the field of force of a word that is decisive'; p. 219e.

25 'The People, A Dramatic Poem' was broadcast on Radio 3 at 10.00 pm on 9 July 1974, with Nigel Anthony, Miriam Margolyes and John Rowe, produced by John Scotney. *Gurney* was published by the IRON Press, North Shields in 1985. It had been written to a commission by King's College, Taunton, during Silkin's residency, and was performed there on 4 June 1984, and subsequently at the Brewhouse Theatre, Taunton and the Drum, Plymouth. After substantial revisions it was again performed by Inckproductions in Durham on 21 November 1984.

26 Robert Shaw (ed.), *Flash Point* (Leeds: E.J. Arnold, 1974). The book includes a significant number of poets associated with *Stand* and who had been Gregory Fellows at Leeds, but also many Movement poets and vital earlier figures, including Gerard Manley Hopkins.

27 Jon Silkin, 'Introduction', *Flash Point*, p. 14.

28 Jon Silkin, 'Introduction', *Flash Point*, p. 21.

29 Ag Jones, 'The Selling Fields', *Stand*, Double Issue, nos. 199/200 (2013), pp. 5–8.

30 Some poems from the 1960s show this switch overtly in tone and mood, for example, 'The Coldness' and 'Defence'.

31 For example, 'growled three stress lines', 'Catching the Audience' [on *Nature with Man*], *Times Literary Supplement* (29 July 1965); 'The Killhope Wheel poems are leaner and more lucid than the gnarled, sometimes clotted and rhetorically over-elaborate language of "The People"', 'Feeling for the Physical' [on *The Principle of Water*], *Times Literary Supplement* (19 July 1974); 'The squeaking of the pump is too audible in these lines', Martin Dodsworth, 'Taking things seriously' [on *The Principle of Water*], *The Guardian* (8 August 1974); 'Silkin's language lacks Hopkins's musicality but has a similar clotted and purposeful density', Tim Dooley [on *The Ship's Pasture*], *Times Literary Supplement* (6 March 1987); 'There's a lot of meat in this book, mixed with a lot of gristle', Herbert Lomas [on *Selected Poems* (1993)], *Ambit*, 138 (1994).

32 Silkin edited Wilfred Owen's Poems, *Wilfred Owen: The Poems* (Harmondsworth: Penguin, 1985). The volume was withdrawn following a conflict over copyright. It was later reissued with changes to the text by Sinclair-Stevenson as Wilfred Owen, *The War Poems* (London: Sinclair-Stevenson 1994).

33 Neil Roberts, Professor of English at the University of Sheffield. Sheffield University Library holds the Peter Redgrove Papers (Archive Ref. No. 178).

34 *The Poet Speaks*, Record 8, recorded in association with the British Council and the Poetry Room in the Lamont Library of Harvard University, edited by Peter Orr (London: The Argo Record Company Ltd, 1967). Silkin's poems were 'Asleep', 'To my Friends', 'Bowl', 'Death of a Son', 'Snow Drop', 'The Strawberry Plant' (recorded Newcastle, 15 September 1966). The other poets on the disc were Philip Larkin, Roy Fuller, Laurie Lee, Charles Causley, Ken Smith, Jon Stallworthy, Dom Moraes, Geoffrey Hill and Charles Tomlinson.

35 The following is a quotation from the current Lewis Silkin LLP website and we gratefully acknowledge the source: www.lewissilkin.com/About-us/Our-firms-history.aspx.

A history of the law firm Lewis Silkin. Lewis Silkin (the man) was born on 14 November 1889 into a family of Jewish Lithuanian refugees, the eldest of seven children. His upbringing was poor but he was determined and won a scholarship to Oxford University. However his headmaster reputedly wrote in his report to the University 'this boy will not benefit from a university education', therefore Lewis lost the opportunity to study at Oxford. Lewis Silkin first worked as a tally clerk in the London Docks. One day he spotted a notice in a window of a firm of solicitors, a notice seeking a 'bright lad'. He was appointed as a clerk and eventually became an articled clerk qualifying in 1920 and immediately set up on his own. In 1925 Lewis began his political career by becoming a member of the London County Council. He eventually became deputy leader of the LCC during the Second World War. He made his way both to the House of Commons by becoming the MP for Peckham in 1936 and the House of Lords, becoming 1st Baron Silkin in 1950. When Lewis' brother Joseph Silkin [Jon Silkin's father] qualified, the firm became known as Silkin and Silkin. However Joseph wanted Lewis to concentrate on law rather than politics – but Lewis still had an interest in politics and so he eventually left the firm. In 1945 Lewis was made Minister of Town and Country Planning in Attlee's Labour Government. He held this position until 1950 and piloted three major pieces of legislation, the New Towns Act of 1945 which created our new towns to provide houses fit for heroes, the Town and Country Planning Act of 1947, which created the modern framework for all our planning law and The Access to the Countryside Act of 1949, which created our National Parks.

36 Information about the Fountain Hospital can be found at http://ezitis.myzen. co.uk/fountain.html, http://www.workhouses.org.uk/MAB-Grove and http://www.workhouses.org.uk/MAB-Fountain. The links, real and meta-phorical, between such places and workhouses, fever hospitals and asylums were visually obvious. There is an account by a woman of being placed in the Fountain, along with a later appointment at County Hall, at http://www2. open.ac.uk/hsc/ldsite/gloria/schooldays.html.

37 *Stand*, vol. 6 no. 2 (1963).

38 For example, Isaiah 64:8, Jeremiah 18:2-6 and Genesis 2:7. There may be a strong association between the biblical in Dylan Thomas and Silkin; it affects the tone of the speaking voice and the sense of strong, visionary speech – even when the speech is meditative or silent monologue.

39 Silkin debated this tension throughout his life. I do not think that the issue was seen by him as merely a *post hoc* academic observation. Choosing the means by which a poem enacts life was itself a moral, political and sensual challenge. Examples of the discussion can be found in his *Poetry of the Committed Individual* (Harmondsworth: Penguin, 1973), pp. 27–39, and 'Imagism, Lawrence, Pound, Read, and Eliot', in *The Life of Metrical and Free Verse in Twentieth-Century Poetry* (Basingstoke: Macmillan, 1997), pp. 30–107.

40 Marie Mitchell, *A Short History of Smithills Hall and its Families* (Bolton: Friends of Smithills Hall, 1995), p. 7.

41 Personal reference from Elaine Glover.

42 Wittgenstein, *Philosophical Investigations*, p. 219.

43 I am indebted to Jon Silkin for explaining Rosenberg's poem in a conversation. I am also grateful to Jean Moorcroft Wilson for pointing to the value of Silkin's comment on 'Chagrin'. 'The rootlessness to which Rodker alludes was some-thing Rosenberg, too, undoubtedly experienced and his poetic imagery is full of it as Jon Silkin has pointed out, most memorably in the reference to Absalom

hanging by his hair.' Jean Moorcroft Wilson, *Isaac Rosenberg: The Making of a Great War Poet: A New Life* (London: Weidenfeld and Nicolson, 2008), p. 104; and her footnote to Chapter 5, no. 42 (p. 411), 'i.e. in "Chagrin", *PPIR*, pp. 103–104. See Jon Silkin's chapter on IR in *Out of Battle*'. I am also grateful to Jean Liddiard for her interest and advice. She is the author of *Isaac Rosenberg: The Half Used Life* (London: Gollancz, 1973) and editor of Isaac Rosenberg, *Selected Poems and Letters* (London: Enitharmon, 2003).

44 'Jubilate' is the imperative plural of 'jubilare', sometimes translated as 'Rejoice in the Lord'. This is the opening of Psalm 100 in the Authorised Version:

> *1* Make a joyful noise unto the LORD, all ye lands.
> *2* Serve the LORD with gladness:
>   come before his presence with singing.
> *3* Know ye that the LORD he *is* God:
>   *it is* he *that* hath made us, and not we ourselves;
>   *we are* his people, and the sheep of his pasture.

'Jubilate' may also be a reference to Christopher Smart's poem 'Jubilate Agno'. Silkin knew this poem, not least as a result of his love of cats. The poem is well known for the section in which Smart praises his cat's relationship with God ('For I will consider my Cat Jeoffrey…').

Complete Poems

My enemy weeps

A: There are many voices in my poem

B: Yes, they are all listening

– Jon Silkin

The Portrait and Other Poems

First published by Arthur H. Stockwell, 1950

The Portrait

The stone face has been hewn by many agents.
The bare surface was sensitive. The scars have
Cut their meaning deep into the cheeks and forehead
On the time-weathered rock. They shape the character
Like no quarry, but mines searching for gold
Set in quartz and crystal; the story is
In the face, grained there until it dies.

But what experiences will blast, hew,
Carve, mould and shape our faces, and how will time
Weather and smooth the various scars that are
Set in stones of different durability,
Until some mason cuts and carves our graves?

Bath

Once people thought it the latest word in fashion.
Now there are other centres. But once at night
Climbing the northern hill, I saw the sudden
Spire of a church silhouetted against the night-line
Of the universe, and thought that it might be an eternal
City. Well now I know different. This sunset, climbing
The hill from a different approach I looked down on it all,
And feeling like God (perhaps for a moment I was)
I saw the age of all cities. There is neither permanence
Nor transience in that place. No, nor any other.
But it will exist in the sunset of our minds
Until the finish of one more star, and then
In the eyes of God, and how long that will be for
I don't know.

Seen

At the commencement of evening,
The quiet evening and the melancholy sunlight,
Gleaming, the railway track in the sudden valley,
The sun stares down as we journey through a Cornish
country lane,
Where blossom clings close to branch and bough:
Or at the end of the short season
After the opening and the bloom and the beauty
When the brown leaves are slowly dropping
When one by one the cricketers depart
The flannels and the crowd have gone
The evenings are colder and shorter
And the pitch is silent
And an English autumn is approaching,
It is to journey
As though there were one destination.

Six Stanzas

I

In the beginning was man. Woman came
Vouchsafed through the formal experience
The parable of living together grew.
The woman perceived the man, comprehended him,
That in the muscle lay strength, in strength lay beauty
Of birth, but was puzzled by the secret meaning
Of the unknown act to the singing of a secret language
In the hum of the blood. The secret has been told.

II

From rhythm sprang the dance the song the word.
In the beginning was the word,
The word was given rhythm with which to speak
In the tongue of fire the fire burns in the blood
And sings. In the beginning was the word:
And the ritual was the dance and with the word
Which was sung.
In the beginning was the word the song the dance.

III

The sea is in the blood
The stone is in the bones

The tree is in the spine
The grass is in the skin

The wind is in the ear
The rain is in the eyes

The moor is in the brain
The sky is in the spirit

God is in the seed.

IV

The dance is in the spirit, the sky
Is fire. The dance under the sky
Is the prayer for the rain and the earth
That shoot up the plants. The bite
Is in the wind that flattens plants.
    The dance is in the sky.

The fire is in the wood that burns,
Consuming the sacrifice to plead
For the rain that quenches the earth,
For a quiet wind that snaps no stems.
The dance is in the spirit.

V

The woman and the man are coupled together
In the agony of the fire that burns
In the spirit. The secret about to be told
Is the woman's comprehension of the man;
Her instinct for strength in the beauty of the bone.
The dance in the blood is the word of birth
In the rise the ecstasy and pain.
The dance round the sacrifice is the living
The dance in the blood will be the life.
The wind in the ear and the rain in the eyes
Are the storm in the spirit.

VI

The birth is the spring the fire the dance in the sky
The song in the blood the stone tree spine the grass
The wind and eye over the moor, this is
The image, the body-spirit. In turn the man and woman
Will move to autumn the leaf in the stream and then
To winter and finally spirit. This is the perfect year.

Awakening

I always feel at spring
A sort of uneasy longing for the indefinable
Unheard of country in the no place mind
A sort of nowhere desire to be, in all weathers
The same, unhampered, without a destination,
Without the knowing where to go, but always
Travelling in the burning country.

One's methods of exploring can remain
No longer constant. Only one's end is permanent
In this world of uncomfortable laughter behind
Bombed buildings.

Vox Ultima Crucis
(The Voice from the Final Cross)

I suppose this is what you'd call the end
The elimination of selflessness
The desire to avoid at all costs that slow pain.
I can't help feeling a first self-inquisition
Is at hand.

    What do we care?
    We care only
    For the immediate happiness.
    There have been many crucifixions
    And there will presumably
    Be many more but
    No one bothers here.

Let us go out into the darkness and crucify
The whole world: or still better ourselves.

County Song

I have seen Wiltshire in the warmer weather
It is the subtlest county. In its meridian fire
June thunders linger in the lonely air
Pressing against the nothing sky. Intangibles.
Another thing; sometimes to look across
A valley to the next hill is pain. I know
No fuller quiet at night than another valley
Filled with mist and distant villages winking.

Many a summer has a negative
In those not dead yet, and many more moments of
Exultation are likely to lift their lovely
Quiet into our minds but it is improbable
That they will live for long beside our tumult.

The Trap

As slowly as I moved, the spring moved quicker
And shut the door. I did not know, and in any case
The room seemed cool and spacious, and when I found out
I did not mind, being blind.
                                    I should have felt
That other presence in the sunlight shadows;
I should have heard the softly rustling arras
And sensed that intimate cunning, yet when I found out
I did not mind, being deaf.
                                    I should have guessed
That after the curtains had parted and that figure
Had stepped out, the danger, but I was numb
With the coolness and the spaciousness of the room
So did nothing.
                                    I should have spoken when I felt
The slow flesh-touch, the brain demand a reason
But I did not, being dumb.

                        How should I know
The ache, the lack of air, the mind's long shock
And shudder, for being all these things I could not.

The Author Addresses his Razor

        We know each other well.
We need no introductions, bona fides;
Myself I'll vouch for you, you are your own
        Good letter.

        You do not flinch.
Your edge is fire and calmed oiled seas. You know
Your ultimate power as I know mine, you are keen
        For the end.

        One slash quick in a flash
Can finish; that's what I like about you. There's
No zero hour questioning in your glance of
        Cool intent.

Amiel

Living in a world of timidity he shunned acceptance
Although he acknowledged the release of love. He knew
The cipher of the heart. He wrote once, 'woman
Believes herself in love if she can give
You all her secrets.' Thus for almost thirty-nine
Years he lived a celibate through timidity,
Accepting the stress of desire without the release,
Believing the sensual to be a fraud and a trap.
Then, at thirty-nine, he received letters
From an unknown woman – wondering

If after all this might not be love, hesitating
And then, seeing for himself. And as if this wasn't enough,
All the maddening lusts and the sense of torment
At his holding back through shyness; and the deprivation
Or rather of his never having possessed a woman; the hopeless
Reading of erotic literature, trying to escape,
Realizing he was only sinking deeper and at last
After falling back on his final defence,
That of misplaced regard for himself and her,
He succumbed (to the woman that had desired him)
More, as he says, out of curiosity
Than cupidity, and fooling himself into thinking
The experience was paltry, or at least
In comparison with the love of the heart: yet willing
To try it again, still getting at it from the wrong view-point.
You see, the folly of attempted segregation,
Of the body from the mind and with it all the unbearable
                                                    reasoning
Out, detached curiosity, softening. Who knows?
And now even when his fear of ignorance had been
Purged, still the agony of lassitude
And apathy, the awareness of age advancing,
Regretting his inaction yet knowing ultimately
He could never marry with his fear
Of committing a decisive action in a lifetime of indecision.

This man thought out the ways of women's hearts
But could not yield his own. At sixty-nine
He died, unmarried, of a withered heart.
One other woman knew him at the end.
He said of her: 'She reaps what so many others
Have so passionately desired.' She kept him in his age,
His constant indecisions and regrets.
'In the hawthorn are the bees. She has
What others have desired to reap.
The bees are in the hawthorn.'

Night

In the unthinkable dark we walk. In there
We move all ways to anywhere, nowhere
Is any place not up nor down nor slope
House, church, stream, tree nor any known landmark
Yet still in the darkness of eternity,
But utterly alone in a mine of reality,
Of this place, that place, there, here, nowhere, somewhere,
Where is was, has been, will be, an infinite
Number of perpetual combinations and
Permutations. Your voice goes ringing ringing
To that other place through a series of doors
And dark corridors. This is the zero mark.

Destination

You shall in this hour still go forward
Where you may see the path through the field
Of grey-green grass, where you may see
The path over the moor of brown-bare earth,
Where you go through a village of cold still stones,
Where there is the face perpetually staring
Behind the glass, diffused and uncertain,
But perpetually staring into your direction
In the evening, as you pass near a church, or after,
On top of a hill where the darkness breaks,
Or again, by the river whose source you may have seen
Springing out of a hillside near a stair of rock,
But still the river turning and winding,
Still deeper and stronger, towards the estuary
Sometimes cascading down a waterfall,
But perpetually moving towards the estuary
Into the ocean: and still the road,
Still gleaming in the sunlight, still in the morning,
Still stretching beyond in the autumn sunlight

Into the intense gold beam, into the burning sunlight,
The living land of a thousand images,
Into the burning gold, into the living picture.
So your land is self won with the fire and with the peace.

The Necessity

We have a tender civilization. The spirit
Is the burning flower whose ashes blown by the wind
Are scattered soon over the wrinkled face.
The trees are easily cut, the eyes are soon
Put out, the lips are burnt, the skin is scarred,
The brow is ploughed. The flower, the tree, the eyes
Are seared in the unfailing travesty
Of our judgment, and we would speak with burnt
Lips, pierced eyes and ploughed brows. Talk to us.

Pointe de Flamme
Grave Light

All his life long
He loved to read by candle-light, and often
He would pass his hand over the light
To make sure, oh quite sure, that he still lived.

Now he is dead, still, he keeps by his side
A burning candle. But he has hidden his hands.

From the French of Jules Supervielle

Unpublished and Uncollected Poems,
c. 1950–1954

'Gentile, Mohhamedan'[1]

Gentile, Mohhamedan
And Jew die the same death
Man is provided for.
There's not a crouched-up breath
That is not joined in death's
Perplexity. I shall
Put my hand in my death
Within a fascist's hand.
Then, all religions shall
Have the one trunk; branches
Of several myths will be
One. Now, upon this earth
The lion and the lamb
Never shall be at one.

Sonnet: Inside

Yet of that fire within which we have burned
    All of our turning, which turning is at length turned
To ash, to palest ash, nourishing the thin field;
O remember: what hell's fires burning yield
    In their cold yelling, which, to free the clown
Whose sharp declension of the bitter noun
    Is loss. Loss. Loss frees also us of this.
By which I know that love of our love is
    That which from fire by fire is wrought. Two flames
    Which struggle in the one perpetual hell
Will heal yet yield to hell; or by the claims
Of that scowling tooth-edged saw-beast who caught your skin
    And tore, by what I know, by this I tell
Grass which is most meadow grows its stalk within.

'Once I put to that root'

Once I put to that root
A particular kind of fire.
My love is so designed
By love it may not be
Constrained. Let this
Indissolubly breathed-out flesh,
Soul, fire or Man, with desire
Be wrought to another's desire
By my own desire. I am
Born that I may not die;
The dying alone shall have loved.

Lyric

Jagged you are.
I know you well enough. Savage too.
Through you buildings lie
Spoilt: I do not know

Quite why it is.
In your sight and progress men sigh
And drown, are blinded too.
The passion of you is

Like a flower. But
How it is you are so vile and still
Daily under the sky,
Its kindnesses, you grow

I do not know.
Somewhere in the south where the grasses sweep
In warm profusion I shall find
Your source and pleasure. And

Life, opening out,
In yourself the giver and begetter,
I shall open too
And surely with my roots
Branches and trunk find
You what you are: both truths. I
Rise and die.

Standing Still

In this garden flowers breathe, and people
Sweetly in this scenery of squares
Stumble in an artificial calm
Of terraces and burning paving stones.

As if one looked into a burning glass
And saw a magnified and different world
Spring into freshness and italianate
Order, unreal and peopled with anxious ghosts.

For I promise you no sweetness in this place.
Only where you thought the birds dwelt,
Lingering among the fuchsias
You shall hear the uneasy silence waiting

For you to end your venture, and your quest
Into this waiting-place where no wings are
I say there is no peace here; only a pause
Between you and the silence and the outer world.

Manley's Hands

When I needed advice
   I would find Manley in his shop
standing, shortly, master over his tools;
as he explained, construed, and defined
   the arts of his calling
      for my working

      my eyes were drawn
to the largeness of eight surely formed knuckles,
and thumbs that rode hugely out of his hands
shaping the line with broad, curved joints
      like the trail of a porpoise.

   From fifty-nine years'
   feeling out the seams
of sanded planks rendered flush,
Manley's hands were wood-worn smooth;
   they smelled of the grain syrup
      of boat-birth.

The Legend

   Be with me now, and for ever:
Until the thaw of this great earth sets in
And the fire of love once more curls round
The frozen legs of nations. Let us be kindled
In that ecstatic bonfire of re-union.

   Be with me in this vile winter
Of cold hostility, this unarmed combat
Of apathy and ignorance which holds
The twigs of desire in a cold still acceptance.

But oh much more be with me
After the degradation of bombs and the stench
Of fire, be with me in the wholesome burning
Of human contact, the handshake and the kiss
Of people to light us into the after-radiance.

Ballad of Bored Ships

This way to boredom. Past the ships at night
Which go pleasuring the treasured isle. This way
Along the seas' highways past any mark
Of laughter or civilisation or swing of sensation
This way into the sea. The submarine
Black endless plunge and only the buoys left
Of memory as shipwrecks on a chart.

This way sir to nothing. The black dread
Under the tunnel of the sea and hearing things
In duplication with a wrecked map before you
Of ships in boredom past their one adventure
Story and ships in wreck under the total
Sea and shipwrecked maps of memory.
This way into the darkness of the sea

And hear nothing, plugged into the night
Throbbing with desire and dirty loneliness,
See the anemone and the claws of seaweed
Or wrecks of bored ships lying along the endless
Shelf of broken incidents past recovery,
Timeposts, there being no time to care with:
There lies a silence at the bottom of time.

This way the impotent journey through the tired
Seas with the miscalculation at the end
No green island the shamrock covered up by
The eternity of waters no other ship
Seen and an utter lonely mine
Our only company and the removed throb
Of our engine bearing us uncertainly about the deep.

And the gulls booming
Out on top and into no cliff but only
The cliff of fog a blanket of desolation
Closing and pressing in again like the sea
And our shiftless rootless drifting dirty ship
Moving through the anaesthetic time
Into the utter gangsterism of boredom

The utter gangsterism of nothing of boredom
The pleasured isle covered up by the filthy seas,
Or, missed on the tired journey through
The darkness of the waters of our time:
This is goodbye and this way down is boredom.

The Exiles

Willing or not, they have all gone out
From the poor charity of this rubbed world
Into a country of undefended places
Which is possessed by a tragedy of faces

And figures in sunlight moving over blazing stone,
Where there lie hidden crooks of landscape
Only to be known when you have entered them
Only to be forgotten when they choose to leave you.

Who made this country? Is it these small people
Who build the barren picture to an echo
Of themselves? or is this spiral shell of noise
Home for these exiles or orphaned to our ordinary lives?

Still, above all sentiment all affection all charity
This is where the mad go, the man born
To be kind of no-one nowhere we can ever
Know, beyond the poor communication

Of ordered words. Make of them what you will
With their land of no laws no king no mercy,
You can ever think you reach them through
A love stripped to perfection. For they are of your flesh.

For a mad child among mad children
(The Fountain Hospital, 1953)

Unwilling, the willing unwilling flesh all moves
From the poor charity of this adult world
Into a country whose sun, that harsh demien

Blazons with merciless happiness his Arms
Upon their faces, ridiculous his gay text
'We are at ease', and they are never so;

Who trudge in their thin valley where the sun
Fills with intense and liquid gold each fissure
In skull and rock, until, even such as

The normal might be glad. I pity them.
Yet in whose name pity what is content?
For could they know to pity would it not be

Us they would charitably bear up in whole arms,
Though with whole minds we distill all worlds into
One world which is a trap; a trap in whose mouths

Spring happiness with pain, pain, joy with decision?
So I must care for them rather than bear
The charity of the mad, who like ghosts can leave

Me when they choose, though I cannot embrace or kiss them.
Beyond the ordered communication of words
(I include charity, sentiment here, affection)

You cannot reach them by desiring this;
But as they smile and touch you, you may go –
No-one can touch till the other desires it so.

Though the mad go trampling through our kingdom still
These children eat when hungry, when they are dead lie still.

The Peaceable Kingdom

First published by Chatto & Windus, 1954

Prologue

All the animals in my poems go into the ark
The human beings walk in the great dark
The bad dark and the good dark. They walk
Shivering under the small lamp light
And the road has two ways to go and the humans none.

The animals in my poems go into the ark.
The fox walks up with his vixen from the high hills
The wounded fly comes, the small dog, the black birds
And the red birds riding on the shining back of the sea:
They all come in from the flood like a holy circus.

The animals in my poems go into the ark.
There are two scrolls on the doors as they go
Which they cannot read. They are blessed for they walk in the dark
The good dark and the last dark, and they know
That human beings will hate them wherever they go.

The Cunning of an Age

The fox sat under the hill.
And all around him the day was springing the earth
Curved away in a style he knew to be home;
The year grew round him like a love, the birds
Cried down the wind

And the air hummed with growing.
He smelt the humble plants at the foot of the hill.
The grass was bleeding like love and the insects stirred
In the air at ease with themselves. The black wind streamed
Over the top of the hill.

Only here had he made a home.
The ways of the world had stopped short of this bulge
On the surface of things because… because it had other
Things to do. And the fox sat under the hill
And all lay still.

Yet as he sat there wondering
How rivers came to be especially
His one at the edge of the world his world, a spot
Of red spat up at his eyes, no more, and was gone
In a twist of vision. No more than that

To the fox who sat under the hill.
The air was the same the year went round just the same
The insects turned around in their aimless journeys.
But just that red at the foot of the hill below
The stream had changed things.

Had changed his home
To a startling place, and below came the horn's winding
Warning halloo and up he was and smartly
Away as the red shot up to his horizon
And his mind's horizon.

And he was away.
No listening or waiting for the will and lust
Of the world but to live and lick his life
From the corner of a world that would hold him easily
Peacefully was his will.

Under a hill of maiden-hair
And grass as green as blood and summer-time
To sweat in his fur and his ways. He was off to save
His life. The hounds were baying the other side
Of the hill. And

He thought as he ran with his name
Of the names he'd been told and the games he'd been called,
                                          but the horn

Whirled round in his head and the hounds fell on
In leaps that distance and time pulls on one, the tricks
The mind pulls on one.

And the wind changed his name
To FOLLOWED from Fox-on-the-hill
And the wind followed, curling his brush. And the hounds
                                        followed too,
Like dreams like death on the hill like birds like grass
Like anything but not

Like fox he was
Or fox he knew and the horn curled round in his head
Slipping over the hill and into his head. But here
He swerved and hid. And the hounds went hurling past
With blood before

Their eyes, and the men and the world
With blood over their hands and a curse on their whips
And a horse on their world and a horn on their minds
Went for a day
        Over down the hill.

No Land Like It

My country is a fox's country
With moors of drenching sunlight and olive trees,
And peace hanging from the branches in clusters of birds
        There is no other country like it.

Its shadows move like lovers' shadows
Its pace is of a dance in passion time
Its birth was thought of underneath the hill
        There is no joy to have like it.

The charity of it
Is like the charity of beggars' dreams.
It has no bells. Its music is the silence of our synagogues
We know no other kindness like this.

Our sabbath hours are as
The calling cathedrals drowned in fields
Of dark green shadows fashioned by those parables
The cornfields hold.

Our lesson is our bread our wine
And laughter in an afternoon courtyard
The sun stokes up. Our children grow up black.
They steal the colour from

The persecution of other worlds
Of all the lands mine is most dear to me
Whose limbs are out of joint elsewhere whose pulse
Whose blood is fevered with

A loveless climate.
My country is a fox's country where
Our lovers meet upon the level
Of a hand given in love. There are no other hands like this.

My country is a fox's country

But I a fox am bred
From out a hollow land of horns groined red
With hounds and men and secret faith and trysts
Beneath my orphanage of angry hills.

There is no land or part of this land for any of us
And no land is like this.

Carved

Two small dogs stood by a dead black bird
And the black bird was very dead.

The two dogs stood by the bird like large lions
But they never touched the dead thing, once.

They would like to have eaten the black thing
But it was very dead with red ants,

Sawing its neck away like stone masons
And the red ants were very much alive.

So all the time the dogs stood they barked there
Because they couldn't eat the black thing.

Something large about that black bird.
It was being eaten by red death

While the two large-lion small dogs just stood,
Barking: they never touched the black thing,

And the black thing never looked at them, once.
It was indifferent to two small dogs.

Maybe it did not hear those large lions
Or maybe the black bird felt sorry for the small dogs.

Meanwhile the dead went on being dead the living living.

A Death to Us

A tiny fly fell down on my page
Shivered, lay down, and died on my page.

I threw his body onto the floor
That had laid its frail life next to mine.

His death then became an intrusion on
My action; he claimed himself as my victim

His speck of a body accused me there
Without an action, of his small brown death.

And I think now as I barely perceive him
That his purpose became in dying, a demand

For a murderer of his casual body.
So I must give his life a meaning

So I must carry his death about me
Like a large fly, like a large frail purpose.

Deeply Gone

for Gordon Wharton

And dragging their shining skins
Across the beach of straddling sands and sea wrack
Scores of them on the high moon night
Came out of the sea

The black sea, with black skins,
Across the silent beach. And from each skin
A naked one diffused with my sight
Their silver flesh.

Scores of them silently
Coming from the dripping sea. The seals singing,
    Incanting, and each one a naked one
        A silver naked one.

And among them as I watched
Behind a lusting fat old bush, a girl
    Slim as shining, precious as sight,
        Stepped from her seal's

Form and her seal's song. And
The old bush shook and I shook watching her
    While the moon watched us all. And as soon
        As she came near to me

I leapt out at her: I leapt out,
And 'You're mine' I said. 'Mine.' She laughed, she struggled
    While I held to her. 'Mine' I said with
        Chromium in my mouth

And silver in my eyes. 'Let me'
She said 'Let me go back to the sea. Once.' And
    I laughed. 'Not me' I said
        'Once gone, gone' I said

And I carried her back
Through the silent cobbled town and away from the shaking
    Bush and the seal skins and
        The seal's songs. I hardly

Could wait, carrying her,
I could hardly wait. I just ran back
    With her laughing like silver in my eyes
        And her words running

Through my ears like lust,
The moon raking the fire in me. And she laughed
    As I brought her home. 'I'll never stay'
        She said. 'Never stay.'

THE PEACEABLE KINGDOM

'Tomorrow I'll be back.
Tomorrow I'll be back with the seals and the sea.
      I won't be here tomorrow and I won't stay.
            I'll be gone.'

'Back with the seals and the singing,
Back to the sea and the swing of the sea and the edge
      Of the black shining world. You'll see.'
            She said.

            'Will I,' I said. 'We'll see.'[2]
And she laughed. But she never saw
      Where I hid her skin. 'Marry me'
            I said, hiding her skin, 'Marry me.'

      And I laughed. 'Marry me,' I said.
'You'll never find your skin your seals your sea.
      'Marry me,' I said. 'Forget the black
            Shining edge of the world'

      'And the shaking fat old bush.
Marry me.' And she did. And I laughed. And I laughed.
      And I laughed louder than anyone, I laughed
            Louder than her sighing

Louder than the bells' cries and
The wind's cries, louder than my heart beating.
      And we married and we married again in my bed
            And I laughed.

      'You'll see,' I said,
Hiding her skin in a different place at the time
      Of the full high moon at the time
            Of the yearning bell

      The seas' bell and the seals'
Bell. 'You'll stay here till we die' I said, hiding
      Her seal's skin. 'You're with child as well.'
            And she bore me

Three wide-eyed boys
Without seal's skins and without seal's song. And I laughed
'You'll stay here till we die,'
I said.

And I laughed. 'Never mind,'
I said, hiding her skin,

I put it under the stone of the fifth rock
The night I laughed like storm. The town shook

And the bells shook and I shook
But 'Where's my skin?' she said. Under the fifth rock, I thought

But you'll never see that, I thought. Never that.
And I went to the fifth rock just to make sure

At the time of the high moon and quivering fat old bush
To make sure, I thought. Just to make sure.

I went to the fifth rock just to make sure. I tell you
It was gone. 'It's gone,' I shouted,

'At the time of the high moon and the seal's song,
The black shining edge of the world and the seas' song.'

'It's gone' I said. 'It's gone' I shouted. 'It's gone.'
And I ran past the world and the shining black edge, I ran

Past the five rocks at the time of the high full moon
With her skin gone. Her gone. 'Her gone. Gone.' I cried.

'I was very happy,' her note ran.
But I'll never see you again, I thought.

The Three Birds Who Were Saints

Perhaps we should bury the three birds again
We dug them up only for their red hearts.

We cut them out and we sewed up the bodies
Now they lie in the open and their black feathers hurt my eyes.

Why did the king ask for their red hearts?
I would have given him mine but to keep their flesh

Under the soil: someone says they are not dead.
It is the crier whispering they sing still.

But the king has their red hearts in his black hand.
Perhaps we should kill him. I do not say that.

I do not say three birds died for singing.
I say they opened their mouths as we went out marching

I say their singing could be heard over thousands of feet marching.
And all for this the king had the birds killed

One Two Three, and their small red round hearts
To stop the telling of them. But their holy song

Walks round and round on cunning voices.
I lay my black hard life down to those birds

This Dreaming Everywhere

The angry fox
Found himself dreaming in the hostile desert.
And round he runs the almighty and bitter
Hand of the sun.

He barks under the shadowless
Hill. What gesture, he demands, sent him here,
Condemning him to trot in the black
Gaze of the sun.

Sometimes he thinks
Of the packhounds the curling voice of the lazy horn
Stirring his heavy legs, and the rhythm
Of the dark drumming

Of the enemy, the
Crying of the red riders and the almighty
Billow of fear, the strange
Grip and fever

In his salt throat.
Sometimes in the desert still the unrepentant anger
The hate for hate the moist smell
Of the running blood

Of the riders' red coats.
But still he asks who sent him here, whose hate condemned
Whom. The hunters have sunk under
The sands

The silence
Of his barking voice over the sea is still.
Yet still the enemy stares
That disc that coin

Crawling over the sky.
He remembers now, the grey morning he set out for
Another country. He does remember.
Now it is winter.

Now he resolves
To run against the fierce sentries over-watching his land
He resolves he steals past he is through and
Halloo it is for the great

Fox of the stolen
Morning, for the red fox the colour of his blood
And for the brutal enemy's lazy
Horn and pack.

This was how he came,
And this is how he has come to die.
For another country is another desert
Another enemy in wait.

The sun is red now.
So halloo for the dying fox of the red morning
For the great red fox that stole the mad
March across his gentle

Sentries, halloo for the dreaming
Fox in the terrible desert of his dreaming. Halloo.

A Space in the Air

The first day he had gone
I barely missed him. I was glad almost he had left
Without a bark or flick of his tail,
I was content he had slipped

Out into the world. I felt,
Without remarking, it was nearly a relief
From his dirty habits. Then, the second
Day I noticed the space

He left behind him. A hole
Cut out of the air. And I missed him suddenly,
Missed him almost without knowing
Why it was so. And I grew

Afraid he was dead, expecting death
As something I had grown used to. I was afraid
The clumsy children in the street
Had cut his tail off as

A souvenir of the living and
I did not know what to do. I was fearing
Somebody had hurt him. I called his name
But the hole in the air remained.

I have grown accustomed to death
Lately. But his absence made me sad,
I do not know how he should do it
But his absence frightened me.

It was not only his death I feared,
Not only his but as if all of those
I loved, as if all those near me
Should suddenly go

Into the hole in the light
And disappear. As if all of them should go
                Without barking, without speaking,
                    Without noticing me there

        But go; and going as if
The instrument of pain were a casual thing
                To suffer, as if they should suffer so,
                    Casually and without greatness,

Without purpose even. But just go.
I should be afraid to lose all those friends like this.
                I should fear to lose those loves. But mostly
                    I should fear to lose you.

        If you should go
Without affliction, but even so, I should fear
                The rent you would make in the air
                    And the bare howling

Streaming after your naked hair.
I should feel your going down more than my going down.
                My own death I bear everyday
                    More or less

        But your death would be something else,
Something else beyond me. It would not be
                Your death or my death, love,
                    But our rose-linked dissolution.

    So I fear his going,
His death, not our death, but a hint at our death. And I shall
                                                                    always fear
                The death of those we love as
                    The hint of your death, love.

Death of a Son

(who died in a mental hospital aged one)

Something has ceased to come along with me.
Something like a person: something very like one.
And there was no nobility in it
Or anything like that.

Something was there like a one year
Old house, dumb as stone. While the near buildings
Sang like birds and laughed
Understanding the pact

They were to have with silence. But he
Neither sang nor laughed. He did not bless silence
Like bread, with words.
He did not forsake silence.

But rather, like a house in mourning
Kept the eye turned in to watch the silence while
The other houses like birds
Sang around him.

And the breathing silence neither
Moved nor was still.

I have seen stones: I have seen brick
But this house was made up of neither bricks nor stone
But a house of flesh and blood
With flesh of stone

And bricks for blood. A house
Of stones and blood in breathing silence with the other
Birds singing crazy on its chimneys.
But this was silence,

This was something else, this was
Hearing and speaking though he was a house drawn
Into silence, this was
Something religious in his silence,

Something shining in his quiet,
This was different this was altogether something else:
Though he never spoke, this
                    Was something to do with death.

        And then slowly the eye stopped looking
Inward. The silence rose and became still.
The look turned to the outer place and stopped,
            With the birds still shrilling around him.
                    And as if he could speak

He turned over on his side with his one year
Red as a wound
He turned over as if he could be sorry for this
And out of his eyes two great tears rolled, like stones,
            and he died.

First it was Singing

        From the first cry
I was given music with which to speak,
        Tramping the staring streets
            The amazed faces

            Turning, laughing with their
Windy voices at the mad singer in the common
    Street. From the first I was
            Given a voice

            To cry out with.
It was music, bread, blood, singing, love.
        Afterwards it was dying
            But it was singing

First.
And from that it was I loved the hopping birds,
    The limping fly
        And the mad

    Bee, stung to anger
In worship of summer. It was their speech and my speech,
    The Jewish stone and the
        Animal rock

    Rolling together that made me sing
Of our common lash, the great white weal across
    Our black back, I and the hunted
        Fox, I and the huge

    Fly, his dangerous wings
Torn from his villainous body, I and the seal
    Harming the human sea with his song,
        I and the bawling dog.

    It was our harm
Made me sing. Afterwards it was death,
    Afterwards it was our death,
        Death of the stone

    By stoning, the animal
By animals, but, first, singing,
    Jew and animal singing first.
        And afterwards death.

Caring for Animals

I ask sometimes why these small animals
With bitter eyes, why we should care for them.

I question the sky, the serene blue water,
But it cannot say. It gives no answer.

And no answer releases in my head
A procession of grey shades patched and whimpering,

Dogs with clipped ears, wheezing cart horses
A fly without shadow and without thought.

Is it with these menaces to our vision
With this procession led by a man carrying wood

We must be concerned? The holy land, the rearing
Green island should be kindlier than this.

Yet the animals, our ghosts, need tending to.
Take in the whipped cat and the blinded owl;

Take up the man-trapped squirrel upon your shoulder.
Attend to the unnecessary beasts.

From growing mercy and a moderate love
Great love for the human animal occurs.

And your love grows. Your great love grows and grows.

Hunger

A woman goes to feed her friends each day.
She moves slowly, she stoops, and in her hand

Is the offering of bread which she hurls with all her love
At the large sparrows, she attacks them with it, but they

Only leap at her as she strides outside her house.
For they know by her carriage and her stooping pride

She is of them. She is full of hunger for
The hand that bears the profound gift of love.

But like them she is inarticulate
She nods and pecks when she would give her heart.

Her body stoops but the straight spirit burns
And while she is dying the black sky watches her.

Never Any Dying

You were right when you said
'There is never any parting.' For although you have gone
I feel your presence still, by
My side, as I walk

Through the roads, passing trees
That would go with me if they could. They beckon me
To stop. But at that moment
Your ghost cries out

Fabulously for me
To keep it intact, to go on, never to grasp
Any other hand, any smooth ghost
Of a body that casts

Itself before me. It
Demands of me to keep our marvellous union
Like a cup, always full
Of my wine.

Somehow love started
When you said you would go. I remembered then
What we had been. In that sense
I was glad you were going,

Glad your going
Had stirred the wounded eagle into the sun
Or to flap clumsily through the roads
Past the amorous trees. And

On my way to look
For you I met the phoenix there. Who was drunk.
He had been celebrating
His new birth.

And I thought how blessed
That was, to be born over again, with fire
In his eyes and wings. So
I said to him

'Phoenix, I have heard
Of your burning.' The ghosts were climbing all over
The tables, the stars tangled
Together as I said this.

Then: 'I have lost my love.
She went into the night. And I am afraid
She has left me
For death.'

'I will tell you
How you shall recover her from the sea.'
My heart hurt and fell in me
As he said this

And I cried '*Is* she dead then?'
The ghosts leapt up like candles into the air,
   'Dead,' he shouted, 'dead.
      There is never any dying

   But go you to the sea
And you will find her nakedness issuing out of the water
   As if she were being
      Born again.'

   So it was, when
The ghosts leapt highest at the word death
   I left, leaving the phoenix staring
      Out of the moody

   Windows, left him for
The bewitched road, which is turned like metal
   To run parallel
      To the river.

   And where it goes,
The holy labour of the profound river
   To the sea, where the sea
      Joins the earth

   And the sky, where
That sea issues forth girls, I followed
   Demanding of the road that it lead
      Me where I would find her.

   The night on
Which I travelled, stretched itself out
   Until those ancient stars seemed
      Fastened to me

   By time, and to retreat
So slowly from me they were not going, but only
   Turning round me like the sun.
      As though my journey circled

And I rode. Would she
Be there when I arrived, would the world's end keep
Its promise to me and issue up
My love? Would the sea's

End tell me the truth and
Saying so, its words turn to my girl?
But no-one can say as I went
I was not glad,

No-one can say
I was not glad the phoenix told me I should go,
And as I went, what I saw
Was the sea, before me.

Imagining I was at
My terrible journey's end. Awaiting the event
Like a magician, unsure
Of his spells.

And in my mind the
Metal road stopped short at the sea's edge, suddenly
And I had to leap
Down from that road

Onto the ghostly beach.
In which dream I acted as the seer.
For there when I
Arrived like a plane

The strip of road fell
Short at the sea's edge, as if the world's metal
Had run out. And I leapt
Down onto the soft

Beach, a dying weight
Thinking: now I shall see her nakedness

Come out of the sea. And I ran to the edge
With three stones in my hands to throw at the sea

To make it give up my love. To make it offer me
Without passion, my love back to me.

And as I ran to the edge I threw three black stones
Hard at the dripping villain, I threw three stones into him.

But he maintained his presence as I had done nothing.
He maintained his black scrutiny as he would swallow the earth

If I would let him.
Then I remembered I thought she was dead

And I turned from the sea that had never given up my love.
And as I turned, a great shadow fell on me

Right over the beach it fell, over me, and over the dumb stones.
So I knew that she would come. Then I never turned back.

I waited. And when she came I took her new hand
Which was wet from the dying of the villainous sea.

For David Emmanuel

I shall pass you the tall moment.
It was on the still day I saw my son
Lying in his laughing sleep.
And the red birds

Poked their shining faces
In the child's small window. That was a shy day,
The sun walking through the mist,
The pale hours

Following his first
Day when we ran into the laughing brass
Bold light, alive to holy life.
And this day I stole

Softly into the small sleeping
Of the room of his dreaming and saw him, half
Of my sure flesh there, strong
To be surer yet

Of his unabiding flesh.
It wasn't the ripe glory of the sun
Nor the dogs grinning below
At a mouldy joy bone.

It was my son. Half Jew
And wholly human sleeping in the curved eye
Of his future. And I
Alone with the great sun

Of the morning, I with two
Large eyes looking into his god's eyes:
He was half mine, half
That woman buried

In the hot raiments of her sleep.
I could not wholly wake him. But I turned to the intruding
Sun that stole so fearfully in
His room. I thanked

It that this morning
It touched my eyes that they were flung wide
To the joy of my son, that he
Entered and shook

My love and took
My heart into his small heart. May love like this
Remain with him, as the innocence of
The sky remains crowned with the sun.

To Come Out Singing

I

I came out singing
And the song was a cry into the green world.
Easily I came into this world.
Then why should it cry? And for whom?
Not for you smoke of ghost, dead chosen people,
Not for you invisible murderers, I did not spring
Out like a cry singing for you. I came
Out of God's six winged folded desert
Because there was promised me one love.
But out of that promise
From that cry, two worlds sprang
Entire, perfect.
The cry is, I tell you, for one of these.
Yet its promise comes and comes bearing a double fruit
A treble cry a green song
A crying green tree a terrible word.
A terrible fruit had opened its division
A fair fruit terrible in division.

II

But who has promised?
A new being bridles in the present.
And that is a promise.
But who has said to you love?
The god inside me promised me
Spoke you the word.
But I delivered the promise
I cried love.
Also I broke the bread
I kindled fire.
I cried the terrible promise of the word love.

III

To whom the six speared star?
You have chosen and you but to whom shall be given
Jerusalem folded over and over in the green valley?
And to whom the sower
The greencoated fleshed ploughman
In the valley? You and you. To whom the green sword?
To whom the tree
Christed folded over and over, to
Whom Jerusalem? You and you.
The ploughman shall take the song into the valley
The greencoated farmer shall bring the sword into the valley
The eagle shall make a cry in the faithful country.
You and you and you.

IV

What may I give? Hours have been
Folded into this decision: others' wisdom given
That the gift may be given. What may I bring then?
That the giver and the loved shall be equal.
The farmer brings his seed to the valley
And neither is more equal more perfect.
What can I bring can I bring to the valley?
Only a green sword only the wish with it
Only my green coat that I clothe my thick flesh with.
And my song.
What shall I bring *into* the valley?
Only my small seed only my forefathers' prayers
Only what lives in me as I lived then in them
Only the green whole song. I shall bring
That into the valley.
I shall be glad most glad to give that,
My life, my love, my Love!

Supposing time came out first from the belly of God
Our celebration of each new year
Or event, or endurance of the holy event
Would be a celebration of him.
And a love, like a new year
Would be of him also, a celebration,
A wind travelling from feast to feast
With the smell of wine and bread on it.
We must be always celebrating love as we celebrate God.
We must always love the new year
Turning in the lighted dark turning like the hands of music.
We must be like ploughmen and farmers in a valley
We must give our love a green coat and bring a song to her.
We must come out singing.
We must come out like a cry into the green world
We must come out singing with the charity of three beggars
We must come out with the marvellous open hands of music
We have to come out like three beggars, singing in the new year
For charity's sake
We must come out singing.

Epilogue

All the people in my poems walk into the dark
All the animals walk up to the ark.
The people are deaf and limping like flies
Cunning shining soft sad they walk,
And they do not know but they walk into the bad dark.

All the animals in my poems walk in the sun
Blinking their eyes and licking their paws they go,
On and on up the proud procession of stairs
Up the proud straight stairs like a holy circus
And they do not know but they walk in the great light.

If all the people and all the animals
Joined dark with light, if all the proud people
And soft-stepping circus climbed their way in the dark
Walked with the black seals and walked with the spidery flies
They would all go into the great light, and they would know.

Unpublished and Uncollected Poems,
c. 1954–1958

To My Son
(about death)

Though being born you can mean
No more than entering
The sharded world, birth does mean
A touch in you, like birds,
Winged if mortal. It means
Keeping the upright world
A quenchable violent flame
Unquenched through violence
To turn through every voice
But only hear that voice
Which is the only voice
That speaks with clarity
About what we should know.

Mortal, swan or child
Cat, howling ravager
Of disenchanted men
Through hunger, derision, be strong
Having all, and suffer to
Enfuse all; then you shall die.

'And on the ground rests like'

And on the ground rests like
The husk of a huge child.
And if two hands would clap
The shell between the palms
Such child's contortion which
The fire had twisted would
Crumble. Frail city too.
Girders begin to droop
And, splayed like a smashed fist,
A-jut the charred ground; so

Pith spits out of a house
On fire as juice out of
My son as he was dying.
If that house were the town
Its pith oozing, the moist
Pity for burning men
You would enlarge that world
You have shrunk, where the wall
With human letters broke
With characters toppled;
The human cry pre-judged
To perish in man's law;
And ecstasy constrained
And bodies held by clothes
And the large world shrunk small
In the law's purity
A snowflake in a fist.
I will leave this heat. From
This year I'll be a part
Of the large world of snow
Shimmering with human woe.
A queen inside my self
And be joined with all life
And be joined with my death
As melted snows intermix
With the pulsing earth below.
Or live in polar flows
Until under the sledge
On paws of the trained wolf
Time's casual runners kill.
Images of the external
Snow subsuade my mind
As I walk from the town
Upon the frozen flow
Of desert ocean. Now
I hear the hurrying cockerel blare;
Through the moon's bars erect notes flaken
Down from his red throat. I walk
Between these luminous desert snows

That now, burning with flicker cold as
The lucid soul in misery ebbing
Such pent-in anguish, it then shatters in bits
Its fingering spirit's cries.
It was on such a night as this
The serpent swirled into the garden,
As life first oozed from the torn tree;
It was not sex grew on the branches
But knowledge of forgetfulness
Whose fruit gorged on the ready soul.
And on that night our garden chilled
And leaves upon their small stalks flickered
To that cold swell our dismayed parents
Universally walked; and clenched
Their minds in anguish to an ice
No human warmth could assuage. Yet in
Night more frigid than that my
Soul is removed on a guilt that
No love can stir nor fear congeal.
Could fear move my glacial spirit
I'd grow on such immensities.
Let the cool flames, which are bitterness
If they must, lick me and
Enthrall me with their tongues,
And make my blood small stones.
I must unfasten the old laws
Taught to me as young girl,
Pinned like a brooch to my soul,
But the wind soughs through the hot
-Visaged temple, round fretted stems
Of rock which had not shape
As through my body lust.
It snicks my will, and the hot-
Structured bones sigh for their master.
      Where is God's will in me
      Where the clear stream pelts underground?
I listen for such cry
Alive not the sand's cry
Even the mayfly's that

With sharp, sullen, poised horn toils
Near or feel I hear
The human cry come from
The cave, like a blow and
Assemble tunes,
Emphasized by a stick
From which notes spring, as breath
From its repetition of ribs.
And going with it that
Voice which seems like my priest's
No matter whose it is
I am glad of its cry;
And were the dead to rise
The tumerous world would not
Know of the dread I have;
For my passion always beats
On the underside of my skin
As though inside a drum.
If this is dying I will
Stay with it, for the sound
Is the human sound all are
Afflicted to need: with no man
Life seems a desperation.
Most voices are loved voices
Purposeful to create love
And love's life's bribe. O human or
Death's cry, then pulse sweet finger
Stick to my ordinance,
So if you're he choose me
And with your moistening
Drive in where I break and
Meet with love's casual seed
Me in my burning place.
Am I not fair and have
I not squatted amongst
The least of your winged words?
Therefore since I'm your last
Of that harsh world we both
Were of, make me your fair
And something, our child?

'She is a milk-tender beauty'

She is a milk-tender beauty
Swathed about my son;
This bud of action's drooped;
I cannot flower to push
Him into death's still valley
No, justice its shadows stabs
To death, in sighs, what sleeps.
Gently out pours his blood
Making her white skin gules,
As after Eve's expulsion
From the garden huge cliffs
And forests rose then fell
While through the moted light
The fiery ball turned red.
She waking sees death and
With furious anguish tears
Those fruitful breasts which just
Before bore my son's weight:
And now my son's blood shrieks
Like red birds from his mouth,
Which when he gets into
That valley named Gehinnon
Where small black birds blind and
Minute noises utter
Their vast parabulas
Will turn small, fierce, black
And pluck at him until
Death has no rest at all.
And now, thrust here, she cries
Scrawling fingers like words
Upon her breasts that had
Submitted and been pressed
Into plunging love's forms.
'And here,' while all the while
Love's blood burns at her side.
She screws those breasts again
Milk-laden perhaps.

The belly floods in gouts
(also of my blood), which
Before had performed love
And she presses and twists
With final kisses her
Whole length like a wave on
The gouges I have made.
I will not give you death,
Live, know what distract
Love of my son is.

White

Voices protected from the dead; they summon us
To gentle love and measureless desire.
I regard your cunning laughter and I have lost
My way. I think of children in the dark;
I was never told concerning this part of love.

And concerning this strange side of the moon I am
Lost, I walk bare-souled, a naked saint;
I am two men running in the pitched dark
With no hands. And the dark has no meaning;
But I look at you and I feel your white smile.

I never was the man for hidden words
But words, like voices, hide from me now.
If I could break the silence of red mouths?
But that which is whiteness more than the flesh
Of children holds my language innocent.
No one in this whole world is free from snow.

The Link

Some dulled, sour
Accumulations of sweat
Which two sweet bodies pressed
    In wretchedness

    Massed on the floor
A powdery, a soft, pool
But dried, and harsh in salt.
    The odour

    Sifting through
The mind, revived, perplexed
Faces held under
    Some people, singly

    Or not,
Re-animated of love
When they came in this room;
    A dark room

    In substance
Not bare, yet substantially
Empty of furniture
    Except for

    Dried salt-sweat
Under a coarse, a flat, bed
And dark, accessible.
    This first is that

    Which we enter:
What is the common bed
As raiments of despair.
    Between such

Bedclothes find love naked.

'A shirt, shirt or night-dress flaps on the line'

A shirt, shirt or night-dress flaps on the line
More frantic than alive, bleached white as bone
Her pegged soul trying to fly. Its wet cloth writhes
And heaves its vivid, hysterical shapelessness
Upon the rope. It does not know that every
Soul, like hers, is pegged as bitterly into
That not one can fly through the unconfined
World; where there are no birds, no ironies
And wrenches on the bitter rope, her raging
Fatuously, disconcerted life,
White arms stretched to more whiteness. It would be
Easier if, like many, she could hang
Identifiably limp and prostrate in
That force which opening up soul, hunts it
The soul – all ways.
Familiarly I would
Handle that white garment, smooth it down,
No longer choked into submission by rage.
If you would hang upon the line, flap only
When the wind shifts you, but retain that strength
To suffer and to submit, not to the storms
Whose signs we are.
Once more; if it is love which smoothes the garment
I would not fret the air hysterically,
Vivid or bare however the soul may be,
But smooth still the white cluster hanging in it
Bottles that you touched, the foods in their labels
You moved, if touching moves, more than you moved me
By touch, your small exact endearments –
You had your love so many times
The kiss upon the seal, the jar with herbs,
That flavour and the kiss upon the side.
The jar sealed tight, these were your loves and these
Received the hundredfold of your square thumbs,
More love than any softness from the belly
Given to any lover. You have had love.
Were you then reasonable, hung and dry

I'd kiss the seal, straighten the tortured garment
That cannot dry, it is always there,
I would stretch gently out,
Your peace to a white, recognizable shape.
Some souls have ropes on which to tautly cling.
I am the adamant to your twisted soul;
I am the line that you are always pegged to;
Whatever tension moves me, yours is mine.
Whatever love you suffer I give you mine.

Relationship

This ring I thread upon
Your finger, not being much
And simply taken off
It is not much to wear
It is so simply formed
No superscription, none
Of flower or cuneiform
Or mythological beast
Or stone
Can tax its worth up.

It is the love pierced through
Your symbol which I give;
And what you make of that
Endows its real worth. And
Upon your small white limb
Such ring as flashes and cries
Invisibly, is much of
The intangible wealth I have
Which I have given you; and
It is a certain sign
Of what you have given how you
Take the ring to you.

Such ring is made of gold
Such ring is artifact;
I give this ring to you
I give this gold thing to you
I put it through your hand
You put that through again;
This ring from me is yours.

Lives in Sand

Now that the mating season
Again disturbs me, I cast into my flesh's
Darkest chamber, the mind,
To see with what garner that barn will enrich the year.

I find none; but fragments of
Such lives other people shed, like skins, upon
The park's frail, papery ground.
I am all lives that coil, strut, fret, fear, are unkind,
Gentle, even brave this day;
I am such fragments as must learn to die.

Yet now as the shadow slides
Its quiet hand through London's brass, its multiple
Large shadow between the grass-blades,
I know like that shade, must mark again time which
The lovers spend to augment
This stumbling hour their lives silt in time's rich sandgrain.

O friends what fragments in my mind you stain;
Though shadows, your lives written through my life, remain.

'Do you see this park again'

Do you see this park again,
Mark its parcel of flat gold through which
Swans pierce;
The stilled gold which, though it seems to, can never move?

Fire from its sun the red earth's breast burns, and
Works its clear will.
Do you see the glittering swans and mark how that fine

Water each touches to
Is burnt, yet each would have that touching still?
Waters can yearn, perhaps,
Love, I yearn for that valley which our shadow dug

On the grass where the burnt sun now lies.
It burns away that first, that last, and everlasting day.

And shall still burn. Well you must mark it now
Though you would turn away,
Pain like a sickness through your mind prevailing
Its ferocious eye.

Love, mark you it well; it was our loving-place.

Do you notice the green with its lake's fire much like our blood;
Do you notice it in the park, a lake that will not flood?

The Confidence Trick
For the Soho Fair 1956

Two dried rubbers drift on the ground, like spent leaves
Over the golgotha of gravel and cinquefoil: and wrap
About the small stones.
Two old spent friends, identical, twinned useless flaps
Of rubber, two brief spasms in the caught air.
Cannot the wolf cry, cannot the burnt lamb bleat or the water
Cry its thirst to satisfaction?
Will the spent things never again
Live? Water that is denied its thirst can never
Be moist again. Nor can the rubber life of man
But drift on the stones in a celebration of tears.
Wine, like a dress, spurts our blood over the paving stones
And we cannot taste our lives for such savour has gone from our lives.
We, the blood, ask only the lightest of satisfactions.
Spend breath, wrack rain; see how we blow away.

Easter Day: Victim

Slowly upon the paving, I
Within the rising day, tread on
An earwig crushed into the stone:
Thinner than the wafer of our God
This transubstantiation of
Ghost into worm raises its head;
Upon these Easter stones where I
Had crushed his body, he stands up.
O thinner than the flesh of Christ
This creature! 'I was never killed
By the fine-throated rose, but I,
Blood upon blood, was crushed by your foot.
Your paper foot turns blindly up
The sun-stoked paving-stones, and through
The casual systems of my death
Easter is our victory.'

Speaking to the Conqueror

To have been crushed, more than
Christ's wafer, blacker my ooze
Than sacrificial blood,
Whatever darkness I
Reptile, soul or the angelic
Transubstantial form
Must occupy, I know blood
Will be shed for more of that.

Whatever death you caused
Whatever that death you will
Die, you are and I am linked
In such a profusion of corded
Knots and paraphrasings, all
The paraphernalia love
Threads through her animals,
It seems from the time when you crushed
Me that we too were involved
Through the coition of love;
But love is different.

The murderer ginned in his act
With the creature he mounts, it is sure as
Death piercing where nothing but
Before the blood pounded, roared
Through the deliberately muscled
Heart, one must die and the other
Go on carrying that death,
And murder will pour through him.
But love is different.

Kierkegaard the cripple, addressing his God, asks to be an ordinary human being

Where the brown thorn is there my wisdom lies
Thrust in my back; the crossed hump like a cross lies.

Through this dark faith I keep my faith in thorns
And where mine is there wisdom also rides
Thrust in my back. The crossed hump like a cross lies.

Old men have told me faith must waste away
Only through faith are dark thorns pacified
And where this thorn is there my wisdom lies.

Only through death are black thorns pacified.

Rock

Dan walked out one night with his mind full of rock
And his hair full of bats and his eyes full of ghosts.
The moon hung down from his arms and a star was
Blazing from his forehead.
Dan walked out one night with death in his hair.
And stars were leaking slowly out of the sky
And in his hand he carried the tin moon.
That was all his light.
And the rock stood up like genesis in his mind.
But that was not all for death had a word for him
And the bats had a mind for Dan and so had the ghosts.

Dan walked out of his mind one night.
But death stayed on. And the rock stayed on too.
To show the third star blazing from the forehead
What an eye can see for and it stayed on again
Just to show death what time a rock is for.
Just to show death.

The Forests

On the occasion of Dr. Schweitzer's visit to England[3]

Saintly, return you to the fist of Heaven
Whose Europe recollects you now, dearly,
As men from sleep, presently remember
Child and then wife, or as the drowning man by spasm
Recalls, in life, death. Sir, we remember you
Sprung from Gunsbach in Alsace where meet the French
And German streams, and where Protestant
With Catholic faith mingles, tolerantly.
The old horse limped, is beaten by the man.
This much the world's misery. Yours also.
From the simple act the good vision came
Sliding in reverence, for these
Disease-beaten. Lambaréné
Contains dark coiled up like the image of germ
Disease in forest, mud lying flat over ground
Claimed by nor man nor beast. Who keeps Sabbath
When that Sabbath swarms flies, when mud laps its coat
Of tongue over the earth? Whatever you keep
We keep also, through the flat example
Of mud
Of breathing forest in whose stillness hears
The crying man sick. In our countries there is
Forest; (for us also) in the forest
Plague.

There is a clearing in the thickened wood
There is a masquerade, there is dancing.
Yet not for this painted hour as between trees
Comes the brute fly who bearing a disease
Utters her sting to the blood. The perishing.
For which sting we shall care, though we have not
(Neither for the limped horse, nor the man
Sick with beating) cared. In the rude flowers
Of the mud you nursed the darker flowers
Whose flesh restored opens, as prayer, word by word
Opens. Or as music opens. By

The simple act of choice the set deed heals.
O Father's care; the blood's flower opens.
Command us, for our actions, this atonement;
Let us see the clearing in your tiger shade.

Example.

We have your actions; we have these words; cut down the dark
Glades. Cut down, you say. We might follow.

War Song to an Ocean Headland

I, perched here at the top of you,
 am perceived as a chunk of mortality
 amidst your eternal cloak of fog.
To hear my war song, you would like to chuckle,
 softly shrugging me off your shoulders;
For your sea roar could easily support
 the rattle of M-16's.
And if a thousand bodies' blood ran down these black cliffs,
 you would think it a soft summer shower.

You: Immobile granite hulk of new found, forgotten peace,
 rising from the sea into eternity –
And me: tense and flighty, frightened,
 I pick and pluck at the lichens
 (far removed from your essence):
 the mosses crumble in my fingers.
We are, then, for an empty moment
 strangely merged here:

You have the time to solve my war-problem
 but the mumblings of your mist laden spruce
 and the whisperings of your wind blown thistles
 are too sophisticated for my short ear.
My fury of choppers and flying phosphates

is to you but a second's flurry of wings
that momentarily hides the sun.
My aching battle alights delicately on your black back
and soon is gone.

'By that house where we met'

By that house where we met
Near where the trees rear their complexity
I bitterly think about
Our meeting not yet foreshadowed. Then you fingered
My name, preparing it
For your love. Flames rose in our spirits as

Sex in the employed blood
Rises to touch, dignified in intensity.
You spoke my name, which sounded
As the sea when it tells itself, 'The Sea';
And I stood in your mind
Upon this same ground, while you as the ocean

Between its waves attempts
To concentrate its nature, you tried to
Involve all that I am
In you; just as the mind attempts to draw
The train as it leans on
Its curve, and then is gone, into it. Later

Where that community
Of trees flowered, we kissed. That was in summer
A month ago beneath
Society's heavy, small-leafed maturity.
But where so many lovers
Have kissed and wished the permanence though not

The dead lives of the stone
To compound with their joy we now no longer
    Joy nor decimate
Our pains as well we might had summer moved
    Us in its leaves' unison.
Some will furrow the tumult of pointed shades

    And crush the material of
Their selves, autumnally. The leaves, the dead leaves
    Will rise in anger with
Shrieking mouths awry against their mutual selves'
    Destruction; some steps tear
A drift of crinkling leaves. Separately

    We trudge in sloughs too deep
For mutual remorse. Better or late
    The world circles upon
Its old, gross hinges and the days seal tighter
    Like graves, our common lives,
Kisses inside the earth. Others within

    The assurance of trees
Waited the liberation of their love,
    Like winter birds stayed in
Those branches, not for comfort only but
    To grow between such space
As a tree takes to mature; they grew.

    We rose and the trees in
That forked moment, in unison forewarned
    Our mutual wreckage, whenceforth
Our lank life has been blown not far from where,
    And it is buried where
Love tangles its pairs of slow heats, yes, where

The trees distil their calm.
Yet though our mutual life died, loving did not.
That measure – though the trees'
Mirthless entablature of our passion
Derides with a patient soughing
The dissonance of desires that were not

Synonymous, nor yet
In harmony with the leaved knowledge of trees,
Birds with their dissonant nature
Search in mistrust for those trees whose growth will endure
Even the eagle's heart and vulture's lust,
Huge and synonymous
With other boughs' maturities than these.

'No tree spreads in this garden'

No tree spreads in this garden
Without root, no organisms in it
Grow but the gathering silence of despair
Slopes through the synodial quiet. I walk in
These unassailed darknesses, and near here
The breathing martyrs' train
Disturbed the drum of the street.
I will not tread this route again; I accept
The stoneness of the world, the broken places
Elided in ruins, and the rural scene
Covered in stone; my protestation is
A cut course, but a dry one,
The bramble of the earth hangs over me
Dried to a bone,
My bones the chattels for another man's pity.
Peace now, clasp peace to you
Dried self to dry sleep, with memory
No more intemperate at the injustice of
Man's stony garden. Fountain

Head nor tongue, the river is now not
Your nature; and that last least is the worst.
A stone out of the blood within my stones
      Has been made of these rednesses;
Through which deserted garden ground the dead
      Have departed, are gone.

Who stand aloof can cheer most timelessly.
But for the step each martyr took I bit
      In anguish the irreducible
Grist of stone; and loudly the crowd cheered
      Not knowing that cheering
To be a comment on their ignorance.

      There is no difference
Between the two; martyrs are self-condemned.

      In that deserted garden
      I tensed my featureless
And glacial sinews, pastureless and dark
      Until I heard the cops' tin whistles
As, toy by toy, they took each saint away
      While through that outrage, loudly
The crowd that day, cheered the carnival
      Long after it had died away.

Park

to G.S.F., in his anger and bitterness[4]

The stream drops through this walled ground, disarrayed with
Leaf, clutching stone, and round large boulders that
Were placed to emphasize, and not mimic
But adorn nature, if improve it.
An isolated garden walls kept fast,
As though it would lose essence trying to
Order the adjoining country's tumult, or
The country take that sweetness for itself;
Walls that excluded all wildness, man broke,
And let nature, with all man, enter.
Some cry, 'man betrayed by man.' The breached wall
Admits a thoroughness it will not regret.
Weeds do not choke, and do not disadorn what
The eye rests on. Rather, this disjoined wildness
In its northern strength, has displaced man's eighteenth
Century exclusiveness with fecund
Disorder, that, once more, falls on the winter earth.

Not quite displaced, either: but added to;
So that it properly shares in changing man's
Relatedness. I have watched the body
Wanting the limb whose use it still asks for; or else
The formal park, though now encroached on, its stone house.
Look round, in startled fear, like the antelope
Who find their covert brake removed by man.
Just as the hidden softness of a refuge
Is gone, so is the house society built.
It was the privilege many suffered when
They reared with pain the balance holding, held by, their pain.
Though some delighted in the harmonies,
The house was torn up, and earth filled the wound;
The seeded tree burgeoned on the scar. What
Man took from nature, as he took from man,
He prospered, and in his protective walls
These partly shared his increase. In the brute world

Brute man and nature grew, till neither needed,
Or cared to endure, the values of the house
So equably built on man's deprivation,
Nature's exclusion. Now the intense growth
In its rough but natural tenderness encroaches
And nourishes what it finds of symmetry.
Each gains. The owners of the house, decamped
Years into the jaws of this moist earth,
Faintly make out the cry of the child with
His bounding hoop, who mounts against the falling stream
Through the park. Men grow more in love with
What is confederate, and the house was not.

Its values disestablish it. Pass to
New isolations. Enriching memories
Like heavy water glimpsed in near sleep, strengthen
The mind that moves lightly against the stream,
Fluent in unchangeability.
Hostile to the age? But if the garden change
The qualities of its growth, be one of those
Who struggles with new complexities,
Though you fight casually. Look to this ground:
The web-wheeled carriage, whose master's taste fines down
The intellect, has passed. Nevertheless:
Individually give to this shared park
The intent of your mind marled with his; and turn
The carriage wheels that bear the intellect
That burns to find its place; the intellect
That spins its own fate, and is its own fate.
The garden out-folds, and the world creeps in.
Walk through the park, against time's plunging stream
Though walking the new, enriched ground is dread.

Blossom

Delight: is it like
Blossoms stiffly distending
Thrusts of blackbirds' tails
On long ends? Or blossom
Whose petal knocks together
In waxen hubbub? Or more
Akin to children clustering
Like fatted petals round
The thick seeds of their game?
I hear my ageing man
Inside turn on his back.
I crouch over my stick;
And in my breast pocket
Absorb the friendly watch.
Else carry over the hill
With a child clutching me.
Damp knuckles with dry insides
Of fingers, hesitantly,
Lead tobacco
Like phlegm from a gap
In my clothing, and drag
Paper across the tongue.
And the wind consumes
This pension, this satisfaction.
I would give it to them
Again, were it large enough.

Things

What activity from
A man, a hoop, a minute wound?
A preoccupation
Of being watched. The writer
Searches the small particular,

The texture of life.
He makes this silent three
Cohere in a kind of damned matrimony,
As if their being seen
Were much for them.
Immaculate sentiment
Of the possessing ones;
A sud of amorous rage
On the lips, particles of
Poetry's divine spirit. He records
The bits and broken bits;
All grist being treasury,
Lifting his tiny pen
As a boy his organ. Possession
Significant since it can be touched.

Those three things again.
They also are meaningful
Which are owned, written of.

They have no energy;
They do not feel, or think:
All that could be done for them.

It is not, it is not.
A barren naturalism,
A 'this is' and 'no more
Than this' settles onto
His nib: twittering, indolent.

Not felt, but observed. Bread:
Still-life of the hungry,
Putrefies; rancid, painterly.

At work the white liver
Squirms with 'perceptions'.
Behind him steals a man
On huge light feet with an
Axe raised.

The Two Freedoms

First published by Chatto & Windus, 1958

for Gene Baro

The facts all belong only to the task and not to its performance.
Not how *the world is, is the mystical, but* that *it is.*
 – Ludwig Wittgenstein, *Tractatus Logico-Philosophicus*

The Two Freedoms

There were two birds today
Broke from their cage and seemed as gold until
    In the dry sun, their bodies were
Transfigured; they hung like ghosts possessed with the silence
    But not with the shapelessness of
Spirits; they, in the sun flashed one gold flown

    Through another;
And then were quiet on the broad, trunked back
    Of the wood chair. They were
Inviolable, with that power and helplessness
    Which sculpture has. The sunlight
Smoked on them, gold were their wings, gold feet; gold sounds

    Fled from their throats quickened by
The winged sun that, for a moment, urged their flesh
    To the transubstantial freedom
Ghosts are. They in the sun became the one gold
    With him in dignity.
I caught and put them back into their cage.

    Surely, I thought, Man is
Ridiculous whose avarice for life
    Is that he must put life
Back in a cage, cage life; he will increase
    The flow of the cruel gland,
Then watch, then feel his power and its rage

    Grow and be satisfied.
I shut the cage door, I looked with a cold rage
    At their stretched screams of pain,
And I thought again of the stairs down which the world
    Turns from its prison to
The cage of the still prison; turns and is caged.

And thought, but it is best
That they fly in their cage and do not learn
    Of that grey, ironic flight
From one space to another, but step down
    From their carriage in the air
To that humble, iron house. Safely the breast

    Has shed that gold
Which has perched, for an instant, on their flesh.
    But as these careful words
Turned in my mind, their cry like a stab pierced
    Me; I thought of my own
Wings, cut and trimmed by my grey God.

Furnished Lives

    I have been walking today
Where the sour children of London's poor sleep
    Pressed close to the unfrosted glare
Torment lying close to tenement,
    Of the clay fire; I
Have watched their whispering souls fly straight to God:

    'O Lord, please give to us
A dinner-service, white, and washed and gay
    As a plain of swan-stilled snow;
Lord, flood this room with your outrageous smile.'
    I have balanced myself on
The needle of the Strand where like a charnel house

    Each man and maiden turn
On the deliberate hour of the cock,
    As if two new risen souls,
To the cragged landscape of each other's eyes.
    But where lover upon lover
Should meet, where sheet, and pillow, and eiderdown

Should frolic and breathe
As dolphins on the stylized crown of the sea
    Their pale cerements lie.
They tread with chocolate souls and paper hands,
    They walk into that room
Your gay and daffodil smile has never seen:

    Not to love's pleasant feast
They go, in the mutations of the night,
    But to their humiliations
Paled as a swan's dead feather scorched in the sun.
    I have been walking today
Among the newly paper-crowned, among those

    Whose casual, paper body
Is crushed between fate's fingers and the platter,
    But Sir, their perpetual fire
Was not snubbed out, folded on brass or stone
    Extinguished in the dark,
But burns with the drear dampness of cut flowers.

    I cannot hear their piped
Cry. These souls have no players. They have resigned
    The vivid performance of their world.
        And your world, Lord,
            Has now become
Like a dumb winter show, held in one room,

    Which must now reek of age
Before you have retouched its lips with such straight fire
    As through your stony earth
Burns with ferocious tears in the world's eyes;
Church-stone, door-knocker and polished railway lines
    Move in their separate dumb way
        So why not these lives;
I ask you often, but you never say?

Baited

On the still bank I shake
My intense line of chosen fly into
    The stream where change is flowed
Into deep change, and tempt the casual fish.
    But who is the bait and who
Is that lilting procession, fish or man?

    Casually reflected image
Fish or fisherman, that heaving minute
    Changes my life away.
Life as sensation baits me to grasp the fish.
    I cast into the stream
And take my chosen bride into my arms.

    Never shall I within
That crystal water net so brilliant
    Or coloured a dancing fish
As I bestride her. I make the minute yield
    Only a meadow's breath
Green, green intangible, breath through my life.

    Gentle as a new bride
The baited fish leaps to my line. I pull
    Its fretting body out of
The unguent water wriggling with breath;
    I lay that fish onto
The meadow where my girl lies, netted in

    Green, green, o a green breath.
It is his death. He lies still through that stroke
    Of my mounted hand upon
His quivering neck, struck, and lies stilled upon
    My red, huge hand;
And such a fish for such a stroke as this.

    Casually reflected image
Fish or fisherman, I hurl that creature

Back into the stream.
Its life, small as a pool of soft blood in
     The hunter's hand it was
Not worth the tremor of my hand to kill.

     As this death hooks our flesh,
He puts his subtle hooks into our flesh
     Baited with tiny flies
And nets our lives away. Death is that dead
     Creature's unworthy kiss;
We are death's fish as we are death to fish.

The Third Death

And coming, they brought with them
The agony of their voices which they placed
Over my mind, that I was glad they had come;
     They were welcomed as guests were,
But in the tenth year of that agony
These reminded me of hell, and my own face
     An object of that country

     That I was not glad of any live thing.
This was the cardinal fault, whose salt agony
Sloed and crabbed my blood; this was the first death
     In the common arms of the sea.
So when I had died I rose out of that sea
     Putting on different raiment

     For new life without occasion,
Being a life of theme and life devoted to theme
As the saint and the martyr are devoted to their death.
     They were the thriving torment of
The second life, yet I was glad they had come
And with their pain brought a devotion in
     Whose fit and the imposition

Of it, I devoured
The pale creatures of the ceremonial earth.
The temporary ecstasy rose from the page
    Like Anaconda, writhing
To consciousness, like spirit out of spirit
And ghosts from ghosts. Then came death
    Whose abstract countenance
    He yet turned from me

Although I knew his hands, and those strange hours
He rides, and the mute instrument of pity
    He stays in his possession.

    He took in his black hands
My son, whose eye did not see whose mouth did
Not speak. This was the second death I saw
    And understood, and then
At the last venture of the tear of stone
Did not understand, because he had died in silence.
    This was the second death.

    In the third life I walked
Through desert, I, monstrous as the illegible rock.
My spirit, in the contortion of the third agony
    Cried out for moisture
Though there was none. And as I walked I spoke
To those voices lodged within the desert of my soul.
    I spoke to my Lady

    The Grasshopper, and the red
Bully of the Ant, and the honourable Bee.
And I pleaded with them, begging them to go
    To leave me to my own peace
And the possessive gestures of the dead
Yet they would not. So then I cried, 'You shall go,'
    Having played host to this greedy

    Faction of insects,
Being not of my own voice yet of their voices still.

And angry because I bade them go, because I
  Promised them they should go, they said
'But we will take with us our brother, Great Language,
With his huge crown and religious body;
    We will take,' they said

    'Your third life.' And they, going, took
With them the substance of that life going as they came
Without honour and without scrutiny
  Without love having no
Identity, leaving behind the dry agony
Of silence. And this only, is the third death
    Which I have died.

And I turned from the inner heart

And I turned from the inner heart having no further cause
To look there, to pursue what lay inside,
And moved to the world not as I would have world
But as it lay before me, as a map lies open
Unalterable through what it signifies, without vision
Or fantasy, yet full with promise. And although

The world as I had know it I replenished
Only with the dreams of the man who lies in sickness
Although I believed in that reconstruction of hope
I knew that world, as replete with misery
As the bowl the beggar raises, empty, yet full
With the dried bones of starvation, as the cup denied

Milk, death before milk; and I turned to the outer
Place, although as I knew I could not hope
To care for those who were there, neither for what they might be
Nor for what they were, meanness scrubbed into the face,
The naked bone of the face in sleep
Not tender now nor cruel but as the stone,

Instrument to be used, to be kept sharp for
The brass fiction of the industrial King
Who is inviolate; but who is yet intact
From Human Agony. So that I cried, Lord,
I am not supreme with your Word, but regard now
Your tin world. Is *this* your vision? Straightway the whirr

Of the indefatigable machine filled the wheel–dark air.
And the worker cried, 'This is the terrible, real world
Of the beggar's bowl, which lies empty, world whose image is
Refracted by a brass screw. Our dreams are wound
Within the coil of tungsten. The beggar's bowls are broken;
But our world lies open like a map of hope!'

Hymn to the Solid World

And thinking of life I turned from that contemplation
Of the inner substance lodged within the spiritual terror
And then from the past whose operation or
                    Whose persistence even through
          The round process of memory
Is like love, complete, because not to be recaptured;

And this was the second life which I marked not now
Dependent on my vision, absolute and total
And because of this, vital, being the cause
                    Of my second birth
          From the salt arms of the sea
Cleaned by whose actions? the salt birds flying
Through the inalienable sky to light upon
The stoning of innocence;

And to watch helplessly, they and it, part
Of the structure of the actual world, to be
Remembered, the past dwelt on as the past
                    The root only of pain

As irretrievable through starlight
As Lucifer to the archangelic kingdom
   And because I turned about neither with hope nor plenitude
And because it was the

Outside I had turned to, I was glad
That I was able to see the actual kingdom
Moving within the movements of the earth
            Substantial, unlike
The Player in the thin air melting to touch
Not more solid than the displacement of dreams
Space taken out of space. Therefore I am glad
That the outer world is not to be withheld, total
      To the adoration of my heart
And the conclusion of my senses.

This Resurrection

My girl walks through the loves of the dead,
      They rise through her feet; weed, hair
Bone, stick and blood rise through her flesh and
      Enter the air.
      These are the world's dark care.

The ant in his brown kingdom blends
      His shape with the brown dead
And all that giant kingdom does
      Receive his tread.

And in the square herb garden where
      Time through the green chive grows
I hear my white-thighed darling talk
      To the oblong stones

Who, in that ceremonial
      Garden where I tread
Hear her pointed footfalls touch
      The shining dead.

Their bones rise up like martyrs
   On the fragment stone; I attend
Those feet that walk through her small feet.
   Grave are these dead.

As the clock in the firm garden which
   With not a small shout
But only by fierce shadow talk
   Casts time out.

Time that remembers not one
   Of the lovers' sounds now shall
Join to that brilliant stitch of feet
   Our own four feet.

The Return

   I have carried for five years
In me, your country cupped with oval leaves.
   It is a land quickened with streams
Which have no confluence, yet they now firmly flow
   One liquid star in my blood,
It is as a jewel there. It is fearful and

   Strange to attend you
For I once fled through your pattern, I who now cup
   Your shape in my palm, and I
Burst from the green veins of your delicate country
   Move into the grey
Borders of the town who crouches in her shadows.

   I revisit you now and find
There is nothing changed in you but myself, I am
   Like a bird
That lightly perches on the angular
   Chimneys of London; I see
The sour hands of that woman folded into her lap.

And I divine I now shall
Not be admitted easily to your source.
      That image of your streams met in me
As the confluence of the stars meets in the one eye –
      This I got when I saw
The white shoulder of your profound hill. Your were

      Then simple to me, but my thought
That now so distorts you, helped by the sensual flesh
      That exudes its particular scent,
The scent that the flesh gives out, and the flower exudes
      As they are loved – the gesture
Of the heart and the movement of the flower are the same –

      That starlike thought of you
Still treads through my head as a dream treads, quietly
      And with precision,
Unendingly real because impossible,
      That thought and that image of you
You now deny. I am refused by you.

      There are a thousand stones in
The shallows of the Avon but must I tender them,
      Become again the intimates of
Your intimates before I begin where you
      Began? The day's
Shadow has lengthened and the red sun stirring.

      Its more recent beams, in the evening
Grinds up its heat still; and in between the sheltering
      Walls of the town
Where the poor's tears are dropped without the leaf
      For their comfort or even
The stalk for their pity, it pierces. May I attend

These stones, as tears should be
Tendered. Say if you will admit me although
    My image of you is false.
Then your jewels, flat and poor, will have my tenderness;
    I will become their friend
Who fold over and over the fragile white rounds
    Of your demanding country.

Bronze Noon

I went into the fields this day and saw
You lying over the earth; you did not see me.
Over the ground, dignified, drifted the first
Fallen autumn leaves, lightly brown,
Which brushed against you. They came unasked for;
Neither by consent did they stay, nor by violence
But in that bronze light you and they together
Lay, you sombre, and they also bronzed.

Across the earth then paced two foxes, barked
Sharp and arrogantly; then they were gone.
No one bade them as guests welcome, they
Did not stay as guests stay or as sufferers of
A common idiom of martyrdom
But slipped redly back into the dark earth
Leaving no trace of their primitive visitation.

Over the ground then a short wind blew
But violently, fluttering those leaves against your thigh.
That too, passed over; but in the climbing
Noon I felt these figures rise in me.
For I am the fox watching for his mate
I am the branch whose leaves are blown against you
By a short wind. And then you stirred. I think

You did not see me, but that part of you
Which always you give to me without arrogance
And without humility twisted over, bronze, archaic
Almost in that autumn, appearing to draw me.
It summoned me to you, and as always I came,
I fell across you in that bronze bell of the noon,
It was without haste you drew me: but I shall not forget this.

Bowl

The beggar's bowl is formed from hands.
Hunger keeps them there, rigid; inside
Crouches a blessing from the sun;
Below; the dried bones of starvation.

No milk; and no wine.
You, into this gnarled hand put
Bread, and drop meat; raw,
Boned and moist, but donate no pity.

Loving

Say who knows how love is?
I am in love, you know.
I turn to turn and go
Yet move into your eyes,
And who knows how love is?
I turn to turn and go
For love will fly; and who
Cares that we feel? You see
Me turn. I turn to go.
I do not go: Love!

The Dark Drinkard

Then what a bony dance claps
　　About these ears, and what
A thin lit lanthorn is the face that
　　Is lashed dark with tears.

Loud that dance and fine that rage which
　　Whistles in the head;
Every mad head that's filled with it must
　　Anneal that winter dread.

I am a fine man sauntering when
　　I am rage, tear and fit
But I must warm the head that holds these
　　Winter tears in it.

For each day's sunday filled with woe
　　There is a deep, glass cup
I am a fine man wandering I'm each
　　Stormed and drugged night through.

For Two Children

I feel the burning of these crying birds
Whose tears drench my flesh and sweat the stone
Of law courts. By this law's destructive splendour

Two children flit through the needle of their town.
Past them, the ambulance on four naked feet
Treads in white fear, its antiseptic breath

Smokes on the patches of the blenched, torn blood.
Dust from the fire like a coat lies on
The rat-like pity of the lengthy dead.

I had not even bread to fill these mouths.
Here are two mouths from whose O terror creeps
Like a thrombosis, crawls like a screeching rat

Out of their net of mouths whose parents lie
Two perfect tongues of ash side by each side.
I have no bandages to dress these wounds;

I see no ambulance on naked feet
Will take these children like two feathers to
The anxious cemetery of maternal flesh.

But clothed in the ceremonial violence
Of fire that with maternal fever those
Burning parents from their bare children's side

Stole, they enter the red trap of their lives
Who are my children. Though I am now no father
Just such a death has entered my two lives

And I have no bread for their sullen mouths.

For a Deaf Girl
(Jean Matthews)

I see you unable to hear,
Although leaves intertwist shadow and crumpled shape
In the sun's flow;

For how silently the shadowing of such violence
Though a subtle stream indeed
That leaflike flow, strikes your still face. Incommunicant

In a world not of your world
I speak of these leaves. Yet still, could you hear, understanding
Would not be what you would hear,

But by rote
The tidal roar of silence in your ears.

To have experienced the murdering leaves
        Their violence, and, through the sharp
Clutches of grass, their scars in the sun and the wind

        Is to be unique. Leaves, voices
Their sounds fill all shapes with protest of your world
        Though you cannot hear

What love is done; therefore do we all remain
        In such silence as you lie lapped in?
For if you are deaf, so are we; though our worlds are different

One sea equally drowns.

Someone I Lost

for a sadistic girl

        One night you did not arrive;
And though the phone, like a dead man, tingled the air
        Your never answered once.
But then I found you lying exhausted in the
        Sleep of the hunted.
You had been with those prim, sadistic creatures.

        Old men and their half-wived daughters
On whom no rod is sacred but for pain.
        So smear your grit about
The belly and hope it sticks in the cut flesh; no shame
        Appeases the ancient cupidon
Whose tongue and whose trunk, its sticks fallow and pallid

By fifty years,
Would split the tender flesh as you would with cane open the cheeks
Of another's flesh,
Assuage you his whips then; there is no scorn like a child's
Scorn no, nor cruelty
The child will invent to perform though impotent to

The globe of love's tear.
Today is as yesterday and today's gift is more pain;
So inflict what you care
To lash into corporeal, childish hate
That temporal hate for yourself.
For I do not care that that whip which you turn through your
flesh

As the moon her shade through your brain,
Swells her flesh, like a deformity into some rose,
Rose, as you would say, beautiful
If red. Yet I know there is never a face but all other
Memory, like a fish
In the dark slips my straining hands; see, your face is a lamp

Shut from this fisherman's gaze
Though his lamp swings close.

From... The Animal Dark

1

Whatever the loss, the difficulty of prayers,
We have to climb up the dark religious stairs
Which lead, not only to a silent room
Shut with dead furniture, but to that place

We dread and sanctify with love. This room,
Light as a candle in a jar displays
Its motif of fruit, firm and free with light.
This symbol is the poet's lemon-tree.

We must attain our natural freedom, here
In this demanding room. And we must grow
More than a ritual of love, as this
Ripe lemon grew upon its desert limb.
This is most difficult: but we must live
The mediterranean figure of our love.

2[5]

My dear, this is a letter to your head
Wherein I ask you back. I do not know

If ever your meaning is ever my meaning
But with these scriptural words cold as Jack Frost

I ask you back. In letters we may write
Only the half of language; so that when
I write the word 'love' and I place love's word[6]

Closely beside you,[7] you may know by this
How actual the power of the shade
Which runs before me in the dusk. So I

Presage the lie of language which I make
And now send you a love crossed through the lines.
When you read this and with your mind work out
Its meaning, that charge may race to your breast.

Death of a Bird

After those first days
When we had placed him in his iron cage
    And made a space for him
        From such

Outrageous cage of wire,
Long and shallow, where the sunlight fell
    Through the air, onto him;
        After

He had been fed for three days
Suddenly, in that sunlight before noon
    He was dead with no
        Pretence.

He did not say goodbye
He did not say thankyou, but he died then
    Lying flat on the rigid
        Wires

Of his cage, his gold
Beak shut tight, which once in hunger had
    Opened as a trap
        And then

Swiftly closed again,
Swallowing quickly what I had given him;
    How can I say I am sorry
        He died.

Seeing him lie there dead,
Death's friend with death, I was angry he
    Had gone without pretext or warning,
        With no

Suggestion first he should go,
Since I had fed him, then put wires round him
    Bade him hop across
        The bars of my hands.

I asked him only that
He should desire his life. He had become
Of us a black friend with
A gold mouth

Shrilly singing through
The heat. The labour of the black bird! I
Cannot understand why
He is dead.

I bury him familiarly.
His heritage is a small brown garden.
Something is added to the everlasting earth;
From my mind a space is taken away.

Narcissus

Through the unendurable mirror gaze
    Like stag's eyes, those piteous ones,
That beauteous face and the entire body's fair shape
    Seeming of maturity.
But it is not. He does not nor ever can
    Fix with those bulging lusts
For any fairness other than his own.

    This was not beauty then,
For love of beauty is not love for self?

Yet though he will swoon only on his reflection
    Be thankful for all he is.
Lest you too overmuch fall through your own eyes
    And drown;
Entirely that vision of him could die.

It is too much to ask for love or even
    Its semblances.

Was there not sufficient punishment even was
There not reward for beauty plunging to meet its face
    Then drown with such love folded
Deeply through that unbelievable
    Pattern his clear lake held?

The Fool

    There was a lady
Who through her mind, green fell the plainted cry

    For all the riches which
A garden yields; while under her budded trees,

    Although she was a withered lady,
I through the tangled maze of hair my girl

    Lay netted in, loved all day.
This lady thought of love as she lay dying,

    Called from her antique sheets;
Flat on the dolphins' pillow lay the carved

    Heads of the fishes that
Crashed through the waves beneath her hair, naked

    And wreathed white about those fish,
As I came to see if she were dead.

    For as she lay she called
'John,' she called, 'below my garden there

    Is treasure; count but the cost
To bury me there.' I buried her that night

Her ghost burst its frail flesh.
The moon, through the mild sky, raised its mouth and

Struck sharply the side of
My spade, and died. It fell, and falling, died;

Like a white child it died.
Then all exclaimed that I had killed the moon,

So that it seemed to me
I must dig now to rid my sharp soul of

Its dark, contextual guilt.
So, when the stars, those multitudinous hands

Rose with their fingers spread
Through the metallic night-sky, I cried out

'Where is that gold, O indeed
 Where is that treasure which you gave to me?'

While every voice cried out
Sharply, for pain, that I had killed the moon.

No argument appeased
The terror of their wide, pacific souls.

For yet the moon, its stars
Of flint fingers, they cry
On me, the night my sky,
Here is this fool who seeks some treasure still.

The Shirt

for Ann

Although I feel its shape could knit my bones
    As the sun's cautery the eye,
Yet by this gift you wove I cannot promise
    Though now I say
Love, eternal love! Death separates: but
    Life too pulls apart

That ancient, faithful, penelopean weave
    Of love's gentle shirt,
Unpicking each web which
    With pitiless care it spins
About the naked, blue – like the hungering sea.
    It is love's curse to bless

And hate; this shirt you net me in will burn.
    For though now beneath these hands
Which press this oceanic shirt round me
    I thrive in your eyes' kind sea;
  That same steady main
    Which through the texturing earth
Is always working its queer alchemy,
Of your curved scalding eye shall bitterly cauterize me.

It is in love's sweetness to calcify; and
No-one yet wove more sweetly than you for me.

The Betrayal

I met a simple boy
    Upon the lifting stair
I moved my look away,
    But he stared.

The next day he was there
    His hand or cheek as frail
Upon the stair, again
    I looked away.

The third day he paused I
    Smiled, he moved away.
Such frailty as this
    I find in smiling.

Yet higher through the air
    Without clasp or rail
He spoke to me 'I wish
    You were mine.'

Such simple talk as this
    Has moved me through the air
'Would you were mine,' I wish
    My lover were here.

Yet when he asked again
    Some voice I could be sure
Did not belong to me
    Answered him 'Yes'.

Meeting Publicly

In the afternoon came her strickened note,
With that its cry;
She would be found asleep
In the glass café.

There on the main street, she
Crouched to her pain
Lay with that attached gaze
Of insolence the

Publicly casual eye
Cauterized into her flesh.
O untiring fingers that itched
In the flower-strewn street.

Who placed flowers on the street
That you might crush them?
O sleeper caught at the heart's
Circling with high

Whirlwind of towered eyes;
O gentle girl
Round whom such simple eyes
Like grey mice, gaze.

Will you not stretch a little
Since they now laugh
And laughing as though that pressure of gaiety
Were a thing to suffer

Casually and without blemish
Without concern even,
The mocking insidious eye of lust and fingers
Which grope and itch

In the blindfold pocket of air
In the flower-strewn road?
The insolence, the assumption blindly placed,
The sniggering eye.

I shook you awake but then
While you lay that I stood
In the brown air thickening gradually with
Both mutated pains,

As you came from but as I entered
Sleep, I knew then
My pain to be your indignity.
For what you

Asleep but dreamed, perhaps, I
Saw then. And making
My pain from you created in you mine.
Say you forgive me.

But of course standing there in the café
I could not entreat this, I regret.

Light

I have not the purity
Needed to judge; kings of Africa sold
Men they enslaved in their wars
In bondage to the English. Who has the purity
To condemn? The chandelier
Of Europe and its bits of jewelled glass,

That intricate glasswork of
Such human fabrication must seem like
Bruises of clustered lights.
Yet entire must be the lilac; peace be our singular light.
It is hard some say to keep whole
What the wind shakes. So too, the Germans found

Civilization to be
Fragile, a chandelier-like lilac, nor hard
    Such multiplicity of
Singular petals to dash in the might of the wind.
    But you would forget that storm
Which bruised the multiple lilac-head. Now as

    I ask you to encandle
Your quivering chandelier into one whole
    Pure and bell-like light,
That smart through Europe bends our crowded heads
Like flowers frail crimson-bruised, harsh jewellery
    Low, loud and harsh;

Much like the surf sliding upon the sea,
    Pacing to storm
Its black coronets. I know the intent of the sea.
    And what single light is not drowned
    In the glut of the sea's dark sound?

To Michael Riviere, for his Second Son, Thomas

    Though you were once the hand that teemed
    The field of Gascony,
    Under your fathers' feet the dragon
    That their king had sown
    Sprang attenuated spears
    Bitterly sharp.

    They from that pasture glided.
    Safely did their flesh
    On the curling ship take flight
    Through the stylized wave and come
    To England, that crozier.

Simply by riding on the sea
Your family grew here.
They found no swallow in this air
But the white gull dashing his laughter
Against the prosperous English rock
Where the crystal stone through which
Gently, flowers poured out, lies set.

And they upon that stone of flowers
Rested and again drew their hours
To that sweet consummation which
This fatigued bird, England, may never
Suffer again to be burned, ever.

Because that stone cannot again
Speak with the voices of the rose,
Suffer any culminating flower,
Stone can become flowers but once,
I incise these words on its quiet stone.

And these are for your second child
Who like a small fly comes
Into a land adread with webs.
Thrash rain, wrench wind; I'll write them out again.

A Ballad

It was a Sunday morning when
    My love would join to me
Her mouth lying open, that the wakened birds
    Between our mouths might flee.

A ship on the tongued waves, I moved through
    The adamantine sea,
And the panting air swept me on though I lay
    Trapped in her combed sea-hair.

'Can you tell me,' she would slip round me,
        'If you will love and if you
Will forever twist like a whisper through
        This spiral shell of me?'

Then she would put her hands above
        My head which passed near hers,
And bless me with her hands which flew
        Like a cluster of sea-birds.

And, 'Will you marry me,' she asked
        'And keep a house for me
And will you feed my children that
        You shall beget over me?'

As our sea-language flew about
        Like two birds through a cage
That from one iron to another fly, yet
        They must contain their rage

Her swelling kingdom of the sea she
        Reconciled to me;
That door my ship grooved through the sea
        I opened it to me.

And I admitted these skilled hands as
        She blessed her hands on me,
And I put my hands on her waiting breasts
        As my mother had let me.

We both stole through that sea-town where
        The liquid in a cup
Is made for drinking from those tears
        A man and maiden slip.

Yet merrily did my love taste then
        Upon another's woe
To try that salt, elliptic cup
        I would abjure to know.

She lay upon our skilful sheets
    Her tears fled straight down
Globing a pain which in her eyes
    She fitfully tried to drown.

'Why do you weep so bitterly,
    Why does the whole sea weep?'
'I have endured another's tears
    And though from port one ship

One ship should sail upon the sea
    I love another more.
This infinitely deepening eye
    The fish-distracted sea

Has drowned within a tear of pain,
    Yet still I shall be true
Till this tongued sea runs dry for it
    Cannot be taken from you.'

I said: 'You are the sea and must
    Consume in your flow all
Those tears of another's woe
    Or else flow not at all.'

'Then kiss me once, but sweep like a bird
    Through me,' she cried, 'and though
You search like a shell for that smallest sound
    Of me you shall not be heard

Through a sea-world, darker than mine where
    Tears drop like gulls
Through two hollow columns with broken wings, they
    Are the darkest tears I know.'

Poem

1

And now we speak of death
Each stress of life trembles, disintegrate of
Experience, several-branched, forming one tree though,
Multitudinously branched inside
My head. Its birds tilt on the ends of leaves
And staunch my stressed wounds, which ooze their green
          thoughts out;
As twigs, spilt by the wind, splinter their sap.
Experience is a wearer. It rubs and will
Split the tips of twigs;
Then branch and tilt my trunk, until all breaks.

Through the silenced ash of night you come: –
Stare as the corrupted face behind glass stares
Stricken to dying, and see world outward turned,
World in one rush turned onwards past those eyes.
The town bird gluts his beak with soot yet. And in
Such stress as this your shape prospers, even
As flowers prosper, and make such argument of
Stress their love. And I can feel your form,
Your glance of shadow sensually ashen,
Your pool of darkness in the evening glaze,
That pure volition of your entire rose
Make love a quiet state of intersection
With time's clay-dust flux.

Augurs of dying, fumes of twisted clay,
Spare, spare, O spare this deep wood trunk, my chair
Of flesh; and this soft, dropping, city-blown Venus
Combed by your smoke, as death can comb the long
Hair of a child stretching it till she break.
Stay your thin hands; such fine, long hands drawn in the dust:
Petal-fleshed she will
Be burned by what burns all women: withering.

2

And if I speak of town, there is more dust
Than I have ever tasted, blown off brick
Over road, on which
On four white treads the ambulance balances.
It is to take the corpses off the streets
We see her whitely staring in the noon.
Scarcely she seems to move; yet in ghostly angst
She glides hideously, Eumenides
White through the quivering skull prepared for death.
The flower, the ambulance and the trees are covered
With dust. Speak carefully. He means to choke;
And weakly the soul would shrieve in soot such
Love left then. My hours turn as through heat
With flower, summer-fumed and murmurous with
The long, black, cat-like cars. And the ambulance
Picks still the corpses. There is so little here
Of summer – for this noon-day is closed, cold
And still; yet motionless like summer still.
Here death attends; here drops his bodies down:
There is no flesh that in dust will not drown.

The House

I gaze into the stream
Where the house in ruins stands, disturbing the crystalline
    Water with my eyes;
For I glimpse below the surfaces of that stream
    Many shapes in alarm.

In shallows my childhood lies.
The burnt house with its mermaiden servants gleams
    Erect under the polished
Calm of the water. Look, from perches children, like fish
    Leap. But short and

Useless are limbs which glower through
That ominous clarity which impregnates the real
    World with derelict dread.
Where this sweetness intrudes with another the proper world
    Again look; not lies gleam but

Destruction. Through the palely billiarded
Lawn now begins to glow the fires chimerical
    Multi-tongued face making urgent
Through glass the scared, white children's faces' throng.
    Begin to crumble such dreams

In the fire's commitment as I
Had, the shrill tongues clamouring for the moist earth.
    I cry out
In several voices at once, for I am these lives
    Which shrill as the sharp fire touches

The tender bone.
Into bubbling mud my childhood disintegrates
    Colliding with dreams
That prophecy of a world through whose white screams
    Of children, drive the dark fish.

There is one house, there is one fire which burns
I cannot lose, I cannot re-create.

Again

I slack on the stonily piled shore
And think of each tumultuous mind
Which gazed on the long sea's stumbling roar
Of marbaline water. And I remember
That this had happened once before.

Stones children sink into the water
A feather lying on the passive
Starfish, raddled pebble;
The weight of the white, battering sea
Trammels into shape
What had a volume once its own.

I dwell on your sexuality
And those limbs tangled
In wrack-clung weed of glistening wave;
Yes, I move to you on the shore
Where the predatory tide
Climbs his white fingers up the stone.
The moon-wrenched tide draws up in waves
The crass weight of the sea;
There is no object which is not
Endowed a shape by it.

Even then if I turned from you as the sea
Rolls off the strand again
You, and before you, women who sat
Still on the tangy shore
Know the sea's limbs will lick into
Their shores' declivities
Again, endlessly.

Upon the strand where flowers of spray
Rinse the stones, I cipher
The purpose of those tides as they
Echo and re-phrase endlessly
'Do not' that large cry 'Do not submit.'

The Victims

for those murdered by the Nazis in concentration camps

Love, when you ask me forgiveness
I see not you but hairless wrists involved
With love's embrace, he a friend the sufferer clasps;
Who is in shackles, whose wrists soar, who is a bird
Wrenched into focal agony. This charged symbol,
Stripped by brutality of fictive detail,
Stark to the pain it symbolizes, wrought
To bird in flight, bone and wrinkled skin, these being
All of the bird pain wrenches into flight –
It moves with such daring the mastery of its flesh
No martyr, less a saint. For saints have been
Chosen by God; martyrs who self-elected,
It was their love of God the arrow charged
When it drove on through thigh and breast. Victims,
Neither chosen nor choosers, but they die.
Action from love, forgiveness from compassion
Issue like glandular fruit out of the thigh;
Though thorns would pain these do not prick to bleed.
I pray your compassion for you know that I
Did not, and could not have endured your pain.

It is impingement makes me feel this so.
The dead raise up their arms like wings, dividing
In suppliance the hardly bearable
Gold spaces of the air they did flap through,
Dying. Their wings were clapped off, their arms were
Stretched to the utmost of their fall. Now still
Arches the sky which quivered once with their cries,
For hard as stones do they now lie dead. Pain
Nor agony nor heart can put a heart again
Into that stone the dead are. The shallows and the hills
Give ground to the dark of the earth and the shades of the earth;
These are put in the earth's declivities;
That is a great coffin. The dead have left
Like birds. Death being no ceremony. Death being
A stone in the earth and spaces in my mind.

Did they speak to you, for they said nothing to me?
Yet sometimes at night in those drear silences
Such words as pity and love are whispered through
My brain's greyed-and-white rooms, coiled with doubt, that dread
Of silent death, by them; so that I know
Entangled in sleep's glade, the bitterness of
The wood as the axe enters it. Those shapes
Colliding mine within me while I slide
Through sleep, 'Whose cry is that' I ask, 'but mine?
Whose suppliance, love, implies an anodyne?'

Unpublished and Uncollected Poems,
c. 1958–1961

A Walk in the Sun

We must always take care
Of men with knives in the ferocious dark
    And protect ourselves
          Henceforth.

       And our children also,
With rigid limbs declared of steel chain.
    We must beware
        In narrow

       Streets that have houses
Hanging over the eager light, men
    Mad to be hold of
        The blade

       Whose swift road
Leads into the little red heart.
    The human cry of
        The knife

       Arrests our blood singing, and
Its cry comes out like a pierced nightingale.
    We must not suffer
        Or allow

       To suffer the blinded animals,
Our children, walking in the atrocious dark.
    But defend our streets
        With fists.

       We may never carry pistols
But with our hard hands strike the attacker down.
    As you walk through
        The town

Watch that man holding over
His blooded eyes a thick tawny hat.
    Neither singing of
        The birds

    Abate his anger. But
Hungrily he will seek human flesh.
    Now with my hands
        A-side

    I fearfully walk this long
Road aware of the distance it takes a man
    To die. I am aware
        As well

    Of the road I may walk
Past the lampposts with the birds singing on them.
    It is the length of life
        Watches me

    And summons my thick red blood
To my throat. I am most eager to live.
    Never before was I so
        Unwilling

    To pass my earthly
Heritage which is a small walk in the sun.
    But the knife blade
        Sings so

    Sweetly in the hot night
I am afraid with all my heart to die.
    I clench my rotting
        Fists, I

    Fasten my fingers into
My flesh. But nothing avails my trembling sweat
    The salt river pours
        Over me.

If there were a dog here
He would smell the fear in my pale thought.
Long is this street with
Fear, but

Short the man's knife and quick
His passage into my broad red heart.
I do not love him,
I do

Not allow him the gift
Of my life. Then up my hands like steel and steady
My thighs and thought
For your strike,

For your knife in the flash of
Exact terror that cuts into the heart.
Thus far fear triumphs.
For I have

Your arm in my arm
And your strike in my grip. Your eyes are over-covered
With four fingers. You are set in
A trap

Stronger than knives more
Intent than the eye of the moon. You yield.
You are right to surrender.
Away

Goes your knife which frightens me.
If the silent dog were in this street
He would bite my
Fear.

So away goes your knife
Holding my bitten fear in its head.
I run the harness
Of arms:

I desire you as victim
To the broad blade that cuts into the heart,
    And opens the
          Way for

      The red rose of blood.
You would kill me though I do not want to kill.
    You are frightened, and that
        Is good,

      For I am afraid also.
Leave we the little thing which lies asleep
    In the gutter. Two men are
        Frightened by

Death – the hand that puts death into man.
Allow the thin vagabond sleep in the road

So that when the dog comes he will bite the bright blade.

'A handkerchief'

A handkerchief
Pleated; a cloth smooth
By an iron's prow palm.
A dry sheet shrunk,
And then boiled thoroughly
Of mucus. An outfit
Laundered of the inward grin
At another's agony.
Now rehabilitated.
A priestliness of maternal
White solicitude.
A carriage for the decencies,
On the palm. A linen grief,
Its silence is intense,

In this instance, with death.
Quite unrelated
To me through the blood.
But since it is his
Mine too, by our kinship.
I move through him that loved
The very nails she scraped
And where she is I put
A hand on her.

Palinurus

His white bones are hushed under the sea now?

Our pilot guided us through the night sea
And there was no doubt. The inbellow and the rote
Of water smashing the grave agony
Of rock and shore did not trouble us,
Pieces of rock and small pebbles since
Rubbed smooth with the wisdom of the sea
Did not disturb the modern throb of our journey
Going into the night. The night springs up
As we enter it, and down, having passed by.
Crowned silence. Our pilot guiding us.
How far are we from land, Palinurus?
But he part of the deep, instinctive sea
Belonging to the sway of the sea trusting in the sea
Said nothing, keeping his course by impersonal stars
Through salt water and the harsh roar of
The everlasting and religious water
Once unsalted come from the discipline
Of the earth. We made our way this night towards
The East, expecting when the first finger
Of the next morning put into the sky
The enormous silence of light, to see land.
There was no doubt. And in our minds arose

That dark serene communion with the sea
Which Palinurus knew. And trusted in.
Crowned silence of the sea. Our ship goes well
Tonight. Peace after storm, sleep after toil.
Profound sleep upon the ever wakeful
Into the enormous arms of the sea, throbbing.
Where are we now Palinurus? Long sleep
As the motor and the religion of the seas roar.
No answer from our pilot. Long sleep.
What kind of men are we? The small ship
Moves through the diamond water of
The social sea. Loyalty to the state.
Why should we make sign of obeisance?
I dream. I sweat. Other loyalties
Tug, tighten my limbs on her, further loyalties
Of mankind, in the deep instinctive sea.
I dream. I sweat. I have a public mind.
O Community, dancing over the waterfront,
To send us off. Girls, limbs open
Rigging of the occasion. O my brother
Your soul too, long now rubbed
Clean as the sailor's garment in the sea
For the purity, for the religion of this occasion.
Others. Others too. Others' voices too.
First: the taste of wine; the taste of flesh
For another. Appetite without passion.
Guns for one. Mechanics of the diesel
Throb of the engine within the throb of the sea
For one. The roaring voices of the crew
And the final murmuring of the voyagers
As we set sail with Palinurus, Master,
And Mariner in the logic of the ways of the sea.
I dream. Murmur of dreaming, lips, tongue,
Tongue to tongue. I am a sailor washed
By the clear knowledge of the passionate sea.
Palinurus! What cry from the fractions
Of Time? What hour, what week, what year, which sea
Are we in? Crowned silence of the everlasting
Sea. Sound of fishes' bodies, in the dark,

Palinurus, cry Palinurus where are you,
Guiding our ship by an old sequence of stars,
Head directed to the indestructible
Routes of the sea? We trust our pilot
He having taken us like children between rocks.
In the thick night through which we could not see, he saw
And steered us with calm precision through
The giant projection of teeth, fangs of rock
Waiting, for the ships. Old enemies. Palinurus,
Where are we? Voices of silence.
Gone. Into the air replete with sea-spray
Into the formlessness of the captive ocean
Gone. Our pilot gone. Palinurus,
Our skilled Mariner blessed with vision in the dark,
Guide; gone with him the rough tiller
Predator of the ship. Male organ
Ship without gender. Gone. We will be lost at sea.
Out of silence the sea still continues.
We do not know our way and the steering is gone
Snapped off in the calm night by his strong arms,
Wrenched with deliberation by
A skilled mind. And a sick mind?
How should we know, who have served only
With skill of crooked hands, fractured with the care
Of small offices? Dreams of the sea.
Home from the sea. The urine smell of children
The clutched hand and the bulbous face.
Ease of smiling; raiment of deep love
And the limbs of the woman opened out in deep love
Home from the sea. I dream.
Loyalty of service, Palinurus,
Into the profound sea that never harmed you.
May it never harm you. But we are in
The grip of the unconscious of the sea
Matchwood of boat in the huge, religious sea
Turning in the increasing howl of the now howling sea
Stateless, towards the East, treachery
Of helplessness and joy of private thought.
Gradually we are not to be harmed.

The sweetness of the sea after storm
The sweetness of the sea through storm
The upturned fury of the faces of the sea
Imperturbable with fury, gnash of stone teeth.
We are cleaned in the everlasting sea.

The Making Act

Haydn bought once,
With what he had, a book
Of music for keys.
Each piece, as he played,
Began intricately to impinge
On its neighbour; the whole
Shaping one growth of mind.
Which, as disease, it would
Not leave; but pressed through
The puscular ooze of creation.
At length there remained some core
Only, and numbness,
Where that deciduous sense
Of the mid-winter thorn
Had been. Blood touched the insides
Of him; then a stiff net
Of lymph threw over.
A wounding heal! by which
He knew the vigorous growth
Was waning, like a plant
Whose sap retreats, winterly;
And whose root, like a withered spider,
Sank off through the earth
To cooling minerals
That once gave life; yet sense
Of life did not come to him,
As if wholeness were death.

He shaped some music into
A 'Farewell', in whose last movement
Players, like human senses,
Snuff and go – two violinists
Gently relinquishing the jest.
His patron got that.
There was no punishment
But the holiday hinted for
In the players' getting down. They did
Leave; journeying south.
Each day as they more warmly
Crawled on the earth's bosom
Seeing Europe's sun
With a more reddish pang,
The blood of heaven shimmered.
They stopped at Greece. A field
Of asphodels trapped them,
Breathing into them a poignancy
Of oils, like stretched lemons
Rinded in colour before them –
Sprang into their senses,
As beetles to the wood
They tunnel, making of it
A food. But Greek girls
Drew up a candled meal.
All this happened, certainly:
The agony of wholeness,
Eaten, and divided,
Though it was his the burden.
Still it was not enough
Until, again, he fester;
Although he pulled the rough-husked
Bread apart, absorbing
Such properties of life
As he grew on, early.

For the disestablishing of Authority

(Poem to be laid reverently on the gown of every University
when it dies)

Dignified since grossly secure,
Authority, a stone limb with root
Transformed compulsively by Man's self
Through vegetating tissue to
Stone, by perfection of the slow–
Fingered command in sententious
Beads of cliché, each dignity
Swathed in graduate calm weathers
Provocation, and smiles in
The rage of sun or north wind.
Chipped into these statuary,
Delinquent in that life has lapsed,
Whose last duty was paid to
Agreed rightnesses, the true
Expressions gleam. Like fractured ghosts
The spiritual shuttlers resist
The flint disagreement is, which provokes
Nothing anywhere in them. What shock
Can these sustain, planted up to
The groin? Show then. No hand, or foot
Joined by levers to the soul
Can be so sure, and be alive.
Forgive others their life and give
If but in memorial gesture, licence
Of choice for growth in the aging spirit
To turbulent young, that they may gain
Awareness through the hard delight,
Else by choking through anguish on the error
I show some live. Untangle the
Profusion of vipers, and let up
The nest of eagles, that the fight
To live, before natural death
Prorogues the soul to its firmament,
May, in decency, begin.

For the Poor: Poem on the City of Leeds
Rubbish Tip

There is a tip near; its roots are trees' roots,
In whose area ball-bone and sharp stem lie
With tipped cinder, that had been newspaper
Or clothes, in compressed fragmentation; have
The memory of the burst flames' inhalations;
Each is put to think of that use it had.
The torn bean-can jostles up to the leg
Of fire-proof trousers; his neighbour has survived
In skeleton, as the perimeter of
A bowl, whose garments of underside are
Pierced by a curtain rod of brass, awry
With anguish through fire, which liberated forces
Mutually irresistible. Who shed tears of brass
In raging heats is at the dry heart of
This convocation of household ghosts. Yes, here,
The lordly lie down with the humble and
Rejoice in their common fortune in poverty. They speak
The essential knowledge of themselves, as each
In remnants, overhangs his wrath on man.
The bowl remembers, such the wanton kick
That let the water, mixed with air, rust its course through
And so invalidate it; the rod writhes
To think children swung on the gorgeous weight
Of curtaining, that, opaque to light and darkness,
It upheld in the ease fire-warmth makes,
And was bent; and it was removed. Ashes,
With charred distortion, speak such eager news
As the huge East in pain, and an unwanted heart
The soul quickly endured, as soon, forgot.
This is the place whose creatures fire drew life from,
Which poisonous nature rank with weed grows in
Nourishing itself on misery,
Contemporary in its collective agony.

      Going on in congressional care the tress bind
In absolute, also devotional stillness the

Infernal dereliction that's man's waste.
The trees are bent on a leaf-taking wind
That plucks attention to their nakedness,
And the trees wrestle with invisible adversaries
Combined in rage. The wind reveals the distortion
Anguish bends in boughs, which lurch mummerially
As though the cold, swollen moisture were a heady
Liquor they had drunk; the trees are together
Profoundly rooted in their sympathy,
Their regularity achieved by being
Grounded in love. Well, though the wind defrays them
Of what illuminates the flower, an oval leaf,
Since what grows must discharge its debt to death,
They give winter succour, bending boughs
As angels with warm breasts would bend over the oppressed,
Above a tip whose lives have been abandoned.
To these who in the confused harmony of silence
Moved alien to each other, when they were whole,
These rooted wanderers give
What life in its helplessness provokes in life,
An individual love to individual lives,
Since life has nothing it easily abandons;
And lift no heavy roots through soil, and stay
Dignified in togetherness, contrasting
That opposite disharmony of the pots
Who lived a separateness suffering joins now.
It is the trees, that with their confederate love
Grow this litter a kind of root, which is
Assured in unity and unified in dying.

Tip

Like a naked man sleepless in love
Light branches turn
In a leaved wind.
In this soil
Trees through care
Put root, tap root
Tuber swollen
With cold, there rests
A bowl, a rod.
Rust has gnawed
Deeply through
It is no more
Bowl than flesh
Rent, the spirit
Sheers off. The bowl
Tells how man
Forced a tear
In the side.
Was put by;
But air took shape, –
Its fanged cherubim
Bit and bit
Out much relief.
The rod
That hung cloths
Had the child
Swing, and bend
His child's weight
On the rod's.
Was put by,
The flames blent
And reduced
Servitudes
And degrees
In this tip.
Paper brass steel
Mildew here.

But the trees bind them
In subtle congress
Of which the rod holds
Grim conference
In twisted kingship.
It pierces
The torn bowl.
The leaved wind turns,
Among light branches
Like a bare man unsleeping in love,
And plucks attention
To more nakedness;
The trees wrestle
With unseen hosts
In visible rage.
The fused eye stares.
It is the wind soughs
Anguish through its branches;
Pain fly as leaves
And tear and tear
To a nakedness:
Yet the spare flesh
Is fit flesh
Of sympathy.
The leaves fly as birds
Deserting trees,
As a man's dying love slips
From the wife he has used;
The flocked leaves crush
To an ooze of love, –
Weightless love
Heavied to an oozing
Beneath its sloughed life.
But the trees give
A slow succour,
And they bend
Their branches over
A tip that rots.
As one from plenitude in

Prison gives to another,
All that he has encased
Increased in the stoneness of man,
Trees lift no roots
Through clung soil
But stay, binding
With swollen tuber, and touching
With much care
A put root
To this tip.
Then, then
In the swollen, in the liquid, years?
Since there were maimed
Still who are maimed.

Conversion to Stone

A living bird huge as grief crouches
On a wall round and brown as a copper tub.
Still, as though inscribed over these stones, yet
Poised there without angularity
Stillness assumes him as death grasps old age.
Yet in his broadbacked silence no one can say
There is no motion to him or procession
Of brown tower hacked from a stone pride.
There lies between the folded gesture of his wings
Neither still now nor moving, in their closed shape
A fat arrogance of brown bones.
You cannot say whose gesture this is, clamped
To a resting place. But pride is his.
Poised on a wall between two thoughts of life
This tiny monument this brown feathered giant
Small as a hand clenched in a square violence
Despising the adulation and the two-legged mockery
Of man, clamps on a look of death;
And thinks only of perching-time and birds.

'The choked bird twitters in the organ pipe'

The choked bird twitters in the organ pipe
The luminous faith upon the clock
Advises the girl whose light-flit memory lies
      Within the naked shade of her hunter
      That every sacred word
      Every stretched pursuant note
Has fierce tense keys that turn with rigid fire
      Strike the shrivelled note to life
And tremor wide the sea-jaw of her limbs.
      Now she sings his words as though swans,
Like wings metallically beat that bronze
        Of air they fly through,
      Brass into the air, divide
The sensual application of his keys
      Until each mode of thought
      Each stretched pursuant limb
Twists through the air, his words, that female bird
Who whirrs her shuddering wings through the Greek air
      Of female swans and Gods.

A Friend

My friend opened
The thick door, and moved
The tap backwards. 'Why?'
You mustn't ask. To interfere
In so delicate
And rational a process
Is... I don't know how
Another friend of his
Defines it: something like
'What has he to live for.'
And yet there must be
Reasons more than this simple

Sporadic deprivation
For choking oneself.
Friend, I am burning.
Our house is very fierce.
The growth of friendship is
Sizzling at the roots. Where are
You? The stairs are glowering.
The hoses of gas vent
Their toxins. With a knife
We'll saw each other's heads off.
Gentle pact of the gas-men.
Are we sinking then?
Pour on those vials of
Profuse reasons your friend has
For dying. Squeeze them over us.
Almond-sweet, friendship going
On among these gas-works.
Should these taps be turned off?

No civilized music here

I mark the engine moving to its trucks.
I attend its master; yes I see him come
To pierce the locomotive that in sleep
Confines the silence of the frosty air
To a white silence that parches the roofs
Of Charlton with frond-shapes. He treads the ground
And breaks the darkness with his lamp. And near
His feet the river glides, I dreamt last night
The net of silence in the dawn
That laid its finger on while we slept.
I had a dream last night. I dreamt that all
The women and the men upon the earth
Had come again to care for her again
Took conscious pleasure in the husbandry
And made its fruits flow through the fruitful horn;

We had achieved community that night,
Yielded the soil a natural measurement.
I mark the engine moving to its trucks.
I'll catch the stars up from the sea again;
I'll catch what seems to dance to me like fish
Although it is the starlight on the sea
The fish are stars upon the dancing sea.
I lay my symbol bare again: I
Will shed the legion of the moral stones
And grow from here of every wilderness;
Grow through my stars of every wilderness.

Passing

The stress of effort
Of the small train, clambering
Onto the Pennines, compares
With one in mid-cycle.
As more of him appears
He seems like a large tram
Charging slowly over
The soil, off rails.
The bare retraction
Of human industry.
Pricked by the earth's hairs.
Softening features drop
Into a fierce head
Placated slightly by
A cold, rounded hulk.
Nearly deliberate
And gentle, in movement.
I do not know this man.
Onto the clogging loam,
The phlegm of the soil, two clogs
Excrete fatted oils
Of mid-age; and further on:
A rounded milky hill.

I cannot define this,
But I believe that it
Is something like his death,
Perambulating to it
As a horse carriage might,
A profuse dignity,
Austere, slightly laid off;
Like a stiffly-sprung carriage.

Painting of a Woman

for Cynthia[8]

Pablo Picasso and Degas, Pascin and Sickert and Rembrandt,
All artists have seen them like this, standing or sitting,
Or lying quite still, but always the single figure, and
Round her room to wander forever, room for a prison.

Now alone in a northern room I lie and idly
Scratch paper, my itch, with poems and drawings, more
Of which lie round me, and on the wall one
A woman I drew this morning stares from painted
Eyes and asks me who she is, and

How we got here, me and this lovely
Femme who is always *assise*, or *nue*, or lying
With her face to a window, or dressing
In the grey dazzle of morning in a bedsit.
Who is close to block out sun, or is seen
In crowd for a moment, or only desired. But is always present.

As when clock saw me go last night, minatory
Murmured "I hate to mention, but eleven," to the company,
Who were too glad to care, and courting
Continued till midnight. Three sisters and another girl,
Three young men, my mother happy playing the piano

Clocks are defeated this way and grow diffident
Reduced to their right place, which is to plot
The shape of to be remembered joys for those
Whose memories are bad, or to preserve the pattern
Of small intrigues, diversions, disappointments.

Which is, to be often happy. In their good time
The young men went on two strokes, sisters
Shared faithful secrets on the way to sleep, and
The ritual bolts of bedtime shot, the servant
Clock was revived by our time master mother, who wound

Us all who are under her roof; in various ways
Has been mainspring or balance, regulator, key,
Though she never knew how, or expected praise
From us whom she first formed. Even the dead
Or now nursed, who nursed her, stand not so tall as she.

So in this poem, and in all my paintings
I mention her, pay due to the always in everyman present
Accepter, mapless, non map needing, stable and ever
Pointed to North, whose law is her nature, and own
Organic, non-errant, evocative, all comprehending position.

And in this painted woman, who cannot adopt
The lecturing habit, who cures all the glibness of teachers
I have exhibited mother and wife and mistress, that's
To say, an important presence and can confess
What we have one and all done. Paintings are often confessions

Though not entirely. Still, to those who loved me,
Who were tender, and were blamed, and abused, whose
Atmosphere was my petulance, half-love, never
Completed and mutual surrender, who
Waited for letters I didn't write, who when

The ice age came made a new start and let
Me warm myself at it, and were not over angry
But pardoned – to these I tender
My lies, fears and folly. I'm theirs
Who made me, my poems and pictures.

'Walking, starved and avid'

Walking, starved and avid, in the heat of love lavish summer,
In streets that were sore from sun, and patterned,
Non-fluent, organised like the grey mud that sun baked
Splits and cracks into blocks and avenues, away
From the huge humour of generous rivers, I stopped as a man
Stepped from a sharp, black, seeming disastrous doorway
Into the arcs of the sun, and carried to a cart a cage
And a bird, while his wife, belly and breast and hair
Bare to the afternoon, laid on it, loaded to silence,
A shout for his son, her child.

And from the end of a terrace answering, from the formal
Entrance to happy lands, the at birth known harbour, open
And island intimate wound in the big bland façade of houses,
Two children, friends not yet discredited came, living
Each in the other's orbit, not touching, but bound
Each to the other's being and with equal and unsure
Eyes on our unexpected pattern, the ominous
Apparatus of departure, stopped in the clockless sun
For a mile long moment, till half armoured against the unusual
They walked towards us together.

The man's voice was quiet, and printed on the occasion
Sending not sound but meaning into the shining silence
"Come on, son. We're going. Say goodbye." Then the steel
Chorus spoke on the road, a road through, rehearsal
For matinees to come, a maze of many partings, and the cart
Parted the street with its blunt bulk, and happy eyed mother
Wore a fox tenderness on smiling victorious lips,
As the children faced each other, obedient, uncomprehending
With small and unbruised till now, not yet troubled faces
And carefully said their goodbyes.

'I have not the purity'

I have not the purity
Needed to speak: the Effic kings sold their criminals.
Those they enslaved in their wars
In bondage to the English. This was inhuman.
This chandelier, Europe,
Therefore, consider, now. Its jewelled glass

Eternally shifts in the wind.
And that chief star, american and lilac
All other pendants collide
Though they stem as one flower. Unenviable that crowd
In the late, continental night.
It is the moral hour now when we in

The intricate glasswork of
Such human fabrications must seem like
The bruises of but one light;
Yet entire must be the peace of our single light.
It is hard, some say, to keep whole
When a harsh wind drives. So too the Germans found

Civilization to be
Fragile, a chandelier-like lilac, nor hard
Such multiplicity of
Singular petals to dash in the might of the wind.
I hear you proclaim in the dark
How violent my words sound. Yet as I ask

You to encandle again
That quivering chandelier into one entirely
Pure, precise light,
That smarts through Europe, as through the crowded head of flowers
Curls its harsh jewellery;
It must seem like the endless surf which bends

Its white crown onto the rock.
I know the intent of the sea;
And that it never could be silent or
    Pace, then be still.

And what single light is not drowned
In the glut of the sea's dark sound?

From the inside of the wilderness

Mad as bells I strode through the implacable desert
And determined there would be no more suffering
Nor further plinth for my wounds.
If desert were my lot then desert I
Would hug to my soul of grit, making from the rock
And those giant birds who terribly darken the air,
Long teeth pulled down as if smiling
A low throne of terror from rock and bone. And mad as a steeple
I strode through the wilderness muttering to that multitude
Of sandgrain. Towards midday the furnace
Of my soul began to seize fire, tender straw of flesh
To shrivel from the inside and the outside fire
So that I cried to the rock 'I will suffer no more
Your suffering or your mute agony.
I want rock for fist and stone for language. I will
Preserve no more the pattern of the martyr, I will make
Friendship with berry and audience from rock and sand
Controversy with beast; communion with bird.'
But not riding to Jerusalem through the flesh
Whose thigh will I clutch, and here, whose
Word talk with? Rock
Are my grandparents.

When First I Saw

When first I saw the rivers of your face
Move through that exultation of the air
Confined by space, and like all majesties
Confined within their natural robes, yet by
Their clothes cribbed like the waters of the Ouse
Which we know must run wider and yet
As wide as the capacious eye can reach,
When first I saw the waters of your face
Move under me, I vowed I would explore
Your source and agent of power, the thin-faced brook
The gliding stream, that round-cast river which is still
An unabused and flesh-cut torrent. For I
Wished in that early knowledge of your land
Knowledge for the motive of the grace which moves
Across your land, sunlight, and moonlight
And the pale fractures of stars whose thin light is
Frosted with brilliance like my lanthorned eyes.
And in that formulated wish I grew
Surveyor of the districts of your face
And body, yet like birds who fret and stamp
The air they fly through, I in that capacious
Element of love desired your mind
Whose still uncharted stages of advance
Ran through the expurgation, of all air
Fire, earth, the watery elements
Un-bound by self-knowledge. I desired the cause
Of the slow movement of the bellied river.

I have been long in coming to that place
By which to another's soul martyrs and saint
Have with slow progress through the air devised
A way of coming to their Maker. But I,
In the dark world where tears are stones and flesh
Is all rant of a burning rubbish, would know
Your flesh, your mind. If my un-asked-for stumbling,
This slow plod of language and these rusty
Thoughts scratch with a slower progress than

Saints and martyrs, though in flesh we burn,
Yet believe slowly I wish this land
For a long use. For I yet wish to come
Into that hallowed invisible white O
That these two minds may move with satisfied fires
Through the indignant paradise of the age.

Separation

And perhaps death and perhaps fear for death
Do not spring from parting. Our parting,
What we have shared, and those things
Small as birds
We did not share, all, all
Are now upon us
As never before. Why, I ask,
Do we make the sacrifice? For
There is no firmer nature than old custom
A local sense of things, a fireside bruised
With cinders? It is not enough!
Somewhere, I affirm, love does exist,
Its human and proud Duchy of the heart
Foretells all disaster, all pain
Suffered beyond habit and beyond praise.
Or why should we question others in love
If we doubt that it exists. But that we tasted
What joy it is to call this square bed ours
In which the custom of our exercises
Waged and clashed sword all night. That was a time
We went to bed beneath those ancient arms
And called it love.
So it was. But now
The petty detail and the private strife
Confirm the insolence of our delays
And that we rested on each others' weaknesses
And stayed most honourably upon those wounds.

And yet our separation
Is surely like a huge pain, a great pain.
Only like, Madam, only like.

Speech for a Politician

Yesterday you were two hundred, dear,
Perhaps even a year or two over.
No one could say you looked
More than your age, grained so
With the many loitering charms;
Here the trim song slips
A bit, since time is exact;
And the old women, and the old men
With hats on straight, garments sideways
Pause, before stepping on
The stairway, age trod into it,
A multitude of human feet,
So many they seem to be there still,
The infinite pressures.
Just feet. Say what you want
Of the human animal,
Man gnarls upon his feet
And when what of man remains
A human condition, merely,
The cerebral bonds of power,
His feet will stump on
As it seems, within stone
An ungiving army of thought
Like the grey ends of hairs of
Senatorial dignity,
If abstracted a little
The way men treat of men.

Europe

The stream is, the roaring stones are
Full of God. The tree hides him
Like sap. He openly smiles when
The bank of violets storms into praise or
Shakes with laughter, provoking the soft sky.
It seems to wonderfully smile but
That is only the blueness, the soft blueness brooding
Over dark dear Europe. The smile from that sky
Is mistaken. We do not see it. It is only distance
It is nothing. We cannot pretend the sky condones
Us. It is God smiles. But he smiles
Because he is full of smiling. We cannot stop that.
Europe cannot pretend to flower every year.
But mark you the breathing violets. People smile
Full of God if you smile at them. Friend,
The spirit broods deeply. But smiles when love darkly acts.

A New Country

Much of Switzerland
Could be put in the church
At Venice. Not the Alps though.
These contractions of
Earth, scraping the mind,
Disturb all balances,
All surfaces holding
Oppositions. Of St. Mark's,
All that can be fitted
Into a house kept by
A Serbian working-man.
For there the cleric absorbs
The world, as a paying guest.
But here, one grafts
His will onto Nature's to meet
Hunger, the boar's tusk.

The locomotive,
Through whose engine perforations
Diesel is injected,
Moves up the mountain further.
And as it passes,
A bulk of powdered stone,
In which consists the country's riches,
Is pressed to concrete.

Further oppositions.
Part of the East comes
Along a tilted thread,
A priced bead. With effortless
Purity it glides
On the waxed string,
Analysing its simple clearness,
Until all forms of life,
All colours, are seen rayed
Off the surface. Here poverty.
And here much poverty
Mixed with some wealth.

Through this diaphanous membrane
Our locomotive pushes
Its useful splendour.

Going Away

1

The canal we purchased before
Is now so choked with weed
All blows derelictly;
And there are plants which trail
Their unassailable
And delicately obdurate
White shrill of flowers.
Time alone, enstationed,
Rules silently here. We need
Not at all, or ever, re-open
These ways, nor need I
Tend
Or protect
You from the advance of
Rank weed. You shall remain
Here, and since never
To be attained completely
You shall be but partially
Wanted, assailed not assuaged
By life's enveloping.
There are
Indeed waterways through
Which some sail but
Yours is not mine.

2

Last night we
Two together crossed
Through the amerced Alps, and
It could not have been more
Unlike what I thought it
Should have seemed: like
Two aerial bodies poised

As snow is poised on the
Enchanted grandeur of
The French-Italian
Cisalpine groves of rock.
For I find now
But greatly to my
Discontent, yet more to
My relief we are
Not now or ever shall
Be aerial as I had
Imagined we were to
Have once been, but must now
Trudge separately the slough
Of self-reproach. It is
Not ever for us the great
Unwearable, and for us now
Unattainable
Ridge of snow worn like
Some collar on the rock.
I may hail
You Alps, sometimes on whose
White crowns bodies may clearly
Even outgrace themselves;
But I hail you as the grandeur of a stranger.

3

Lately, as we passed through
The patois, whose restlessly groping
Tideless waters stringed
Themselves against those shards
Of hollowed trees, our ship,
I was pleased to remember how
A wind, glacially as
Nocturnal caps of ice
Blew, harshly between
Us, that same wind which
Moved down from the clamorous

Perfume of olives to
A small ship in the sea.

O you, a dialect
Of that sea, through whom my ship
Spurts, the wind that urges
Me through you
Is olivian, laden with
Promises; I hail you.
Hail and farewell my love,
My poor and sweet, my tideless
Olivian small sea.

4

I watched you as you were
Dancing contained darkly in
The shuffling earth's Greek heat
Which is brown and aerial
More aerial still beside
The blue-lipped sea. What if
I knew, like the wine-blue sea
Which is not wine, and there
Is no wine coloured that way,
That all between us is dead;
Can nothing be saved? Swiftly
The mountains of Greece like a
Huge bird terribly swoop
Between and between and between
That dream of me and you
And give me what is real
From what seemed beautiful.

And I know
That mountains cannot lie
That the lips of the sea and the shudder of the bird in the hill
Are not lies;
And I know

There can never be any of what
Humanity cries loudly for;
There can never be any love.

5

Greek words and their glances
Pierce, even through
Dusty Athenia, the white
Imperturbable fury of
Sun-fired marble for what
Goes through is not fury though
You grow what the tigress has.
It is your tenderness goes through
The hardest substances.

Wherever I go I must take
What of viciousness you replace in me;
Astride the bird on the sea
Sharp in the crisping waves,
I scrape the earth from me
And my ugliness falls from me;
So I take only across
The drop of your tidelessly
Lipped sea, Ipsos and, skeined
As a thread in the scarf, its strands
Thickening a love for which I can
Only say 'thank you' and leave
Without saying goodbye because
Love is incapable
Of complete separation.

A Space Together

Then soft as thoughts within
Love's companioning, she nears,

And bares silently
The feet she came on.

And like a fawn moon

Subdued in brilliance
Of lustred fawn snow

She bares all herself.

The moon is full size.
The planets on their leap

Round the unhorned edges
Of her soft side.

They press their maleness on her
Who wait; like me, wait.

The heavens in apprehension

Glisten about her
Their inviolable passions.

Only she waits. She.
Not quite alone. Nor I.

'Listen to that sensual muse or paraclete'

Listen to that sensual muse or paraclete
Who speaks your lines as perfectly from the head
Or groin as even the desert grows its sand
Or river its water or the rain its rain
Or any beast or substance with no thought
For thick complexity endures the sad
Irony of its nature. You be formed
By him, and the gentleness of a dove
Then turn your nature to the pain, compare
The rough sweet dirt of love, entice your head
To thought for every creature, and endure
The pangs that knowledge from eternity
Make, from stars, from suns. Examine the length
Of life you have, and live as you can live
According to the will of your formed flesh.
The desert, the wood, the figures of your future
Calculated in the stars. That blind goddess
Take to your heart and hunt and struggle with her.
All is most endless that is new.   Listen, see
Hear, understand. You are as blind as me.

'An image conceives in its meaning'

An image conceives in its meaning
Other images;
This earth begets some
And prison is made, a tiny
Pulse of cage of love.
It holds what is known
Has not yet been held;
But love removes to power
Cruel in gleaming fits,
In joys of possession.
Yet this is of no avail:

Since man may not cage his love.
The banked fires smelt
The bars; these in prison
Vanish cleanly. There is
No such thing as a cage;
Chain, shackle, and ball are fools
Of the foolish days when we,
As a vein injected
With the fumes of power,
Closed with a cold rage
On those we had charge of.

So shall their fit discourses
Charge entail.
Redress the innocent.
We clean ourselves that sickness
Drops like the white spots
Of leprosy.

Living[9]

I melt into this room.
Mirror you have seen this flesh
Between the accretions of other
Feathery lives. Tell me
Through the lucid intervals
Bird-past skims into you,
As I stand in you, naked:
Have the thighs grown, or tough
Buttocks made sorts of progress:
The face: in what change
Of particulars might grace
Lurk in the hair; or under
A bit? But slightly more
In the colds of the ferocious mind
Stare, and evaluate,

On the air's whitish silences
As frost upon moist glass,
Since only I will hear:

A sense of largening
Of the big body yet
Of the heart perishing.
Which in this moral shrinkage
Man despairs of himself.

The Re-ordering of the Stones

First published by Chatto & Windus, 1961

for E.C. Gregory

The Area of Conflict

Searching how to relieve
The piled cacophony of
My spiritual unrest, I
Mistward that morning went.
Everywhere on glass it
Had globuled moist hands.
And though behind doors sleep
Hung webbed, larksvoice with
Spit glittered on the glass
Loosening fear's cloy.
I moved like a doomed leaf
Taking a path alight
With dew, which crept into
A field, burning with flesh.
I said to one who raked
Up arms and teeth and hair
And human bone and hair
And human teeth and hair
Into that fire again
'What are you making here?'
Though he did not reply
Turning apart between
The cold heats. I asked, 'do you see
This flesh still lives, clinging
To its life, and is loth
To slide from its lapbone?'
He raised up to his mouth
The sneering lip we dread
Closing his fingers on
A complete silence. Sky dropped
Down tears in blood, I think.

The Measure

We all cry for love;
But what if we get it? To hold
In sex, and affection,
The adored human creature
Making of both a unit
In love, and procreate
Which is the end of love,
Drops one small image into
A widening universe.
Man's love disintegrates
In the space void of him;
And gradually he comes
To know that he is small.
What is man's love? To hold
Into despair the loving creature,
And propagate an image
Is the utmost. Beyond his tides
The chronic invalids
Of broken universes
Wait in derision on man.
Yet he was formed to love.
Earth cries, sun cries,
With the stark, hapless Gods
Phenomenal of matter
In space, to this end.
But when man reaches this
And grows into himself,
He dwindles to his size.
His spaces melt into him
He occupies no area.
Love then is the space of destruction,
And but for the harmonies
Of despair, he is nothing.
Weep, then, to be a stone
Or a cold animal
In servitude to something
Other than consciousness

Which love brings; since that shape
Or measure, in awareness
Through love of what we are,
Is that measure of space death is.

Astringencies

1. *The Coldness*

Where the printing-works buttress a church
And the northern river like moss
Robes herself slowly through
The cold township of York,
More slowly than usual
For a cold, northern river,
You see the citizens
Indulging stately pleasures,
Like swans. But they seem cold.
Why have they been so punished;
In what do their sins consist now?
An assertion persistent
As a gross tumour, and the sense
Of such growth haunting
The flesh of York
Is that there has been
No synagogue since eleven ninety
When eight hundred Jews
Took each other's lives
To escape christian death
By christian hand; and the last
Took his own. The event
Has the frigid persistence of a growth
In the flesh. It is a fact
No other fact can be added to
Save that it was Easter, the time
When the dead christian God

Rose again. It is in this,
Perhaps, they are haunted; for the cold
Blood of victims is colder,
More staining, more corrosive
On the soul, than the blood of martyrs.
What consciousness is there of the cold
Heart, with its spaces?
For nothing penetrates
More than admitted absence.
The heart in warmth, even, cannot
Close its gaps. Absence of Jews
Through hatred, or indifference,
A gap they slip through, a conscience
That corrodes more deeply since it is
Forgotten – this deadens York.
Where are the stone-masons, the builders
Skilled in glass, strong first in wood;
Taut, flaxen plumbers with lengths of pipe,
Steel rules coiled in their palms;
The printers; canopy-makers –
Makers in the institution of marriage?
Their absence is endless, a socket
Where the jaw is protected neither
Through its tolerance for tooth,
Nor for blood. Either there is pain or no pain.
If they could feel; were there one
Among them with this kind
Of sensitivity that
Could touch the dignity,
Masonry of the cold
Northern face that falls
As you touch it, there might
Be some moving to
A northern expurgation.
All Europe is touched
With some of frigid York,
As York is now by Europe.

2. *Asleep?*

Today, I want to speak
Of human agony.
It makes most men
Very sure that pain
Can be eliminated.
If pain were suffering
This were so. But such agony
Is not a passion, but persists
A bruise in the being,
Because human tenderness
Is insufficient, or love
Which is not always tender,
Even refutes this passion.
What shall we do for pain,
Man's agony? If we wound
Only to kill, we are mad.
Deny love, and we inhume
The hunger we live by.
Yet without tenderness
We die. So we must live
Complexly, as befits
The bedraggled human condition
And being vigilant
Experience much of man
In the fibres, in these moral fibres.
For man's life in its pain
Is something like a jungle
Where everything that is
Is agony, in this sense:
That things war to survive.
Pain is complex, something akin
To a stone with veins of colour
In it, that cross and cross
But never reconcile
Into one swab of colour
Or the stone that contains them.

Three Critics

I speak of three critics.
The first is the most considerable;
Yet for some time has been pre-occupied
With lineal purity,
Just as if syntax, that
Interlockage of human action,
Moved on the surface, merely,
Despite the medium.
His own verse is clenched
In morality, and cold
In the triumph of a voice
Supposedly neutral.
The second is one
Who asserts a belief
In the impersonal
In poetry, great poetry,
Suggesting the moral glimpse
Is suffused and obscured
By the insertion of
The 'I' in the text.
This can be so. He also
Wrote some verse.
The third still writes some.
He is like a ball
That lightly swerves, or even
In a high wind, is turned
By whoever blows, in contraries
Balancing all with civil
Hand. He has returned
Where he never came from.
This last, in some ways,
Is emblem of the first two,
Their stance cautioned
By the transparencies of intellect
Rather than intellect
Coupled to the embraces,
The convictions, of feeling.

And these three together
Composed in cold entablature
Reflect society which
Has little warmth, much arrogance,
And little firmness.

Respectabilities

Many liberals don't just
Make love, they first ask each other;
And either is free to decline
What the other wishes;
That is, unmitigated
Possession of the beloved's flesh.
Nothing hasty, nothing unconsidered
Catches the liberal by
The hairs of lust. Nothing.
And this consideration
For those feelings
Of the approached one naked
In love or in hunger
Is extended to all.
He will, for instance, ask
A starving man if he
Would eat, pressing
For the particulars
Of hunger. And enquire
Why he is deficient
In bread. All men are treated
With such perception as stones
Get into subjection to
Their shaper, as their use fits
To his. Men are chosen to meet
That judged compassion which
A liberal has. A wounded man
Receives the ointments of love

From matrons, with respect.
Sex, the inhuman hunger,
Demands courteous
Submission, polite domination.
In fact, the turning world
A stone delicately
Veined with acceptable
Colours, deficient just because
Another stone has gouged
A bit from its flesh
Demands the liberal heart;
Though a different stone
Brutal in the untamed
Components – a misshapen
Tongue of useless rock –
Merits, and gets,
A frank dismissal.
And this, too, is fair;
Though more than half the earth
Is denied purchase on
That delicate conscience
Cash gives: a fair if privileged
Mind veined with gold.

The Liberals

Nothing was beautiful then,
Nothing is more than beautiful
Than it then was.
A building I knew nine
Years back is modest yet,
Abrasively puritan even –
The National Assurance Board.

It is where the state speaks
With some of its poor

Of their intimate problem: cash.
It all resolves for now
In that; a man's sex, his wife's child
Melt to the half-a-crown
The board gives or withholds.
Yet if cash preserves men process
Of change does not. What seems beautiful
To some, tiny dogs sniffing
The hind quarters of time,
Seems so being past.
For the bad times are here,
Again, in the Exchange
Where some men queue for dole
And get a bit, and some
Sit in that other harshly
Disinfected place.
I cannot quite make out
What the cashiers are saying,
But paper money rustles
And metal money scrapes.
More metal and less pulp
Are what the poor get.
Why not loathe everything;
Why not! The earth is defaced still
With the same moist-fleshed men
And women, like grains
Of impetigo. We foul
The stones we have sprung from
That we share this modest space with,
Brutishly refined
In plucked skirts, and stiff pants.

The Book-Purchasers[10]

Subjected to various
Pressures, in particular
The barren potencies
Of his society,
He bought, and kept,
A book of girls photography
Gives parts to, but not textures,
With breasts as big as Balzac's
Computations of interest
And went to bed with each,
Finally with five at once
Interchanging the parts of each girl:
An arm, buttocks, the smile
Re-pieced together as he would
But not as he had:
And this crowned
A mind as lustred as those
In the poor south.

And it was worth it since
For two-and-six he got
Purchases in lust
On several hundred nights.
Only the dissolvent of sex
Furthered his disintegration.
The copiously inflamed[11]
Multiplications of lust,
The inflictions of sex
Overcame him. What follows?
This follows: pain
Of barren sexuality
Suffused his soul.

The days sealed tighter[12]
Like graves, his hot lives,
Kisses inside the earth
Which gradually suffocated him

In their profusion.
And then, to many men
Variously like him
He offered the purchase of loose sands
Deleting from sex entirely
Love, that those following
Fell on the clambering grains and gave
To a dry planet drier lives
Eviscerated of the desire
To create anything
But the compositions of death.
This final perishing
Is the intermingling of man.
Weep for man, who can die.

Culpabilities

It is a matter of opinion
Who killed Hitler. But my belief
Is that he was quietly assassinated
At night, by many men,
Rather in the same way
I mean, without much noise
And over a period, but still,
As the six million Jews died
At the instigation of those
European guards
Whose desire to procreate
Changed into a labyrinth of cruelties,
Assisted plentifully
As always, and on this occasion
By miscellaneous
Poles, Magyars, Ukrainians,
Though this time not the queer English,
The exemplary Danes, nor the small
Pathologically heroic Netherlands.

So who can blame the Nazis?
There merely inherited
A European illness,
Embarrassed beyond morals,
Beating the flesh until
The rods, keenly stirred
Begged more. And that mystery
European nearly
Remains virgin of solution
As much, indeed, as society's
Ills pursed on a sick wind,
Rotting it, making a liquid
Of the poor body.

Genocide

Something is deeply fair
About justice. Those who raped
Tibetan girls castrating men
To prevent a fruitful Tibet
Are accused of genocide;
Yet what can sustain
The act deserves
This name; as a leaf
In the river is 'beautiful'
To a European
Seen through Chinese eyes?
The flesh of the thing
In the mind is beautiful,
If the mind perceives that.
Yet the truth is
That the small testicles
And the large head
Were severed from the flesh
They were part of.

The answer seems that power
Is possessed by those
Incapable of asserting
What they believe. They cannot tell
What was the true nature
Of the Tibetan death.
But the whole earth is touched
With this; and it is turning
With what is terrible
And what is delicate
Upon its back: fair opinion.
Like scales of fish sticking
To this tissue, and to each other,
Are these dead people
Slain violently
Having something of the Chinese
Leaf in their death.

Deficient

A degree of self-criticism,
Of self-hatred even, is necessary,
Like stones placed counter
To the foundations if
These are to hold. Such self-critical
Society of opposed stones
Does not obtain in Hampstead;
At least, largely not.
Some believe that the spaces
Of earth can be so changed
That it will become prodigal
Where before it was fecund merely.
They plan this seduction
As though like the sunk silences
Rosenberg speaks of
These molten caves in the earth

Could, by speech, entirely
If permanently be changed
And made to pleasure them.
The piles of stillness
Are massive. If men pride
Themselves on being informed,
They change little, hardly supporting
Their bookshop. Silver is rare
If expensive, paper money
Unobtrusive as is frequent
The second-hand trash.

The area is deficient,
Largely, in a class
Familiar with hard work;
I mean the kind of work
A labouring man does.
With all the piled agonies
Of a delicate conscience
They cannot defer sterility.

The milks of pulped grass
Are purse-mouth: the leaf-spreads
Of sycamore cover this ease
With shade. Pity these whose spaces
Are without force to resist
Their ghostly easiness.

The Centre

My ancestors made love
In the hot pastures of the near east
And got me my seed there.
I should be drawn to
The Mediterranean.
I suppose I am. Greece

Was the shudder of the bird from the high hills.
But Italy; those with gold teeth
Are plucked of these by the Italian;
His main industry is fools.
His landscape gathers on the surface,
Not deepening into
The scents of heat, that delicate
Strength which breaks through
The white, Greek rock
In veins of darkness
That smell of the mineral
Origins of men.
So there is Greece. But my mind stays
In a place I saw little of.
The river drifts through
The town, falling massively
Under a low bridge.
Geneva. Was it fixed
I should choose your cool streets
Hinted of by the south?
Round this place move
The ornate schisms, intertwined
And made fast by the vicious and costly
Emblem of puissant Europe.
Is it strong only? It is also
Absurd. It is a continent
Caught in its intellect
At which centre it drops
Into a great lake;
Like some bath with its plug out.
And it is here I am
Constrained by having both
Prevailing intensities
As locked, and as formed
As the coolness is formed here
In precision from the clash
Of oppositions. Such firmness
Seems pre-determined
And intertwined to a gap

That is the weave and the space
Made by Europe in struggle,
Where choice flickers, but does not choose.
It is where the tensions meet
And wear each other away.
The life of a great
Intelligent continent
Falls through the space
It has made in itself
With too much intellect.
Or was it the intellect
Sought for a bride
But found only itself
Sufficient for its appetites, –
Say a poison this chemist
Fatally delivered
And tasted, and decayed on.

1. Warrior

Some division divided on itself
The parent world, in imperfect fruition,
Conceived as child in her children. All men
With all women, split between their single love
And their multifold, were born in thought,
But before them, thought as division was born.
World fits like a brain. God, making himself,
Since being made makes the flaw, is divided
On himself. As if air were a discord
We breathe division. What is division?
Man lies on rock, in a barren splendour,
Disaffected from himself, from rock,
Even division. Despair shall come,
And shall clutch him, and tear him
Till he is bits. This is division.

2. Drowned

Disaffection, like a germ, has entered
Man's breast. Then straightaway he was sick.
The delivery of man from this is certain
In one sense: there is not much of delivery.
Disaffection means letting go what man
Had in the way that soul, a fabric
Of experience, is disentwined
Be he Man as thorn, Man as candle.
Even love, in each particular
Like a piece of material the lonely tailor
Sees for a moment, a comprehensible
Spasm of light, folds and crinkles.
And as it falls, it becomes like drowning.

The Wall

Living as though a wall
Had been raised between
Each of us; we would speak
With the other of those spaces
Of earth we call him to.
Yet, by compulsion, we share
These stones. At which some men
Would call this a failure
In communication. The fact is
Not Babel, but mutual despair
Separates us, since each
Through love, detachment, or exhaustion
Is himself alone, though each one,
By nature, lacks what the other has.
The walls remain. They are
A possession no man surrenders
But he perishes. And in his loneness
He beats on the barriers.

It is the agony
Which seems supreme, as stone
Triumphs in what it is
Though its manipulators
Give it whatever form
The conscious use demands,
For man is agony.

The Breaking of Rock

Against this fact
Of you, intact from pain,
All that is mine
Smashes as fragile shell
Spumed on a rock
Piercing the torn sea.
Each scrap of wrath is
Grit on itself
And falls through my life
As sediment. For what else
Is rock, but to resist
The changes of the sea
And break what it is.
Nothing I do quite
Rids me of you.
Not love, but hate I pour
In freezing tons of mass
In seethe. You resist it.
You nestle an inward weight,
Pounds of you intact –
As my harshnesses
Slip off you
In tiny suds of noise.
Yet in the way of me
You perish. One day
The weight of coldness

On your motherly palace
Takes sternness from you
To resist. Down you go
And pulp, as bones would;
Prayers for strength remove
Malicious rock, a crown
Slipping among heads. And gleefully
My waters almost shaped
To the divide you made
Of me close wholly above
The bits of dereliction,
Paying the decent stretch
Of the entire compassion for peace.

Black Sand

Volcanic islands hold
Your memory. Black sand sieves through
Its red, at sunset, a
Last jealousy of your sea.

Cast your net in the depth
And number your catch.

A fish with blue fins,
A many-pincered crab,
A lost engagement ring.

Gulls hide their eggs in black sand:
Night spreads its net over yours.

From the Hebrew of David Rokeah

Bonfire

The clock stops its hands now.
And the sea;
                    Only the sea beats out
The pulsing of your fear.

The gulls abandon the cliffs
Used for keeping watch from,
Before the day, which
Drifted listlessly,
Has become evening.

The bonfire's flames lick at
The twigs, and catch of fish.

Wanderer, prepare to feast;
And turn your back upon
The sea that waits for prey.

From the Hebrew of David Rokeah

Mother and Daughter, and Huntsman

By allurements to be trapped for
Some girls get this kind
Of man; they make stark husbands
Who eat your pulp; and you feed

On his devouring. His hands
That seem gentle, and are cruel –
Merely the delicates of his craft,
Never letting slip what they catch.

He pierces you, to the backbone.
What can you cry, but that
He has ginned you on your love.
Remember you expect no mercy;

None; that man you have got
Is not assuaged. Winter
May spread some leaves on him:
Rage increases in earth. So, precious,

You know what to expect.
If his flesh makes the earth swell,
What hope have you? You become
Like him even, in age. You will

Be generous, but you'll be haggish.
Yet where you lie you will
Be temperate; the spaces of earth
Are prepared for your kind, as for his.

You may even check him, slightly.

Go: marry with him.

Depths

Textures. Why always textures?
The fuss. It is enough
You take and hold the thing:
That being warm it gives you
A special sense of permanence.
Since but for the whole shape
There would be no texture. Despair
Has texture. It is constructed
From a total helplessness.
Despair is texture; without it
We should not know how to face
The thing with such certainty
Of loss. But touching it[13]
We very gently feel
The whole paralysis

Of agony give way
Into the steadfastnesses
Of reality,
The differing planes of surface
We cannot avoid contact with
Which employ the sunk depths.

Savings

I see the government
Is suggesting that some
Of us save money. A woman
Sitting at table with
A pen on her lips,
By her side the snap
Of her fiancé, writes
A letter: 'if we both save
We may have what we want
In a few years.' The order
For torturing wires and straps
A man and wife may use
Is already placed.
Meanwhile parliament debases
Such foul coinage
As these two save
On massive armaments.

I want a small clock;
I want a bed, a wardrobe
To hang my trousers in;
Also a kitchen in
Repair, for I want food.

But let me stay my soul
A little clean of her,
With something of the compassion

A strong woman has
Decently gentle. Death infinitely
Comes close when we are old:
Death of the soul is like
A pan of boiling milk,
The heat thieves it away
And something of the man
That might live after death
Precedes his flesh into
The soil in particles
Not smaller than dejection.
We are born part of the way
Death goes; but I pray the angelic forms
Help me to stay that bit
Until I die.

Sacred

I have talked with respectable women
Many of whom declare
The several fingered dew
Laid on a man's parts is love.
More naked is love; some say
Pure, like a glacier:
Yet congruous as despair,
Or rather something
Meaner than vanity.
For one with coarse-grained hand
Ties her sharp ribbon to
Her hair while, binding him,
Yells, 'love O love,' though she
Takes with an ancient care
Ever to give what is
Part of security.

There are others too, numerous
As sand-grain who sweat for
Not ambition but bread,
Having all but the seminal part
Of coarse men and cold men
Unenamoured of love
And love's perplexities.

So here, besides the cash
I give you a steel necklace
To be worn near the flesh
As conduit, a flow of
Hand-made steel ornamentation:
So many lesser than you
So many professing love
Less capable of that
And who are bought, and know it
May not pretend to passion.
Incapable of passion
They move with a rigid glare
Beneath their horror.

Nothing of tenderness
Will ever touch in them
For child or animal
Much generosity.

You to whom too much
Is given, but no love –
It is so much you give me
The tenderness you give now
Though that is bought from you,
That having little to offer
This much of you is more
Than others surrendering;
More than respectable women
More than such practised thieves.

For a Child, on his being pronounced Mentally Defective by a Committee of the LCC

You are not like them.
Men learnèd with women, with rigid souls are pleased
To measure what gaps your brain has.

In those unstopped spaces your laughter howls
At their pure probing of your defective mind.
You shrink from

That heart defective of pity;
And you shrink from intelligence that with
Use of brutal wood bricks

Is decided, whatever
Lacuna impedes the delirious message of reason
You are subject to the wardress's care.

You are to throb in a house, where God's spat blood
With coughed bone, though mewed up in man's frame
Is not sinewed to intellect

But to memory of each flawed
Soul – confronts your passage out building a cage
With bare bars of the iron

Some caged brains spattered
And the blood cursed
As it cooled on the metal.

The chill mind sits in the perfected
House, carefully pronouncing madness.

Yet how may the cold heart be sane;
How shall the naïve intelligence be sane?

Since the pure mind that would love you has
Become discorporate of its love.

For the rooms they examined you in were loveless;
And the faces shaped like the pitiless wood
Were cold, inquiring, with that madness
Which understands not the purpose but
The applying of what it learned to do.

The chill man once more approaches your searched house.
Only may he perceive how to unlock the door
That conceals what you and he crave. The way
Through mind is a passage through doors love opens.
Love, only. If without love, he but glides
Through the cool strictures of his immoral intelligence.

But there are no locks to your house, child. The blown
Straws of man pass through you. You are howled through by
                              the elements.
Your love, and your fear which is fear of what is not love
Are detained by you:
But the heat and dispassion of the world press through you.

For though lit with your love, your soul
That is not intelligenced yet
By reason, a darkness we increase
Detains nothing.

Without darkness you strain nothing to you.

Perhaps the intelligences must darken
What permits the uncontrollable
Radiance passage. But love which
You have, remains
Undiminished through what madness ever light is.

Dedications

1. *To Tamasin, aged six*

White as a new-made cake
Tamasin, with long hair
Darkly hung slack,
It is little you ask for
Or any can ask: to speak
A few words, and be answered.
To solitary men
From isolated women,
But this much: with child's hand
As you, to hold in the clasps
The scant human affection
Rare as bread in the starving
If sun-clasped coasts of Africa
And hold it tight, a moment,
And never let it slip out,
In the clasp, like a hungry eye.
For the eye is the soul's eye
And this food that we give
We eat, whiter than you
Or children yet spotless
Having as purity
Their simple hunger.

2. *To My Friends*

It does not matter she never knew
Who Pater was. What is rare
Despite the encirclements of marriage
Or even the political relationships
Affianced beyond parliament
Is love, which breaks the breads.
The staff of women, the dread,
The hunger of men, it is not
Just what I am capable of

If mature; it is the force
Behind those intimations of our senses
Progenitor to more growth,
If anything is. Remember,
The moulds of rock perish,
The flower so delicately formed
The minute exactness seems meant
To last. What does live
In the complex fabrics of air,
Uncoloured, and always nubile,
Is this man-like attribute.
So very carefully
Consider what you do
As an action related always
To this eternal motion
In man's leathery breast;
For the way we treat each other
In private is minutely
The way we deal with wives
And they their men. Even stones
Wrinkled in a contempt
Of their manipulators
Lie in some comradeship,
For their sakes. And for Man,
Men matter, whether that God
Who made us, and the stones,
Is watching us, or bored
With human agony
Lies in immortal sleep
Terribly locked, not witnessing
The outrages of human hunger
Bearable only because
They must be, even these uptorn
Grains of love that are burned
In complex and primitive agonies
In concentration camps.

The Possibility

I accept all
Of what seems large,
The ship in the sea's unlovely
    Pressures. We cut

By as much
As we are pressed. Water
Begins its unsmiling hurts.
    Behind the bay

Shifts small if
Clear, a past become
What it is: detached, seen, despoiling
    Its richnesses

If ever it
Had them: houses
With love in bed weaning to fullness
    Its moment.

But sun
Puts forth the light
We move on, a track from past
    We leave

Through sea's
Incessant hiss of
Collision on the boat
    As it pushes

Sharp, taut way
On tormenting waters.
If we turned back, what past is
    Preserved through

Itself would be
Made bare of fact as
A scoured shelf is first deprived
     Of jars

     Then
The skin of dusts
That vaguely obscures the first white
     Cleanness.

     What we fear
Is such past which
Not destroyed yet now falls short
     Of what we were –

     As we move on
Light, a track that leads
From the town shrinking like a heart
     In moral danger.

     Where we lay
And took, as bird
Rising in flames takes
     Victory in pain.

     Only less.
Small but hard the moment
Of indestructible heart.
     Which is burning:

     Caught, stilled, held
Through its own pain.
No other terms. Nothing more
     Or smaller

     Allays, increases
Whether or not it
Be burden, or kind of crutches.
     If the boat

Cuts the sea
It is waters also
Persuade it to cut, clenching us
   The further

   We rise over
The poised lifts high
Of salt rent through which
   The misery

   Pours in,
A weight
With mass without sense
   On, on

   What hope had.
The heart with love.
We have no heart. There is
   Again the moving

   Out from, the pause
On the tip of piled
Waters, the fall, then
   In departing.

   We must be
On, having now
Less than there was: the land
   That we ever

   Constantly held
In belief, a claim
In substance, less now; and we move
   From it. Yet

   There is this:
When the limits of pain,
Ecstasy, glimmer up, showing a frontier,
   A kind of

Pure hope; pure
Because it cannot
Be chosen, nor be anything
    Other than

Now what
Despair makes it, neither
Made nor imagined otherwise.
    The kiss on

Your closed eyes,
If this is despair
As we move from what we knew
    Over water

We did not
Think as tented, pulled
In such upward wrath of earth,
    Then it also

Is hope; as
Under my kiss you
Ask if this is possible
    And I say

Yes, this is possible.

The Wholeness

Tiny stones
Have misery
Unforfeited though bound with
Good roots.

The continual
Sway, deeply rooted,
Of the branches of solitudes
Shares pain.

Stones in
Their large or
Minute splendours, or the olive
That recalls

Its inner
Shape, even
The hand that planted it,
Bring little

To the flesh
With that
Spirit it nurses; we have
Small contact.

This olive,
With the hand
That scooped earth for it; masts of cedars
Poised high

In thought –
This sensuousness
This getting of images
Was never

Sensuousness,
But handled, merely;
I am a man waiting his dead wife's touch.
    And I wait

    As though
This getting of richness,
All unctions of spiced Asia,
    The animal

    Oozings of
Gums, salivas
Of odours that leaves yield
    To touching,

    Is nothing.
Truly this seems nothing
Compared to the modest touch
    Of the hand

    Gently
On cheeks, places
As curved, but laid modestly.
    We did not

    Share in this
Touching and yielding,
This courting sensuousness
    Of earth.

    If then
I was content,
I should be glorious now.
    I partake

    Of the olive;
I plant and reap;
I have sharing in grinding of
    What I gather.

Yet having
The harvest I
Do not possess it; it seems
    Its granary

    But not grain.
It is increase
But formally, mine as
    Stones are.

    I therefore
Distrust that past.
Many gathered seeds without issue.
    We walked

    You, the soul,
I, the flesh, speaking
As with finger-tips held up.
    And though we

    Have use
Of these, they
Are as if rented; no man's.
    And they

    Stand from
Their wholenesses;
We are two-selved
    Creatures that

    Each with
Self-violation charges
Under the strange, live sun
    Its destruction.

    The tiny stone
Of creation charges
The fluid in the crude oyster that forms
    The pearl. But

No precious
Creation nor wholeness
Of charged pain beautifully
    Entire

Is of me; I have no commodity.

The infinite charges of the flesh
The commodities of sensuousness,
The olive, pearl, stones of creation –
In their sensuousness these tear us.

    Yet the mental
Forces billow, and joy,
If it is joy, as we are torn
    Quickens you to grow;

    Not as
A quick seed in stone
But as you never grew, swellings
    Of wheats,

    And then
The billowing of
The entire meadow of curved stem.
    Silent in

    The stirring
Crop, the predator
Is dismayed, and takes flight.
    I perceive

    Your growth,
In which
Perception plant my grain.
    For I

Lived before
Through flesh only,
As it were, on some infinite score
    Of images;

But on these
As the eye
Cannot touch and the hand touches,
    Merely.

As the seed
Struggles with
Soil to flower with assertions
    Of more seed:

We rear with
The one the other an
Infinite sensuousness of wheat
    In commodity.

The dying
Body in paroxysm
Turns over: we turn
    Away from

An older
Disaffection. The branches
Stir above the healed lovers.
    The huge halves

Of this life are one for once.

Unpublished and Uncollected Poems,
c. 1961–1965

Great!

I wish, I mean – I want
A war. Yes: a war.
War!
Said flushed, grace-white Charles.
And after him, somewhat
Below, of course, as befits the English tradition
                              and its working-class,
Dark and bony Jack.
Though if you want more,
You'll have to say it.

'Much did you think'

Much did you think
Of the mutilated creatures
That move in my poems:
The fly that is torn, and the sharp
Fox who is followed.
Now you speak of how much
My verse stays with the jews:
A pool damp with blood.
Yet of seventy three
Poems three alone
Are of jews being killed,
While a further three make
Mention of them, merely.
Is Silkin demanding of
Thwaite[14] overmuch? These deaths
Outnumber our protests to
Their murder. Think:
Were even much of my verse
Formed in jewish protest, how much
Has the christian theme been
Beaten thin as gold
Leaf and laid, perceptibly,

On the lip-wounds of its martyrs.
It seems I press upon
Your domesticity.
Why should I not protest though?
Shall the foxes be denied entrance
Because they are turned jews?
England has a lid
Fallen over the pupil
That gave mute assent
For asylum, by petition.
This is not sufficient; I ask
That you understand there has been
Murder of Jews here
Murder and hatred christian-wise
Intertwisted in heraldic concord
To make domestic an emblem
Where all is clean.
All is not clean.
A beast is intertwined
In costly emblem
With its prey's soft flesh
Making with such softness
Of both mawling ferocities.
If a man is
Trapped under a car
With blood gouged on his belly
Or foot, do you condemn
The pain? The accident
Of birth is human to its pain.
I ask not of your pity
A generous response,
But a less hidden one.
If you will be supple,
Resilient, like the deer
To those large spreads of curved
Air pressing between thighs
That overleap the swift spaces
Of diminishing air, if you will
Make your mind this supple

To what I am saying,
I will make a pact with you:
Just as long as the pain
Of this insolence
To us remains unadmitted,
I will speak of the jews.
But when, soberly, men
Sit down together
Under the strange, live sun
That moves the strangeness in men
Into a recognition
Of common origins,
I will stop my voice.
And this consort is
Possible, is it not;
This befriending of
The isolation in men?
What do you think to this?
Come; make a pact.

Nearly[15]

As a child
I sat, with buttocks
Firmly planted, legs spread
On the pavement; and held
A marble on my tongue.
An oldish town; hair
Drooping from its mouth. Besides which
If I swallowed it
I was mad; and I
Was mad to put it in
My mouth. The slightly
Sweet alkaline
Spread through the small undetermined
Body it dominated.

I was addicted. Soon,
My grandmother called.
The dinner's sanity.
Our sun's dry magnificence
Is a normality.
The eastern sea is clawing
At the grit, and threatens
The plant-life, further on.
I feel the fibres of
My brain heated
Away, each filament
A small snapping-note twisted
Into two separate threads
The air moves naturally
Between. Two points, air like
A soft broom pursing
The dust left in a pile
That will pass on nothing. That will
Not nourish a thing. But the cleared
Spaces may.

Why We Are All Socialists

Heart of the heartless world
− Marx

Not as common in the polar areas, you can nevertheless see in the sky an exact reproduction of the land in front; the image is upside-down, and joins, touches, the real landscape.

I

Inert, like a star fish, roughed tissues, but skin still,
In an unnatural element,
He is by the gas-stove.
The bill will be heavy. The anguished
Capitalistic paper−

Redness in the print
Dry with weeping, has passed
From his eyes.
'Can we do no better?' But 'no better'
Colloided, half-drowned, in
Too much beer is
Released in violence
Like a punch in the head. It breaks up
His small, blond, flapping life.
Another instrument
Is sharply visible:
A bread-knife at the belt.
On the stone floor,
Peaked, broken glass
That will not be swept up.
A minute chip of glaze
Has been bitten from a mug.
An intense wound:
The whiteness of earthenware
Blood, whose lip is missing.
A coat bent round the leg
Of wooden table.

There is comradeship
Of broken pencils, teethwrenched.
The academic frame
Is torn, without sadness.
Are we fighting for this?

II

There is also the friend,
Bent as a pocket knife.
In the troughed face rill
Seventeen manly pints,
Like ordure, moving towards the cock.
'It is his business:
What has he to live for?'

He will regret that.
And in comradeship urge
That gentle pint, which makes liquid
The lets on 'certain aggressions.'
His eyes are nearly closed.

III

If you look upwards, in the arctic sky
You may see reproduced
A flow of exact spar
Of ice;
And furled, enclosing snow
Turning towards you. Upside-down.
I think that if I could
Perceive through his eyes
I should begin like this.
Two images reflect.
Flowers of ice: spars that
Burst the sweet form, bud, glint
In the frigid air that tumbles
Meanly and helplessly
Round them. Soldier-ice.
Workmen that flint it. In
The sky, an image grows
Of this until it is
In exact reproduction,
And greedy for possession.
Two ice-peaks touch, and there,
His figure is: a clenched-up.
Works at the changing world
To shed its parasites.
Works at it that men shall
Govern their labour.
The change is slow, like carts
Hurled through mud; grit and clay
Oil the axlepiece,
Turning on itself.

IV

From this resolute
Coherent arctic ground,
Passing through his hot mind,
An earth of labour
Against its inverted self
Breaks into storm. There snows outfurl
In soft, stinging shape
Flurrying onto him;
Buffet, fan up, his
Exact fires. Notations of revolution –
Scraps of Winter Palace
Eructate through the cries
Of armed sailors: 'Onwards, on, onwards'
– Crack, with the mind they stained,
In freezing contact with
The snow – crushed into his flesh
Its down-turned peaks. He has burned,
And then is frozen in
Cold wastes, shrinks up until
A flake's size;
Each remonstrates with him
In angular stricken cries,
In process, for their world
Whose produce is its needs. And the mind
In outwards contact with
This earth, frozen in fact,
Is instantly frigid, splits
Like parted glass.

There is one to help this:
Eyes that through envy have
No lids, in envy scorch,
Peel a bit, from the fire's
White slab. Eyes would shut
The glare of energy
From them. He has no skin there.
What he wants burned the eye

That had now to look on it.
'A mind chooses,' he says,
For whom 'psychology
Is bunk.' Then tries to disarm
His friend who grips, with terror,
The kitchen implement.
His pale fires are gassed.
Why should he do this thing?

V

If we could have our bread
And tea; if that mind would
Incline into sleep.

The mudded wheels clang,
And are still. The axle breaks.
Black birds flight it. Our man
With small eyes is generous;
He will not let our friend
Keep on the taps – 'but philosophically,
He has the right', is how
He shows his intellect;
If intellect is what
That mind is, aware
Of his friend's roughed hand
Turning the knob of gas.

Were these two together,
Wrapped in a cloak, married
As the law tells us, – by concepts
They nourish with working with
The worked men. Wounds
Of a mutual infliction
Weaken the impulse. It drivels.
The down-turned peak intrudes
On two men trying to forge
The tiny spring of change.

Each individual man is
Forced individually
To act: from its whole
The rat-like part gnaws out,
And what it is is made
Larger, more fang-like,
By working in the world
Where, like a plant-owner, greed fingers
Its seated swollen belly,
Fobbed with a hunter-chain.
The flesh bears itself on.

What Each Person Wants

Surely activity of politicals includes human relationships?
And where it does, don't these relationships suffer?
But there isn't yet an end to others' suffering.

i

Three men at study: ocean vessels, turning
Over the waves' leafage.
While we were at it, women
Visited us, and were kind.

ii

Stare down, and focus.
Through the air, at height,
The serpentine malice of
Waters, the straight
Bluff-harry chimneys of
Manufacturers
Seem the size of a man
Digging the road. It is the action

And object acted on
That enlarge.

A chair with a straw seat
With wooden arms; bare wood
Clothed arms stretched over.
He lay in it. Taps were
Pulled on, the air gassed.
An ostentation which
Sometimes is loneliness
Pulls inwards the human
Frame, as if wrenshell,
Filling that emptiness.

That night there was no sleep,
Save his. Kitchen knives,
Waxed, marled cords, were taken off.
No need for grief; it was
His point to rest at last.

iii

In the afternoon, the day,
Like a sphere, is round us.
At work, the labourers
Cut bricks in two; birds wheel
In toothless hunger. There's no rest.

All starves. We are hungry,
Mother: feed us, we ask.

He is awake, and pulls
His baby smells over
His chest, for some disguise.
Odour of feet, soft, scopping-out beer-smell,
Putrescence of studious mind.
He rises, like a child.
His twenty-three years, small,
Swaddle our anger.

Toast-rusk and milk-drink absorb
And mollify beer; the muck goes.

It is all flushed away.

iv

'Yes,' the third one says,
'He has recovered; yes.'

The fight against the bomb
That will destroy us; the fight
Against those persons, then,
Who want to use the thing;
And for those disemployed
Whose coat is lean, slack;
And for those dying
From hourly deprivation
Of grain, bean, pod;
And whose beings are wrenched
Until they are not sensitive;
The fight against man's work
Continues, as it did.

When the dark comes
And another kind of gauntness
Melts into us, I think
We are a bit afraid
That in us a gap,
Where love could thrive through us,
Is growing. O, my comrades,
We shall see to it;
We are not going to make that mistake.

Reality, and other places

A town of biscuits and huff, –
In which, like savage wires
That put the eyes out
To make the bird sing
Wilde was put in jail, –
The place is composed
In swords and boots
Intertwisting in heraldic concord
To make domestic an emblem
Where all is clean.
One thing disturbs, though, which
Is persistent, comparable
To burbling smells of mud
In the hard-working north
Merely a lavatory,
Disjoined, and without cistern,
Troubling a soft-bricked yard.
It is demurely splendid.
Yet what if it should start,
Since coated with man's slime,
A disease. As if the beast
Intertwined in the city's costly
Emblem moved deeply
With a cold wrath. For men here
Have concealed
The mawling ferocities,
Like a claw festering
In the pierced flesh.

Confederate as blades of grasses
As naively unfeeling
Let those press them that press,
While the strange, live sun
Quickens the mild, the savage,
In neutral splendour.

'The poems of Clare's madness'

The poems of Clare's madness
Are not like the tough stem of gnapweed,
Nor is the slight purple flower
As the fury of Blake.

Why not? Or rather, it is like –
Tough as some poets are
On the outside, soft within.
I can't love all nature.

Does despair make some compassion
The tear moving to set on
The muscular, gentle hand?
What is it made of?

So salt, so moist, so indescribably
A fluid of the body,
Water that you would not drink.
What depth has it?

When you are lying beside
And the child wells in my flesh
As the force seems to gather within a wave;
O, love, what is it?

Put your hand into my hand
Being careful neither is set aside
As separate entities;
By the frailties

By a human tepidness.
A large tear shall contain us
Like a membrane of self-hatred
Tears of rage

Against what is done by each other
With actual cruelty,
A band tightened round the head
Till that bursts.

Some Changes

I saw the wind lower on
The earth its queer head
And blow; the cropt hair
And flat, small, childish ears,
As was their custom,[16] still;
While all the features of
The land, rocks, poles,
Were chipped, or broken up
As bitterly as husks
By the flailer.

An embittered justice
Carelessly retributive
Could rip up pedestals
And all the careful planning
Of sanitary man.
Not only just wind, but what
Perpetually shoved
The idle mind's defenceless
Ease aside. Over
The road I saw were blowing
Some poets, who all the time
Protested that the wind
Would not change them: and yet
Not like grass were they bent,
But rolled, with much contempt,
In all directions that
The road permitted them.

And still they cried 'I see
No change', or if they saw –
'Poetry', they said calmly
'Is the manipulation
Of filaments, a drawing forth
Of the imagination;
As such, freedom', they cried;
As if that were the thing

Which if they chose they could
Avoid the wind with.
And pity, like a child,
Which is a fashionable
Thing to write about
These then preferred to leave
With all the other issues
That blew like sediment
With intermittent fury
Through public areas.
As though this cooling earth
Wished to see the human
Mind feel and act on
The elemental pity
And rages it gave to
A casual ignorance.
'Our homes,'[17] they said: and then
A spider in the bath
Was seen by one of them,
Naked, cool, derelict,
Like some mind burnt through.

'I am angry, which means little'

I am angry, which means little;
Poet's words, flecked seed.
Why not all people's? Such ownership
The landed gentry are awaking.

They will be pushed off
Hoed, hacked; if they don't share.
A pity. The consolations
Of nurtured objects that the eye
Scrapes and is scraped by:
The costly sensibilities of possession.

These are what we wring:
'Ant' from sinew that is wasting.

Re-form, re-group;
Share, or they will not have us,
Or any morsel of us. They push back
Our not insignificant rubbish,
Driven up the wall, pierced into it.

A savage, soft-lipped people
Pour hotly onto us
Molten in their rightness: raised hands
Cleaner, and softer, than
Tissue inside the mouth.
Gristle, kneebone and head
Tool and cohere their rage.

We will give nothing mothed
But a live thing: a bean, berries
Fruit from the stone north.

We have offered nothing that they want.
We cannot push off with
Our failures, as they justify our death.
The grass-root, the subtly tough
Fibrous thing, the thing that threads off
As you rub your thumb over its sullen length,
That they wither under the earth,
And the earth itself sours; blisters.
I shall still keep to this.

Circus

The servitude of beasts
Is the condition with man.
The belling circus day
Admitted three camels. It is
A fact that man laughs
At his inner image. Their steps,
As though the ground gave heat,
Made of misery
An inarticulate tread
Bedraggled in servitude, and branded
Of laughter. Earth offers the astonished
Scorn of northern children.
This is man's condition
To breed derision upon himself.

For the Dead Woman's Husband

The swiftness of dying is the earth's
Speed, turning. As the soul inclines
More steeply than the earth is curved,
The thin flesh begins its rigors.
Then spirit with utmost violence spirit
Can make, contracts from flesh
That was as equal an instrument of it.

Ah, the rude growth of man's body
Whose flesh drops away in flight;
It is dark into more of such darkness
The flesh cannot retrieve itself from.

A woman's pain was the whip
Of disease demanding its true
Recognition. Later she died.

The bough deciduates,
And the main trunk fails, as if pierced
By the herculean lightning
The sky's tensions form.

And as ever, the dead tree decays
To the strength the earth nourishes with.

Beyond this, there is no knowledge.

Yet the complete death of self
Is unimaginable.

The sun blackly causes
The laceworking of leaf through brightness
To repeat the substantial leaves.
The shadow lurks in piercing
Grasses, after the sun
Has charred, and leaf torn
A space from the air.

Dress her in the garb of death,
When you think of this woman
You stir a coolness that rises in you
That her shadow brims the clung surface
Come from undrowned depths.
This way you give life to
A memorable pattern of lace,
But her lace is unthread.

More, if we think of her, her shade comes
Alive, and breathes her life delicately through us.
Think, one breath makes many lives,
Though her death is frost. For then she takes off
Though she is permanently in disguise,
The person of death, which makes all one,
And breathes her life delicately through our thoughts.
Grief mend yourself with your grief.

'A girl danced, and she seemed'

A girl danced, and she seemed
Untouched by any life;
A freed point of aspiring
Incomprehension through
Her being.
The proper image is
A runner. Many are similar.
She is air impelled off
A gnarled scree in that the processes
Of men, in making money,
Manipulate her.
Nothing of choice made her
Magnificent: yet nature
That made her is deprived
Of feeling.
Touched in the groin by sentiment
Her being rejects its natural
Clenched, glittering heat.
Insistent hard-skinned fingers,
Pale, slight, slightly filthy,
Immaculate, and small
Press the thyroid's sensitivity
Garotted a bit: these
The enterprises of cash.
And, like these enterprises,
Mindlessly dispersed
Through a delirium
That knows no weight, nor hardness,
Nor hair, but its own hair,
Furled over the stomach in that
Abandonment, which is display.
Nature's depths are a surface.
Only the flesh is sensitive,
Growing away from some point
Bright and indeterminate,
The parts of it that are
Touched, by common assent;
In conduct, more intimate,
Less animal, more anonymous.

The Landlord

'All tenants will
Do as tenants will do.'
This remark is written
Over the fanlight of
Our house, at whose gate
We tremble with mirth. Unfit
And condemned for living in
Our landlord has just put
The rents up –
'To meet' he says 'the rising
Costs of living.' He should know.
To which he adds: 'nothing
In the house must be changed
Or shifted, but through me.'

When shall I ask for grace,
How know the moment when?
I rent a modest room
In which eleven flies
Shifted slightly as he entered,
Like thoughts of lust conceding
To conscience room for love;
Poor, slight, foolish love.
But they remained avoiding
All but the obvious
Temptation. Thus a book
When opened, disturbed
Two fat ones embracing,
So that my quarrel with them
Lost much of its justice through
My landlord's sentiment.
And by the flex which goes
Down where the wood runs,
By my bed, a cluster
Of eggs appeared. Yet
Suggestions to the landlord
About removing them

Produced a rebuke.
'Since being fair' he said
'Means with the tender conscience
Of the artist permitting all life.'
And in the afternoon
Brought a large bowl of flowers
– Painted I should say –
To show he had this.

Then soon I was
Disturbed with the filmy
Crackling of membrane
As the huge summer flies
Burst their eggs.
With thick short legs and eyes
Moist, round and cancerous;
And their bodies were larger
Than my foot. It seemed
Hard to be sharing
Such a room as this.
I hated it: I loathed
These creatures he loved
And I decided then
That if I dared I would
Burn them to death.
Too large, too frightening.
Yes: some accommodation
Must be found between
Myself, them, and the landlord.
My room is small and dark.
I am afraid, my God.

The Bugs

Here comes her landlord whose
Eyes swell into a greasy
Flare over the pupil.
The smuts burst – satanic,
Male, and Roman; the eyes
Hap on her. Oh splendid!
As if in his soft patrician
Sac a potent life thronged.
The other night, I stayed.
And in the morning, he took
A ladder and stuck his head
Through the raised window,
To see if we copulated.
And yet his concern
For my girl's virtue, and her fine
Body, joined as if each was a thief,
Could be lulled on that bed
He rents to – any lady
Out at work. He compares with,
For the sheer spectacle of
Others' cash drawn from the groin,
That writer whom I know.

And he copies the plant louse,
Manipulating himself
On the hairs of the stem,
Sucking the milky sap
As he can. He bites, then sucks,
And voids after feeding,
On the fine hairs of the stem
Tiny black globules of shit.
Then again he draws
Himself up by those forceful
Arms, which grasp the hairs
Of the stem, and strain minutely,
His tiny spiteful legs
Rubbing upon each other.

Sometimes he fills the eye
Making me thank my Creator
In whose reduced image we live
That man, a splendid bug,
Though tangled in the hairs of nature,
And like a traveller through
The moving swirls of fluid
The milky oyster balms
The gritty voyager in,
That man lives also upon
The flesh of his kind. Fine! Fine!

Choosing

Speaking of love, you said,
'Not morals, but passion entails
Forms from the shifting splinters
Of processes – from which
We say love is stable,
Permanent.' 'Love' I said
'Is…' You completely
Leaned forward, and kissed me
As if you were naked.
The chairs, that kneeled under us
And others who sat or lay
In their perspicuous
Assemblage of chaoses,
Like bits of gyring light,
Persevered in
Their service.
You stretched over one and
I put my body like
A garment upon yours –
Joined in the undulating
Process of generation –
Not distinguished by size,

Or depth, or anything of that,
But the slight movements finer
Than subtlety, more pared,
Less conspicuous
And altogether full
Of the severe energy
That honest with frond-like
Insistence draws into
The broad moral mind.
This mind 'is its Age':
A large, bow-fronted
Window, gazing through
Its transparency, pressing
For the whole view, upon
Its nature that does not choose.

This Man in Pain

If that is what pain is:
A decent lack of the whole
Muscular agony
Man once tore the ground with,
He is it. What is more
He knows no more than this.
His sex, his smiling,
The filed apprehensions of art,
Are acts of blindness, as a blind person
In all he touches –
The stinging lemon oils
Or the waxen, odourless flesh
Of the cactus are rubbings
Of blindness. The well-lengthed back
In its nudeness as it reaches
Out to pull a flower
Is slurred in the breeches.
See how he smiles:

Smiling is bits of acute glass,
A menstruated shape of moon
Peeled from a mind tormented
In disintelligence.
This is not wholly intelligence
To be wholly with pain;
This is not wholeness
To be one's pain, only;
As if this earth were compacted
Into its agony –
Taken for that only.
This causes the stones to protest
And the droves of flesh to cry out
That their pain is burdensome.

At Durham

To have come to that point where we do not know
What passion is, we are as stones
Hewn in love, but laid
Back in our nature. If you are
Not friend, but some being
Piteously incoherent,
Wounded as though in wings
Which lift you from a crushed,
Distempered self, you are
As I know I was. For once,
In the provocation of what
You create, havoc of friendships,
As one mad, I cut
You to the ground
Making you whimper; not I,
I say, not any of me,
But you – to a creature
Without redemption. Why must
There be roles; let us dispense

With victims. To be victor
Is to be without spittle, numb
Where the victory was to film the palate; the blood
Frightens, dismays, defeats
What does not conquer. If we were each
To travel the common way
A great stone might to that
Infinite point at which
It feels its depth from love,
We were active as the God
Who made the incandescent
Mass of earths from
His casual soul. We are leach
Stones in the soft church
Above the river Wear,
That the wind, mixed with our dust,
Constantly rubs at. If we could
Perceive, we might see entirely through
This town, that the great church
Is uncentrally poised, and not once
Stops the eye's bounded search.
Are we not of one cast
In variety? Made numb,
To die as children
Unloving? Let us touch
One another, unfriendly christian,
Before we die
The common jewish decay,
As the mad, sorry in death for
The space they grieve in the flesh
Of others. Since I am with you
In nothing if but this.

The Expulsion of Pain

What kind of obscene
Clothing must a church wear?
Christ for a christian
Is crucifixion; bone and blood
Is crucifixion; to rise up
Is an act nurtured from pain,
Which save for it were nothing.
Christ's sap, Christ's ooze,
Man compared to a tree,
Nothing. The christian, it seems,
Wants a constant renewal of blood
In its shedding. I am afraid.
I abhor that christian faith
Which worships the human form
Men killed. When holy men
Worship the Divine in pain
Who will they not select
To keep alive the sacred
Gland of cruelty?

Men in Asia who knew
Poverty as a disease,
And the violence of nature
A sickness, whose epicentre
Was man, worshipped no cross.
They were too occupied
Fighting starvation. The condition
Created by the Divine
Was life, which man accepted.
Yet some would take on no image
Of complete goodness. For a God
Comprehended in every thing,
Was a force that sustained and destroyed,
Creating the image it ravaged,
Shaking its large beard
As the earth shakes its hair, we entangled
In its streaming fibres. Consider

The Hebrews whose germ produced
The Christ. All Europe took him
Until he was with them
A prosperous disease.
Is this how we balance our Divine?

Man's image laps on nature.
Yet in response he is
Yielded through his blindness
A metaphor, his illusion
Merely. We have to examine
Ourselves the way a child
Inspects his flesh. Then perhaps
We shall glimpse what is not man,
Yet hope to see ourselves
In a more adult way;
And cease praising this image.
It is time to disrobe
From pain. The buildings in purple
Decked for the occasion
Reject their dress. Yet we
Must be watchful still
As a man, summoned as guest
To supper, looks to himself
Through his host, but is vigilant
And critical, yet glad
Of his host, the supreme, host of hosts.

Lindisfarne

But who does hawk at eagles with a dove?
           – Herbert, 'The Sacrifice'

'Brought' over the road
That the tide covers means
Men 'brought', and men cut
The stone which they loaded
And horses carted.

Over the uncovered bar
Red sandstone, and white stone,
Bits of Priory
Isolation swallowing the yelp
Of gull, the arctic duck,
Geese.
The religion of the self-isolating saints
Eating fresh water.

The island is small enough
For the sea to shake, sufficiently
Firm for the castle to stand,
Moated, grassed short
By pasture.

Some men fish, which needs courage,
And shoot birds, which does not.
Life is taken where men live,
Where the saints live, no life.
The fish inhale the sea.
The saints are confined
Their whole life for the mind
Drawn to its God judging
The war men make. Mild to these,
They squeeze their life into
An odour, pungent like an onion;
A spirit, separate and concise,
By example alone.
The Danes come and smash it
Smash the church. Mildness comes
To no good but its own.

Which Kind do we Belong To?

A participating
Disruption organized
In small clusters
Is what nature seems.
The insect with its carapace,
The small sand snake
Minutely venomous,
The ant in his fixed world
Of enormous labour,
Rewards, punishments, –
All are ordered;
That is, each within
His own kind. It is therefore just
We expect of man
Who is a subtle organism
With a large brain and hard feet,
And a proud vulnerable heart,
That he live at peace;
At least, with his own kind.
As unlikely, and as horrific
In fact as Hughes' pikes
Mouth jammed into mouth
That neither can withdraw.
Intellect has sharp teeth;
And the heart seems made with thorns
All pointing inward.
For man subsists, not with his neighbour
But himself. Beware, then,
Man, since you are fittest
To live with the hungry fox
Or the sharp twitching of the asp
Who complains once. For each
One in his kingdom
Is a law as fixed as is casual
The appetite of men,
Who would swallow stones if needs be,
When the colour attracts; a confusing
Of swollen indulgences.

Going On

I think of all the toughs through history
And thank heaven they lived, continually.
I praise the overdogs from Alexander
To those who would not play with Stephen Spender
                                        – Thom Gunn

Thom Gunn wrote a poem about Spender,
That gentle poet, who changed sides.
He wears a space suit, perhaps
As sign of toughness. But man
Is too near to his destruction
To imitate a forced strength.
What he has forged, a few blades
In a packet, and a paper bomb
Whose heat burns hotter than newsrag,
Should make one deliberate. The sling-days
Of David, even the comparatively
Contemporary hours of Lawrence
In Arab outfit, are gone.
It is as much as we
Can do to be ourselves.
And compulsively
The blade moves too near
The vulnerable flesh
And we must see each other
As plainly as we can,
For the hunger in man is tragic
I mean, to grow himself
Into a powerful image.
But, complexly, the soul
Cries for some nourishment
Of a different kind. Who nakedly
Plays with images of toughness
Shall experience the blade.

An Age of Copper

The touch of
A feather lowered and raised
Off one pan of the scales
You gave to justice. It
Seemed beautiful: the preened
And graduated hues
Of each fawn branch
Undulating in
The stroke, the moving air,
Like the stag pressing through
Its head of glistening antlers, –
If the forefinger and thumb
Holding the feather had not
Disdained that dear vision.
  But when the assembly had
Returned to their stiff sheets,
You rose and struck the other
Pan with the heel
Of your palm that the shaft
Rose up and kicked the beam.
The blow was violent:
And scoring the thickened flesh
It nearly destroyed
The balance; yet I praise
The act that with scruples
Expressed your nature.
Though in the double part
Self-honesty must play,
Many Congolese
Were shot, or starved.
  If that part of the land
Seemed to desire secession
From the main government
That drew your interests
In copper to the larger,
Purer share of people,
Who blames you for sullying

Minds breaking away
From the white spirit that said:
'A share in the lands
We but graze with cattle'.
    You forced the civil split
Wider apart. Then men
Were pressed by the heel of
Your palm into the balance
Until their scrupulous weight
Fused with the instrument.
    Not much is wanting.
Those who were hungry lingered
Hearing the copper wires
Scratching the plate which rose
To catch what was let fall,
Not knowing whose the weal.
But that the taps with heads
Like gawping Cherubim
Spew over the face
Their molten services
In fluid diamond
I see. Pleasing and chaste
Is the design of these
In which a master swills.
And since to take on credit
Is predatory all
That's chaste has been paid for.
Even fertility
In which the poor believe.
    Your wife is bearing: from her
Body innocent as milk
And youthfully as smooth
As the soft breast of it,
Pieces of unformed flesh
Drop, clenching the bits
Of hair and rootless tooth,
As if these would observe
Their native ancestry.
I pray they be adored by

Sober Englishman.
A praiser, let him
Hold up this dully fierce
Burnished morality.
Let us, with gladsome minds,
Praise what is copper, the man
Falling beneath its loads.

The Island

He came down
To a shore where evening was made perpetual
By ancient, absorbed woods,
And walked
On, drawn by feather noises that
Were mapped above the shrill
Pulse of scorched water,
And he saw,
Drooping and flowering then,
A ghost.

Turning to go up, he saw
That it was a nymph,
Sleeping upright
With her arms round an elm.

Moving in himself from
Image to real flame
He reached a field where the shadow gathered
In the eyes of girls
As evening does at the root-foot of olive trees;
The branches distilled
A lethargic
Fire rain of darts.
Here sheep dozed
Under the even warmth;

Others browsed off
The glowing surface;
The shepherd's hands gleamed
With a slight fever, like glass

Warriors
(Echoes of human activities)

The fourth willingness between the two,
She being satisfied, he knelt down
Wanting prowess to be vain, and from behind
Gave certain pleasure. A shudder of infliction
Motioning her even distant organs
Into a need he did release.
She could not see, but feel what he did to her
And for himself, he felt briefly, an extinction
Of flickering prowess, which had persisted
Because subdued in a rivalry
Of separate capacities. He did some of this.
Their organs were oblivious, and she was fruited,
And given the produce he was incautious of
The visible, helpless life borne of willing organs.
Which every creature has. With more surety
His mind being cautious, she would have composed both
Into mutual quietness, his growth poignant to her
As a fruit, to be reached for when ripened.

Ruthlessly

She, being audacious,
The perturbed planets relent
To the curved, lucid size
Of a drinking-glass, which inverts
Those fixed pressures on
Her conscience. Viscoid, cool
As greyish liquid, what need is there
In her intricate leverage
Of tenants to be fair
If she be just?

A delicate god. Some god dispenses,
In due course, all the properties
Tenants pay for. Thus a chipped cup
Is healthy on their lips –
Whose foul gifts turn fair
When lent and paid for by them.

As for the bits of hygiene
Her soul is clean with
They are her sacrament,
She is kept in idleness.
And breathes, and gluts
Her rent-paid flesh
In tenant-worship, and that soul
Performs its goodness.

But for whose good is
This breath breathed in for?

Oh the charity of white teeth smiling
That half-bite the low, benign voice
Which exudes its goodness;
If she be a pious god
Think how the hierarchies
Of the divine system should clash,
One god on the Next:

White milk against white teeth,
Biting the sweet cud
In horror, with gnashed
Righteous hatred.

Are you over her, Lord?

The rod has its blackened flesh
Whose burning is only for good souls.
Is just; there is no other.
Its tenants are dirt.

The Terms

Something insists that
The other part be told.

What had made him like this?
Was the earth partially dry
Or else the root defective?
It needs just a small
Nick of a disease
To make a deformed thing.
He had grown quietly
Forming a kind of life
With something like birds
That shrill in winter time.
Though this was not like pain,
Or else that kind of pain
Which is inexpressible,
As a contorted piece
Of stone will offer hardness
Over the contortions.

Did I do this? It was
Early in winter that
The breath began to show

On the air, with not much whiteness.
Then the child gradually
Gathered its senses up
In one intelligent
And variously deep
Fluid over the eye
Until the mind no further,
Or the skull, or the eyes' lashes
Could restrain it. Then
From the eyes slowly burst
A great moisture of life.

Did I do that? Did earth
Slip that attention which
It breathes into most minds
Formed with its energy?
Maybe not earth; nor prongs
Paired onto the lifted skull.
It was the two of us,
I think, that made him like
A nearly perfect thing;
Not that we did not love
But that we did not know
How to maintain its growth.
So that imperfect feelings
Defected the child's mind.

And it is this that makes
Me want my humanness
Inward, silent, devoid
Of anything but what
The mind needs to grow on;
Because we made the child
That had a separate life,
But then he died; therefore the mind
With moist, with long tough roots
Must search for honesty
More than it might have done,
Knowing the thing it cares for.

'Was it, you say, because'

'Love seeketh not itself to please,
… But for another gives its ease…'
So sung a little Clod of Clay…
But a Pebble of the brook…
'Love seeketh only Self to please…'
    – Blake, 'The Clod and the Pebble'

Was it, you say, because
You loved me, or did not
Love me, you therefore loved
With him, and again with
Him? Although you now
Say you were not in love.
How make light of it
Saying 'It was unimportant,
It is unimportant now,
It is finished, compared with you.'
How, unimportant? The broadness
Of me in my love
As it is with you,
Should not be made smaller.
To conjure with that pleasure
(Which almost equalled ours
In a week's absence)
Making it small, makes ours
Less. Let me have big threats
To shake a large thing,
Since casual implements
Cut down my dignity
That I come to you with.
Do you wish that gone?
What size then would the trunk be,
And then, the monstrous head
After the trunk had gone,
To roll over a field
Crushing the sharp grass-blades,
Alike in helplessness.
What might they even then

Know what I was cut from?
I can frame a forcible lie
I can conjure the pleasure
But not the subtle warmth
I have in knowledge from you,
With another. May it be for this
Blake made the small stone lie
Within the yielding clod?

Two Women and a Man

My enemies rejoice that I am in pain.
All my enemies are Christian;
Friend, this is simply explained.
The Christian tells me that if I
Am struck on the cheek,
As all Christians deserve
As a part of conversion,
I should turn the other
To the fist of wood.
Thus the Christian rejoices,
Not because he is joyful
But because, dutifully, he can
Strike twice. All of which
Is perplexing and Christian.

But then, the persons that I love
Are Christian also. The Jewish God,
Moreover, offers no solution
But the bare choice between them.
So we are caught hanging
In the curved eye of our future,
Specks,
Seen by what we see.
This is certainly perplexing.

O God, cry for us
Because I cannot.

Hatred

Gothic creature, calvinist to the tips
Of sense, three things disgust me in you:
The first is in this: you discreetly inquired
After my flat during that relationship
Which is not ended, with my woman,
Through which gap you pressed hoping
To hasten departure. It never happened.
Your friendly wife, and your two children
Came no nearer. In my division
The owners were solid with their tenant.
The second thing that I loathe you for
Is your conceit. It is a germ
That wastes your being; little else moves through
Save an occasional piercing of misery
As you forget your self-image. Then
A fawn bat shades the air. You are here
To remind yourself what you have not failed in,
A predetermined belief in your verse
An agnostic, blunt, sense of power
In which but for it you would be contemptible.
And you know it. Then the third thing,
In which we close together, is pity
For which I hate you since I must pity you,
Vulnerable in that you do not perceive
How much distaste you create about you.
It bites you. You do not feel this. You have
A disease in which all the delicate nervous
Apparatus of sensitivity
Is numb to the otherness of the world,
Delicately harsh. In this you are helpless
Which is my pity. You cannot amend
What you are unable to perceive.
I see you would give small mercy
Yet I must share such tenderness
For the creature pinched in hostile jambs
Whose door shuts out that exacting world
Which depends from your existence.

So we share your life like a useful virus
That keeps quick a position strengthened
In consciousness. No other person
Gets such distaste with me as you.
So stay a rigid calvinist
Predetermined from warmth, having the flickering hatred
That shuttles between the human areas
Of cold, like a bitter wind:
Your conceit will perfect what it cannot change.
The little woods which lead so much
Into the tangled thorns of hell
Most men cannot be intact from
You make simple: Their loathing is not yours
As your pain is not. Scrape there a grave
That you slackly lay haunches in.
Yet the earth, you know, hates a fawn rat.

Crocus

The crocus eases apart
Granules of warmed earth.
As unmolesting as a rod drawn through fluid iron.
A petalled thing, almost closed,
It opens six spearheads
In cautious sunlight, thinly veined
Through their erect soft flesh.
On one stem. When dead, the wax sifts
From it. It lies flat, and shrunk,
A shred of pigment, not skin even
Which dead flesh leaves.
Alive, the flower is an empty bowl
With ginger stamens, a dense orange stigma
Intensifying the steepness of the petals' curve
That shield the fierce colour.
The flowering long ball rises, its weight upwards.
They are in patches.

Mildly return where soil
Was churned for an arch
Lifting a road up, shrinking distance
In concrete, the vernacular
Substance for now mixed firm.
An ease with physicals
The tamped layers seamed
To each other, as if nails
Were struck in to fix still.

We are on it; the crocuses' colour
Paled, forced precisely out of itself.
Its pallor an index of flight.
Thick upright cylinders passed
Turn their heat round, a dulled light
Ashing a thin spire. A grimed curd
Is air, frost, dust; thickening.

With brick, with more brick
With the brick, with a man's hands,
A kiln makes brick.
A brent darkness with heat hovering
And lightly split on protrusions
Of bone, or puckers. Dust is inside.
One skin irritating the skin under it.

Forced to hire their bodies
Their land contracted like a skin over the country's lawly bones.

The earth has heaps of itself.
And streets are runnelled
With shit. Bodies are contused
With iron; that had split open the clod
Where anthrax lurked, waiting to dart
Through the cut skin.

Their children make cotton.
The fluff of the hemming thread
Spurts
Drifting noiselessly into their quiet lungs.

The crocuses increase.
Their stems fatten into
Succulent trunks, with grasses notched and flickering
An edge that cuts an ear off.
Their hardened globes clash;
Their soundless pollen
Jolted out, big as rust splinters.
It's as if metal could weep
Or inch hair. A matted shit
At the plant's base. People tauten
Like a twine of cotton, shaking in
The crocus breathings, getting their shade
Tinctured with yellow. A berserk iodine.
They are unhostile, huge; the toe parings
Of some large creature the sine
Of one petal's curve.

Sparrow

The boldening scots sparrow hops
On claws; insolently knits
Into its beak a morning's chances.
Then a threat melts into
The punitive eye;
In anger that fears itself
In others. Its chill concentred hatred
Moves in three bounds upon the earth
As if stitched there. It's a brown spark,
Struck impotently on its small girth,
Noiseless, feeding.

The arm of Scotland grows
Through mist, gaunt and haired.

The sparrow's cry is air; all of it,
Crying for territory;

Space also, livelihood.
It is the first creature to appear
The first to die,
That deep green dew
Moistening the ravelling grass
That mats up the sparrow
To a ball, grieveless.
That depth of green
Sparrowless with sap, a fluid
Stiffening into age.

Our Country

Two slopes are trenched
For the railway deeper into the earth's cut.
Its sounds nestle in the rocks,
And rise, like sprouted rod on the grass.
Each bird defecates a blotched ordure
Through the sound, and onto the stone.
In oatmeal, in bread, and more bread,
In bread, and shortbread, in scone,
In herring, for every provision of suffering
There is a flour milled
From the grain union has got.
Our sewage is seamed in pipes the size of a man crouching
To where the jellyfish opens and shuts like a flower
Concerting day and night in a handful of seconds.
The smeltings of war stay. Poverty is courage,
Its nausea, the more we lack
We nourish pride poor as
Up-country soil in which
The mountain daisy tufts its roots, binding up the grains.
We have two eyes for the flower's one:
Our lords burn heather, making pert
The shoots for grouse. Soil shifts,
Granule and moisture.

Some nose apart the thighs tuppered together
Where the pulled skin of one flesh pulls the other to it making
                              a curve like a petal's.
Each of us is a flower, desolate, upright
Concerted in one soil.

The System, or what it said last

In the stone body hairs
Of stone thread the centre
With minute channels. The juice
Drawn from the soil moves
To feed the centre
Because the outer ring feels
The inner ring's helplessness.
The ring outside copes
With lice,
And a band of tightening wind.
Inside, the column of stone
Grows denser, stronger to demand
The juices it first asked for.
The centre returns protection
Of some kind
For the outer brunt's trunkly frailness.
Spiritual frailty.
The whole organism
Is growing stone.

The second is seeded from the first,
Its boluses winged and hard,
Its progeny a tight green
In their case. The pith
Grew in a soft column:
Dryish linked series
Resting above each other
The upper an integer

Of its lower. It grew thickening outer rings
And fed them. And the servant is
Inside, it is said.
Rustling worshippers, of a kind,
Absorb and change light
Into breath. Each grows,
The inside held at length
By the outer; and what
It supports, this gives
In return, the idea
Of spirit; the elder part
All soul, dryish.

These two, succeeding each other,
Breaking together an idea
At all cost, good;
Unflinching
Sacrificial as the jabbing bee.
They demanded of themselves
Their labourers' gentle lives.
Or brutal, at any rate,
In peace; and making war together
Are very loyal.
Born conscripted.
And for another thing
Their lungs were hurt
By Europe's steel, or their faces were,
That had contracted them.
Spirituality
White,
Folded in paroxysm
Round that steel bit
And held
Noiselessly, at length.
Generous as a cup of water.

Nature with Man

First published by Chatto & Windus with the Hogarth Press,
1965

Nature with Man[18]

The lank summer grass
As it is, bent and wailing;
A scorching wind
Scours a whole plain of it.
Dust still oppresses.[19] Then
As if the earth received
A bruise a pool of brown
Slime erupts slowly
From among the stems. Summer mud…
Hot and stagnant. The grass stalks
Stand pricked without root
In the rimless mud … in what eye.
On[20] some field of grey stone
A white sud of saliva,
So fine it seems a mildew,
Agonizes over the crop.

But are the humans here? Nature
Had a human head. The mouth
Turned on its long neck, biting through
Scale, sinew; and the blood[21]
Carried through the flesh
Beyond the ends of veins
As the severed head
Rolled into the bullrushes.
This limp and useless
Going off among tall weeds
Has soured the earth, whose body
Decays and perishes.
As for the pain
That suds onto the stone;
That, simply, is pain.

How much else is there?
There is only one head.
But it has several minds
Which still give out

Great reticulations
Of ideas, nets wilful and sharp
Over it; binding it[22]
In pride and thought that cut
The smiling face of pleasure.

'O pity, pity, pity'?
But the weedy soul is shrinking.
Nor can it see how
To join itself unto
The membered flesh. The whole[23]
Of nature is turning slowly
Into an eye that searches
For its most developed
And treacherous creature, man.
Monstrous and huge eye:
The entire process[24]
Of nature perverted
Into the search for him.

A Kind of Nature

to Leonard Clark
for Leslie Norris

Keats' vision of Langstone:
Land and sea separate,
The first, sorts of mist. Sea fumes
Through a ship in sails
Coming thinly on.
The land fumes; so it seems
It too sifts through the ship.
Men's made things, images of them,
Replace what we have learnt
Of trees that hold the soil,
Or flowers, seen closely.

Their beauty still remains.
Not nature's, but the eye's,
Whose ligaments and moisture
Contain flowers that were flowers
Seen often. Oils of seed
In liquid chain held in
The lemon's crystalled sharpness
And green pulps of simple cabbage.
Great England. O what laughter
Of water ripples into your vegetables,
Or slender sweetness through blades,
The delicate grasses of sensibility
Purple, pale violet, or lilac,
The three leafed clovers
Spread into curtseying
Demurely nubile.
Take care of Nature. Keats'
Vision must stay: a trope
For critics, merchandise
For types of shopkeeper
And poet; and be the sacredness
We use in churches
To justify 'the benign vision'
Of an indifferent God
Swollen with pulps of man.
He is our carnivore
And we, His feeling plants.
And that's the complex part.
For if He cared more
We might, like children
Put on trust, treat one
Another with more care.
For the price of having the Father
Would be obedience;
His images, our flesh.
But if we are alone
Like stones in a huge field
Stupidly brutal,
Where is the trust, that fine

Sharpness of moral care
Inhered in each recess
Of lemon consciousness?
Nothing will guide
The pressed stones open
To the waters of heaven
That erode us, as we nudge
Wear and crack each other;
Though we are a beauteous
Gift of each other.

Soon

Our boat gorged up
Between shores, whose vines
Held light, pushing it onto
The sea underneath.
Nothing spoke. The cut
Waters spent themselves
Inches between the craft
And close shore. Grapes tangled
With the mast, and fell.
Through a chasm of plants
We emerged, and there,
Wanted breath. Our sides,
And foreheads, creased wetly.
We lived, we knew. And then
Anchored into the space
We came on, without speech.
And of one movement
Went onto land. Through woods
Where dust with green
Spines of fir passed
By the shoe, we climbed.
We came to tilled fields
Whose corn had been grasped,

Or whose nuts, & vines,
Waited a man's hand.
But nowhere was that creature,
His mule not seen. Until
Over a plateau with
Some cypresses we saw
The temple. The queer thing
Between us was the silence
Thinning the air; its clearness
Bore the sun on us.
And here, like flies, we moved
Distractedly, with membranous
Hands raised upwards.
And each of us, I felt,
If he could have believed
Would have spoken; admitting
The cold nourishment of fear.
Fear we had not:
Save for our half-fear
Stronger than all. Tired
Of this I moved up to
A cypress, erect, tapering.
And picked up from the ground,
With fangs open, the ends
Shaped like small clubs,
A cone. I lifted it:
Emissions of seed spilled
Over my hand, infesting
It with seminal decay,
Leaving on the core inside
A speckled whiteness.

The Distraction

for Ian Hamilton

Yesterday
She gathered flowers into
Her arms; and though I cannot
Tell you what the life
Was named, I know that these
Were last flowers; some final
Intermission of colour
Before the season falls.
So that in this poise
In which a woman took
A mortal thing to her body
There seemed a poignancy;
As though the figure of
Proserpine near Dis
Breathed into that bent form:
One flower entering
Another at her breast.
And all the time she gathered
The fairest delicacy
The dead nourish in nature
Nor for man's delight but
For the whole exacting process
Of growth towards the earth.
Yet from the earth
Some pincering insect form
Emerged, as if it would
Draw them and death below;
As though the cold did not
Contract the spines of life
Closely enough to death.

The Religious West

You tell me the Christian religion must settle accounts. What accounts?
I see none. It has helped create a life fit even for pigs.

— Priest in Old Play

One sees
But a heap of shoes
Beaten to trash.

Not one ritual's deterred.
Since 'pigs will always be pigs'★
And a knife help
As ever:– a pig for a pig.

'Light on a bare side,
A little tear of blood
And a cry: what could we want more?
If having these attributes
Of the martyr.
                              I see one
Shoe of size, big as
A lap-dog, is moving
Out. Down with it.
See the sun, how it
Goes on illuminating
Its fragment central to it.
                              He does live
Among us
Whose rigid desires made good
Aggravate all that
Perplexes man,
Fluttering within his flesh,
To unanimity
Through worship, action, attention to
The meticulous problems that taunt
The spirit. Borne against
The sun is some loose blood.
What's that? An ounce or so,

It would appal its kith
With its meagreness
As eggs their fly.
What's that, that is borne
Against the faultless sun?'

Slopt in wet, tugged loose,
It sprinkles through the seas
In tiny eggs of mud.

Slowly the sun,
Like half the face of God,
Seethes through the stained west –
Exultant, smeared, and tired
Of its labour, gorged on, and relished.

* Bialik, the Russian-Jewish poet.

Defence

for Ann

What 'one-in-five' can do
No man can quite do

She arrived late, with this motto:
'Time used in reconnaissance
Is not time lost'. Useful hint
On how efficient our defences
Would be. Sent from the *Home Office*
On 'Work of some importance'.
And 'The first thing' she said
'Is that there will be four minutes
Of preparation before
The thing is dropped. You should

Instruct persons to stand
In the centre of what room
They like – for the blast,
Unlike the bombs of the previous war,
Will draw the walls out.
There will be no crushing
Of flesh. Instead
On all sides walls will reveal
The citizen unharmed.' Here a question,
But 'No' she said 'we have
From our *Intelligence*
Absolute assurance
Our capital is not targeted.'
Total warfare, by arrangement.
And she was sure, when pressed.
'But there will be devastation
As we now suspect, in radius
Of forty four miles.
The water will be infected;
The light from the thing, astonishing:
Which though surprised by, we should
Not look at; but shelter
Behind some object "to reduce
Damage to the tissue"
From radiation; or shelter
Under brown paper;
Or, if you can, –
Sheets soaked in urine.'

So women who crotchet,[25] stop that;
Men labouring whose issue is
The two-handed house, set that aside.
Girls big and delicate
With child, turn on your side;
You will melt. The ravelling spider
And the scorpion whose prongs itch
Will fuse in a viscoid
Tar, black as a huge fly.
The whole of nature

Is a preying upon.
Let man, whose mind is large,
Legislate for
All passionate things,
All sensate things: the sensuous
Grass, whose speech is all
In its sharp, bending blade.
Leave not a leaf, a stone
That rested on the dead
To its own dissolution.

She left then,
As if she were with her feet
Turning an enormous,
If man-made, pearl
As a means of locomotion.

Community

You said 'you make love to me
Like no other.' I did
Not ask if that implied
'Recently'. For if
The dead are here, now discomforting us,
And though no one at all
May be so daft or childish
As to gaze at the wiped knives
And shuck the dead off, into after-life,
Yet there is our sex: and this,
With the abusing of it
Through urging it, and also
Threat of companions in
Our devouring, remains
A direction of bodily energies
I call 'love'. Such a word
Seems cynical: the contempt

Of the emancipated,
It hardens the mouth of every
Adolescent woman
Seeking marriage. I use it.
I saw: I felt the flickering
Slender muscle strain
For completeness, and forcing back
The sheets, you under me
A determination of movement
With your vagina's lips
Taut as a bow – and the hill
Of living bone rush to me
As if the earth shifted.
There are no areas of
Our lives, isolated,
Life-giving, like benign
Liquid on the sand.
There is this: a creation
I am not yet ashamed
I helped to make. The dead, even,
Put to death by creatures
With a crude cleverness
More immune than instruments
That tease the genitals out,
Do not make this seem wrong.
We imitate, basely, but we imitate.
When I die I want
No ritual, only the strengthening
Of the passion to create love,
Not hindered by some mourning,
And perpetuated by
This simple image of
A pervasive hunger.

Processes

Not flesh; and spirit is
One part of this.

It is a softness not easily abraded;
Whose play, a slipping out of the summer's fingers
Detains me.

If it were
Your kiss fixed on my body
Not all of that
Would suffice.

Something that can be thought.
Though that smelted into
Mind's cold, yet
Upon the fingers.

Its pressures sink onto
The man inside the flesh
Who gropes after union.

So that the manifold thing
Is like the body which
Poor Plato whirled about in
Sick as war.

And you can feel that what
I'm speaking of is love.

I touch you; but mostly those
Charges your smile grows from

Until you are a gathering of forms:

The rose in mildews
Whose trenchant whorls
Of felt shape self-perfectingly
Cause to char inwards;

The idea itself, perishing
Against its will, like a man
Enlisted to fight
War's contradictions.

It is these things you seem like:
All of them:

Even the man.

The fatherless body melts
Of its enormous wounds.

Though if we'd bent over
This dying man, such care
Would be, like the adult's finger
Closed over by the child's hand,

A form of permanence.
But he has turned apart.

Evening

At the foot of the evening's marches
A clear water shifts,
The colour of an olive.

And reaches the short fire
Whose memory is a space.

I hear the crickets and frogs
Through smoke

Where grass shakes, delicately.

From the Italian of Ungaretti

Death Pain

To die
Like larks thirsting
In a mirage

Or like the quail
That has crossed the sea in
The first thicket
Because it has no
Wish
     any
More to fly

But not to
Live
On lament like
A blinded goldfinch

From the Italian of Ungaretti

Watch

A whole night
Thrown beside
A slaughtered friend with his mouth
Turned and grinning
To the full moon.
The congestion of his hands
Penetrating
My silence,
I write letters filled
With love.

I have never been
So fully
Attached to life.

From the Italian of Ungaretti

Rivers

This mutilated tree gives
Me support, left in this pot-hole.
It has the bitterness of a circus
Before or after the show.
I watch
The quiet passage of
Clouds over the moon.

This morning I stretched
Myself in an urn of water,
Like a relic, and rested.

The Isonzo scoured
Me like
One of its stones.

I pulled my four
Limbs together,
And went, like an acrobat,
Over the water.

Crouched by my clothes
Fouled with war, I inclined
My head, like a Bedouin,
To receive the sun.

This is the Isonzo.
And it is there I
Most see myself
In the universe
A compliant
Thread.

My pain is
When I do not believe
Myself in harmony.

But those hidden
Hands give as they knead me
A rare joy.

I have relived
The stages of my life.

The Serchio: from
Which have drawn, perhaps
For two thousand years
My country people, my father,
My mother.

This is the Nile
That has seen me be born,
And grow
And burn in ignorance on
Extending plains.

This is the Seine; and I mingled
In that muddiness learning each
Part of all myself.

These are my rivers confluent
In the Isonzo.

This is my nostalgia
That in each
One shines through me, now
It is night, and my life seems
A budding
Off of shades.

From the Italian of Ungaretti

No More Crying Out

Cease murdering the dead.
If you hope not to perish, if you
Want sound of them again,
Stop crying out, cease
The crying out of it.

They have a barely heard whispering,
No more than the increase of grass,
Happy where no man passes.

From the Italian of Ungaretti

The Child's Life

He lived, or started, to
Grow as a leaf. Thorns
That bud in mid-winter,
The jasmine whose pointed smell
Picks at the senses, and elicits
Secretions of eagerness
In the hanging basin of the loins,
In subdued weariness
Die off. Some different growth
Where assent is denied, where need
Admits and nourishes its creatures –
This growth became
His measure. Like a leaf,
He spread shade under him.
His humanness changed to
Plant vigour.
It seemed to him as if
Speech were constriction,
A crushing tight of silence;
As though he could speak
But would not. As though

The human form and its
Consorting were a forgery
From Nature, poorly thieved.
We made him; and some of
Our anguish filled him, burst
Slowly from him, as the moisture of death
Intelligently released,
Moved away quietly.
A stiffening quietness
Showed through the face-skin, such as
We had not seen. He had
The impassivity
Of the veined leaf
To blown grit and smutched rain.
He grows with the soil.

Burying[26]

It is not in the face.
That force has broken off
Which pressed through the ducts the liquids
Nourishing your life.

And absolutely as
You had not before been, with a
    Marked stiffening that

Composed your short frame,
The flesh settling noiselessly onto
    The compact bone.

A bricklayer tooled that space
You drew the entire process of your growth in
    And died in, gradually.

With no bodily pain,
But with grief, akin with the agèd; your face
    A mass of sea weed.

And after you had died,
Thickly pallid. I could not think
      There was no breath left.

I paid a few pounds for
Something to case your flesh, it seemed required
      By trade you should have.

Chewed pulp with fibre
Crushed into shape by the corrugation of men's will.
      A child would not have

Perceived the poorness in that.
You preferred nothing, with a likeness of absorbed
      Wills acting separately,

Such as the buriers have.

The psalm, as a shade
Of flower, touched merely
      Where you were.

I think that if I could
Have paid more for you,
There would have been more persons[27]
Standing above that hole.
Much good might that do still
Although the mouth has gently
Chewed your flesh into
The ineradicable
Humus, the thriving muck[28]
Which feeds the things we feed with;
For you were not honoured[29]
Except with a thin box,
And the soil, which fastens
Each living thing to itself
Without ceremony or hate
Or anything casual[30]

The Child

Something that can be heard
Is a grasping of soft fingers
Behind that door.
Oh come in, please come in
And be seated.

It was hard to be sure,
Because for some time a creature
Had bitten at the wood.
But this was something else; a pure noise
Humanly shaped

That gently insists on
Being present. I am sure you are.
Look: the pots over the fire
On a shelf, just put;
So, and no other way,

Are as you have seen them; and you,
Being visible, make them no different.
No man nor thing shall take
Your place from you; so little,
You would think, to ask for.

I have not denied; you know that.
Do you? Do you see
How you are guttered
At a breath, a flicker from me?
Burn more then.

Move this way with me,
Over the stone. Here are
Your father's utensils on
The kitchen wall; cling
As I lead you.

It seems you have come without speech,
And flesh. If it be love
That moves with smallness through
These rooms, speak to me,
As you move.

You have not come with
Me, but burn on the stone.

If I could pick you up
If I could lift you;
Can a thing be weightless?
I have seen, when I did lift you

How your flesh was casually
Pressed in. You have come
Without bone, or blood.
Is that to be preferred?
A flesh without

Sinew, a bone that has
No hardness, and will not snap.
Hair with no spring; without
Juices, touching, or speech
What are you?

Or rather, show me, since
You cannot speak, that you are real;
A proper effusion of air,
Not that I doubt, blown by a breath
Into my child;

As if you might grow on that vapour
To thought, or natural movement
That expresses, 'I know where I am.'
Yet that you are here,
I feel.

Though you are different.
The brain being touched lightly,
It was gone. Yet since you live,
As if you were not born,
Strangeness of strangeness, speak.

Or rather, touch my breath
With your breath, steadily
And breathe yourself into me.

The soft huge pulsing comes
And passes through my flesh
Out of my hearing.

The Continuance

Your head had grown onto
Your knees; short arms were raised
With hands that pressed against
The temples. Each part formed,
It was fit to meet pressures on
The natural, linked flesh
Of yours inside hers.
The vessel's maternity stopped
Its involuntary, concerted
Nurture of your body.
You were expelled.
I think you did not weep;
You were red, smooth, raw,
Reliefed in your growth.

Something is asking to come from me
It is a mind that has no flesh.
Leave it. Leave it.
Something requires ease
But will not have the touch

Which first pervades the thought
Of one's own flesh, and is
Put then onto the child.
Something is weeping. It is no longer weeping.
It shall be left without
The hand which gives the flesh
Its nourishment. It feeds
Its cry with another cry; it weeps
Upon the bone, and sinks
Its separated pain
Into the bone, starting
A potent, tearless, grief
That had begun before.

Something has been Teased from Me[31]

Something has been teased from me
Something insistent and tentative, as grass is
With soil; each binding, each nourishing, both.

We together were like them,
Knit, as the insistent roots of grass compact soil in a field:
A system of thread holding soil it eased into particles.

Their strength crumbles stone:
You allowed penetration. What can't be stopped must be
nourished –
Pervading like grass,[32] a sort of fire.

That would not quite do.
Grass does not feed itself, soil is bound by roots.
It is a composure the grass gives.[33] You asked

For some change in me; insisted.
You shrilled, were acrid to the touch; but grass cannot change
its roots.
It seeds itself in the soil, needing it; but is not soil.

My roots offended:
That tentative strength from which I pushed
Tall, seeded, sharp; whose webbed anchorage held you.

What could I have done?
I was loathed for what I was best, filled
You with liquids not yours. I seemed not good for you.[34]

And slowly, I became
Undesired. What you needed,

You stopped me being:
A thing that cracked stone, ate it by means of roots.
I became reed delicate, a set of porous fibres.[35]

It is not natural to
Grow by separation.

We did.
We pressed each other off, and grew through that.

The fruited thing persists.
It is corded, and thickly braided,[36] like the unopened bluebell's
flower.
It grows in you. It demands shape and blood
As it thickens to consciousness.

A single thickening sharpness lifts
Through moisture. It is nearly to be tolerated;
It has to be. A part of me fastens in you.

Grass sucks water and salts in,
As if it alone existed. This thing is more swollen.
But it is grass I think this bone and blood

Is like, persisting as grass, a blade of bone and flesh
Lifting to consciousness. It integrates
Into a flexible and feeling flesh.

As you lie down to
Give it its way, you turn on your side, lifting up
Your right thigh, shaped like dropping moisture, to your breast.

It demands strength
From you. Heaves. You heave. It is coming away.
It is good; it is to be endured.

It has to be. It comes away,
And as it does, is given breath.
Milk trickles through the tubules.
It lies beside you, put there. It will cry out.

And be nourished by you.
And grow like grass, wastefully. For now,
You hold it in your arms, and nurture it.

Dandelion

Slugs nestle where the stem
Broken, bleeds milk.
The flower is eyeless: the sight is compelled
By small, coarse, sharp petals,
Like metal shreds. Formed,
The puncture, irregularly perforate
Their yellow, brutal glare.
And certainly want to
Devour the earth. With an ample movement
They are a foot high, as you look.
And coming back, they take hold
On pert domestic strains.
Other's lives are theirs. Between them
And domesticity,
Grass. They infest its weak land;
Fatten, hide slugs, infestate.
They look like plates; more closely
Like the first tryings, the machines of nature
Riveted into her, successful.

A Bluebell

Most of them in the first tryings
Of nature, hand at angles,
Like lamps. These though
Look round, like young birds,
Poised on their stems. Closer,
In all their sweetness, malevolent. For there is
In the closed, blue flower, gas-coloured,
A seed-like dark green eye.
Carroway, grained, supple,
And watching; it is always there,
Fibrous, alerted,
Coarse grained enough to print
Out all your false delight
In 'sweet nature'. This is struggle.
The beetle exudes rot: the bee
Grapples the reluctant nectar
Coy, suppurating, and unresigned.
Buds print the human passion
Pure now not still immersed
In fighting wire worms.

Lilies of the Valley

Minute flowers harden. Depend
From thin bowing stem;
Are white as babies' teeth.
With broad leaves, immobile;
Are sheath-like, and fat.
What have these to do with beauty?
They must take you with
A fingering odour, clutches the senses,
Fills the creases and tightens the wind's seams,
As noise does. The plant is equipped.
Even then you don't like it.

Gradually though
Its predatory scent
Betters you, forces you, and more than
The protected rose creating
A sculptured distant adulation
For itself. This insinuates, then grapples you,
Being hungry; not poised, not gerundive.
Hard, and uncrushed, these flowerheads;
Like beads, in your palm.
You cannot destroy that conquering amorousness
Drenches the glands, and starts
The belled memory. Glows there, with odour.
Memorable as the skin
Of a fierce animal.

Peonies

It has a group of flowers.
Its buds shut, they exude
A moisture, a gum, expressed
From the sepals' metallic pressures.
Its colour shows between shields,
Cramped where the long neck
Swells into the head. Then they open.
They do it gradually,
Stammer at first. It is a confidence
Permits this; push aside
The shield, spray outwards,
Mount in height and colour
Upon the stem.
They claim the attention up there,
The focus of all else. Not aloof at all;
Brilliantly intimate,
They make the whites of others
A shrunk milk. They must draw
To them, the male ardours,

Enthusiasms; are predatory
In seeking them. Obliterate the garden
In flickerless ease, gouging out
The reluctant desires. Theirs is one rule,
And is found everywhere
Feeling transpires – extends
Its tendrils, helplessly grappling for
Passion of a different order
Than the peonies'.
What will be looked at,
However fleshily adequate,
Conquers the amorous.
By nature, a devourer. Cannot give.
Gives nothing.
In winter shrinks to a few sticks,
Its reversion, bunches of hollowness.
Pithless. Insensate, as before.

The Strawberry Plant

The rootless strawberry plant
Moves across the soil. It hops
Six inches. Has no single location,
Or root.
You cannot point to its origin,
Or parent. It shoots out
A pipe, and one more plant
Consolidates its ground.
It puts out crude petals, loosely met.
As if the business of flowering
Were to be got over. Their period is brief.
Even then, the fruit is green,
Swart, hairy. Its petals invite tearing
And are gone quickly,
As if they had been. The fruit swells,
Reddens, becomes succulent.

Propagation through the devouring
Appetite of another.
Is sweet, seeded, untruculent;
Slugs like it, all over.
It is nubile to the lips,
And survives even them. And teeth,
Insane with edible fury,
Of the loving kind.

A Daisy

Look unoriginal
Being numerous. They ask for attention
With that gradated yellow swelling
Of oily stamens. Petals focus them:
The eye-lashes grow wide.
Why should not one bring these to a funeral?
And at night, like children,
Without anxiety, their consciousness
Shut with white petals.

Blithe, individual.

The unwearying, small sunflower
Fills the grass
With versions of one eye.
A strength in the full look
Candid, solid, glad.
Domestic as milk.

In multitudes, wait,
Each, to be looked at, spoken to.
They do not wither;
Their going, a pressure
Of elate sympathy
Released from you.

Rich up to the last interval
With minute tubes of oil, pollen;
Utterly without scent, for the eye,
For the eye, simply. For the mind
And its invisible organ,
That feeling thing.

The Violet

The lobed petals receive
Each other's nestling shape.

We share the sun's beneficence:
Frost, men, snowdrops.
Then the violet unfolds. Not an uncasing
Of the corolla, each petal compliant
To the purpose of survival, obedient to that; but as it feels
The sun's heat, that puberty
Pushes out from its earlier self-clasping
Two distinct, clenched halves. Stiffens them.
These fluttering portions that made
The bud, separately elect
To be the flower; the violet
Halves itself, pushing apart
In two separate forces;
It divides up itself, it becomes two violet portions.
It is not a conformation of members,
Each petal a tooth, an eyelash.
On the other hand, the violet is torn apart.
Its increase is by dividing;
Its stiffened petals push further apart.
It adheres to its nature; it has no maturity,
Other than this.
It requires courage, and finds that
In this unclasping of its self-worship: two palms tentatively
Open. Going both ways,

They absorb a huge circle
Of violated air, an intent
Movement of embrace;
Created, exposed, powerful.
The air is coloured somewhat violet.
It costs itself much.

Milkmaids
(Lady's Smock)

Ridging the stalk's length,
The pith ducts. You'd think
The leaves found by water. Their openness
Guards them; a giddy, a careless
Effusion of stem. That is strength.
From the topmost, a flower triumphs.
From each undomestic
Flare, four petals; thrown wide; a flexible
Unplanned exuberance.
A veined fat is under
The svelte integument;
A kind of vegetative warmth.
From the centre, axial, determined
Extend the stamens, long by usage
For survival, and grouped
Round the curt stigma. Nothing less enslaved,
Less domestic to man, they are twice free.
Will wander through your plot in whole families.
You will not cut milkmaids down.

That tender, that wild, strength
Sucks the untrammelled consciousness up.
They mount the incline breathless
Pale violet. Their eyes wide,
They halt at the wire. This is the camp.
In silent shock a multitude of violet faces

Their aghast petals stiff, at the putrescence
Of the crowd wired up. This halts them:
The showing bone; the ridges of famine,
Protrusions, want, reduction.
Silent also, they confront with their modesty
Of demeanour – the stiff fatigue
Of the sack jackets something altogether different
From those who supervise
In their soft, rigid, cloth –
The prisoners confront
The unservanted faces of the plants.

Between their silences, comprehension; like the wire
Halted, staked, live.
Crowding through the tented cloth
That locust detail, to each person.
For the flowers, the forked,
Upright sense of human
Creatures wanting patience, pulped, compounded into their
                                        children.

Moss

'Patents' will burn it out; it would lie there
Turning white. It shelters on the soil; quilts it.
So persons lie over it; but look closely:
The thick, short green threads quiver like an animal
As a fungoid quivers between that and vegetable:
A mushroom's flesh with the texture and consistency of a kidney.

Moss is soft as a pouch.
There are too many shoots though, boxed compacted,
Yet nestling together,
Softly luminous.
They squirm minutely. The less compact kind
Has struggling white flowers; closed,

Like a minute bell's clapper;
So minute that opened then, its stretch seems wide.
The first grows in damper places.
With what does it propagate?
Quiet, of course, it adheres to
The cracks of waste-pipes, velvets,
Velours them; an enriching
Unnatural ruff swathing the urban 'manifestation':
The urban nature is basemented, semi-dark;
It musts, it is alone.

Here moss cools; it has no children;
It amplifies itself.
Could that over-knit fiction of stubbed threads reproduce
Defined creatures?
It hovers tentatively between one life and another,
Being the closed-road of plants,
Its mule; spreads only its kind –
A soft stone. It is not mad.
Reared on the creeping dankness of earth
It overspreads, smears, begrudges something
Though it is passive; spreads wildly.
It is immune to nothing;
You cannot speak of misery to it.

White Geranium

An astringent sweetness from
The veined leaves and round stem
Scrapes inside the nostrils.
Each part is haired,
Standing against dust. The Geranium
Shakes stiffly in the moving air.
Its stem, that has thin brown skin,
Extends a straight green shoot,
Unjointed, with five buds

The size of swollen pips.
It is the leaves' odour
Picks at the sinuses.
I want the buds to bear more than this.
Each small, tight thing is
Too formed to change much.
The haired surface protects
The thickening stem, which hardens
On its replenishing sap;
The leaves' smell
Is nearly incontinent.
The plants suffer themselves to be potted,
Warmed, conserved. They will
Shed whole branches;
Their size and quantity
Less than a shrub's.

Crowfoot (in water)

It is found, rooted,
In still water. A leaf,
Shaped like a kidney, floats
Leafing the underside of air, over water,
Taking in both, each side.
Inside the water
Are filaments of flesh-thread
Hair-drifting.
The flowers are white,
Simple, articulate.
Nothing smutches them.
Mouths of cattle, large
As sycamore trees,
Eat and compact stalk,
Leaf, stigma, and pigment
Into their food.

Shapes that no flower bred,
Not like any contour of nature,
Are piece-mealed
To a sponge of surging parts.

Articulate plant-speech does smutch
The ridged palate, bellying towards
The organ of hunger, minutely impotent.
The chopped articulation in the throat, –
Cattle's throat, – the woe
Is devoured. Crowfeet concerts
Its parts in a webbed cry.

If ripe, the seeds rear in
Dung casually dropped.

The rest persists under
The pond's rim. Can be devoured
To an inch of its life.

Small Celandine

Its petals close onto
A bland, contiguous sleep.
When open, they shoot from
That part large with organs,
Hips and face merged
In a thick, capable frame.
Its high crutched head is genitalled
For survival by display.
Flowers' conduct is supreme:
Fruit cankers, but petals age.
Insect life feeds on
Not it but its ripe seed,
Excreting over it; shard, rind, and succulence
Pinched by the sharp, smooth jaws.

A flower survives this. Small Celandine
Has sharp petals, its intensifying
Of their length, a self-absorption
That desires no further object.
Its lithe, green underside
Governs, with its greater thickness,
Each petal's direction. Leaves swaddle
The stem, as if near water.
It is indifferent to light, persisting with
Little sleep. It will
Not open or shut with what
Strikes into its senses.
It is insomniac.
To that, merging it
With its form that presses little
Of itself on our minds.
We are not its leaf, its breathing.

Its adults, consciousless
Roots concert the sensuous
Nourishment of earth.

Goat's Beard and Daisy

They are closed, by noon,
Their petals held upwards.
In this sense, sleep is tension,
The closed tips of petals strained
Together, carefully.
If fertilized, they close earlier;
Conception achieved through
The stealth of a third. A plunderer
Covers the rooted creature's face.
The flower's silence is
Taken for deafness. As the insect hovers
Its passage is tautened through
Two kinds of organs' needs.

And what they have to give
Is as the bee nectars. Then they close.

The daisy has its mode.
It will close at night,
Or when rain gusts;
The soft, pouting stigma takes
The pungent, oily stamen's yielded pollen;
Grain is crammed in the gently
Insistent opening.
What the flower does it may do alone.
It will be beaten down, rather than open.
Rain squalls,
And sheets the swelling ground;
The closed daisy is fertilized.
When light comes, it responds,
Watching with one eye
A tree's bough
Wet all over, the antlered form
Stiff through girth, not pride.

Iris

Three extended tongue-like
Petals fall outwards.
A black, finely haired purple
Covers their extremities.
This colour suggests sap,
Like blood, gathering in pressure and staleness
At petal-ends that hang
Unable to sustain
Their weight. Where the joins
Of those three start
Are three smaller shapes,
Not striped like the first three,
Above these a further three,
As if a mimic of the second,

Suggesting consciousness.
A ridge is on each outer petal.
It is a fur of stigmas
Curved over the widening tongue,
Between three uplifted pale violet portions,
A coarse furred ridge, and like
One furred lip of the vulva.
In the curves of the flower
That are like an ear
One smaller ear listening advisedly at the larger,
Is the stamen, erect and white,
With its anther white. It is the male part
That is hidden, the female proffered.
Its colouring is determined,
Powerful; one band of it
Repeated, enforcing itself.
The species is prized for its shape,
Its chosen periodicity
Of flowering, a man's mind
Propped by growth that does
Not choose to grow.

Harebell

It is not bred by nature
To produce a succulence
With a seed nestling in that.
It is related by name to the Bluebell,
Which has flowers clinging
Like a braid round its fat stem.
The harebell is one flower,
Its solitariness
Bespoke by its colour, not blue
Nor violet; hovering between, precisely.
It is a spare delicate bell.
Inside it are three pale sugary stigmas welded

To each other at equal angles,
Not seen until looked for.
Its stem is thin as wire.
The flower looks down, and if
Lifted, looks fixedly
At the admirer.
Its silence halted between primness and beauty,
Its shape is wrung from the sounds of life round it
As a bell's sound forms the bell's shape from silence,
And resumes its demure integrity;
More precise, more shaped, than the bluebell;
More venturesome. More stirred, ungarrulous.
Stern as a pin.

Note on 'Flower' Poems

These poems have flowers as their 'subjects' but they can only loosely be called 'flower poems'.

The method is to take one particular species of flower, and to look at the flower quite closely. I also try to characterize the life and process of the flower and, in making all three substantial, to suggest certain correspondences with human types and situations. Yet although the poems are not only, and not simply, about flowers, they are not only or simply about human beings and their predicaments. They hover tentatively between the two, although whatever object or situation they temporarily absent themselves to they never lose sight of the flower. I am trying to find some common denominator that will pull together these two kinds of life. Even so, the poems do not poise themselves centrally between the two. They concentrate closely on the flowers, and it is towards their centrality they tend to draw *human* life as, in *The Peaceable Kingdom*, I was trying to draw human life in the direction of certain animals, and a peaceful consortium of all animals.

The poems work by describing the flowers but also move through them, re-creating some of our own feelings and attitudes, and where these differ from the flowers', suggesting sometimes possible changes in them.

Nearly all the flowers of these poems are wild, undomestic. The cultivated flowers are subject to the care of our hands, grown for our pleasure; cut down or rooted up if they're weeds. But if they are weeds, and are also insignificant, they may be allowed room. Such an action would flatter a man's vanity; it would permit him to praise his own compassion; his moral sensibility would be self-congratulated. We don't use the word 'pride' today, but that obstacle to honesty still stands.

These plants were all observed in the garden, the small hinterland where domestic and undomestic plants sometimes co-exist and sometimes compete. I see the garden, in fact, as a kind of human bestiary, containing in the several plants earlier developed and anticipatory examples of human types and situations. The first poem – *Dandelion*, for example – sees its subject as a seizer of space, and asks for political parallels to be made.

Moreover *Dandelion* and *A Bluebell* describe the flowers partly in terms of machines, machine shapes, or made objects and substances. The second poem (and I would pair these two) brings in explicitly what was implicit in the first: the theme of nature being a 'preying upon'.

The third and fourth poems are female in their analogizing (I'm of course only speaking of flowers). *Lilies-of-the-valley* – the flowers are seen as predatory, not beautiful. Their scent forces itself upon us with a meanness, and with something near to vulgarity. We succumb, and they conquer through being predatory.

The Peony might seem to be the same kind of flower as the Lily-of-the-valley, but it does not triumph through its odour; rather, it traps our sight. And whereas the Lily-of-the-valley means business, the aim of the Peony is to subjugate and enslave the admirer, and devour not only his attention but that of the whole bestiary.

The Strawberry Plant is in some ways a poem different from all the others. We cultivate the strawberries in order to devour them not look at them. This controlling fact places these creatures in a different relationship with the humans. The human appetite is roused; and that's an altogether different thing from looking at flowers even when the looking may lead to abuse – cutting them down for our rooms, or perceiving them as useful illustrators of 'human character'.

The next three poems are about benign flowers. The *Daisy* is closer to my conception of innocence, that is, an awareness, a complexion, got through experience (the opposite, therefore, of naivety) and where experience stands, largely, for vicissitude. It's the uncompromising simplicity of the Daisy's appearance that I'm trying to re-create; and it's the uncompromising quality that makes it so rich in this simplicity.

It is this uncompromising power that relates the *Daisy* to *The Violet*, a flower that for me presents one of the most complex of natures. The Violet is seen at first in its chrysalid stage, folded and self-absorbed. It's the tenacity of this self-absorption that individuates the flower. So that opened, it's this tenacity that carries through and dominates still. Its petals do not form a corolla subservient to the whole flower, whose purpose is survival. But in as much as the petals were, before, self-absorbed, they now spring apart and go opposite ways. *They change only to invert their original process.* The tenacity, the lack of uniform performance of the petals, which are the whole flower, visually speaking, characterize the Violet; just as what characterizes the activity of any person who makes something – an object, or a child – is the tenacity and the variety, not the consistency of the total activity.

Moss is a poem concerned with urban creatures whose sensuous shrinkage affects their capacity to propagate. Like the mule's, the organ is a shrunk thing incapable of increase. What is important here is that the stuntedness and sensuous diminution is caused by the cramped, base-mented environment. I am trying to characterize the stunted quality of these creatures, a quality that becomes eventually a barrenness.

Milkmaids differs from the other 'flower poems' in that it contains a direct confrontation between plant and human, instead of the implied partial analogy between the two creatures. The poem, I hope, avoids any tendency to anthropomorphize the flower; it tends to assert that the plant and the human are two separate but confronting parts of one society. The confrontation joins the creatures – what joins them even more is the total distress of the one and the capacity of the other to absorb this distress. The exchange is made more thoroughly because of the brutalized condition of the inmates of the camp; it is their degradation, but their will to persist also, that makes it possible for them to share their own and others' experience. It is this brutalized state that permits them to deeply perceive the openness of the Milkmaids, and, for the flowers' part, to absorb the condition of the humans emptied of 'the capacity to be patient under suffering'. Nor is there any reason for them to be patient. The Milkmaids absorb the experience of the human being and are changed – one creature's mind changed by the condition of another, so deeply, that this change is inherited by their children.

One last point. To remove nature, to isolate it from human nature and then write about it, is an extremity as unproductive as the one which sees all nature as a (symbolic) version of man. Man is a part of Nature and to isolate one from the other, or to slide the one over the other, is to miss either the (related) complexity of both or the 'solidity' of each. The two are contiguous; and that is what I'm trying to get at in the 'flower' poems. If seen as contiguous, they can be seen as two components of a whole capable of mutual enrichment.

I ought to repeat that the majority of these poems are about *wild* flowers. The state, or monopoly capitalism controlling the individual's environment, this, I suppose, would make the (apparent) choice of the *wild* flower seem an acceptable symbol to some – if that were my meaning. But I don't see it like this – the wild flower as a lonely, isolated creature (there are, in any case, too many of them) standing for the isolated individual. There are these overtones, but I am not trying to anthropomorphize the flower. The wild flowers have a strength and tenacity that sometimes contrasts with the domestic plants; I am concerned with the former's vigorous contribution to the domestic land, their proximity to, not their symbolizing of, human beings and their activity. (*Nature with Man* would be an example of this; man grows from Nature and remains a part of it yet by virtue of his intelligence grows apart from it.) The injunctions of the state are an obvious enough possible danger to the individual, and society as a whole, but, of course, it depends on the state. Much social conformity results from the inability to resist and to change attitudes that have never been formulated by law. Some state practice, or sanction, like that of Nazi Germany, seems to have resulted from a political ordering that exacerbated certain forces it either permitted or deliberately brought into prominence. Not everything with a natural root has to be encouraged. I suppose I should add that I anticipate a time when the state will wither away. In the meantime I'm continuing to write about, among other creatures, wild flowers.

Unpublished and Uncollected Poems,
c. 1965–1971

Water Dispute

The hills' shape, in hard, and dry strata
that flake slats off their top plane,
immerse their image in lake Tiberias.
They fill it, and start moving through it to us.
Not so; the water's surface, alone, starts
to travel its flakey depths in thin layers.
Which disturbs the treatied demarcations,
their surface eliding ours. It touches us now:
their hills lick in pyramidal springing peaks a reflection
on our shore's sanded patience. Their hills
aren't to finger ours. Yet that eucalyptus,
that growth of an odour with which nothing is to be done
but breathe it, and unlike the pigmenting, loose petrol,
it breathes over the lake. From fierce
Syria, Arab smells irrigate our glands,
dilate and secrete, conflict with an
intelligence of what a plant is that is Arab.

In our flexed glands, such
melting away
of but their sense

with but our fears
watery as our intelligence of them
inside our doubts.

The Jordan brims us
with a fertility that's a
contagion
of them in us

the mortality
of water;
the fear
in it.

Seeds of Lead

A grey roof of tiles, slanting.
And bullets sally bean-like from it.

Close by the wall, lay fate
and my brother Yehoshuah protecting me –
ramparts.

The sun stood, stolid
and silent, like a bull,
shining through the wide open mouth of noon,
and stretching
for a pear ordered to serve hedges of hawthorn.

The wall, a gaping womb, abseiling
lead seeds,
I'll sneak out in the early morning
to see how in her depth
the stars, of
silence, are born.

The faces of my fate and my brother Yehoshuah,
are made up distance
as if thousand year old statues.

Many years later this became clear
to me in the parks of large cities
and in the museum.

A Forest Tale

So, in the forest, into its hosts of trees
where the pit's darkness is seeded over the surface,
and where many bandits are haunting there
to capture the princess, sleeping, who will wake
suddenly because, at the right moment
the light will flash up.

Thus, in the forest, the darkness
having the vitality of old men.
An abrupt discovery of some clearing, – a sparkle
of memories that were cut down,
and the sleeplessness of sixty men with courage
who know all the ways in, and out,
and who at the right moment will not be turned aside.

The verge of the tree-tops and the spires
of the tips of trees;
the maces of light as lightning curls about a branch;
the image of God is large
in our watchful eyes – a fledgling's finding itself in its wings
so that we will live and
continue in our love.

'Concrete'

Concrete
and brick.

Therefore I bought an apple tree
but as the wind blows on it, I can't
hear which of the
sounds each makes.

And not 'makes'. Comes
spiralling along the widening
thread
of wind.

I am
against music.

Because, young, the tree has no gender
and is closer to an animal than
when a full tree – even so
it squanders some shade, and some
branching noise,
ligamenting it to you.

And creates nothing but itself.
It is a silence, and if
torn, is still heard.

So I move with it since whatever
it is, it is part of
how the tough creationless motion of vitality
hisses over
the red haw globbed on hairy seeds.
A huge chest, filled with vitality, blowing
this through the dene
across the back-yard, which drain-pipes sink into.

Not played on, or playing with.
The breath of a man muscly with intent.
The tree, about to rise and get on.

'Kevin, can you remember'

Kevin, can you remember
      that setting posts in the yard
we crossed them near the ends twice with
          two-by-one slats
   as that foreman said.

   As if by doing this before
trowelling the concrete mix
          into the holes
     for the posts
we attached roots. That's
how he seemed the third time I saw him
in his cottage, sunk in the incline's
foot, where trees – I mean rooted in
a spare fertile contour, the short bole
of him, upright, as if he met
the posts we set in, and each took from this
pre-made determination. Whatever
         his stems from
you would care for him.
Impulses in each of us held, in him
re-intensify the livid
rings the mind tremors with, impelling growth.
Here, hand me the hammer, those nails are in.
         Which isn't to say you
          mightn't want
        to measure the stir of
         the leafed branches, as they flex
   from the root here.

Sea Anemone

Fastened to as if grown
Through rock, it tries eight
Threads of muscle, in water.

Creatures are born into their condition
Do not choose to be plant, animal.

The sea flower chooses both.
Its flexed tendrils move with more suppleness,
In the sea's currents, than tree's branches,
With a wave moving in them
Like the movement of something live
Moving inside the body of a man.
And then not moving, but moved by;
Moved in the sea's tendrilled dispersions. A speck of salt
Grasped at. Or an insect
And the sea's thick small grasses close
Contracting its clasping threads
In a slow spasm of casual hunger
Tightly inturning the animal in this
Until splintered, crushed into the flower's gorge.
It absorbs the creature's flesh
Its life dismembered into threads and body.
A sucker, a knob of flesh
Pressed onto rock.

It works like lips, a mouth insistently,
A brown vulva softly clutching the stopped finger;
The erect finger, bone not muscle,
But then tendril, not vulva.
It exhausts its tendrilled mouth,
Eight strands compacted upon me
Sucking something small into something smaller.
When the finger is pulled off
Reproduces deflecting one limb
Onto another, a stringy petal
Coiling a further member of its body round.

It is a plant animalizing
Its members, an animal
Cautioned to the rock, stuck there
For food.

Snake

1

Some low-branched ling
Enlarging the heath's stretch
Not curved as the sky seems, you must tread on it
Disturbing the viper, its flat triangular head
Forward on its limbless body.
It has poison in it to bite you with.
You should be frightened, its forked
Black tongue bendedly jabbing at you.

Its jaws don't open wide
As the boa's can, dislocating its hinge to swallow
The creature's life it has constricted;
Breaking up the ribs, its wide mouth hooded
Over your face.

The viper bites. It has a pair of teeth
Sunk in its flat gums, which are
Hollow, and through which the poison
Is pierced into the body.

It must pause half an hour
For its venom to gather again,
Which is the period the swelling poison
In the body's disagreement much have antidote.
It dies otherwise. This timing is precise.

Their scent is prodigious. A man
Who stepped on a snake's egg was pursued,
The man running onto the afternoon
All limbs, shouting; the heavy limbless beast
Melted the dense crowd into open fear.
Catching the man, she bit him. Her rationality
Is a whole instinct. They are not generous
Beyond their own preservation, or their kith's.
They do not need to be. To be bitten
At the root, for a long time; and be numb,
Faceless, slackening into fat, wasteful,
And paralysed below the plexus,
The man must look to the serpent; fanged,
Biting with understanding, communicating his bite.
His flesh thickens into a fatty slackness.
In any case, unfeeling; poisoned
At the root. Falling, when he does fall
With the unction of horror that cannot prevail upon
A curiosity about death. A cool limpness
Which the bitten flesh endorses. The smiling
Flaccid muscles untie from the bone,
The ligament uninterested as a bit of burned string,
Listless; visible, but its substance consumed.
The muscle itself, the fat and meat passing into
Each other, looses character, and disperses
Through the complacent body. Not pungent;
Odourless. The snake's jointed slackness
Locked inside its whole visible power enters
The curved earth, to descend where the heat mounts,
In decreasing intensity, in increasing separateness.
The bodies of the dead linger
In the earth's fertile skin; she moves
Towards the hot centre, where substance is molten,
And rests, coiled like a slack whole spring,
Waiting to be tempered.

Waste

Gathering wood, I saw a tramp
And he was poor. On the soft earth
With his knees up, I was aware
Of him when he spoke. He watched
Me fill my bucket up: I saw
That he was poorer than I.
His clothes were unpatched, and the bread
Not whiter than his skin except
By the throat. The cold dug under
My nails. I took my fuel up
The runnels of the street for our
Two rooms. My child on her mother
Dug her gums into the breast;
She cried out, softly. Pressure
Of a man's hunger solicited
The tender, parasited milk.
As if she shared her child's food
But could not ease the man with it.
Other men, sullied of my kind,
Pressed through his shape for their subsistence.
That twig-like breath, holding open
A lung, which is half of a man's trunk,
Relapsed, pressed them from his own need;
The trunk vigour, of its assurance,
Dropping inwards. My child had fed.
Some of these men sit with their knees
Drawn up tightly to a chill
Jupiter-breasted trunk, and want.
And as they want, soft splinters detach,
From their richer neighbours, eaten out, like old
Saplings, that still should be younger;
Sift into the earth a morsel of their strength.

Amana Grass

First published by Chatto & Windus
with The Hogarth Press, 1971

The bare declaration of political watchwords does not constitute political activity. On the other hand, the struggle of opinions as such, or the bringing about of certain changes in the social consciousness is political activity.

(Note on Stawar: a self-educated writer, was born at Warsaw in 1900, the son of a working man. His literary work began in 1924 with sociological and historical essays, and literary criticism. He (has) published articles on Marxism and art in 'left' literary journals, one of which, till its suppression, he edited. He has been in prison for his journalistic activities.) (J. Needham)
    – *Othello and the Mangold-Wurzels* by Andrzej Stawar,
        Scrutiny Vol. VI, No. 1, June 1937, pp. 27–28

This spot is notorious for having been, for a long time, the residence of some runaway slaves, who, by cultivating a little ground near the top, contrived to eke out a subsistence. At length they were discovered, and a party of soldiers being sent, the whole were seized with the exception of one old woman, who, sooner than again be led into slavery, dashed herself to pieces from the summit of the mountain. In a Roman matron this would have been called a noble love of freedom; in a poor negress it is mere brutal obstinacy.

        – Darwin, *Voyage of a Naturalist.* Ch. II, p. 19
                (Oxford World's Classics)

Six Cemetery Poems[37]

1

In Iowa, we rested, seeing on a rib of ground behind a lighted field
a minute cemetery, without church. Flowers lie at the heads of
                                   lengths of turf
held motionless by the dead; flowers at the neckline[38] of
                                  headstones chipped or not.
Of twenty, cared for, half were lopped, the material token
hacked where, below, the neckline was profusely tended.
Through cut grass roots of trees rise, at the surface burnished by
                                   feet, or by a roller.
The dead's place, combed here, and decked, by lively hands.
They are present, you said; why, if such force passes between
                                   your body and mine?
as the record plays, does your hand open my lips again?[39]
what figures does the mirror keep
and the camera secrete of what the eye and it took?
These have died. I said: that woman remembers her daughter
quickened by her above ground.
I am not consoled, you said.
I want to keep your form which holds my flesh from bone to
                                   bone, open.
I am holding in me the breath of the dead; their breath, only.

2

From the road, I saw a small, rounded bluff, a cemetery
tufted on it, churchless, and squarely contained by wire fencing;
one more field, increasing in it a short, thick tree.
Its branches emerged, multiplying densely, compacting
an opaque bud of wood and leaves not chinking
light through, or air; populous of itself, impacted.
It had been planted among the dead, or grew
with them, first there perhaps, the dead
put about the tree, in urban grid-like plots.
Since void, that had tissue and bone from them disjoined

into bland nitrogens the tree burgeons in.
Burgeons and thickens, the graves tidied
emptily on its root-veined lumpy wilderness;
the graves in distinguishable order,
their territorial bitterness lapsing[40]
into the dense acid wood. Lingeringly
it darkens, and I feel the headstones' life
lengthening past the dead's lives, or any trim, lively care.
The stones split into the shape
the roots strain under with gregarious presence.[41]
The fence's tension snaps, with the grid's.

3

he made the rampart and the wall to lament;
they languished together
                              – Lamentations 2, viii

The face, in several sweet bones, fitted,
to her skull's, the bones shaped into its form,[42] is fleshed in joy
delighting in itself which issues joy, joyous to feel.
The hair congruous and abundant from pleasure springs
down her face to her knees, her legs folded beneath her, the
                              hair, its grieving length,
over the floor. I expect your cry.
A tree, as if its branches are of hair, bends
these, trailing them to its necessary pool. Stops there.
The hair of the tree fluxes to water.
Your hair, in branchfuls, the tree-shape
bends and flows through your face: the tree[43]
in its all-eyed shape nurtured
by the untearful pool[44]
shedding no jot of itself.
Where is the reciprocal shedding
from the faces, working in grief, the one for the other,[45]
or between even you and me;[46] your hurt
working its face from mine,
your tear in a metal-like

leaf, tugging, at the eye of him who'd weep, for the one
weeping herself.[47]
Nothing weeps here that does not weep, for itself, alone,
the tough small disc of grief
shuddering the body, the joyful hair leaping
like water to the ground in a cry.

4

In Anamosa sandstone is cut for a prison by men from Iowa.
Space fits where the stone was, at its top a tree hangs its naked
root through.
Below, they are sawing blocks; at the saw's teeth, nerves catch;
and skin, and hair at the fore arm, and dust congeal with sweat
a mucous not sensitive to its own touch. Slits in
the jail walls sense a division of light straiter than a chapel's.
As much width as the weeping judicial eye admits
of light at its mind. The prison honours the free men,
who work earth for corn. Here's a farm, a grain barn,
and at the limits of it, staked, a cemetery, every man
that is here on his feet. No weight of stone
keeps the man under earth, or headstone attributes
him. A stone column its head shrunk to it, a skull
bevelled and elongated, each as the next is, without
ornament, and no jot of name. No burial has been here,
earth cut, flesh wrapped, and the soil again heaped
on the flesh as though you felt it upon your own.
Each grave is uniform in the signification of death:
no grub hatches at where the flesh turns putrid, no smell
of flesh softly green insinuates the haired nostrils.
I feel the garb of each man's life, erect, obedient,
and stronger than the death of his body.

5

It has taken breath, but of that it seems to have none.
As though it had drawn breath and died, that, and its cage now,
                                                          stiffened.
The grass bank swelled, is swelled and though rigid, is glad, an
                        unadorned joy falling slowly across the incline,
that has yet being dead a winsome thing to offer.
On it neither flower nor beast, unless a man, treads
but in the rising, then flatness the slope bends into, mostly glad.
And at the crown, a house, not joyful, holds
in place that fluid continuous pleasure the ground
though dead does not hold back. As a man keeps
place with the peaceable, austere beasts he is disarmed by.
The house, in wood and white, shimmers, it dances
the government house, ample and consolidated, jigs –
in foreign substance timbered into American earth,
various and fraternal. American Indians
dwindled into margins of plain flat under
bison with their bent horn the Indian must have,
that the white men bulleted. In Iowa
a cemetery is planted out and fenced on the town's margins,
square and strict, newish, the Jews', federated
as the wars demanded, or age did; the Jewish American
dead in earth, in rows, neat, decked with small limp flags.
In form, native; breathless, voided in the fecund
corn-belt, wanting memory: doctors, farm-men, dead soldiers
merged with clart particles of soil
that can't grasp spaces until wormed
by flesh that's American, dead, preponderant
and exalted. The others are scattered
boneless, and wearied of their individual substance
blent and lost near the cemented onrush of crank-ridden highway,
the fast interstate mindfully pressed
between two steep flanks of heavy soil,
one dwindling slowly to the cemetery, a loose iron gate to it,
foundling, amnesiac, the most recent.

6

for Paul Tracy

Miners dead inside coal seamed by fire, under Pittsburgh
or between lead, from poison that touched and made stiff
the liver as it opened last: what the flesh failed of
employment caused. Prospectors, their wives, and issue
come of wiving, they are each dead
who obsessed, impregnated, and made the retina
gravid with images of silver.
I found evidence of them on a hill below
where the cage had ceased; no church by them, or metal.
I found more dead, fewer though, near a canyon
named Sucker Creek, east from that, and in
a field, the green square it contained staked with posts
erect at the corners, holding wire up.
Few dead, where few were living, and against
their solitary gentleness, or brutality, as some
fetched a tendon to their neighbours' throats, a farm cart
with four large wheels, its shafts erect, dark red
and stiff above the wire its carcase
is tethered at; living carcase; the arms
raised in astonishment, and fixed
at joints stuck now. Perpetually agape.
Together, the dead are crustacean, the large
crab of the soil, pincering its track under
earth that will fracture, webbed by micturating roots
dregging earth of its nutriment. The dead heave it open
and move with vulnerable hugeness on it.
A four legged slowness that is a limp almost.
I hear each ligament and tendon working
to print back on us what we let them have
as they aged and sickened. I am afraid
of the jointed, vulnerable, crab-wise dead.
The cemetery waits, contemptuously patient
at their congealed practice. Listless crust about soft flesh.
The cart's arms jar, their load to be re-assumed.

Brought Up With Grass

1

Brought up with grass,
Fastens under the doorstep, and catches
Between the toes. Not far off
A cut in the earth's moistened skin.
The fall's head disinters
A glutinous liquid congealed
Round air.

Many dismissive hands
Are like this dropped water.

Another gorge is close
Touched with the first's weakness –
This sheerness
A dizzying proliferation of dark, green moss
Dankening the acute
Corners of shafted stone.
At the bottom are ferns,
Spored and moist. The roof fell
Inwards, and over it, gathering water
Moistens the dissident slab.

It is the water drops.
A man, occasionally.

Here also, a cave
Like half an eye in the ground:
The eye, out; its space, left
With falling into it
A jet of water that splays
Its energy, downward.
In and through which his father
Could be seen.

The tractor draws
The blade a foot's depth. The cut
Worm is writhing. This plot is deficient.
Inches food up to the maize stub,
Into fibre matted with gruel
Of colourless nitrate.
The soil gives, he whispers.
Gives as it can.
A person, three of them
Sustained by its cumbersome wit.

The house shifts with wind
Inserted in ill-jointed planks.
More wood is in the forest
After cutting to be dragged
Off land wet with frogs' sounds.

It shall provide, he said.
Thrashed the grain. Small rocks
Gnash each other, who were one stone.
The wind has its heart.
We are more than stones; nature's produce
Choice, intellectual.
We adhere to her. The pine with swelled
Roots, a veined creeping
Over ground nutritiously furred
With needle's and bracken's tongues;
The split violet chewing
A knob of stone to grit.
The small wren bladed
With protective anger pierces
The intruder on the moss.
These are our fatherless
Coercive elements. Give us enough
To eat. The frost chars
The fatness of lobed blossoms.
Their death is ours. Our daughter

Sickens. I want her thick
Veined fat round the flesh, firm.
I want her speech to sieve
Into my breasts panicking milk. I desire
Her sounds over my face.

3

Nature pours onto the
House a burnished, lucid rain
That sieves through the palms
Of Hemlock.
There is no rationality
In her giving; breaks
Up or nurtures. I want moisture
For the ribbed palate; on the skin, warmth
Where the frost teethed itself.
I want consistency.
The wind desires lebensraum,
A small stretch of causeway on
The obtruding texture of the earth.

The brilliant frost
Champs its minute teeth into the blossom;
For some months, its last delicacy.

The shark forced by
Bereaved fishers to take
A poisoned sea urchin –
For seven days that melts
Itself out of the gut.
A disinterred spike works
Through the muscle.

4

I am an ingredient,
And expect the impersonal
Pressures on a thing
Trying to survive,
Among what seems malice, or is beneficence.

The stung asp with its
Acidic portion, persists with it,
Is a nail, a scratched pincer
Of my thinking. I am shaped
Crab wise; or as a fly
Infecting with vomit and
The orts of virus
A bit of carrion.
Tusk of rampant fish. Or whatever
I am I am, too,
Lens-like to
The skin's infection, its movement,
Transist into the meaning of
The configured shift of burning wood.

I will work to survive
With what will work.

I cannot bear not to
See clearly.
                    I qualify
Others by their concavities. I form that whole
Of creatures creeping together.
A bit of metaphor
A clear one.

Amana Grass

The leaf of your hand shall touch but not cover me
— New England proverb

Amana grass, its spikes of hair rayed as branches
from long stems, is sucked by three locomotives, their haul
filling space over tracks. Wind wraps its length,
hot and dieseled, through spaces of stumpy grass, barely green
over long slight inclines. Air in varying pressures blowing on
the train
sounds fiercely between houses, where space, holding
other spaces, of human loneliness, meshes.
The same in that wildness locomotives haven't seen;
beneath earth filaments of root, everything, tangle.
The train links points in which the human crouches,
is found, rejoices. Wind appears to feel out crevice,
and surface. Does not feel, no pain at all in how it contacts.
The sun's light, without visible sun, sinks coldly through frigid
wind.

A leaf turns upon asphalt treading through the park.
Wind picks at a face rising and sinking on long legs
stockinged, their tan rushing to compare with the net's colour.
Nearing, she seems to compose her face, the air being frigid.
Slim, as the legs are, almost a woman's; not fleshy yet, or coy now
the thighs swelling behind a skirt now short, the hips
larger than they were, composed, each, into tentative prominence
the mild fury she receives of her intent frail hulk.
Of the mid-west, in bulk, solemn, a flat grandeur under its
heights of corn,
she strains little to her. Of what is there,
a train's horn contracting desolating space.
Of what she is, something ribbed; of what she has, nearing,
the rib enlarged. Of who she'll be,
the clasp that broaches two minds, hasn't enjoined them.
The face's sadness, tenacious shadow, melts into resolution.
Speak louder; shout, for I should hear,
the wind asks, each creature begged of it.
Each thing is to its need, not much remaining to implore.

Space the train threads grasps for more; in it, a tree
shakes leaves rustlingly at grasses naming them sharp stump.
Grass tightens fierce roots on fractions of soil.
The soil, from stone, in passivity, grins; is to ingest all.
How, among nature's divine egotisms, to grow
her especial fronds, antennae sensible to another.
To enlarge, amid these natures, whose heraldic egotisms
                                    silently conflict,
she must fight. Earth's fullness, though,
may be shared; fleshy needs, feathery demands, requited
'among the stained emblems under which the stiffened flesh
fragments. On the bits, vultures perch that, gleaming
on frozen blood as if armour mirroring the dead enemy's
                                    conquest, rip the flesh
their image flares on, captive since to what they strip,
flesh, not stubborn or curious.' Brown grass ends are as limp,
and thinned, as crystals of falling snow are intense:
experienced and dense, the aged spirit sheds itself.
Appear in the air, edged; bitter against nostrils and cheekbone.
Wind stirs it onto each creature unremembering of earlier needs
to be requited by what creeps and grins against its knots.
She tightens her coat onto her breasts, scarf lightly to her ears.
She'll get home. He moves through it, sure he'll find her;
white powders, some of heaven's properties, sift over the sidewalk
bonily cramping the foot inside its strict shoe.
Treading he sees in virgin snow someone's feet printed
towards her house, before him, his, exactly. Snow
lifts into his face, melting flakes caught in clenched eyelashes,
blasted on edge to him it is adrenalin charging
the mind's eye to dilate over the prints. Calmness
then. He turns, from tracked eddies of feet past
her house, to her, feeling for her ornate small key.
The evening star, in fruitful magnificence, rises with moistening
                            splendour, towards the sky's taut, precise limits.
He approaches, the counterpane unpuckered, smooth for the
                            crushing of heedless, fruitful weight.
No evening meal. Thought of food prepared by each one
broken down, as if by enzyme, into other hunger.
Pancakes nurtured into floury presence; stay-in-bed hash; sauce

biting its butterscotchings sweetly into cream and cake; these, gone.
Her lips parted as if breath, passing between, stirred the loose
                                        hair shaking past the forehead,
she summons the first kiss to her body. He parts her lips, his
                                        tongue stiffened into her.
The spirit dilates; the fleshy circlet starts its flow.
Older, he prepares: on his breast heraldries of self-power
                                        chevalring love
stain him: on her breasts, prints of the stain.
He presses her down, she helping him, parts her, and enters.
She won't move. Forced to him, and pinned, she can't.
The spike piercing the belt that holds it as it stiffens
upon the bar; tightened upon each other:
so he in her her, so she round him. Malely and femalely
they are clung by self-swellings they can't slip
of a sexual love ending in each other's
mirroring vauntedness. 'For whom do I brag?'
Then stricken to tenderness, minted, as if to the doe's hunter,
he asks of her: 'Did we make this, of our intent hungers?'
She fears it may be worse. She, feeling pure, the dew might look
sullied. The purities in her chill, condensing her heat
to drops that lustre her success, or, if she fails, rebuke her
that she melted in their dewy script that
in unsweatlike nature gleams through the skin of women.
He gets off her, hot and distanced; she faces up to the ceiling;
her thighs are separate in distress and coldness.
Flat Iowa is stretched in snow, through which her Vermont
                                        hills rise
strict as her mother's breast, wrinkling the torn flats they break.
Her nipples lose their stiffness, her breasts not thickening a milk
should have milk were a hand on them, be smaller than his.
A strict, sweet whiteness, purely of her breasts
is, for her, the milk achingly sucked by her child's lips.
Unlike her vaginal whitenesses, or a man's sperm, flukelike
at her itch; her breasts' exclusion, each one.
He turns from position onto his back. Wind like pricking metal
over the surface of another exclaims a passion
length-like as the scoring on him of hair naked.
Like the pressure of touch, the wind's, her hair scrapes her silence

through him its length. It is to him as to a beast
that working four he puts a hundred feet down
to his mile of hillside's inch.
Her silence teases her apart, forming distance, cars
slithering from each other. She separate, he distanced.
It is England's width, soon, the north part, stone,
where the silver mine fills, on chipped quartz, chipped
                                    limestone, earth, wire,
lies, at any rate, choked, – the plants at this segment of earth's
                                    carefully spun rim
rubbed small, low, wiry, red; car-rush whirring such colour
rearward of the mind, darkening, with the sun
                                    melting
through north England, its heights, flat as Iowa's,
dark, extinct, which he travels. – As she moves away
to Vermont's hills, shrunk, folding as they cooled
into claustral heights, wooded though, familial.
The New England heart is contracted in virtue
                                    durably
to itself; as a mistress to her heart's blood-holding loneliness
attaches herself. The ancient stems of plants
dilate to water's ancient tractability,
averting our care. 'Haven't we, at least,' he asks
'nurtured each other?' 'Yes' she replies 'and been weaned
off each other. I have. Although you, I see, still
think of us as creatures, creatures or plants, in symbiosis.
I want nothing. I mean, I want purely
on my own, strengthening my especial substance
to grow itself, – a plant thickens its xylem
from water for more of it.'
Her strength, a boiling fluid,
wells to her vessel's brim; she spills not a dram
through hatred's surface.
'Why bear with me? Haven't I hurt enough
what once I seemed to value?' He feels tenderness,
as if excremental, evacuated from her.
She feels herself a mountain creature, exalted to permanence
of the rock-born species. At the door she backs onto
she asks: 'Am only I culpable, or are you

AMANA GRASS   315

some guilty creature also?' 'It's as though,' he answers
'your strength laments of itself, or the attent
sinew finds "no" what most charges it.'
'Isn't that what you want?' she asks. 'I want more,'
he answers her, 'as you do.' 'Then want's
our portion.' 'Need it be?' he questions.
'My attention makes small, yes and lucid the plenitude of us,
the water-seeming fall of hair, gathered, then braided to a
                                    gleaming length
seamlessly twined, into an image feelings breathe themselves in,
value insists on, until memory fixes, prints and shows as experience.'
'That's not like experience,' she recoils. 'It may
be how it works, but how it works is theory,
and I want the thing, and want it mine.'
'We're not machines,' he goes on, 'and how we work
is how we value what works in us.'
'I don't have value'; her hair glowers
on her copper skin, anvil and substance, clashed
into hissing and cooled re-formation.
'Listen,' he says; the space between them pauses:
'when your mother had you and you were pressed
through the tract a stranger to her womb had eagerly before
                                      approached,
after you left, with a body of wrinkled skin
and no more, except for the initiation of breath,
as if for breath, you turned to your lung-like past.
Of anything gracious, firm there, and mild, didn't you add
the sinew, flexions and tendernesses, you and I
had from each other; your mind with such light from this
in your skin it gleamed, lustring the undewlike sweat
that from your body's heat expressed your shape, stilling you.
In that decent stillness we did nothing that day.
As though over the moss, each plant, each flower, we lay between
fitted the intent self to a peaceable kingdom, toxic leaves
and petals, by lively consent, being sucked
of poisons by elements they had with care selected
and compounded into wrathful and frigid bitterness.
It was consent. So it seemed to us
in the vacant wilderness. Your eyes shut

in concentration, mine alert through me
a wakeful quiet…'
                              – 'That may be so,' she said
stepping from the door.
                              This, this reduces to the nub
                                                        events
through a tumid spring to mid winter;
                                        the thorn,
with sporadic sheen, budding in the mid-west's spaces,
the lustre against such nature. Wildness
abhors space filled unless more brims it;
Physics denies, wrongly, in this case.
This is not a love poem to do with love, not,
what goddesses of love exact, for love, of their gods;
the complex swelling of bud and root, the crossings of branch
                                        and leaf, prolix in nature;
nor in fiery points synoptic verse, distanced, entailed,
with sensibility at the fingers' ends, in men's folly.
It is not, either, verse for someone; though a poem
of love I experienced, whose image is troubled
in America's: brutal, shankered; a magnificence
of Roman cloth umbering an Etruscan shade.
With vital parts, also, touched with self-doubt. And still,
the following lists of attributes, in this disorder:
fearful, isolated: what men cancerously die of.
What more to bite on? What is more than enough,
what is in plenty, in the widths we congregate,
of estate, insurance, its probity; or else
the unassailable defection from honesty,
isolates, or aligns our sly feelings,
at our circuits, pinched into our chosen
antipathy or liking. The intrinsic being perishes.
An animal keeps his passion; we aren't of them.
Perhaps I can tease of this plenty nothing; not of America.
So that of the two, of this single image
in two metaphors, love is rendered, that gracious abstract
passing through the naked upright fork
of hell and heaven, scathed, through that quaint background,
but, now, advancing. And since witchery,

the sapphired and webbed flesh of angels
is now unseen against the sky, elements
of love tinged with fire and pasture loosen
annealed unearthly cries
as rigorous for our earthly needs.
I have never controlled it, a quadrant
I am an interval of. 'Love' I cried
once, 'love,' between the markings,
and was quiet; with little before that
to say, though it comes now. It presses me
to revalue what is in obedience to me
and think of control, again, its limitations
its constant limitations, against openness.
I must know that something like you is alive still,
something quick, something tense at its quick, at the quick,
alert, and with that, making the sinew bright and sharp,
the whole tendon and muscle on the bone with no
hint at death, or scent, or thing like that.
I must know that there is no death on you; that of you
more beauty stares than in your image.
Therefore you shall stay alive. I need clarity.
I need the image of you bearable
by control, and within my courage;
or my courage to grow, matching that quick in you
paying out the veined, the thin, lines
of your shape in durable contour.
But that is exacting. So the thing I want
is that you with the passionate elegance of a beast
into the man's love breathe yours; in age, holding
your value to your body, move, as you must,
in some reluctance, to your death.
— A night past I dreamt of the hire purchase man
asleep with his wife; both seemed young and pliant.
They lay naked; his arms clasping her waist,
his head rested between her supple breasts.
I saw that he dreamt, and what it was; and that
not of his wife, or of some other deeply
moulded eager girl. Belshazzar-like
he dreamed that, fanged, he, on hands and knees, crept

with open salivating jaws on the poor
and negroes, lively victims, in his right hand
the papers of his wealth-to-be laced
with the strictures, bonds, enforcements that would ligament
them to him. His wife stood naked
and grinning among us, papering the ink-smeared
visible body with signed bonds,
but mostly, about her cunt, she pressed
the papers, wadding and girding her fruitful organs,
shutting her sex from view, and access. This was
her assent, her husband's dream, and my containment.
I was speaking of love, and America; and how
I value it, as I knew you did,
when you wrote: 'I want to be a woman
to a man so badly, I can taste it almost.'
I was speaking of value, I guess. Of what
knits in the spaces, where wind
creases its frigid movements into the face
as it swerves on. I was speaking of you,
and of love once more: warm, intelligenced, exacting;
of more immanent value than Hebrew parallelism
or the Anglo-Saxon metre.

A Word About Freedom and Identity in Tel-Aviv

Through a square sealed-off with
a grey & ornate house,
its length bent, for one corner of that,
a road leads off, got to down steps:
wide, terraced, ample.
The road's quiet, too; but nudges as
the square did not. Walking
some below the city I heard
a pared, harsh cry, sustained
and hovering, between outrage
and despair; scraped by itself

into a wedge-shape opening on
inaccessibly demented hurt
it can't since quite come at;
imitative, harsh, genuine.
A pet-shop four feet below
pavement level; in its front yard
a blue parrot, its open beak
hooked and black, the folded wings
irregularly lifting a little;
under which, dull yellow soft plumage,
the insides of itself, heaved, slightly.
Its tail was long, stiff. Long in stiffness
that at once bends entirely
if bent too much. And as it
turned in its cage, bending the tail
against the wires, it spoke
into the claw it raised
at its hooked face, the word
'toràh, toràh' in the hoarse devotional
grief religious men speak with
rendering on God the law
their love binds them with. Done,
it cried its own cry, its claws tightening
onto its beak, shaking slowly
the whole face with the cry
from side to side. This cry was placed
by one Jew inside another. Not belonging though;
an animal of no distinct race,
its cry also human, slightly;
wired in, waiting; fed on
good seed a bit casually
planted. Granulated, sifted,
dry. The torah is:
suffering begets suffering, that is.

The Torah consists of the body of Jewish religious knowledge.

COMPLETE POEMS

Reclaimed Area

Walking up sands, offal is gaped from a tunnel seaward,
                                        muddying its edge.
Bowels ceaselessly open, add to the sea, not much. Broken
                                        tackle drifts
up, shored. The sea sucks off noisefully. Many pieces sprawl
each like the carapace of an insect bent open and then made flat.
Concrete slabs improperly founder in sand. A brick.
A way between stone is pressed by the hot foot flat, although
                                        dry. The sand ends.
A boot disconsolate of its wearer. Mourns him. Nothing
                                        mourns. Each thing
is individual and broken. The fresh sea is impounded by sewage,
                                        bordering
a domain where refuse in such profusion grows the eye is
                                        astonished at our potents.
It's all battered. You go over it, straight. A road starts
with houses on it of the English Mandate: substantial
walls fortressed against heat. Some windows pointedly
shaped for the Arabs: a concession. The Arabs are ruled again,
not by the Turkish mind, this one, a flower with petals spiked, broad,
sharp, bashed out of a sword and planted, has displaced the earlier –
was tempered in the north. Some houses have broken; others, partly.
Washing sweats. Peels, stalk, pot all lifted to the sweeper's barrow.
The road is pared to its soil, scraped to where the ant
eats in bent and long-legged splendour, scraped brown, having
                                        our waste
or not, as the broom lets it. Further, at the town's focus
coffee is tipped into the mouth, lips gripping the glass.
No wrinkle, or flexion from it returns the darkening pressure
                                        of the lip.
The mouth affords the town's prices; skin is regarded for its
                                        texture.
Waste from here mingles with the others', bowelled into the sea.
The ant from omnivorous takings distils
its formic acid to bite with as its unregarded jaws grow.

Jaffa, and Other Places

Towards Jaffa, foot-dragged sand is flattened, and pathed, the
                                 hardened grains
fusing then to a road, on which the fallen foot stifles. Houses
                                 shake into dereliction.
A flat incohering of sand with bricks, remaining feet above, stays.
A gulley cuts through these levels down, sprains in its sides, between
which pours brick, charred wood, tarpaulin, stopped. Inertia heaps:
mound of boots, motionless and brown, remains of the mandate
                             army, dispersed in England now.
Done with in worse places: shoes, crutches, irons, many
                        oddments, each similar, the inert teeth, ash, hair, dust
winnowed between grains of soil or not winnowed between them;
most of each category useful, separated. The flesh gets isolated
                                 from these,
the goods and its body harrowed apart. Each item heaps on
one of its kind, itself buried. Wardresses help sort each class.
And not the negro, his hunted skin finding each shadow not as
                                 dark as he
offers an absence as blank. Shortly the spider
is trained to bite at the organ; the bone round it liquefies, the lips
of it attendant and limp. The Reich's swollen architecture will
                                 be less dank.
New immigrants near this ashy zone, pacified and burnt.

What Are the Lights...

What are the lights, in dark, doing on water?
That is fishermen, intruding nets
sifting into, and pulling from, in pairs.
Lights, also; fixed on boats that
in moorings heave on water tugged by a soft moon.
All cheese; while fish squirm in hundreds.
There's a fear in that light giving
the bleak water a foot, at least, of green and depth.
That's excellent for sight; in it
the mind shakes, working out one thing,
known; and the other distracting it
from being so. I know what the men do;
what if, precisely, they aren't doing it.
In darkness, light opens the eye
as the eye opens a distance out.
Though not at all. It only seems to.
How if they only seem to strike
nets for fish; the fish go on perishing.
Lord God, I am afraid.
Then better. Speaking on you I
feel comforted you're not at all.
Not, that means, at all.
Although, I still can't tell
if these men are doing what
they seem to me to. You will
tell me, love, if you seem loved.
A long time, I leant on myself,
the stick, short. You are quite near now.
Tell me it is you that's reached into by me
and not by you, as I delivered myself to me.
And yet, please explain, quite slowly,
why it is that, giving love but which the other
incorporates only slowly, that then this other
becomes distinct; and why it is the force
you are the nakedness of
gives us clarity. Perhaps
you can say why. Or I'll put
my hands under you again

Conditions

Shabbat: the sun is slithering into earth, now; the molten tip
of a pole, searching; the synagogues open; renewing
its heat detached in the earth's; from that, a ruby smelts.
The synagogues light, redly. Off one,
a room, its volumes half the size of a man, erect. Does God
live between spaces defined in the Hebrew script crushed upright?

So much oblivion in
such librarianship.

Part of me feels as though
it would like to believe.
Care for after death
seems a balm swathed over the terrorful
body that, with life,
was beautiful as a god;
its fluxing gleams resemble
the wick that constantly
sheds with its lightful wax
their immortality.

Three conditions diverge
their singularity.

Comradeliness, where terror
at death is sprung into
a thread, stretched to fixed points,
staked, where each friend stands.
The thread that's stretched absorbs
the other's tremoring.
It burns along itself;
it is the news that one
constantly sheds of himself.

The second is death, which cramps
each creature in his pain,
and is joy's measurement.

Both seem gifts of one
divine, offered up to death,
which is the flame exacting
the tallow and cord into
their own magnificence
and an extinction shrunk
under a flat, black vault;
as in exchange, the fixed
remedial care of God.

The third condition is where
a man sees by his flame
whose dark he shrinks into.
And each gout of permanence
is used, charred extinct.
I feel some terror here.
The small individual pool
of tallow hardening in death.
And taken in the lump
nothing much comforts it.
Or taken, anyhow.
Courageous, animal.
Melted with others' lives
into a wax flame of
a small magnificence.

Ayalon

Let the sun stop
Let the moon stand still

They have halted, sun and moon, lit
and congruent on us, and discover
the smutch granuled where tissue
crept together and healed.

They have halted: no thought
has clothing;
the hair of her flesh cannot help if it is seen.

It is seen, it is seen
that an Arab village its Arabs left
Jews brought explosives to.
The stone lit against each seam, and clasp
where the fluid silica, developing privacy,
rippled and set

as if the olive stone were opened on a meticulous nut-like seed
white between the fingers

a baleful spike grazed the fine, dismal stone.

May the eyelid be a curse until now, but may no further sleep,
or what passes for it,
let the nerves ponder
in a skein upon the bone.

The moon with a
swab of cold.

She and he are to move as we were grown to them.
Their light needs us,
decked, restored and lively
with each other; and we
the periodicity of the eyelid
drooping over the lashless eye.

Bull-God

The earth's not round at all
it holds no poles flattened to it:

a bull-god. The haunched-up limbs,
not bothered any, flex clankingly against
a rigid stomach, at the tests poised
for rut. A clinkered heaviness. The head
is groomed, hair of it and face kempt and woven
making the face smile with huge moist power.
As religious Jews wear it, their hair though not as thick
which coils and hangs. His hair is their conqueror's.
And the wings, nilish green come
of blood of the river's reptiles expressed into a scale,
stiffen us, nightly, into them. By day we scrape
and irritate the unearthly shard-like integument
into substance that we'd have with moisture, as dry clods.
Trees rise to the diameter of a hair.
Night folds again, as wings, screening together
the light pressed between them, corrugating it.
The moon, lit, has been glimpsed; it is much
incompetent grappling to cover, wrap
her cold thighs in translucency.
Her unhappiness is a cold swab, internally nursed,
a perpetual thin white menstruation
by rote faithful to childlessness.
We have none of her eking light, wings
about our crouched forms in Babylonian ribbing
vault our soft-shelled, glowing flesh.
The impish grin of the dead, white-skinned
succour their malice on us. There, in the earth, there,
through it, I mean, their faces emerge, or through
the mineral veined, white flesh of others
dead, they smile. Smiling, the matted square beard
hardens in its sleek undulatings. The dead here,
and other than here, in their spiritual progress
deflect the material offering some make
of the obsolete piastre lustring its worth

upon them. Stamped both sides, without head on either.
Much immunity serves these dead; for us it assembles
in us, the living, a stone in us in our organs
that they were once like us.

Divisions

Cedars from Lebanon, in community, move into the swart,
                                                    pointed hills.
I don't say many. On two legs bound into one,
rooted into terraces between drops of rock-face, in sparse soils
cornered where wind pushed that. Layers of snapping pointed
                                                    stone shift,
one can guess, like whelpings, about their roots.
These roots know what they are about. The trees came together;
                              tall, fleshed like a wax feather,
their leaves green throughout. And as the sun changes the trees
                                        don't; sharp, slim.
Not many know what sex these creatures are made of.
The whole tree comes into the folded integral hills
of Judah, one of many, towards a sea struggling
to erode from the land its form into the shape of Africa.
Creatures with two legs come, and sit against a Cedar that no
                                              longer moves
forward. They spread a map over their legs, engross a frontier;
a document embossed by lines that divide one bit of land from
                                                    the same bit,
the first of these trees from the last of them. The line is
arbitrary as a fish-hook. As if two iron hooks
stuck like picks into the ground, and their shafts pulled,
until in the earth a gap opened. A small, neat structure of stones,
in fact, marks the hostile step which it is death to step.
Judah's hills do not stoop, they are said to skip; those trees
in Lebanon do not bend; their mild, emulsive
sharpnesses advance through the nourishing earth they compact.
A hexagon of dirt is trapped back by a leaf into the soil.

Suddenly the landscape, one might say, is startled by
a man in a blue shirt, its greens, its ochres fixed by a depth of blue;
as if before these changed but now were frozen by the quality of
                              blue that they are not.
He crouches; what is he speaking to the wrinkled olive; what disdain
for the tree's agedness as the plucked creature furs its oil on his
                              salt fingers?
The hills shimmer; also, the tree standing in them: a trembling
                              on one
point from inside. A haze, in dots, condenses over the
                              contracted earth.
Past that tree, there, that shorter one, two men are dead.
The sun is pushing off, the trees persist inside their shade
eating deeply on the earth. Opening the clothes you see
among the groiny hair, the useful penis, in the heat distended
                              slightly.
One of the men's has a head, circumcised; a chin, a ridge
that visibly hardened as its body's blood gathered to it intently.
Alive, a bit of marble with a ruff of skin, in folds; thin, brown, slack.
The other man's is hooded. Each had its fissure that as it entered it
the lips folded back upon themselves, the ground moistening its
                              entrance.
Now the vulva, slightly swollen, its hair local, remains closed
                              however.
The lips closed, in a pained sleep: the female part ruminant.
No: the female part mourns the unique instrument it was to it.
The faces of the men show that death, which each divided on
                              the other's
body, entered the left ear, and then the mouth. In leisure.
None attends them. The sabbath intervenes like a blade.

Snow Drop

The blanched melted snows
Fill the plant's stem, a capillary
Of heightened moisture. Air weights
Round a white head hanging
Above granuled earth.
There, are three scarab-like petals,
Open, an insect's carapace
With a creature in these, poised.
It does not move. A white
Cylinder with two
Thin bands of green, broken
Away where that part finishes.
There is no more.
The sun's heat reaches the flower
Of the snowdrop.

Worm

Look out, they say, for yourself.
The worm doesn't. It is blind
As a sloe; its death by cutting,
Bitter. Its oozed length is ringed,
With parts swollen. Cold and blind
It is graspable, and writhes
In your hot hand; a small snake, unvenomous.
Its seeds furred and moist
It sexes by lying beside another,
In its eking conjunction of seed
Wriggling and worm-like.
Its ganglia are in its head,
And if this is severed
It must grow backwards.
It is lowly, useful, pink. It breaks
Tons of soil, gorging the humus
Its whole length; its shit a fine cast
Coiled in heaps, a burial mound, or like a shell

Made by a dead snail.
It has a life, which is virtuous
As a farmer's, making his own food.
Passionless as a hoe, sometimes, persistent.
Does not want to kill a thing.

Creatures

Shells are now found
Of creatures not still subsisting,
Chipped from the hardened mud under
Which oil lurks.

Men came with their chipped diamonds
And a pole with these smelted onto it
To bore rock. Oil broke out
Into the clear American air.

Barely noticed at the time
Among the soil screwed from
Above the crude useful oil,
Shells, about half an inch.
They were whorled, and chipped from
What they had been hardening in,
Falling through the glistening mud
They filled with; the spiral
Wriggling creature gone from them.
It is a spiral horn, silent;
And shaped like an inert
Clammy-skinned spring.

They grew property:
An amnion, a house;
Their grave no more special,
No more particular than
A pattern, a repetition of curving
Continuous shape, for survival.

Flatfish

1

It moves vertically through salted
Pressures, with a head that sees sideways.
The nets are submerged, which it enters.
Nothing to come for specially. Men want it.

The white flesh powered by a tail filmed with skin
Sways its mild hulk into their fold.
The white flesh is food. When boiled,
It flakes easily off the bone.

Is this love? God created us
For the toothed shark, the molestation
Of two jaws hinged through flesh
Onto each other's hooked teeth.

Its ethics are formal, determined.
Otherwise He made the mild flatfish,
And gleaning mackerel that flatten
On the dead's helplessness strengthening its rancid colours

He made the flatfish, their eyes
Naïve as a bead drawn from a leopard's skin.
Their white flesh is flaked into the mossy,
Acidic belly, just hanging.

The good salt, phosphate, each dissolved
Into flesh. The fish are left to gasp
In ships' holds, mulcting the air
For air moving in the gill's membrane

Miserly, useless. A gradual pain
Until the fish weaken. Could they cry
We might gas them to concert
Their distress. Nets are men's media,

Their formal, knotted, rectangular intelligence.
They survive on what the fish weighs, their welfare
Accurate as a pair of scales.

2

We are not going to change.
But husband the sea, planting the fish spawn in
    The frigid heft of plot-water
        Grey, but not stone.

Mackerel will gorge
A sea parsley, its flowers sprinkled with a white, granular petal;
    The shark will eat mud
        At the sea's foundation.

Though to reap will be by net,
As many fish as grains husked from their flattened case,
    The ear raped of its oval bolus
        Folded into itself.

The precise allotment of fish
A growth in kind; pollination by a brush tasked
    Onto differing species
        For the flesh's good.

The flesh's good. Elsewhere
We seized on our own kind, not for food. Each fish
    Glides through a forest,
        An oily lung

Of sea weed, the swell
Moved in a land-grafted integument of sea plant. A uniform
    Thicket moon-masted, its foliage
        Begins to lock

Fast with sea-forester's
Skill. We evolve with our hands and brain. The pad of each
    Hand, moist; the nails sharp
        As a grown fin.

Poem

At Laggan, iron
bridges the Spey's banks, water
on these, snowed. By Daltholly though
Spey braids into a small loch
again closing on a clump of homes.
Bridged with concrete, then, the road marches
ranking trees keep the earth soft and pine-smelling.
Light crosses the earth. We come out
between higher walls, of mountain white
as with sky, that shelf indistinguishable
in white; the black gaps glower.
From the bare peak bluish light
tilts, where life isn't, showing upwards
each facet assured and monstrous
of bent and pointed squareness.
Wind opens the tense parts
coolness contracts the mass, enlarging
on it the water: one impulsion
with two effects on the rock. The upright heaviness
will shift, snow stone and sky break
from each other. Here the bridge is rock,
rock cut that cut stays rock:
a curved stillness in air raised between two banks
of fanged rock eroded to its bitty sharpnesses
themselves un-shaped. We cross Garva bridge,
the three stone arches subsumed
to what they are built in. The river
harshly slopes down over red shafts
of stone, milkishly tinged.
We tread in Wade's road, where other English
soldiers meticulously abandoned their minds
among rock, Scot and revolt.
The mouthing shapes of red-dressed ferocity
stabbed, burned, and slit open what was there
until, by a stream spurting
into a crevice, then
scattering onto a shelf of rock, a dead man remains
who does not tend sheep, fence valley pasture
or grow to kiss his wife.

Northumberland, for instance

The stream, thin and stony, has flint
in its bed; its shape was heat
and hardened in each splinter a kernel, frigid and smoky.

In chill unextinguishable water.

And over it, a bridge
mounded on two jambs forming an arch, no door; its feet
in talons gripping
the shallow, evasive water.
They don't. The aimless clarity
funnels mindlessly between
that gap-clawed power. Not between villages: links
serves and remembers. Its lord's power.
And is shafted in the gregarious effort
of two hands and a back in one muscle
of several men. Several men
made this new bridge, the road bowed
up in concrete, each of its feet
twelve seconds apart. It is boneless
and has the sinew of many worked into it
fluid and tendon filamented into it.
The first bridge is heraldic; the beasts of the master
struck into his sign in virtue of their strength.

The bridges straddle water; and crossing
either, we are
permitted: by who built them

and are each a colony
in stone glaciated into
each other

who would be contributary,[48] a distinct
step, a curve, a heave of laughter of itself

Meetings

I walked from the town in
Mid-morning, by paths that
Pierced the exhausted wheat.
Stone and glass lowered beneath
What I climbed. Its blue haze
Gave out, and the path, sharply
Cut into blackish earth. Trees began,
Raising branches, their leaves
Touched with stiffness, hale though.
One with thicker leaf and trunk
Grew separately. I could not
See men at the back.
Another, I had not seen,
Turned through the gate before
Me, moving the iron through
Its railed arc, and he left
His hand clasped over the top
Bar as he moved it on.
　　It was not gentleness
Nor age, entirely.
And after he was through
He pushed the quartered metal
Back on its arc, which shook.
I might have stopped, a pause
Of courtesy for age
But did not, and nearing him
He seemed to have forced his
Stooped walk to my side quicker
Than I to his.
　　'This the way into
The town?' 'Yes' I answered.
The question seemed to shake
His flesh; as if the voice
Of intelligence were firm
Even in shrunk frame; smiling slightly,
As if the thought of his
Expended shape contracted

Mine in his. I asked
If he had eaten. 'Yes'
He said, crossing
His hands across his stomach to harden
His curved shape. Some earned
Hoard of thought nourished him.
　　'Across that field my strength dwindled.
I took from the earth my frame's
Energy, tended one, with the other's.
I am this now.' I noticed then
His eyelids were too small
To cover the stiffened muscular
Sight. Came close to me,
Lifting his face to mine,
Elaborately spat onto
My mouth a thin milkiness.
　　I would have hit him.
Some self-tenderness in
His body prevented me.
He slowly moved on top of
Grass trodden into earth.
From that tree he passed
I heard a core of voices
Casually bent
On profitless violence.

Tree[49]

Under the yard, earth could enable nothing, nothing
opened in it. I smelt it once, when the floor
was up, disabled, rank. I made boxes
and grow mint, rhubarb, parsley
and seedlings that lift a furl of leaves, slightly
aside an unwavering stem.
A friend dragged a barrel off rocks, we took it home;
I chose a tree for it. It is five foot
with branches that may stretch across
the wall, with minute fruits, of hardly any colour.
Its leaves point open, and down. The whole tree
can glisten, or die. It is dark green
in earth mixed with peat dug by a lake
and dung I crumbled in.
I can't fudge up a relationship, but it gladdens
you, as the sun concentrates it, and I
want the creature for what it is
to live beyond me.

Opened

Take from
me this ring
straightened open, a length
but, once,
contracted on your wrists.

love love: cries the
ring, straightened.

And again,
entering you.

What you have
taken off, you take
to you. The shaft:
the force
reciprocally.

Our Selves

Without fash, your body admits me
mine stiff with blood, its pressure
accumulating to my penis

your menses distant
as the sun
from the full moon.

Tenderness, with what draws my part
into you, hover within your skin. Its pores dilate
as if each lived a separate, identical life
like a flower rising, and opening its milky jot
at the skin, where there the threads of feeling
softly crave, insist for it to be driven in you.

My years compress to a man's substance.
The lips of the child remain untouched.

I rested between my relative's sheets
in a house close on yours. In that pupa
my fierceness turned in on me.

My aunt was fastened by a cancer, her replica
grating through each tissue whose shape
of her she settled into. The kiss
dry on my skin, inlain, there, as if a trace
of white wood were chased into my substance
by the years in the surface of a kiss

she drew herself into, I have put
in a box, with flints ignorant of friction.
That extended, that principal, Judaic phase
has left off. The candelabras
branch into some sort of magnificence.

Unpublished and Uncollected Poems,
c. 1971–1974

Lovers

Safely desire me; the sun
And every instrument upon
The evil pathway of the Ram
In his black course
Is gone. O feed with your jealous hands
On these thighs and come to this door,
Only to set your burden down.
My Love, with your hands
Unlatch these tenderest of valves.
Make our diverse feelings that
They mount like creatures in the sky
Mount, and are gone:
But, Love, stay; I desire that I
Be yet desired and possessed,
That not a word your burden is.
Love, ravish me!

I have no care for death.

'My marriage day dressed'

My marriage day dressed
slowly at nine. The hairs of grey mist, touched
by her fingers, shivered lightly. Abundance
from the springs, which are this land's roots,
printed a malformed, huge moist flower
upon the street. The circular assent
melted through us. Those ceremonious
words, in two breaths,
wrapped, momently, our two forms
in a single garment.
Where is it? The retracted waters,
the springs, which, as if to freshen themselves, withdrew
to the source in a gap between two stones, they flow.

Wanting better

Frost, water's mildew; the sea comes
in still.
                By it, we stood
upon shingle; or, on sand, shelfing
into the watery smells in the chevrons
of light. The herring shrinks its element
salting an oily flesh. The eye dazes.
One great stench of the elements is here.
The earth's variety, its filled plate, tipping
gently into the water's rustling
or clack of pebbles.
And you said: our boat's clinched
at the hawser's ring. No, what thing did you speak?
No wharf, or hut; no human particle
stacked into the integument of earth
and mad for water, little bowing men
trying the sea. For what you said was: we
aren't near to any human. So let's fuck.
And anyhow, we did. We stood upon
a found tenderness of skins. I did not
ring your finger, but what we found
on fly-bitten sand, which was rowed back
in a boat, prevailed only on sand;
or over worn staring pebble crushed
under our bodies, slaking tenderness
between them, the dinghy's curve
pressing into the salt integument
which occupies itself, rubbing down stone,
after the flesh, no further pressed by flesh,
restored its natural shape. Sounds shaped of bell
split on the rural air, strewing the town's
tarred road with brass; the law sprinkles here.
I thought I saw the Maine coast, with spiked trees
rising off stone, raise its flank up.
Vacation, like a rented house,
is crooked into the gentle earth. I and thou.

The Clay Image

*In the beginning God gave to every people a cup of clay and from
this cup they drank their life*
                    – proverb of the Digger Indian

1

And so, Love, if this is the flesh which wraps
These fullfed dead in vessel of clay flesh
I, being dead, one of those dead who glide
Through the city like angel fire-torn with
The burning multitude of shrapnel, if I fear
That I may be asked to that feast of the dead
Which is before the fairness of my death
I fear to tread where the real dead have been.

And if I hold the clay
Which bears the water in its wandering hand
And veins this innocence as milk is veined
Within the breast, I walk and share the growth
This clay first made, from which I drank. Because
My eye would see
What each eye relishes before its death
That deathless world where each stream and its reed
Resemble their perpetual soul, where each beast
And each plant in its paradisal image
Interlocks one life with its next, I therefore
Joy to walk where the true dead have been seamed
And wrapped inside the grave cup of their clay,
Because I dare resemble my healed soul.

And if I am of those dead in pretence,
Tricked by this soul to strut like the dead, which soul
Has been licked with fire
That I fear to tread where the true dead are, where birds
Perch in sylvan ignorance across
The fallen merriment of timber, therefore I now
Walk across what is both cup and grave

Where in that hollow springs life and death, there gives
To every substance growth and to that growth
The pale brown shroud of death. Therefore where shall
I pass into, whose hollow satisfy
The flames which spring and struggle in their heaven?

Birds strut and rubbish perishes.

O gentle air, in whose death I now walk
Grieving the city which once pierced you
Spire and sacred tower, from this clay
I talk with, which itself builds up the city
Cut down by fire

I am of what wastes, and in its wasting perishes

By the deed of the Fire
By the act of the steel bird of Heaven.

2

MAN
I have been given hands that I may know
The gentleness of plants, the moisture which
Clings to each leaf and clips within its bowl
Light, and all raying elements of air
Which congregates inside that glistening O.

CLAY
O brass O steel and golden Man that drinks
The water which I hold, whose swift intrusion
On my liquid property is careless
As sound twisting on water, millhand man
That shining ant who takes the glistening rain
From the possession of its grass is more
Enduring with the elements who uphold her
To her cast-brown image than you who drink
From my outraged and forcibly shaped flesh
A mortally tragic cup.

MAN

Two-natured clay
From whose forced O two knowledges are taken,
Although I drink
And my flesh is unparadised, I bear
Your tragic water joyfully in my flesh.
I am a wound in nature you may not
Heal. I on your breast did suck the rose
And she provoked my growth; that growth provides
My death, although I pulse with finite joy.
Feed me less mortally that I may plead
The mercy of my innocence in my stretch-ed hand.

CLAY

Go; do you.

3

Coiled in the playful frail entanglement
Of weed stone raises crutches from the ground
For the crossed hunchback who binds to that back
Her shuffling cross. And up two steps, which twist
Into the air of heaven a tattered man
Claps his dumb frozen hands with neither heat
Of fire nor heat of love, into the air.
And where the fire-stumped spire is cast down
Among the riding of the stony earth,
Where thieves and drabs and beggars roll in sheets
Of frost-dried grass, I put into the air
A new town made of my imagination,
Whose soul is made from scab and thief and saint.
I bring the fountain back into the soul;
I fire the snow and burn the ice, unlace
The tears tied in the praying bag. I bring
The water back we spilt the clay cup held;
I bring back what we killed our neighbour for.

Feed me the carcase of the Spanish bull.
Let me feed on the dead, disgorge what has

Ferociously been burnt by the steel tongue
Of twisted metal singing through the air

This wind's song; this preposterous metal soul.

4

I was drugged, I was urged on a bank of clay
To dream this life again, to raise this town
Where I then slept, and where I slept put yet
A ceremony of spire into the air.
When I created sin from clay, and killed
On the same bank I sleep, enemies, friends
And put out the young eye of child in solemn
Rage, this Adam's part dreamt that I yet
Expurged that past and resurrected from
The clay, dead lives, housed and clothed and fed
The congregation of split tongues. But this
Dream I now forsake nor yet upon
This air, or any other oath build up
Tower, or spire by moonlight, for a brood
Of tongues or cup of gold. See, there's not here
A slum palace or tenement bricked from church.

How shall I build the test of this burnt brick
To a well-read town? Let the builders build again
And let the fishermen pull out the breath
From that harsh fret of water, the scaled air
Of fish. Let me throw from me my dreams as
The traveller in the hot eye of the sun
Leaves off his cloak; let me leave off my dreams;

Give me my sight again. I am new risen
O Sun, O my Lord God of the still air.

'Beneath the hedgerows'

1

Beneath the hedgerows, the songbirds are dead.

Old heroes are bones and legend now;
gone to dust.

It rains the grey rain
of still-born January.
Arthur, centuries dead,
drifts timeless amongst the mermaids, for we
preferring ecology
and birth-control, have given up believing.

No more, no more, my love –
only the noise, and the words;
The noise, and the words;
The voices, and the words…

Monstrous verbiage.

Ah, come away, come away…

2

There is paucity in the land;
Many are unemployed,
and we suffer at the hands of the police and the military,
and some are interned, and some die in the streets,
and there are always new wars,
and suicides amongst the prisoners.
There is paucity in the land, and overpopulation;
let them die, let them die,
for they did not wish to be born.
There is terrible paucity in the land;
we suspect the communists, blame the black men,
and in the mouths of the mighty

there are rumours of an international conspiracy
of jews, and it rains ever
(the grey rain
of still-born January).

3

I have seen the roses, too,
and heard trails of distant laughter whispered on the wind,
known the musty smell of autumn in the rotting leaves;
the will-o'the-wisp shimmering
over the reeking fen:
and the mire
and the quicksand
and the internal bleeding.

Day by day, moment by moment,
myriad insects hatch in the dung.

4

There is no horror, no fear in life;
only the slow dying,
only the slow death,
and the souring of milk,
and the gasping breath.

Emperors and lords
are sick; are weak; are weary.
They do not care, do not care anymore;
for there is no horror, no fear in life –
nor joy, nor beauty, either.

Incongruous men,
from sterile ships,
walk the empty face of an empty moon;
let them die, let them die,
for they did not ask to be born.

The emperors and lords are sick,
glutted with blood.
We shall kill them, every one.

5

Monstrous verbiage.
Sweet words flowing from the mouths of the mighty.
come away, come away, come away...
The concentration camps are out of mind,
the slave-ships long forgotten...
From sweet words flow
the sewers and open graves...

And shall we kill them, every one?
ah, come away, come away.

Fiery images devour the soul.
I have seen them; struggled to describe, define...
Inchoate,
mute before the knowledge
of ineffable essence,
the essence of ineffable knowledge,
I have seen these things,
I have seen these things,
grotesque, and unsubdued...

Let them die, let them die.

There is only the noise, and the words,
the voices, and the words,
the noise, and the words...

come away, come away, come away, come away...
I shall be lulled by the waters of anonymity,
while my memories grow long in the tooth.

6

Sheets of grey rain blow across the sky and soak the land.

'The forehead rises a distance'

The forehead rises a distance, grey hair
in the skull, continuing this, but then, swayed back
as if reluctantly, touching the mid-crown.

The skull living as
the body's cup.

And other images: the haws, and
ochre grasses doubly thick; cut,

                               the symmetrical carcase
of a straw field.
Some thwart-wise of colour stooped on the sheared hill.
The brain:
originating, declensionless.

Mounded earth, stone in
it, supporting this.

And for the third time
seen, no change in him.

Sporadically some twitch of arrogance
sprung in neglect,

And animation, the harebell
clapperless,
flickering and blue in the eye.

The machine binds up crops
some grass, some streaked
straw-stuffs. The soft-stalked hair, grey.

A bird gulleting seed.

Then: from the skull unslips
a braid
of creatures in a union

of men working. They throng, and are streaked with
some winged or grainy flutter. The hands turn
wheels into a track making for the steep
brow, and again down, the field bulging
with the hill's shape in it.
This is the shape, and the work takes it in
          as that man would the old
          or work-maimed.

Life in the field

Chestnuts in the mild grass,
in diastole. Father with child
on Hertford's field in mild joy.

'Father, the field is a sea.'
Stanchions of flowering. Sea
nevertheless, with poles

of flower that deliquesce.
Can chestnut stanchions branch
calyxed forms to a bass

strum of words? What language?
Oh, none. This mealy, fondant
mess pauses the eye.

With a soft shrug of breath
earth lets huge energies bear
candles in stanchioned forms.

'All-eying moon, fury'

All-eying moon, fury
of livid stone, female justicier –
'yer said what?'
'You'll hang for this.' 'But why?'

Early sun is kind for plants. Rooted
or on the trot, we nab
its incremental touch. Between
us and it, foists

the moon. – 'Yer but a gob
of silvery phlegm.' – That's how
though our earth lifts
round the sun, we get

but just half a day, and grow eyelids.
'You are going to die; the Emperor
and bad art don't mix. Either
the perfect jar, or a dead,

mutilated craftsman.
With the blessèd shape mingles
the Emperor's love. But a bad
shape is death.'

'And this is justice?' Industry
reflates with brilliant
craftsmen, and ferocious
blood-filled ghosts.

'So make it good.' 'My gentle Lord,
your handservant, dear God,
the man's eye demands
each multiform perfection alone.

I can't. Cloisonné, the blessèd
shape in jadeite
et al. My breath's white
shape over glass survives me. Have

I no life but yours
in the next world, all
that spring away?
Lord, answer me,' I ask

The Principle of Water

First published by Carcanet Press, 1974

A Strand from Caedmon

Now we must praise heaven's possessor;

I cannot sing. And silent, as at first,
left the feasting.

The holy Shaper, first he fashioned

as a roof the heavens, and the middle earth
this eternal Lord, he after adorned.

I cannot sing. Silence magnifies
the creaturely, livid dross of flies
pricking faeces.
             Our almighty King,
this glorious Father, the everlasting Lord,
wrought the beginning of wonders each one.

Near the farm, voices encrusting
tree-forms of grass bitten by deer.

The air opens, the cuneiform voices
wedging praise. Also to be seen

the harrowing angel, his still wings'
extended denunciation

Killhope Wheel

Tree[50]

Under the yard, earth could enable nothing, nothing
opened in it. I smelt once, when the floor
was up, disabled, rank. I made boxes
and grow mint, rhubarb, parsley
and seedlings that lift a furl of leaves, slightly
aside an unwavering stem.
A friend dragged a barrel off rocks, we took it home;
I chose a tree for it. It is five foot
with branches that may stretch across
the wall, with minute fruits, of hardly any colour.
Its leaves point open, and down. The whole tree
can glisten, or die. It is dark green
in earth mixed with peat dug by a lake
and dung I crumbled in.
I can't fudge up a relationship, but it gladdens
you, as the sun concentrates it, and I
want the creature for what it is
to live beyond me.

(Untitled)

Small hills, among the fells, come apart from the large
where streams drop; the water-flowers
bloom at the edges, or in the shallows, together,
and are white. Whoever comes here, comes, glad, at least
and as they look, it is with some care, you can feel
that on flower, may tree, or dry-stone wall
their gaze collects in a moist, comely pressure.
I feel this, but slog elsewhere.
Swan Hunter's is where we build naval craft;
they emerge: destroyer, the submarine

fitted, at length, by electricians. Their work
is inspected; it is again re-wired. In the heat
men walk high in the hulk on planks, one
of them tips, and he falls the depth of the hold.
It is hot. The shithouses are clagged, the yard's
gates closed for security. The food is not good.
Some people in here are maimed.
I am trying to make again the feeling
plants have, and each creature has, looked at,
demure, exultant. The man who has fallen
looks at me, and looks away.

Centering

At the West End, a bridge.
Coaling houses, shutes, and among such power,
contrived, at the top, a little lever
which would unclasp the heavy trap.
All the ships come for here is fuel. Few come.
And none, further.
Near the bridge, each side, houses
struggling to cross over.

More east, seawards, a further bridge.
The trains bend that way, then, turning square,
cross the whole river.
Below, the quay, meant to focus
activity to it.

The maritime offices, craft
moored from Denmark.
The masts' shadows stable on the customs sheds.

No centre can be formed
here or by the next bridge. The trains
pass on a tier above the road.

Nor here; the road belts between
the strength of the region fused into two spans,
gone.

Two precipitate banks, where water pushes
within a moment of the quick of you, bituminous
and rank.
If you were made
at the river-side
you have to be a spanning, at least.

Killhope Wheel, 1860, County Durham

1860. Killhope Wheel, cast
forty feet in iron across, is swung
by water off the North Pennines
washing lead ore crushed here.

And mined, here. Also fluor-spar.
In 1860 soldiers might kill
miners if they struck.

A board says that we're free to come in.
Why should it seem absurd to get
pain from such permission? Why have

I to see red-coat soldiers prick
between washed stones, and bayonets
tugged from the flesh?

Among the North Pennines what might
have seeped the flesh of miners, who chucked
their tools aside?

I can't work out what I have
come here for; there's no mineable land
or work of that kind here now.

Why does a board, tacked to wood,
concerning my being free to visit
nourish my useless pain?

Like water. I am its water, dispersed
in the ground I came from; and have footage
on these hills, stripped of lead,

which the sheep crop, insensibly white.
The mist soaks their cries into them.

Strike

The earth comes moist-looking, and blackens;
a trickle of earth where the feet pressed,
twice a day, wearing off the grass.
Where the miners
were seen: a letter blown damply
into the corner of a hut: 'Oh dear love, come to me'
and nothing else.

Where are they?
The sheep bleat back to the mist balding
with terror; where
are they? The miners
are under the ground.

A pale blue patch of thick worsted
a scrag of cotton;
the wheel is still that washed the pounded ore.
They were cut down.

Almost turned by water, a stammer of the huge wheel
groping at the bearings.
Their bayonets; the red coat
gluey with red.

The water shrinks
to its source. The wheel,
in balance.

Spade

George Culley, Isaac Greener?

A want of sound hangs
in a drop of moisture from the wheel that
turned and washed the ore.

A rustling of clothes on the wind. The water does not move.

I have come here to be afraid.
I came for love to bundle
what was mine. I am scared
to sneak into the hut to find your coat.

When you put down your pick,
when others wouldn't sprag
the mine's passages; when you said no:

soldiers, who do not strike,
thrust
their bayonets into you.

They were told to.

The young mayor, shitting, closeted
with chain on his neck. I want to

push my hands into your blood
because I caused you to use yours.

I did not die; love, I did not. All the parts
of England fell melting like lead away,
as you showed me the melting once, when you and the men
with you were jabbed,

and without tenderness, were filled over;
no psalm, leaf-like, shading the eyelid
as the eye beneath is dazed abruptly
in the earth's flare of black light
burning after death.

The spade digging in the sunlight illuminates the face of my God.
Blind him.

(Untitled)

Concerning strength,
it is unequal. In a paddock
by Stakeford, slag, with bushes dripping
over stone, a horse crops, slowly, his strength
tethered into the ground. The Wansbeck
shivers over the stone, bits of coal, and where
it halts a pool fills, oily
and twitching. Closer to the sea, it drops
under a bridge, coming to ground
where the mind opens, and gives uselessly to
the sun such created heat, the air
cleaves to the flesh,
the bench facing the water, sat on by old men.
If this goes, nothing; this clearness
which draws a supple smell through old skin
making a pause for it. Houses and scrap will heap,
and flake, as
if organs of the soil clagged
with shreddings of rust.

Platelayer

for J.M.

'I did not serve, but was skilled
for fifty years, laying plates
measured as carefully apart
as seedlings.' The line came
west from Morpeth, crossing
the third road for Scotland.
At Knowesgate, four houses
group on a bank, set away.
A station was built there.
'I laid plates for eight miles,
but short of Morpeth, sledging chucks
that held the rails; kept them so,
although this has gone now.
Yet here are four pines of
the five I put in. And here
I helped to concrete that
that was the goods bay.
My dog has sixteen years.
We both suffer the heat.
And yet her owners had said
that she must be put down.
I did not say that. And the lupins
strike through the platform;
with a better chance I think
they'd have not done well.
But what I think is that
my work was finished up: five years
past the track taken apart.
No, not so; now we've cranes
to hoist the lengths that we
laid down, form on form. Also gone
a certain friend, who finished
when I was made free.
I shan't work any job
twice. And this is strange,

having the letter from the man,
although it was not him.
Yet surely as like him
as the bolts drove in.
"I can't think of your name
or what you are. You must
excuse me and I have
nothing to tell you and
why I am shut up here
I can't speak of with nothing
to speak about."
But still I am certain
the track we built was skilled,
although you can't tell that.'

'The bird is ligamented...'

The bird is ligamented without a soul; it is lifted
in a wind, blasted from the silica furnace.

The People[51]

A Pennsylvania German Pie Plate

Hand-wrought-and-decorated in 1786 it is inscribed, 'The plate is made of clay; when it breaks, the potter laughs.' When he's dead even. He turns over as it breaks, and laughs; unless he, like the plate, has baked in the oven.

> *Pray thee, take care, that tak'st my book in hand,*
> *To reade it well: that is, to understand.*
>
> — Jonson

Onirique

FINN
I melt to sleep on my left side
and dream
of archaic beasts, baring a white honed smile;
unpunishable, alert, and pacified
in mutual consent, their quirked grins knit
a peaceable, brilliant continuum.
Which goes.

Branches are cut, and cross-piled in a square
to eat the flesh up of a heretic.
Each has a defined
nick in it; but why
I ask.

On my right side I dream how
by an inn, God molests
a tired man, austerely erect.
And cleaves the flesh, but that those halves each time
melt whole again.

Once you've the knack, I shout, the fun in it will come.

A dry voice answers that what I say is
more in its line. Like death, I say. And it:
you're not about to die yet, nor is he.

My God, I thought, that is as well. I am not
about to find
any screwball
sticking by me.

'You're premature' the voice said. I got dandled
onto a cleft in rock. The voice disposed
no face, no comfort I might draw from it.

But as in a dream felt
the hand, fitting
that one likewise upon a shelf, as if

but bored, too
much with it

moved off.

Brief dream. But under the cut pile
of branches, an odour
of soiled, fouling life

more murderous than this God

gorgeous with light

that light incised by smiles
at the teeth's edge, by men
turning to stare at it.

I turn, waking, and reach for Kye who sleeps
in first pregnancy. I catch
up my breath and kiss her.

I. Growing

FINN
A dog howls over stubble fields, where smoke
wavers between two straight trees;
no sounds billow frost-marked hedgerows.
Yet he uses distance, his bark dispersing
as smoke in the lull after harvest before spring,
that taints, by London, the country air.
I turn off to where my wife will labour soon,
gravid in blood, spinal nerve. And quit
heavy winter sharpness, with sullen empty light
reddening grass-tips, hair on fruits' skins.
What is at home? No sound mixes the door's
jarring its hinge. A voice. Yes, I answer.
Each thing here is childbirth. Metal bowls
cambered like shallow buttocks, the heavy slope
of another is her stretched belly in the weighed
drop to her cunt, that opens. She calls.
The pouting track's soft firmness dilates;
jugs gleam, wide-lipped, prepared for dropping
water to grin in lolloping mirth; the stable, working pan
will get the flow bent onto the wheel turning
to wash the pounded ore.
Come up love, Kye asks. The stone and wood room
having winter flowers, a fire banters
its tongues onto their erect blue flare.
One other is here, her friend, large-boned: sit, she says,
in your own house. Laughs. He'll not be long.
How do you know 'he'? we each ask her.
By his size, by that, with his slow turning
about. But there's the kettle, and ring the nurse.
Kiss me, Kye asks. Her brow gathers
moisture in the furrows, ploughman's sweat.
I wipe her and kiss her.
                              Below, fire heaves
behind iron, intently heating a pot
and sinks into itself, moulting ash.
Its vitality itches terror into the wood it eats;

flesh deciduates in passion. I love this girl,
who is making our child. The nurse comes;
her stiff apron is white and terrorful.
I am upstairs, Kye asking to hold to me. Warmth
beats across her fear and mine. Her fear
is of what makes in her, mine's a white subtraction.
Yet she holds to me, as I touch that swollenness.
'Now' she quivers 'he stretches me, love.'
'Now hangs back in me.' Yes, a hump,
and sullen, feeling no joy rooted here. But we
wait for its first shove, as it is
to issue rushing, cord knotted, cut,
and reversed into the navel. 'Now' she breathes. If she
pushes, I can't tell if he does, or it's she.
'Hold me,' she insists, 'no, don't.' Fastens to my wrist. I suffer
no hand, but its grip. Sweat shakes off again.
Her bowels move, and open. Then at the parting
of strange lips,
her child, clustering, heaves a gulf open. She pushes,
now contracts, heaves wider, and it is going to come.
It is. 'No.' A pause, renewed, for its coming,
rushing out. Has it? It does, and the spiral wreck
of abdominal life terminates, the creature stirring it.
Even as he's lifted, lightly slapped
for his first cry, I know I shall not
see him unnamed again.

Kye, for his necessity, from hair to feet
is specked and salt, its glistening
moist as placental amnion.
Now it is, for cleansing, the water's turn. Poured,
capable and clear, into the cool, a milky
fluid dripped precisely, and her body washed; never
as helplessly lying, cleaned of excreta and blood.
Sponged gently. As grass is plaited in a crown
for the May's queen, queen not of herself
but of each one's May; as, blithely, in equal parts
each of us is the May, so she is washed.

THE PRINCIPLE OF WATER   371

He howls. 'That's hunger. Pick him up, here,
he is yours.' The nurse smiles. Lines in her small face
crease her labour, with others', on her;
midwife to each child she lifts him to Kye's breast.

First food passes his mouth;
then he lies quiet, and is knit to her
in such sticky entangling he will unpick.
                For now, the arm
grows large she holds him in. Cinders stir.
A dog barks, splintering light.
The pans are hard at rest, we would be glad for as much.
                        Coldness stands up
and, full of care, puts both arms
about the solid house.

STEIN
                        At eighteen,
my first journey, at length, though not specially,
with one pain. Opening gates,
the signal, its painted alpine station, with beyond
numberless circumscription.

I've my circumcision,
with, in Riga,
the same shit:
loathing, the gentile's
stare backward.

It comes, love, again;
we are to be plucked, much
as the mouth, fastened on pain
rejects its tooth.

England, a stable calm,
crosses the road. I am
a step from me to those
two whom I love. But then?

I am a great way off from anything.

A wind reverses each cloud through the boughs,
notching the tips of this adjacent moon.
A nimbus incompletely haloing.
                              Past this
third house, I see a neighbour. A light wind
tightens her skirt above her knees, tanned lightly,
and creased. She is political, she says,
and, formed inside the party, used, who would
be used, taking from her her youth, as if
a ghost despondent of its flesh. It is
the cause. Is it? For now, perplexities
in certainty creep onto the small mouth,
tampering the vigour prompting its bare skin,
that wears as anxious to prove serviceable.
Ruthlessness pauses lightly, knowing to get
and score her generosity away
it seems, until the bone is at its skin.

Stares at a number sweated
into my shirt;
naked, I'd swathe my wrists.

She has no child, and I,
in me, spores of grief
shield their eyes.

More flesh: the furnace eats,
and sweats dust.

Columnal fierceness of some brilliant march
from Egypt's swamp or grit. We undo the bland
obedient waters of the flat red sea,
the hovering walls, balancing God's natureless signs.
Bad nerves thread distant, but avenging, forms
displaced, a time, by God's mild crucial hands.
Burnished armour, and strength stepping in it,
this crosses to some locus where its face

THE PRINCIPLE OF WATER   373

is crossed upon another, glimmering
in iron. Each pays.
In Europe, the Jews
pay definitively.

Lying in Buchenwald, as the British moved
up to us
in slinging densities of ash, one man
walked, dressed in brown, through it, and lifted me
up in his arms. I felt like a mild plant,
shame cringing me. But he was crying. That one
should be cried for, as if a plant had worth
beyond its fruit and serviceableness;
outside the staked wire, heaps a pit, and spaced
an equal area from two further ones;
a mass grave, and the indifferent botany
of herbs branching a pungent sullenness.

Those whom I touched, I left. No weeping,
that salt drawn as in work, sweat fiery
through labour, frozen
bolting fuselages

with her who ceased.

Why should I not have been born as a word
sprawling inside a Yiddish lexicon.

I cried 'love' once; no person answered it.

I visit my friends now,
their house, rooted
under a hill of cropped grass, and by
a farm: Adam
and who made him.

FINN AND KYE

What is it that will not eat mash from a bowl?
that lets the spoon come to its lips, then ails
and weeps, or, if the spoon pries past them,
weeps and chokes? Or being fed
vomits his mash entire.
Earlier, as if that mesh of him were
my making only, and that he won't eat
my care alone, and I could, alone, unpick
his belly's tightening
she flung him on his back, hard, over the bed.
He lay astonished. Then huge tears swelling with
the eyelids, came away from him. Silence
breaking with moisture on his cheeks.
I felt what he might learn. Much anger, bruised
in hatred, he got thrust down with. From me,
his wetness on my stubble, cowed by her
that he could see. Deliberately, she asks,
why is he silent, and, why does his food
not stay with him; what is his quietness?
I can't reply. She smiles: it is as if,
she answers, he's made perfectly. As if.
As though perfectly made, but in him, life
moves very little – love, it is not there.
Then hesitantly, but then, instantly sure
she lifts him,
holding him to her with such tenderness the slight
widths of air between them, as she slowly brings
him to her, yield and tense in supple
passion endured by both. Instantly
he cries to her, long, slow, insistent, rising
to screams, as he tenses his head from her.
She lulls him, his pained flesh swaying her with him.
It is as if, she says, pausing, in him
nothing joins. As if that tissue in us
that forms an Adam, or a Finn, has not
met in him.

I might tell him; but how might I, blithely
as my lips on his penis, or as

with brimmed a softness on his quick as it
is tight in him? Why won't my sweet intent
not pass from me to him, as I took in
his well-planted, minute, sturdy seed?
I want the child to take breath into him.
Yet how, love, – where, I'm asking, in him is
the tangled sense laid
as nerve-web in the well-held inner bowl,
a bowl supping the discontinuous
splashes of shape and feeling on him, that form
the memory that is him.

She tilts her head; a grin, being obdurate,
edges the eye and mouth sharply. Some mirth.

I am, yet what I am no man has touched.
I was made slenderly, you know; and fleshed
over the buttocks.
My hair is long, and light, and hangs.
My head draws at the back into a curve
that implicates a mind webbed in a brain.
My fingers are long, and small, and my waist
tucks in over my hips. Two men
were there before you, and no other one.
Yes, but this should not flatter you, for here
I exercise my choice. Love, oh my love,
you touch my breasts and they excite. You kiss
my flesh as if you loved me. But my lips
force a smile sometimes I do not half-mean.
I loathe this. My mind is not dainty; tough,
perhaps, and pert pert as a bean, yet, so,
irregular. Love, if we do connect,
we have a child fresh as white berry –
I speak no more of it; what we have made
is beautiful, I know; and tenderness
will sour in me if your neat courage deserts.
Whatever he will make, he should grow soon
my literate intelligence, with it
your shrewd imagination, sharp as sand

and newly cut, edging the mind's thin blades.
He should have – love, lift him, and see if you
find in him our minds, joined up in that new,
that lithe, unbaulked, hurtling intelligence
so beautiful to see; see, there, I think I felt it.

II. History

1. STEIN
I tailored three suits, which hang
empty of me.

Come kitty come on kitty
                              my three
cats
wail in a curve formed
on each other. And leap on.

A string vibrating three
versions of one plucked self

        Some life goes on
        no one said it would not.

2. STEIN
A tale-bearer
                treads the horizon
and we converge.
Asking: which emperor
                              did Tacitus loathe?
History has limits.

I write down nothing of experience
I was combed through, like the head-louse.

I made up nothing
                         from others' print
nor satisfied
                    the need for some key-figure

but in extremity budded
                              and was pressed
between leaves. I made up
history in the lump
holding it in me.
And what of that I was I can bring
upwards constantly. No wreath of judgments
pricking my forehead.
                         Uncertainly I'll promise
to bring an opinion, after I am dead,
as a mild ghost stirs benevolent for talk
on earth, beside a steaming hearth-fire.

The numbers stamping
                         my wrists
derive no mystical insight
                              and, if seen
will not touch a soul.

I wear what is marked on me. Suffering is not strength
wanting,
              or down-payment
                         on survival;
if it implicates
                    spiritual qualities,
that's accident. In the pitiers, even so
pity in action is dead.
                         I survived
drinking my wife's urine.
                         And again,
the rifle's thud.
                    Additionally
a foot burned, the death of every beloved:
many in there were beloved.

Oh my love, virtue was not dropped
from between God's thumb and finger.
As we went for it, the shell husked
small droppings from the worm, as if
who should be virtuous.

Problems heap in amongst the remnant.
In each case men say 'He is a Jew.'
                                    One says
'Jew' in Israel, implanting their difference.
For whose sake, 'Their deaths must not
diffuse through mud.' Who is mud, I ask.
Our monument's barb
                            steadies in rock
Jerusalem is
            a stone over.
I'm not yet dead;
                others may have wished
intimate remembering.

How how? Monuments
                        absent the mind
excuse it, are not
ruth, not pity, nor sinewy discourse
in the here or to-come of us.

Again my life
            fines to a point
pressing here

on four of us. Kye breathes
in this place edged by fields.
A tree that sides their house
taps at the glass and scrapes
thick spicy leaves onto
transparent barriers,
chill and brittle. She is
as if my daughter once
removed in blood; she smiles

and nods, but fitfully,
on my words. Adam, not
not my child but take in
a deeper breath, love, than
you have done yet, and touch
my mind, as Finn touches
the child in me.
What is to come, I want
to know, of me and them?

3. STEIN
If my people were to forgive the enemies of my people there would
be no forgiveness for my people. Mother, Mother!

III. Testing

FINN
These are London's consiliary
offices of stone, edging
the river with a prospect of
not flowers, pilasters of hope

in bloom. Each stone face is firm
with rhyme, and echoing a confidence
borrowed. Rectangular stone widths
group upon the forecourt

disdaining the river. A lower wall
silvers tidally, with, in traces
the sediments of us, dirt
the dried skin of London, forced
off into the stream.

The way to enter is
through front doors; we are
going to, with Adam, for
doctors, whose tests

relieve ourselves each
of hope and, with it,
unhoping care.

No trees; water that
is to the building
what the building is.

And we who caused it, in
whose service it is —
and those who work in it
stained with tea, compose

a fleshless soul, the extremity
of service,
of utter purity, slightly
gone off.

Mother, Mother! these buildings
with us in them, integers
zealously conflated in the common good.

The common-wealth magnified
by each of its hand-servants
to the power of one.

KYE
We have sat four hours, with Adam,
that tests may be made
added into such choice
he can't know we make.

The trailing corridors, lights regularly
spaced between mahogany doors. One is
opening for us.
Adam feels cold, sweating lightly.
The temperature is lowering; the anxious
chronometrication of London's business
in this slight chill, where we live

netted in its jurisdiction.
Adam is sweating, coldly. Almost a year.
In the marble jamb a fossil
unfolds a shape we enter.

KYE
Up on his toes, it is amazing how,
the man creeps from behind our son, and brings
before him a huge bell, clanging it hard.
Adam continues smiling. On the couch,
naked and tranquil, no jolt of his breath
until, a minute after, a thick sigh
dismaying the held silence, shakes out.
Startles us. But not him, nor him. A bell
with no responsiveness to it. A sigh
shaken out from the child's watched silences
elapsing then, definitively shuts
this winter's interview.

What silence, with what effort. The ringed finger
barring the lips, his voice quavers through phlegm
blown off the lungs, the ejaculatory
opinion, fined by logic down – the forms
imaging science, and colourless as dew.
The earth breathes out. The business, as is normal,
shut into words that close the test. The tone
is natural, and sparkles decently
with worth; the nifty instruments replaced
unneeded as unused; writing is done
niched in behind a desk, as London's madness like
the waters of the Thames through London's council drifts,
and is checked.
                              We feel,
in glances, relieved, his work certified. But Adam
is proscribed. And we
being young, with no further obligation, entered
upon the state, its ample lap, its breast
moistening him.

It is what I have done. I feel, used by
using these instruments, what this man feels.
Adam with smiles is grasping seriously
the adult finger in his palm. Is love,
using this knowledge, love? let it lie there.
This is the letter, which the hospital
will take him in with. Leave him there. And try,
with that life in you both, to grow whole with
a second child, but not identically,
I mean. He stops. Conceive another life
since that is what you must. Rises, and stares
over the oiled, and sliding wateriness
whose soiled dispersions pour onto Vauxhall.
What may I say? I do not know the words
of comfort for you. Goodbye; his outstretched hand
the nails round, their moons lightly white,
a circular cleanliness. I pick Adam up
weighing as much as I, smiling again.
Give me the letter, I say; Finn gives it.

FINN[52]
Air that pricks earth with life, and turns as it
returns to darken, in the year's midnight,
thins in a chill distraction. Winter sun
burns a low arc through the horizon and
is absent. As we trudge the area where
our child is lying, this soil is trodden by
the mad, who, at the next spring, that is
at the next, may, with its flexible sense
elide by that stark light the vacancies
in their maimed circuits. If no world unfolds
these dead may rise to, if the flower half buds
a flesh that does not know itself, and does
not open in a separate flowering,
and touches signs which touch without a trace
of healing correspondence, in this world
will have to do. She, who drifts with her group
of friends, as if we beckoned, leaves, and is
behind us both. Her shape bends gently down.

Her large quiet hands, her breasts hardly there,
an independent mildness, at the mouth,
branched past the cheekbones, brushes to the eyes
widening in hunger.
She gazes, and lifts my hand up slowly to
her lips; then kissing it, releases me
with care, gently, and leaves. That gentleness
forming, without submission, as she kisses
my hand gravely – who shared in that kiss –
in which instant sane or defective; shame
at my dividing question. Walk a bit
on to the ward. Out of its souring brick,
bird-like, the mad alight, shake, and fold in
their movements to their bodies, gazing queerly,
or quiver in recognition, timid, but pressing
on us to touch us over our hands, or faces,
or touch us with their eyes; while everywhere
their mild untrained gaze forms the unsure part
in creaturely connection. And as I feel
her hand, earlier forms shed their flesh, leaving
this bare. Twelve almost, to test
my sanity, I squatted on the pavement
and put a marble on my tongue, closing
my mouth on it. If I could swallow this
and die, I was insane. Or if I left
it balancing on my tongue, then I was mad
to do this. Our child for them is mad.
We reach the twilit ward. Adam lies in
a bed as if an adult. Through his face
his blood, making the skin chill, dampening it,
stirs. He breathes, yielding a changed breath.
We labour it, and press it, the lungs
that can't be relieved, letting it from them.
She rises, and slowly, as she brings her mouth
to him, her lips widen. Lightly, and light,
as if she were withdrawing, as she sinks
beside his silence breathing, she lifts up
his head, and lightly kisses his eyelids,
his mouth, then, as she puts her finger to
his palm, turning his head to us. The eyes,

eyes that are firm, breath in a changing form
moves through them, with a flickering softness in
its shape. Over and not obscuring that,
the moisture of his body
swelling the eyes, and widening them, brings
the life that concentrates, searching itself,
to grow connections in him. Forming him,
formed, and held like this, it connected us
to him, holding us until
that moisture pressed with a thick
movement from him

IV. The Chair

KYE
                              Adam's chair is cut
in lions as arms. An amphora unfolds
a vine that flows up, straight, enticing to it
two massive birds, within whose wood beaks
a wooden leaf is shared, linking the chair's
wide back. Two griffons, standing, weight their front legs
over the higher branches. It seems dead
to me; no, it is threatening, and I must
move it.

My fingers stitch; a pink
nubile obedience silks
its floral vacancies.

A mimic pause between us, then – all this
bores me, Finn adds. He lifts a glass up
and, with a little shrug, releases it.
Crash. It does bore me.
                              Branches in bud
outside the pane, touching, with dried bloods.

Yesterday where in the war bombs split
I stooped in the mud: a can with rain in
advancing rust.

He does not now hear, causing me to wane
against his ear. I love him yet, and loathe
what in me's teased the vulnerable. But watch
the muscle tighten, with the flickering
under the eye, signing a violence.
Not that he'll see, I flinch. He waits, he pauses,
and lets me be. A precious flow of joy
through me, then shame at this. But more comes from him:
the house seems barely ours, is passage
through which our loneliness drifts; with nothing else
I would still want the chair. And I would watch
it squatting, four-legged, in a ploughed-up field.
So much, I think, for images, and am sharp
and hard inside me, listening to him
say we cannot avoid our pain

                      can't we,
I ask. We can do more.

                   Perhaps, he says
and will, I tell him. It is our pain, which
we cause each other, or, do not. I had
the labour, the stretched terminal closenesses to
our child. And that suffices; nothing in me
created it

           we did, he says

                 then I
do not remember it

                 or anything,
he answers. And cuts off the music there.
A dried tune, in the head, is thwarting me.
All happens then, He slides the chair to me
hands clenching it, white as the face behind
the spaces in between the birds and vine
that light onto the garden he stares at
unseeing.

           Sit there, he says. But I do not.
Sit there, he says, or is this dead too?
Is it? A pause. If it is, watch me then.

What may I answer, and must watch, to see
him raise it. As he lifts, the facial muscles

fasten a little glare, that switches through
the neck; he lifts, pauses, and swings the chair
against the wall. What then? Twice, I think, twice
and smashes it. I hear it splintering.
The flapping birds drop through the torn vine
rasping its leaves; the fruited, clustering vine
and tendrils spread upon them, each of these
winces apart, with every imaginable
tenderness we had our marriage-day.
And lie, flinching. I will not see. My face
weeps in my hands; salt is one white, death makes
another in us, by our child. I was born
weeping, into this.

STEIN
Treading the snow, and pausing at a shape
to scrape it clear, a man is trying
for hard wood to make a chair from. The lane crunches.
Snow squeals. And images of war move in the snow
raising a commune recessed in the brain –
traces of snout, vixen's teeth, crab, us
smeared through the cells the mind remembers in.
The chair plants its four legs, and grows; it is
not shaped like men cut down, with sprinkled frost
tipping stubble, but a harmonious
and peaceable clop of feet treading work on.
Scrimmage of tensions in the mind form by
yielded accession on these images,
made solid in a mind perching a bird.
Chipped out, and in, creatures appear, and join
a pact; archaic ferocities remain.

Now's wood for winter fires. He took the chair
and broke it easily.
                        Stammering naïve blood
was loosed once more, the little mounds of dead
snowed over. And no blood there. Here the flesh
delights to die, teasing the appetite

with helplessness, dropping into itself.
A synergy of claws agreed to meet
and lie in mildness. This went with the chair.
Teeth sheared the mild flank. All that again.
He saw, or did not; broke it, anyhow.
And no restraint, or compact, stayed. The chair'd
no strut, or style; austere harmoniousness,
simple to break. Reluctant of itself,
he broke it, and each creature so detained
by art, free with its all-eyed strength, sniffed, stepped
and tore, its one eye splinteringly glazed
over the panting flesh, whose piteousness
sheared in a mouth of spikes. These two unclasp.
Pink, with no use, their torn selves want their halves,
whose heap of neatly sphinctered grains of soil's
a small exuded heap for burial in.

My eyes sweat, watching. The blow thuds across
the leafed-out woods. A scream ends in screaming,
folding the violated air round it.
The scream, the testicles, are leafed out.

It is done, and they tell you it is done.
'Duty', they say, and 'fearful for us'.
A snap-shot of the scene, wafer and host,
as nourishment. The mind tenses and arches
a rancid gaze over its phantasies.

There is no language, some say, that could speak
of this. And some, no language that should speak.
Hush. Pure language, language must be clean
of blood. A fine incontinence of love
will not indulge the sufferers. Then wheesht.
Language is pure, has autonomy,
a life not to be tainted, and its sense
has pure separation from the thing
referred to. Words choose, and they do not choose
a moral valency for blood. And others
'save me, save me', they stammer, who reject
the blade they would not use. Tendernesses

runnel these folk together milkily;
the bitter herb regales a rawer flesh.
And again, language, they claim, tarnishes
lugging the obscene weight. A great steel
from its self gleaming, keeps its inner life
pure of rusts. Wipe it. Faintly I hear
more of this, but not much. A tiny cough.
The throat flicking its ease; dust from a coat,
a ledger of the saints, flick, it is gone.

See, it darts. Quick, firstlings come. Grasp them
before they vanish. Threads that gossamer
I did not spin. Take firm, gentle hold.
Use us, these forms repeat; as I am, so
shall they be. My past at the junction with
their separating lives, I must use quickly.
Guards coughing; the cold bore down their words; I lived.
I should make that mean something, if for those
whose lives despair. I will try.

FINN
In my own room, I am, in paint, anxious to prove
all feeling survives its facts.

STEIN
1.
As if I were
their copula

as if

2.
if if

Nausea

nausea
of me

nausea

KYE
So that I must,
therefore, unpick
our marriage.

Death has crumpled Adam. This man does not like me.

And with that other man,
he will love me, not not
at all but if
I touch my husband.

What is this?

and

I cannot be forgiven my child's death I did not make.

Merely, that man would forgive me.

God, thou shrike, who
at me pried, pert
as a bean, I had
not even an orifice you wanted
but a slit
you probed in me.

I forgive you
not much.

A woman sweats God
out of her

and

the garment is, in halves,
laid by.

When death is a guest, those relatives sit in mourning (shiva) for
seven days; candles are lit and burned through, it being sacrilege
to extinguish them.

STEIN
They must, for our needs
cleave, as my words will
together
            the curved spirts,
its spray, the impulses
of the fountain
                    folding
into their provident source

in this instance, pain.

A candle burns its white
deep-seated thread, the wax
of hot soft light shrinking
into itself. I have saved
a remnant, the terse stub
of this light which cut light
over the murdered through
the dark there, for myself.
I save it to deplore
what I have lost, and as
it finishes, I will be
a pool of hardened wax
wanting thread on a plate
whiter than me.

So then there is no point
in telling anything.
I need light for this and
need such, as will not last
beyond this, to outlast
itself, that I may live
from it. But then
the simple gout will flick

its spot of fat into
my sight, and drop in through
its dark.

I should do this – insert
a history of leaves, torn,
lifted, turning in air,
then softly
dropped, where
ground banked and pressed us
under its fall
                    that two
unloving animals
find mercy's image : love

for my reasons also

in their house.

V. Camps

STEIN
As each of you sits, hear me, please.

Which is, two images. A town clustering
over a stable bluff; of desultory
brown rough clay, and stone. Houses light up
above the river's tidal gleam, unslips
ocean merchantmen in on the sea.
In gear, tugged; blithely salt spirals off
the stable wave-form prow. Prepared enough.
Pointed north-east into the Barents sea.
The second is a park, bedded and clipped.
Laurels unfurl loose bloom. A bench in wood
upturned, its short iron legs uselessly stiff
and pointed upwards. Screwed into its back

'for Aryans only', on a metal strip.
Closed wagons are drawn in line through wind, and stop.
A melted cry behind a sealed door.
Some hush. More then, then, more, and more. The train
jerked on its wagons, covering them with
its steamy patch of roar, billowing the park.

It came. The Polish engine, sweating, among cold;
its steam breathed over snow. Wagon doors
pinioned back. Mostly the guards with dogs stood,
as we filed in. Patience, and our murmur, wavering.
Neither the young, nor the elderly, wept. Once, a guard
gently helping up an old man who faltered.
Some vomit, softly, in lumps, falling past the edge
of a wagon. Prayers made. None bidding us safe conduct.
In a woman's back
the butt's thud. Her body gathered, and chucked
into a wagon, with the doors pressed to
sealing the cries that pressed their shapes on them.
        A jolt, and the train started
its riding inward on a plain of snows,
black in a straight line, scissoring this blank in two
erasable and equal whitenesses.

Urine and fear; the fixed erasure over rails;
stench ravelled through hunger. Three days, round my watch.
Food, crammed in our pockets, as we had thought to,
outlasted by shared thirst and hunger. Neither heat nor chill,
stuck in the darkness fixed to earth that paused
over its sullen axis. Occasionally we halted.
Nothing. One further stop, the double note,
someone said, of a plane, many, encroaching.
We were bombed. After, the grinding on. I could see
nothing. My hand in another's, or my arms over her
as if dancing. Sleep, torn at length
by a last halt. Voices in German pulled
and pinned back doors, and she and I stepped through
a huge space, as I dreamed, of emptiness;
        with here, a bird, pecking

in snow by the svelte guards; their neat
white alpine station, the signal shut across our route.
The station-master in Austrian railway toque.
I thought that I must laugh. We showed our documents.
Barbed, through the snow the high dark live wire, staked.
Fear, my breath dense in me. I smelt
the crushed ooze in the hair of one, that gleamed
shell-like. I stepped back; struck me; stumbling
I thought
I have nothing to show.

The women were stripped before us on the snow,
whiteness skimming a whiteness, dazing me.
Running, as ordered; such election for
what might be seen; what could be seen I watched.
Some fell, with cold. I stood there, but one man
ran to a young girl. Laughter. A nod; the blow
let blood into the snow. Some girls were jabbed
to run, no breath to cry with, and they dropped
abruptly, caught in that soft uniform,
the prick drawn stiff against the trousered leg.
My mother was not seen, nor she I held
through darkness in the train. We were not notable
enough to sift in the first choosings from
this forced community of Poles, and Polish Jews
mixed in with those who sold us, but were yet
included with us. I was glad of this.
For as we were defiling to our huts
I thought I saw one man who lived a block
from us, and who, in hate, discovered us
to those cleansing the soft snowed earth of us.

We left, or dropped. One marched, searching the step
none kept. I could not quite touch her, as we,
too marked to try to seem unnoticeable,
were led, flanked by the guards, into our huts.

Some nights breathed in the shortest days. Air
speckled with carbon. Huts, inlaid with us

in double-layered bunks, continuously re-filled.
We were filed, by district, as though we were a map
sections of which, as the figures melted, emptied
the signs whose grid crammed tightly on more of us.

One night, blood between us. The knot stirred
and came away. She was gone with what
thickened in her. A space came
from a space. Then nothing.
Shalom, some cried.
I sickened. As she could, her mother nursed me; my own
cannot be spoken of. It breathes
into space, flecked with ash.
Peace, some said.
She got that. I shrank on my frame, and clung
to it. Her mother got my food to me,
as others watched us. She sat, touching me,
making flexible a body thinned
by the blood's loss.

An image of a ship sails, with two more,
milk at the salt prow, nearing. The sea
blinks; in its eye a tanker stretched off-shore
turns on itself away. I watched three ships
sail in through Christmas, wind churning the pier,
that flaps the sagging cloth. The masts slip bare.
Men with their bags step through the deck, and swing
onto the stone quay, past the figureless crane.
The hawser's taut, clinched at the capstan's iron.

These images being not deciduous.

STEIN
At times raw soil grazes my eyelids; I
need death to take my shape, a cleric that
might fasten me to it, or, possibly
the doctor's care. One touched me, once; I winced
in perfect health. One fractured the camp.

Each smiled. The first, with powders and advice
tended us. The other, with a rack
of probes, stared at the flesh never anaesthetised.
And guards made sure they had a health unflawed,
half-matt red, like rouge over onion skin.
The snowy bank sweats; smiling slits the heap
of shapely whitenesses, unfastening
the flesh. Formed by some blade a fistula
stops up the blood.
The mouth curves to its mirth. Extended wings
shrink, and the feathery flesh flails, and drops. Some
argued his skill. Flesh struggles, but it yields
a virgin figure of endurance.
He found its point, and did not move past it.
In terror the flesh split, with pain; and ceased.
Or was deformed, unskilfully stitched up.
One of them used up half an hour of pain
helped to her bed. And in my sleep an astral
shape gas-colours, flickering shabbily.
Changed beds. But then the guard discovering her
rising askew from it, beat her. The first five
lining the huts in coupled layers got beaten
every dawn. The blond intelligenced
vigour of the morning guard, my hair
silken as his.

A leaf appears to move
under the eyes. There is more

I told them. God was struck by this, suffering
imagination's growth. I think I glimpsed
a quizzical, wild thought pursing the mouth.
Once I saw how a guard, while shouting at
a boy, pulled from his tunic half a blackened
bread, passed him it, mouthing 'juden juden,
arbeit macht frei.' No one is sure. Some thought
God levered on an elbow painfully off
the floor. And those who on the noon's dot
walked to the chambers and did not walk back

said that the quick of Germany went still
and, listening, heard its cry. I heard nothing.

I stayed my mind over a heap of pistols.

What seemed the point was keeping the whole mind
intact, stopping the flesh from withering.
We were not so much to rat or to a thing
that wanted sustenance. I kept two cloths
as handkerchiefs white as I could, white as
is said a whale-bone is. Crushed flat and squared.
They were the whitest square inside the camp.
A tear has impulse, none there; a movement,
a moving out to work, falling to sleep.

But wasn't there, Kye asks, one person there
loved by another. In all this, she said.

The word is scrupulous, and has a hinge
with fear, fatigue, or boredom moving it.
True though. A man, holding together metals, stood
by a woman who bolted them, observed by a guard.
Sometimes in their work they touched. The guard
flinched as he saw this, sometimes hawked, and moved
away, or he would bash one of them. Both
endured the blow; each was of the same town
married in Catholic Poland. They were Jews
with black hair, deicidal.
In the camp there seemed not a second pair
more careful of each other, or, of a stranger, than
these two, aware, at any instant that an unfelt
chipping of care, some little blunting
of sensitivities eroded them.

They were a silent gathering-point for me.
A paired calculus of intent human
scrupulousness linked in our mutual drabness,
by which I, and others, I felt, could measure up
our actions, so, humiliate the self
by suffering the inequalities

of selflessness.
These two bore a seal of privilege, given gladly
despite the thread of equal fairness and unequal
needs common to us.
                              Once the guard found
her working alone; a dram lacking counter-weight
sunk in herself.
No rape; he offered her for her husband white
fresh bread; which she took and gave him.
He ate; it was white and fresh, asking nothing.
But just that portion lifted in him his flesh
a gloss above hers, noticeable to her.
She smiled; some muscle pricked over by a nerve
tensed her. She waited. And the guard approached
with more bread, pricing it. She took the bread
and not its price. He struck her, hard, over the mouth.
She, cupping it to her, dropped. No one was there
watching. This, also, her husband ate. She feels
the cells that once multiplied on hope use
and go from her, as on her arms he touches
the down greying.
Her upper lip grew thin, to him fragile as bone.
It came. A fixed proportion of us to stand
and line the chambers, while the rose sublimes
its shadows of zyklon. He heard, and she.
As she, her flesh weakening shaped her choice
and, as it shaped, chose her life, shading
hers from his. She lay still on her bunk.
Although as he smiled, rising carefully from
beside her body, held by her, she heaped
into a smile all that she could, softening
the face into as much of what they each
had felt. The shadow left her then; that smile
travailed its face for days, hovering like gas
on the mouth, on the eyes.
Such dreams, such exercise of abundance, cover her face.
That little life, Finn said, as if it could
have saved itself. You do not know, Kye answered.

But Finn is listening. Dust at the eye,

and dampened by it, smears its soft expanding
shape over the pupil, smarting it.

A second pair worked underground, and bolted
metal sheets, sleeping in the hut by ours,
as equally crammed and as consistently
sifted by gas. These two met in the camp.
No joy in her. She had coiled her hair, tying it
into a huge, fair, glistening knot, piled heavily.
Her left hand had no middle finger there.
She'd brought to wear a broad belt; buckled brass
hooped up a woollen, grey, stained dress. Round him
as he absorbed her gaze, the air went tight
and fastened him to her.
She had a child by him and it was dead.

No quickness, and no moisture; but a thick
vitality. She was alive, she loved him.
All of her face was thin, and like a cry.
She had a brother here, who hated him.

He had been picked out as gauleiter in
our group, choosing the Jews, a Jew amongst
more Jews; a scholar in authority
with no weight, queer with theologies
wedge-shapedly tapering to a blunted edge,
insensitive as less sharp. He sorted us.
He pre-arranged the sequence that we filed
the chambers in; some cried their needs, he used
a deft and moistureless logic for the queue.
He was in education, it was said;
able to calculate, an integer
of their device, recurring terminally.
He drew the good meat, queued by some hatch that
we did not line and, pliant as a limb,
food, pliancy, and reading melted him.

Smoke rises off the stacks; feathery soot
catches the wire. A man walks, hands catching

his thought between them. Guards rose, noiselessly,
strapped to their rifles. Those who had said 'no,
they would not go', were taken from there.
Some said his ledgering was correct. Gathered
among the next figures was Elsë. Her face
ached with vitality. Yes, she said, death.
It was that. She erased the name she loved
with hers, as the good signs
have it, where there are signs
to speak of.

He stood wiping his hands, his cap in them.
Passing she almost glanced at him. He stood
between us. No turn changed with hers.

        Her breath
pressed through us, and stayed
her in us

VI. Some Growth

KYE
1.
The moon disposes of
much fierce light, in sky
erupting desolately.

2.
My body and its shape
have no rectitude.

3.
And my limits are these

STEIN
Oh, for some natural
simple propriety

yes yes

From human rectitude
anthropomorphic beasts
work to be rid, and quit.

Yes.

The avocation of
complex and sensuous
imagery deforms

or, sensuously enacts
some subtler honesty.

At home such things thrive.
Domestic truthfulness
sardonic, compact, and pink.

The household turns on
its livid flies. Domestic
deformation clears
itself. Dross softly
falls through the air.

KYE

1.
Hair amasses. Thicknesses
root off the brain,
its shape,
its fineness; helmeting
the skull's bones.

2.
And he advances.
It is a gentle, a grave
absurd insistence, coming
to me, taking
my face in his hands.

Stein kisses
me over the mouth.

Not sex, not near it even.
Thankfulness glowing
from release.

The points of hair. The liquid dots of flesh.

3.
What meaning, Finn asks then, his tone cool,
dabbing the brush lightly, the touch, precise,
what meaning can this have? I did, he says,
and covering his voice the boy's small plea
which once I took for innocence in him,
I saw images of flesh; rightly
I suffered; isn't that sufficient? Must
I suffer them once more, unlike the dead?
They left, their pain died in them. Through no fault
but patience, we bear some of that in us.
What were we made for? My dead, touching me,
open my care, by right; and as I look
past Adam's shape, it is mine stares through him
at me. That is sufficient, it is all
the grief I need, as I can gather in
my hands to give him.

4.
STEIN

Your little child, as if he could take
his thread of injury, and hugging it
to him, creep off. We show the dead pure gifts
that, living, we did not offer them; our grief
come back is comfort to us. You could give
her love, or if not, gentleness, which is
respect dabbing the pain. So much of care
pressing the dead is simple. Even simpler,
the earth wrapping their flesh, its dampness
insinuating nostrils with a grub, – to scythe

flowers at the waist, that stem the granite vase.
Some generosity returns to us
and with love, disguises our own wounds
as we dress others'. Perhaps if I know this
the mind's not so in dalliance with itself
thinning a pure self to fragility.
The neglected spirit
                              suffering by you,
Finn asked. Yes, I said, promptly, and from you.

5.
KYE

Slowly this young boy put back what
little he had, with care, proffered.

1.
FINN

A voice, as other voices, stilled
by accusation; I find yet
something in me needs hearing.

Wales had me; and it was wet
over familiar stone. Town Hill
hastened my father down it. He flushed
bilges, as the ships came.
Work, indifferent to the peasant
over pitted hills, required him.
Ships vivid with rust cut
the Tawë, rustling ore. Fastened then
under the hill, off-ending
what smelters in South Wales got
and made pig of. The life we gathered
was round a rented table. It was mine,
I did not want.
Out, I begged it. I left my blate
originating root there.

Tarred wood amongst sea-flowers.

Love, oh my love
my gently abandoned roots

nothing in me like those
faces that lean through him

and no more of this.

2.
STEIN

She touched Finn's sleeve, but what was it she touched.

The modesty through Finn glances his cheek.

Yes it is possible, I thought. And felt
my form, touched with her care, increase: a small
insistent rising equilibrium.

She stood shortly, she turned from me.

And tough and lucid, formed
an independent shape.

I breathed night-musk the plants breathed out, which scented
the house. Dark, then,
touching our fear, crept rigorously
between branched spaces.
                                Childlessly the night
comes upon long legs, and puts both arms
over the house, with her placing cups
in our preparation turned
aside for a further thing.

A Shetland Poem

At Grobsness, a house
mild-visaged above the sea
had three floors; the roof
and its wood hold.

No other beams.
A minimum of elegance spared
in stone. Twelve slabbed frames
admit all that comes.

Dung stamped hard
onto the floor gorges
the blank mouth of the hearth.
The house fills.

A shelter for beasts
the best they may have had;
when we disgorged
from the steel cavalry, our crofts'

flesh thinned to
water and shards. Wasting
grasses spindled some wool
skeined loose.

The wind staggers itself.
With stone broadcast
on low peat slopes
touching water.

Child-absence, absence of women
and the dank flit
of beasts useless save
to the industrious visitor.

But by what we had
before, not worse;
and the slaughtered had not
this good dirt.

Shouldn't we have, by
a tally cut against nights
chilling inside the moon's
crubb★ of frost,

wanted, and got, more than
a pinched nissen hut,
fish, skin flayed, the storm's
goring shove.

The ribbed vessel, with sheep
was lifted, and jiggered
clumsily on rock; a creature
stricken beyond repair.

The doe of the sea.
We were not. But what we were
worked under hundreds
of moons icily lugged,

we were slow asking for.

We got from each laird
the fish's head, the crimson liver;
now we have the whole lot.
But less the dead

the depopulating
war, the multiplying thickness
of the Atlantic magnitudes.
Of the sun, a flake.

A pale ameliorating
glüd★★ quickening
the coil, in us it stiffens
and presses up in mirth.

The throat lusts for its oils.
Joy, joy – spills, and makes free.
We are going to drain, drain and crush
the spent beer-can.

Civilization eats out
the blood from the heart;
the laboured gratitudes
between us and earth

make a lace-tented shawl such
as our women excruciated from
threads marled round bitterness.

★ *crubb* circular stone wall within which cabbage seedlings are protected.
★★ *glüd* the glow from the lights of a town seen at night through mist.
Note The two glossed words are from the Shetland language which is in effect
Icelandic.

Three Shetland Poems

1[53]

In upraised hand, the stone house; its good father
and his flesh began their weakening. A monument
to cared-for-acreage – he leant
through his son, his words urging their release.

For his son they were legal; they were the will, codified.
He listened, his heart not in it. Prescience told him
these things will endure no alteration.

The farmer begged his child to be sparing
with breath. It was slowly done.

In the house a diligence of objects.
Ships replica'd, coin; layered sands in tubes.
And in one authoritative portrait, a dead woman.

The hair dankened.

Your mother, your two sisters; the house
of stone. Promise me you will keep intact
lathe and plaster. Let no maculation spore
any part of this. But, he said, in a smoky whisper
drawing off a little, pulling aside his son as if to command a secret,
promise me the most needful – that the mortar
be always skimming the house.

The son smiled, abandoning inwardly
his whole self to its shape.

He sifted the elation, through frost, from
Edinburgh's red stone. In Rose
street the ruthless abundance of waste, the patrimony
trickling in silvered filth along the gutters
of a street mantled with women's breath. A tiny
fish swimming in the island's hospitable voe, he watched
himself agog for the silver hook as it pierced
the dangling worm. He became his father's
whole life-time out-of-date.

2

If you had to choose, I asked her, which of

them would you have? One tongue, at least,
dickered upon the palate, the words,
like fish in a creel, packed on each other.

In the late summer, its small startling beauty
touching her hair, she answered. Their meanings
skeined together, her words were clear:

I would have both worlds.
But choice forced on me,
I would have the best of each.

Through air sloping past the voe, each still
thing seen, a car rode, and, altering its gait,
reclenched on a slow third; its exhaust
smutched the air, the fine machinery
breathing perfectly.

With a smile she turned from this. Walking up
the low slope, she re-entered her house, and took
to herself her solitary form.

In the summer wind, with no haste in it, the smile
dissolved, and the wind reflated earlier
contours of itself, its tress blowing
out over three miles of water.

3

Beside a precise, working model of the Unst water-mill
in a corner of the Shetland museum a man
was reading the sharp uncial Hebrew.

As a child, I said to him, as a Jew

He smiled. He closed the book trapping his
fingers amongst its pages.

The hammered tools of agriculture, commercial
and marine activity were pinned, and the integers
of work showed up. An odour from two
centuries breathing irreproachably.

He talked; he would detain me. There was
nothing in it. His words had little
purpose, either Jew or Gentile. Not uncial,

nor cursive, nor anything at all but the acts
of a man wishing to detain another. He shook
my hand. The skin was dry. When
he spoke, it was mild and nasal.

At five Saturday evening our boat moved
from Lerwick drawing thirty-five feet of water.

I could hear the man in the Lerwick museum
with salted, cursive breath, annunciating
Shetland.

Some Work[54]

1

Wide as a man crouching[55] pipes sulphur
a stained shore. In shelving brine
opening, clenching,[56] jellyfish squeeze day
with night: a handful
of electrics.

A tuft of mountain daisy
prods threads in knobby earth perching on what the plough cut
past, white and untoppled.

Two eyes search at the flower's.

The skull caps
its cells,[57] thread to thread. A brain
originating
declensionless.

With, sporadically, a twitch
of arrogance, sprung in neglect;
but no change in him, seen
a third time.

2

Distantly, the harebell tense
on one foot, clapperless, it wavers
through his eyes, spurts
of blue touching up
intense radial blue.

Seeing this much, his mind
endures a feeling recension.

A machine binds up crops.
Some wheats, and grass–stuffs.[58]

Birds gullet spilt seed.

3

Finds its way in. Sensitively the brain
ennobled by a chattering flash of muscle
working, droops, reminded of labour
it did and did;[59] the spirit inch by inch
its muscle cramping
on bone, humiliates.

Electrically tremoring, a bird shrikes
in the black, nearly frozen soil
its gold beak and jaw.

4

He minds again the labourer's
loth, merciful energy, that slices
clay for a green-topped root.

The stubborn life stubbornly
tugs out, lets fall, perhaps, flashing dispersions of creatures,
and braids

them together in work.[60]

Another's hands turn the wheel skidding
the machine through the brow's rim,
the field bulging with the hill's shape.

This shape, their work takes in.[61]

5

Each of us one fibre in what he braids.
Feels an aged stained clay skin rankling[62]
its flesh on us; a tithe of succour
from us gets offered.[63]

The light hesitating deliberateness
from old fingers, its hand, stained.

One might shrive a tenth; the act
squats in me:[64]
Do that again, it says.

Yes, the flesh repeats clearly, I will.

6

Hands, the hands. Salted grease on
the wheel held still whatever that
protrusion, stone, lump, gnarl of root, frail skull
he hits,[65] slurring over.

Dragging the hissing plough
about from the hill's
jagged crown into the rejoicing
bedded broad stretch of loam
foliating spiked oats.

The work, though, the hand:

Have done, it cries, jogging the hoe;
finish up

Three Poems about a Settlement

1

I picked up a stone
in the settlement, planted among
trees in an oblong;
sounds brushed onto them touched
the intricate vague mind.

Between trees, some young, or fallen
and partly buried by grasses, I fetched up
a flat stone with marks.
It heartened me. I felt relief
that it had, shaped by hands
and incised on,
come through.
What did it read, in words
gouging a vouchsafe
over bed, or fire?
How shall I
be communicated with,
now, here, between trees? A further scratch
might be enough,
a meaningful incision meant
to show up lastingly.

2

Finding the settlement
and lying in it.
'It lets us' you said.

A friend not known by you now dead.

By us, a reservoir.
Birds' cries, touching.

The ditch is amulet
circling the hill. Water or blood, away in it.

Once though; that is not known. Once

lust, cold stone; and a few cries
violent with smoke. An intruder
is bashed. And the cry
craves its self
rushing from it.
A dwindle of blood. The bird
hops and sinks.

Amongst trees, and a herd of geese,
those, from unnatural causes, now dead,
patched a life
in flocculent snow.

Militia, the linked, harrying
mail of this kingdom
skimming the earth to break
into fine separate grains
the upturned bands of soil
weaken, dechain, and sink
under the plough.

A chain of mail, harrowing the earth,
left the earth.

How much
forward do we look?
I asked you.

3

Haste is two roaches, darting
onto the carpet; one
with belly swollen.
Mice nest in the foundations, and pitch a shrunk language
our voices weave through.

Can anxiousness
wean itself?

We are moistened, under trees
by each other, in this settlement.

The stone was flaked to shape, placed, and clustered
a group of heads over
the newly-born.

The breasts' filaments glisten
with milk, and the cry for milk.

But this went, as it does, violently.
Fractured blood is a ditch
full of it, let
by soldiers, with their reasons.

For what? Yet despite this,
an Aenean moment, elate
and suppurating fear.

From between trees hedged by stone,
nothing, no, something: a man
bent, streaming from here with, under
his arm, in skins, a package

that wails. Which is seamed
in the creases, each with terror, to the man
clutching blindly another's child,
running with life

THE PRINCIPLE OF WATER   415

The Malabestia

Malabestia (thus the present name of the village Acaster Malbis, by York) was the name subsequently put onto Richard of Acaster. His actions were an off-shoot of an incident in York which is, despite the City guide-book's coy paraphrases, fairly well-known. In 1190, when Richard I was crusading, barons used the king's absence to erase their indebtedness to the Jews of York by the direct method of slaughter. They stirred up anti-Jewish feeling to the extent that the Jews took refuge in Clifford's Tower. They were offered safe conduct if they agreed to conversion, and some few who took that risk perished. Not all of these few, however, since three Jewish women got free, and were baptised. The majority of the eight hundred, however, rather than test the citizens' promises, committed collective suicide. Finally, Richard of Acaster, who was one of the indebted barons, killed the three women, afraid that he might otherwise be forced to fulfil his debts on the king's return. The women were mourned by the local community which regarded them, at least nominally, as Christians.

I

1

At twenty water sinking in me crossed
my flesh;
my soul ramified
into some huge dove, quaking hugenesses
of air
along the North Sea's watery nausea:
a central and preposterous saltedness.
Its sullen magnitudes touched me and flared,
then slid back. My curved woman's flesh
by spiritual fingering was worked
like lace the church refines its edges in.

Grease moistens lowering eyelids; the Lord watches.
Let him; the tenancy is his; I am.

2

A blank quietness shading foliage
circling itself; a circular morass
of pond with-out. Mud adheres the flesh.
The principle of water stirs through it.

Mud is not much. Placidities of it
collate the still-life in its vacuum,
digesting three lives. The end
came and lay still.

II

1

The naked Malabestia. Wild garlic savours
the church area. Stumbling inside.
In wood, in marble, and, with death, their image
focuses into beatitude.

Baptismal life, sloughing its dried skin,
the paid up souls out from their stone row squawk
in whiteness to an upper clarity
not much fashed with who water a lent soul.

Others go on, renting fecundities
of land glacially flat; who have in fee
stone on it, ale-houses, corn, pigs, and men
let out to hoe the soft muck thickening
an arable. Their strips of northern work
induce a fertile lot. The spider hid
in the grave's corner bells death's quivering sharp
maternity over the life we have.
Some power goes on; marble and wood die off.

2

The Malabestia, naked. Wild garlic, stiffening
the penitential air, its rural church
is bolted, until
the crinkling blare notated for the ear
the dead use, opens it. My Lord: Doomsday.

Get up. The bones clink, and the heaven-forged clasps
fastening them, thud rustlingly onto
dank clay. And what remains of screwed board
squeaks as this resurrection, with force
not imaginable to the flesh,
erects the Malabestia's progeny
into a detailed everlastingness
of what they did.

III

1

Eight hundred Jews in York, fearful of Christ's
demoniacal laity. Labouring men,
with splayed stubby palms,
offer on secular hands baptismal rights
in everlastingness, with temporal
extensions *gratis*. Worth considering.

The church gapes, this impure plenitude
promised it.

The Jews won't. All that church-space gets its breath,
and stone grinds its pure habitude again.

2

Love, oh my love, cut in me, here – slitting
the bleb of flesh, one blade
was beloved by us all.

In common preciousness, the righteous blood
heaps off the mound perching the tower we are in.

Three Jewish women accede baptism
and slip free. Judah's blood liquidifies
the earth since inured to it.

3

Water sprinkles on us; the ceremony
gleams through our hair. Not a drop stays.

Grace reaches for our minds, but thankfulness
releases us. Mother, what is death? Sullen

stillness. Two Gods melt my soul and link
their wraths together in it into one
central and pressuring displeasure.

IV

1. What the Malabestia do

Gentleness moves in wools, and pity is
naked in furs. Thus they tread, their dress
fearful for its riches. Much afraid
my father's patrimony, that the king
did not stoop for,
will accrue to me.

The Malabestia have debts. Who cut
the life ties up the purse strings. Let that come,
if it will. The Malabestia, who might
but will not hunt the gentle hare, and tug
its body quiveringly through the hands.

The gentle hare, the Malabestia.

He nears, closely the blissful sun unfolds
and draws the eyes that get and turn this light
back on itself. The knife thrusts and sticks.

Baptismal life shrieks to his God, our flesh
is thrust away.

                    Prayers of wood
are said by rote. And beads told off, greasy
with fingering, these soaked in paint slick
with unceasing use. They hiss in tallying
over the wire, clashing the farther end,
beads on abacuses, bearing our souls
in flight across the penitential wires,
fingered by spiritual men. The beads
rest between fingers, but the souls in them
are elsewhere delicately acquired, and tagged.

Our bloods flow; steeled in christian terror
we divide the mud clinging us.

2

My failed desertion, my gently abandoned roots,
oh my love, where are you; if that
is not presumption since
we have not met still. I'll draw on
my self my failed
desertion to meet one God with.

One God, in one sufficiency.

Being Christian, might he conclude
my brief soul, levied over death?

Ah my dear father, my blessed God,
since you are he,

would it have cost you so much to have raised
me in your arms, and brought me, dead, that brief
and necessary distance, to your room?
Its moderately gentle space commends
a sprig naked between my breasts. You did
not place that shape there, just the space confined
itself. A sullen pungent odour breathes
care in the mind, of which love presses from it
renewing much. What space, what terse delays?
Care, oh my love, prompting a fingering
of mercy. May my first God see to this?

It Says

Thinking on my life under
the smoked glass, I come near
its substance. As a man watching
another scraping light
off grass, dropped by the sun
across it. As if
he very carefully thought
which blades he should not
deprive. So that each time
I brood, it is not on
my own love, or another's
merely, since I touch
now, even, the fiction which
in the Talmud speaks
of how a man each night
works at the book. This is permitted.
And each night, his wife
attends him, but not just
because she does not read
the Hebrew. It does not
say if this married girl
is beautiful; each night,

the book insists, this man
brailles at the Hebrew's uncial
text. Here, the story slightly shifts:
it is another night. His wife
weeps lightly, so lightly it is
neither against him nor
upon the Talmud but
for her lacking him.
The Talmud hardly speaks
more, but, as if sun
closed up, momently,
a few scraps, a few
hesitations in grammar, adding
that for the tear she dropped
the man dies.

There Are Four of These

1 *Persisting*

As the rounded skin lews
seven clustering berries fruit
a yew's branch-tip.
Fastened to wood, whose sap
slows through fibre, they offer,
by inches wintering through
the year curving from sun,
a fireside the mind
absorbs warmth to the cold
sore lesions by. I took
into me their jovial
separate reds the banked
country road was lit
from hedges by. I was glad
for their distinct warmths, not
their offering, but that I
might take, and never let

each bag of tough fruits
know why I wished to.
As if misery
healed very slightly.
I did not stay, but such red
is cordial in me;
I saw, as I years
since opened this fruit, small
silkily combed seeds
in white nylon-like threads
distinct and oilily
together nestling.

2

In the lane, dangled berries
of yew ripening a pink,
a lit cheerfulness, as leaves
on the chipped stone sprinkle.
At length, the house,
cut in Palladian
with, for twenty years, life
not forming in it. My eyes
take no comfort from this
and stare at its huge
empty modular.
Only as
half turning, the red,
the whitened red and lit
ripening of berries, as if
hallucinatingly
across my eyes. As though
looked at, and wanted
to be looked at, and touched;
lightening in cold a pink
and clustering cheerfulness,
their bulb-like warmths a consenting
illumination among
unlively greens, specked brown, with dubiously

inactive earth
topping Northumbrian
stone jammed deeply
over a central, molten,
slowly turning
point of crucial fire.

3

The house climbs up and spreads
its taste into the year.
'my hands, my hands' he said
staring on them, and then
over his lord who watched
his hundred workingmen break
their stone out of his rock.
He had his craft; they had
their labouring gratitudes
helping starvation.

Harmless as a winter tear
the red berry outgrows
strictures of windless frost.

The yew-tree here bares its fruit.

And I am glad of the shapely
heat the mind picks
of these seeds past need
of sun, or care that would
develop between them.

And by them,
two onions sprawled in grass
rotund and sensual,
nestling contiguously.
Who came here, and who put
them here to take the frost's
notched teeth?

Mildness that dews, deforms
in mildews of grown frost.
On glass, on breath: out from
the wood, in spores, bedding
two iron distances.

A locomotive sweats
and whistles: the forward sign,
which is 'enter the junction
triangulated under blue
incessant lamps.'

Northumberland, Northumberland.
The pain, that pain.
'Take it away from me'
you said.
            I am not capable.
That of me which derides
the match flared carefully
or, not even flared
on studs of glued sands,
moves with less warmth to reach
the practising wound inside you.

In Islington, you cover
your floor, where your father
is not, and you live by
the practising, continuous
warmth searching the forms
of reciprocity –
of which it is all you
and not me, and which bares
my hand upon your breast.

Northumberland, Northumberland.

Filaments of wind;
a tarred and plucked sea;
the berries, the fruit, and warmth
hung from a yew-tree, each
disfigures and joins into
an image of madness giving
no warmth and crept onto
by frost that coughs inside
the street-cat's throat.

Disposed and windless
strictures of frost;

your four limbs fold
in sleep's thicknesses.

Come away, come away

Isaiah's Thread

1

Cry. What shall I cry: flesh is grass.

The billow stiffens; the wheats are no longer supple.

Whom are we to send? One we relish
as fresh image of us; he can petition
the little widower.

Then I said, here am I; send me.

The almighty Father, Prince of the grazed fields.

But I saw the fly, its life webbed.
And crouched on its alphabet a voice, crying,

shall the axe boast against who hews with it.

Go go go, it said. I flew into the earth's rim.

And grew cautious. No indeed, I answered.

2

The lion sniffs the moor's hair; straw-specked wind
upbraids saplings into the trout-mouthed voe.
Out, it said.

What shall I cry? Cry. Why must people by people
be torn?

Yes, I said.

I undid my hand, and fastening to it
a stone dilapidating from a house, crouched
in the grass's time.*

I was astonished. Shall they abuse
the creature melting through the field.

I waited with open eyes. Men automatic
with rifles defiled singly across
the fragrant and depopulating croft.

It is a question, I said, of love, and gripped the stone.

The fly will be appointed, the sweated ox;
and a furred leopard, over the kids it has pastured.

Lie together, grin, creep, pant, assemble;
convene the kingdom.

* *the grass's time* – Jon Glover's phrase.

Unpublished and Uncollected Poems,
c. 1974–1976

'Where much grass drinks from its side'

Where much grass drinks from its side, Shap's hill, an unbearable
                                                                    figment
of lake pushes against its roof, grassy desire. Shap stacks granite,
is trod by blackish crows; and streams, whose reeds prick the
                                                          portioned-up spaces
these dispersions collide, twine. The streams don't conform to
                                                    the land's puckers.
Constant to their pressures, and weight, which drag them into
                                                            the earth
but for stones they have floated, and then dropped in a cleft
furred, lumpily brown. Worn off. Bog cotton and peat are the
                                                          fruits, acids
of rock only a bit mouldered into soil, held by grass knitting it
                                                    up. Sheep crop
with a mildness that feeding, without stop, turns voracious.

That rock is not conscious of itself or of anything other than itself.
The stream probes lumps off the hill; the hill drains itself of
                                                            water; grass
coheres soil in its system of roots that is indifferent to it; crows
                                                                  magnify
above water. Alight, feed, shit, are black. Darken the darkening
                                                            air.
There is no thing here. Not quite though. I stood off the road,
                                                          moving
into a hollow that was dug. How else was the space made?
A sheep with two horns, crumpled, but pointed out, stared
not hostile absolutely, its horns at me. As I moved to
the road again, it was sufficed, turned its head once more,
                                              watching; trod uphill then;
white, territorial; inside a ringed oiliness, a wool coiled like
                                          hoops of muscled electrodes: a strength.
Belongs here, dies, here. Then's pecked, torn, chewed in balls of
                                          woollen meat in a bird's crop stocks.
Out, shat.

The river Tawe muds banks which a factory's struck up.
A shed of metal sheets clangs. Nothing's in it; the air it can't
                                              hold. Its girders, bare. Rails
incline into tarmac that thins. The Tawe ablutes
manufacturer's sediment, the body's dilations, beyond saturation.
Can't expel much. Worms fuzz the mud. Plop. A fish
squirms in chemicals diluted by the Tawe once fresh, the sea not
                                                      fresh here.
Bricks pale. Nothing is here that lives, yet all is humanly made,
                                                      stood up.
The lives are discontinued. No bolt, because of no door. Metal
                                                      walls
part from their girders. Clang again. Not much stays.
I step on Tawe's banks built up in brick, then concreted;
two piers extend the stream into the sea, [accoursing]⁶⁶ it that it
                                              gets there. A surety.
Where are the men for this, their boats
Glendaver, Lord Boyne; trawls, chains; a net; berries thorn by
                                                      the wall;
the brown, grey sea froths slightly, as Tawe's skegged mud
         pollute the salt broth that works the bedrock it swooshes on.
The gulls scream: clean fish, a mate. Splatter rocks washed into
                                  hygiene by the sea's moonly neap.
Ha ha amongst the mud. Coated. But not sunk much into.
There is the Galbraith's tanker working American oil to the core
                                              of his anus.
His ship seems not much to like humans, spewing out, clearing
                                                      itself.
Cash, carry; the cleanse. All on board's this way.
Clang. The shed are falling off that are not now used, where
                                              grain came
for the millers. It's now Swansea. English to the willing Welsh.
                          Conquering bathers;
since once they had a tithe of Welsh bones, they shall gorge now
Welsh haunches whose cunts wrinkle in nationless passion.
You can stuff your lardybread, cock. Who said this? Where is the
sorrow some could weep its purity into the Tawe and not have
                                                      it tainted?
The launderesses weep on the banks because they have no

                                        sorrow to weep for.
Therefore, they are lonely. Therefore their grief, isolated from
                                                    sorrow
without intimacy, and with no depth
of object to be miserable about.

'The map hovers open'

The map hovers open, whose slender
memory, the lute,
twists in its sharp disposals, like
a lemon squeezed into the mouth,
plucks her father.

The cloud of longevity
scuds into Owyhee.

The other's sister entails
a husband,
the worst man on earth.

Bluebells silence the woods
from which children spill
mauve hair.

The Little Time-keeper

First published by MidNAG/Carcanet Press, 1976

Gifts Against Time

– Ella Pybus

1

On the insufferable flesh
over the creeping haulms, light

gauzes with saffron; and the limping soma
yields its psyche. The petite desert woman
crouches;
death's parched foetus.

Vulnerable hand-maiden, stay.

2

Who stays? In abundance
torches of sable light, in pustules soot
on the dump of after-life.

The livid melancholy of fat.
Extinguish
the greasy flambeaux, death stays.

3

Spiritual contusions:

serpent of roots, whose stung shape
writhes upon the earth lashing
with the prowess of miracles.

Be Moses: throw light on the wriggling bronze
over rock divine with water;
get memory quick with pictures
for our aching forms. I take

responsibility for
the fleshy images
I bring with me past death.

Four Poems, One Northumbrian, and Three of the Hebrides

Borrowing Light

Earth, borrower of light. The rural institute's
fly-blown low-watt bulb spots the congregation
no root
for them. Tedium of earth, frustration
of bitter dahlias. Milk's sour breath deforms
by day the meadow's rim, the night's tense pupillage.
Their fly-blown memory is a lighted corm.
          Donor of light. Rank silage
laces the voids, shoe seizes its numbed foot.
Milk runs udderless, and the dawn defines
spillage of light, with frost ferned over cold soot
as bird-like sleep wakes in the long beams of the mind
its darker life folded in consciousness.
Prophecy is an ear coiling on entropy,
a bird receiving news with a thin lilac cry
rankled and stained by the physicist's black fly:
truth grooms with listless hands its darkening stuff.

In the Place of Absence

Winter's burnt light. Islands of stunned hills
in Gaelic smokiness; the calvinist spills
a bony lava of ill-natured prayers.

God of voids hanging in silence; human years
sweat and distill; an oaten sustenance
mottles with earth as memory despairs.

No leavening weight, of sand or flocculence
to make the peat bear up the joined barley's light
spiked granary of demands, no long-thighed elegance

rustles the nerve. Libations of potash; grain
the fibrous mind to dust it has been led to feign
expectation of. Harvest's undulation

silk fish sprawl the quay, stars forge the night again
whose exile's passage tilths the screwed milk of the sea.
Lift up the veined bay in lamentation

in consciousness; it's grief distaffs the hair, mother
of sons. Squid sea, marble and indigo
of loneliness. The town's plantation sows

magnification of pain. Huge elisions pass
through the eye-rimmed sea.

The Hungers of Commerce

A minister's watch-chain hugs the cloth's paunched grain.

Where the wing rises to the gun, by harsh decoy,
an income is stuffed, like a spiked ear of rye.
The spirit's mash distills
the visitor's mind, ghostly and lyrical.

Raise up the kneeling deer. Bewitch the seas, and hoy
fish off their winged nets; the hotel's stormy pots
tint with salt blood of fishermen, that spilled
like lentils, like crabs and prawn mashed in the sty
of watery commerce
under the moon's tug, on the belly's tide
the wave's considered battering;
obstreperous needles stitch the tweed seas brushing Skye.

Weighing Out Loss

Fortune weights
to earth two heads, coppery
ill luck

on lilac hills.
I hug the sacked peats I'll
lift

humped
to Lewis's malicious pibroch. It
opens Seaforth, first

of the earth, onto
Monsterless broken seas:
the Hebrides.

My tongue names what's
a whole lack

the supple magnetisms
of the thigh: to whom, to whom but
wind could I

offer my stunned prophecies?
Down the gangway bent the foot's
emigrations my

body cast
off its shades, and bespoke my drunk
   phoenix exiled,

   on the boat, of loneliness:
in the dense estate of the Glasgow
   plantations

blood's the slighter tie of warmth.
   As at the first, was

I done for in the plummet isles.

Australian Poems

Tolstoy's Brother Plants a Green Stick in their Estate at Yasnaya Polyana. It Has Happened Before

The woods at Yasnaya Polyana.

Eyeless leaves
rustle their neighbours' faces. Sough.
Sough: the wind. Tolstoy's brother
plants his green stick.

'If ever you find
this carved secret, Earth
will have greened a Paradise.'

Green, green.

Black men, abiding their wilderness,
scorch the defoliated, wriggling grub.

Whitely the ferry chunters us
between bays. In oiled dispersions
of wateriness we sprinkle to our rest.

The cut religious stick fades
among first plantations. Wind heaves.
Wordlessly, it vanished, bearing
what the hand gave, of brief warmth.

O supple Paradise. Integument
prime as our mother's breasts
folding milk.

The pouched marsupial intelligence,
its care, its teeth, stained with grass,
its leap to the peaceable kingdom, that,
that and not other thing, where is it?

The greening of a cut, wordless
Australasian stick. Wind lifts
like a huge leaf. Lovely questions
foliate the Pacific.

Sydney 1974

Jarapiri[67]

1

Mama-boijunda: the spider cries
from below ground, Boohë, raising
life through earth.

Wanbanbiris, people of wood-gall
Latalpa, snake, and the death-adder Wala Wala women
blind husband-snake Jarapiri Bomba.
Wife Jambali, tugging her sons.
Each to the haired spider's word.
Scorpion Garangara pincers his itching prongs.
Our pleated feet cling
to the centipede, Jirindji.

Spider re-enters earth. Splintered
shale his legs, excreta
soft round stone in a heap.

2

Grass rests the two women, by whom
fire, lapping twigs; the waterhole flares.

Graspable, Jarapiri lies, huge
and toxic. Wanting him, they creep
through dried grass, like mice.

Jarapiri listens
to what is heard:
dry grass fastens to him.

No, no, he cries. No,
coiling himself,
his length fanged.

3

Jarapiri Bomba, blind, created blind.

What can an eyeless snake? The eye
attends to the dancing with voices tuned
for life's increase. So be it. Bestirs, coils
slithers to the dressed plain, where flesh
supplicates. Blind, but not deaf.

Can keep step, but cannot keep place;
trips, throws each dancer. Blind Jarapiri.

You fracture
our dance. Quietly, we
steal our life from you, since no entreaty
begs you home.

Wives, children, praise wetting their lips, all
evacuate the plain. Heat
of fire shimmers the vanished feet.

Silence calls out.

I die of loneliness.

4

We grasp our journey and walk. Jukalpi
the hare-wallaby, the egg-swollen women;
lice drip from the wood-gall.

Haunted by two women, Jarapiri
will you coil and sulk? 'Old creature,
we'll hale you by the head.' So say
each of the sons, raising him. Jarapiri
lifts his wife.

5

How else divine how sand-hills, and the snaking creeks,
otherwise became? The sand plains
'clothed with eucalypts, spinifex
and the desert oak.' In nakedness
we make friends with an odd-faced land. The tale
unfolds at a touch.

Strange nocturnals gather the air.
The little birds shriek from their branches.

6

Poxed with beasts, the white schoonering men
unlimb our myths.
We have no figures for this.

Sydney 1974

Honey and Tobacco

1

A flat disc of earth. Light, dripping
work, the sun burrows through tired ground;
travels by night through musk
of she-fern, ochre, milk-stone, and oozes
on the cavern's face black light.

The Rainbow Spirit coils there
harder than the baler shell. Be still.

The moon gets up, and the Saucepan
pours out black milk
from which stingrays, turtles
and fish – quick, tomorrow finds them.
The spirit child chooses, swells
the woman, whose pain scatters
armsful of sparks frost hardens.
The spider Mamu-boijunda, upon
two hands: cries like an owl.

Honey and tobacco: the good and bad meet
and our child thuds at its opening. Croo,
croo fans the spider's howl. Sun
raises herself. Quick, where
male fern and woman fern spore in dew,
gather dew's liquid in sweep of the bowl.
Water for the child, and woman, quick.
We tread north between tree-ferns.
Our forefathers' spirits, painted
in the same rock, get praised
and kept in their place. Shark, turtle,
sustain us at the sea's edge. The disc
slops in its compass. No change;
the Dreamtime, perfect time of our Creators,
touches us, moves from us

1790. A year of conviction
for two apples, bruising the hold
the lowest bid contracted.

Calvert, Camden, King: onlie begetter
of us thousand fleet-winded
by our dear Lord's grace,

the tracks are Cooke's. Sydney's shore
inlays with brine, and the soft
judicious sandstone heat chews.

Wait. A hundred as good as dead
from food or its want. Stench
waylays the jagged rat: feed on us.

I touch our child, where nothing was
is something. Your flesh is coral
live with sweat, the sweet honeycombs

the strong. *Calvert* and *King*
paid to transport us, was *Camden*
bought to deliver us?

Save us, we beg: curved through
our flesh is the Earth's
fear at our axis. Listen

the prow's hiss subdues; Mary, hold
your milk to you, our child
is dead. Two-fifty dead

is the makings quarter us. Raise
us to the earth. Three

salt canvasses of their charge
wilt at their poles – a withered heap.

Off the shore, Commerce
evicts our dead.

3 *Mary is told Population is riches*

Property is theft; but some theft,
some taking back of earth's property...

the aching human form turns
through its flesh 'to God'. Ah
for such honey we dance
backwards who for our country probe
the sweet from the bitter. Gold

in England's Austral sun, our labour
combs another's sweetness; the grub
half-starves amidst honey.

Property is riches; what
is more property? When the white ships knocked
upon sandstone, all was poor.
'Copulate,' they said
opening the iron from us:
the rhyme breaks.

Fireside of the cove. Men fight
for us, women
suckling with gin the infant
desire for men's one possession, Woman. Begin
then we cried. The women
derived rum from the ships' masters,
feeding that, then their thighs; and withal
we come to it. Fire blows dew
off stone, this early day.

A kangaroo leaps
in its distance.

4 *The wanting*

Will we have a child, Tom, a second child?

My breasts so tendered with milk that touched
they'd burst. I am marsupial
and our child's mislaid in my belly. Find me.

Three-masted schooners stiff with drink,
their twanged rigging's the tarred voice
of Port Jackson. Even such music conceives.

Let her manage. My breath comes salt,
my soul's vapour on the quay grits
of crystal the sweated workshoe scrapes.
Drowned again, be under no man's foot,
I'd breathe my salt contagions through their flesh.

The thefted pastures lie
fat with the lambs of God.

The little birds shriek from their branches.

I thank God and ever shall
it's the sheepe has paid for all.

5

Earth gives: and the fruitful sheep stuff
the grazier's eye; desert grudges
its spidery paths. As black men grimace

the white creature tilths his furrow. By water
fluffed wattle dots the air. Here the black
tears his portion: 'a white child

enters our woman, water laps up
the white man, and the shark eats.' Mary
with second child white as a plaited loaf.

Passion turns over the lovely earth,
and ships fleet under the arc whose steel
barters train for train. 'Grace us,' we ask,

'span us.' Surely. We sometimes ask for
sometimes desire the contrition grace nulls.
Who, us? In separate sentences

we moisten our breath with theirs. Whose
selves darken? the bay with sun splinters
and blessings of a kind glance the white man.

Is it our sullen-hung selves numb us?
The grinding wheel unrolls tracts
of the New Earth; with forked lamentation

scorpion and snake twitch their insulted
flesh from our rubbery mileage. Give me.
Give it me. The flat unchanging earth.

Sydney 1974 – Newcastle 1976

Note to 'Honey and Tobacco'

For Australian readers, the few factual references may seem patronising.
When the white men landed on the Austral continent they met with
Aborigines. Whether or not the land is now shared, it is viewed very
differently by black and white man. The poem attempts a bi-partisan
view. The first section offers an Aboriginal view – of the flat unchanging
earth. The last section collides the white man's round view, and its asso-
ciated ideas of progress, with the black man's flat unchanging version of
the earth. Section two names *Camden, Calvert and King*, a London firm
which offered government the lowest tender for transporting the second
(1790) shipment of convicts to Australia. Since in the contract no stipu-
lation was made by government that the convicts should be delivered
alive, the transportation became murder.

South Africa's Bird of Paradise Flower

In flower it is an idea of self
as bird; two nacreous tapering ears.
Nothing tappers in them. No hammer and no drum.

The neck flexes. Its cerise bird's-head
gouts its juice. It colours cerise.

Its ears plume. The head is a lower jaw;
the upper beak, a spindle with blue flanges.
Why no matching? Five rivets stud
and pair this creature to its under-half.

It unfolds deception. Two plumes listen,
and a silent beak emits lucent gum.
In Africa the black skin is black.

Not two plumes now, but swells, and pricks
a further pair, a second violet beak;
two birds rejoice over one neck,

and the body replicates huge leaves.

So fine the mode of words is its ghost.

The flower is its first idea. Rammed with
so much of itself, it furthers other selves

that multiply. And will not take flight,
rooted in austere bright irruption.

Sydney 1974

The Excellence of an Animal

A sombre cat outstares
mild food, and that absorbs
the tentative black cat.

Your cry – its calculating
delicate balance of abandon

connects: your jaw fangs
with milk white hairs.

All your excellence has left you.
That is not true. Footprints

tacky with life pursue
their owners. Winter noon

strikes through its brilliance.
You are a black leaf

the pavement steps over.
Maythorned or grimed the car's

grim elegance consumes
the road, with a barely

apprenticed transfiguration
of lust two people quench

in the gear's change. The straight
road hits you; his woman's

moist basis transfigures
the breast's fleshy compassion.

We prised open your mouth, and there,
a little drench of blood
between the tongue and the palate.

Cat. Cat. The small head
eats out sight, as winged fleas

quit their host: as sin drips
from our dead.

All creatures with their ghosts

in any form, bring
yourself free of the wheels

Alive

Up trots the cat, and on
the bed three spokes array
a rimless wheel; and if

your mother's gone, softly
the radials of her care
dispose you; it is hard

to sleep, and hard to abandon
the mind's lucidities
stained to its under-self.

What is it? Candlewick
in your hooked claws; sleep is
a snapping of night's threads.

A bird cries, and worn flesh
refreshes in worn sheets.
Embalmed by sleep, allowed

our life by it, your gaze
raises its agate qualmed
with milkiness and stares.

Impudent pissing cat,
licking its penis that
is a bud tapering,

a soft barbed thorn, you are
alive in forms that cram
their sustenance through you.

The Polish Girl

The moon never
had amnion, but of parent
    ripped

    herself; your walls
chalk with pain. Nubile and single,
    your face steel

    and lightness.
Your father Polish, your mother
    a space:

    a waterfall
of hair is your roots. Bride
    without groom

    whose fingers 'd raise
bloom on your loosened thighs;
    how should I know?

Your smile opens
care; though skeined with no groom
you shall

lust and
none of me suffers
your bloom.

The skin tells it; take
joy with thirsting. Skein

and braid water

and may the hands, may those
that braid the fall, probe, and be mobile
as the soft waters of Poland.

We Use the Language

Paired leaves, sprinkled with rice
and a black mouth,

Nature's dish. Mamma, what
is it? On the thatches

smoke the Portuguese.

A scream in ashes, tumescence
of gnarled blood
resists the thorny insect.

Ash drips, a deliberate
smoky unmanning of body. Go by:

cradled in her open belly
the half-born child, its valve of breath
pulses with labour.

The word 'portuguese' in English
translates as 'ally'.

Blessèd language, O blessèd be it. Cover
the bits of flesh

bring within the ribs of your word

gently my dear father
my gracious Lord, with much tenderness.
Like a leaf.

Again

Friend, the blackbirds words, they dart 'wheep-a-wheep, wheep'
                                  so high up

not sufficing.

We have not met still, aren't about to.

The word I can't say
is, the waste.

And I don't.
Why did we never meet? the right
word, placating pain. No:

but the word admitting
your grief was correct

therefore acceptable.

Dead within
your own hand.

No, it's not true;
not the wrong pain, not, either, the just pain.
The pain.

Through the space I will
not pass, a few words

unacceptable, unbidden.

Who is to come to you?

Yes

Abundance hoped for of
the springs, off which the heart
glebes sharp, hard water. Breath
through a heartless earth comes
heathery, carbonic. Dress –
get dressed by nine; our car
flows to the Registry.

Few ceremonied words
civic and unchurched: two
breaths wrapped our single forms;
marriage's double yes
effective terse and ringed
is the bare copular
of two assents. Bare flower,
tough willing alpine plant,
I hope. Springs that withdrew
as if to heft a fresh
gout of pure water braid
and steer onto the plains
benignant and alive.

The Plum-tree

Our grave spittle covers his face.
Afraid I insult my God
of my poems I'll say little.

We married in late winter.
Mild as a pear, whose succulence
lured its priest. Yes, I said,
I believe; and miracles
balanced on pumiced hands. My door
glided shut.

I speak of the six million
and do not shave; no iso-rhythmic
evenness of mind temper
the blind compliant ratchets of industry;
and for the earth I work off, I earn
how much? We consider, and feed
the excellence of three cats.
When the sun undoes its pure,
fierce hands, I talk with the plum-tree
in the dene where mild limestone
kneels to the ice-floe. The tree's
incipience of fruit makes plump
the maidenly flowers: to what is torn,
wrenched, shot, or beaten, it can bring
nothing.
The dene's light crumbles. Of no use
if beauty affirm the techniques
work anneals; and, what droops away
is beauty as consolation – in the flame
work is of cash drudged for.
Barren are the plum-tree's flowers
fleshed as they glisten.

Two Images of Continuing Trouble

Fountains Abbey

'For Christ' the rose stone avers.
Chaos of snows. Poured milk
of disharmonious stars.

White thongs in white commandments.
Like masons we cross our roof
in fixed devotion; which is

prayers' ideologue, image
of man changed to his praying,
the abutment to God's fleet[68]

northerly hail. Shepherds pray
God come in gentleness.
The Crook forms its own question.

And it is gone; leaves clog
the chiselled epitaph.
The Cause pleads for a wreck.

The vanished crown flows
in dull rose to the earth
and stone gives the shepherd

to the face of coal. Do prayers flock
and cringe in the flaked
snowy vortex? it's as,

my God, you said it would be.

A Prayer Cup

As if steel, but a silvery
tar creeps upon Isaac
in Abraham's hand. Our Bible

is clasped in darkness. And for wine
three inches of the blood
of six million. The cup

wells Hebrew, and my grandparents
have tracked their kind into
the lake over-flowing

our curious feet. I who write
a factious poem want the means
to bless a christian. Breath

from the two locomotives *Work*
and *Freedom* steams over
the numbered faces.

Arbeit macht frei ('Work makes freedom') mottoed the camp gates.

Untitled Poem

The perfume on your body, and the musk of it.
The second is on me, I smell the first
on you as a sign.

I wear the undelicate odour.

Shuffling through the city, my mildness deceit. Hungry
and light-headed with venom. The adder silks
to refuse bins.

Fastened to the street: the working men's hostel past
two bins. A man beat me to those. I was afraid,
and the pulps he left stayed unfingered.

I had not thought of you: timidly
I spent my pence. In a dormitory
my body covered my trousers.

Along your flesh drifts your hair, a tree bearing
concupiscence, and your smile shows.
This is enough almost.

Your arms are slim, your fingers' amazing strength.
The tree's whole self blurts through long hair.
It's not grief, not joy; saffron spills
milk on the road.

A friend working through television gave
me a brass thruppence;
I bought tea with it, bearing nausea.

In Jerusalem the hills, bare; soft-haired goats
made of teeth; all the shoots are champed.
Hunger drifts through plains, over the declivities
of London; delicate smoky flakes of it.

On the rock splinters cold air; a coward
felt another's bruises in his groin.
He fears the cold air, its true match. Love, I love you.
Can I mean more?

You smile among four friends; three of us speak
and you say nothing. It hurts; your speech
is a silent woman.

Each night the kicked man screams.
If I help you. If I can lift you. His stain
over stone is blue, feather light.

The feet of police emboss the sidewalk.
                              Linked
by my penis, our child could grow.
                        Fear
synchronises with us.

I enter you. Local as a root. I wait
for you to get your breath. We measure each other.

We are prepared, lassitude melts. The hair
is naked, the piled spaces of hunger, and I touch
our candour;

the flesh in abandon robes gently
the tenderness. The candle's flame curves
round its inner light.

Your hair is sea-weed. You smile monstrously.
Memory flushes me through.
Your salt skin rustles on me. Of love, this entirely
is not what we were taught.

Thin black coffee in a pan flicks
beads of heat. The flaking city mounds
stillness, and amiable sleep
spreads our flesh.

We will not last, love, as we are. Love,
I would have us stay, ever, like this.

My conscience, my fear, and our sex, stir.

We Want to Survive

Sundown. The candelabra branches
seven flames. Sabbath is a taper.

The half-world douses sundown's fiery
indignant moral forms. Although

(surely) earth at its poles, flattened
like an orange, where blenched winds

precipitate with no end – earth tires;
inside that night we are its fires.

Is it against fire that one prays
each seventh day? Is every prayer

subliminal with earthly fear?
It's dark and the candles spit lightly.

Like hotel functionaries we hiss
with insulted life, who shrink with fire.

The cantor vomits wax, grease flares
his eminence. Six days worldly fat

burn on the seventh's consuming thread;
is fire the meaning prayers endure?

Admit the mind through fire. Of no sex,
on the burnished silver flame assigns

as equal mild deliberate fire.
Look, Isaac; and do not touch.

Self makes its fire. Each outer flame
selves its next flame that bears a fire

gravid with inmost flame, no flame
that does not burn, is an unburning

inner moist wax light. I bring

my grandparents in an image in
inside the inmost flame. Old men,

someone's grandparents, though the sons
and their sons' sons are ash, someone,

some old man holding to the slack
rough skin of an old woman prodded

past child-bearing, some old men
are still grandparents. And they putter

their Hebrew as the cuffed wrist bares
and passes moist bread, that the hand

has blessed and split. Take it, Isaac,
since you know the language. The moth consumes,

and Hebrew prints the wings that sheet
in fire. An unburned darkish moist

prefiguring resumes the life
of memory that neither loves

nor does not, linked in dissolution
to what dissolves, but does not go.

Not just yet, Isaac; no, not yet.

———————————

The Little Time-keeper

Entropy at Hartburn

Between the hoof's cleft loam squeezes;
so beasts enter night-fall. Steamy
presences; the dunged breaths falter.

Hartburn divides night on itself
with a shutter. 'Mildred clamp out the dark.' Cream lace
embroiders its holes.

The huge energies untwine, and stars
slither away on the braids. The wagging stems
of sex slather to inane fruitfulness.

Not a thing to comfort us. The holly's fruit
taps at the church's stained glass
where solstice clenches its day,

and small energies out-thorn, the profusion
of winter at mid-night.

The Holy Island of St. Aidan

Primitive light streaks the sky.

Lindisfarne: wreckers clang their matins
and shine the guided light; the sea gulps.

Dawn lowers its leaden rose, the negative
sinks in the developer's tray. If men
are pierced by want

Holiness conceives murder. Midsummer
storms the sea and the hulk under
the long shook rope of waves

surges on Northumbria's teeth.
Mortal things. The flop, the cracking of them. Day
wipes clean that slate. The mild castle,

church, priory laced in Ionan
leaf, chevron, and the stone grape
smile to the sea. Mortal things.

The moon in its system, the connections snapping.

Riga, or the North Sea's Berwick

Light fleeces the Tweed's mouth
where there's no work. At this solstice,
the sun opens its hands.

The relationships. Ah, we remember:
our monument fathers our founding prince;
rears his stallion, that the balls

hanging to it glare at the people.

In the nineteenth century they were cut off;
Edison lit his bulbs. The white swans
work in them the city's ordure

to a kidney of stone. The mouth open in pain,
the river messes the sea. Stars
quit their diurnal circuit.

Entropic: the sprung clockwork
runs from itself. The animal's
equipment's been soldered back.

At Nightfall

Night-fall unfastens the door, and the font
baptises the raw body; womb
and its flesh pule to each other.

The mother's milk: clear and sweet
dropping from the soft pointed opening.

It's the stars count, and they flee us
inundating their absences
with our terse lives. When we die
we are dead for ever.

It comes clear finally. The Milky Way
vents its glowing hugenesses over
what's not there. The galaxies
pour their milk away.

Nothing's going to last

the clear baptismal water, twice welcome,
like two good hands

like the olive with
its stone of oil.

Shadowing

Upon one straight leg each steps up-hill and burgeons
through a year's ring;
their leafs breathe.

'Clothes'. No, not clothes.

Arboreal men, shadowed
by leaves, so

shadowing us
we sliced our flesh from their shades

that cut away, the trees lie
acquainted with the shadows of death:
for which there are words
and no language.

Give me your branches: the woodsman
handles their deaths: a blade and its haft.

Then us. Earth washes away. Leaf,
leaf leaf

like treeless birds

Shades

Cheviot: makes silence of
life's bare soft maximum,

fluxing not much. No, hangs

its milky fluid in
Henhole's vacancy; plump

bellies of cinquefoil mixed
with the Barren Strawberry ooze

their lobed flesh at the cleft
Cheviot turns into;

and through the soft
crushed odours, what trees?

The Elderberry and
red-berried Ash, not here,

in the North's summer dense
with shades. Do they

grow in us; do our selves form
on theirs? The Oak's

rooted head branches joy
with leaves close as wood-grain

with between them birds
numerous as mustard grain.

Not here. And yet here, even
so, the passions of form.

I need you. Who else,
who else but you?

the huge strong soft presence
with roots; robust

musical presence

your shape
of noise ghostly

with permanence:
                        Tree.

The Marches

for Isaac Rosenberg

     the half used lives
lift in strong hands an image
of their blooded faces off the freshet's
watery layers

death's ill music creeps
its heathery silences
upon the ear's lulled smithy.

In silvery ounces the Rede
waters through wedged stones;

we are two
in the forest's numerology,

where the mouth casts up trees
numerals
the rip-saw chews;

papery type informs the novel's
symphonic lexes.

To write a poem
from which breathe
the silences.

For Some Time Yet

Where Catcleugh soaks, turn
by ballistae pilfered. Dere Street

is running sprucely. Striae
of the North's Rome

where flesh blanches on the short sword.
Fleeting death
mouths peat and amnesia.

Like blood, the sharp wrens
drip from the hanging tree.

High Rochester, the square common
in fee to no-one. The sun
bathes in its gorgeous Sabbath.

The Sabbath dove puling in the wall.

The square's greening of the fort.

In the edgy grit springer and cap
groove a gate's masonry. Dere Street

leaps off the eye. Three staunch houses –
and the wall, staggers some yards: domesticity
dribbles to earth.

Sandy heat, and russet
hens in this place of white eggs.

Cluck. Warm comfortable upright
hugs the brood; their mush heaped.

Black agatey eye blent
with Sabbath's heat.

The sun's glance plucking time;
a hen pecking it.

Jesmond's Well

To give the water shape
as water forms us

at whose well–head, into
which water braids, *Gratia*,
is carved:

for this source, thanks; at which
to give it that we say

'St Mary's' where it comes
to light, pulsing over

the ground Quaker and Mason
have made a grid; a couth

grim elegance subsumed
by brick in plots. Water

streams a costlier fragrance, Earth
of the ratepayers. The principle:

stealth, care, interest

the flesh white as milk, charitable
as warm bread.

Centre of Absence

Names for one street: Pandon?
The same course
winds hesitantly to decay.

Pampedon is *Pantheon*. The Roman site
opens a Greek name: *pantes theoi*
all the gods. Oh, yes;

the city will scrape this
from itself. Mender of graves and teeth.

Clop: the worthy feet counsel
speculative contracted powers.

Stars burn in the simple dark;
our dense lives fly.

First, Jew-gate: rain sluices silver
braiding usury on the stones

with workmanship. Newcastle buys
the Jews' expulsion. The King

is all gold; Judas bit small
in the coin's realm. So, the King's light

clatters upon the streets. 1656,
'Come in again,' Cromwell stutters.

Jew-gate, in traceries
of despair

the systemic fountains
of prayer and flesh

Trade's filigree rubbed
of instinct; the steep street

slithers through vetch and ground-ivy.

Over by the Quayside, as if a hanged man
cut to morsels, size of a dog's mouth,

nothing. Decayed commerce

transacts melancholic Scandinavia
in desultory amber beads. 'Ye divvent

knaa nowt heor.'

Breaking Us

1

Moss sprinkles its cry; in the bowed
fields of wheat, poppies
flutter themselves.

Love, come on.

We hand-cut stone fruit
in the lintel over the door.

Blessedness in that.

2

Turning its arms, the caterpillar flails bricks.

This section is almost ended.

Tears that would come
press back their springing.

A cry flutters on mudded tar, its road
a wheel that unrolls, hastening.

Street sellers of innocent fruit
are touched by the police.

The lintel with fruits, splits.

3

Smells of tea on the shut
curtains. Winter's light
puts its arms round the house.

Touch me, she says.

The rug at the fire, and the fire
warm us.

Love, our child conceives
amongst wool and the milled
white bread touching you.

4

So much spills. The look
you gave the house
goes down with it.

The wheel drives downhill, mudded
in under the Tyne. An oiled rag
stretches to brine.

Our house, love, done in.

Wind dusts dust with it.
Their plan unfolds in a flat way
a flat road, where the rug
laid our thighs.

There, dust off clay blows from
the despairing chimney breasts.
Nichts, love.

5

What we have been given.

Given? Brick for chalking on;

the rush through the eye
of the summerless high-rise,
each jot of dust rented.

Dust off the armaments
smokes into our heavens. Consecrate this
constructed at the rim
of the city's eye.

The cheerful councillor's face
gleams off the earth.

'All power to the constituent city assembly'

No tree, grass. The caress
of it at best the going
drab daily.

Love, we are dust, owing rent.

The rag stretches to the sea.

This section is also done with.

First to Last

1

The Milky Way: a chart, a conducting
of white bodies
lit by time in darkness. Off

in another place, spirals of milk
curd that darkness. If we fell
to where would we fall? Prodigal forms

that pour away.

There's no grasping them: no name
reveals the parent

in heavenly nakedness.

2

Here sprouts Meldon: *Moel-Dun*,
a hill
shimmered by cross, by cross or sign:

to house, to haven; in 1242

the needful light.

Church as a long room, chancel and nave
one plain intrication. Snug house

a round low vault of stars
ceilings in blue crosses, blue and blood
shadowed with gold.

Were we gentle, so would this be.

3

Traumas of smoky shadow.

Bolam: of two names one
forced on the other: swollen ground.

Creation names her groin.

But before this, where we cut
their shades from us, place of the tree-trunks.

The likely pastures char.

Sheared from Rome, the Causeway
runs off. Poind and his stony dog
mark the foot's emigrations

grass persists in. Mound and stone

ponder the North's shadows:
the acreage of green farmers
under huge leaves annihilating
in shade their greenest powers.

Amongst the tumulus the short
dolerite coffin, grained with soot
upon the lumpy

glutinous flesh. I can't say.

For what's there, what is it? eyelid
bereft of coin, no bones
tumbling through earth. The grave

envelops no name. Death
has burnt away.

And smoke, lingering.

What Can We Mean?

who didst stretch forth Thine arms upon the cross, to draw all men
to Thyself... give peace to all nations
— The Flodden Prayer

1

The prompt field of battle

is a chart, on which
men deform each other

a well, course-pipe pulsing
its lush onto the soil.

A proud Prince, through England… a King
etched over Scotland: the drums throb
upon the furled heart's beating
in equal brotherhood of pain.

Blood paints blood; is this
to be human, above mouse, or the oiled
fur-clung otter? Flodden

notches the ranks, and the rank
is a gap in the tumbling line.

Cry, what shall I cry? Our flesh
is grass, a withering
its clause in the syntaxes.

Soil recovers its right mind
however heaped is ditch
of blood or burial;

the living are a wound one
upon the other. Sunk flesh
and the tried soul perish

one in the other. 'Flodden'

the mind bursting its soft
root of blood

3

He harries another. There breed
no wounds to the battle, none,
but the shared nuptials of death;

slowly haling the body
from itself, that bespeaks
its mutilations. Stop that.

Sopping the green worsted, blood
pulses on, whose bare pain
death shags many ways. Enough;

but pleasure's innerness, silence,
voices lust's fury, his body's
very breath. What does

it matter what we do
to our lives; the stars

will freeze their milks apart
in equilibrium.

The soul nourishes in blood.

4

It is the discipline
of strong men that clasp
the weak into strength's ring.

Clap your red hands, our pikes
devour their flesh; jawbone
brays in an ass's shape.

Were it in us to be
as God, and break his covenant,
we'd rive soul
to the spongy equivalence
of torn life. O, then,
by all means, purge and disperse
each nucleus as if
a blooded soul. Donor of light.

Life through our pikes, we cast
our arms wide.

The Church is Getting Short of Breath

Sabbaths of the pensive spread buttocks.

Conscience, the size of a dried pea,
chafes over the pews flesh sweating

its Sabbath juice.

Douser of burning wax: old man
hugs remorse like a first wife. What labour
will such bridal pains be fruitful with?

First night of marriage wakes the bride
to shimmering kindness; our hemisphere
dishes the Sabbath, dead prayers,

the dulled rose of texts, desert mica.
Air breeds to the shy nibbling tourist.
Work-day fingers the rosary of work-days.

Work's necessary bead; the mechanic
wrenches the thread by which our lives
fasten to us.

Coming first to church, sharp
as the warrior wren. Morning dews
the prompt mind, tourist of the holy
places pious with no use.

This is the true debating-ground,
and here the praying hands consume
the life they build. I shall do what I can.

The question loses its memory,
and the dense shade, in the spaces, runs
to hydrogen

laconic as its dull copulars.

Sneck the latch-door; Adam from sculpted
wood raises Eve with himself
to the bridal shapes. Love congregating

the bench will have its forked play
of their clasped forms: I have come to an end

of the ancient days. Laboured tweed
surplices the rich man.

My lovely parents, when you shaded
each in the other's thought, and flesh
pleaded one anatomy, of life,

endless life, death's frail nucleus
sweated to come alive, its soul
in our flesh. I loved my origins.

But you mid-wifed death. So I became
man, and as others judged me you
I judged. O gentle God, with both hands

you lathed prayer, a chariot's flange, God
of hope. The stars' system contracts,
that, or they flee us. Of such fountains

we lie in the solar ground, and the question
loses its mark.

Late Poem

Cheviot's milky calm is summer's
dis-playing paradise. The hill

swells, and pouts until Henhole
opens, whose fluid strip

hangs in air, a gravity
out of nature. No trees;

its bare flesh grassed, stocks
the smells of a pharmacy.

Long gentle flesh, solstice
of deep hot contralto in the air.

Nature, in friendliness, gives

the crucial means stir.

Behind light, the darkness
to be believed, in which

sparse hydrogen

lethargic, as the mind
of a successful graduate.

Stars: the systemic fountains
of plural milk pour

away, not
for ever, to

dead equilibrium,
the system indifferent

as a dried hand. Here
was our flesh, and love
moistening itself that burgeons
perfect form as if

it could not go.

When we die, if we
are dead for ever, it must

be of no concern; the planets
will lie apart.

Thus the architectures, desponding
of joy; church, or the camp tower

nesting a vigilance of fire.

I think of light: vertigo
in light's dynamism as

it flushes between folded
hulls of concrete

through hidden glass, motioning

death's volition in me, and bellows
upon the concrete.

No, not that way, even
as architecture elegances
huge chill grace. Three things:

an inward clashing sound, as
of love; to have lived
is something. Equalities

of tenderness no thing smutches.
Sleep before two deaths, flesh
of despair, as the mind weeps

its disemployment. We smudge
the echoing humus: the stars'
heavenly system annuls.

We reach, we reach in

measurable loneliness

unless two shudder on the body's
richest extremity.

Fountains of prayer decease.

Note to 'The Little Time-keeper'

If the universe were stranger than it is we'd go mad. Flodden Field indicates Northumberland's role as the Poland, or marching-ground, of Anglo-Scottish relations. When there were no wars there were feuds, and with or without feuds were the moss-troopers and reavers. Cattle and horse stealing were a rule. After Flodden, while the English soldiers were stripping the Scottish dead of reparations, local people got into the Earl of Surrey's camp and lifted the growing plunder. The Northumbrians were more thorough than the Cumbrians, Cadwallader Bates suggests in his 'Flodden Field', and what better time than when arms were busy elsewhere. The English army was as moral as the Northumbrians, and if the latter were more devious, they had endured the trespass of too many armies to keep active a sensitised compunction; theft, they might have argued, cannot be made legal.

There are other ways of being provincial, and the collaborative root shared by Northumberland and my anxieties about space are here locally enacted. Even so, the root-expression is not a technical means for supplying the existential substance of an abstraction. The local is an exploration of becoming; it is a means to habitation. And for all that, Wordsworth's altered phrase evinces the connections without showing the needs of the anxiety. Thus I call the group 'The little Time-keeper' because that's how man works for his security – by computing his presence in relation to the planets' motions. The Aztecs got it to such a pitch that they could compute what day it was some two million years previous.

You can travel the area with Pevsner's and Richmond's *Northumberland*. Its compact 'history' provides a mind for the eyes, and the remainder of the book defines what the eyes see. Even so, there are the inevitable gaps – Middleton Hall, for instance, or the Meldon church's ceiling. Yet to mention these is to point away from the real gaps. Architecture may be social history but, one might ask, whose history is it? Pevsner answers that question when he writes of Wallington that it was a house 'built by Sir William Blackett in 1688 out of the proceeds of coal and lead mining, shipping, and Whig convictions.' That isn't all you need to know, but it's a great deal, and it compacts all that an account of the region's architecture must omit because it notes only the fine-looking, the worthy and the beautiful. Behind the beautiful stand the cooks, stone-masons, and the brutally underpaid who worked the mines and shipyards. In this sense architecture is a social history in default of these. They are truly present: the houses they built or paid for, with their labour, are more truly their monument, in more than one sense, than they are ever those of the Blacketts and Armstrongs. And if the Armstrongs, the Ridleys and their peers had their house built, what did they 'build' for their workers? To discover this is not to read about the beautiful-as-the-leisured. It's to read pages of bland indignation, and these are texts the middle-classes will buy only if their professional occupations require it of them. These are the properties. And these are the deficiencies Pevsner's and Richmond's work entails, as it were, by definition, and it must therefore be a tribute to their work that such deficiencies are so adequately delimited.

I find the other deficiency in myself. The fear of eternity started to grow in me when I was about eight. The fear isn't unique; writing in 1933 William Eddington noted:

> It is true that the extrapolation foretells that the material universe will some day arrive at a state of dead sameness and so virtually come to an end; to my mind that is a rather happy avoidance of a nightmare of eternal repetition.
>
> (*The Expanding Universe*, 1933, p. 125)

The fear is made up of a crux. On the one hand there is the terror that after death 'One short sleep past, we wake eternally'. What in heaven could one do with such time? But if that is fearful, look the other way and perceive entropy. There, the fear is generated not out of traditional beliefs handed to one like some awful gift, but by that traditional substratum put under pressure by the new physics. And it's both problems that bind together the fear. My background is a mixture of rationalist agnosticism and dilute orthodox Judaism; the bases of my spiritual clichés are identifiable in the familiar approximation of anthropomorphised eternity. If I disposed of God as though the problem were intellectual, I also believed, in a childlike mode of half-assumption, that all I had to fear was death. When I died, my spirit, and perhaps some version of my flesh, would rest in eternity because, by definition, that was its provision. I could merge my existence, if that's the right word, in eternity in the way that a child merges its existence with its parents'.

In 1865 the French physicist Clausius reversed a crucial assumption about the nature of cosmic energy. Prior to his formulation it was believed that the energy deployed by the stars and their planets was limitless, and that therefore their life was as infinite as time. The stars' limitless energies and time's eternity were one.

Clausius formulated the idea of *Entropy* whereby the energy of the planetary systems is not limitless, but finite. Energy expends itself; it is self-consuming and not self-perpetuating. The universe, to use a perhaps misleading analogy, is like a clockwork motor and its impulse is finite; when the planetary energies are exhausted the heavenly bodies will lie apart in dead equilibrium. Energy is disequilibrium constantly if unevenly moving towards total expenditure and rest.

The analogy is negatively suggestive. The clockwork can be re-wound and set in further motion if, by implication, the hand of God is there to do it; what the system cannot do is re-wind itself. Clausius's formulation crucially effected the removal of physics from tacit co-operation with theology. Thus if energy does turn out to be limitless, and if the entropic view of the universe is at the same time correct, then it will be the hand of God and not physics that does the re-winding. The entropic view does not support the optimistic if terrifying belief in a cosmic eternity. On the contrary, if theology is committed to a prospect of eternity, it's a view it will have to advance without the aid of physics. Theology might reply that it has so far managed very adequately without it. Is it more adult to trust to faith or the new science?

Bird

You flew into a rage
but against glass

your wing grasped its mistake
and broke. Wing and hand

in pure helplessness we step
through that oval, the eye's

thin stoic fluid.

Pitchblack
and dense

grows the flickering will to live.

Off the anaesthetist's slab,
the mortician of gas, hop

through the ranks
of men.

Your chirrup

all gold
on three toes. Black distinct intelligence,

from the mishap of gas, beat
through men's ranks

slewed
on Boxing Day.

Uncollected and Unpublished Poems,
c. 1976–1980

In Mary's reign Justice Barton convicts George Marsh of Protestantism at Smithills

for Elaine and Jon Glover

I regard you: a farmer's child
soiled by Earth's pieties, the least ounce
of which is fertile with the word.

The people hungering for it, the church
retaining it; the wind amongst corn
whose presence you were an ear of. Grace

as unassertive as this got proscribed.
Justice Barton gave his mind at Smithills –
you were not to; at the stairs' foot

you stamped, once, and fractured the delicate
flagstone with your charred print.
And fire. And more fire. Mary's flesh

strips the bone. Born again with
pain, the unbearable midwife, you were
sieved of your word. The flesh in ash

brings its soft rage to Barton and scours
its foot print plain to the day's eye.

Samson's Hair

I could never understand Samson's hair:
the strength of it, the Nazarite secrecy,
the (unblameable) conspiracy of silence concerning it;
the (constant) apprehension of losing the great stuffs of hair,
                                        the terror
when Delilah caressed them, lightly.

On the other hand, I can understand Absolom's hair.
It is beautiful, clearly, like the sun in its fullness, the moon red
with vengeance.
The odour it exudes is sweeter than the sweet musks of women.
The chill and sly Achitophel

must avert his eyes as he sees before him the cause for David's love.
This is the most beautiful hair
in the kingdom, the justifiable
cause for all revolt,
and then, the oak.

Six Poems from Metoula

1

No ancient
glory, not Jerusalem. But very
beautiful, very

beautiful. Here a bird treads air
with a smaller bird, her daughter perhaps. A woman

tourist leans at her husband's ear
from the deckchair, in English
so that I shan't understand.

2

In this air, where I would dream, shapes
are flying, sharp, cut,
this light, almost painful.

So this is the Lebanon.
A plant-lined valley stretches
from here to the whitening canyon, opposite, and the morning

breeze reminds me
that I promised to unite you.

3

a black
dog
like that
must belong
to someone
what
will be done
unto so much
darkness
and what
with the hair

in the greying fur
of a black
dog drowsing
in the pepper-shrub scented
garden
of a hotel
in Metoula (after
long illness)
what light!

A place is not empty. You
fill it. There's

the Lebanon burden, and there
somewhere (unseen) Syria. And Pongo,

lazy dog that he is rolling upon his
tangled hair. So that's

the life-story of the man
in the shirt embroidered into an orchid. Sir,

what are you discussing there?
Plans?

Lady?
Everything is brown
here. A place is not really
empty. Everybody
fills it.

Venus did not emerge
here from the sea (no sea).
Antaeus did not wrestle
(no partner) and Jacob's ladder
did not balance here (uneven ground).
No mythologies grew
on this hill
nor in the valley spreading
beneath it.
But every every one watches
television from the Lebanon
and a moon like the one
climbing here, red,
over the mounts of Syria

could not have been more seductive
even in ancient Greece.

6

The holiday-maker says 'what life,
how terrible their trades union House.'
Lady, why must you sit
in the trades union House
when you can sit here
in the garden
in Metoula,
in the *Hotel of Cedars*?

Else Lasker-Schüler in Jerusalem

1

Almost one year
two years, *The Land of the Hebrews*.

Oriental harmonies:
the longest, most unnatural hair

a geometry, with lines wavering
stone.

In this small wind
shaded grey, not a wind almost

a touch of wind, breathing:
Else Lasker-Schüler

in her rented room, in Jerusalem
is drawing a cover
for her book.

2

Your flesh buds:
geometries in a Tibetan Carpet.

Daylight burns
the clothes on you.

Since my loneliness
never
a spring
like this

in the pallor
of whitewash, wrinkled:
a mirror.
I could say more

3

I don't know the language
of Judah, nor
how to
catch up with its haste
I can't decipher
the clouds, coloured olive.

Night is a step-Queen.

This bitter root
this
estrangement:
if it could only burn once more
in the incendiary's fire,
if only
for a space.

'A black sun streams its fresh medicinal'

A black sun streams its fresh medicinal.
Faces mummer cries tearing the skin
whose kissing twists to mouths.
If you want life, go, croons Antiope
naked as her child.
Theseus by the laundresses'[69] tub
kneels, a wave
of women half-risen –
mixing plasm
cries, the split hand of the clean.
He loves his male child, its small mouth quirks pain.

The laurels bend honour to grief's subtle thong.
Hippolytus spatters Phaedra, raucous lily
Of pain, with purity
for the cold election of Aricia.
Venus's sly hatred twists apart
her thighs clench and a dart fastens their need
pure as a wren, to bridal its year's blood.
Neptune ravels him
in space, his horses fracture
in mixed thunderous air
the body of love's pain.
So like the father droops one lust in dew
Neptune through Theseus.

Dreams rise, and sleep
smears the lamps.

'The tram runs, and the soft flesh spills itself'

The tram runs, and the soft flesh spills itself.
The lacey stone clops with a farrier's hoof.
The flesh seems like an eyelid, clashing on
the tidal rampage of energy.
Fatigue vials our death. But poised by strength

you are a bird, whose thermals raise you up;
you make the rondures of air's faint flesh.
The clicking registers with downy tongues
strew a depraved north. Wheels gulp water
sluicing the jagged braid work fractures in.

The soft remains of energy spill free.

Scraped faces lingering on black glass.

'The back of the heart empties'

The back of the heart empties;

    the hushed logos
cleats ribbon and alphabet

    in one synapse
of us, but as if one had
    died, as this

    day he's
a column of air, off which spine the head
    withers hardly.

    Letters strike
through the head; is it love's price
    for a room?

        No, no, it's all
the cost that's true. Nothing, I would say,
        emulates truth:

        as he is dead
so I am dead for you. Our fleshly
        charges methodize

        of pain fit
for angels, a hymnology they whizz
        easily through:

        that clacking
flight of the beaked skuas
        they change to

they're virtue's flensing tool. No,
here is the space. Of that heat
transacted in the open wildness
the heart knows; to love
counting the webbed knowledge
winged over the heart's blood.

Condemned

Forty one is the age for suicide. You chose the right time
after this, death will not tarry.
Desdemona refused.

Othello, the moor, bent over her to put an end
to the scene. He had little good, after that,
to say for himself.

You were not Desdemona. Not from Venice.
Your father did not object. Calm, he brought to
matrimony, daughter of death, who could have known,

daughter of dust, slowly, slowly you made your choice.
Forty one years you waited. Then you hurried.

The Psalms with their Spoils

First published by Routledge & Kegan Paul, 1980

Praise is comely
— Psalm 147

The Cathedral Chair

Of a skip: of a monument
of hollowed burned space; outside which,
   brayed rubble.

  With buttress
and saint air takes shape. The skip holds
   a chair,

  its swivelled
body quietly nesting, whose tubby grandeur
   carts

  to the knacker's.
Without murmur; the arch-bishop's diurnal
   track slid

  about this swivel
on God's terse demands, or between
   a man's buttocks.

  So gently
I lift this thing, and I strip away
   rexine

  buttons
and the soiled studs, and, in ounces,
   the tattered mullions of leather

  and the wool
until the wood frame in its muslinned flesh
   – it glimmers,

  it is a god peeled. I give this figure
skin, and sit cupped,
in its thinking the idea sepalled

  of the most dear absences, and which
unfolds in the ventricle of lithe air.

A man, a woman and a fan

What the fan beats
odourless of a dried space once
was sweating air.

The fan now
spirits nothing. Upon her breast

the moist fractures of his speech.
These two propositions: the agitation

of unripe fruit, the olive
whose births flex the husk stoup of oil.

Differing rhythms: 'Yes,'
she answered, 'for love of me.' The fan agits

its half-bird's wing
aghast for stability. The breast
heaved gorgeously.

He got it, plucked
to the hot proposition, penetrating

the declivity's lush: she
of his love for her, staunched; he, that loved her.

So the fan
worked between

'and neither of them might agree till death.'

On the batlike integument
the half-fleshed, the twilight wing
speckled with lace:

'I worked for ninety years and lay down then
beautiful as ever.'

Resting Place

In…c. 1230, John le Romeyn, then subdean of York Minster, recorded the sale to the commune of York Jews of a plot of land in Barkergate adjacent to what was already antiquum cimiterium Iudeorum. *It is therefore on that site, immediately west of the river Foss and now under the tarmac of [a] civic car park, that archaeologists will no doubt one day disturb the posthumous tranquillity of Jews who can have rarely been completely tranquil while alive.*
– The Jews of Medieval York and the Massacre of March 1190
by R. Dobson, 1974, p. 47

1

Where the camshaft weeps
oil, where the pained axle
contracts

over Barkergate, what there is is still in pain.

The car, the cracked plated animal,
these oils weep by degrees back from their cells.

Their crouched forms
tremble above our graves: Judah'd with oil
their iron drips into our mouths.

What is it then, is it nothing?

Earth's justice
cakes the skull with the clay's
bronze confections,

we are
oil creeping to the Foss
where a sword rests its two edges:

it is not nothing to lie anywhere
that they will let you. The sword
rusts like a child,

the Jewish child, the gentile sword; earth
    sells itself to us.

Camphored in oil, I lose all memory.

2

Church minds its force and men nurse souls but through
each passage, hope, a furled lamp casts its beam.

Of that Church, John; by whose furled lamp I sold
our loam for dormitory to the Jews.
Earth hold them gently, and be gentler to
this woman than her child is, nursing her
each part of death's submissions. To mind so
the flesh is nurse to death. If more life is,
then they must each become a door of selves
each enters by in suppliant need: their own.

They never heard of this. Angel of death
made of desire and mercy raise your wings.

Jerusalem

This 'good plan, fleshed in childhood'; these fruits
raised out of the lintel. Meagre light

smoked the aperture where Rome, elbowed
in brass, illuminates the war-caves

the North's bashed out of; but not Israel,
a stone sumptuous with carved light.

Hollows fruit under the olive tree, pith
to cram the black seed. Every creature

works out from the dark: miners
cough in Solomon's emerald caves, scooped

by lust for delicate Sheba, in whose flesh
the fertile cock never sates. This good plan.

Without which no God would be adored, none to
raise earth's pillars, or the North's mild orange brick.

So much of the world is as this, fine
arousals of flesh pinioned in spirit tack

through ginnels: the soft wood-pigeon.
Sieged Jerusalem runnels on the sword:

like wind famine clings the canvas walls.
Yiddisher flesh concaves; children, mothers

in seed lie like Babylonish reeds
wailing outside the wall, whose stench

spasms Roman muscle. Our temple's
the Sabbath candle,[70] and our prayers

disperse in rubble. This wall is a straight
piece of misery whose root like babies' teeth

's a row of tears that blench and harden, altogether
changed from grief; and the small figure, god,

undone of clothes, stares doll-like on ashes.
I can't tell you.

To think hurts. It hurts not to: still
I can't tell you. Jerusalem, olive

and white; light glutinous against
stone. Flesh sings as if spirit;

would to God it were, but then, no. All
I have to do, where clashes

of serene absence whiten blank stone
is lift you to where this illumination

overfills with space.

Into Praising

1

In seventy C.E., Romans
mauled Jerusalem. For three months
Jews stubborn with flesh that ate
the spirit, then
nothing whatsoever. A fiery tooth
the temple.
No commander
might restrain their trooping.

2

The word surrounded
so by light

that when

the Jews began forming aleph
in a crab-like uncial,

they compacted with God
two signifiers; first: that all

good poems be made of prose.
Then, in after-thought,

Jerusalem the shadowy
celestial city be fleshed

with the earthly. Yes, He said.

3

These three conditions, in which
we are human; to love
and be loved past
what is reasonable. So we do, and would
be done by.

The second is to be tortured;
and not to love's the third,
the half-life half-lived,

where to be born we risk
for sure, one of these. The thigh caught up
with heavenly nakedness.

4

At first, David's shepherd-city;

but where did I meet you, you
with the coiled hair, the black
bounce of sheen? Is it Ruth's

spiral entangling;
Solomon's wisdom is an emerald
in triumph, sex, and the doused riches
of slaves.

The composure of lust the discomposure
of passion in triumph in you.
Solomon's passion, joyous
as emerald, unfolds her.

And He has his way, God
makes sure whose forehead
the tiny jewel lustres. Even so,

where flesh is, the spirit does good
masonry; the two Jerusalems
compact branches of stone and soul,
a huge stark weft of praise.

In it, a black sheen,
mortal, the earth's vivid lie
of terror conceived and conceiving
love in love. Jealous God

abandons his altar and kneels
to his creation. Jerusalem

is praised.

Acids

From earth's acids comes
the soul of praising. From the lemon flower

a nub of scent, that discloses
like the musk at your thighs.

You require astringency – nub
of as much response: the pink bruise

dawdles moisture. You beget
the wounds of taste: acid, acid

too far in to annul. The membranes,
that praise consciousness,

are mutually of
each other's consequence:

a nub of lemon flower.
The earth brims with its juice.

Praise is not overspill,
it is the blessing turned

back to itself. Praise, praise:
praise with sufficiency

free of blight, of spirochaete.
The lemon flower fused of

two tasks, two appetites
that mean no harm.

Going on

They wail their souls for continuity
— Isaac Rosenberg

1

Tugged from your fallow, my seed chills.
'And there won't be kids.' It is your mouth's
o exclaims two presumptions.

2

Be in no other place; no no
never any than this.

Our spirits' lumpy unguents concentrate
to this idea, and you smile.

It's the structure of all, all smiling.

3

Obscene tenderness: belly and torso
mix in sure-sexed stillness. If there is
more nakedness, where would I find you?

Is there more? It's where God's first
soft shrug of death's nucleus rubbed.
So small a cherub of fear. Yet whatever
it is, love, love, make our child.
And, in any event, you.

Love in War

1

Could we dry
off our lover's face one winged kiss
what a fly-by
powdery fluttering.

What did Eve get? Napoleon's kiss
flakes like mica. His woman's
lemony assured flesh
jilts her marshall; her sluttish
flesh, her pouting flesh.

Her flesh.

2

The wrecked vapour of a kiss
and a battle. The sleeping tanks
bedew with summery rain, and the flesh
ragged like parsley. Her kiss

tissues its salt trail
on the lidded eye.

3

Did Eve get prose? Welts
of dashed light at the thighs.

My kiss endures your intensity – you
aren't ever done with, not your kiss,
not our originals. What then?

What's bare underneath
resolute nakedness?

Meaning Something

1

I hear the bald yap
    of air under Cheviot – peat
    is the day's palaver

ashen in a twang
    of skeined smoke. The daisy
    shuts its numerals.

And Harthope's wrinkled waters
    peel the glum stones
    of wrinkled age. The sunken

witnesses drip.

2

Life distraughts, in love
    or leaving it, yet
    a sprig of heathery stars

bespreads this truthful day.
    What if it left us? Yet
    bare summery rain

and palms of bracken that smell
    of the pious blackberry; we
    recount our numeral

among countless pasture.

Wife and man

We were contractual, each
child opened the ring: Love got
this holding. I am

getting strangered, and the heat
in me violates
this ringed structure. I'm space

made of absence, whose children
were blooded with me. Stranger, smithier
of my time:

so I am molten, so it comes
to me, tenderest
muscle, with obscene muttering.

Isaiah, ploughsharer; of lithe
mensuration, the fleshed inches
beat to me. I'm children

open of their bodying. But make
a ring of me again.

The Old Version

1

The scaffolder gets iron
I get the height he makes.

2

Our words bear Tyndale's word
back on us. And as these men
carry their raptness to
the fire, pain inspirits
determination in
a rage of pity.

Language got up and walked;
and the tree sprouted where
a blade had drawn its sap.
His word spoke and grew with
the language we denied.

3

The Jew Mandelshtam
grew into Petersburg.

4

The Authorized text rejoiced
its patrilineage;
wind in the ship's masts
shags the uprooted pine.

And we rejoice as much
with space as substance. Of
which now it's said it goes
to moth. Such substance is
alive with holes.

5

Love, stand nakedly;
the new version says this:

'every mother's son' for
'He who pisseth the wall.'

It prefers it prefers, and you can hear it.

In your small breasts I see
the veined membranes. Until
death, the Old Word 'flesh of
its flesh.' And it is right.
It's not me saying this.

6

The stalks are milked
the stalks rise once more.

When you leave she said

When you leave she said I turn
to my self that stays. It's the book's finger
beckons me; let the quick kiss go.

The book engrosses a page, or so.
But let my narrative take hold
in this dismal century; the modest rush-light

burns for all it's worth. O heed me.

I write to you

I write to you, standing,
at a square foot, or so, of oak. It is enough;
and in any case, no more is here.

My letter to you
is well-made, and speaks of love.

Making it

Between art & money, London – volatile
as gas. The pigeon's feathery
limb grins at the cobble-face.

Mild-trained as the falcon, raspberry quartz
rings the palm's acquiring limb.
Never quits. When we die good
for the vault's primary life, soul,
that burnished conscientious lamp.

The soft blood and the raspberry
leak from us, and earth stains
with life. Flesh abandons its mind,
that garnet, hard avid and shadowless.

Leafgold

The people, as always, paid the taxes you claimed were due
— Bertolt Brecht, 'Song of the cut-price poets'

Blood and raspberry, the true mash
of London, bare of all else
save a fine palaver of leaf-gold.

Across the truck-driver's thwart shoulder
and the small-bosomed typist marked
by flickering alphabets, leaf-gold.

Their weal and ours, it's all one:
a fine imposture the State sheaths
on our worked flesh. How can I wonder

we stuff that blotched gut until it bursts.
What of that? Idly, our bare souls
sprinkle the bare earth, like leaves

beaten to airy thinness.

The uses of man and the uses of poetry

With pleasure I read
How Horace traced the Saturnian art of verse
Back to those peasant burlesques
Which did not spare great families, till
The police forbade lampoons, compelling
Those with a grudge to develop
An art more noble and air it
In lines more subtle. At least that is how
I construe that passage.
        — Bertolt Brecht, 'Letters about things to read'

Gently the moist worms adapt the soil.

It's not always like this; I've heard
how a man visits another, hired
to teach poetry in jail. Some smile.

Not so the warders, who adapt
most to the rod of discipline.
Talent burns its crap away: the man

in jail, fast as the other learns
how to teach, grows to write;
he leaves the fine rasp of lyric

for satire. In the prison yard
the willow bows its decent head.
Wardens pick out their man; he fixes

them in satire, as freezing water
Russian soldiers the Finns drove
into the lake's grim medium.

This cold fixative. Warders bear
their prize to a quiet cell and here
beat out their limits of his endurance.

He is finished, and the wounds eat him.
Even so, pity the warders with
feelings much as another one's

and weep for the uses of poetry.

The Lapidary Poems

Brecht's War Primer is written in 'Lapidary' style. The word comes from the Latin lapis, 'stone', and describes the style which was developed for Roman inscriptions. Its most important characteristic was brevity. This was conditioned, first, by the effort required to chisel the words in stone; second, by the realization that for one who speaks to a succession of generations it is seemly to be brief.

– Walter Benjamin, Commentaries on Poems by Brecht

The chisel grows heavy

The chisel grows heavy, fewer words
would lighten the hands; and to keep
him who wanders this hard ground
like scurf, scurf the size of leaves,
or who grazes the mild squares
of London is unseemly.

So who is this?
Earth's fingers revolve earth. Those
who search
will pass through me.

Lapidary words

Lapidary words: for it is hard
to chisel stone; and to detain
the reader at the tomb
softened by moss, and the lichen's bruised studs
of gold, is not seemly.

You, too, would not want
to take from the wanderer
grazing the mild squares of London
his time you now bear.

There's no more; the lichen's nail innocently
feeds its point
into the child's burying place.

The Lapidary Style

The *lapidary style*, brief as a cut
in stone, for it is hard to cut that.

And for such words: to those spangling the road
like wheels, to speak brief is seemly.
A long life of the short time; we all try.

Out of such a day, the day blazes
of some soft shade its great viridian
branched at the vitreous brick. Fed of

the body's plight incandescence, that works
every inch of this little yard
clasped to the road like a dead bride.

———————————

I in another place

Faustus
How comes it, then, that thou art out of hell?

Mephistophilis
Why, this is hell, nor am I out of it.
Think'st thou that I, who saw the face of God,
And tasted the eternal joys of heaven,
Am not tormented with ten thousand hells,
In being depriv'd of everlasting bliss?
O, Faustus, leave these frivolous demands,
Which strike a terror to my fainting soul…

Faustus
For, when they die,
Their souls are soon dissolv'd in elements

— Christopher Marlowe, *Doctor Faustus*

('I in another place' – a phrase from Keith Douglas's 'Dead Men')

1

I saw earth taste lime, of sweetness
a type, but not its purity. Good if
this to your composition put a form
different from you. My pronged tongue seeks
your mouth's fiery constant, truth. You'd say –
'feel it?' – but 'no'. Leapt off the train, – the fall
did not destroy me. Earth cracked there; and hell
sooted its light on you, unrecognizable;
but then, your lips with blame drawn thin I could
not miss you. Yes, you in duplicity
your sullen aura blenched in tenderness
you turned bashful of your thin nakedness
and to you, practised, drew me. As I stood.
Your milked breasts pouted but, touched, they release
starry milk-spattered origins. 'Of joy
a murderer, you rasp, a murderer
of lies, therefore my murderer.' 'But life

allots one mate, I stuttered, that is – ' 'fine –
you think I'll want to stay in hell?' Her drooped
breasts, suckled, nurtured still. 'Are you here
for good?' 'Just so.' And, smiling, 'are you?'
'I'm visiting.' 'Don't count on it, we who've
a use for men with souls – ' leaning her back
on me, the heart's shapely narrowing –
'where is he, I asked, lingering
in hell?' Something at that went shut in her.
'Summer's wings jigger tidal arrows
through the licked Thames, of flossed waters;
his suppliance is heaven's that is all.'
'Dullness, I pleaded, works. Spiritual
fingers salve death's gash, and more than here.'
I who had not an end nor good end missed
the dew sleeping tanks glinted with
in the war's years, where the sharp slobber
of men's bones pierced the barren river-bed.
We're children who plead for justice with barbed tact;
silence judges, as love douses once, and again,
flesh with its numen – ecstasy. 'He did
not blab, he was discreet, discreet until
you read those letters.' 'And then?' 'Then he's what
you thought he was until you find he's not.'
'Is that the truth?' 'Better it's true, even.'
She said, 'you make of hell, tedium. See
the naked, yea, stones even, through whom
love blurts its energy, in snow's blotches
flower a sane petal, a spread torch
bright as any intellection mind
burnished with frost aspires.' 'Is he then
in heaven who would be here?' 'That's heaven's part,'
she cried softly. 'Made of absence' I thought;
though tact, left-handed finger crossed the lips
restraining the word (sated, powerful, even so
elected for silence.) Some are.

Our train darts on hell's arteries, flint-ringed
diesel through which it fissures: on which
judgment divides two guesses. The first
is love (perhaps), face lightly strained
at the mouth and eyes, hair crossed by wind,
fecund on vision. Our train lamps violet
and climbs. The second guess tampers
with your vitality, taking judgment
on me of you linked with another. Righteousness
swaths through criss-crossed blades, dividing
bad from good; it would be simple. Finding
it is, judgment flickers,
and sharp webs grandparent the woman's face,
painful to gather, also, meaningful
to few but her. Of her kin, her *kinde*, their kids,
the shut source; the egg chafes its yolk
to fluffs of pert chirrup, the hooked chin shakes
and cereal nods its spikes. Creatures fasten
in the ark to the sea's volute, deep-chested
as a mountain-threading bird; we flicker in hell
on its leaf-like metro. Cindery
and prejudiced, we helix the flanged tor
(time's metamorphic). Apprehension
turns judgment, to us never adverse, or but
each is its flattery, to be glad we judge
(can judge). What averts self's torse of light
can't bring to use our mutual incidence.
The train lurks, white-chested hoyed thing
clung by the angle bent by eave to wall –

                            we saw three
hold up a boy – about five years, – and two
gripping him, the third razors
the penis. The end tappets blood
in urine. Howls over the kicked thud
of engines revved, the sad bikes sprung.
Pictures of naked men by pain arrayed

some bear the images of these on boards
that squeeze them in a vee, vice they shared with
a squaddie's mirth at images of pain.
Mirth, bird-song, – break from a rotted
string: pearled teeth turning carious.
But gasped vowels lithely unfurl
their knots and circles, the letters
kicking their serifs, the upright stalks,
come to the ear's sensing –.

    The train reclenches a gear, I, glad to abandon
the damned; yet distance sickens. We climb
a satyr's beard like crabs; a lecherous wood
here blooded to the roots of Daphne's pine.
These masted ships, affianced to earth
blurt their root selves to the curved wind. Our rested
train moves up.
            'But you chose him.'
'Many flicker, she said, to the light like moths,
like spidery moths tangled with light; I was
with his needs moth-like. You should have loved me,
have chosen me, although I chose him. Or
then killed me.' With swollen hands, she,
she beat me. Crouched beneath a rising tower,
we wait, until, as distance turns its head (and not
until) we rise. 'My punishment is this,
is a stained spirit, or none. See how a stain
anatomises its cause, drifts for residence
to its flesh. I must choose flesh
without spirit, or the body suffused
by a stained soul. Heaven creates of
no choice, either your wrong flesh
your right soul disdains, or self
painted with its wrong soul. That yet shone, trod
eagerly to scrubbed regions – a doorstep
daily scoured for the wage-man to step
on his backward trudge. The white step
forgets the sooted brick, yet heaven places
this blanched slab the reconstituted soul

must first flit over – a new bride. She
slow as her patient flesh ever was reaches
the threshold inflamed with torches – our penance
in imitation of that azure context.
This will not change us into good men.'
    'By intercession,' but why advise, 'with prayer
that fingers providence, beg: to death to spill
heaven's quick waxy creature. Then catch him.'
Excitement and her, two pieces of being,
stitched – 'I want his spirit bodily.'
I thought nothing
of mercy, my limbs furled in terror.

3

'Is mercy one earth; does the shimmering melt
of phoenix squawk effective hatchery?'
She asked, 'Is it the earth?' I said, 'Fear's dank
Absolom tangles haste in the boughs;
a boy unpicks him. Like spilt blackberries
coals heap the miner. Where the Hart revives
iron's fine element of clay burns free,
it thicks the smithereens of excrement.
The silks the poppy crimps amongst the wheats,
wrinkled silks, delicate engorgement
of men in loam; a jagged fire sustains
in blood's murder. So the stark leopard pads
with milky feet to staunch the guarded earth,
distraught garrison; earth that is sewn
with metals, for a good earth.' 'Yes, she said;
but where's the hell men won't go to? I guess,
though who's to know, since torment's designed
to maim the spirit to obedience,
all must pain. Hell is our single place
all like the neck of a bottle crush through.
A double sense of wrong yet think that I
would do it over: two senses
of one action like a candle's flame

you cut with scissors, yet it's one.' Pauses.
'How long to wait? joy's true garment
of his sixty years sublimes flesh, if it does –
ah, my love, spirited friend; from heaven
you come, to me it's heaven you come to, blessed
animation of spirit, acquiring flesh.
Lit glancing panes heaven obliques on
each other, light's split – hard-faceted
to make plural singular virtue. But not
in that obedient place no virtue's in,
it's said, in hell. If love is here, quicken
time, make increased velocity off
the back-years. Make time lighter – dancing,
a pipe, yes, timbrel, a soft clash
of raised cymbals, with the scraped goat's-drum,
– like hunting men stiff with their affixed spears, –
or brushed cymbals, bells rustled. I will
dance. He is about his way, I, mine,
and both, together, since we are that way
the Lord won't spoil, since it's the Lord's joy;
we are love's operation, its strong feet
run together, a single limb
danced on its energy. We're that bright
peculiar ancient eye, prayer-bead...'

Three days a leap and an
informed spasm
whirling slowly from the azure
in nothing, a derangement
quicksilvered on hell's mirror. Bloodless
light mouths the gates – glissades
of waxy rock, marbaline lard – shocked open
as light rushed to meet itself. Hell's murky torches
grin in a row of soft-tipped teeth and freeze
his body. Multitudes
with their sins clamber
rock dewy with sweat, and peer.

to make quick
a man's appetite, permitted; as well
to lust, if women do so. What I fear
is if a man, by lust – not bred
to subjection – is, by her need for power, led
in powerful subjection, his desire
her power; her absence
is her touch on you. She's
not passion, but passion for power. Love's
pith crammed, care's unction:
to the stoup, pleasure, off the shared hand, balm,
in satisfaction couple: the seeds, the oils.
We did not know this. We came on
hearts, palms, tongues of herb, their thorn-hedge
speckled with grit. The sun clarifies
its terrifying hue, and pain admits
not loss of love
only, if it is love, but a loss
of love's worth, that slow, imbrued
pang of nard. Here,
by refraction, mirror and glass, we took youth
and our unlulled forms, both,
through mind's cold discerning. Tacked
to the banyan, gouting root, the motto: test
your sight. Touches of flower wreathed
my hand at your breast. A river refracted
insistent forms of water. I said, 'here
is heart's-ease, pale blue flower, few want,
making of pallor the image BELIEF, which mints
value, glimmer of small fires.' 'Ugh, you
said, that's heaven's kind voice.'

The sun fires mildness: flickering, lurid
on chalky faces. Poppies flutter

their engorgement of blood. In hell men
who turn to stone, fulgent their passion
their selves weak. But the garden
where this half-light soaks the foliage
unearths our forms:
she, who hungers-without-end, and he,
the fire's cherub
tangle their profiles. Clarifying
urinous light, in which
a limb clunks the stone tier. She kneels
haunched, kissing his hands.
A little breath taken, slowly, beneath the heart;
the rest, stone. 'Save him, save him.' How
can I? Melted animosity, pity's sting
confuse to bad blood.
We become blind with open eye, like owls
by day dreaming the actual world. She embraces,
kisses stone. Eyes that weep
beg mercy, love's mulsed fragrance,
its nard. He roots in earth feeding flesh
to stone. She cries: 'you
love what fits your desire; I,
of him, the bees furring promiscuous joy,
a sweetness in strength. He
gave himself to love.' Her body against his knees
to fondle and kiss the hands,
fragile as they consent, and implore: the beggar's
bowl, to grease
with heaven's drops of myrrh. Then the head, dry,
and hairless as an ochre nut lolled
on its shoulder; the rumpled torse
of flesh its stone.

The flowers lily with stigma; the lamps
fulvid. Waves sprinkle
the dead with flowers of sweat. And lifted seas
froth the rigid sea-front. We kneel, for pity,
residentially pure.
The sun hoists its familiar destiny

like a bribed coin. What we would
and what we must, these two
fight inch on inch each other
to earth. 'I will not let you
go, except you bless me.' The sun's

spavined rouges are lost energy.
What purpose and what purposelessness, then?
Mend, I'd say; the spirit, mend, mend.
That flake, and that flesh: there's no difference.

The Barbarians

Ohio's field

Ohio's field sprung with chilled fallow deer
– nuzzle the glass that separates our heats
that separates our hungers. We can see.
Our forked cry turns its snowy barbarous head.

A satiety of spent juices, complacency
that might be named *fulfilment*. No; our needs
from theirs disjoin. We tread those roots of ice
where congregated heads of wheat before
us turn, white as judgment. Mercy has roots.

The far kingdom

At 4 a.m. the phone chirrs. Over
the Atlantic's
ageing locks of water disinter
his fleecy messages. Between his lips

there is a truth
and truth between our flesh. Which
is this? The plough
turns the earth over, its bruised
melted swords.
The plough still a sword.

Holy holy holy, the far kingdom.

Water[71]

Makes a lush canyon of a rift in hell,
this blessed water; lucid mantle
on which the pert chive's long-fingered

indifference depends. Let it go
which way, like quicksilver it is
love's sacred infamy, it is that

fondant moisture stiffens the terse cock.
What of it, love, what of that? It's if
not all we are, yet what a great prince throws

of deep confusion into certainty,
his watery prison where the chamfer sticks.
These are the works, this is the praise love gets.

I dare say water is the least of it.

The separations of grief

Tenderness and the blessed tension of water
are elsewhere adept. Water's secularity

is a tap, a toothless mouth asleep;
can rim vacancy, or torn laughter;
will pour its welfare upon the downright hands
of gratitude. Waters of séparation
are inseparable. And so is grief.

The presences

Your tongue's wet narrative in my mouth
moistens no history, it is its presence.

The fecund cave veins with your sex
vessel complacent with another's joy.

I'll change the metaphor.

★

Thwart presence, opened from its trunk,
in being, simple, it devours gratitude;

that is its hunger. But absorbs handsful
of its plain food, gold, in a kind of suction

from rushing light. Returns tokens
of that gold immersion in dipping greens.

Surly boughs unfold from their trunk.
Some streams vein, fan-wise, inward.

I see I've changed subject also.

★

Snow terrorises the land. You lie
white to whiteness. Soon rains will charge

their benefacts, disgorging
winter, its crystal spars. This fiction

of love vanishes, the teller melted.

The deformation

I am a form disgorged: magma's forms pelt
their splintered mineralogy. The souls
of angels suck the rubied tracts of blood.
Crystals turn ichor in the divine mouth.

But gentle rains discharge their benefacts.

★

First innocence is simple, and shepherds
handle him gently, knowing how hard the crook
be gripped as winter comes to snaffle it
and sheep on twisted ears of corn made fat,
fat as ripe wheat, from their indignant grasp.

Abel knows the earth better than me: God takes
his blood in gentle hands. The smug flesh
success imprints, I hoed, I put a mark
on every part of him. The earth's fruits
abound, magnanimous, heavy, at the sky's-line,
the mouth closed.

★

His success deforms innocence, mine
in its structure rucked, grins. Nature prefers
another. God, as if forked with lightning,
ignites the fleering tongues, that drip with gas.
I'm for the smelteries, a new button

fondant with decency. I keep none, for none
to their heart's imagining exalts me.
The half-failed fondle their half-success, flesh
famishes on its soul's pity. Holy holy.

Finished

A coin in your tongue's wet hollow...
into its pitch, Lethe's, stutters memory.
A garment clings the prow. You,

from your memory, discard us, lining
ripped from a cloak

dark, ample cope.

★

Freedom is the deer you out-fleeted.

The dank Absolom of fear tangles haste
in the boughs: free me, free me.

How can I? Your hair tangles with juices
your life from the boughs suspends.

I can hear your cry, I cannot find you.
Out-hinded by freedom is the gentle

majesty, its defeat mild and huge, –
the wedge into my life. Absence

and immanence, like marble, swirl
each space into the other.

Urban Psalms

Here is my watch

I say: here is my watch. Ineptitude
has torn its spring, or age – filing the spine.

Lymph saps from wrist and neck, a bomb that's rucked
the beautiful terse forms… We stand in rows
and piss the soft beer of Vauxhall away.

Homed

Flower-bitten glass with cursive Arabic.
Furred in insomnia, tea sways milkless.
Sleep, in whose pulse truth performs; this rich house
drifts through Shap's quarried rhythms, paving-stone
that interlocks and locks in waves. I house
like a pale lyric. See, the great bear's watch
breaks up: soot, darkness & lethargy.

Armouring

She's a glass cup by *Yassin's*, receptacle
and space, ovular. She is a menses. When
I tilt my head, she tilts hers; and lift up slim
pellucid flesh, bracing apart thighs.
She is against death's naked taking-form,
her bare ounces of warmth.

Restaurant

Her fan trusses its scope. An eagle's wing
melts of its succulence in fire. We eat:
the sun's sure-footed mileage, desert shade;
the soft-mouthed appetite glides in a dish.

Light bursts shade against a tor splintering
this mouthless residue of flesh. And salt
savours its grains, and quits its ancient form.

The wingless broiled sun sheds its residence.

Pain and innocence

Trachoma's spark, it taunts the weeping eye.

'Take me,' she says. My thigh blanches with cash.

She is the innocent one, she is, she is

Lamp

A strike: chalice of steel splutters with milk's
hot purity. An unfurled day: mirth's flexed limbs
play in a thin sun micturating snow.

It is enough to make you laugh to be
a labourer, this mill-race shuddering.

What can we do with it? a labourer
chafing hands, thinks carefully of power.
The brain weighs its own choice: tatters either

a mushroom hung with gills, or opens to

a gallery. The furled lamp casts its beam.

Psalm 23

I hear you speak with it, tall-boy luminous
with physique and health. And if you draw its tongue
to write on, the substantive word will feel
and thought be fortunate. It speaks like Eros…

it is Psalm 23, beside the still waters…
shadow of death. Fasten its voice in it
as shut cathedrals with plague shudder. I owe death
no charity, though the flesh suppurates health.

Debt's papers mouse, yet purely husbanded

sharp starry linen there hoards table, bed.

I wish this family prolonged life.

Joy, lined with metal

joy – joy – strange joy.
– Isaac Rosenberg, 'Returning, we hear the larks'

Seeing all the movements of hesitation

It's winter. Upon sleek rails a gloss
of crushed frost, the sugary mess esteemed
by earlier freight sliding north. The train
pauses for breath. By a burly stream
stroking the earth, then dashing its stones,
a man tracks with an unwatched look. Through light
hung in the mist's long skirts he trudges
as we gather up our force and go.

    His name tosses in our bulk's wake, its cry
through our muddy century, its burly water.
A gull's call, tossed dihedral, feathers
the stream where the long-nosed fish dive;
thick-waisted time flies slowly away.

The bleary stream

The bleary stream from stone to boulder lurches
and stirs and traps feathery mud. Trouble
is not its watery language and it voids

like a drunk woman, as overhead burns
an oily furnace tracked for Edinburgh.
In open shirt and jacket a man plays

between a river and the rails, blossoming
his tin notes. They are solitary and
they sprinkle desolation. Without office

he wails his tin flute where the stream pisses
over the verges of this century.
A big man fingering his tin flute.

A question asked about love

Where a bridge fastens two soaked banks
there clayey waters braid; and a man plays
a tin whistle, in an open shirt

and jacket. Is the mind a loving form?
it enters the stagnating air, and breathes
it is the breath, the only thing.

In this raw fecal place wanting
occasion or office, something revives
the soured virginia of the mind that prints

the little consequence I am among
the wary spaces of this flute's cries;
jaunty, particular, the spidery feet

writhe on the margins of this chafed mud.

Hearing oneself

A shabby stream that's dunged by Lothian
has grass chewed to within an inch of life.
A heavy forked tread; an overflowing

task of milk will swell the cow's bulk
to lowing tenderness. A large man rests
his tin whistle between dark lips.

Haddida of notes, then none; a whining
of plangent tinniness in nasal cries.
A man hears only his own loneliness,

and if he cannot hear then he must feel.
By this sump of fecal spillage a big
Man plays his flute for all he's worth.

A meeting-place

He plays the whistle's pert male form, which is

so easily fished out, and clearly blown
of shrill evasion of the lyric. I hear
warily by the paddock's edge that curves

into the soiled vexations of the Till,
and is a broken retina. He blew
nothing upon the air that changed into

a serviceable noise for power; he got
it right. His flock of animating cries
fetched up the fur-anointed beasts; they feel

a bruised expansion of their congruence.

A peaceable kingdom

1

They crept to hear all that he had to say:
long-leggèd bird and leopard whose power is
with sensual beauty spotted, all converge

upon a man with a tin mouth. And there
crouched with her temporal power a naked girl,
a beast haunched on long thighs who takes thought to
those cavities of birth and mind. Pick what
is dropped off a tin flute, thick stubby petals.
The shaking mice scamper between thorned grass
their thong-like tails swishing in fortitude;
but sumptuous music, nuptials of tin, which
they cannot wait to hear. Authority
creeps with its mouse-like thigh, portfolio
of skin amongst this wildness congregated
with white salty flowers like stars.

2

from the arctic's pursed mouth
the white breath howling nebulae, of which
noise is the greater, stars the less. And still
the mouth's milky obedience, cherub of storms:
the north's machinery blows itself on stage.
The blizzard tugs apart, a fudged clinging
at the ploughed rutted features, a damp
six-sided polar clasp. Earth's kingdom sinks:
the snowy animals convene and die.
The mouse's soft rasp of nail on snow
does not avail.

How pity was first made

Drawn from the horse's mouth horse-hair: and not
like eyebrows, or to fatten up a chair.
Of the fly's eye, blinded majesty
the loss indented by a fed pin.

The mind's awry, its baulked energy
transepts the brain's cathedral, purity,
making a cruciform of pity's flight
altarward: ah we say, that is true.

The blinded mind in an excess of rage
pardons itself of every cruelty.
It is the mouth prays, the seething heart
walks on long broken legs into hell.

Little swollen pump, love's angina.

A posthumous life

Mid-winter's pregnant with
a form snow hunches on.

Mid-summer frost, aghast ghost of heat
dissolves with light; and fire that was light sinks

quenched in earth's shape. John Middlemass is dead
whom I knew little, and liked more; a ganger
who separated man, and field, and beast
with commerce distance linked. He drove of men
and cattle a branch-line.

    It's gone; no spurt of droving
    or passengers. Lupin
    dissolve stone; the nailed light
    and nailed wood loam.

The plough's volt is its furrow. Rev & sweat
spatter the wrecked saints of Lindisfarne
walking in fire on the torn sea.
In jets they whimper on the crabs' burial straw
where white-faced tourists crunch the cheeks of shells.

As walls drip with honey
so waves litter the pebbled shapes
of star and moon.

The fields bury with wheat
with barley the earth lustres.

Sharing out the maundy farthings

For Edinburgh, the train rises north
then slurs west, as a bee dances
sideways to its hive in. Fan north:
either Dundee rivers its silver or
the highlands' seamless garment without man;
the Gaelic mountains snort there, animus
of blubbery flesh, circlet of bees rustling
the marram's antique honey. Such options.
What you do is stop, where the flute
tacks the air. The lilies' spotted tongues
poke through barbed grass the beasts ease past,
spectrum of clawed slinked power in a space
of animation. With a charming tongue
and nothing loth. No stuffed moralism
but a blessed honesty known in advance. The cat's
small breasts succour her children milk. She is
music'd & glad. It is the cared-for flesh
covers the bees' workful limbs porting
honey grasped from the sweet tip. And dogs
flicker a ragged bark. As I look back
to my hive, my hexagonal
wax childhood, of such malleable
tensile accommodation, London's
my honeyed nursery, vatted, and glistening
on six-sided amber. The beasts trot to
where music holds them. Play in this other place;
we'll put our farthings on the saucer or
a tithe of pleasure calloused to your hand,

your finger tips hardened with covering
the flute's breathy holes. Such sediment
of lively music spittled through the tin
where among bristling oats you spiked the air
musically. Behind me, worshipful of
our Russ-lives, London of the onion-domes,
packed memory of the honeyed delicacies
childhood circlets. These sweet farthings
industry like bees through the chill
of startling beauty, a woman with raised
fingers at her coiled hair. This work
hoards me in its creating hand. I take you
through my future, I share you out
lush, my lush, my dearly won nursery
of adult honey.

Of lace and stanchions

Stations of lace on stanchions trains climb from

over the Kentish frolic, but its fields
are summery and bare. A young girl wears

her legs unstockinged through the year. Laughter
fills her mouth, ululations of bent

spires, malted torsions of green. But poverty
is hierarchy. And if you're beautiful

and have your hire, it is not anything
when beauty steps out of you. Poverty

is hierarchy. I am creatured this way,
to fumble hefted bricks into a stack

a skilled man constantly depletes. Cold hands
callous their flesh upon the year's first-born.

Something that silence can't be

1

Mind, fabric of its clan's blood,
stains with need; after burning
the flesh is its mind's lily.

We prepare each other beds of ash.

2

The wings of a herring-bird
gasp and bespread a foliage of ice.
What a fan that is. A bird's foot

webbed with water gets clung
by leaves skeletal as a leafless tree.

3

Like a wing's spiked flash, our stars
start away. Later, the fan closes
upon itself: the lacquered stick.

Here am I: a speck of dust, grinning.

4

Ice melts its foliage, and memory
frees love. Blameless scatheless
the flower opens its silent mouth.

Wildness makes a form

In Memoriam the critic Merle Brown

1

Spring's tinct is urinous on the heart-shape leaves
marsh-water's flexions cringe. With reed and bird
in mutuality, hospitable
to each one's sounds – music is sound threaded
on each one's listening, amongst wildness,
this sluggish jamming of impatient forms,
this enclaving of form
in authentic dishevellment.

★

Gaudy practitioner, sedent – plots, enacts
co-ordinates of our growth with that wild growth;

a purged barbaric wildness what I want,
accessible, authentic dishevellment.
Not too purged, yet not so dishevelled as
to parch to salts a modest potency.

A voluble small jar in Tennessee.

2

Paradigm of belief, with what is.
If you are affirmed, if it is holly
goaded by tongues to probity in thorns
gleaming from verdigris,
the burial is decent; but the worth
of the hot mind delivered to the approbation
of forked tongues destroys.

Selah, I'd say, selah; but not amen.

3

The self is from its being taken out.

4

The winds that you might see are tangled grass;
trees by their gleeful bursts of force thrash down.
Spindle of flailing but chopped lengths of trunk,
as if someone had bashed a wooden pole
and it had whorled in pain. To forearms flailed.

The silvery tree-pieces of the moon;
the wind lies bent – a plough, a knee broken.

The studs of lichen pledge into our flesh.

5

This wordy poem, grief's fabulations,
howls under quartz cliffs, with blood tinctured,
to hang in moulds – the fern's tribulation,
authentic dishevellment. Stammering tongues
are by grief made clear, of which spillage
death encrusts stone: Merle, Merle,

this is the very kingdom, artifice
of survival amongst strength in disorder.

The great tree falls away to the ravine
dribbled with bent cars. Words among branches twitter
in dishevellment, but with speech.

If you would have it this way, so would I.

Unpublished and Uncollected Poems,
c. 1980–1986

Filaments of the plain

If the shagged sun is fierce mild water brings
the speckled fig sweetness, sweet hyssop its fuzz,
just as fertility will flesh itself
a child. Holy, holy, these wild springs
a devil sings amongst. Innocence, in bands,

of thick steady arranged flame. Air folds
like paper. Like branches, our arms flail
burning and tangled. From the thick creased stones
made smooth, our lives spin loose and flop
through earth, a shout terse and final. Why?
and the sopping knots of scarlet
thud and snap. Over fields, a fiery bee
scrapes chrysalids of ash, shiny fur is
a murmur of starvation,

and fear and gentleness trot like paired cats
aching for home. Earth holds down three spaces,
three pools of Solomon's, cupped to filament
a sensual wilderness. They crush, with an idea
of God, like fiery skulls.

'The broad Ohio'[72]

1

The broad Ohio, with barges flocking upon
a livid energy, they foment

steam, a soft dynamism,
on the fiscal buildings. Blond light
hungers for the shapes, the dense

precise imaginings, the restitution
of mutual need.

Preponderance of hair, that blond thought
streams the pillow
with tense intimacies, hands listening
on bellies.
Intricate melodious sufferings
and joy, I can touch bewilderment,
unfastening a pretty band tight
at your forehead.

3

Intermixed and casual,
the daisy, its blond tuft, unclasped of petals,
stirs, shifts open its light
deranging possibilities. Blond, streaming,
the daisy masses its form
with the particles, the substantial
light.
Mild and lucid,
of active lingering, a true
inseparable form.

4

The hair freed, the fillet
if you remove it, it forms the blond thought
of mutual lucid heat.

The idea vouched in the fingers, a lithe
thinking the kiss flickers with, in me,
in every crevice thinking vanishes
into, the blond
disruptions; on you
the wave sinks, the foundations of waiting.
With that, tenderness brims
the form of innocence, residue
of the kiss that broaches us.

Imprint

In frost the daisy's light, greased seed turns to
melodious sufferings, sticky substance
fast on the eye's look. With tense intimacies,
hands listening at bellies, Thetis, her head
an arrow-shape, his broad docile face,
imagination interfuses each
with tenderness: the kiss's double-mouth.
What is is disappearance; in slow
fiery permanence through renewal – the imprint
of the wedding.

Of love's composition, upon linen and pillow,
her hair streams with tangles, and it is
in filaments, blond inundation, light.

Goddess of light, goddess of animals,
takes the space, filches the space that imagination
sees her hair with: blond hair, its blond
changed for the blond imaginings. Thetis,
who did not let go of him, that simple
stiffening, death – a snickering behind
that partly raised hand – took him to
behind a shed, as police take one
to be destroyed. Then she threw light
in soft spokes through his flesh, death separating
him from Thetis. Noise, fragrance, the stiff
magnitudes of frost, and oil, heaping
the earth. His spirit comes, mewing for home
as if this rushing, fastened earth could be home,
as for these stormy mites it is, each one
struggling to fold itself. The shining bug
becomes a shield, clasping its spotted wings.

Opposed to death

It is precious to your sight, if you
are You:
a day
amassed of ragged viridian.
In the vein, a sugary contagion
rasps with aniseed. Does nothing

fail? By the cypresses,
their combed arranged viridian energies,
from nail to elbow the pepper-man, weighing
his hot soft ounces, is red; his 'fear death'
inflaming his desire
for more hot life. The amalgamations
of 'fear of' with 'desire for',
death mild as talc.

Mild as talc, also, gentleness
drawn through desire's heat.

The father

The misery blood unlooses –
a grill vents burned air, a susurration
cut

on the rotor's blades;
my city's pendulous food shapes
the belly.

By the Monument
my father gathers cash, that those
the lathe's nib,

chamfer, or docker's ton
has maimed may survive. The mind's a grid
    bevelled to fit, workmen

    flickering
at it, a mulch, mishap of leaves pressed
    in the gardens

    of industry. Devils
fork in the owners' flesh. No,
    I hear my father say,

    that is not true.
St. Paul's clashes its shapes; by stealth, on four
    bent legs, we creep,

    the tongue swift
and soft in mouths, moduled to fit
    each other, as
we reach ourselves, each cry
    is pierced flesh.

Tenderness[73]

Its water crushes from ice. It lifts
and the eyes follow it
in a dark lilac gleam, a band
of tart jessamine wrapped across it, and as it hits
the spill off the pool, where the cliff is masked,
but not in lament,
actual, wingless falls
plummet to squares of rock, pitched over, unbroken
by pelting tentative liquid
shaking in several directions; and always,
as it bathes and splits on shafts of stone,
a blind mix

of escape and power in equal weights, like a hand
coursing another's thigh. Its name
is the bridal veil I am permitted
to raise, its gauze, it concealment, its ounces
that fall in chaste
frail abandon
between us;
the heats, the unfouled tenderness
inching to an act it begrudges and postpones.

If tenderness is a staring lamp
and your hair is naked on me,
the stare of the lamp
is the hand's model.

'What if I love you? am I not permitted to.'
'It is in order,' she tells me.

The Ship's Pasture

First published by Routledge & Kegan Paul, 1986

The achievers

Behind a front-door
stairs, without turn, or landing, run to a back-attic
in one flight; breath and breathing
go diagonally, as if
hand in hand
through the house, red stair-carpet and hall lamp
separating two walls that build
like stanchions
of light
into the roof.

This is Jesmond Zamyatin made
in his *Islanders* a Russian jest of –
shifting the tedium of yards, as he oversaw
the construction, and constitution, of Russian ships.
1916, the pole of the year: its ice.
A dithering of Ocean; the Czar's icebreakers
furrow dark water.

In a front-room
siding the stairs, a boy fingers
a flute, and a young woman, circumscribed
in a circle of light, shed from a lamp like a green bonnet,
stands a little
to the side, back a bit,
and bends above him to read the notes,
their closed dots and fins
silently filling the page
as stairs
fill the house, climbing
a magnitude
of soft despair
and achievement, coming on.

A paradigm

Here, mother, are a few words of love, meant
for Christmas and unfinished. But, mother,
I mean to give you love, a window in you in which
I see myself younger than I thought. Is this
love's face, I, who love, seeing none

but mine? Rather, a crooked tree,
its wood sawn from another, propped by
an engine's metal shaft, of the intricate
machinery of steam.

What use have I for the figure, its indice,
the closed dot on its open page? A *Kennedy's*
Latin Primer held shut in his hand,
the rosy cheeks recited a paradigm

the tongue cherished with ruthless Latin.

'A little naked son'

A little naked son at his father's shoulder,
with white belly and dangling member. He points
his father over the shingle – cog and mainspring
in grandpa's hunter. A town murmuring

in the cliffs – from on top of them,
a rope shaken its length, the eyes say,
with bees here, the flint, that look like bees
watchful over the vats for their multitude, rising
to amass honey, flickering continuous sheen
of labour. All the hive gets fed, she says.
Summer murmurs in her wings.

The boy faces the sea and won't enter.
His father puts in a foot; anguish at
sharpness of cold, at what he would
have his son perform, who waves his limbs
like a leaf, or aphid on a leaf. Christ,
his father mutters lifting a foot; he pours
a pailful of grey sea on him, and laughs
and asks if it is cold. It is cold.

A soft shrug of tears. Between leaves
and shade is a kind of concourse
where two can wander, unmoving. A hoard
of pale light off beige
mealy flowers – a linnet
his tincture of three notes she hears, her breast
faultless with his singing,
her feet squirming, the small vees – with wings
springing open. It lingers between them,
the birds that intertwined
with beaks, with energy, lifting away.

In the shade, the tree gives them as equals
as equal listeners to the flown birds
a temporary middle harmony
like a branch
of open blossom.

Taunton – Newcastle 1983–5

The government's comic

The ghost of a flea
          – Blake.

If his mother bears
our child with
a torn brain, shall she die of it?
I'm the government's comic, my brief
to make people laugh. My existence
is a thread of spittle in their mouths. Here's
another version:

you are a droll beast, I its flea
an itch in the legislature,
my jaws out of proportion to my small eager body.
You shall be aware
of who I am

by my stipend. Where's the shaping life in me
to form my laughter in your body
in its long, spiritual laughter?
Where the blood in me, to help me feel
your laughter? I bite
you between the balls, the smell
excruciating…
the sweet flummery of blood
my child will have of me. On the day the sun

in its storm of making whole appears,
vivid and huge, to shuck
the shrunk, fitted iron
that bands the earth – and reveal
union and boundary, and raise
what isn't quick, until it is, I will make our child,
as they all are,
whole again. My Lord, my dear life, breathe
into me, until my limbs are astir
to lead him to a table, where the stamps – hinged
on sheets – I have saved for him

are no hobby – stare, stare away,
like the Minds of Nations, in profile, strong
as the gaze, the eye's
bearable magic. The bow!
God, bend your bow –
the underpinning of the eyes
the strong yielding bolt of the gaze –
and make the mind endure
all it has learned to fear.

Under a lamp

What was the dream, what? I searched
the mind's oceanic magma for congealed
recognizable substance, muck,
for a spindle of meaning.
In the cerebrum, a phrase jammed
into its echo, 'Saint Pierre
et Miquelon.' A page
for colonials in an album,
a muted screech
of black children.
I tried to imagine hunger stepping
into their hunger
with my body.

A dream wash'd in sepia. I guard
a puritan in the civil wars,
blind vulnerable Milton whom
General Monck's victory would punish
with death. Milton? This man with me, his eyes
frightened, patient, is absolved of murder
in the peace. I bring him over a brown,
hardly lit passage, light
the colour of brown smoke, 'Sir,' I say
'by here,' into a room where squire,

a blind star, offering light
but seeing none, enemy
to regicide, not unkindly sits
in the king's absence forming sentences
on a soiled bench. My arm
on his shoulders guides the prisoner
before our judge: one blinks at his hands
one stares at the other, mildness
and mildness. Light streams
up stairs behind him. 'Sir,' my arm
on thick stooping shoulders, for fear
of death. I said, or looked. Or if I said
or guided the man
before his judge on whose side
I supposed myself,
against death – this soldier
like a shadow under a lamp, is white.

What are these stamps? Saint Pierre
et Miquelon
I had thought
in the Pacific, tall people
with a black skin; these are islands
off Newfoundland, made cold
near the gulf of Saint Lawrence.
The head on the stamps
inclines, and drops slime from
its mouth, and then a gracious smile
of one who would kiss
those whom luck has vanquished.
Sir, I touch you before you die,
on the head, and press
you into an album. St Pierre et Miquelon
your finger-like children
clothed in hunger
and a polar fur,
their skin misted in the dark winter –
mahogany. A dream of care
inches across snow. The king of the poles
watches, with the head of a white eagle.

Autobiographical Stanzas[74]

'Someone's narrative'

no man ever treated of a subject that he knew and understood
better than I do... in this I am the most learned man alive
— Montaigne

For a man's head

1

Leaving his eating-house refreshed, my father
carries the flimsy cash, most likely in
his inside pocket, buttoned to admit
his fingers. It is for a man's head
crayoned by fumes, a page of shapes
over the foundry wall.
And will the head come with me, and will it
concentrate a nation's charity?

The animalizers, benched in an eating-house
stare at the faces outside pressed to glass
whose grins are sickles. 'No,' my father says,
'that is not hatred.' Must I love these forms?

2

How shall I find my best way in the mind
this jittering world changes constantly?
The self is from its being taken out.

Acetylene: evacuated to a house in Wales, lit by gas

For gas, the house waters carbide, often meagre
for burning, though our lungs cough up a shred
of acid that we sicken on. Up at

plastered stone, flaky and gravid,
the sheep butt; smudged with an orange dye
wool inside mist wastes at the mothy house.
Then gas heaves. Quick, turn the spigots
across their limp flow, and ignite[75]
this powdery whiteness damped to gas, a flame
that looms, raising a brightness edged
in a dark blister to a light shaped like
a woman. In this midst of war we see

a foliage of thorn, holly, as if truth
would have us pilgrims. Pollen off the grass
sprinkles, in dots, its future over us
as house, school, and jagged hospital
subside. The cracked dews prosper
in war's electric.

A sprig of berries, blunt and pupa-like,
oozes its juice on the ragged sweetness of
the ferns, although this crude mummering
lifts flame fretted round that first discourse
of gentleness, light.[76] Our placid veins murmur.

Over the kitchen a bell widens its mouth
and closes it, each life between its lips.
We are to survive war. The bronze lights
its soft rigours on white, ribbed flanks
raked with scratches, as we lurch past –
small evacuated scars off thorns
pierce a filmy latent skin, as we scarper
beyond a hill. Death vanishes amongst
its stony quiet.[77]

'We were evacuated in the war'

'sinking below the level of himself
to mark the insides of his head, like glass.'

1

We were evacuated in the war
not working with language, a dull shrift
of possibilities, and sprinkled our piss-pans
with fool's gold. By us, two mines rusted
with real gold, quartz churches the Romans
split – septuagints that enriched in small[78]
heavy handfuls. A queen's ring opened
a new mine, fifty feet under
unpumped glistening, a watery shaft
the eye retrieves. Invisibly air folds
round branches,[79] delicate mainspring about
the sun, a sprocket that flicks up dew
at the flower's lip, misting dull gradual curves
of pasture. Like sweat, itching drops
barb this flesh. – I'd stop the Welshman inspecting
our fool's gold – Judah's pyrites – grained
by fanged sawing. If I crush and pan
valueless sediment, smelt fool's gold,
pawn it, and run off, I'd still saunter in
haphazard grass, bulbous blackberries,
swollen multi-eyed spit; even this house[80]
dishevelled, I want; cursed, it is said,
to frizzle; on its flagstones[81] blood speckles
in polish, where a master got knifed
balking a servant's marriage. For true gold,
authentic nature in dishevellment,
the hand abuses quartz to extract
fingers of gold, modest and noble,
splitting a Jew in Christian doubleness
of love for the community he serves.[82]

Shy looks of England rust in the fool's gold.

So in dishevellment nature forms golds[83]
neither as brutish as the other is.

3

I sniff gas —[84]
carbide watered to light a dim house
where I am clean in a fee-paying school,
a pure scholarly, a large-kneed boy
whose brain squats, in it a carbuncle made of adamant;[85]
not kind, bullied as bullying; a Jew
paying for to be educated in
the Welshman's English – an inauthentic metal,[86]
whose herring-bone lines where a fat saw cuts
the lesser pyrites, at spoil-heaps.

I crush a childhood's Welsh indignities
of self-hood and inauthenticities.
Their fighting, brave: my crudity, a dishevelled
outsidedness, in large knees. Those boys
disarrayed merely, but yet authentic
in it with real gold, easy-natured
and brutal.

Oh, if the sun will arrive, top-hatted,
spangling each of us. Love lamps safety,
but I'd love genuinely, father or boy.

The woman's curve lunges at me, whose fruits
fasten my fingers to her.
I think this is the way the bush sings
at its growing.

Anxious with gifts

Anxious with gifts, they laboured between ruts
their ridges toppled, wavered over morsels
of quartz, the mudded drive parallel
with aching trout and salmon, trees diffused
between:[87] came toward pond,
kitchen, gas-making shed, and turned right
to where I waited, clad dutifully in
the weave beaded with rain, that stung my thighs
like piss. 'Oh, come on,' they said; I came
slowly, as if in sleep, to them. I kissed
my mother solemnly, father solemnly[88]
and said, 'Come on, father: mother, come.'
Children with parents cram the house, as energy
swarms the creeper, a leafy electric
that we, here, have none of. Only gas,
diffusing a wet pressure, not burning,
of soft poison. Yet tables line
with heads of children, each a forbidden lamp[89]
at play, supervised by teachers eager
to make their togged charges presentable
to parents. I said, 'My microscope-set, quick,[90]
hold the slides, fine as insect-wings.'
She didn't. 'It's my birthday,' I cried, midget,
disconsolate, the tears powdery.
'That's enough,' they said, 'we're your parents
you've forgotten, re-making you in our
memory of you, and will even snap
your gradations of intelligence.'
Centred diaphanous gratitude, a web
to which I fixed.

The drive in ruts, with sifted ruinous
mud, wisped at the mosaics of
pebble – their hands huge[91] and linked, mother
was radiant with pain. Ribbons fluttered
love in inducements, eager blandishments
of my dependence. Through the knobbed woods[92]
the river specked with flux, a snake whose prim
triangle of raised head gushed clammy forms.[93]

'Here is your knife,' he said. Second present,
with a silvery tongue.[94] I drew its flash – and missed
the shrieking wood. 'You've lost it,' he decided.
My parents in interdependence, me – I hung[95]
in whims of re–appraisal of sons,[96]
feral, yet forced to return in need[97]
meanly arraigned for its ingratitude.
But love is prodigal, poor, dependent since
the knife is lost. Its blade, shedding
drops of light, peters to nothing. So presented[98]
to me like a toy, lost love re–formed,
its tears tied to each other on a string.

I come to you directly, out of love.

'The shrieking wood', but with a different sense, is a phrase out of David
Jones's *In Parenthesis*

Romano-British

'the war, the war'

1

Faces inside the wind's gusts smear us,
and heat lights in a bronchial mist; at twelve
I, like a pale face plied onto a stick,
a pole, from the hedge's swaying, witched
conical tufts of grass, but it cost me –[99]
as if turned witless. I watched Rome's soldiers,
an infantry negotiating shafts
of rock, in patches of lethal shine; but not
much interested, I turned, suffused
with home, its rooms mottled with gas. So I
flittered over ridges, splayed tracks
linking my feet, rubbed up with diamonds,

platens of quartz, that joined and flowed upon
a courtyard, the cobble serried in
a jaundiced, diaphanous sun.

2

We ached with sleep. Waking in a faint
dot of screams, I rose up, passing
between upstairs walls, finding in them
a solitary room, its flowered rug
toggled with sweat. Over a narrow bed,
in white cuffed sheets, celluloid as dresses
a matron wears, I wrapped myself. Boys
rose in a line to be beaten, and, faced
from me, their buttocks drooled whiteness, on
thin attentive legs. The light, eating
furious dust, sprinkled a carbide light,
the carbide, that we damp to gas for lamps.
Violently a door slid. I lay
behind myself, in doting innocence.
And all the night would form in discords of –
not roads, or a silence on them, hung
in livid strips – was a train[100] metalled between
Llanelli's columned slums.

3

The bricked riveted balcony at which
a door kept sliding clumsily – the supernatural
is rarely deft. Each boy had a red weal
bobbing its tiny jabs with blood. Spaces
of night throb, with artillery
aimed for planes. If I could tear my body
from this space, where my life thrums
vibrating military enthusiasms, I would,
as a man lifts weights not before
lifted, be strong.

Leaving

Like the beads of weft meagre
on their warp, war came apart, slowly,
with fatigued strength. I was fifteen. A dinghy's husk
lay awry in tidal light. Father
let me go.
As if I could.

And running to Victoria, its flaky theatres
of women, its fish-bars,
the salons of lost-property, here I unearthed
a cheap room. My tenant's mouth
creased in the landlord's eyes. 'I'll leave it'
I said, courage wetting
the granitic curbs.

The armed

the actual duties…are not in themselves unpleasant, it is the brutal militaristic
bullying meanness of the way they're served on us. You're always being
threatened with 'clink'.

         – Pte I. Rosenberg, 1915

what an impatient landscape

         – a traveller

1

Like dew, spotting the hill's edge, lumpily
I left behind the town's lamps opening
like eyes, their insides; or rather, the insides of
a bird's crop, with its spurt of muscle that portions
a mash of stored half seed, half grit, onto
a sinewy gulf its effort concentrates.[101]
I had this sense, leaving a place of coal.

2

Effort in winter.[102] I was returning to
the camp, conscripted by the infantry
at eighteen. Coldness, pricking moisture
in slivers, I began a run, for camp
frightened me. Charge,[103] sentence, and clink
at eighteen; odd conjunction of fear
with boredom made a threat,[104] which the army
materializes, replica of exact
brutality, its mintage, boys. I turned
amongst light joined in shreds of continuous
blobs of light,[105] which suddenly did not
exist, as if ingratitude had caused
its orange nubs to melt. The road curved to
my deviating straight tread; precipices —[106]
all that was sheer, I felt, dropping onto
my knees to negotiate these imbedded[107]
curves of blackness. Shame speckled my lips.

3

The instance became representative.

I came off leave, with a friend, reaching
the same village by nightfall; but this night[108]
was hung up on the moon, a zinc nail
glowing curiously. Viridian forms[109]
zig-zagged erect; oblongs[110] of darkness
that the strip of road hung livid in had lakes[111]
in shreds, gashed indifferently with[112]
the land's edge. My friend, fearful soldier,
with long legs quickening from me, though I
begged him to wait, scissored his lucid shape
into the frozen valley, a form bobbing,
khaki beret, its badge lingering.[113]

And I, judgmental without sense amongst
this plain light.

'Given a night's kip'

Given a night's kip, I had to climb
steps, to enter my bunk.
Bare women stacked by me, their pubis
and cunt like naked faces whose moisture
dripped off the page. Of what
use the women flat in journals,
my splayed fingers
fastened to their page? The phallus rubs
erect before an image.

Venus stands the other side of my mind
white, and shaking lightly. Her legs are stiff
and like her lips, apart. Her kiss
is enraged.

A hand[114]

You came, a howl nearly. I said,
leaving for three months, 'you aren't crying.'
The bus piped, in starting, drops[115]
thick and vaseline. For what does the phallus
quiver? the hand simulates
a fig, with my tenderness
in your image.

'At Hardknott Pass the startled road'

for Gavin Ewart

The startled road at Hardknott up among
the rocks fingers the contours. It is like
a waterfall. And jagged cyclamens
shake loose their forms, and pour them each side of
a milky cataract, pelted and itching
softness, wild cyclamens. You turned, lifting
your right thigh shaped like dropping moisture, that what
was made in you fruited itself among coils
of temporary life: wave-like and then
as calm as milk. So that the daughters live.

The mother draws her flesh up like a wave.

Absence and light

I shall get so used to absence I will be brought to more absence
than you from me.
It is a tree, a dim flossy absence
and a tongued florescence of wood. Take me, take me
in my absence,
you who know nothing of what it feels here,
you with your own absence –
apprentice stars
that saturate a dim chunk of space

and soften in flight like sodden fruit – fingers
with their touch in absence fallen;
stars out of blackness from their limbering masts;
but you, open
your mouth, speak, darkness of a sound
I cannot hear
you, silence, you awesome light that is loose and limb-like;

as if a tree, its opaque acid flesh,
its rings, perpetuated a radiance
in our two forms of one another's lingering.
A ring of acidic flesh biting in the soul.
And then the light, ashen and radiant;
this place of absentees renews itself
its space from which it grew, this radiance
in place of absence, if it is in place.

Given a Flower

A field of grief
— Ella Pybus

1

In the violet fixes an acid leaf
through the smaller of two petals:
this life,
its exact strong
smirch of pain. You said, look,
these petals,
their mauve scuffed paper, a hue
getting pale. From your yard

each mauve flinching shape of light, you said,
mixes with the pale, the pallid
dark of a spring night. Look,
holding out your thin hands
the fingers bent, whose flowers,
whose the mauve, dense
fictions of twilight, streaked
with fingers,
the pale, livid nighttime?

2

An inseparable form
the mauve petal, its hem puckered – the mauve flesh.
No, you spoke, no. Furled
huntress; not as the bee goes for it, but virgin,
and like a priest,
you admonished love. The violet
shuts, in the verge in which it roots.
A whole earthen cavern of music
a vacuum of it. With dreams
of lovelessness
as the moon's shade peels off it.

A field of grief
in this snowy, glum light. You said, 'This is not
a future.' In this republic,
aching with snow, you walked
unsteadily away.

3

In this tarnished leaf printed in the overside
of the smaller of two petals,
matched and different,
the violet's life flickers. The flower
extinguishes like a lamp.
It is a penitential bloom,
the spring's want incessant
as the giving which famishes.

It is never nighttime. Its curd, that is a kind of dew,
is pain to the male sex:
I have nothing to do
with the acid sex of the violet.

Forms of grief
asperge the southern night, its salt sprigs
of blossom, dogwood,
the twisted star-shape, in whose hollows
salt curds.

Louisville – Newcastle, 1981–2

Winter bees

1

Winter bees, finding enough blossom,
of the sweet, small copiousness they cram
winter – frozen muddle – with amorous pressure;
the acetylene flare of bees, nectaring
in suffused purple light; the honey
cool moral, waylaid by feelers.

2

Flickering sugary flowers, their doused blameless
substance a gelid intermittent veining,
like strands of wintery heat – the bee hunts them
for liquor, jabbing a superfluity.
Veined blossom flickering, scalloped clouds, these consonant
sharing forms, a bee their suffering link,
is also a heated wire, quick form.

3

The zone forks its electrics, the sky, fanned
in ridges like a shell, splits with the flash;
the bivalve in a half form, coy fissure.

In cold this unceasing flare is work
a prisoner of honey slowly unwinds
as if it were a spidery filament;
oozed sugary superfluity
the jasmine hardly notices it yields.
The face is winter's

plum-coloured, a huntsman's hung up in the fog.
A doe, spotting soft grass and briar, her breath
gassed in exhaustion, inoperative limbs
tied as a thicket is, green liquid,
greasy manufacture you recognize
is gangrene. Recognize these shifting marshes,
the horse's buttocks, the man's slighter ones
a contour upon the animal fixed like
a grin, blood misting the thicket. Remus,
with fierce light, with struggling blood, as if
you ploughed up North America, tune your horn
with fierce light, with straggling blood – as if
the evening's silvery flanks, the gashed flanks,
the simple sun, gashed. Hot star, rise up, see
your furred contemporary, curious nectar
of the lonely; the dead wings, without weight;

the embrasures of honey, the queen's furred kinsmen
in rows and layers, effigies for the spider;
pointed receptacles, corbels of honey
fluted with dust, scum upon amber fluid.
The young boy shoves off for lunch, whistling –
his little pipes, the unbroken larynx, are reeds
of cheerfulness, earth for him so much down,
fluff, a mantle, on the bellowing cheeks.

The Wanderer

Fumes mist of gun-metal, with bits pricking
into a sunk light – I need
one to speak to in this murk,
my fiftieth year its archway, with fog

off the pole's lumbar region.
You fly folk,
I fasten on you a spidery form
quick as bindweed. And I can't

help it. A month back
the redcurrant's orb hung
two seeds, like a kid
supported in its womb. Rain

spots our linked hands – a sharp-witted
heraldry of love. Old stems
bear the redcurrant, new ones the black,
and memory is both. Half my life

I starved the womb, now I want
what she doesn't – who gives swaddling clothes
with a folded pram to the neighbour
swollen with redcurrant.

I've spent my memory. I'd rather
the staring wide-eyed world as bride.
The Thai funerary ship, rouged glass
on huge watery wheels, scores the street,

and smouldering flesh – the emperor's – his coat
is a black fuzz: the flies
are tickled to death.
I will admit, I prefer love.

Leaving *The Free Trade*

Ah, that's the heart of it; if we
could have free trade. A bar… yet what
bar is it?… one that
was a house. You stand close
to your lager, lightly warm. You smile.
Politeness is all the rage.

A tree that's grass, serrate leaves prick
off a stem – within the top
thick dots of deft, light
green pollen. The smells
of our class:
beer smoke and envy sift
between the strong lax fangs of leaves.

'Shall you leave early?' 'Please.' Wan smiling
in a white demeanour. Your heavy
animal grace. 'Do you prefer
this one?' – my grin stared at. 'What
is it?' as you turn
thirst to lager. As if a thing
in a painting, I'm
a trap, and rat smiling behind slats,
its head, that had
chewed its tucker, lowered
between the two scapulae, fur thinned
at where ears stiffen. We are
docile, becalmed. You: your moist
mindful, animal tenderness
is smiling.

This house, its ceiling
in lozenge tracery, a rose, is slicked
with murky pink, the bar

a furniture one must step
round. 'Love, throw the darts.' The board
chuckles within its rings, zinc
competitions – 'I will' you
tell me – bull, zero,
thud of points entering rings. You put
your hand with mine. It's The Free Trade;

the eyed male minimum changes
to amenable companion, of a double nought
paired sequins, the two
nude bodies – us – heaving
that has scraped thin, paint
chipped off wood
in a pub with ship-builders
in a front room
of a seventy-year house built
to be modest –
humbling pain, the sweet
hot alteration, tenderness,
amour. I touch you. You are good
to me. 'You shall not,' you say 'escape
as easily this time.'

The ships all
shift from their moorings – in
a big swelling flight, fill with
departure, sail-ships
stirred with the wind – move down-hill
into the sea, through the arms
of their double pier. We are on the sea,
we are ships, from The Free Trade
the great chill amours of the north,
with lamps winking, gone.
The waves are furrowing themselves,
a sloshing aftermath.

Poems concerning Salome and Herod

Herodias was married to Herod Philip, and they produced a daughter named Salome. Subsequently Herodias divorced her husband and married his half-brother, Herod Antipas, but the marriage was condemned by John the Baptist on grounds of incest. The story of Salome's dancing for Herod has become secular currency, but it is sometimes forgotten that Salome was no more than a damsel when she so pleased Herod that he promised her (mother) anything Salome should ask for. The price exacted by Salome, at her mother's instigation, was the head of John the Baptist.
– see Mark 6: 17–29

Salome's life

Look, she said then, made thin and small: I'm still
a damsel. Look, have a cigarette.
Ah, I say, no thanks. The mutant air weeps.

Go on, she tells me. 'I think I feel afraid.'
Well if you are, then, don't. The bed-shaped room
contains a primus and a fire. Chased limbs,

thin face, her buttocks fondled to thin moons.
– But kiss me, please. Or see here, a different prize.
She kneels, and, from a chest under her bed

she lifts the Baptist's head up to the light.
If you might wish this frizzled appetite,
I got it from my mother, beautiful

to any touch. And I will give you it.
She puts my timid fingers to her lips.
– It's in good nick. Saliva tissues at

the jaded casket, lips spout the preserve
of his mouth's wordy spiritual – death.
– So do you want it? but kiss me, I beg you.

To her thin fractured person the designs
of misery have touched her with, she pulls me
– but put yourself in, gently, and lie still.

She croons from her shrunk litany as much
as in her extreme youth she thought was fit
to serve and save herself.

Salome's Herod

His mouth jammed with 'incest', a lamp unfurls
its lurid flesh from darkness. That's so.
I steal strength from him, and in me
nurses his fragile time.

Now a'm a damsel, how old is a one?
ma foot havers, couldna keep still
th'thing; it clambers
and speeds, dappling
his eyes that are big
with th'Baptist's. Ma clothes flailing
a'm two powers to flicker
smiling
and ma feet, and to flex him
in my wavering blade-like movement.
I stop
and take off everything. To me
I take the Baptist's fluttered cry;
and into me
the King's products.

Salome's self[16]

The rooted crystal lake
bleeds fish to the line; I'm tied to myself to flutter
like a damsel,
a breastless haired puberty. What
thing am I?

Limb and eyelid work, upon the tessellation
where ibex and fish preserve in the floor's pictures.
My hot self is pure space,
but his heated eyes dispose of me
in his darkness, whose energy silences him
in me. I am freed
upon another world, in which my silence
is a halo of ash at the wall grief
can't touch. Pity
and self-pity divide me up.

Where is the mother to abort or save
me? 'I will,' he says,
'be good to you.'
The disparaged soul dances, and dances
its disparagement. The opening
flower's parts were good enough.

Herod's life

Her self's innerness encrusts with
my liquid.

Breastless bare flesh, a painted smile;
and the haired mount
nests on the fork of thin limbs. The damsel bares her
contour of frail machinery.
Frail eyelash, her bleak future

in vials, a sort of perfume,
its stoppers irremovable.

Maternal heat shimmies her. I
come on spidery male
legs, a little haired spasm pure
as an egg, to take my ounce
of delirium
with hers. The mother has her daughter
to do
the end of women.

In excruciated heat I run pure
of God's foundry, and cool in a falling
eyeless shape. To me
she's good.

Salome's John the Baptist

Where a cistern weeps lobed flowers
his absence and innocence
blur against a wall. The lily's tongue is full
of his truth.

The Baptist's flesh shakes away its caught lovely head;
I am the blood. Herod spangles with sweat.
My desire is rimmed by the Baptist's eye.

And 'no', he said. The body of every
man will be torn and reviled.

Herodias

e fango è il mondo
         – Leopardi

'The world is dirt,' a poet says. It's the wind
drops a crystal with a black root through water
to where toothed fish nose. The sink whirls up its mud.

My breasts are magma to children's wishes, and I
desire my provision. The Baptist spatters
Israel's veined lily, with a mouth of snow.

But I don't know who I weep for, or why. She
has work in dancing. Over the pictures in
the floor, performing on the tessellations of wheat
she bares herself. The soft immersions of
the Baptist inundate after all with his blood:
my forms of rooted water work free.

Three Poems about Grief and Fear

A socket of plain water

A socket of plain water. On my hand
the lake's obsidian congeals. I draw
a fish
a bearded wrinkle of fear. 'Immerse me.'

'Mercy is in the blood as much as blood
lingers in water. Torn from water, mercy
lies in your hand:

replace me in that sweet obsidian.'

Innocence barbs the lake

Hot hands: their fetid mercy sweats bread.
The palm hungers with its bribe.
The bread is a hook, and the baked meats
of slender grain lure our mouths;
this is the travesty of love
sodden with our element.

He stares at my face, mingled in his:
water, the eyes' strange pastoral.
Our bodies throng, touchy and phosphorescent,
like dew
at the flower's lip.
Innocence barbs the lake.

The sun's body, resting

Where light frisks in the shallows,
splintered flints in the water's radials.
A grin comes,
a flickering of darkness's mirth; the flower here
says it will live.

Bread is a burden on water. Here we thread
ourselves in fear to their watching: here
a flower is opening its waving spikes.
The flower is strong, it says that it will live.

As if soul were a glimmering aperture
the sun's huge body rests. Sacred with fear
we share each other's hinged timidities.
The flower is strong, the flower says it will live.

Envy of God[117]

Fig, date, and balsam fringe
two pools, where shields rest
in Judah's desert… with gazelles hurtled
by fear, by fear checked.

Fig, gazelle, shield – words resting
by water, in desert where
that small king the asp grins. So we wait
by water to be at rest.

We are enough for Judah, and the shields
will suffice us. His psalms pluck
at our praise, that gleaming capacity
filling our jealous mouths with His name.

He made the wild places, I, too, form songs.

Climbing to Jerusalem

for Moshe and Ziona Dor

The locomotive, a short
satisfied fierce horse, scores the plain
after which five carriages jangle.
At the mountain's jointing, with anemones
that spot blood, glimmering orange fruits
like memory tumble. A stuttering olive
pierces the terrace with age, being adored
as if a woman of a hundred.

The denser patches of anemone blood
the higher we thread – you abandon us.
We strew energy as Jerusalem
helmets its stone; the herdsman, His shadow

fractured with sheep.
Pure absence measures
the plain we leave –

its celestial wounding – where the stream moils
between trees slender as astonishment,
their long flanks
dressed with fingers. Amongst
glimmering wheels of fuel
the sacred catches fire with the world.

Footsteps on the downcast path[118]

This poem is not concerned with heroes or martyrs, but victims.
And in that sense, it is intended as a history – not so much the
'lachrymose … martyrology' of … the Jews, which would, in any
case, now be unfashionable, but a selective history of them. This
history runs from Roman Jerusalem to the sewers of Warsaw. A
Polish leader recently remarked that the current troubles with Soli-
darity in Poland were caused by its Jews. That there were at the
time something less than 2000 of them must therefore attest to
their ghostly presence, something the Jews would not altogether
discount. History is ghosts, troubled ghostly presences. So that
even if martyrology is not to the exact taste of most Jews it is an
ingredient produced by history, and can only be ignored. It cannot
be dismissed.

The poem is in the main concerned, historically, with the Jews
over the period of their dispersion, although it finally rests in Israel
as it is presently constituted. When the Romans destroyed the
Temple in Jerusalem in the seventieth year of the Christian Era,
they destroyed a view of the Jews, or rather they assisted in a change
in the view of the Jews as it was held by society. Thereafter, society
saw the Jews, in their dispersion, as anything but the people who
had created the Bible. Cromwell's invitation to the Jews to return
to England was an invitation based on their linguistic ability with
Hebrew. The creation of the State of Israel has once again obtained
for the Jews a fresh view of them.

The poem begins with the dismembering of the Temple, and moves through the expulsion of the Jews, from England in 1290, from France in 1394, their partial destruction at the hands of the Spanish Inquisition, and their exposure to hatred in Russia and Poland in the nineteenth and twentieth centuries. It rests in Israel.

What the poet must be careful not to do is trade on history, and to deprive such a history, as it uses it, of its factual truthfulness. There are many ways to distort such a history, and one way would be to use it as a justification for aggrandizing violence. Another would be to use it as the basis for claiming a superior moral stature, and as a demand for further studious suffering.

The protagonist of the poem is a Jew. He sees crucial Jewish events re-enacted over the walls of the Old City of Jerusalem, as he descends into it with his antagonist whom he has by chance encountered. This man tempts him along the lines of 'you may as well squeeze enjoyment from what you regard as the abuses of power, it's … they are – enjoyable. Isn't it, in any case, self-righteous to be a moral being? Aren't you likely to claim an unjustifiable, preferential treatment if you see yourself in this superior moral state?' The antagonist may raise some of the right questions, if for questionable reasons. In a mental sense, at least, this figure is bent on destroying the self-narrating existence of the protagonist. It is for the protagonist, this good liberal indignant Jew, to answer and not deflect these questions. Business as usual.

If history makes people, we, in our turn, try to refashion it. The poem is concerned with that attempt not to abuse this capacity, and with trying to survive it creatively.

I was not aware of anything mystical being intended in organizing the poem in six parts.

1

The tormented in a sullen privilege. Now
they are captors, and bind a naked man
to a wood horse. Then, they beat his soldiers
to his body, dappled with fear.
And for sustenance, in any case,
they tear him, beseeching forgiveness.

'Men at their torturing,'
a man said. 'These troubled soldiers, gulping
their leader – does it disturb you?'

The wood flinched,
as water flinches with wind; the aureole
is scratched off his chest.

'Anguish cleanses,'
he said, 'and it's anguish in these men, lapping
his blood. Come on, all it is is torture.'

A tree shakes with ice, fear shags me;
the fir innocent, his sharp grin sagging.

'Look,' he repeated, 'at this feast,
the eye innocent, the hand not.'

'I don't want to'

'but you should.
What a housewife you make. Doubting Thomas
passed into earth, and it got
a larger helping than he. These men
gasping, you can feel their pain, they feel it.
It's the way we are, each, contrite
for what's done.'

We get a move on, patrolling
this city of steps with a soldier's
muddy anguish. On each side
house-walls shop-walls
with moustaches,
sold calico, silk, the desert's spiky
rambling wool, and the stone walls
quickened on one side of us, or the other: chiefly the left,
on the left, always. Here is the first
stone visitation,
a tableau. 'Hear me, O Jerusalem,' I mutter. You,
heavy, petrol-fumed

like silk. We watch,
with sweat panic'd into the buttery stone,
a stone picture, the slab growing quick.
Women are hiked onto blocks, soldiers
hold open their thighs, as Roman flesh comes
in the woken belly.

                                        'Look,' he said
'they are beautiful'

                                        while, at their back,
the temple sputtered like upright matches,
the doric'd flames a burst tangle
of burning cries, the folded paupery
of bodies flammable
with soldierly hatred and rage, curtains of torn light.

'All joys are sexual,' he said, linking
his arm with mine.

                                        'No,' I said, 'no.'

'Are you virgin, the coy sabbath resumed
in prayer? or something'

                                        still pumping my arm
as if to spurt a ragged juice.

                                                       'Yes.'
'And not attractive to you?'

                                        'Each woman has…'

'All women are; never dishonour a cunt.'
And what else but squeezing the spirit
to tighten the candle's hot feather. 'Oh, my God,
what is preferable?'

                                        'This is torture'

'To not have is torture. To have nothing
is a mockery of creation.'

We walked more downward through the city, its crustacean
vaulting ragged. There was a second picture
in stone: three boats – each, a round prow,
a breast lifted.
Raised up to the sun, that between it
and sea, the English pennant shook its cross,
I mean blood. As if waves caressed
the wood's creaking sussurations, two mailed figures
lift children, with their frail
nuptial of parents, in gentle unction
to the sea's usury. England expels Jews.
The date crouches on its flag: 1290.

That first picture undid the temple, seventy years,
its squat fragile ghosts.
'History,' he mouthed, 'is wonderful, is its own pentecost
the brain of God exhales. Such suffering,
such parleying in stone, that batters
a skull someone's hands have carefully,
with consideration, put at ease.
Look, you speak as if your fruits were sugared.
Are you a decent man? kiss your arse then,
your lumpish testicles frumpish and sinning
as any.'
                                    I turned away justified;
and as his purposeful destruction of me
sustained, we saw a third picture –

                                    a stony hill;
in it a ledge, two men on thrones wearing
their gold, each head fitting a heavy crown,
with white hair, floss conferring sanctity.
In the soft mouths of Fair Philip, and Charles,
a torn shout – 'Juifs, Juifs – turn again, for you
pity is France.' So the ragged speech,
as trucks judder, when a locomotive startles.
A troop of families, at the alpine face,
half-exiled, alive in exile,
start downwards, like spiders clinging
textured crystal. The movement, hardly

set into opposition to itself,
than the mouths, 'Juifs, Juifs' –
stencilled a delicate 'no, go away.'
Families at the clambering seams. Two kings shout: 'Juifs,
this is the kingdom; go. No, do not go yet;
I mean go.' Open mouths at the dainty
air, the sun crashes onto a tor:
in cold desolations, splintered alps
speckle with figures. 1394, the date
freezes in air. Praise for my God
fills my mouth, frost, that spangles me.

2

In this hot country there is a dotted winter, hoar
baffling the mind of paraffin: a weak nucleus,
soft, hollowing forms of gas. The lamp fluxes a burning hand.

Virgins come, wisdom mingling with fools.
The big hand strews its quartzes of terse life,
hard structures with soft fuels. Careless and intense.

Spilt wax itches the curious hand Psyche searched with; foolish body,
her person charged with curiosity – that waxy
illiterate conjunction. 'There's no release
from foolishness.' That's what he said. I answered
'let's have something to drink,' 'yes' he said 'yes,'
and we went.

3

Two separate events, two feet in two shoes…
the march, the slow protestant amble;
a pair of feet, many, like pelting rain – but the sound
in the lamp is like ash, its dots identical
and every dot comes out of the same flesh.
Bruised puce, bruised heart, the sea pulsing in it;

THE SHIP'S PASTURE

the salt is the same, as water is,[119]
crossing its bed. To the bed it's the same – many stones
uprooted in watery flight. These ruined facts – ah –
as, ah ah, to a stethoscope's black cup.

A dais, with Torquemada, the face, plain,
its invariable smirk hot and boy-like. A tongue
pushes out lips pursed on mirth's quick. Quaint bi-sexual mouth
of lisped lippings, an orifice, a hollow jointure
of mouth on tongue. His candle the thick root
of his mind, a martyr's bed-light, singes so many.
Christ's proxy wets the hot earth,
staked into which not a cross, wood, – its projecting
metal length glansed, its tip a penis
on which men, the Jews, rest their genitals. Soot and melting,
the Vatican is ribbed vanes, a vacuous spirit
its night-piece, mucky fluttering angel. Weep,
like Ruth in the corn, having no home – weep
for Christ in innocence, for whom pain, they say,
and death were made. Jews sit on this metal jump,
corded by their necks to the upright –
a cross without arms – and their tongues protrude.
Look at the picture, if I seem to lie.

As the hands of dark sisters death and night softly wash this
                                          soiled earth
the remnant searches a fresh portion of it,
as if who in this ambling soil could root. Who, and where.

                            4

This ragged city, a thallus on a pole,
blotches white the even-coloured psyche; at its foot
it buries in our soft dust.
'You are what I need,' the city spoke, like a girl
in the dormitory of a hostel.
The city spoken for by a single lamp, Jew or Arab.
'I need you,' she demanded, hair

wisped on the sun-burned skin, the blanket rucked
on the hostel's black-painted iron, a bed
braced with dreams. This city is a hospital,
sickness pitting its joints, with its split bags
of lavender. Its matrons are ill-advised
and ill-fed, but, in the market,
jaunty with spice and fruit.

Dreams in a ruck-sack. 'Oh, look,' he said.

'You again?'

                      'Yes,' he admitted, 'this city's
soft-spoken ouzo, like an old client
whose eyes are milky with pain, won't disperse me.'

The stone devises another scene
as dust devises life, its shadow.
The lives of Jews dissolve in Russian, a lamp,
its flame lightly blue behind smoke. It bristles
with cherubim, a spume of exultation.
The Empress Caterina's bronze candle-sticks
spatter.
           'Wax is blood,' he said.
                            Her Cossacks –
her riders' legs riffle, and bridle bells
flicker, softly jangled. 1881.
The Russian tongue is a strand in the officer's braid,
in his zinc badge – its artifice
a cock on a weather-vane the wind shakes through.

And then a stairway of familiar
more recent likenesses. Of Poland, its wars.

An archway links two terraces of homes.
May frosts its eglantine
that is not maytime, spring
dancing its thrush upon tawny grass.
Fire arrives, a horse brandishing flame – a mane

of thick steady arranged bands – catches
at shrieking wood and crevice. Girls
in a row, on fire. Hot sheen, blood
in ashes beside that. And wiring
that trails, then snaps – the blue cobbles slashed.
Armour's chain rickets on the flesh.
Sinewy cries, anfractuous crying; sweat, petals, shit,
and everything that one must do, to resist
in a Polish sewer. The House
up-ends its beard of flame, Warsaw, feathery
with soot; a fossil
gets smelted to a wall.

The working flesh of Polish gentlewomen
steps the downcast path. Spiny cats
trickle the streets, with lean inquiring faces.

5

For Jerusalem start the train with fifty lirot. Then, springy, dili-
gent as a goat, the locomotive circles the hill's aureole – the
buttery stone of which has a nub of fudge-like decrudescence,
viscous and sweet. We spiral – as if, by reverse motion, we sank
down; as though the down-spent mind were, by stuttering
connection, an urbs suckered with flittering minds. Not so:
sucked and dabbed at by moths, we climb.

Under Jerusalem is a sea. I purchase an unattractive boat but
the oars are made of Galil Cedar and give off a wan dismissive
smell. Lucifer abandons this cavernous water, his fire dark; it is a
cloak he has shed. No littoral and no tide, but a number of crisp
shells pallid for want of light. I go to tie a hammock under the
speckled orchards of citrus – these fragrant cheerful lamps. This
is a mendicant corner of the Turkish empire, its moustache fine
as an arrowhead.

At David Street, a man weighs heat, from fingers to forearms
a soft hot red, its greasy powder hairless as his skin. This fear of
death on him enflames a desire for more, hot life. My friend
smiled faintly when he heard this, as if he were my diary.

Returning once, we stopped to extinguish a fire that had seized another bus. After, I was afflicted by the ragged viridian of Cypresses that, notched with a grim demeanour, step up-hill. If death tastes like this I may find it bearable. The pepper-man dispenses his red touchy ounces. My friend laughs on David Street. The talk of the evening sputters in Aramaic – Christ's year, with its wings of short stubby feathers. No more trees with the hinged mechanism of the cross, no more men springing fully armed into martyrdom: I want the cross to fold into a featureless stick. On the Temple's Jebusite threshing-floor I know that the wheat is about to explain, 'I am eaten, I am alive.'

6

A simple quantity of Hebrew spills.
'Is this a pogrom?'
                    'it is not' I say.

'Is all that finished with?'

                         The timbrel
in orthodox voices as they bind their shoulders
and pray. No, it is her hand dancing, her nails
that swish the light. If I'm alive, stone, not music
gives me my energy. I form a language
of chips and indentations in rock, scratches
and little pressings of momentary rest
the may-fly in her flight north left on it,
the bat of cherub wings, the family
pressure of angels disturbing the desert pebbles,
in their variety communal. I form words
and become stone. Praise for this to the designer
of letters.
                Dropping through this hell to a shaded field
I scrape another stone. The jerboa
fixes its little teeth into the side
of something smaller. Sparse cindery flowers
rub bees that like the insides of the plant,

the sweet wax food, spiky fractures
of blue and lightning, each feathery spike holding
a flame inside its own. I wait beside
these acid pauses, flower-like, my eyes
wide with surprise. I fondle surface, and its veins
smoky with tenderness spread, binding themselves
with bitter strength.

My friend smiles faintly, and his smiling is
a patch of bleeding on the tufted sand.

Drink, nightly, a small measure of dry wine.

Jerusalem 1980 – Newcastle 1982

Communal

for Dennis Silk

Prayers and rifles mingle[120]
like legs of sleeping soldiers, like the mingling grains
in a stook. The weave sees
the competence of its collective life.

The café's a tattered flame, its fence
creosoted
in a distraught Mandate.
A Bible in one corner kneels,
its hassids
lust's tumbling Absoloms.
In reciprocal absence – both a space
and a grief –
some girl waits.
Breath from a great-coat speckles with the frost.

A man from the shipyards

*In the process of becoming a Quaker, Penn, still in the navy, asked
whether or not, or for how long, he should continue to wear his sword.
'Wear it for as long as thou canst,' Fox replied.*
                              – a 'Quaker story' from *The Quakers*
                                   by A. Neave Brayshaw

In the destructive element immerse
                                   – Conrad, *Lord Jim*

Penn, from the shipyards, bears a sword – 'natural
to a man of war'… 'what must I do with it?'
'wear it as thou canst,' Fox answers. Thou is
thou yet, although that natural, aching
psyche in its wet plasm of snowy
righteousness requires, 'your life for my child's'.
That some women
are not made more compassionate than all men.

As if for arbitration, with his sword
Penn leads the beasts – a forest clearing, by leaves
melted to twilight, the sword
like a bird biting
the leaves to line its children's nest; and not
much different, she, a human animal,
pulling his senses to her breasts, annuls
jealousy. Penn would change us,

the soul's light standing to its flesh,
its sleek shape, as charge;
he would merge the natural with the common flesh
as leaves with light merge,
where a community of stealth, of mild and fierce creatures
and dangling hair touching the breasts, gathers…
'not that we can't see,' Penn says, 'but the pain
because we do,' his sinewy mind
all-eyed, spotting like
a candle in snow. Penn and Fox

smudge with earth, lying between
friends, digesting the consequences
of hunger. They speak their minds, each day –
the leafy day, the branching night
in harmonious succession
– natural, again, most natural,
as when at length the living God
like living water
lifted his creatures up. Natural.

Penn took a fork from his pocket
as if he had meant to swallow meat. At which
the creatures shuddered in their forms, yet did
not creep away to weep. And tears,
which are the edge of grief, started, like blood,
the animals whining in upstart pain,
abandoned now, to be love's careless victims,
in that compact never to kill. Of love
they thought but little after that, as if
love, a watery human element – *in that
destructive element immerse* – were fit
for breaking, the lesser magnitude than care.
Then Fox's tears dropped,
the land held in his thinking
of rocks, sand, tears.

The Makers

*He imagined that he should be transported to scenes of flowery felicity, like those
which one poet has reflected to another; and had projected
a perpetual round of innocent pleasures, of which he suspected no interruption
from pride, or ignorance, or brutality*
– Johnson's *Life of Savage*

Lives of the Poets. He who wrote them listed
by, opaque as ink. Awry smile, as if
knowing the English Makers he ambled with.

A kind of honeyed community, worker bees
corbelled in their queer hive, who danced
in syntactical unison – he could feel
my eye on them. But though I hailed him,
the man who made compassionate sentences
held his smile wry and erect, and no syllable,
as if it were a farthing's worth of grease,
slipped past his lips. Discreet
as an emptied cup, or a churn made white
with used-up milk. I wondered, since

he would not speak – was it death
forbade communication, as Jews
have an interdiction against speech between
the living and the dead: no, it wasn't;
merely, he would not have an exchange
of touch or of words with, for instance,
– and in that instance lies the wretched fact –
those English men and women who have killed
the Irish, and sleep easily on it. Like wasps,
and not like bees, who sting and sting again
as if labour were not a jagged instrument
to be defended and broken, but poison's lance.
For whatever reason, not a peep
or smile could be got from Johnson. He left.
In the hive, the acid honey, a burr
of sound and work and feeding succulence,
lay in the vats, till our delicious innocence
should be more modest of itself, truer in sweet
atrocious delirium, and in
reluctance to be eaten, save as food.
Johnson had gone, I knew.

What we have held

for Jessie and Sylvia Epstein

> *Here the patient stag*
> *Breeds for the rifle*
> — Eliot's 'Rannoch, by Glencoe'

This basket is a weave of rushes,
its sides steep as the rushy creek, with rushes,
a weave on an Indian
woman's thumb-nail, ninety years,
the brandishing wanderer's
nomadic plants; a funeral basket
containing those whom the English scuffed, their being, these
                                        squat fragile ghosts,
their temporary essence, scuffed,
like a rubber on a pencil mark,
but like a hand brushing water
speckled with light – the light stays.
And even so, they breed
as if for the rifle
of the voluptuous
revolutionaries. This woman's labour,
of which who is to speak,
is like an emboss; the impress
is hers, but the paper is that
of the people by the Skokomish
speaking Twana – a basket
with nothing in it, and fit
for everything. The woman's name
is *Louise Pulsifer.*

Crossing a river

Three barges, their decks of planking stabbed by nails
with gleaming oblong heads – their noise is moisture
from a horn, on offices, in which inky fingers
blotch the copies of claimants' letters. The river
they divide is a vein of filth, taking commerce,
with the sun dipped in it. I see pity crossing

the water. A town: pity stoops near it;
a cloud with sun in summer stoops with
a lumberman whose spine aches from his axe-blows
and the cutter's soft rasp. It aches, he says.
He and fatigue, two spoons in each other's shape
– work, workman, pity in one shape
of two spoons. I see the image and I see his shape.

Ajuga

In fine rain, a flower pricked
in tongues, off its stem.
Delicate virulent blue,
a bitter red-brown veining
the leaves, a hue Norwegians stain
their wood houses in. Blue, may-blue, sturdy
in all gaiety.
Ajuga: made of mercy,
never to pierce, in aimless torment,
its fellow.

It is to survive
from Europe in America, hid
in a small sealed box, its roots
such as they are, wrapped
in moist scraps of towelling. As I turn
from it, two roads

form a T of metal, welded
in blue acetylene light,
dismal dark roads, beside which sandy earth
hugs dry lumps of quartz,
the T rubbered in a skin off hot tyres – the mid-west's
colourless summer: bleak sun
on pale earth,
the mottled festoons of withering.
A man's torn mind holds
in his porch-seat swinging from
thin chain.

But here, thin pipe roots
of blue dark flowers
glowing like labradorite vessels used
as ballast – ballast-flowers,
like medals, like hearts, like a cat's tongue
poking. You advance
in delicate strength, in joyful
meekness; in me, like ducts, the swift
inturned evasions feeding
the soul's vena cava. Root your ghost
in me, annul violence
here, none knows why.
In this frosted garden, this icy suburb,
in great bleak notes, triumphants
of winter – hot blue flower –
Ajuga – comedian, voiceless
in the garden's clenched hand.

There is a wood, shingle house picked
in scales, a cobalt evening
a dry dark seethe
in milky sands, and a thread
of gannet's flight
with feet extended: the blue flower
as intense here.

This chronic disposition
these sounds of life together.

Four poems from the Chinese

The garden grows darker

Energy clarifies in the twilight
in dusk's shade clouds straggle and settle;
the curtain of twilight with a light breeze freshens
scraps of light glimmer the green and blue wood.
In the window, this light goes out.
The garden is touched with desolation,
its green pool flutters white, the white of pain fluttering silk... birds.

A cold noise is the feeling of autumn.
If one loves, the beloved shares an identical love;
strings of an instrument become concordant: wine gives a transit,
a journey, dispersion.

Unused to

Autumn wind is crystal
and white dew turns to morning frost;
at sunset branches are pliant, by dawn have stiffened,
yellow leaves that had in the day a green life.
From clouds emerges a bright moon... as from a cliff
and causes a pure flow of white light, a flow of plain silk.
The balcony can watch a forecourt,
'ao-ao', the hungry cries of geese during the day: up they whirl.

A clear refined vision over four seas, the empire's territory;
the lonely disemployed one meanders within an empty hall.

The heights of Wu mountain

Imagine Mount Wu, which a woman – the shaman – possesses,
and a thin mist over a crooked terrace that faces into the bright
                                                      south;
coloured mist rolls up, rolls off,

monkeys and birds stop their speech, and start up again
… such beauty – as if it could be anticipated.

Waking confused words, confused within your gaze.
We sit in each other's mutual longing;
a green courtyard discolours with an autumn wind.

The passes

Mist bulks the space between mountains
from amid bamboo, the sun falls;
birds lift into the spaces under eaves… the wind is free
of the cloud-forms the pass holds.

Crossing to Europe

As hovering – seen – through fog –
– Emily Dickinson, 'A solemn thing' (271)

Light with frost burned, a natural doubleness
to which the mind shapes itself… and drifts…
the frail boat, insect, of mast and cross-parts
with haired rigging. In the cabin, three
hands, doggo. The bare mind makes
what it can of itself – the prow in
unequal exchanges with water pierces
never tears eternity. Work

is the ship's covenant, with oil.
I lie in my cabin, astute, under lamps
whose brassy discs of light soften at my cheek.
It's what work becomes, melted in love
to ease, though the double human creature
produces pangs of birth that men escape.
In the nature of water I'm absorbed.

I know I'm salt, thinking oblivion;
this swill is my life's transforming, and I,
full savour of it. Flaky with it
I begin to harden, through and through I'm salt
in a middling petrifaction; but to what

I see preferable, Europe, a tassel
of greasy lights – its congregation of
flesh making ash, enough to stuff a house,
though in burning they say we renew: and still
the wispy soul reposes in another's death,
so that as the ship hovers mid-channel
it chuckles, as if its keel rasped pebble,
as if the channel's shallows rip, is it, the thin
limb-like underlife of our craft.

Almighty God, I mumble, mercy on him
mercy – who carved the creature from its shade
the whale's torn shadow, from the whale – mercy
for the spotted larceny of flies
and for the tingling mollusc – its wet beige

Naming souls

An hour is held deep, in the underneath of time.
In the religion of purification
men's innerness
stands stripped of garments in the dusk
and prays to see God's image. Ah, if only I could bear up
the cup of bitterness,
my eyes turned inwards, I would drink to the terror in the eyes
of soldiers, brothers whom I fought with
and reached the Sawa's water.

They fell, tangled on the wire,
their feet raised high,

and that wail, essence of their dying, lasted only
a moment; they died, then,
very dark.

I stood on my own, the last
of the species that fight,
seeing these brothers, with feet turned upwards, growing
until they reached the sky, in death,
to kick it. I saw
the moon like an animal
rub a silver face on the worn nails in the boots
of upturned soldiers.

This fearful glowing on the nails in the boots of the dead
who kick at God, electrified
my being with a terror
that shone as if I were dying. With the flesh's
eyes, I saw the divine
in fear's mystery, in men falling. I cried
then, as if I were the last to cry
who never again in life
will cry what I wept
on the Sawa's water.

Translated from the Hebrew of Uri Zvi Greenberg
by Ezra Spicehandler and the author.

Before Mundheim

A man comes towards me, his sledge-hammer,
like a toe, slung at his shoulder. Serving
time. In Norway, servitude
is freedom bound in usefulness. He sways
with the pale blob of his hammer that presses
his gristly shoulder, and collar-bone,
on which the haft, shining with use
and sweat, rests. I fear him.

That is nothing. Promise of esteem is nothing
to him. The stone is his, length
of time, length of haft and line
of cleavage in grey green boulders
strewn by what is fugitive in
a fighter, the huge chunks
of explosion. If my father dies, he says,
I shall forgive no one. In a lake

not deep or sufficient for the salt
dimensions of a fjord, there stains
fir-clad hill, with large
thorns of conifer – mottled savageries
beauty in deep water turns to,
God's bristling things, this image
clear as the thought that rubs until
the factual roughnesses go;
no death for the image beauty turns
to in deep water. The reflection

sees hill, trees, grasses like hair
climbing against the sorrel,
milkmaid's knee, if it
exists, cow-parsley – the man
with hammer walks through me into
the foundations of the lake, punishment and crime
drowning, in Norwegian water that holds

what it sees – a village eking out
its mild nature, white and spiky church,
three houses, with loading lofts without
pulley and block, the stream
gliding onto the lake. I cling to him
in his drowning, in fir-like water,
my crime as nothing in his death.

From GURNEY: Gurney's poem

How to make a jib that lifts the maiden fern.
If a spray of leaf,
tooth, or hair, abandons itself
to the claws that should be hands, –
intent on handling – it will crush.
The leaves crush foolishly and spray in handling.

How take nature in modern hands, how give
the dockland man, his hefty male child
and cheeky painted daughter, the bent contour of earth, –
a pink campion
stepping on black soil. The barge

sifts through pasture, its working man
smudges his fag in oil and clay, this tandem
of dirt.

The lamps of home

Do my ears burning, does my face, mean
you remember pulling-to the door
of a flat, so close to the lines the traction
of locomotive and freight went
through us, our moist coy sex minted
with another's? As if you
were a house entered, a soft rage
of three in two pairs, of stars,
spearheads in a scuffle
of metal. 'Absence,' I exclaim

like metal scraped on itself.
The word lights up a terrace house,
or barn, that houses warm cattle
with their baled grass. Some small regular

gift is made, a sandwich cut
and wrapped for a wife leaving on her night-shift.
She nurses
the morose septic hours.

A car travels a coast-road. Flimsy light
from its lamps mixes
the driver's life in misty strands
with this absence of light. He sings, a high
cracked tin sound. The border
brings to his homecoming
two daughters and a son,
whose lamps disperse distance.
A son with red cheeks, their hue
in the blood.

His lamps turn the mist; but on
the moon's cracks tides fill
in, as if death approached. They swish
in denial; not so soon, they say,
his energy is theirs. The ruff
of the moon in tides swelling
across her face
in icy boisterous movements.

Newcastle 1982–5

The ship's pasture

In the sun, the leaf, hesitant but active
this florescence of plain wood; with joy
I saw the fields of England, as new, chartered
shapes, bargained for, and so, snipped
with standing sheep, their snowy garments
by the limestone walls, bulbous fossils,
their thick inert forms braids dangling

the soft wealth of England: Selah. Except
some people here are brutal, the fist,
because of standing in the wrong place,
at the cheekbone. Fist, or snide
arrowy word.

I rose from England much refreshed, but returned
at evening; much undone that was once good
prior to this mean juncture. It was joy,
beside my self, to see the new fields. Whose
is this land that, like waiting flesh, turns
with a kiss, domestic, but yet is
a local habitation with no substance or name
sustaining it? It is the ship's pasture,
its interlinking husk of submarine,
sea-spike, the sleeted fields of destruction:
for payment, for emolument. I am
a part of this – the bee, cutter of wood,
whose timbered house is unimaginably
hospitable. This is what it is. Northwards,
a new Jerusalem with the lamb lies separate,
its shade dense and lovely. The woman
starts again, as though each portion of this
were knit afresh.

We stock the deer-park

for Vincent and Hiroko Sherry

We are the deer-park, this truth is
self-evident? So that war, your
next one… in the plane, you,
a long-legged rodent,
are angled in the seat, limbs trailing
large brogue shoes that splay
frog's feet. You grip

a manual of war,
the finger nails wanting blood
their moons a misty lunar white.

The rat's bubonic
swelling under the eyes opens,
with odourless sticky threads, the matter
of new wars. 'Yes, sir',
his whiskerless face at ease
with obedience. And soon
the results of our obediences,
the groin's swollen stuffs, the armpit's broken
lump, arm that can't ease
against its well-shaped flank, and chest, the whole trunk
in its disposition of gaiety.
I have seen
the sharp, physical
shreds of London,
after incendiaries. War,
its intimate plague, creeping about
like the rat's whiskered
twitching sniff at us,
our intimate parts exposed.

Ah, sir, study elsewhere;
if we change our needs, you
aren't needed. Gas, like dots
of plague hidden in a rat's fur, loses
toxicity. We lie

down gasping, and the huge
host kingdom, of love's long-legged women,
and their men, stare
at our death-dancing – sharp breath,
and the slump of one mingling
in another's – the genders
are bare and swollen. In their health,
their nectared pleasing disposition,
in their long, spiritual laughter,
they stare at us.

THE SHIP'S PASTURE

Light needs certain gasses and the dust in the atmosphere before we may see by it

In space, space and light is passed
through dark, but in an atmosphere of dust
and breathable gasses, earth's mild
ball of space diffuses light. The bird
tramples the air.

As I look back, the island drops through
light and changes to slate, as if air were sucked from
the daytime, leaving space dark.
Before us, with the ship rocking as if
pleasured, light hazes as we come on
to the headland, its jut; in hoops
of mist stooping hills, their laps
and shelfs made as the land sat down. Underneath
the earth in discs moves
and cracks, the sea
so blue it smells of blue, open deep spaces
of it, where by the shore small fish
speckle like sand. Their shadow gives
them away. You saw them
and touched them, as you have touched me.

I draw apart the shutters. It is you says,
up. Between island and mainland each sound
turns back, turning upon itself like a cat
upon its tail of swishing fur. As the man
clasping a bow of stringed music turned
and in an instant of torches
she was gone. And he, forfeiting
the sacred grief of others, in
his unnoticing grief, was torn
in pieces by the women of a god.
And if air changes
its composition, we lose our life,
as a language alters and the poet,
that small fish in aspic, mouths a silent

verse where his failed language, words
in odd shaped pebble, spatter the earth.
And here, if the mild community rages
a torturer smiles at his labour; he struggles to
be worthy his hire, the organ
sheared, the feet first as a man tied
to a stretcher is fed into a furnace. Greece shimmers
into the air. The science of light holds us.

I see you, I touch you. Insects with
feet and stings ready help
themselves to that small captured piece of field,
a garden. A bird flirts a speckled wing.
In his shrine behind a door of glass – my Lord God,
emerge, please, from the small silver figure.
We've been born. Share me, have me,
friend, daughter, companion.

Postface

I read Frank Kermode's *The Genesis of Secrecy* in 1979 and found
there what touched off what are now 'Poems concerning Salome
and Herod' but which I at first called 'The Salome Poems'. In one
place Kermode pauses to ask, 'how old is Salome?' In the poems,
she is more than one age. In the first she is, chronologically, about
two thousand years – though fixed in early middle age when the
most extreme point in her predicament as a woman, trapped by
early experience, has been reached; with neither age to console her
– if that is what it does – nor youth for her to enjoy. In other poems
she is a 'damsel' but, as Kermode suggests, the term is dim and
ambiguous. In the end I felt that when Salome suffered Herod she
had barely entered puberty. She had in her her mother's feelings
and ambition, as well as her own early mental tumescence. With
this equipment she was easily the prey of Herod, and Herod had
nothing in him with which to resist his desires. Herodias and her
daughter formed a double pressure on Herod and his authority and,

together, they exacted from him the life of John the Baptist in miserable exchange for very little.

It stayed in my mind that Salome was the instrument of this, but was also acted upon by the experience, altered in such a way that she found herself, as it were, in a room without window or door – not a blind room, but one without exit. And that having drastically changed through the experience, the alteration that she had undergone permitted no further change or growth. Thus the harshness of these poems comes in a response to the pressure Salome both applies and suffers when she is still a child, physically, spiritually and morally. If there is a bitterness in the poems it rises like gall from a still sense of how Salome – the damsel – is simplified by such pressure and in that state finally obtains harm for others and damage to herself.

I would not want the Salome poems to represent the nature of all the other poems here, but in one respect a number of the poems share the preoccupation of the Salome group – which is to do with transgression and its pain.

I am thinking of actions and their irreversible nature, of which war is an instance. It is not only to do with killing, but with the appetite we may acquire for it, the presence of mind working one way towards more of the same. We need no reminding, for our presentiment of these things is painful. So many have so often noted it all in these years, when the extent of human unhappiness, and misery produced by war or aggression, has made some ask if we will survive as a species if we continue as we are. I merely add to this that the timbre of these poems, and their preoccupations, are, all the same, connected with a different possibility for happiness, which isn't a sin. To re-enact in a certain way the condition of pain may imply the possibility of growth and happiness, and in doing this, in a poem, it may both contain and focus them in reciprocity. That at least is a working theory, and the containment of them in a poem is a way of transmitting their value to our needs. If as a result one may enjoy and value a poem, that is something, for such a close response may help one in turn to mediate between oneself and the world.

Unpublished and Uncollected Poems,
c. 1986–1992

Alpine

1. *Her*

Red coarse sand, coarse like gold, and blue alpine flower
in a well-proportioned leafy stock;
in the dips of this sandy mountain,
steady and mild as her back's hollows,
pools of bent snow
in hot unwavering light.

2. *You*

Your tenacious, unmaternal
poison in my psyche; me against myself.
Your face shivers in maternal lament;
a simian craft evasive and legible
in it, its want of magnanimity
the compassion your genes have smeared in my blood.
I remember you,
the flower's unthinking, mild magnificence,
our tribe's harsh-footed abandon.

A woman from Giannedes

Pines burn on one side
in winds crossing the plain. Village people
with dark, green living evergreen
and prongs of dead twig. Cells wink
and brim resins.

I would stare at the dry
spikey plains, their chill switching
mist to smoke at evening. I was a girl
and enjoyed it, except as rains
twisted men and women into rheumatism,

a stutter of black
lightning. War: my father

fled the mediterranean's width
like a Jew, leaving my mother
to a German soldier they shot as fighting
ceased. They shaved her head, each
week. The porcupine. Is this why

my sister opens the window of
a shrine, and lights the wax
stub in a bowl? Christ stares
past her, his lustre silvery
and mute. In this
crude, gentle bowl lolls
the plume, baring rock
and trees, touching sins
like numbered friends. God, what is
this, but to say I bring
my evil to you, in words you pass
into the flame, blue potassium
harsh homely blue, quickening with
sin, wax, oil, those portions
of life I replenish. I never knew

Mister Eliot was a Jew-hater. He is
a clean man. I see to it.
He sees to this. I iron his shirt
and shake the dust off what I've ironed;
I pull the crease into his trousers out of the hot, flat
triangular metal the stove heats.
And what is not in any contract,
I tender his sadness as he crouches
over the gas-fire at night.
Smile Christ in
humanity, if we will let you.

The pine is the natural crucifixion.
Its pious resin drips into the sea

like an icon exuding blood.
All the pines are men, and women
the resins they shed.

In 1934 Eliot published *After Strange Gods,* the Page-Barbour lectures he had deliv-
ered the year before at the University of Virginia. 'What is still more important
[he wrote] is unity of religious background; and reasons of race and religion
combine to make any large number of free-thinking Jews undesirable.' The library
copy, although frequently underlined, has no mark at this point.[121]

Chrysalid

for Pamela and Robert Woof

Her meek flowers she rustles
in the hall, with its life of moths, raying
shivering luminous forms
in strands, that wipe her shoes
and guide her steps – perfume
the two of us smile with;
or she's a bodice of flowers in
not her house, with me, the shadowed *ipse*'s
self-doubter. Where the gas
tears its mantle, a web, fine
and industrial. Fire with less light
then, a few dark stamens,
her face stronger
than this flitter.

I enter her daughter's room,
the jambs holding space air drifts
through without collision, her eyes,
blameless and recognizing.
The front door has closed the hall.
From youth's huddled chrysalid works such a self,
age, the terse fluttering life

more of that than
cut flowers. She is presence

and absence. I say, better to die
she, better not to: and as if
I had asked, 'drive me across
the boundary, its stark twisted
chain insolent upon the road,' she stirs
her flowers of pouting light, 'read me,'
she says, 'now read me.' Everything
that I am not
is reversed upon me, the secular
flower of her existence.

A box of seeds

The lamp's tilted lens flings light
at you. And shapes that the soul bears
enter your eyes. A swelling of earth,
in its adit a half-tilth
of bone and masonry. As, Mick,[122]
in a controlled chaos, that girl's thinking
in her milky eyes
winks into her glasses. Such life!
like a cat squirming in your arms. Is it
nothing, with these forms breaking
into your eyes?

Thin-legged slim horses
in a truculent harness, eyes like lamps.
Soldiers switch past, their turbans have a swath
thick as a bull's penis, the horses
like bare, haired Chryslers.
A man smiling at his sword, another's
hand, spider-like,
crouching
and stiff.

We do not belong, and have nothing;
neither the haw, small lamp
of silky seeds wrapped in furred thread,
nor the beak that knocks open fruits
upon the nod, then the next
instant, the nod does not lift
its head. Yet we feel the making
out of nothing an act
that changes nothing forcibly into
rented precious life. Dust

hovers on the soldiers, and sweat
or misery rims
a wetted white under the eyes.
They graze the watchful flesh of women,
and like fingers
their warmths mingle, a grainy
scentless pabulum.

It is passed on. A sweet
blue green
bitter adhering
in clay. In London I tended the dead
with a sickly, shortening grass,
and spaded the soil
over paupers' flimsy bodies. What else
was I to do? It became
my trade, my living.

You've stopped smiling. The writer's
tongue, in its flesh's webs
and driblets, its moist roots,
is a hesitant creature.
Work, work, Mick!
the mind in
its waterfalls needs
no hands on it. It spins
the armatures, and attention
relishes another's offering, a calyx
of constant flowering.

Veining

1

Before morning has wiped the sky
I lay thinking of my family: those
made by a generation's lust,
or a clapped-out duty. Unlikely though.
My grandparents, in a house called Rookwood
my aunt, close by;
other Jews, with a bit of solvency
a street, sprinkled with Jews,
the bay reverberating light
that it curved around. Trams swayed

the hissing lengths of the bay
where milky-haired prostitutes
waited in one's in the moon's chink
to fuck on the quiet sand of Wales
one, and then another. The sucking
illiterate murmur. The salt of the sea
rubs its eye. Lift the night up.

The tides, the frail pincered scuttle
the people elegant
the people half-naked for each other,
no, beautiful in the curved reverberating light.
I knew something was up
beyond Parkhouse, his bat's wholesome soundless
hit, in Glamorgan,
as the trains no longer struggled for Liverpool.

2

Transient as the feet of mothers
and fleeing sons, the sand edges, and sprinkles
earth, it sharpens the sea's fronds
prehensile as another's touch. No: the sea takes

what is closest, and kind
as its appetite, with its liquids,
plankton, tissues of algae,
cucumber, and a whale, works at
and faintly harnesses
into a gift, its choice, as it takes
portions of slithering earth into its suck.
I love you, earth: I shall be unhappy
to not know how you go on
after my filaments, their membraneous sticky thread,
like a snail's track, have dried out.
I want my mind in yours, the sea
rips up your coast.

3

I stare, like a fish,
at your bikini tightened into your thighs
above their tapering.
As the garment to its flesh, the hips,
the fruiting of its form, so
the brace and lift
of your cunt, its nature pressing
into the gathered cusps of the cloth's
diffident concealment. So you hold,
smiling, the veined structures
of your sex, lengths of hair,
to your head: as if a delicate tree,
the loosely grasped veins of sense
the mind is made of,
the cavity, its containment, the tree's shaking
of itself slowly. I touch you lightly
for fear of public places. The bay's curve
is like a crescent moon on its side,
a salmon-coloured mare
in an emerald field of soaked grasses.

The life that is marriage[123]

In the house

Mice chew knots for resin, and a shelf aches
in the airing-cupboards, where my hands find
two papery birds, warm on the feeding-ground
of our sheets, their treachery the rinse washes clean.
Her shape his eye's, her breathing proportioned
to its change and stare, watery scales
that spew a fluid, the sticky spread
of his thinking is this: two can lie
apart, and lie together. But she
who will not come again, though I might search
our sexual bedding; he, who never leaves,
and trails his pubis in a sac, broods on
his betrayals, the marmite, the spicy pot of that
which he's not done, and what he has, moist acts
in another's fur. His lemony feather
is loose, imbricated, fish-scales
at his crop's bleb of seed and pebble;
a small eagle head, the beak closed
and petulant, shoulders the cone-shape
of a mountain. Clicking with lust, he's turned
from her, whose love's unbearable, she, the cone
of volcanic melt. She fades and deepens,
the rose that comes and goes, like dying, his freedom
measured in her wings. And what
they have, he of her, is space,
the lives they've skimmed through – perched now
in the security of mid-air – a cobalt screen,
which is their past packed as coal, a black
rinsing light, stuttering sheets of bird-song.
Its dot and texture
is a raised honeycomb, granular sugary acts,
with flies' legs, and morsels
of feather in a jelled fluid.

I this house-owner ask: 'shall I think, not

of my her, but the she-bird?' She's hinged
wake-up eyes. Like them we die
for want of a bit of bread, shavings
of partly-sweet barley, its spikes
bled in the wind, this
before sugar was born in the mouth,
its drying succulence, pale
and makeshift
as unleavened bread.

Thief

In my hand a piece of chrome, wrenched
politely off a wrecked car-door, windows diagonally slashed.
We, thieves, whose brains the police, firing
rank on shivering rank, have made their muck.
In my other hand (I've both)
a wind-screen wiper, that's shucked
snow to rubble, its gums and teeth
crushing the blade to its brace, like a flag
frozen to its staff,
the stiff ribbed droop of its salute.

I smell the wrinkled opals of gas suffusing clay
and water. I break into a house,
put my hands, fearful of the vermin's rasp,
in the airing-cupboard. I find two birds:
a yellow cinder, like a bangle on the other's neck,
one dead, one not. Here, whoever
is this stranger whose life I prise open, a house,
its blazing sufficiency of glass, – here, on your leafless sheets,
I would give half of one life to the dead one.

I unlearn the worth of a chrome
door-clasp, a blade's
pitted rubber contused
by its rasping-off
of snow, the hyperborean speech marks.

Snow is dashing at the architecture
of burnished steel oblongs. I, bird-thief,
his talon in a sugary flan, I'll die
like a bird, and the stranger will have those two
dead and alive. The snow will refrigerate
my body, until the sun burns my enemy,
winter, a patch on the struggling lung.
So, this leafless story: goodbye.

Words from below the level of speech

This summer evening I stood without you
in fields of concrete. Below, off river-mud
men picking bait. Ships, torn in the war,
in flashes, deconstructed like half-armoured wingless
insects, on the quays. By a little hut
like an alpine cabin, in a bed of tea-leaves
from three years of tea-breaks, a rose-tree,
its single confection a strong bloom.

The wife cleans, and the welder kneels: his heat
works the good patch from the holed. In Swaledale,
by logs hot in a stone cottage, limbs naked to hands
and fire, two weeks a year. It can be made
to be enough. His smiling is kind.
And this night in summer I stood without you.

But a friend is dead, who researched arms,
the sustained piss of electrics dislodging
everything. A man on tall legs
came and spiked him. In the dene's small trossachs
of pointy shrub and thrush, the welder pricks in
imaginary plum-trees, for death is the finger-lengths
of a boat in torn waves. This summer night
I stood without you.

Our curtain lifts blossoms and bare women
through a window to grass, where a climbing-rose
from the wall's snapped webbing, drops its scent
in clematis and blackberry. My friend's conscience
is a nail and batten
raked down face and chest. He teaches
at a jail, his ear a specialized instrument,
having the lively rumour of others' speech,
their connections with his speech, snapped. This prisoner,

his client of pain, 'This,' he says,
'is the screw's talk, "another one off, sir"
– of a mail-sack dropped away.' In the normalcy
of our language from outside, he speaks
of their dead,
below the level of teeth and tongue.

Love, we're in the thick of things, yet not
blown away by secrets, or the screw's words,
the whitened roses spattered pink, this summer's night
where I stood without you.

'A leash rests its chain and clasp'

A leash rests its chain and clasp, the dog
a moth's lightness in his basket. His owner
is a body of stems, not stiffening to the creature
pulled by scent as moths to light. The stems
jointed, like grass, his energy lilac-loose.

Who will ask him what the body-weight, of the blur
of roan, the calibre of each hair,
of the fractions of sorrow, the creak
of mutual, tender deference?

A growth lay on the thigh, his pink gender

veined and furred, squeezed behind
the buttock's muscle. His shag,
its gentleness, denied us as if
we were not creatures, but a franchise
of God's, pin-striped actuaries. When we die
like the smell of shaking fennel,
its rasp and web in umbels, its planetary heads,
or a train-noise away in a tunnel, it is (mainly)
the hurrah's of Satan's foundry, his slave-angels,
rentiers, their solder company of buttons
in fading rings, our quietus in his bleb
of melting lead. This dew-lap of us
is Satan's triumphant add-up. There is pain
in everything: genderless broken-off cusps
of celluloid collars, a dead burned-up child,
the fire of our times, his master's voice
in the spaces between his master's speech.

Neither hears the other, the bell
on the mountain-flanks, its umbels of noise
stemmed in gentian and ochre stone, in hill-silence,
its fierce impersonal quiet.

A tyrant changes the body

A tyrant is making the ear, again: above
the neck, a fortress,
the ridge
that entices our blab upon
the untiring translator
of noise to meaning, past the globule of the hammer –

this flat lily of our body
its mixed forms of intrusion and reception
is an open box
of fuses,

the ear's ridge a stashed
bar half-thwarting the hole – it is

to be seen, this failed
militarism, swags of clay, redoubts
slovened
to unserviceable earth. The ear's idiocy.
I see plaintive limbs, a box
of miniature prosthetics,
the bones of a child, its chances in the mother's flesh.

A soldier visits home (L'étranger)

A train's aerial mast takes mileage
off distance, like paring an apple – to where I home.
Everyone's badge, I, a soldier,
my disposition of homelessness, walk between
the sufferance of houses. Where the street ends
in branches, salmon and milky,
the moon dies.

Where is she? the tranquil moment that's breath
misted over glass? Stepping to the flat roof,
a naked girl, supple pale leg testing wind
and light, Venus with her hands tearing atmospheres,
her male tagged in briefs lies by. Lie, she says.
She sways pretty haunched knees. Her limits stay.
She laments the sun's just opened. That red sea
with its obligations to rejoice, lies
with its parting, closed.

Time frightens me.
The moth-like train eats its time, and the sun's altered flesh
hangs fluid and dark. After his torn orbit
has flung him aside, who will dare, who will fix wings
to his shape, to whizz him over his, the sun's, pressures
of crushed space, like grass beneath quick feet?

I am such a creature as must be tender,
even good. Meanwhile, between the mushroom's gills,
a slatted, mossy, acidic breath gets its life
from the silence hung above mountains
and fields of grassy animals grazing off the earth.
I defend things, and I kill things.

My father's language was German

Our Fighters bled shade on father's arms,
'this is a war.' Along the quay where a serpent,
the [skilled][124] eel, of Sargasso and weed
the docile eyes, its moisture whose cistern of hate and fear
hatched skin, diamonds fluffing carbon,
menace with pity,
my child's brain weeping for it:
Father, sister budding
five years more than me,
the years like blond steps, laughing.

War despairs of not killing. It lifts
off wagons concrete fabrications
obedient to hold tested space in which
faces pale in gas. Fingernail, eyelash
scrape the chamber's roof – 'love, hug me,
suffocate me.' The gasser presses
naked eyes to a glassed aperture. In goes
his vision. Suffering will end some day.

Isn't it war's cruellest wrong that lets
a child live, not its father? The Allied
bombers share
us with what we make, 'splinter us,' we shout
at the sky lit with dim lamps,
little, bloodied worms. We beat
our strength through bolts, quivering like hammers.

In the printer's chase crushes Isaiah's verse.
The mercy will never deliver. I was born

a creature with uneven wings. Kiss
my boy's cheeks. I'd be a father.
From the bunk surfaced
with grass, wind thin as a camp with no food,
I listen as the fuzz of noise withers
for the short-legged, fortunate
dust. I'm your ear, your silence.
Darkness travels on, it amuses me.

Hospital

Coming in

When the city is tungsten
and saffron, she whines, and as air whirrs round
a humming-bird in its nectar, in coils
birth shakes out.

This red and grey form sluices through locks
valved to have it in the sea softened with pure water;
a serviceable hurtling male craft
hugs the mouth it tilts past, rounded corners
of wood caulked onto its stone lip
like wedges of an arch. He enters melted seas
with fresh boisterous water, tinted like
grass sprung off slate. He's polite

and vigorous in a devious world, and gives
a simple 'yes, I am' and 'I would be
here, in this world, with you'. Everything
that will, in this hospital, grows towards a life.

Save you

Your blood is to be taken from you. Dawn breaks
several times. Later you were saline
tasting yourself afresh.

A ward

A bed with no mattress, then
one with blankets, and linen spotless
as a washed body.

The third holds a woman, her face
thin, tresses weightless
at her cheeks like a faded peach. The nurse will weep
when she dies. She gives black swollen grapes,
and is in love; the nurse fits her shape
of mercy, crouches, touches the sickness
that grows more than life.

When she comes home, lilac;
its four lean points, a slither of colour,
whose odour studies the sick
in whom the bitter crab
makes slime of the liver. Her term is
for as long as care, and medicine from shops
doing its trick, staunches her.

The blaze of infant life pitches
over the roofs; in her wind-scratched eye
folded polythene and cans drifting off
the pavements scrape the cambric
and sodium commemoration of the late day.

A puffy-cheeked
smoulder at the horizon. Decease winds down
a restless lamp.

The sick themselves

In through the viaduct,
behind them, the little mashed groins of hills
terraced with swags of flower
and vine ripe for harvest. As they come through
to an arch shaped
like a slab of bread whose grain
is like solid ovals of water, what stands
in quags above them has no swab of algae
fish can chew; eyes like gob-stoppers,
mournful and greedy. As they come past,
bristling refineries, translucent piping,
its fountain in a sealed system, lamps at each bend
of hard grave plastic. And all this
grows negligently. In old
stalls of manufacture, new supple power.

On this water, three
linked barges with demi-johns of chemical
which, if it spills, the brickwork will lip
with stalactite-like stains.
These drive within clear sight
of the hospital, where nothing heals
today but as the body can. Slicks of ointment
in whorls of frigid sound. In canisters
the shushed traumas of ancient men shrieking,
their noise slashed in creases
dug into the cheeks. Breathing,
on plum-stained tiles
and blood in tubes.

From the nurses' palms, grief
slithers over the blobbed and messed long chambers;
the venereal groin
the fluttering lungs. It's Grim's Pass;
we sink into ridged, steeply sloping mud, sodden creatures
of nightmare.

Prolepsis

If he breathes and if he builds
atoms in a crux pathogens will release
and be eaten by, give the wrists
in their supple activity, use the needles
saintly against pain, devoted
to prolepsis and hope.

Arthritis stiffens in our structures.

We glisten with health upon
the bristling moors dewed in work coming
towards us with folded arms.

Hatred and generosity

Souses in hatred of itself and of the different
flesh sifted through a moist-skinned Englishing.
Flavourless bodies
rolled up, and shoved in a west indian drum,
their moiled bodies, the hollow sounds, when banged;
dulled by what's in them – quiet musicians,
noiseless platonists
for whom essence palely imitates
the Messiah's splendour, if, in the back-lane,
you see him, a latched gate,
its sneck lifted
by fingers drifting, ineffable
in their odour; that breath
in hospitals. Of whom the generosity,
the self-preserving impulse, bringing warmth?

The shaded forms at dawn, pattering the curbs
of granitic half-resolve, the tread over
white bristling moors, footprints patching intent
in frost. Why is so much breath here,
and no more? Where are
there sufficient beds? Snow is filling them.

Duplicity

Teresa Almond in an increasingly bitter
DHSS shredded her code of practice
which instructed clerks with
'they must eat less, give charity and cut
income unearned; promotion
that toothed shadow follows.' Hard code

to live with, simple to work, the poor
as they never were, since she took
the Ministry, its descent to hell whose walls show
moist watercolours of the dead. For this, the heart's
systole and diastole grew
apart like a leaf in
and cut of sun

and she died, leaving nothing
in indecipherable hand, betraying
neither colleagues nor the poor. But where
she had ranged in the portal, inked paper
a clear xerox of the code, shaking heads,
their negative wafts of air, she grasped
the law's designs and gave
her suppliants and her claimants silent maximums.

She became a thinning
thing, ounces of herself, pecking as little
as those she felt sorrow for, feeding
her body with her soul's hunger. It is
the truth of her life: ours

is different. Someone's raised her fountain
in the conservatory, a mansion with guards,
its art, silver you pay to envy
where a pump blossoms water, over
and over through a curved returning spout. May
she for her duplicity, if it is, by water
remind us, the shaped head, the headstone, cut

in its surface braiding through a pump, integument
fixed and mobile: remembering
if it is duplicity, or if it is not,
that lingering commonwealth.

Daughter abandoned

Things alter me, I melt in
the pelting steps the Cree takes, in it, the moon
on her back, shivering and pink, the flesh of melon
mother gave me before both left. The night broke
like a bridle of hair, the female decent animal
stopped, and would not eat, the huge
considering head of maternity turned away. So how
be but water, in the Cree's stream, a female
creature its stones lift, and tear to lace?
as in the deeper love, of anger, my parents tear
apart, never to join, again, as I will
come to myself, after the stones bloodied
with the gaffed salmon, have flowed backwards
from me. I rise, patching mist's damp on the many
calls for help maddening the telegraph poles,
I dab creosoted wood with acid peaty vapour.
And up the hill dawn bursts behind, woods entangle a school-girl
of mists: by noon she's water, again,
the sun in it like shattered china.

Will my lace be gracious to my flesh, will it become
my body, will it be flesh, again, not lace;
and not be clothed in the torn flesh, of lace? What is lace
but to make the body attractive before death?
to cover a whole flesh in plenteous lace.

The Gallovidian martyrs were drowned in faith, the robin says[125]

The bird has few words to spill. His legs
are bold. The robin's breast is on fire,
he tears the little metres of air. There's no milk
on earth for birds; chicks feed with frost
and the dire consequences of faithful love,
a stone and a worm. Something else that's here,
light, whose carbide water makes, the earth's
modern lamp – acetylene. The robin's feet
are retracted in fear. He has told me.

You can think what you will of water that makes light.
So, the robin says,
undoing his silence, smallest of larger birds
stabbing crumbs in the yard, where a sump bleats
with rain, flood and clears.
Choose a human's version, or the robin's,
his companionable dismembering of crumbs:

Faith brings two women to conviction, whom nothing
moved. Dulled faith fastened to a stake
the body and soul of them. Slowly the tide walked
whom the moon pulled without thought but with
the mechanics of stars, up the beach, and, as if
in a dream of itself drank them. The nightmare
the horror of actions with the selves in them
that unfold their petals. Some fidelity
comes like a guest, folds its wings like an angel
and his staying is like pain in the wood: it is
and is nothing without xylem, its flowing stutter.

Fathering

The shirt on my chest's lung-like hair
dark at the nipples. Father and mother
I kiss you, which is like the grass
I scythe as it blossoms. The blades' wet is helved
on earth. Waiting for loving-kindness
we have wasted our lives.
For grass rises, flowering lilac hyphens
of chromosome. Is it permitted to touch you?
Shall I be requited with an answer?
My child Adam reached out, and touching her
died weeping his mother's grief.

His lilac chromosome renews her pain.
My lovely parents, if you come again
if I gather over earth, as primitive, as befriending, as grass
whose seed crams with broken-up lightning,
father, gentle as you are in earth, how will it be,
my mother, who is earth's?
which I will choke with, as if my skull
gave something living a habitation, its complex
energy like the crossings of a snail,
spidery harmless tissue, that makes a swab,
a timid emollient gauze with what it trails?
My parents, will you come upon me again
and I kiss you? Shall I be Adam
and the crux be swabbed
and the mouth touched? Tell me
what you believe.

Grass

My head pieces broken-up lightning.

I'm amenable to the June-bug's whizzing head
and a perching fly. Mosquitoes dammed by glass
inject me. My blood no use to them
divests their poison of venom. They crouch
then surge amidst swishing wings,
their horn of plentiful warning, a tug-boat's,
that's an ant on the rippling wash-board, in its deck
nails drinking
God's unsoiled light, the immaculate mortal sun.

I'm His fraction, breathing ounces
that with my tranquillity
synthesize the beams.
I am of use.

The Lens-Breakers

First published by Sinclair-Stevenson (1992)

Urban grasses

With a sickle, I tended the dead in London
shortening the grass that had flowered
on their bodies, as it had in my child's.
And I piled the soil over the paupers' flesh
in their flimsy coffins, which split. What else
was I to do? It became
my trade, my living.

★

Earth, I shall be unhappy to not know
how you go on, when I'm like those
I tended, shearing the grasses
above their foreheads. I felt tenderness
yet I did not know them – and how should I re-assure
that nothing, and say, yes, I care for you
because you are nothing now. Yet you are nothing.
Could I have dared tell them?
and therefore I remained silent.

Four related poems

for Ed Kessler, Richard McCann and Henry Taylor

'A black huge butterfly'

A black huge butterfly, – I stepped
from its lashing progress

of frail sheets, no targets in them, the wings'
brushing circumference, its true gender

from chrysalid to darkness, in the air,
that serene blue fluid; it, too,

indifferent, touching things with darkness,
itself so brushed, those lashing silent metres.

Flypaper

A fly sinks into these adhesions.
Only by tearing a strip of abdomen

or its fiercest organ, the eye, from itself
can it lift away. Us, thieves

of its creaturely flickering wash, the feelers
striking off faeces, the residual

protein, more crucial than its gender,
its face grasping at ours.

Beings

Two minute flies, beings back to back
join with a long black particle.

One of them bigger, its wings raised, holds
both in tension, erect

held perfect connection
for hours, with legs firm over paper

sufficient for them. Their long completion
on white stirs

a single memory, of how
I, too, being with you and by Him

imagined, yet imagining, left
to be, in dire amazed

double shared control
were, on the eiderdown, a feathery creation

of us, palm to palm,
the wings flighted as with joy.

Aching to survive

We fly people, with a fly's hand
clasp fly-like fear, bitter lungs

professing care. So, do you mean
kindness, I asked this fly? Scratched me,

the wings unbroken, frenzied
as a butterfly's, a lashing whiteness

from the basking chrysalid, of two flies
tangled, in the sly mentality of lives,

of rasping bosoms that ache to survive.

The frail flesh simulates a caress.
It is turquoise and worry. A slither

of snake-forms in the wings, veins of dirt
whose lashing stills itself. We preen,

for dirt, too, wants its looks. Sucking creatures that fuzz
into the sun, that anxious silent

fortress of light, the good trespass
on a whole fly.

The sad might of minute
life, the tenacious hyphens

that join us in love, in all rearing storms.
So we march to die of each other,

the smell of abomination in combat,
tumultuous vulnerable wings.

Intimacy

I watched a woman feeding
birds, until
my soul went like light: not I (me)
struck on my pulses, but humanity

hammer of light stricken with itself

itself anvil and hammer
hammer and sheet–metal

or, if not it, that hammered
light, not humanity

then you, love, feeding
the menacing forms, their acid hunger.

Paying for forgiveness

In a Trailways, shaking over red clay,
wild poor shapes hang in a sulky wind
of glazed polythene. As we start,
a child bellows softly, she mews at
her mother's breasts pressed up into the v
of an ill-made blouse. The gaze is cheerful,
her repose her daughter's sleep, father

unfolding in it like the soiled shapes
of duster he cannot sell.

The planted rows, the dead all men,
their adversary stain bruised
like mulberry on red clay. A barn
of warped, bare wood pinned in it,
nailed to the shape weather splays. Pines,
their branches held down to gain height
for the bole. The poor lift their arms
and sniff the armpit's sour
compelling familiar. The bus shudders
as clutch and drive engage. 'What's here for me,
the wisp, the grin scratched in a dull pane?'

With a friend, long-tailed males,
gobbling Arab food baked in the fanged
bevelled taste of pine-nuts – taste
of trees in mist – I watched two women
enter the restaurant, the shorter lifting
in the s shape contour of her dress
her silked thighs, like a hind, light
deliberate steps, yet steps full
as the body of a hind as it steps.
'Gentlemen, please,' our guide pleaded.

The engine cuts. Over tarmac
diesel has messed, the journey
unwinds its head like a ball, a twine on which
dead soldiers dawdle
like beads. The lovely energies subdue.
In one hand
the sopping brain
and dead grin, a weed in the other,
its bud in milky blue triangles.

The serpent, none to pick its fruits, creeps
under the bush, to lie up stiff and straight
like a new stick stripped of its bark, coloured

as brilliant as spiced, poor food.
'Hower yawl? I'm white trash (it mimics)
better'n the black.' We grin,
stung like asps, to hear our thoughts
made plain and English. 'How-er yawl?'

Dead and wrong. Those souvenirs, bayonet
and webbing, greed for our fingers. The serpent
shuffles in the bush, the skin, bound to its jaws
in filled triangles of quick shapes
gets stained in blood.

The sepia plates of slaves, the bidding fixed
in their expressions, the flesh exemplary
in servitude. On another plate, mildews
touch the hanging lamp of a rail-junction,
the criss-crossing of rival companies
tracking the prairie, winding the lush anchorages
of lilac brandishing its mourning shapes;
the lamp that grows, the only lamp that grows
solicitude. Like threads a spider runs
across a field, the tracks combine and draw
men keeping farm, or the ashy furnace –
its pour of iron, its granular heat.
Abundant whitenesses of cotton and steam,
their shushed energies serving a head
canted in one direction. They gather
to feed the gatling, poised, bored
on its tripod, ready for the hands to grip,
the face behind it
pieced together, like the seams and cooling-chambers
that make the thing a possibility,
a well-made thing, cunning
as a horse. Like candles, carefully,
firmly strapped to form a barrel:
the grin on triangles, firing blood.

The train has lost the junction, the wagons of men
up-ended in battle, the torn mixtures

of many bodies
hanging from spars, flung against iron castings.
And all the time more pulsing engines sweat;
their heavy boilers, their couplings; the flanged sun.
'How c'n I see yer that ain't he-ah?
We paid reparation until we're white,
to nineteen forty-seven. Now we're fergiven
what yer can't be fergiven of.
For losing a war, like a clip
of a bullet. Ma dear child, the farm
lays in the grass, poverty lays in the grass.'

Gypsy Moth

A Gypsy Moth holds a castle of bruised rose
in its sights, the engine beating like a moth's wings,
but the moths beat against or tumble over
the walls, across beams of light, on glass,
and in the windows – their sensors,
their furred heads, winged bodies with a burning sense
of the bulbs naked over the readers.
Lightly they wipe their webbed flesh
on our cheekbones, and we imagine
ourselves winged.

The Gypsy Moth's self-enchanted drawl,
its music in two notes of self, regarding self,
throbs in the pilot. Satisfaction
secretes over face, mind
and brain, until he is aglow
to do it, to bomb. The readers rejoice
their arrowy targets in the castle tossing spires
through a Gypsy Moth's night sounds.

I hear the Moth on its tarmac, I rejoice
and dream, but imagine death, my head

huge and burned as a moth's. In a field
by the glade furring the gorge, a farmer
sprinkles Shell's nonchalant toxin,
friendless friend, hearing the Esk splash.

Civil War grave, Richmond

for Dawn and David Latané

This pit is eighteen thousand, where scythers,
uphill, wound coarse grass. A father's kiss
covers the brain of his fifteen-year-old
in a wet handkerchief; the trees' beauteous
philandering grief bursts the sanctuary.

We kiss, we taste a boy's forehead
and our kiss: mercy sees the merciful. And the
victors kiss her hand in a chapel
of wingless moths.
Nothing tarnishes, but kisses: not
victory, not mercy at the
eye of her logic, its futile music.

If you're dead, if you've lost, couth
prayers and silent rifles, are something,
to be flung in a translucent pit,
its jar of suffering. Why

does the body touch us, even
the lopped spiky hand, an elbow's
club, the haunched infantry's shoulder, thorax, hacked
under the nipple? Touch
even these you may not kiss. Brush
them with lilac, and pour on soil.

No smell. Earth soaks it into its musts.

Mercy returns to us, she has altered
her mind, and puts her bony fingers with us
on our arms' hairs; the inch
in thorax, chine, hair and nails,
the eyelashes, of her tenderness, it
is a burning thing to be touched
by her,
and be her ghosts.

Trying to hide Treblinka

for Jon and Elaine Glover

Blessed is the lupin sown to thwart
what our soldiers' hands raised to the light:
a camp with no architectural style,
with a name like this, Treblinka,
and the unnameable, blessed be He, God. *Schlaf*,
as You must, in sleep's grace
of abandoned bliss. And you, God's sweet.
Blessed be He.

Maculate flower.
Blessed the lupin, thick snappable haulm
with innocuous hairs; blessed its noxious seed,
petals, a bird-shaped milky blue.
Blessed the lupin, with no mind to choose a soil
but what sustains it, and what flowers
its unending ignorance. The animal God,
this salmon-spawner, blesses.

The camp, a hole in the eye; its zone, the flowers' assart.
A hill swells with breath and flowers: some blue,
some faded blood ones, that sink their roots
in shreds of carbon made visible
with hours of damp archaeology. Unappeasable
the claws, as they travail
that earth their hands trowelled.

Juniper and forgiveness

God unfurls the atomic cries
of arrowy birds. The land smells,
pulling apart tenacious waters.
It is re-creation. Noah gathers to his body
the tender Father's, pushing out
the sprigs of hopping Juniper, 'go, go on,'
through swarming grass.

It is a new earth, and I like it,
with everything that steps from this ribbed ark. Through adhesive
layers of air, one integument
breathing with another, shade struck from Ararat
darkens the trees that hurl between grass.
These lacy leaves. 'Attend to us,' they beg;

'yes yes, we are going to.' God's pairs of us
sly and connubial from the old zones,
with a rustling, delicate sense of children.
In sin we see a new vision, leaving
in twos, taking as we must
the smell of Juniper and forgiveness.

'Through leaves and fragmented light'

for Margaret and Michael Mott

Through leaves and fragmented light the cricket flakes
her shaped notes off wings. Crouching
by a woman in pain, in the hair on my arm,
on wood, or its faecal ash, she has made visible
the idea for a spring hardened to tear, slowly
apart, our bodies. She is not
that idea: a contralto, her oily discs twanged
into our lives. If what it is
to make pain, what more

to clash this soft battering consequence, lyric
percussion, a pebbled
softly rattled water, that unfastens the two selves
of one mind, to stiffened facing flighted wings.
I search for, find your body-sound
flickering winter in ash's doldrums, the atomic drowsing
in a hearth. And with you
waiting is remembering, where none need
rise in the dark. Tell her, it is so.

In two spaces

One space death sledges holes through, and this other
nurturing our exchanges, breath and touch,
that impregnate the sufficing space. But how?

As I worked in London, and shovelled
loose earth over the flowered coffins, I felt

that the dense space, its substantiation
made with the grasp

of limbs endowed with taking from each other,
stayed unrelinquished. Uncertainty
like ice has covered this.

★

Space, with the holes death sledges. In you step
to a different space – a chair and a bed –
breath and touch substantiate. So here

are both spaces, neither relinquishing the other,
swirling translucent wrestlers. How could I

with leave-taking embrace your coming in
this room? Like blood, the space with life
clasped in it enters this impure world.

Moses Harris and the butterflies

what can thought but devour object and self

Butterfly and stone, in shade's calico
disguise each other. This ghost-catcher (we eat ghosts)
tenses net and desire. She rises alive
but mistakes, surrendered as Job
to Satan is she to him, with her God's gold moons.

He depicts his trade: 'what I do
is not who I am.' Yet in his nets more tensile
than sea, unless weight
is strength, her wings flummox and tear.
No end, he gasps,
to the times she must be beautiful – like love
catching in the nets.

So this tender fake of beauty
treads with yammering noiseless pulse, etches
a pin, and presses it in the mid-stream
of a moth's thorax. The spidery fur
and fluid nick with air, its sharp
inaudible rush a snatch of dry odour
in the chest.

By a feathery pool
of beasts considering God's dream of mild hinds,
he shoulders aside a branch, enters a silent quarry
of cyanide and zinc, God's uneatable delights.
His airless creatures lay out on slabs. See off the ghosts,
Moses, Moses Harris, you, depriver of wings
and you, deprived.

Moses Harris, an eighteenth-century lepidopterist, produced a book of butterflies
and moths called *The Aurelian*.

Cherokee

On sandstone, barite
makes sand-roses, cabinets of them
in a year of dying. Close, but not close
in kinship, so as to keep those they love
in sight, in the world
next to this, distant
as the odour of plums tossed
in summer wind. The blades of sand-roses
glint, as if touched by mites. They gasp, and smell
of bituminous air. They were
the Cherokees, their drops of blood
made stone in God's washing tears.

They open and don't breathe
in the air's
generative lulls. Wherever mercy
is human, don't look
to pity to come like a child
weeping its maternity, perfect
between the hands of the rushing form
of the Shekinah. Creation is
an Indian fury, needs art for its pain,
statues of hurt.

I smell frankincense, pity's herb.
We'd do right
to be scared of it. If I want
another's sacrifice it must be I need
pity manifest. With little faith
I chafe my hands; tenderness
rubs perfumed between them,
the best, most weeping of grasses,
the least form of life I crop.

Shekinah: the female principle of the deity in Judaism.

Inside the gentian

for Rodney Pybus on his fiftieth birthday

This gentian is paint, its form
seeping in coarse paper. Off the anther float
the pollens, mysterious wingless
birds of fertility. Veins of damp thread
stitch its flesh. This is the size of magic,
a deformation of spells: the petals
sudden and huge, their slender cliffs and space
with birds in them, stiff as pencils,
the teeth clenched, the pubis trailing in a sac,
gold discs of pollen a guano of unmelted frost
on their quills. In the gorge a glow rises
from the self buried in its anguish
of self-hatred. Its cat's teeth bare,
its false matrimony of self with self
a wet clinging garment. Find another's face, for eyes
and light would beg for blinding
if your smiling had no hand
to touch its mouth. Above me,
voices, a parliament of indecisions
like animals with no speech,
its grammar, its voice and pitch
violent, as if for murder. I hear
in the faint percussions of the stream
a brass band, to their necks in mud and water,
a regiment with our *absentia*
scratched on their bullets, their arms raised
with rifles. These lives pell-mell,
with extinction certain and distant as light
in the satanism of night's indigo.

We stand in the fickle dome of light. Where are the fruits
in their preserving straw? In the hands of the blind.
She put them there.

Praise the gentian, her gravid form
for the printer more visual than a kiss

the hand, its brush of eager pigment
the printer's blocks, his adhesive inks
and the platen's waiting tray.

Praise the gentian. Praise her.

Famine

for Kevin and Trisha Fitzpatrick

The dips of this mountain, mild as her back's hollows
have barbs of moss in splintered quartz. Three luminous peaks,
close, like tines. Dabs of coarse wool, on paths
that hold the pastures fat sheep tear, as if
the grass would starve back to the pebble it has split.
A dead fox, its mouth of saw's Vs, the ants
are sawing off her neck. Someone who'd caught her
had trussed her back legs with stiff, wax-like cord
of nylon, used for tying sacks – their cruppered shapes.

The cruelty is palpable and simple
the fox's teeth jagged as glistening rock
the fox's mouth open with pain. Yet God fills
the parted air, the helmet of foliage, and requires
His clay creatures, at play with animals
models of His designs. We kneel: his grief
is sudden downpour
we're sopping with. His tears make iodine
tracing our acts, staining the print scratched by
a kidney stone, small and blunt as a match-head.

The trapper, that little one in Yankee plaid,
his mouth, its collusive decipherment
of what is vulnerable, has ceased its mirth.
The lips in strata dried like a shale, half mud
with a tobacco stain, and poverty.

I see chevrons on the milky herring, their blemishes
traced in salt. You drift, and I with you in tilted seas.

*

He cut water and mud. This was creation,
Ireland, its pudgy apple blossoms roughing
each other, like tribes.
Curoi Mac Daire, with a body white as death,
has spread warrior thighs. His son's face
tilts with regard, taut smiling mouth
watching his father's sword cut the softness
of cow-parsley. His wife is Blathnaid,
has hair never unplaited, and hugs
a bolster, made of flock from their sheep,
hot and belligerent.

She esteems Cuchulainn. He's like a thistle,
a flower that slakes her, its mineral nut-like juice.
He lifts her husband and her son – the long blade,
the bodies, screaming. Where, she asks, in the world
will tenderness, a lingering female god,
be again?

With feathers greased, limbs pinned back for long flight,
the air behind in oiled streamers, they lift up
their wings in sexual preparation, tiny swimmers
inside a howling, and a scrupulous space.
She, he, him – arrow-shape, containing
the druid that her husband cared for. He preferred
all three: Love to his Lord – meat, bed, and fire.
His wife, her wit – its sweet sheer taste of her smiling.
The boy: because he loved him, future lord
of his experience and tutelage, his winter's bee
in a small exposed hill-fort. He leaps, with her
in his arms, off a cliff. They lift,
the breakers, the bashed green turtle rocks,
the mottled treacherous blood splintering
in algae. White warmth and red hair

tangle with daylight,
the light in curls, flesh straight as a stripped stick
is white.

★

The tribes, like blossoms roughing each other,
let in the Danes, bringing their prow-heads, cut
in delicacy and ferocity.
Then comes a Norman face, his metal nose
fitting his visor, the chest's width armoured – no part
uncovered, but a hand, white, tapered,
pointing a sword. His frame
is slender, and trained as a whippet's.

★

Grasses rub the furred necks of horses, their joints
large with succulence and flexibility.
Behind the half-circles of gates, England's pasture, Ireland,
her soft wealth a fleece, a thread,
as if from God's strong hair. The Gael
has a huge obsolescent head; it tilts
to the Norman's willowy stick.

Mild Gaelic chews its delicate address
in diphthongs, worries at its survival – shall it,
shall Gaelic, die… be as spit
in the futile grey of the Atlantic's?
Their uncomely hands face upwards. Rain is it,
or grace? In a flaking sun, creatures;
in a moist air, their steamy forms: pink mouths
with delicate froth. Some pray nearby, where the cut fields
have rows of heads – men who watched spears of grass,
and the calves of herdsmen pricked by them, and saw
their dewy infantry. This is Cromwell,
England's soldier.

When he has found the trembling hare, its silent gasp

in a shook, or last triangle of standing wheat,
he scythes the fields, again, he hugs mountains
where the god's a shielding stone, and rain's poignant arrows
scratch the cliff, lapsing in a lake of black and rose.
I tremble with the height. Below,
a boat, its stone hull
upturned. With praying under it.

★

Chapels in the grass's time, themselves blossom, with primroses
and straggling vivacious eglantine, like wire. Their flagstone
notches the sky's blue, a slate bruise-colour,
and hasps a ring to heave it up with. Were the saints
for to suffer our suffering? This it seems

we asked for: generous blood in the heather,
lanterns of it on stems, blobs of litany.
Music hidden like a hare, their two lines of singing,
a double hymnal of men with women, a paired foliage
of pliant acanthus. Praise us,
for surviving, greedy for our neighbour's love
to the touch precious as bread, the moist
dead sustenance.

'Shall Gaelic die?' A poem by Iain Crichton Smith, written in Gaelic and trans-
lated into English by the poet.
'The grass's time' is a phrase from a poem by Jon Glover.
Curoi Mac Daire was a chieftain who held a hill-fort on the Dingle Peninsula in
south-west Ireland. His wife, Blathnaid, betrayed him, and her lover Cuchulainn
murdered both her husband and their son. For good measure they took with them
the household druid but, loyal to his Lord Mac Daire, he took Blathnaid in his
arms and leapt with her off a cliff.
Cuchulainn: in Gaelic literature, chiefly the *Ulster Cycle*, this Irish warrior of pagan
times figures as a great hero of legendary feats, and is sometimes described as 'the
Achilles of the Gael'.

Energy is the basis of morals

for Bill and Ann Darr

A stag tears the lilac horizon. His fear
compounds the energy of dogs. He billows

as they leap, and subsides, his spine kicking
in the torn lungs, master smiling, 'eat.'

He has starved his creatures. His webbed gums
large with blood and saliva, the sud crushes

on blaeberry lips. His dogs consume the creature.
I tear my soldier's khaki, its opals

of blood, and stitch leaves for my body
because the Potomac reflects me naked

and I want the dignity and insolence of nature's clothes
on me as we kill. I have seen

my father stoop and swill the frail marble
of his shoulders; my soldier's blood runs,

'dead,' I hush to myself. As I feel
men's thighs exalt their horses, I ask

what grains the xylem, what selves
the gene in the harming, mystic blood.

Thirst

1. *Gratitude*

With a mouth of glowing mist, the harvest moon
urges our silent voices, body-dew,
damping the hammer-beam with soft, bat-like
nocturnal hymns. We thank Him for the grain;
its short fractured energy
like broken-up lightning. His harvest's metal hook
feeds our mouths.

These are silenced voices. But by them
a forest, its howling speeches; cones thrash
past branches. A thief alerts: his jacket tight
on his chest, like bark. He bashes old dismal lives
for brass. Yet this is the time to stray through houses.
Our doors hang ajar; cut in the balusters
hearts beat with gentleness, through which a cat
noses dried honesty, stemmed in a vase.
The back lane cries for rags and fur; fierce as ginger
he treads, in the currant bushes hung
with his piss. We must thank ourselves
who are alive.

No no! gratitude's the way, touch God's virtuous mouth
of herbs, the bashing circuitries of seeds.
Slyness filches to the forest-raspberries,
by imitation, the grass's lightning.
His admiration is a mouth of leaves.
He glares his black lamp; thief.

2. *Praising*

We praise the harvest, a swirling helix of leaves
stuffing each other's mouths, gentle tornado
of glut. Gratitude bites the underpart of God's mind.

3. *We are cared for*

Energy, jagged clinging force, lying in
the thief's first life, chose a priest's.
Small lower lip, sensual
large upper one. A little mirth soldered
to the corners, plural vulnerable delicacy,
like a leaf grazing another.

The passover salts them together. One man is,
and the other, said to be a god.
A finger-nail dips in salt. This is Judas,
not a Judas yet, touching
Christ's fingers, kissing his moon-lit cheeks;
the light of the world will char his soul.
Christ shouts, 'I've chosen, Father,
but will You melt to an uncorrupted
strategy of light?'   Judas's lips
dry as silver.

The oval heads of nails, hammered to unnatural
duty, fleck with blood, and weep
in Christ's wrists. Their shining is over. Envy tears
the mind's salad, Judas destroys his body;

and earth renews its cruel gland. The priest cares
for us, to the ends of the earth.
He draws a line
over water, without termination, his vessel fleeting
in seas bifurcated by the polar cap.
His strong adhesion is to pairs of us.

4. *Green wind*

Green wind shakes open the trees' heads, their isolate
voices, a tissue of moaning
in unbrotherly solitude. This is the harvest-time; be rejoiced.

5. *Good chance*

Work out what to carve, between mind and the fractures
in the butte's snowy happening. Stand and smell
the wind off its corners. From the noisy grass,
twin-tracked by tyres and feet, be fortunate,
pick up the horseshoe, its thrift of motion.

6. *The way we choose to live*

His people thought they were his progeny.
Their praise, shaking upwards like smoke, he deflected
to their God. No sacrifice in blood;
they choose, litanies with mashed herbs,
an oblation of leaves. Even this they regret
but sense God requires something. They provide
no pacification of brutal godhead.
Thunder is a goddess. Tears are ours.
Their elegance, a modern gratitude,
a thankyou in their mouths, the leg sturdy
on its considerate heel, the instep's tenderness.
In the yearly tabernacle, a trembling horn
ushers in the hoped-for forgiveness.
'There never was a promise broken,' she whispers
to her husband, 'but was redeemed in pain's
massive later time.' The judging, tremulous horn.
The halcyon ark bobs in the steps of
one with a mind for God, spittle flecking
a mouth of pride. He kisses his fingers
and touches this disrobed sacredness, as it
flings by. The priest flowers his prayers
over the year.

The hems of the acts that lift the scroll
to the congregation swish the chosen one.
'We must have forgiveness,' they shout. 'You have it.'
He unscrolls leaves, sewn, not for nakedness,
but vulnerable words, prancing before God

like children, uncertain if to be grateful
or independent. The fig-like mind
fleshes with trembling, its hopeful generous seed
proud if it dies unsolaced.

I lie half-dead in a tug, that smokes like a man's
dark, furious pipe, in the Ohio's sluice,
beating nightfall with pudgy disdainful wings.
Slow, thorough, the bastard Charon.

Take heart: the last this body sees, 'Oxo,
good for the brain.' I die, advised.

The priest gathers the wasting languages
spoken by a handful of fingernails.

7. *King Hezekiah, the spring, and a water-tunnel*

Night's dim herbage tense and feeding stiffens,
like creatures lifting their mouths, with fur beaded
in surprise and water. Hezekiah kneels, cupping his thirst.

If water tastes thirst, if sweetness finds
thirst's shifting delirium, if it is sweetness
as much as thirst, how is it thirst resists?
If thirst is water, it must show disdain,
except for dry mouths. Hezekiah drinks
as if he would die: the amused water spills
pink solitary thread. To tame thirst,

to have and quench it, with pipes that thread
water through his house; the cats mew
at doors, for portions of religious meat.
This whole sufficiency, this was modern
this modern water, its sufficiency.

Yet water springs away, untamed. Cut thirst's
obdurate highway through the flaking mountain; turn,
biblical water. Don't stop, or be poisoned.

The city's families, in loops of aching rags,
cloth subservient to the day's thrift, wait
for the king, to surprise, to garland them with promises
of liquid: thirst stands, in flowing water,
imagining it passes through the rock,
its linked fingers
of liquid concatenated,
pursed and braided small puissant spring
headed for rock. 'Say it,' the stone tells him.
'I say it,' Hezekiah, unused to mountainous talk.

Water springs off its coil, insects fuzz
the sun, Hezekiah, seeing the plan,
their thinking, how it concentrates like leaves
shaded on each other, concatenations
of taken light,
dilapidation of winter leaves
shedding summer's thirst, shadow hanging on wood,
densities of wood and leaf,
an upward darkness piercing the light.

'Shall I be soused in sweetness, they in their loops of rags?'

The entanglements of grass with earth, and beyond
the stain of water, salt chevrons of sand off the herring.

'Water,' he says. Agreement swarms like a fish.

Hezekiah, twelfth king of Judah, diverted the spring Gihon by tunnelling through
a hill, thus bringing the water to within the walls of Jerusalem.

Grass called barren, not barren

It bows lacelike barren heads, it is not barren;
its seed, short fractured energy
like broken-up lightning;
a scent of forest raspberries wipes the grass awns,
my mind stores their lilac's softer scratch.

★

The cost of giving, is giving more.

Dead nations, their mouths bitten by hunger:
in mine their ventriloquism suppliant
as a chained cat, the tether
of his spurting cries.

Heads bloom in their ancient coins;
on the obverse, seed wedges in the crook
of three awns, like supple, nonchalant
kicking legs. The people's bread, goddess, their sex therefore.

Dead sex, in billowing forms scratched
in the brothel wall
you step through. You are intense. The amber
you wear glows on your daily nakedness.
By taking thought, you can make a child; as simple
for you as the man lifting a shell
to his armour-piercing weapon in its turret.
His tank is hit: its iridescence peels
like webs of broken light.

You give birth. Your sex has nothing to do with it,
the opening of heavenly flesh. Five stars harness
their plough hid in flagellant, pulsing light.
Your hand is stiffening
its milky palm the outlay of female giving.
A man's love is tender in you,
you fill with humanity, blessed grateful goddess.
In place of our sacrifice, you adore us.

By imitation, the raspberry filches
the broken-up lightning of the grass-seed.
Grass will have none of the fruit: it is a pure self
that knows its acts, and magnifies none.
It is its gnosis, the secret soul
that dies in immaculate completion.
Your grass my flesh touches, sensitive goddess.

Woman of grass, if you are generous,
I shall prick in the coin's fecundity –
those bashing circuitries
held in the seeds on a nation's penny –
a bullying comma. The reverse side is king.
Goddess, bless me,
in my having been alive, although I can't lose that.

'if before'

If before it were surface
now it is not, with you,
and I felt it was still deeper that it must be
as the plane roared passively
in the tolerant spaces, these iced blue clarities;
afterwards the aircraft murmured,
but that was not too late.

If fanaticism, the little dust of madness,
a dust
like the aircraft's burnt mineral on snow,
if love does not dare willingly
like the eyes of politics, its assent,
or grow of itself.
I care, love.

She put him in and he
began that long, exquisite journey of mutual satisfaction.

Flowering in winter

I cut winter flowers for a stone jar
hoping to hear from you: two of each – heartsease,
with faces like the twittering dial of a compass,
its magnetic tenacities
filamenting ships, in water bifurcated by the polar cap –
and the five tab-like petals of jasmine
children leaning through a carriage window –
I sifted in the stems
of winter blossoms, the wind's hurrahs
tearing like the ends of hair, to flowers.
The asymmetric aggression
breaks into harmlessness.

Where are your words? your face
unpetulant as dew. You hope for the best,
and bud as constantly as the moon. I put my hands
up to your cheeks, the flower
of our hurt, for fear to touch
you elsewhere, the bud precious between sepals:
my hands, your face. There will never
not be the moon, flowering a man's hands.

But love, its dignity! The moon, her mature
belly, is a Jew wandering the night sky;
his gold is beaten to her silver. Her light's a forceps
she gives birth to ships with, tridents that crawl
over her livid heaving face
of sea. Is it sorrow?
The extreme of love. Go on. The tides whamming
against the vessels they raise:
it is love, it is.

A psalm concerning absence

The glade is an eye, a dense unseeing space
holding that preciousness, absence.
The heavy trees have their thinness,
the leaves, the jagged swivelling ovals.
Shanks of birch
have untangled muscle, untapering widths
constant as this absence.

The lucid forest eye hangs blind
as the huge, feeling elm. Nor can bough or twinkling leaf
make this eye blink, or the eye hanker
after a trail through firs
mixed with autumn's deciduous mist.
Through the twittering mosses

rises merriment's smiling lip,
wide sheer cheekbones, and teeth
your smile quick at my stag's heart. The hand
sheds its touch constantly. This this, flutters the bird.
Please, I want my hands at your face
that flowers bewilderment, in whose midsts I beat
my male wings into the thicket.
We are the animals devouring absence
and the humans that transcribe it.

Fidelities

She stewed the plums now
that in the tree's plenty
we might have some in the
winter when there's none

Climbing through a soft tangle of spring growth
the air fennel prints is hard to breathe;
I climb further slowly. She's not here

the sexual scent off my screens. But brick-smells
and tar, like cold in a tooth's nerve.
And the sea's tangs – fish, petroleum,
and the horn of a liner, its cabin-pricks of lights,
the hot joyous worlds, or money and the dissatisfaction,
dance-music; nothing I can touch. The captain's smarm
touches off romance. A half-bared shoulder.
The sugary ooze of plums, a cool taste
hot in the pans. The girls are held
at their thighs by the v-shape pleats. You tasted
the honey. You fucked, and I didn't.
I didn't choose, and you did.
Treachery comes out of the sea
like a goddess, her fur is dark
as the mouth of a fish. Sea-smells
in the dawn's cobalt and pink. And the soft-smelling complication
lining everything. The starched, empty sheets.
Running to a hole, the water wrinkles.
It is a question of unfaithfulness,
the promulgation of light in her hair
the designs of sex, the steps up
into fulfilment.

       The sea's drying waves,
cake-like apartment-houses
of both sexes, and the slithering torsions
reflected in windows, the menace
of evening pleasures, deck chairs bent double
in anguish against rain –
the soft smell in itself. And finally.

Like a blunt nib the bus tugs
from its inkwell a contour
of wavy road between cliff and sea.
And fumes drop after it
a smutch of powder. Powdered gas.
A spiked undulant and the railway
enter the smoking cliff – its space, a dull odour
of electrics. Which stall with a number

do I piss in, what disease pollinates
its sticky, star-shape plasm in this hall?

Italy rejoices: the pumiced glimmer here
of release from the German clasp
forty years earlier, when I saw a soldier
refuse a man water. Everything
that is War is evil, they tell us.
Do we speak? the clever
are the quiet ones with no harm
in their syntax, who whisper into chambers
where the living catch fire (it is untrue;
we burn gas and paper). Faithful to all victims
but her, my mind murmurs. Beware the unfaithful
hungers, and the wispy hilarity,
the trenchant clinging odours, a smell of water.

Translated from the Gaelic

for Iain Crichton Smith

From where he was born on the island of Harris he lives
fifty miles, which, across the water, is so near you might
plough there. But this is brine anxious for blood, so that to
be near is not to be close; although this sleeve of sea can
sink its fractures and lie guileless in placidity.

Whenever you turn to watch him, he is facing away from
the island, its old geology which gave him as a child some
joy, and permitted the midnight sun to have its woman's
bony fundament. Lord, the island is many witches, laid
one upon another. Yet even the lightest wind might bear
him home, although that would be premature and
mischievous. Look what I've done, it might say; and
surprise would fire the abandoned labradorite, as
unusable as sadness, although its blue was once the

weight braking the ship's scudding velocity, a ballast of
laminated gleaming prodded up in the cratered vicinity of
Hudson's Bay.

Strange blue grin. He, too, would be surprised by the
wind's acts, and his protest would sound like those voices
spraying across each other's psalm, which the precentor
initiates, its laudation the parabola of distance without
measurement. Perhaps; for the region's unkind theology
has instigated a secular mind in a religious being. He
knows that the soul, in, or after, death, or even before it,
may be filleted by a priest's after-dinner rancour.

And how will those without teeth and situated in hell, he
asks me, wail and gnash? Teeth will be provided, he sighs
lightly. The sigh is a prism. What he smirked at is a part of
some unimpedable yearning. The prism is a sextant, the
sextant an astrolabe, which before that was instinct.

Which is what it is now, and he could home over water
with instincts like Trojan soldiers forcing Greeks into
trenches of spikes. But in that first home the God of
rationality sells ten to hell for every one predicated on
heaven.

His wife understands every fragment of this, and laughs.
Stark sunlight blesses his life. A foliation of archaeology
enriches it. Shall Gaelic die?

In Norfolk

The yachts graze. With long necks that stoop
to crop, they suffer us
as their teeth stain in grass. Frugal hands sort bricks
in a sandpit, their utility, heft
hue and shapeliness, broken. Two fields link corners

above it; the owner stands like still wind,
with his daughter, her sensitive gold. The white barley
a collective of old men
with hair lifting, he touches her. She will mate
a Nelson,

the girth of Norfolk's stags. His men steer wide horses,
their intelligence wastes
in petrol, as they plough
v-shape screams of birds. 'Magic,' they smile
as their children stare,

and the stars drop on their tables one night
a month – Orion's disentangling silver.
But they're harrows, knuckles smashing clods,
in their eyes
meteorite flints.

And as they die their houses suffer
not the soul's brief flit – but this, a shunt
to a builder's pit. It's here, in their pitch
of scent I can't sense, the nettles
entangle butterflies, a cloudy opal that dusts
my eyes; the lepidopterist, a male
venus, nets in his desires.
I smell houses broken; a nimbus
of humid fertility
in pools; and the half-used life
of the prodigious cross-beam wastes
diagonally across the pit. In my hands
is shoddy mortar. 'Uh,' you say, its dusts
on the long plaza-shapes of your foot and instep.

We are twittering birds, we'll beat our wings
out of this; the prospect is a fragile scent.

Amber

In Poland, pines
blob their moulting pitch-like sap
into the salt: fossil, fossil gum,
a resin the State lifts
like intense, red fish.
Intimate elegist of
life's raw, Catullus grafted
into his mind,
like a wort,
a staunch, for the soul's bleeding,
the love that pained him, the stippled
fluttering wings that found
a sparrow's warmth
in her breasts. I've threaded
a chain with this amber.
This little wear-thing,
round-the-neck garment,
its loop and comma, will indent
the left of your right breast
and the right of the other.
Dandle this substance, that's slow to warm
but warms right through, its flow
hardened in salt,
between your breasts.
Not that,
like hands round a sputtering match
I don't want mine
to hold you, but that
when I take them away, this pine's drop
will touch you, not
like a sparrow, but with
this other warmth I say
is mine: but is
the amber's, this rubbed
electric that will
limber alien
compatible energies.

Yet if nothing threads us,
like beads pierced
on cotton, keep this alive
substance as token, as warmth,
as if we were
to have had love.

Such as five pelted, shivering
almost unclothed
Welsh saints found one night,
in Pumpsaint. Not love, but a warmth
nature's bitter soulless hands
could not take from them
that night, as they sheltered
their heads on stone.

An inn. Refuge smoulders
a chimney in
this watered valley,
this Welsh paradise before
England cantered
horses over it.
The river Cothi turns
straight from the farm. I touch your mouth.

Woman and her bread

What I cared for was not bread, not,
in our road, a van's doors pulled back to feed
hunger, but the two, inextricable, with men lifting
panniers, whose days were also youthful.
I was glad for the man's smoky breath caught
in my boy's jacket, its forked gender
of economy on my girl's body.

I'm cheerful, and inspect
the day's loaves like fishes, hundreds to feed the thousands

old as me – a peg, rammed,
and split, on a clothes-line, with garments flapping
like married lives in a violence
fire exceeds. Is this the jubilee
of each day's bread he bequeathed me? This
it is, and I'd bless each loaf
lifted inside the shop, for the till's medals
and tabs to rise, on the day before yesterday
is shorn of its lamb. I'd die of bread,
its pitted textures, its magmas
of dark confectionery. It reminds me, baker,
of you. You rose early,
and died, the cross of this morning,
its wood to be assembled, for the day
to be the day it is, not yet
put together. Although, surely, goodness and mercy

will come to me in the next life. I love you,
baker, and hope to see you. If I clasp
my youth's joys in age's adoration,
will you recognize me, will you kiss me?
I am God's citizen, a staunch believer
in hunger, appetite, and, in His mercy,
fulfilment.
                    Then praise Him for your bread.

Durham bread

for Dave Bell and Jackie Levitas

Streets of terrace houses cover
the hill, the sun's tufts and hollows
in lilac smoke turning stone
to honey. The railway steps
through on arches. This is Gala
miner and minister, bands that break

lugubrious cries. The hushed brass,
its softly hurled quick touches
a friend's death: yes, I loved you.

Living, like smoke
on stone property, patches of brick
darn a worn fabric, its patch
of small-builders. With stepping
between, a miner,
a lawyer, fragrant and striped
as a cardamom. A tall bird
uncurls its neck
and rises like a figure
off a tarnished penny.
Its streaks of bodily black force
drift at the dun stone
of church architecture.

Some choose not to have
that church. Christ so imbues them,
these workers of Frosterley marble,
their fossil columns, they drop
their Christianity
in heaps of languid clothing
on the river side, swimming until
their bodies with tiredness fill,
naked as the soft opening
they started through.

Walking, what I see,
the air lifting between the stepping arches,
is how their spaces
are like the thick slice of Durham bread, cut
against hunger,
slices like generations of boys' mouths,
this boy, Dick, even
now, cramming his
with white, thick unbuttered bread. He feels
that bub, that generative, pert

tenderness of his wife's breasts. His hands
echo her shapes. Durham

bread, as the trains wing it, where
some have neither bread nor love. Slovenly
clothes crease the frail height
of a man buying his stamp,
whose monarch's head removes
a letter to his friend. Take the bread.

The levels

for Mick Standen

Past Quaking Houses,
on the bull-neck of the north Pennines, that has no head,
in a flat torn sky,
wind circling among hills, like a miner
with wide shallow bowl, panning –
above Alston, I went with my nets
to dismal grass-blobbed flats, reaching
into the Solway's firth, soft basement
to rubbed, soft water
not poisoned yet by fission, where the fish frisk
in a dismal sort of way. Their tails lash
the brunette forms of the sea.

My nets an impediment over shoulders, catching
at knees, or scraping the back of calf and thigh.
On a journey not so big as a rushlight,
the bog's rushes smeared with sheep's fat,
I went. The quaker graveyard still scythed
of nettle and its remedy, dock. At Silloth
I threw my nets into the sea,
their meshes chagrined with a dead
exposure to air, and no fish.

Nets that weighed on me, hiss in the floating sea.
For hours, against the sea's pull
tugging like any fish's mouth, green flimsy
triangles of salt wrinkling greek characters
on sifting illiterate sand.

At length six fish obliged, as if for pity
flickering over meshes they can't pass. I pulled
them out gasping against the heft
of frigid water, with biting mouths,
scraping upon the element they leave.
And their doleful eyes and breathless gills
tricked of their pasture hang in bodies
laid by on the denser lingual
of a mudded slab.

The silence thickens
and turns to water: lives that bite
the shining levels of mud,
the creamy monstrous air, teeth that gnash it,
are dying. Teeth and eyes hook
with a presentiment of my death.
I have taken your lives –
delicate adroit netsman.

A man and a plant in a house

You on a ledge in the sun's co-active
diffusion, with seeds furred
in orange berries, I, with a bed, each capable
of seeding, we start fresh in this house,
being womanless, mutely wailing
continuity and warmth.
But my eyes, these foolish witnesses,
had forgotten those with nothing.

In this room I'm to speak little in, you follow
those gentle battered forms,
your confederate equals, trees the wind sways
open, spreadeagling stormy birds.
Like lace fidelity is lovely
between us. But the flimsy pain of those
I betray, shakiness mine from birth;

for now the modest tender colours weep
at me not strong enough to staunch their blood;
I hear the angels of rebuke, those scratching the glass,
whom I must admit, familiars of dread
sawing ice from a blue pond
for the refrigeration of souls.
I must perish or speak with them.
In the world, not a leaf is guilty.

Psalmists

She is she who will not come again,
though I ransack the sheets, two canaries

that drop fluttering speech, he,
with his *cantare*, 'two can lie

apart and stay together,' his moist acts
in another's fur. His right of return,

safeguarding in a sac his trailed pubis
frosted in delirium, female with male,

a wing weighted on another's
in mutuality. Here's dense granular night-air,

which is the dead in their marriages,
the silent sifted flesh of wife and man

a granular air, wife husbanding
their love, like honey, like coal
sweet pitchy tar that bubbles understanding,

in front of which this canary and that one

hang from a claw not visible,
translucent howling bear of light,

prairie wind, seen
as a lover's impress on the sheet, wind

swathing wheat, the silk
lying under His unuseful refreshing breath.

★

She has hinged wake-up eyes. They sing
as if for want of bread, that partly-sweet

grain, this before
sugar was born in the mouth.

I praise the God who is marriage.

★

I will feed them, though they never feel
the outside translucent
serene blue. In winter's morning
I leave my house
wedged fragile and large
in Bradford's hills. A concave inverted pond
of blue douses light on me.

★   ★

I am a thief. In my hand a piece
of chrome, wrenched
politely off a wrecked car-door. In my other

a windscreen-wiper, that's shucked snow
to rubble, its gums
and teeth crushing
the blade to its brace,
like a flag frozen and adhesive at its staff,
the stiff ribbed droop of its salute.

The wrinkled opals of gas in clay
and water! I break into a lonely man's house
and put my hands
in his airing cupboard. Two birds,
a yellow cinder, like a bangle on the other's neck,
she, dead. In this residence,
this blazing sufficiency of glass,
with one bird's dead life, such inclement unequal
distributed being, I unlearn the worth
of a chrome door-clasp, a blade's pitted
rubber, contused
by its rasping away
of snow.

I steal his yellow oscillating wings.
I will feed and keep alive this male.
My song will learn his, we will both subsist
in societal agitation. The bird is a male harp;
I, David and King, take and strum the lifetimes of his wife.

Apparition

Damage

Is it the top has screwed
from my head, like the cap off a grenade? Screams
rise from me, who's missing my lid. I'll screw
to myself, what I must find again.
He throws the best cup

in the house, not at her; the wall
breaks into china
the handle in pieces dribbles to the skirting.
I've my hands to my ears, to scream,
shaping to a question mark. I am trained
into the serifs, ridges, and hollows of letters;
I am a watermark inside paper. No, I am something;

the boy fastens to the back of the couch
fingers like silent tongues. The voices of father
and mother make of my silence
this question, who will be hurt most?

A man with unclenched fist

They chase about the table, hate, that takes
away gender. Her hair swishing cheeks,
that was the darling of his fingers.

My brother will die of their shouts. He weeps
and I must attend. But why won't they stop, who have
more energy than a child's? Why is this night

different from all others? How can
the four of us, unforced, hold each other by the waist
to weep contrition and love? Unlovely mother

and weeping father, divorce, the church's
legal knife. There were chairs and heavenly cups;
a man, with unclenched fist blessed me and vanished;

it was as if I thought I could not die.

Douglas of Sorbie and the adder

In the village of Sorbie a boy called Douglas regularly shared his bowl of porridge with an adder. His mother overheard him speaking to no person she could see, until she finally understood that he was talking with the adder. She called the farm-labourers to destroy the creature, which they did. It is recorded that her child died of grief, and that for many years after children came to garland his grave. This story is recorded in Tales of Galloway *by Alan Temperley.*

A snake mouths a boy's hot gruel – 'move across,
grey beardie.' Over steps, feeling the sun climb
upon darkness, its filaments
filleting tracks with light,
sharing the boy's food an adder raises
its bars and curves of body, a boy
waving a spoon, the snake
a boy's smiling pleasures. The mother

in her pleated skirt watches. We move
in a place of designs, a crust
of gas, and hardened gas, a helix, like chasing
butterflies – or on a concourse
where stars lash, and play,
and fall, like a chain of bracelet, on a kitchen-
table, each month. Abandon, or the spokes
of a wheel plugged into the hub, like us,
formed for work?
Would stars rive out another's gravity
collapsing the life, to make a lesser system?
For less work, would we?

The mother, her ovum, her twist of feckless gene,
watches her child touch a snake, she
infatuated with his future – a pleated
sun success opens, who will give her child
to Georgian London, anachronistic
huge casual brutalities, the houses laid
along grasses and a resting sickle.
The double-breasted widths of the rich
swarm in fine worsted.

She tip-toes, her moulded thighs swish to barns
where day-labourers thresh: 'Fetch hoes,' she says.
A snake is harmed. A boy screams, piecing
the dead flesh, a snake's papery
eyes bathed in venom, the evil's counterbalanced
justifying hesitant smiles of 'let him,'
from hired men, like entropic stilled planets.
'I will eat grass'
he tells his mother.

Her totemic sculpture that swoons one face
above another. His will faints in hers.
He whets a spoon against the slab
a snake bit to shed its poison, like taking
stamens from a crocus mouth
to sweeten bread. The soft selfless gullet of sunrise takes
his grief and intelligence.

Children who are friends, and friends
who did not know him, garland his marker,
discomfited, petal-spears pieced to
a day's tufted eye. A sister says,
'Michael I must take you home, mother is just now
putting up the lamp.'

Galloway's religious killings, and the lonely language of Gaelic

The tide woke, lifting our estuary mud
the Solway tasted – river, like a fish, sucked
it in, hated the taste it vented, but slowed
as salt and mist kindled the Machar's breast.

In neither fresh or salt a stake rises;
Wigtown's to drown a girl. 'Oh recant,'
we beg. No, she was sorry. Gently
we pull, and with her religious hair
tie her to a pole. The flower struggles,

twisting her rims with the invisible
fearful moon's untwisting a flint-hued
watery skein, that billows her dress,
and steps above her,

whose gasping delicately fills me. Not the clash
of her precentor's psalm;
or the miscegenation
of her people's voices with his. Her 'sorry'
is mist in our windows' cavities,
not in our Gaelic, but the tuned
bitter second tongue, not our flickering schwa

but speaking in English, of her clothed form
on a sea bed (my daughter's face
fine and lone as hers). We speak

of a girl's *christe eleison*, the chants of pain
her panting, breath, bubbles smashing in air,
not acts to heft in Gaelic's lofty storage.

For weight our tongue with crime, in its over-plus
of delicacy, its lyric the tussle
of a lonely language demented

with heroes, burden it with our crime,
and Gaelic, the gentle immaculate tongue dies.
But English, frequent shit in its grass, puts spears

of lilac seed through the matted crime.
Their mind's broken lightning in each fuzz
of soft-spoken seed commuting to earth

the generations of its success.

I ask the depths of hill snow, Who will be brave again?

I read in Alan Temperley's *Tales of Galloway* that, in the period of the Covenanters,
Wigtown pleaded with two women to recant their faith or die. They would not
do so, and the two were tied to stakes set in the estuary and left for the tide.

Galloway is a complex historical area and it is nearly impossible to separate out the Scots and Irish components, although the term Galloway Irish is far from being a fiction. About a hundred and seventy years previously Gaelic was spoken in south-west Scotland, and I suppose, in the poem, that the population indigenous to Wigtown and its surrounding area spoke Gaelic first and then English. I am not sure to what extent correspondence between English language and race existed, or if it could ever have been determined.

The silence[126]

As I close my eyes, I can see
the village and its plan, askant
my line of vision. Tilt this, one melts
to its plan; lift, the village is
in one piece, its existing life[127]
from limestone, its diagram a street
in which no car dare pass[128]
another. A donkey's ambling width.

As I pass, their stare catches me
by the shoulder, their shadows gone still
as a lizard in flight changes
the lines of its short, tailless life
into a radiating mass of lines waving
frail limbs and feet on stone.
All stone cracks, all
cracks form lizards.[129] No sawn blocks
but rock scooped, as a natural
prison is. No grass, or tree
through which a bee treads
its shadow, counterfeit
of self, over the leaf-blades.
Man, animal and woman stand
stripped of shadow among the stone;
its pargeting flaky[130]
as a blister dried to its face.
I stare at my palms, their milky
abrasions, the pale veins

in the wrist, the whitened
character and life-lines.

Sea and rock
caught together in a concurrence
of stone and tons of soft salt force,
the trapped unshadowed
sea in anguish. These faces
break their alien stare on me. I'm the same,
all skin and body, my shadow
buried in their stone. Lord God,

I am a bit of the sea:
I don't believe in you.

Gifts

In medio ramos annosaque bracchia pandit
Ulmus opaca ingens, quam sedem somnia volgo
Vana tenere ferunt foliisque sub omnibus haerent.
– Virgil, Aeneid

A sunk plot, in this city
of nurseries: the herbs, flowers
and branched forms moistened
in their warmed sections. I stare
at what will shed
sugary plums. 'Take it' – smiling –
'and plant its union
of stock and scion four inches
above soil.' In this spring
where breath is distinguishable
from thin smoke only in
its having no scent,
no sweet, destructive odour of cell
in flames, I took

the tree, disentangling
roots, easing from the tuft of struggling forms
feet, the bituminous soil
in soft morsels.

By May, flowers: their hue
wings of bees, their exposed parts
a sly feed sucked by a head
with winged legs.
Latched in the shed, implements with
teeth to the wall, their grainy poles
smudged with sweat,
the pale wood softened
in winter's blotch. Wasps
held by raised wings bite
out fallen plums.

Winds streaked with cold lift
branches, as a girl stepping
from water switches her hair.
Fixed in the skins of plums held
to the leaf-backs, dots of pink
fleck and gather, like fish
in chevrons of water. Winds dissolve,
the raised and half-raised branches
disentangle and hang
the hard fruits dripping sugars.
Tawny persuasions of light
on leaf and skin.
Smeltings of a sugary sun, the soft
succulent feeders:
for which I meant to use you like a slave.

Forgive the trespass
of my hands in your leaves;
your barren presence, if it comes to that,
I will leave standing in this sugary sun,
its mildews, its hoar.

Semite

(my name is Ratcliff. Why do they pull it apart as if I were a Jew?)

'Ratcliff.' What did he mean, to rile
my name? The school screws seven to a bench.
Lap, works the tongue. Cutlery
stinks lightly of metal polish. I lade jam.
In a great hall at war shortages
cry out for silent heroisms. Fingers
of food-stained wood tighten their flowering
in intricate desire on lozenges
of lilac glass. 'Rat-cliff?' As if
I'd pissed me-sel', or that his soft-eyed pleading
that mocked my hauteur, since I'm of the south,
was not enough to make his fellow-cogs
lifting knives of jam howl.

★

She married dark hair. Margaret hoped to see
her face raised on the water's medal, in
the well, but she got me: a child.
Long thighs, long fingers – a skein of time's
cottony dangling. We bud a stem
too dried to make a child. Her whimpering ceased.
A d & c took it from her. This one,
darlin', I say, the next is yours.

Blasts of black smoke. The city unpeels
a burning fetid tyre's softening forms.
Conscience softens. We're slivers
off the Metropolitan Railway's carriage axles.
It's hard to be unimportant: harder,
she says,
to be conscienceless.

Constancy eased marriage. In earlier solitude
I formed the lips of friendship, kissed

the glass, and made nothing. I,
a brand-new kid, came in my fingers: howled.
Were I a cat, its gender cut from it,
my fur pattable with need, and soft,
I'd roll in dust letting it sift in me
and better every life of mine I have.

★

I dreamed of constancy. A hill
spreading a field curved in an s-shape to
a stream withered with pebble. A bank
of earth and boulders, behind it
our dead; a cat, a tree, a woman tearing
soft hazel nuts into her mouth.
The land mists, the furrows spun off
the blade so deeply, they hair this corduroy.
This sighting along England, critical
of it. I see what I shan't have, women
with their quick. Between its teeth, then,
death took me, but dropped my mind, a bone,
litter for a small fold of earth. In this
subtle field of England, I drown,
streaking, hissing
in the flecked candied flints. My fingers
turn something that's light and sheens, not
swart pebbles pressed to the eyes
to see inside the world, sight and opacity
making vision, but a matt unslithering
oblong of glass, transparency, thinness
I drag two fingers on preparatory
to setting it with the slicks of spit
in a microscope – the father's gift I broke
before I'd used it. In my mind this time
no breaking; constancy is clarity.
A mottled green drifts in the glass; is it
our constancy, through which her character
stains my new-found conduct?

We both, in two. A head butting, a fish,
splutters in her, but scared of too much sea,
of that authentic element. Of any.
I am a Jew, who claims his English form
is bogus, a self the candle's flame
envelopes, with a flame standing within,
pleading its dignity; some christians
abhor the temporary miracle:
a constant dew-shaped form, holding both flames.
Dew weeps, and the self vanishes. I aspired
to a fair-headed saxon elegance.

★

A Jew is teaching Poles Yiddish. They will
use it as part of their language, a part
of Polish (of Poland), as expiation
and scapegoat – mixed tallows that point
a single fluttering, with every part
of the soft pennant, this flimsy orange cloth
sure of extinction. Should this be?
The letters are Hebrew, many of the words
German, with ash in their chests' tangled widths.
Brush it off. It can be brushed off.

They'd better hurry. No Jews will be in Poland
to speak it with. I burn, my heat a deft
clumsy mismanaged constancy. My body
like chalk on a blank patient slate. I cover it,
and her as well,
with words that vein with a substance proper to
their innocence. I find the hard word, hope.

Polish fragments of dust
(between Poles and Jews of Poland)

'Too many to hide.' With flimsy rage
we climbed into the hiding-places you created
and showed to the Germans, your occupiers.
We hid in coral, in the helix of shells. True?
In ovens, rain-casks, in the water
lithe and forgiving, in mothy folds of camphored linen,
in others' beds: no –
in soiled clothing, in the chambers
of gas,
in the spaces of our *absentia*.

★

We dance-stumble in the cellars, fingers
softening our fontanelles to baby's blood.

Children pick the struggling hermit-crabs, and you,
with Germans, take from their sockets rooted stars,
the earthy sky in dark concaves, rock-pools,
these gymnasia of survival.

★

In Polish snow, she lightly touches a German:
'one pistol between five Jews. Who wouldn't
kill those we hate, like you?'
In the moon's biting halo, two humans
white as gathered moths.

Can loathing and accusation be gentle
as a cat that noses the spaces of balustrades?
The poem's language, but the verse's burden.

You desire ships, your scudding power
with its unceasing speech, that inward stammer.
They bucket teeming seas. They'd be carriages

on land, dipping through hollows, stuffed
with Polish berries, the little blueberries
that have no scent, and break the heart.

★

To ask to live is blameless. Your ships,
their machinery is frosted echoes
I bite through. You are Sebastians
and Christian infantry
with arrows in your flesh, as they are
in our quarrelsome bodies, which are homeless, too,
as sin disremembered.

Freedom clings to you like a shirt in holes,
a wet flimsy headless shirt. My Polish
soil, my Polish Polish air, Poland
touch our ghosts with care, they will scream all day,
and you'll be in tears for ever, whole angels
in the religious skies, where they use
the time for petitions of injured souls.

Yet on earth destiny cries out, kisses you.

Now cross the ice in bliss and peace.

Tangled in war

In Stornoway a shack, two stanchions by it that drip
the news of war. In this stub of tower,
tongued vertical planks
under a glaze chipped like nail-varnish, homely Norwegian
smokes on faded wood, a language
that the storm, which suffers its force,
aches to mate with. Our sword, the hilt
a dragon sinuous as vine,

is better-made than any sightly implements
the farm uses, that Viking ship
billowing between the glen's flanks, its tree-mast
a head of clustered antler. Christ torn in it.

Everything is war. The share is beaten back
into a sword, the storm is a house
that splinters it. I feel
the house's beds of child-birth linen, its tenderness
daughters' exile in cities, cunning in exile.
Theirs is the child-freshness. My hands lie
in the house's space like a wound, its innocence
a past woven as a thicket into its present.
The shadows blood like thorn.

Linked by their acts

Up through a field of stone fissure the gentian's pudgy blossom
made from parts
of bodies, a cheek
kissed, kneecaps, the noses
of assassins. Where crannied hills
skip in God's smiling like lambs, these flowers
light death's route. We, the first fingerings of spring,
would make couples of ourselves. The half-ounce
of scorpion un-nerves us. Its pebble
oval like an eye.

What hankering translucent forms? It is early ghosts,
the man, a dog snuffing
urine, a wonky nail splayed on a fence;
its kidney shape concentrates
in the dog's left medulla. Like a fish he tightens
the leash rubbing his sodden master's wrist.
Oh oh.
A bleb on the dog's thigh. A man chooses

you will die, thin alpine-pink hair. The crab
in your thigh. Peace to you.

The linked plod of eventual ghosts,
for after death
memory makes spirits of us
to asperge our beings. It touches
Emmanuel, the God waiting in us.
Memory, like the wind that jolts open the heads of trees,
and swells them, memory, like the aureole of a woman's breast,
that transmits care and stiffens the nipple,
its deluge of milk,
memory touching sprigs of hopping Juniper
put from Noah's ship of wood,
memory, its web of instinct, strong as sex
and more greatly innocent. Like nuts honey splinters
and pieces together, memory like halva,
memory a nimbus rainy with its moon
in our illusion of its tenderness.
This dog leashed to his sodden master.
So much happens in the sky.

Jews without Arabs

Did we make them leave, did they turn the wheel
of dispersion? We flee
through desert prairie, those grasses
that never flower, though the cold at night
is the thought of the day's herbage
glimpsed in heat. Where are they, and the grasses?
They left, as if
we were boys to be shunned, without our sex,
miniature unicorns, but flatteringly;
like guano, like the bats' cave.
Their absence is our loneliness.
A fan full circle. If we stepped
into our shadow, we'd have no breath.

Here is a provision of bread the sun bakes,
a space in rock hiding Moses
God seeks to kill. We're Jewish Pharaohs
flicking water, whipping it. Canute's deathless stick
that parts the sea – fringed with Sinai's bog-cotton,
its flags of small dissension. All soldiers,
weapons, manuals, sweethearts
in kodak, sink, with the claws of a tank's tread
and the howling metal roar.
Ezekiel has bitter signs: in the lilac sky
his wheel turns
its inner circle in reverse. I free a soldier

like a fly, into desert meadows
of pebble, pale and fine as sugar. 'Unacceptable,'
in delicate abandon
in fine shunning wings, the mayfly cries.
She, the humming-bird's constant intrepid companion.
Theirs the mixed family of creation.

Our enemy's absence, which is the spear of loneliness,
an undying son we each have,
the unimaginable, unsought-for child
with us by a sandy spring, where we substantiate
our constant debarment – it mutely hammers
the dreaming part of our lives: a bruise, an inescapable
panic of inseparable pain.
The milk in our mouths is burnt for ever.
Friends, friends, what may we change to?

Secret Service

(between a Jew, visiting, and a police agent)

We meet by Ovid's grave
exile its greening, its tree, lament.
I slough off my boots
and rest my back against it. The tears
distant as thunder. His suit light-weight
as skin, 'brother,' he says
and gives me a *Genesis* in Hebrew.

Lemberg 1825, sisal knotted on each signature,
its end-papers eau-de-nil
and torn. He eyes me delicately. The book
warped, as if under a stone
in raucous swivelling sea-water,
with, in indelible ink, 'Issac Elias.'

★

He takes two strides, 'I'm a Jew,' (he tells me)
'so I give you this.' And 'brother,'
as if he knew
I knew no Jew was in him. He prays
in Hebrew, him and me in the synagogue
of the Sephardim, me silent.

The prayers fold back in their books, Jews' smiles and hooked
                                                    fingers.

Theirs is the feast – thimbles of spirit
and half-sweet cakes. We caress him
with Jews' morsels.

It is Family Family: an aunt
prints lips on a ten-year-old's
brow rising a forest of blond hay.
The air, the skin smells
of youth abandoned.

Jew and Colonel. He stares, and, with his thinking
transforms me. I've the fuselage of a mouse
and hooked wings: me, bat-like
in his Transylvania, his packed sentinel of conifer.
'Warn the Jew to be no Jew,' their aphoristic murmur.

He spits on me; this sud, a vaccine
of Jew, puffed like ash into the blood.
'Inoculate a Jew with some Jew; he'll be no Jew.'
Oh he knew, this client
of Hebrew.

Oh, oh, yes yes, Issac you indeed
is it, in indelible ink?

★

In the spaces between God's star-like fingers
with wings slatted either side of my flesh;
with these crooked battens, these bones of fragile evil
that trellis the sun's wrathful face,
my form whizzes home
crinkling like a zip, or a rack wound
upon its cog. Which breaks my back's
listless ease
with my wife's welcome I'm not worthy to receive.
She spreads angels arms
jagged and wing-like. 'Elias,' she shrieks
in the Hebrew I've none of. With her small
hand-embosser she gave me, I impress
my name in fear
the investigators will come
upon me, in Hebrew.

Wait for me, I say.
And I wait for you, 'my sweet perfumed self,'
you tell me as I lean over you.
This earth of wives and ashes.
And fear and defeat soused with sweetness and love.

The hand's black hymns

In August I began to love you.
Two islands, yours a scorpion stinging
in sea's acid, a divine, consistent, serene
blue fluid to the sky's.
In my fields of poppy separation undrowses me,
flowers' deaf phones, their veins twitching
oblivion, mouthpieces of an incontinence
brine rubs through. In their tidal roots
distance rocks each land, and separates both.
Distance is smiling. Faithful

as air, where are you? Or is this
presumptuous? In tufted forests I wander a finger
discharging its senses in maidenhair.
Less flexible than building-steel, wind
bonds to this island form: its Roman word, its lost
Roman meaning, *vectis vector*. Innocent
stinging messenger, I follow you like
wind its message. Poppies rummage wheat. Because
I want you, are you less absent?

My hand's a member, a clover's flower
in waiting. 'I can touch you (I say)
you, who lie in the next room.' I say what
deceives pain. It's our voices mate, by phone.
Japanese terrain, the ochre-skin, toad-smooth
hue of the stung creature, in lulling acid,
the scorpion, its lovely innocent head;
and this island the springs tether,
its inner brain the sea wrinkles – is 'venture.'

Our airmail: yes, sweet, we live off the trees
made thin. Refugees are like dust, and all
we bear is absence. Please, put out your hand, if
you touch me, I can. Yes, love, yes

the airmail paper on which we sigh
grins at the words, my fountain-pen that tugs

black hymns from its crushed reluctant sheet. Your fingers
hold the poem, your idolatrous desire
perfects mine. The hand
that reads the poem is more beautiful than it.

Mr Lloyd's life

Being a child, I moved with Mr Lloyd
slow, his leg taken in an earlier war, and reached
the others,
each equal as the next, like flies. That war rose
half translucent, like a cliff
the flesh of soldiers
dashed on it.

'A great day for the race.' His joke cultivated
laughter, like flowers heaped
over more, on wood, a joke bestowed,
asked every day, a child's man the wars hurt still.
'What race, sir?' Lloyd's boys who walked by him,
his legs covering earth
in another war, instructed
to have an answer. 'The human race,' Lloyd said.

Men gassed and watched, suffered the children.
We waited to be destroyed, the gasser pressing naked eyes
at the chamber's aperture. In goes
his vision, through the lucid Jacob-glass.
Lloyd's hand easing his thigh
in equal paces, in pain, as I now understand,
learning to take English, from a good man,
tender as Shakespeare,
in both wars, their midsts, moving from the hips
that could bear him.

I watch this war. It is another's blood is poured,
as if I came to die
and stiffen. Under the feet of children raging
with distance, he lays the fire of Welsh hills
that have cooled to grass and milk.

To a lighthouse

After years I turned home, self-hatred
shredding my leaves, my feet huge
as horse-chestnut's leaf, dray, Clydesdale
useless for loads. How I forfeited self
with hatred, how I stabbed it over
and planned death;

for to have deceived
the self, was to make a shyster
of the body's innocence. So I tricked
my mind to accept murder
from me. 'If you wish,' the mild being's
shy smile shook the spine-pole of messages.

I pictured my head in a landscape, jigsawed
the whole, the skull shimmering
from its environs, bony hills, with trees
pinning them. And if you looked,
a hare, huge and electric, earth's force
transfixing her.

At the back of my head, blue soil, me, inching
timid suicide.
The method: to take the body
from embraces, an angel's even;
the means and cause: fear of wings. And search
for hope, a lichen, such as you might enjoy
to find trees murmuring with? No.

This resort of ships, my home.
Between the privacies of break-water I fed
self-hatred, as I was fed
madness and seaweed, left by coward tides
cinched round earth, moon's bitter, ungraspable
girdle. Subject to jigging water,
I, a sad, lonely man, licensed
between home and marina, entered a boat, clacking
the heads of nails that pierce the slippy planks.

Happy, ever after, to run
for the lighthouse blinking
its existence. Until one
comes and sledges out its light, those pupils,
élèves of light, disciples, disciplines
of guidance, and trust. O the dear blank eyes.
They have not done it yet. They think to.

Pity, a machine-gun huffing
air, swivels from me.

When I showed the townspersons
jasper, in a cube I had lifted
from waves tossed wide as dead arms,
they commended
the self-interest,
that had
stooped to find it in milky waves,

this cubed apostle, this quartz learning
from godhead to be impure. I rejoiced,
who will not pawn
the cubed jasper. Or if
I did, I'd lose my mind, as much
as a wave looses its hand
on pebble, oolite, hematite, the teeth
of granite gliding molten pools: the belligerence
and splendour of a form.

I think of marble. The dark waves
in it are Masons flitching the town's market;
the white, bird's guano, is youth
voided after their labour; they mewl
bitched tears.

Lord, you should have inserted
your ghostly hand between sperm and egg
in the sanctuary of a woman's body, to prevent
me. I am a gem-collector's stony
tit of facts.

The land tips squares of quartz.
Prong, here, the theodolite's
three legs, spy in its protractor
the scythe of its heterodox
gaze, Ireland and Kintyre,
kingdoms of the Gaels' sad diphthongs,
language a gull hovers
of shadow on a wave.

The lighthouse keeper tags a
bird, its barbed flight in his beating mind.
My feet, clop
on cubes of stone, under the beacon's
other side of night, blinking
constant vision. Mr Donald lets me
lie in darkness as the light sits up,
washes, shines the self, is trustworthy.

First a craftsman's solitude made
lantern, then lenses. Mr Donald says
they are bullseyes. Only the light shoots them
rubbed in oil
on diamonds to get consistency
of vision;
stupendous, brighter than day, to guide
ships through
a sour cringe of providence and waves.

Ships fleeing
between nations,

swishing the furred indigoes
of oil on waving crabs.
This performance, its entirety.
Speckled cancerous herring, a dark-footed
sun, prancing upon sea. Now I will save my life
in my hand.

Decent God, you need our love, as all
need, helping you through bleak necessities
of love's exchange. Or else, a lonely smashed God
a gull's ambiguous death, in rigging
a feathery casualty; a broken angel: one of yours.

Lens-breakers

Wood ash stinks a cat's fur, sweeter than smoke, wood
cut, hovers a scent like chyle or sweet vomit. Fire,
in the wedges, hides in smoky quadrants of agate.
Ash sugars the cat; his wedge-head with arrowy fangs,
eyes half-closed pebble. His mineral
distant gaze is topaz. Fierce and red
in the lap, hunger turned us up for his
thin lucid fire to be fed.

Since I'm mad, approximately, I yearn
to be kind to some creature. Our cottage hawthorn
leans on, its grime of white smelt
in petals. The meadow sprays red-currant, apple,
dusty plums, echoing the tides' salt. You can't
be sure it's brine or sugars
dotting the skin. From the sea I pick a cube
of jasper like a turquoise fly.

A track of scurf (I mean the reader
no harm by this) shakes, slowly,
to the point, that empties from its throat cubes
of pink granite; below, this bitter ship,
Deutschland. Its wrecking tries faith in their God;
if the spiky fingers are like splintered
arms, their arms are fingers.

Lloyds pays. Many nights of one episode redeem
the dear bonds. But nostrils do not now
bubble air through brine. Once I lulled a cat
whose nose spluttered blood, a car hit. Lloyds
pays, and charges rise to honour the future.

My love, I'm saying men
step off a truck, whose half-haul
tarpaulin hoops to a stop, handing sledges
to each other, like buddies consigned
to courage in war, bringing the lantern
to earth, with mercury vapour behind
reflecting dutiful glass that twists each scrap
of wandering light through the lenses rasped
on laps, in water and oil, until the bits
rubbed into the lens comprise
a consistent vision.

They wedge at a sledgeable angle, and splinter
the eyes, like a peacock's feathers' eyes, their alert
serene mercury heating to a chlorophyll
in a leafy beam of fifteen miles,
that cannot see. The light flutters
like a butterfly, I'm sure.

On hammers, blistered glass.
The ostrich digests iron; the loch's
wary salt shunts glass under it. The lighthouse
wears no eyes.

If I'm petulant, I'll bash sea-shells
on the difficult track threading to the sea: no way,

no way, my wife, cats, my smashed
decibels. The lenses have their ghosts tripped
from Edinburgh. When electric quits
(it quits) the ships wreck, and raise costs.
So it goes, a trinity, of ships
insurance, failed light;

the lantern, the strophe hammered apart, the hymn, the Jupiter-eyes
beaten thin as air-mail paper.
The men of divine darkness, spattered with drunk vomit
after their work. Tools
lean in the corners of housing.

Honouring the father

A river town presses moonlit circles
from fish-shells, buttons for blouse and shirt
sex separates by gender. I am grass
whose seed crams with broken-up lightning,
procreation's lilac forms,
eyes dropping through earth. We are confederate grasses.
The wind bending us is God's sequence of hands
whose leafless transit gives us birth, turning
to nothing.

It is a question of seed, as the moth stubs
its life into the charred light.
My love, my parent, my moth rest
a little, father, your rubbed generous lightning,
you, ageing magnificent sovereign.
Is it permitted to touch you? You have
your father's life I have been allowed
of lilac fluttering chromosomes.
All night the shop is open, with its eyes and lilies.
The candles bloom with moth and daisy.
Come a little this way, I pray you.

Cleaning the light

My father sits by the screen, each of six contestants
made foolish with knowledge. The compère smiling
at a woman's naked shoulders
and timid gentle mouth, his body between pulsing wings
is absent, the mind
beating in its bodilessness.

Father thrusts his merciful beak-like head
and light hair, which is beautiful;
the screen cannot receive
father. 'Oh you fool, you clown,'
he shouts at the bodiless form.

A ferocious light unspent in winter's branches,
barbaric, judgmental, orange
distinct over the bark; it is this world
and his mind at it. Like a lighthouse-man
fastened outside to the lantern
and its beams of light, a broom swathed
in a torn overall, shoving off moth-like clinging snow
suffusing dark in the lantern's octagonal glass.

It is praising light to clean
a bare harsh existence
of the spring-like dark. Such my father,
his retinal intelligence.

Tenderness

Not trusted with a key, I jar the front-door's lock,
its nice prevention held in my parents' hands.
A woman in the hall points flowers, scent and tungsten
showing grime in the tiles, their earth-hued triangles
of trunk, of bough, fruit and blossom making a tree.
The house is my parents' sanctuary,
therein
the woman, our hall's solicitous familiar,
like an oyster-catcher jabbering
a red bill for her endangered young.

My parents form a pearl
fit to pass through a space, to hold the staying loop
for blouse and shirt. May I touch you both?
We cannot touch. We speak of ships scudding to Palestine,
male Jews and passionate rigid woman hoping
we will connect. We have wasted
our lives, waiting for tenderness.

My parents, my lovers, pour the tea
and let the swollen belly of pewter cool. The shop will stay open,
like a bulging lamp,
a topaz ossuary, its jovial thick-set beams
fuelled by the dead. The light feels barbaric,
this quiet rape of darkness,
a moth's wings clapping itself into life
that burns up right away.

Father, mother, your moth-like lives are never spent,
waiting for tenderness,
the nape of the neck will be kissed.

Fathers

My father's determination
was to be ash. With my
mother's submission
he is burned. 'Yes
Ash that is not
like thread, or snow' she said.
In her
like nothing.

But that is kindness. I opened
a box. A dead mother
had limpeted a green
blue globe of thread
to the wood,
like mould, which
as I touched, her
glistening kids volted
from, colonizing the white
piny zone, leaving
the father's spiny fibres, by her
chewed to gossamer,

his consubstantial self in her dry diligence

the father my ignorant
finger made dust of.

Testament Without Breath

Previously unpublished poems from the limited edition
pamphlet published by Cargo Press, 1998

Arum Lily

for D & J H

Arum lily, white petal peeling
in a scroll off my thin ochrish pistil,
am speaking of Titus's acts, his dust. Like Josephus,
Jewish Roman, scribe with a light sword
of deference. 'Beat me down (I think)
like a nettle, if you must.'

He writes (I speak) of Mary Eleazor
who finds space in Jerusalem crowded as a railhead,
She brings her cash, and child. But then
by the road that winds truthfully about
the hill to Jerusalem sleep the half-bodied tanks.
Rome puts her armour round the city
that helmets its stone, the great helpless Herdsman;
His shade fractures with sheep. The historian
is a Jew picturing for the brain of Rome,
Rome in its electric power,
the Jews of Jerusalem starving. Rome,
beat these Jews; you must.
Josephus flutters his light sword,
his swift-footed infantry, talent. I,
witness, not historian
flower, not journalist.
His pen has fine carrure.

And Mary Eleazor, not inactive, in
hunger, with fury, kills, or is it knifes,
her child, and eats a half of him.
Arum, be fair. Yet how? How be just in a desolate place?
And as the Jews soldiers, their muscles,
like Laocoon, flickering about starving bones,
smell the food, Mary, with a voice of the lamb
says 'Eat. I have eaten what I produced,
feed on what remains, you, Jews, lily-like spinners and weepers,
you, flowers of the forest' – the soldiers,

writes Josephus, who was not in this place,
'slunk away.' His fine carrure scribes in Rome.

I, arum lily, by this dry water,
who am filled with witnessing, unable to die.
Josephus, apostate, touch me with your darkness.
One summer's evening fills with history's long spokes.
Mary, in the recall of all, hurtles like a message from God
                              through my rooted being,
God of limits.

The Mimulus Showing Itself

The contents of a poet's will is the entire body of his or her work;
but Testament *will be your most important codicil because it is dedicated*
to your religion and God, and we don't often get that chance.

– Derek Hines

I have died, you said. Your will is no thing,
but your testament is the release of your image
in my breast. Tender love is my recall,
Mimulus. Yet in the yard, now, you raise
trumpets, in papery silence. Save for the blood-orange tint,
you look like petunias, your returning upon us
is a ship woven into the ocean,
upon Penelope's skein indifferent to an ending.
Clash clash. But never, never that at all.

If you were an ark,
shrieking with scrolls over the flood,
but you are no covenant of law – a return,
not in pairs, not in pregnancy.
Your bond is your life.
And everywhere, in split time, your testament is your leaves,
like a pair of out-turned feet, with a single heavy-seeming flower
almost clumsy. Across the battered

rootless flood, an ark
nests the mimulus-like testament,
a scroll to hope with, and live by,
despite our petulant vengeance against the accountancy of our sins,
mimulus, opening a filly-like wavering vision,
fragments of a fragile God.

Making a Republic

Edited by Jon Glover

First published by Carcanet Press and Northern House, 2002

Editor's Note

In preparing this volume for publication I would like to offer sincere thanks to the following: Jean Allen of the Sheffield Academic Press for initially commissioning this new book by Jon Silkin. He asked that it be called *Making a Republic* just before his untimely death. Rodney Pybus for advice on the manuscript, and the interpretation of the poet's intentions, after a long acquaintance with his working methods, and to Sarah Rigby, Michael Schmidt and Neil Powell of Carcanet Press. It is hoped that this volume will be the first of a new series of Northern House publications prepared jointly with Carcanet.

We have attempted to establish consistent punctuation and use of capital letters. There remain some ambiguities in spelling and the use of inverted commas. These include the poems 'A Gentle Hare' (the word 'cheek' may be 'check'), 'In the Lithuanian Forest' (the first occurrence of the words 'Goodbye my lovely boy' may not have inverted commas), and 'The Poem' (line 28 appears as 'My son, my Absoloms…'; we have made them both plural). Capitalisation was clearly a sensitive issue, as witness this appropriate quotation: 'Beyond the Kingdom stretch the fields of the republic, arid and terrorful. But not everywhere, and not constantly, so.' (Jon Silkin, 'Edward Hicks, 1780–1849: The Peaceable Kingdom', *Stand* Vol. 19 No. 2 1978).

Jon Glover

The Soul Never Has Enough

Sitting by you in the yard as if
you were my child, mountain ash, I see
He has chosen to have silence in your mouth.

Wordless beatitude. As the snow dominantly
smells, of snow, and you lose leafage,
the wind's noise hones to notes on your physique.

Soul, soul, grief's slippage
is your silence. I must not speak.
No end, and no more. With the wind, darling, you engage.

Permission to Weep

My ego is a futile black lamp, but glowing
and removed from death, grieves the composed spontaneous lilac.
Its congregating flowers crush my being, my lumination
chars, but that dark, scratched against darkness, updraught
of sheet clinging to wavering flimsy dark, rises.

My future and my child's are mortgaged, bereavement
is a fresh lilac word. In a suburban carriage,
on waking, I ask, 'Who is he?' My flame, at the terminus,
hesitates in the station portals, inhaling
air's horizontals. I have the feelings of grief, missing a son.
I have the means to weep, and shed light
without cease, to catch existence, and peel in florescence.
Portals of grief and life. Does exit
and entrance create no distinction? That is untrue, that
is not the case, for living flame destroys itself,
flame, our interval
of fierce wavering light, coming aboard.

All the trains of consequence crossing the bridge, flash.
Why is the salty river full, and hungry people

camping in boxes, by it?
Heavy rain splinters on concrete.
Where is the government agency for heavy rain?
Walk straight into the food shop. Eat and weep.
The plate is white as snow. And the swan
of grief has vanished straight into it. Child,
I will not weep and shed you. You are grief:
and your eyelids slender, like her limbs.
In this is no palaver. You are dead, so relentlessly.
Here the pricking flow of lavender takes the yard
with its working day's smell,
yet as if each second refuses to be borne, where rain,
with gusts of dampness, freshens.

Lament

In the kitchen a gas flame
blows away. Hissing toxicity. Mother
is in tears, yet the oven
has lamb, the minted potatoes
have an alkaline myrrh.
A bowl
of haired loganberries. In summer's
loose bridle father prunes
roses. In the corners
of three mouths our
triangulation
of harmony. Yet unrelinquished blooms
in the gentile city, I, child
in unredeemed Jewishness. Light
connects with three lime-trees
and white lilac
in lactation, business
and law not
yet apparelled
in money. Where are you going,

mother, father, so soon
departing? You have hardly been
here, yet you
forsake the lilac.
For how
long have we been speaking
English, positioned on laminated
deep clays of London's Yiddish
which rests upon Hebrew.
Some Jerusalem! Stay,
there
is a little
thunderous dew,
so silent
this late summer
morning.

The Inheritor

Under modest dripping limes father said, 'All I have is thine,'
his house breaking up. Niece and nephew,
you finger the rubbed silver, dishes glazed with birds,
their unceasing heaps beneath linen father and mother lay between.
Put them back, put it all back –
these ancient pictures of hell, teeth stolen
from camps, strands of gold hair off a rabbi's pubis.

The Shekinah, her six foot, enters, her wings rooted in delicate
                                                    scapulae,
they, like a tree folded, fill the room's top half –
earth's physical circumferent messenger
who will prise apart the dead jaws
so the marble be inserted under a lifetime's fleshy tongue,
for even if we speak very little, it is muscular.
'I am closing off the heart's valves,' she says.
Sportif deft mortician,
living female Hebrew God.

Father, I saw you in the holy land by the Gate of Mercy
by which the dead, buried in their hope, wait to open. 'Admit us,'
like lifting leaves thronging the ear. As the Shekinah
does her simple task, father asks that in due time,
which is not long, he be burned. Yes, she says.
And sifts his soul from him.

Father, your purest acts informed your soul. We are
what we do, as our flesh is what we eat.
When you read, that English rose in you, our Hebrew spoke in
English,
the relinquishment of its tongue pacing back and forth between
the Bible's English and its Hebrew original.
Not that the church cares.
Father, if you wished erasure, then what was the reason?
The phoenix fleshes its smoke, the soul is yeast.

Fire

Over the neighbours' faces, a house in twisted girders
is burning. Bareheaded and bowed, the friends create
a circle, like a strange wedding band of 'conscience,
care, integrity', as two firemen direct squirming water.
'Amnesty, help me,' the mother cries,
also, with quieter voice, 'forgive me.'

★

In a suburb a car, on melting stones, I, afraid
of its poor form crouching in fire. It was surprised.
Like short-winded birds, in the city core glass splinters. Earth
has this at its axis, we humans bound in the armature.
God, give me grace.

★

Father's coffin went with speed into the furnace – surely
too quick for your life's double burden of sustained love.
Daniel's friends in thread of coats and hats, in the molten mass
gave nothing, not even the triumph in which they walked
the man-fired heat. The king watching, obtained nothing.
In dismay the eyebrows twitched. His odour smelled fearful.
Father, listen, after you were burned, I met you
one evening in a small room, off a party frolicking.
'How are you, father?' 'I'm all right,' you answered smiling,
we both knew you had died. What I want to say is this,
it is true you were burned; it is the truth we spoke after
the event you had designed for yourself.
Despite the slightly scrutinising cast of your smiling
the sanctum of our warmth lived in that little space,
costing you to construct. Come again in my lifetime,
where you need not speak, as often we did not. Father.

Tasogare

(Cousins of a lifetime quarrel over a wedding gift given
to the parents of one of them)

'*Tasogare*? who at dusk stands there?' She,
a removaler. Her teeth, lined, like rain
sliding off glass. Her breasts, large as her need
for tenderness. Small empty hands
sidling, flirtatious, to find beauty
in value. She is green jags,
in double-spike cleated energies, like pairs
of married bulldozers
splitting skulls of clay.

The canteen, its forks jangling their tines,
was hand-made, for my father and mother,
given by my father's brother
for their wedding. Knives, slotted in glued blue baize,
in this community of instruments

you look to from my mother, now she has no house.
The cutlery for fish, a carnivore's
implements, the salad-eater's,
the cheese-man's, the bibulous
delighted mouth, the eye, and notorious
canine teeth, she touches my parents' canteen
commissioned by my father's brother.
Everyone is dead here.

In this marriage, little
armatures of design, silver splashings,
set, not in the shapes
of food we'd munch, not fish
jellied to seem a fish, or shaping
in a fluted basin

                              – One hath broke
ope the Lord's anointed temple, taking the life:
well, no, not taken, ah
– no, not the life. But then?

This cutlery's designs and hers, they move reciprocally.
For where her emptiness opened, then their designs
touched her with life, in her body.
The suckling love she bears in imagination went
when summer rose on the dewed bench of sex,
drying an imprint of rumpled dress, no further to be caressed
by a mother's hand. As my dark shirt
never looks for a mother's fingers – hapless
unwarmed relative.

The fork's tines rise to handles of dolphins
to fit the hungry motive in the palm; the fish knife,
that's no saw blade, flakes
laminations of boiled fish. The spoon
is for Cain's fruit. The whale, huge, from God,
and the Leviathan. His mucky torn favourite,
they spread, they set into the ladle's handle. The implement
turtles its scoop

with the boiled shelled flesh. As you reach for the set,
the community of cutters and scoops, tenderness
lifts this fabulous gift in your arms that never are
to have and hold the soiled
sheeted, delicate bodies of my parents.

You raise up my father's brother's gift, as if to draw to
the congregation. It jangles,
has its movement, of fish flying
dreamily through the glaucous
altering canopy of frangible brine.

These implements
of life, its dietary hebraic law
in silver, counselled
and hand-made in it, for father and his bride:
It is, and Everything, into thy hands
in time, you, the sweet seeker.

The wedding forks, the cutlery for my father's wife,
hang in your arms, like an aquarium.
You have taken our love,
like a chipped shaving mug, into that space
where personal things are burned, as my father, in
his collapsed flame. As mine is
and your life is, vaporescent.

Tasogare is Japanese for 'Who is there in the evening?'

The Offering

With a day's leave I tapped at my aunt's sash window –
the slender breast of Swansea bay. Her father said,
'Soldier, don't come this way again.' Honeysuckle
was my childhood's visiting, her smile disremembers.

At six, I disturbed him and father. About my waist
he scissored his thighs, for my stillness. I hardly
breathed, father silent. What can the Psalms provide?
What, but death? no no, never think it, falling
off the stairs in my father's house. But he lingered,
and with the fingers of a mechanic the Shekinah,
her great wings pinned back as the hair with a headband, undid
                                                    the soul.

I must kiss wet lips, taste of sugared lemon,
the top lip a white bristling. 'Kiss grandfather,'
mother said. All that the child did lacked generosity.
Like the drive-belt on a nineteenth-century loom
relatives, from the distaff side, move in line
and ask for love, such as I have not to give.

The gates of the Psalms open, I hoping I may
be blessed, that I may bless. In these unlocked spaces
with black crew-cut fur and violent teeth, property
of the Hebrew kingdom, one pads with a sign from his neck,
'Close the gates, your aunt is washing her hands and feet.'
On the toiletry of women I have not intruded –
but find what you have not given, and offer it
with strength that does not countervail delicacy
and put a small blue flame of rosemary
in flower into her hand.

My Father's Mother

for Catherine Lamb

I squirmed in your seed, father, that deceitful
fake haven. And from Lithuania's forest
your mother trembled with eight children
in London, by its docks, and its gaudy ships
with infirm structures. And died young. Your father sold fruit
off a cart, and taught Hebrew to those who loved their Redeemer.
You brought me to these grasses, Joseph, the mushrooms there
like birds' graves, the house bordering this field
the mullions of which flash squares of glass in the evening sun
that peels our sight away.

If it is Isaiah that bloods in snow we say nothing,
making torture cells; clerks, welders, citizens, all in collusion.
Father, my love's failure is in ashes
in the crematorium. Shall I write poetry
for another's instruction? But now I promise
you will meet your parent, and, like the crocus that helmets peace,
she will open, as the lighthouse filaments
a chlorophyll beam that shakes butterflies and moths
over the sea. She will be alive I promise you,
in the next life, for she was with you in this.
When she died she took something of you over water,
eye by eye; but this moth redeems its head of light.

The Fathers

A dog-lion's haunched triangular fury
guards the dead. He says, 'Several things;

first I bite, then in death I guard you.'
'Besides, I don't want it,' I said. 'Then forgive me.'

'I'll guard my own death,' I say. So then
he bites me. Meanwhile a little swooning

in the blood. I tell this dental fool,
'I am the right, and fierce, creature,

the insects gnaw my veins, my newly rived flesh,
I find the Jew in the scrolls. I nourish him,'

and I dispossess him like a father.

It is the crime: I lay two sandals down

as if it were my mind, its occupancy
for the foot that shudders fitting into it.

It is that gentlest act, I was given.
Shall I be nourished, in my giving?

Hearing a great beast cry,
I am called to account.

Father, a Son

1

A Japanese mistake has taken bodily
my Hebrew being, and, re-incarnating it,
has pricked it in Man Body mountain,
a shrine refracting joyous, sacred light –
this the fragile, foolish, gentle prophesying
where I root.

Melted snow splays upon
a ledge of humped stone dividing

a stream, whose separating, flowing weight
in unequal distribution harms
no one.

If I'm felled, with my pith and muscle
clasping this inner life that's not mine, yet
death cannot take what I have had
into what I will become, this being I am,
a cedar's gentle unabridged mass,
shimmering dark
on others' darkness. We are chastised idiots,
endlessly punished until death, who transgressed
and dishonoured our parents.
The dogs piss our roots, and wear their suburban chain
where we are feral. The trees are in some splendour
of male tresses and female locks.
The double condition constrains. I have a self.

2

My ceased, my shuddering and sobbing father,
weep all you humanly desire for yourself,
with none to question you in your conflicted loving,
where you are inadvertently in light
because you did not transgress her, loving
her who loved you.
Oh that is something we can't calculate.

We can't withdraw love, we
may obstruct it,
love, springing in light,
father, which is virtuous;
don't you feel it is,
or maybe you do not feel
love is virtuous;
the filament of guilt heats
the aching bulb.

Yet please, accept
this filament in you that lights in me,
fragile wiry light inside a docile bulb –
being what I cannot see
with which I do see –
receive this gratitude I made from light
which I give back to you, you, invisible,
whose ceasing I did not see.

Father, remember who I am.
To love we come immediately. My God, if it is true,
I do not speak about it, walking
the promenade, ashamed amidst
the couples in laced-up gloved forms.

In my Father's Books

In my father's books I touched the naked women
I dared not, at fifteen, and I desired
their complex flower would touch me.
Yet who makes tender acceptance of such
a one? The women are smiling still.
Father, I say. But she
lies bare upon his knees, and sups the tender proposition,
whisky, that's to suffice their happy night. O happy happy night.
The black tresses of a woman's regal supposing form.

My grandmother allowed me a willow dish.
In its glazed hue, a withy, its head, like a hundred gently opened
taps,
spreads its pool of moral tears. Their jets in promiscuous dedication
eke the blackish blue, and swell a pool of unchanging white,
the finite blood, perhaps, of a tree. But the white pool
is a gentle sexual puritan, spreading beneath the tree
on this dish, one of many fired for the masses we are.
In this pure pool, with its foulness there of birds and insects,

I am afraid of immersion, and see such necessity.
So we come here and hope to give what is not
to be forsaken, love, fading timelessly.

A Gentle Hare

i.m. Matilda Bau

God smokes the sweet compacted flesh of wild woodbine,
small yet like cut-down trees where cold fissures
their periodic rings. It is like our flesh, but what are we to those
cut down, their flesh sepia as fur? By a track sashing a hill
a hare waits, to slip through hunters, these creatures
of their hounds, by threading her evasion back between
their advance. Strong cocked ears,
sonic twitches tuned to earth's rumour,
in gentleness she eats thin grass.
Winter lumbermen heat their patch of cold
firing wedges of live creature.

O, I cry, is God smoking us? 'Some day,'
I cheek him, 'you will die of us.' And he, equally,
'That is my privilege, for all flesh is sweet woodbine, as you learned
in Japan, by the lips of the volcano, its flanks of ashen grass.'
Among such ash I remember the few Fridays
gathered and tied into a small dry herbal sac, a candle
another flame wicked upright in a saucer, and grandmother
who suckered my drawings to slippy panes with smudged
                                                    ancient spit.
And when as a child I thought I was turning mad
took me in long arms, and lightly lulled me beside
the phone-line my distant parents sat by, in their different frenzy.

In love, the self in fronds gives away its fruit. Like kids
who frisk by the rails, a freight's beam on tender eyes.
Why am I afraid to put my arm on your waist? Am I, then?

You with a hat, in its broad rim like a crown of straw.
What is this drowsing awake? Is it the fat tap of love,
an obsequious candle? Not really,
it is strength being modest, like the huge sepia hare.

In the Lithuanian Forest

She had said, 'Goodbye my lovely boy,' his prone hair,
with its unabsorbed moistures, barely a thatch.
I had thought she meant, 'Goodbye, my lovely boy,'
who had meant 'Goodbye,' the familial energies
still pulsing her gentle brother
in his famished veins.
'Watch for your legs, I am the scyther,'
sharp as grass that cuts the lips of the unwary whistler.
How wearing it is, and how different
from the puissant shafts of pungency off lavender,
the zany pinnate and vital dense leaves.
Shall I bare the tooth of levity?

Yet the sister and brother, the man concerned,
'my lovely one', in all human mouths.
Lonely, then, in his waking season the child, this watcher
                                        woken, seeing
fleeing stork-like birds, bearing away filaments
of us flowing in their bills, soft as hair entreating the church
                                        meadow;
it's an earthly hair darker than grass
bastioned at Harlech.

The bay mare, colt, and stallion, they are cognate,
they nuzzle and weep; if their kingdom is hurt,
it is not broken. Uncle, your large chemical head,
your veins, soused with our family, in distress you,
the friendliest, hold your door open
in whose recess light creeps

to touch the hall's tiled fruit in the mouths of perching birds.
The tender side of the family is dying. My old, lovely boy.
Did pines in the Lithuanian forest
where we sheltered, without protection,
comb the air with affliction? I listened
with my fingers, I touched my grandfather's hair.

His Cat

Fifteen and adult, I lift our tortoise-hue cat
to a glass box, a doctor's phial twisting in mud-green vapour,
and like a kid a winter's sigh comes at mother's 'Gas her.'
Doctor asks, 'Will you stay and watch?' Am I afraid?
She raises her docile head and smiling fangs, asking
'Cease killing me.' She looks, and then she dies.

I flee to the priest his mouth dabbed with angel cake:
'But child, she has gone into the world of light,'
where, under the church's arch – O, hell, O divine
promise – I find no mercy for myself or her.
My failed self and a gassed animal.
The arch is an arrowless bow, wanting desire.
Here's where I stand.

In my palm is a mute bell, her name,
a collar, some tangled hairs. Stood on a railway cutting,
do I suppose grass restores? No suicide,
still, I trespass across the electrification
and reach the station's bridge-form, 1864.
This war takes boys to France with makeshift steam,
the schedules cramming the mooring-place by London Bridge,
the soldier-killers heaped in tears, the carriages
like coffins, flickering over rails to the horizon of battle.
The destruction of the resistance to do it.
The jouissance at the gun's discharge of souls at each other.

Who are you to say I am too young to kill?
I had a cat nine inches tall, of indelible grace.
But the boys, the flag of their disposition,
fragile, stained, aching flag. I, a child, succeed.
Blade upon blade of sacrifice, even of grass.
But will the creature forgive what I have done?

My father is not a soldier to praise or blame.
Nor is my God, though his church says that all may wear guns
and deliver gas shells into another's right to life.
When I stand at sentry, the voices of bird and cat
and breathless mule, and the sigh wrinkling past the septum
of the horse tethered to a stake;
I, having no less right to life,
Hear that the mud is silent as earth's depths.

Are They Both Dead?

Peter, your eyes stared in hers, and her sight was retrieved
yet Peter, the cat, your mother forsakes you.
The dogs' yelping vibrates in you, for you it is meant.
They canter over earth; your mother yields no cry
in tuition, she is absent as refused love.
Nor is it only her that is gone. Your protector cat,
large as a sumo, is not home. Here they steer
their push-bikes and their cars like taking sex. It seems
everything moral has bereft earth; the beam of a lamp
torn from its wick, the instrument derided.
This ground the cold opens discloses its newer mineral,

where, where are you? They got your throat and pulled out
your breath and stomach. Of course you are buried;
where is your protector, that is the point?
The sun's delicate lust is gold, he weeps upon the moon,
he comes as near to being moth as the self can bear its heat.
He stays his course, and weeps. He keeps on.

Where between the interstices of pity are you?
Can one pity morsels of flesh, like clothing torn?
It is gentleness in Christ the uncrowned earth misses.

In this late spring the cuckoo-bird jars two notes
in its hemisphere of theft usurping others' nests.
Milch isch ein ganef, milk that boils is a thief.
My grandmother said this, and smiles. Death is the thief.
Death is endless, like children.

Printing Radio Stations on Glass at Lee Green

The cylinder revolves across the glass sheet – 'Leave
it,' he shouts. Splitting, it avoids my foot.
Radio stations print over this deck,
from which I get the finely tuned sex, focusing
the radio finger on each station,
but shadowy things creep on me.
I find the beams of hacked-out sound,
the thoroughfare of coherence
Beethoven is fleet on, yet flees its enabling widths
of marching-violent feet, the rifles' stock, the beating
of hands in a clap, striking cherry,
hardest sweetest wood in Europe.

By Lee Green, we printed station names, against loneliness
but a glass sheet cracks upon a glass speck
of an earlier breakage. Between the sheet and platen,
the openness of which pleasures Beethoven – a prairie's grasses
                                        and flowers,
its topped-over tall yellow, the self-cultured reds,
and the spiked grass – it is a world hacked-up
between the platen and cylinder hissing print.
We print, that the young girl hears Schubert's *Sylvia*;
it is the silent box, the silent wired-up block
of constellated dark that takes her soul.

By Lee Green they knifed a black screaming man, 109 stop,
the red bus sweating to Eltham,
where we printed the beams
for music in its lambent coils
that wind the coppery wires of partnership,
the rows of wiry power drawn from the structures that do not
need us.

The young man on his bed, sad as a clerk, waits.
Like Sylvia, who with unmated limbs
presses her single bed,
and hugs thin shoulders in long
thin arms with large cupped hands.
It is their collateral music, hidden in a lucent sheet with radio
stations
that crumples, I left, never to print on glass again.

Yet woke once, in a train, by dark St John's,
struggling, clear as glass to be printed on,
shouting madly – no one
in the carriage – 'Who
am I?' and if I am
a glass sheet in Lee Green, what is it worth?
where young men knifed a man whose flesh is black,
he with no glass, light, lucidity,
dropping by the concrete upright
fluttering a steel enamelled red and white bus sign
'Put out your hand, stop me.'

I sat on a train, with a single shoe
for the atomic genes of electric,
like a timid moth going for the light that strikes
disclosing a lens of feeling petals,
lifting and opening up the clement form.

A Noiseless Place

On a bridge separating school-towers, my students
not being early, I, beforehand, smell the wisteria.
More pungent than the flower, a man in grass smokes,
the sun's heat having racemes and fingers. Is what I see
a second manhood? Dead and conscious
as a child, raw, bitter, as damsons, vociferous and gentle,
I carried, like a dead animal, the wounded child
in my arms, to a noiseless place that he might grow.

Shreds of dying tobacco, and a leaf's featheriness
in smoke release me, in manhood's child, to prise
open the wisteria, its adult smell,
and disturb there the foetal man, his unused wings,
shrouding the papilionaceous being.
Is this narcosis? Is this simple, do I suppose?
My seeded manhood bonds and stirs in pain and brutal chance.

In gravitation, a field of thunderous dew,
the stunned drops thick and fast, I come alive
with pity for another. And fear makes
this childish soul into resistant flesh. I will
not pass away, and death will have to kill me;
and even as earth pulls
me to my curse, still
the fritillary energy. The wings lash
in metrical air.

The Fireflies of Minsk

Frail monoxides from retorts of coke haze
to chambers, and gas. As two men
uncoupling a shield
from a spy-glass watch these lives, who see
themselves watched,
as they gas.

Spectral collaborative chums, gassers
maybe forced to it, but they work,
Ukrainian, Lithuanian
specking mortuary counters with these gassed fireflies,
the humans, not more delicate than a lit insect.
The gassers can't know who they've gassed,
'What name,' they cannot ask, 'which insect,
with stiffened feelers, were you?' Nor cry aloud
'This is she,' gas hovering
on stiff eyelashes, or antennae. One man sees
these ceased invisible jerkings, these human
fireflies of Minsk, inside the cupola of marriage and death.

The gassers beam fiery light
into cellars where we hide from their death, with those unborn
sprouting birth's soft hair in her. And she, like all the others,
gasses in concrete space. As we know.
Space in the cupola of Minsk is fireflies,
is firmament, is creation's starriness,
the chambered gas, a star-filled cupola.
And one gasser from Minsk, thinks he is a butterfly
and one is from Ukraine, hugging loaves like a wife to his body.

In God's ancient, child-like mouth
his mother's milk mixes his childhood
with ours which we never had;
this stinking spattered weeping God is insane. Oh, crash crash
the beams of gas fall. 'But child,'
God says, 'your mind is clothing itself
against me.' 'Me, too,' the firefly stings darkness.
And the gassers beg, 'Come, with your adult mind
and do not judge us.' And the firefly
pierces my brain with mercy. Still I would refuse.

Two Poems Concerning Jews in England[131]

for Emanuel Litvinoff

The Jews of England

I have spaded over the Jews' field, of London,
how fresh with the dead it looks. Yet in
which coffin, what stone
cast over, and where then forsaken is she?[132]

Among minute untended
flowers that will persist over graves,
in the hundred versions of grass, in the common multitudes
of comely growth and style, covered by soot and dew,
she is she who will not come again.

★

She is my father's mother, her flesh a fragment of middle
German, whose principal hesitating
speech shakes the mountains, fills the trembling air;
'Kill them.' What is the question she has no need of asking?[133]
In fenced adjacent plots, England's dead
and English Jews[134] have rotted
in enmity. We fill the earth, and we are poor[135]
as people who flower must be.

We cannot fight for each other
who fight each other. It is death that's flowered
our common hatred, and unshared sorrow.
Sometimes in my weeping, I taste their salt.

The Jews in England[136]

I had no voice, and borrowing one I made English harsh,
which is your tender complex English.
It is your language, and I must look for mine.

Hear my speech, love, take notice, and stay within my acts.
I am your tender gentile woman, and you, Jew, have brought
                                                              us this,
a poem that is a single note, of praise, the psalms
fresh as a changing glance, a fragrant look,
in an English we had not, but on our tongues
makes our lives new. Yet now, she is she, this tongue,
who will not come again, although I sit in grasses,
their flowering, their mutual forgiving allowance
of space, like feathery cats at a dish – the prairie,
with its miles of sound, which adjusted to each new comer,
until it has been cast up by the spade, its mattocked web.

I have no notion of how I shall die. I saw it die.
I see it, my brain, nails, digestion, all to decay into new earth.
Revolving its cutting edge, a thresher,
where wheat, stalk, haulm, and staff of floury seeds
like torches, stand, each eye broaching the same vision.
We face our God. And eat.

The Life of a Poet

i.m. Isaac Rosenberg, in the First War

for Dennis Silk

Rosenberg, you do not talk easily. You write
and life springs up poems like warriors,
in the war, which killed you.
Lion-tongued enabling
angel who seeks
the incarnate female soul, 'Shekinah,' you cry out
as the steel fragment enters you.

The creatures with unicorn
fabulating tongues will never die. No, they never shall.

Only their flesh melts in gas.
The Female God stands like a great trunk to heaven
whose salt splashes your supine torn person.
The small fierce being, you, midsummer frost.

The Poem

He who would not be frustrate of his hope to write well
hereafter in laudable things, ought him selfe to be a true Poem.
      – Milton, 'An Apology for Smectymnuus'

Where we were few, the flower audible
our blood not tense or gentle, we were poets.
Us, contemporaries, the ego a pastry-hued ghost.
Its twinkle of ukulele, yet
a grenade's smash. The sun gives the heat
it cannot feel. The poet is on all fours,
misty skin finer
than metre, though syntax in his pact
of understanding
with mercy, supple as a baby's wrist.
From God's sinewy chromosomes,
conscience invisible. We, bitter-seeking
animals must make conscience. But touching
whose pain? Slovenly light burns
from a pure heart, I say.

Words about a horse, a cycle's milky
lilac spokes? But jagged conscience, a soul
of broken-up lightning. Majesty
with pride, without conscience? The mirror titters,
the face a tense narcissist.
Now comes darkness, its teeth of noise
the rifle's dental anguish, a man with slugs
of lead dotting
a woman through her waist.

The air paints, yet the sea wanders
the music of this island through the ear,
but the mowed women, the bitter
pregnancies, and their unborn
asphyxiating in the cellarage. My sons, my Absoloms,
keep your flesh, and do not go killing. The bronchial foreland
hoists its pines, their fragile arms of lace,
toppling like refugees, the piney cones
in succulent aristocracies of perfume and victimisation.
Their lacey leaves, their ferned breath.
This is Croatia, we are poets, from abroad.

The Pain is There

When soldiers with the regiment's flashes enhancing
their shoulders gave him tender freedom the camp inmate
spoke up: 'Thank you, even though you're late. The pain
is in my eyelashes. I will close them now.'

Primate

Trembling monkey they experiment on you, your value
as a primate. *Air France* and Belgium, its *Sabena* –
feathery metal, angel-flesh, since nothing else
crosses the sky – bring you, the pilot,
the navigator, stowing their craft, torpid
indolent moth. A featheriness
of mildew and morals. The technicians have strapped you to
                                                    the head
in a clear globe. You see and shriek.
I borrow the language of collusion.

Gift

for Michael and Kathleen McKeon

You gave up this slip of rhubarb, its literal leaf
dying, head like a naked brain. Orion
nightly casts a greeny light on it. It's eerie.
'Get an ego, I have one.' Yes, brave Orion has one.
Rhubarb transmutes the horse dung I forked in. With my few
words of Japanese I greet it, 'O-yasumi nasai,'
the evening violet and copper, my smiling
falling about it in silver paperiness Orion eats.
To the day's light the creature adds a radiance,
using and releasing it without diminution.

It is like the sea shells one gathers to pay
another, its common opalescent worth
passing, pressing, through succeeding hands, accruing
their warmth and the coolness of rooms where they lie about
in careless tender temporary lodging.
Is this old fashioned to recess in a poem? They do not
linger, tranquil brief and precious residence.
Which is like the love one might, any day, be given,
if one is a lover.

If There Will Be Hope

Servitude to fear that not death but life takes life from me
is like two trees with their crowns roped – a man, head down,
an ankle bound to each crown. You nubile poplars,
not long to be freed. Yet what release is this?
I ask money from you – you, dead, do not set on me
starving flies to syphon my blood; for I must feed
my partner and myself, O risible words.
Self, let me be conscious, O hell, outside my self.

And now the greenfly insists on its milky crouching life,
and light in summer's night sky refuses extinction
since either the sun, or this light, stays high, property of our Father.
I think it is the language of England in this night-sky. No, no,
it is modern radiance – my daughter smiles at me
as if I were childish. It is light, deeptoned,
Rachael, such as I have never felt; it is perhaps
the speech of England's Jerusalem, waiting to be worthy.

Printer

Any day soon the sudden pictures I tip into the linguistic eye,
images I print having litho-intense surface,
a man with a woman, he naked with her beside
a tree its bark clothes. Look, a ginger money
spider climbing. God is now. The vicar
who likes fingers of toast raises Him to congregated eyes.
And the rabbi, heated to a pitch of hatred, being afraid,
I also am a Jew, hating and afraid,
they each raise Him, the universe's tenderest heart,
to eyes forsaken in and enduring midsummer radiance.
It hurts and it is true it will not cease.
In what phase of this will I be dying into your creation?

Suburbs

I

I carried the dead of Lewisham, into
refrigeration, and I took care, never to jolt
these hospital clients, who might ask, 'What is this place?'
What should I have said, before they were burned?
The senior porter told me, 'Go home, now; I'll bring

the suicide from the electric rail, what
remains of him.' How be grateful
to mercy, or to a woman struggling to turn, to help us lift
her to the trolley? The blood
of her ward runs with the surgeon's blade.
My task, to be gentle. Through south London
the minute speedwell, in passion and terror,
flees towards me.

II

Young girls whitely
in the night heat, on the paving, lean
against the phone's lit kiosk. Legs spread, not
in debility,
but power, like phone cables conducted
into the blood and nerve of lively insistence,
passion's, despair's, over sun-heated slabs
of granular pin-pricked darkness.
Grass-flower and brick raise these suburbs.
Local power, local pastoral.
Their new world is coming, out of nothing.
The moist tongues, of languid
roe-like girls.
The aggression in bent knees. Nothing utters. None of it.
Over them fork sullen bitch-like elms.
Certain of love.

The Silesian Weavers

> With gloomy eyes, no tears,
> they set before looms and reveal their teeth
> Deutschland, we *weben* your shroud
> we weave into it a three-worked curse –
>   We weave, we are weaving

A curse on that God we all prayed to
in wintercold time and hunger's time;
we have hoped, waited, no use,
He has mocked us, deluded and deceived us –
      We are weaving, we are weaving

For the King, a curse, that Reich-king of the rich,
whom our misery could not touch
who has extorted from us last pennies
and like dogs has shot us –
      We weave, and we weave it

A curse on this deceiving fatherland
where only disgrace and shame thrive, and
where each flower early dejects, un-forms
where decay and foulness enliven worms –
      We weave, and we weave

The shuttle works, the loom crashes
diligently we weave, *Tag und Nacht*,
Old Deutschland, we weave your shroud,
we weave into it a three-worked curse,
      We are weaving, we are weaving.

Translated from the German of Heinrich Heine

Respectful Question

Where a bird folds in its wings alighting, a cab
rubs to the curb, two
getting out. The bedraggled older man, like a cash-point,
pays. In the acidic red
tenement, shots crack the sky granular
as honey, making sure. 'They paid,'
the driver of the faded blue
saloon testifies. One tongue makes a jury.

Violent distress urbanises the city
of God's fresh hand. 'Do you want to die?'
A pulse of moisture cracks the air,
and wrapping the duvet round my body
in His terror I drop from sleep.

A Short Poem for Hiroshima

Over the steps of a bank
flesh melts into shadow, no,
for that is absence of light – into concrete,
by a severed atom
of America and Emerson's over-arching world, no,
by fair, be fair: poor Emerson.
Yet the institutes of democracy.
The tea weeps into pouting cups, its infused drops,
a servant girl, dying
to attend her master.
And where, in pain, is he?

Country Water

Cold spring, an unwithered petal, finds
winter yields to it. Amateurs take the fish,
the river takes your grandfather's two brothers,
the niggard appalling water
they enter, as if they might drink it all.

A sly blistering country river heads
for Osaka quay, flickering both on old news gangrened
in a sturdy green fungi. The quays, the quays! turbines fan
their diesels to Kyushu, fire island,
which craters melted fire, earth's first substance.

Taking Ourselves to Heart

All creatures that on earth do dwell
Sing to the Lord with cheerful voice

but if we were life-forms, prior to our births, what pain
in that waiting, which infects the quick of every thing?
how be copious, with a forthcoming love,
if pain darkens the glass?
When I was a child, evacuated from bombs,
in London's nerve and tangle
of fighting back gravity's instant
of bombs dropped from their hold, rickety sensitive eggs –
'Why,' she asked, 'make yourself vulnerable,
why flaunt your body in the raids?'
my minuscule terror – 'Here, get out of bed, quick,
under the stairs is safest,' my mother just pregnant,
I afraid, in the tissue of adult terror,
to be ash and still alive, before dying.
So, if I speak of dying in the artistry of another's hate,
how, in that dark, with justice show creation?

At first, a flea tears a jawful of space,
whose metabolism makes blood of such a meal;
it becomes a furnace of dietary minerals,
earth's lovely tragic body. It is feathery malleable clusters
of lead smudge crystal. Clear is amethyst
and lead is counterfeit. Before life breaks into itself,
this bird, hovers in vacuum, sweats oxygen,
pure amethyst jay, prognosis of its type, in brute frustration.
By it, a pearl curds from a white belly,
seasonal malfunction, its silence first pain. Like childbirth.
Where the child hooks in the arms, pearl lulls in the hand.

God scours himself in cold Norwegian falls.
God, irresolute space-lifter, hi, hi, it's God
unfolds like a spider miles of interstellar
arms, and trees hoist huge limbs of solid water.
Solid idiocies lull in boughs. Amethyst jay tightens

its spiral flight, 'Create me,' she implores. 'Make me alive.'
The panther's blast, the scorpion poisonous and nervous,
the amethyst jay does not rebuke her maker.
It might. Sleek damson arrowy furbelow,
squamous phlegmatic energy,
this peaceable feathery fledge.
The scorpion pins its venom in stone, 'huzzah,'
delicate rose-stone utters. Humans we are coming alive.

We blink alive; Moses, hoist threads of water from stone.
Be precipitate: make gratitude, adhesions of goodwill
in insects, mice, us – bitter lamenting frailties,
the mice, with soft hoofs, in bitter lamenting frailty.
'Clop' is the fly's step, its ulcer of filth.
Horses and spidery flies, four-legged fingery racers.
And then, again, she comes, dragon-fly with hinged legs
bumping on the crusted oils of the maker,
who might not hurt a picture in a holy place,
whose acts and frail loopings worship her God
by depiction. God fondly moulds the aching breast,
fountain, whose giving body creates the mind's piercing, double
generous pulse of self and the child's suck.

For this warmth pricks a benjamin-face flea,
heavy Semitic jaw, the weight of which, I, Jew, do not wear,
unafraid as a box of knives. Sharpens its teeth on bark.
Our torture of the helpless is in view. Like apples, fallen to earth,
these intelligent drops that beg gravity, please,
to not heap or bruise
their pendant rosy weight, the dropping
sad defeated fall is like a son's evil
twisting from a flowery mouth.
In clusters stars beg to be let to shear
in separate dartings, and stir homelessly
in the huge friendless act of being alive,
like a slow local train, that passes under a sheltering lamp;
masts drag from the catenaries.

That gentleness creeps home is not helplessness.
It is the need to give a hangar's space shelters oily beasts.
Its silence and the beasts' assent, for weariness. Weight for weight.
At the wheels light prisms mercy in chill water
like the soul that often tears its bleeding source,
as the prism bleeds its cancelled light.
If all energy will fulfil itself,
obdurate as insects, our momentary flagellations
of wings, rancid drops of antennae;
if a child curses its parents' act, yet, creation, be tender.
No animosity should prevail, yet we
admire a flea's necessitous energy,
that swells the belly with blood.

We are children, beaten to independent forms.
The child that lay in ashes, from the fire-bomb –
we need to make trains serve people in gentle
quantities of visit, 'How are you?'
God of the templates, we are coming alive in ourselves.
You dead, burned in the fire, won't you get up?
You appear lazy as roses.

Snow Flies (the Yuki Mushi)

God rolls a smoke, saying, 'No mafia filiation,
they're the rose's worm.' And leans to watch
girls stepping against a bus–lit pool.
His arrowy spiritual moisture,
the workers' drops, salt and physical.
He is not physical, and we are flesh that he makes,
Liliths or Eves, grasping our tongues of sex.
Such making is generous, without calculation, it is his growth.
God, grasp this strength, maker of men in lament,
brutal people, in tears with what they have made,
temple-women, silent musicians of snow, in pale blue myriads,
cold for the sex put in them.

In your plunging atmospheres, God, you transfix me,
but it's the human I love. When you made us,
gracious intrusion, lilac rubbed into our gene,
so that we cannot say what we are, but know
we are not all human, the lilac in our soft-blooded constitution,
with the zany snow-fly, the ephemera, in the lilac's physique.
It shows ten days before snow flutters on us, in Hokkaido,
in electric assembly dancing, grief spilling
from a fly's mouth, sugary ginger-stinking rosemary;
these hopeless infant bitches, yet next year, flies again, like
                                             sperm, in myriads,
hoping sober compassionate lilac gives them a day more;
for rosemary has an adult scent of ginger, caring and capable,
but lilac brandishes arms that end in light.

We are writing last wills. The flies mass in a globe,
flies, only flies; no flies, that with
minute thuds precede the life of 'was', with a pasty, luminous blue,
and in a blur, dancing, they approach and fizz
at my face and in my hair,
slowly, I am almost alive with snow-flies.
It's like snow, their pretty wings batter everything,
the electric ganglia, the susurrus. Fading like old soldiers
past their killing time,
and if life is not in them, where to look?
Blue, that's in the wings, having life and death,
plangent like a Greek shrine, with its candled permanganate light,
blue, the tiny business-like wings.

Three Poems to do with Healing

Paternity

Crab-apple: wild apple-tree of northern Europe, original of the common apple.

1

I sniff your fish–like slight scent, crab-apple,
aging on grass no more swiftly, as she gathered you,
who would sit with you in her lap all hours
but for the day's mild howl of obligation.
Red pinks your filmy skin, father apple
of North Europe, you, a bit of chancre,
softening with perishing, withering forth
births of down, root and capillation, in co–extensive
gentle congruent laughter, trickling
acridly, to death. Your others hang
in the swirl of wintering tree that the stone house
had snitched, in barring our common
path, with the alphabet's 'no trespass'.
Which fades the labourer's footprints, restores that first silence
your little bosomy shape ventured,
excrudescence, nucleus
and flesh, acrid, sloe–like, but yes, sure
primary apple of the north.
Europe's bitter wintriness suffuses you, winter as pogrom,
humans going bleak as Jews, destitute, where the ice–floe
cracks in fins of emerald, mist steaming desolations
tumbling and rising, each way, in nature's malice.
Yet you, magic crab-apples, Palmer's joyful lamps,
little puddled lamps from a crucible,
your tree is hung with marsupial life, external
ruddied dyings, to come again, out of earth
now privatised. I see the metro changing
its spinal signals green, chirr of square vulcanite wheels.
Sheltered in our room, you, on jade-hue lace – summer.

The smiling kids might show things, but shyly
stand away from the fence between us. Slide,
eucalyptus pole, painted Australasian bush,
construct a halcyon. Private land.
The fruit tree of common ground is barbarised
by a fence and the commination, 'no trespass'.
Acrid harsh molten fruit
off this unaltered tree which rose,
to any hand, by a path that flows and dries
in common air. Now the labourers' footprints
fade in a privy silence that divides
this airy conduit, where 'walk here'
is also 'fuck away out of it'.
If we forgive the house's trespass upon us –
but from us they seek nothing, and shun
the variorum of creatures. This becomes – private
from common ground flowers a cicatrix
of stiff improper tissue. We are menace
and we are harm to each other. England, given
the chance, you charter earth, fence
massive wild orchards, enclose paths, arteries
feeding the land we then culture.
History is not fraud, for in each voice
is the other's story. But then you can tread here,
and the potent scattered marsupial apples
on private earth. Will the dead coven and ask
'Is this the better way?' For here the crab-apple,
inoffensive branches hanging aged rosy fruit,
growing through winter, was grafted to stock on stock
to make these acrid apples sweeter, in a range
of marbled integument to skein a sweetest flesh.
Nor has it surrendered its paternity.
I hear the Lord humming on private ground
and the stinking crow jabs blind earth;
but bless us, I beg Him.

The Horses

City, bless me can you
amidst flowering grasses? since but for your ghost
in my fifteen years' grass uncut
where father were you?
From a red-head teacher, nubile Hebrew rose, I tasted Hebrew
                                                    syntax.
Eight years old.
Where am I, terrible enfant, like the cone of a house's fumigant?
I want adult seed, these slivers of light on a grass's torch.
Give me a glance at the tapestry, made of silk-worm's
mulberry deposit, re-worked. Hi. Hi.

Oh, hi. Now I will filter earth, washing grass's small ovals,
I am folly's *folie*. Yet these miniatures
with wobbled nuclei holding mercy.
In my circumcision, beneficent
unchosen loss, I re-start,
my cells holding a bit of God that enfolds
my back-to-back parents. O wrathful, short-fused
deity, you did me up, a child's legging's hook and eye,
so I turned to your physical world of bosomy subsidy.

Hear that sound – not England's, not Japanese,
not Kyushu's unearthly Mountain Aso;
its extruded magmas, those volcanic flanks, green
and succouring, that graze the brown wild
knotted-by-kinship horses, no 'horsy horsy' for them.
Together they mouth fine grass from stinking lava,
and the unroman spring escapes hot
into the town's common pool of men bathed naked;
we stare at each other.
And the active gleams of armour
(loaned to another country)
off the mountain lake blister in winter's icy sun,
its blades, seismic metallurgised
oxides of light.

Will you listen, self? I can hear a flaccid
undreary voice, a note peeling itself of air.
Is it grieving? Margaret, Maisie, Alicia?
All your names' dainty robust syllabic breaths,
touch me, I beg you, I beseech you, let me touch you,
most beautiful of all faces. Falling water.
Falling water exuded from earth, and tumultuous magmatic horses,
in their fluid fear of the human – upright unnatural horse –
yet the horses' courage grazing by fire,
mouthing grass's volcanic blades
(where the railway's gantry and scalloped fence feel the swift
                                        passaging of freight).
I will be part of earth's normal particular growth,
won't I? Not yet the failure. Look
at the horses plucking succour.
Expect fire.

Orion and the Spiders

Enough giant to be a fool, I, Orion, twice
had sight taken from me. Am I like Lucifer? He,
a god of soft contraries, torn from God's light
and his own shadow, in filial
vertigo, he plunges akimbo, turning
a dark three-legged form,
hugging one knee, then quivers upon a slab;
not hell, nor mortuary, amidst dark spires of forest,
the chant of Gregorian branch-forms. Here,
as in any place, Lucifer
in his ego's gentlest prongs, in his soft contraries,
is modest lumination. A crashed projectile. But I flaunted about.
Everyone, forgive me. I abused
a woman who gave me love, afraid to dab mine
on her cheeks, her arms and body. Stupefied
in a taxi, or striding through starry woods,
where the flies hide in the roots of things,
I embrace my sad healthy flesh.

God smiled, and burned away my vision. A gaitered physician
whose clothed muscles glanced my naked arm, handed me up
the mountain, grasses needly as rain, with stinky goat-figures.
I wish him well of his mercy. Clasping
my shoulder, he faces me toward the sun's opening gates
and light lenses my pupils. I receive
a blessed sliver of ego,
lightest atomic substance.

It is like the ganger's lamp inspecting the rails of the plain, slave
and wheel-slaves. I weep because
the felloe-bearing tracks are fixed.
I weep for iron.

It's as if everything prepares for adult love
but I am famished with parents silent as a piano-leg,
curved muscleless bone and foot of knobbled toes.
Then with my claws and their shields, I find Artemis
huntress and god, and pace in this tandem,
her hair bare and free upon us both
naked of society's envy, ha. We hunt the squealing mouse.
But we gasp at the ocelot, mostly she's grey, tinged with fawn
in naked ovals, her lovely glistening polar underside.
Who would fire into her belly? Who?

God's mouth is chaotic. 'Is this your love of me?'
I wept with fear all my own, and his mouth
tore at my eyes, as a beak scored another's liver.
My large insane being became a citizen in a dark space.
What is despair, but a darkness? So take me
a short way on your arm, to the hospital,
through the sanitary odour of long-flanked pines.

On the operating-couch God's ocular gift is rodded-up.
In my modest room I plan a luminous future. I read
in my friend's book of a pond, a basin of glowing
freshets filamenting earth's pure liquid. I stare

through a stand of trees. What hangs there?
It's an active spider, her asymmetric mansion slung between
                                                    two trees,
her child, is it, with her. Flicker, hesitating
importunate pleader, a scuttle, pause; her tiny thorny male
of tremulous flaxen legs, who does not weave. She flutters
her abdomen at me, 'Fuck you.' The pale-apple and black
of her being minatory on her shell. Swollen
with digested flesh she webs her nest's graveyard annex.

In every dream is the chaos and fruit of all dreaming,
– child, and nest, chaos and webbed light. Some prefer
their house to contain all the facilities: she,
abattoir and dining-hall, made from dreaming's twisted wires
                                                    of love.
There's a thin child, with instinct larger
than any fly, past-it aphid, bigger save for the stumbling
ingenuous dragonfly, his perfect tender levers.
The mother's limbs pincer, her mate is tremulous
affectionate, sexually mistaken.
Instinctual widow, the crash of her mouth
and forepaws abases his liquid skull.
Her isolation hung in gossamers
is the single state of women. He in these streamers
is death's slovenly patent.

A woman with large breasts in a damson sweater leans
from upstairs, catching the presiding mountain's gasps of iced wind.
Gusts take the spider's nest to the bleak trees
undomesticated by sweet and pleached domesticity
where in their carpet chestnut and apricot toss in verdigris
and break apart. This is black, the moon bites
into arachne's space. The tips
of her legs feel for the balls of my eyes, but what use
to this spider on the loose? This winter, I heal and heal.

Orion

*Orion a giant slain on account of his ego, was restored to life,
given vision and light, and put with the stars.*

Lilac's congregating flowers perk, ignorant
of death, but my body is without fragrance.
I did not nurse the crushed miner, nor was I one
to a havering woman, helping her shit.
Nor with faded-blue breast, a parent
having the moisture and smell of authority.
I want to use my childhood, not derange
a river's migrant track, or crush
the tree-lined current's milky undertow.
A softer radiance would be OK. But I would become
Orion I was designed for, my vision
of light with intent eyes.

Here's summer, its solstice, people
raging in happiness, red currant, feeding the season
a trickling viscid juice. I am lonely.
Look, the iris's flimsy visage,
and the common lily, ours; it goes on,
dies, comes to, from deathly pale to paper incensed life.
I, too, if you please. I strike through woods
making the leaves volatile.
Dabbing and laying my light on your cheek
I disclose your dark skin, with mutual delight.
And you touch me unawares. I believe, humans,
you have survived yourselves. It is the gift.

The City Being Us

And when she did not arrive, I went and bought
silent fleshy violets the city smudges with benzene,
dust, and a tang of peppery filth.
And as I bathe the unhurried form each night
her shade purples my hand. Whitey, she mouths.

Beauty is magisterial. It will not
tell you what it will do, it does what
it will to you. She, over me, overplussing
my affection with an urban tremor,
anger, violation and gentleness, more than I ever knew until now,
and I learn reciprocation. Whitey.

For They Are Beautiful, in Many Languages

In Baltic fields hurl these whales, murmuring
with Lithuanian, the tongue 'they
are beautiful'. And the same
in Gaelic for the deer 'they are beautiful'
whose lives he took. And they hide
in mountains, from the envy of the world. Please, remember,
for the fawn against the russet, it was
a poet, Duncan Ban Macintyre, in his
mother tongue, 'they are
beautiful', who killed them.

Like rock's climacteric, in its duress
of pressure with heat, where the speckled
life dulls, until the granular sparkle
in cooling silence restores, so these unwrathful
hookable Leviathans, whose nature keeps our speech
going, their suckling, crooning
mammal intensity. The sea cries
giant maternal tenderness, not since heard.

But the ring-pigeon dies in air's
burnt branches, for eating crops. They
were innocent, we killed
in our error.

Pulcher est, hoo ye fè toh-ar, 'they
are beautiful', the sea's mammals, whose blood
I can't trope with wit to a language
resisting its weight:
they are beautiful, they are creation dying,
with our words which they mistook,
these creatures, lovely without guile
using our words as if we meant them.
The world is the literal world of beauty.
All the whales rear upright from the north's chill pasture,
giving their flesh to the hosannas
'Praise him, have mercy on us.' Once
in a lifetime, my God, to witness this, and trust
our tongue. Their blood
floats to heaven, and their seed conceives earth.

Sylvia

Schubert is Sylvia, the tiny fly hears,
when she was a maiden, having no language,
and if she had what good did it do her?
For this is Sylvia, tangled in the strongest threads
adhering from one pole of grass to another.
Death twists the fly onto her wings, the legs
folded to her body, and the wings shear memory. True?

On the ledges amidst the slow
heart-beats, I count
you, love
who suffuse our period.
I will not die

in a hospital, the mortician's
ledge, linger
in a mortuary
refrigerator, where I handled
the yellowed stretcher-borne flesh,
until I have remembered everything about you, the hair
you cannot see, threaded in some hidden part of you.

But she, a fly, Sylvia, the fly who has listened to Schubert,
thorny-haired, little suckered dead foot.
Her magnitude of eyes, their lordly depth.
This is love, this is she, living, beyond death
who has heard Schubert being love, who has listened
as intently as a spidery chancellor, Sylvia, she.

Visit for Ever

At the end of August a moth came at
the white wall, shut its black wings, and listened
to Handel, quivered its body, as a man
whistling common tunes, touches in his feeling – I think
it was August, and it was Handel –
and he was able to withstand and sustain
passion, clung on the wall, in entrancement

for if we may, then this furred guy with
still wings also, for the virtue of his life
and deep black constitution
which autumn has not taken the heat from,
by stealth, or through gradual decline –
in his dynamics of ecstasy undisturbed by the catchment of the lamp
the sleek bride of light –
open and peaceable in his soft immaculation.

Elain

This is the day when something else shows,
the falling ill, irretrievably, of one near you.
I am not, Elain, expecting anything.
It is the time to concentrate upon grief,
what you have done, Elain, the sombre wit of your paint,
refusing to be confined by yourself. These are the main
designs of energy, waves of traction from a magnet
inducing the sensitised filings, to disclose
the actual force. This is the news.
And quite different from that of Reed Books,
a firm working, not – perhaps, on the calculations
of cash, personal oustings, the determination
to futurise profit – if it is or isn't in books –
and add to this the illness that sees
poetry, of all things, an obstacle.
So one grief is slanted across by another's pain.
You have not gone from my feelings, Elain.
I think a poem, properly, nurtures its defence
and self-criticism, working with justice as it can.

Endomorphic

This has to be sorted through.
You can't tell me anything about love
who said I am to be comforted.

I saw you ended, with isolated white flesh;
the mouth pursed, seemed to be complaining
bitterly of something. Had you pain? The nurse
nearly wept, 'You come three hundred miles late.'
Your white body unbreathing, you have conquered.

Your mouth had minced words, they were like scat,
you were tired, were on *schpilkers*, grinned

with intent knowing eyes raised upwards.
'Drink,' you asked for; your hands
tepidly clutched mine round a hot cup.
Any fluid did. Then you cat-napped. I mourn.
Dare I need you? – the last papery intimation
of protection taken off. Mother, this love
has crept down the bore, the substratum,
and denies the velleity, which claims tenderness.
Teach me how to have loved you,
my ancient dear.

I am not weeping. I make this complaint.
Of our first child, 'He should never have been born.' So you spoke,
denigrated our produce, with my first her.
He dropped a tear, died, this almond-headed child,
his clearness in the kitchen of enamel bowls keeping watch.
Nothing can gladden anything here.
I can't focus you, mother.
I put my shoulder to the car door
and shut the husk,
I, genuine unmourning article.

They knifed my silk, my only silk
shirt, that my lady had bought, little
yiddisher knife, insisting on death-grief
in the Hebrew way, me,
your blood relative, son & co. But at this time
I love sex, pure uninfant joy, her
who receives me. No interminglings,
mother. I feel the irritable plucking,
and scald of the cry, 'Child child.'

At the grave, she and I touched your box
before you lowered in. I shovelled morsels
of earth, as I had done on others,
which these three young Jews, earth-spading
Jews, now put upon you – the uncuppable
bread of this earth, soil, thuds
of it. Space taken into itself.

They can say what they like;
the death certifiers did not authorise
your leaving, all they can say is, 'Yes, it's true' —
your unscheduled ceasing; the collar-bone
of a hare is no more delicate
than my sentiment for this her.

Mother it is time to be lyrical.
There was a saviour,
and such was his unaggressing nature
the constitution of the kingdom was set up to accept all.
Don't even think it. No king ever was,
only the idea, his grief over each parted soul.
Don't be afraid, don't even
be angry. Go where the feasting tables are,
and decay, courageous then as thou wast here.
Shall we converse again? The clock runs on.
The archipelago, wet from tenderness
itself like spume blown. Permanently.

Watersmeet[137]

In Northumberland, by Hexham, where the North and South
Tyne rivers meet on their way east.

1

The railway arch views a trinity of water
one stream, and a second, then, each in the other.
Here a walker hoists his pack, a tree
hanging a troubled burden of fruit, off one
to the other shoulder.

Precious this water is to my tiredness.

The tracks are taken up, the tracks endure
the pitiful life

of objects omitted from the future.
In the absent railway, the catkin spills her pollen
where a man with roots walks. She is the first
to entice life to hers, after
the short-day's solstice.
Christmas light spills glad-shouldering hymns,
the carols' large glib cheer
we stoop to, that omits irony, foe to men,
that is men,
which stars the ginger shape of biscuit, nips the tongue with
all-spice.
You must not spend all the candle until the year dies.[138]
And was it kind,
God's child entering[139] an ancient world?

2

Waterboatmen dent one river. A spiky-bone trout
flickers by, slim, insouciant.
A second stream, simmering volcanic water,
sways on journals in the turning globe.
And when the magma bursts
over which this pointed water runs,
its gushing mineral scrapes life off, a toss
of sulphur, men's little forks turning
blebs of soil.
And who am I stubby suburban grafting
behind a white-scented privet,
its leaf catspiss,
but a moss,[140] in dried
wavering fingers of summer?

3

Two rivers join, and how
decipher in whose character the other bathes?
Is character tested by the ego's smoky lamp,

the paranoid, blocking out steady generous feeling,
that, riding in each other's flow, is the only certitude? This,
of marriage.

As if in marriage, its papery certificate,
its papery water wrinkling calm and simmering water,
which is the ghost of all that is marriage,
water that is marriage, each ego modifies
to the other. This water and that flow. Both flesh.

And they are all that other, which is,
in all its character and boisterous ego,
what nature is. Each emboldened in its form
in exuberance. Creation sprays of itself,
a stubby plant that creeps close to earth,
how should it grow? or the buried taro,
fluted rough potato, the alpine sea-waves
of bitter grass, the spiked straw-hue marigold
its triangular space meticulously hoed
and pressed up to the house, a diadem of wood,
the tiled ceramic shaped in quaking movement.
The liminal and aching fields rule out
bamboo whose root system grips earth as if
a man in a woman, with frail sheds
of black pine, and red pines, the mecan trees
lamping small loose-skin orange fruits,
their sweet fleshy segments loose, in a tremor
of spiked leaf.

So it spreads over all volcanic earth,
seismic fertility, bitter smelling narcissus
and twisted matsu, all
water's exuberance, all character
and the ego of plants, unlike the human,
that does not vaunt, brag, or shoot.
It is as if only cemeteries are fertile
if to be human is fertile.

If you speak so much, God, can I hear myself?
Only in loneliness, that privilege,

I burn and share myself. But like water, I mingle
and exalt another.

4

Two rivers meet, union, unpromiscuous, by chance,
and sport in each other. The saint kneels with one vision
and offers by this water
with unpresuming ego his thread of gratitude
towards his spangled God.

Are rivers sprung only that we may receive them?
Is fertility our only garb? (Some dress in Chryslers).[141]

The air is smelling of our thankfulness.

5[142]

If you had churned water and earth to mud
but withheld the flash-flood, torn with stony jags

> *it would have been enough*

if you had flaked tarry plutonium
in which a modicum of moisture

> *it would have sufficed*

if you'd withheld tectonic mud
its diffident treacherous plain

> *it would have been enough*

if you had melted the sun
like a cube of sugar
if you had pressed the lake like a stud, into earth
if it were virid, if virid from harsh pine
crammed to its scummy rims

> *it would have been enough*

if clean water from a tap
and the glacier had retreated into hiding

> *it would have been enough*

If it had been milk on a teat,
an unfailing tap,
the snow-melt unforeclosed by profit
the flash-flood out of the ring of mountain
with sulphur, the swan-reflexing glib
sleek-feathered lake,
the salt on the teat
in thirst, that had once not been thirst, love,
the mountain, its celestial drip
plutonium, again, warped in tarry flakes,
the tectonic mud, and the water-drop
of the republic of ants

> *it would have been enough*[143]

It was enough. For there is water
sinking through a rotted gravel, short
of the sea's rims.

It keeps an ancient freshness.

But the sea, *Into me with you.*[144]

Water sinks through stones, and discloses
rose, umber, and jade, quartz, picked from our fields
chipped from mines, or scooping a cave
where a defeated huntsman barks like his red fox.
Or there are stones of no colour. There are always these.

But if waters flow in each other
without consciousness, from Watersmeet,
yet are themselves, as we cannot be

only ourselves,
we, without the single, watery, blessed state,
are yet like water mixed

the sigh into gravel, I make, touching your breast.

And if your breast knows that water lingers
in its milk, let me touch you
and postpone the sea, and defer the sea's licking
my feet, for as you know, all of this
meeting is where we have been, and when stopped
cannot be taken from itself.

Holywell

A pool of pure water with a spring, built either by the Romans,
or by Saint Ninian in the fifth century.

Ninian, the man in stone, lifts his hand to bless
a pool he formed from a spring, hesitant as a small cat,
gingery abandoned, making its way. Touch the man,
as the pool, like an earlier marriage, bleeds away
though her brother's and my dead parents' mouths speak
under the water, and each is well pleased
with the other, by where Rome strode across the body of the North.
Touch this man, please, put your hand on his stone flesh
and what he will not feel, you will take.
Lichen, I say, just lichen on him. Touch him, please.
Penicillin, you ask, smiling?

We just and only just, but just established
taste the spring's released sweet pent-up water.
Our languages don't mesh but we have come this far
by the water's foliations, constant uncombatting
head of water springing, which we sip, fine and sweet as the lips
of God.

Like salmon in heaven we break the barrier-mesh. Let us be free.
Whoever in these ungentle times hears this
will turn, bored, from us. We live beside each other's blood,
you, like the stork that infibulates the sac of birth,
its neb that hooks swaddling, a child in it, her fingers lightly uncurled.
The man of fourteen hundred, in his genius, blesses all in his zone,
this place of hurrying water drenched in mint.
God credit us with truth. We are your children.
No, no, we are adult, afraid like children
and learn to take what is given. Here's no grabbing,
no expropriating of a portion. We have not demeaned water.
And now we listen to water pulsing to the village.
Tonight when they swivel their taps, it will spurt into their palms.

Shaping a Republic

We busse our wantons, but our wives we kisse.
                                                    – Herrick

Reciprocation, active sharing
you do more than me, Japanese, yet dark
like your mother. Beautiful, as if you stood in shade,
and the leaf's chlorophyll, with the light it occluded made your
                                                            colour.
I have so little of your language, 'O-hayo gozaimasu,'
before rising, many times. You write and speak English.
        To busse, to kiss its meanings, the tongue doing both.

Your son, 'Learn her language'. Yes,
though your English comes better than his, who is teaching it,
the intense snow-packed winter buttressed up to the school
                                    room – Hokkaido, where
blue flies, before the weight of summer gets pushed
by spring to melt into winter, come
        one day, and die that same one.
            Which means snow soon,

suffocating all smells
      but its own scent.
'I was honoured by their coming upon me,' your
    son, his maiden companions.

I feel your intent steely complicit
smiling silence. A sweet smirking.
And dark, yes, tree-shade
    and heat.

If I could source my aggression
    I'd bathe
it in your shade.

In a silent Newcastle night, whitey
opens the carotid vein of a black.

Now you've finished mothering, I beg
please don't mother me,
    you, feelings' gardener, diet's steward;
dead, our poems will, in amiable
opposed passions, discuss each other; poems that
  are made once, talked
    about, again.

We try England, but you
won't forsake the car, darling vehicle,
rigid love outside, puffy with it within.
I suggest, 'this little parish church'
              cruciform
  miniature planned precious one
that constellates a few houses, sparse mild universe;
in the spaces of that Other is the energy, which clapped
our world into being. 'I don't want,
church smells of death.' Even ornate Bethlehem's,
its universed jewelled inside, its recesses of fearful unending beyond,
the filament from God cast into art-love? Tosco?
    Answer me.

You can stay, the Home Office admits.
What's it like, Alien? In
Japan, my agit was for, not England – it was: for
a suburb's mildness in bronchial evenings;
but I missed English, being my speech,
what else for a Jew, but another's language?
Tosco, some make of us aliens, ash
die die, no, we are safe fleas in UK.
Back to United K, we're not to be lulled – how
might that occur? All's changed. Borne
on the rapid transit,
this intricate fuselage of wood-lice circling
    our root–system: terror.

Seeing one flower, solitary and regarded,
flowers I see, caracolling, reared up like horses
menacing, but soft swollen belly of vulnerable energy.
One flower, ionic, with head bent. But a human beating
another's head with a bar, flesh like roe.
Flowers are rearing like horses, like prayers made
each year, impressed in each other's shapes, in floral communities
of flower-like assemblies, aspiring and restrained,
flowers imploring we see and not uproot them.

Sometimes I speak and you do not hear
sometimes you don't then do speak, I unhearing.
These flowers always hearing and silent,
the pansie freakt with jeat, Milton wrote, listening.
And as he listened they grew
      and as they grow he hears
  a magisterial dance
  an insisting meek energy.

At the Wayside

I sledge chucks for rails leading beneath the sea
to Hokkaido's island, where dispirited Ainu
shape fierce bears in wood, and have Japan's passports.
I have serviced the trains' motion that is all.
What residue? My body's dirty muscles
breathing with less blood and oxygen, the skin
flaccid, bearing stretch-marks as if
my flesh for the birth of others'. Foolishness,
carelessness! The bitter milkless coffee
I have each work-day
is my wife's gentle flask.

My mother died, who was my last shield.
Directly, I face the wind's trying
for skin, hair, muzzle. For three days she possessed
no being or residence – broken Jewish
princess – in her transit to a new place
where angels with wings without shadows career
over heaven's basalt cliffs.
Nothing changes or cancels, save our lives,
and what we give lives through earth's continuation.

I could not, like Abraham
from smithies of sacrifice, bring lament
to her death, yet she, spunkiest
sardonic being, in these hurt days,
and her work became, though her spine fractured.
Creatures that root in the wayside, as if a nation
flowering, I have not their capacity.
Like the withered statue of feckless Ovid
by Rumania's Black Sea, I bleakly stand.
O self-complaining fool.

Yet my frame continues for the needs
of the rail and chassis, from Honshu
to beneath Tsugaru's straits,
for the majesty of common velocity.

O lulling waters of the north
I want to be moving, if to connect
with common neglect is akin to this. The arousal
of flowers from amongst stones – I shan't tear
any from the dieseled graded stones bedding rails,
lulling waters of the north. Ainu, Ainu,
take heart, for whatever the blood in you, as in me,
there now begins silence, and the answer to it.

A Woman from Japan

I

1. *Blaming the Photographer*

A fly chafes frail impudent limbs, bites silk,
is bleak delicate adhesive, watches
the photographer, shy pornographer
with a box of images. Is amazed, agitated
at the man fastening body hair,
mammal down and smiles, in a box. Who pipettes then
a little fluid, fixing my past
in his future. Who did not know,
or did know that a soul can smear – liquid on a slide –
which has blocks of aery possibilities,
but somewhere knew, and detained them in images.
Ferocious visual hold, impresses like a heated grid
in floury egg, or a punch in paperiness.
The photographer seduced an image of me
as I was vain, and am still that,
although I do not care to be young, again, in my shame.
Though I stood my ground in the precinct,
my silent garden, as the obstinate flash
took place with ineradicable determination on me,
squire of carelessness.

Love, that's then, this is now.
Little warrior, sculpted female, guard your legs,
for images are scythes of time. The photo-taker
caught my being in his lenses,
my actuality in his swollen convexity,
a crushed betweenness, frail as lepidoptera.
Long maned neck, subtle legs feathered in fetlocks,
our lives mingle, slowly, in which a clash.
Large spread of hands, compact body,
you hold beautifully. I ride tentative, but OK.
In grief, or deprecation, you spread
your hands, large, and plant-like,
a little desperate, in the midst of our fighting.
Touch me again. The concaves of my heart
your haven, boat with eastern wings.

2. *Meeting in the Temple of Refreshment*

At our first deliberate meeting, we came by the river,
Asakusa meaning 'light green', meaning 'spring meadow',
though Japanese spring is cold, is biting florescence.
An arcade lit off water fuming generous light
sells clothes for every precinct of human flesh.
Decency! whatever freshet of mischief dashes
with merriment, careless of honour. Foul, strikes the clock.

We pass into the available Temple space.
Drumming fiery bells, two temple guardians in fury
in alive wood; tenderness fangs this precinct.
We purchase incense sticks, plant
in a tank of hot ash: the dibble glows.
And I am instructed by you, knowing
I shall pray to this god, me, a cloud in trousers,
whose reply travels my spirituous ley-lines.
Mirthful silent thunder. Huge head
and savage agape mouth, 'Yes, you shall have her.
Now back away, human.' Love, I kept this
from you, being instantly afraid for what I must,

and how I should. Stockings sheathe your legs.
The river exults piteous light. We are guilty
adulterous persons, coupling in the sun's futures,
spidery flies attached to our web.
A god allows us, to disclose the meaning of our act
to understand and act the act: *Je ne regrette.*
I hunger for you. I touch you. Precious
fertile redemption, I say.

3. *Conversations with the* Hebrew *God*

And you say you're not guilty? I say I
am not innocent. *Paranoid?* Not that.
I heard you admit it. No. No springs
incise in that fluid direction. I am
what I did. *Surely.* So the God and human
in unkilling combat, one that will die,
one that cannot, unless the mainspring faults.

Lord, the innocent tree sprinkles its refreshing pinnate shade
on our hot words, thinking our speech heated foliage.
The tree believes leaves spring from each of our mouths.

What do you expect me to believe? Sir, it is the affliction
of vanished democracies, mediterranean lavender
darkness grows athwart. *Blaming photographers
for your adultery?* Punish me then.
I can't. I won't. The man's nitrate deforms
my outline. How shall I act?
Help me. *I repeat what I said.*

It is hard to speak with a God who withholds
his visibility. But I tell you, sir,
his shadow of me fills my airbound passages,
the avenues that poplars flank tenderly.
I like poplars. I desire to be an unburdened tree,
a decent trunk. He smears, this magician of thumbprints…
I hear you. As your skin tautens,

your body's structures, having reason,
deform from balance. Your reason oppresses you
out of sanity.
Sir, for your theorem of my well-being, thanks, my case
is desperate; please, I must clear myself of him…
fingering mortal,
you expect me to be a father? I am not
a temple deity, but creation's mind's passion
– if that's not too lofty –
I work to wince creatures to integrity.
Sir, help me.
Silence silence silence.

4. *One More Try*

Eyes are the soul's vision nestling in her black hair,
hair stillness upon her naked waist.
If I could only make
as much as the photographer with his fingering
and talent, squeezing the bulb, creates. The box exudes
its flash on me. Visualiser!
take his images off me, sir, let me have myself.
How shall I meet, how join, with myself?
– foolish middle-age child.
Sir, allow me a bridging-loan.

II

1. *Shinto*

In hot sun winter chinks apart frail wood
of a shrine. The roof's shingles warp –
a hitlerean look, askew with hasty mortar.
Shrine number one-eleven has no chest
or air, for the long breathless night.
But now delicate hope, which filiates the infant year,
    someone has re-built the chest. It breathes.

We pray, which relays to a god's small dedicated ear,
the air itself and the act, delicious,
apples cinnamon alcohol men sprouting chest hair.
We boil fleshy roots for celebration and nutriment.
Slice the lotus root, and glimpse through
to the new year. Tapering magenta root
a softened bitterness,
arrowhead, burdock, cognac, meaning 'devil's tongue' –
these in mid-winter, the sun
diaphanously about and about the precious child, new year.
But oh, our acts, presumptions, the bitter
past, like a burst spleen. Have in mind
the Jew, Miklos Radnoti, his black notebook
of poems, filling on a forced march.
Grief is the sprig of remembrance.

2. *Your Parents' House*

Tosco, your house and childhood, of frail rooms. Slide
a wall of mullioned glass, space adds to itself
solid space in a cedarous atrium,
its roof of tiles that quakes, a boat in its rough pasture.
Rice, and a sprig of persimmon from winter's branches,
which also fruit. Toast and mecan
and cooked rice. Buddha, won't you eat?
What ails the tucker,
hungering abstemious god?

Your mother kneels in a small
room; work,
bed and isolation.
Her calligraphy is haired like a comet's tail.
No detrimental
stroke injures her preliminary snow
of paper, – ink tasked in
induces shivering
characters, sleigh-strokes harnessed to wolf-dogs
over snow's snarling acceptation – a coupling

with energised black. Dark as Sheba, she,
mother, essentialises her creation
in ink strokes. That's what it is. Prayers
in equal duration and
unequal weight
for her brush
and you, Tosco. One might
say, but I don't, thou
sacred hope, mid-winter sun
for you, love's small dark apollino.

Pillars of trees that won't flower the house's silent atrium.

3. *The Father*

With unwithered petal cold spring will persevere
with winter and see it out. I want that now.
Tsk tsk, fool's impatience.
On the heated carpet for visitors your father
lies, draws up legs to his chest. Men, mother yourselves.

He teaches children the position and swing
of stars. Are they music? Do they whizz
like arrows? Case by case, for each children's
hospitable group. But now, he is an anxious sprig.
Has he enough for those who survive him? Always
the others' silence treads
in his footprints, or lies with him. Tentative, stubborn
elegance, hair, a spiky flower
unclasping its corolla on stamens, 'have me',
sexual flower-parts, 'take me'.
Ahead, a black
fountain re-cycling performative energies. What
it is, he knows. Not yet
a table in green pasture, two little porcelains of saké,
father, not my father, your stars,
your daughter, and no envy.

4. *Forage*

Winter sun, blood on tar-green leaf. Who
runs ahead to buy bread? We pass
over narrow roads
pressing on us leaf and cringing bud. Who
is risen from his bed, striped pale pyjamas?
Should I know? You break away, and run,

little naked Ceres, three times mother – without you
nil growth. Homing in the air, sudden spurts
of flying turn you through sliding walls of glass.
The cyclamen you bought your father has fleshed pink flowers,
kicking roots in earth. Japanese father,
your earth, stars, daughter.
Sir.

5. *The Passions of Exile*

Tosco, you are the Jew in exile. In Israel.
Not to each other, Tosco, but we are aliens
in this spear-shape country. Hebrew ferocity.
Enemies on three sides, and Mediterranean
waves heaving like horses; their flanks splinter stars.
Tiny rivers moisten this petulant
Christ-risking water; small Yukon
twists like a gentle worm into it.
Pharaoh's life treads in water.

I walked this fortress city, and at day's end
I picked up a hurt pigeon,
that was in Disengorf, I, childish
and responsible, gentle, being timid.
At home put the creature outside
in a night pricked with mosquitoes. Sleep, I said.
But morning, unbreathing heap of feathers,
a burst pillow, no flesh, or ticking.
Jeering boys' voices sissified me

as I picked up the dove, Israeli grey. Ineffectual Jew
in pointless tenderness, by romping jeering sea,
its clenched nearly closed mouth drinking
at the openness of other pools.
O shake my hand,
violence, be disarmed by plucked strings.
Naked fingers
tick over the tune 'home', for peace,
no brooding wingless loose featheriness.
This time I said, what will you do, we
manufacturing war, the right hand
losing its sensitive finger?

If my people... you've just said that. The humble
part of the sky shook its thundery feathers... have I fed
the fainting plant, the strayed stalking cat,
the alley's potentate, or clothed a child?

I have lost my nerve, Tosco; we're back
in England, my home, which is your exile.
In England, you are the Jew – 'Yes,' she says,
'I love you. In the fainting moment
of death, your partner, will live after you.
My voice is in you as yours will live
in me, untwistable-out, no roots, no stitchings-in.
Tear your voice from me, you tear my flesh with it.
It's worth it, love, everything worth it,
our beds of ragged growth, the meek yard
of brick walk and slated-up earth, with redcurrant,
firm tentative violet, mint, lavender, these pungencies,
tendrilled active sweet-pea, nine inches up
thirty centimetres if white, if pink, shorter.'

'This house survives to you...'

but she, 'That is not love, just now, love
is touching me, preparing me
to understand my nakedness. It is strange,
but having children, making them,

bathing his dying parents, in their veins
a cancer from Hiroshima's big-bang, I did not
discover how to be unclothed.

I would find it with you, have you
found it with me, or I shall have never lived
to be who I might be. Love, who am I?
It is not ventriloquism, my English – please
answer me in the urban meadow,
festal arcade,
or temple, in beyond the guardians
with forks and judgement,
for if you do this, faithfulness. Naturally.
Wills are for afterwards.'

Unpublished and Uncollected Poems,
c. 1992–1997

Two Women

1. *The silk-machine*

A.C. 1991

Apt for weight, thread's tensile reels from
each silk-machine. Perfect. Yet once again
fierce Earth (forgive me, Angela)
flecks headless nuclei in the silk.
And who is She?

I forget. But 'you've a way with creatures.'
This kindness, spoken in a farm's cobbled space;
nor did I tell you how
the cockerel spurring my shank bruised
our smile with pain.

★

You spoke of Earth's spontaneous cruelty.
And she retaliates. 'I dislike' she says
'your writer's fictions, underpinning me.'
Earth mouthed this spleen, and in
you, full-length woman, reproduces the headless
disease, laying you low.
I put my feathery licence by yours
just the same, in honour of your silk-machine.

2. *A Quaker's death*

J.K. 1992

Judy, modest Quaker, you have died. The fledgling, too,
that lifts a downy menacing under-coat. To retrieve
nothing from grass's spears. In the Norwegian's
icy experiment, you died. The face
is blameless.

Winter's bee, silent and brave. But now, on patches
of nettle, unstung, in her lightness
of being, the butterfly, with soft dots
of eggs, drops between acid spurs
her babes of custom, with wings. You bear
an idea of your self to our violence.

Jubilate

As the plane slowed, my chest
as if the Rockies' huge brown lit spine
we cleared – my sense of you
as one your land still feasted, opened.

Not Scot or Saxon, a skull
the hill, Northumberland, is a fox's
head in grass, lapping the Poison Sea.

It must be like the bone of you I love
if I could ever get us there. Whose fault, whose grave
indecision not not to love, but be
incapable of double form? Mine
if you care to say, I can hardly
breathe speaking of you. I enter, you,
huge cloud, a chill coal breast. But your spine
like the swan's tearing open water,
bashing black watery rings, this prairie
of water barking, *Prairie du chien*,
its tiny bluish berries and frost
pricking independent branches – you, lovely
amazement of limbs, are wife, preferring
to be that, with perhaps more name than touch
and lash in our breasts. Is it that we
are too much for each other, hill
of bone too much, like earth's breaking open
pain that spurs grass, the lilac cereal?

Who ever you are, yet who
but you, your sullen widths of heat
in buttocks hesitating
between pear and roundness, full
sensitive duplicates, you are
vigorous, hesitant, all-deserving
amongst lilac seed. Or amongst
no child, but three cats pissing
in urban soil plums
are flowering. Where will
we be? O, jubilate.

Into the triangular yard

A locomotive drawling wagons through unstopping snow
locking in hands that lift a coat and scarf to snow-fed faces.
The cold has its heart, clenches. Now, a mauve
potassium lamp suffusing
a country station. They pelt stones here, hard
as skulls. There are no ruined stones. The locomotive's
energy turns over,
while some freeze. And despite a house
of railmen, sleeping, with one, or with two, stamens
nursed in their heads, as if innocent as hair,
pushing off, the train
loses the Buddhistic light of the halt,
with those snecked in, in silence.
No female mutual God speaks in this.

*

'Who told you you were naked?' He asks.
We stitch leaves for clothing, made clumsy
and insane, breaking this
herbal mechanism.
'But who told you, of nakedness?' The voice

weeping in the dusk of its question. 'I shall
not come again for fear you kill me.
I will die with you, children of my madness.
Children of my naked body.' But we will not die soon.

Selfish cruel God, wait, for the triangle
of inoperative tracks, and the light's shape
starting to voice hatred of us. Collect us,
then, like gassed verminous insects, dumping
our lightness, if you want. We have been of value
to our selves. Warmed by chafing old skin on disused hands.
There was some mercy to us. You
the ineffable wedging light.

Useful poem

Reading poems of your country inventive
                         yet dull with cruelty
I must read everything with greater care.
            What, did you write of love?
       whose theory, and in which furnace was your soul
cast? I may not exist in your future. Must I?

Japan, exposure

I

To the convenience-store, the shortest pencil-shuddering path
stutters across macadam, trenches grass, quickly now
slantwise over parking lot's uncoupled ceased batteries,
wheels without drive, a road-disc forbids
entrance, torn off its street. Trudge
the unofficial wriggling line straight to the store, to boys

with printed-up amazons. The clicking lips,
voiceless, of unfledged single men.

Elsewhere, shanties. I have lived rough, but here
the dried shit quilling earth, like halva. The disc
adverting a sun-fed honey girl, slit and bracketing
a corrugated roof. Live rough and black: the violence
of white and black miscegenated in fear
in a white's house resisting seasonal change. But in Japan,

here, the cat's children grimace in influenza,
blood off the eye's lens weeps past its cornea – helpless
mothered animals, whom we dose
shreds of anti-biotic spurted into
staring, held-apart eyes. This bub, this ring-eyed child of fur.

Shanties almost everywhere than here. Cats
half-advantaged in Japan.
They shall not die.
Nor will the riches partly-consumed hold off
their being dumped; while over the air-strips
the unaging rice fields ghost and spatter
through undercarriage and fanned exhausts of 747,
the trundle of carts sagging with rice
these were the lands, after all. To where
shall the growers have gone
in their ghostly expelled lives?

II

As on a transverse pulley sun falls through aborigine earth
it lifts a hemisphere of light into the dark, spreading
pale textured glass, but no, no glass, moist pale
lilac, slithering to ice-slate; that tinct,
an aviator's suit, footballer's shirt, sky,
its Moscow Dynamos combating Juventus, a cloth of air
with populations of knobby-kneed light. I watch,
in a homage to dust, this game. In silhouette

the caretaker walks home, gentle knowledgeable
half-educated prophet, comprised in gifts
for carpentry, fixer of afflictions, but most, one
who rasps steps with pumice or be the caretaker,
makes rolls having sweet chopped beans:
for this alone he's a hard wood seat in heaven, worships
all cats: mother, child, the male,
simian, long-armed, simous probationer,
nabber, pilferer of meat and eggs and milk;
enters the female from behind, always; nervous
short-tailed sex-sinuous russet and silver Cypriot,
maker of kittens, colluding with students
behind dormitories, fed by girls
with eyes of does, who ride bikes to class.

The creatures know one stratum in the campus. He,
of dormitories, has fuller knowledge: 'Kindness',
such advisement tack to his door. Lives with one daughter
wrong-gened in skin and lungs, allergy
for fur's dander. So cats may not stray in,
where mother sleeps in a zinc bath.
Paddock of aspiring trees. This man-permanence,
with student-flowing over a smooth rock
of man-kindness, Students, year by year
with the same man. I talk with him through her,
of how 'cold February wakes all animals
the human cries, in life's hatchery, of sharp-throated sex'.

His kindness deftly survives. The nation
with rules, which you must find with one to break all.
Upright as a Welsh dresser, with saucers tilted
behind beading matching cups of willow and stream, reclines,
that open, occasionally, on this:
cruelty, shogun-striated appetite of slashed veins
no other violence can slug, or conciliate gentle.
None disarms this violence on saucers
and the halved soldiers whose brain
spills in the pale tender willow-blue
on the cup's side. Look for instruction,

with the God of light, salmon-vested footballer,
aviator clad in naked lilac. The sun
has dropped, sideways, from the sky.

Three poems

I. Opening the voice of the hungry

A foreign voice valves its noise with shyness.
Mr Philoninjen's, cucumberry
at my throat. Ginza's night-women
finger each client into the dark. 'Women'
their madam says, 'shower men from
your lovely valves.' On a street close
by Ginza's, Mr Philoninjen
nurtures hunger with pity.

I, arrowy from the West, Scots herder,
small education, thistledown
from a Glasgow yard, blown
amidst this kingdom of peace, where shall I lie? For Japan
wants food. Mr Philoninjen,
after the war, even his books
are hungry. His passionate notes
project a dairy industry.

Under snow peaked on Mt Iwate
after a stump of summer,
sheep flake wool, flaccid cows
holding milk, urinate.
Their legs carpenter

in patience. A bird's thorny calls
shiver berries of ice.
Patience
suffers a child's death.

Japan's a kiss of salt. I want

to pay for this information:
his friendless hand returns mine outstretched to my side
as if to heal the West's speared, regenerative Christ.
My milky flocks of Ayrshire
I harry above Stranraer
are creatures — belly
on the hill's spindrift rusts
standing to the scythe, like any beauty
in naked readiness.

His polynesian triangular skull
gentle and asking with intelligence
moves amidst a nation's warrior magnificence,
its active patrician sex, I've witnessed
between matzu trees' spiky hairs.
The bewildered foster-child, sex,
even the child-harlot.
Ginza's fortnightly clinic syringes
disease back into the nation's female cave,
the male glans and duct adhesive
and black in its heresies of love.

It seems Mr Philoninjen would
kiss my hand, but travels
these fingers to a black Spenserian book,
no knightly and daiseyed stanzas,
and in this sullen allegory
earth is a pilgrim that winds down.
Scotland's clan-blessed rose
is religious? who knows?
Here they feed each child every
other winter's day.

In his book of death, Japanese names
hang from the language's razory feathers
in its characters' straggling lines.
North of Morioka

summer's indigence
farms against winter,
and the fins of the fish of the sea,
dainty doily fret, are God's offering
for our succour.

In patient suppliance
Japan slumps with hunger. Mr Philoninjen draws
handbooks on starvation to his sloping floor;
the dead names spill
their infill.
He says, 'If you travel north'
and in my brain I experience
the tightened obi sashing a waist,
her child undressed,
his muscular squirm of buttocks slipping across, and falling from
                                                    her thighs.
The brazier's eye glares at an empty cot.
All day the blazing sun travels without milk

II. Travel by the night-train

Snow has wounded the train. As it must.
The woman opposite who raises herself hangs
between the shoulders and folded lap: the lamp
that read of murder's mucky blood
sleeps. Tragic virgin of desecration.
But truth is soft-thighed. Conscience, the moon,
holding the sun's lust in her, stays.
I lay my hard life down to her. Dear self, I'll help
all I can. I, tree-inspired farmer, the wind, indelible,
        the indelible wind in the tree's head opening,
I, a farmer, tree-inspired, start to learn
not sussing this country of thatched-looking characters
that forever hold the China War, the Chinese rapes.

In every schwa, a signal, as I wish?
In my pitchy narcissism, the mordant quartz
of whisky's rusted cube; but the bell clanging

from utopia's silence
to a woman's swollen hunger, and blood-spike
stabby stabby sex, and hungry blood-drained child.
Hunger's to be fed for you came to do this.

Her belly's insistence of child, swell and droop
no flower matches. Why, farmer, do you envy
love's anointing conception, or sex
whose quills instrument the female peeled
across a bed? Wide sleeves and disdain,
her journey. She drops her paper. 'No retrieval'
she signs. The thatched characters
of Japanese open their bellies. She sleeps
in her husband's absence he in her smiling.

Morioka Morioka. The cold trumpeter
shouts open our doors. The train
destroys its fire, cancels
its poles of electric, the gantry
collapses, and the caetenars finish up.
Polythene, faeces, oil. On the ceased track.

III. Moon snow

The train drawls upon an elevated bridge of trussed struts,
my Scottish formal language, not, I trust
selfed by my ego. My home is unmoving light in shifting water
meeting tristesse with innocence, in praise.
I, unmarried farmer of Pinwherry, having laid
my virgin self by the wayside amongst the Pulpit
and Elder flower am a lonely man, Jacked
with frost and nakedness. I read in medicine
and the poem by Henrysoun, where she,
leprous… or of one streaked with infanticide,
but I know milk, and its tubercular thong.
I would work in Japan, helping anxious creatures
to form maternity, and be milked.

Not me, but the pony prints snow affixed to glowing hooves,
her stringent unafraid muscle, head in oncoming darkness
that the stoic beam of my acetylene opens
on the road alienated to rock, feral
with giant ferns of grotesque cold, obeying none
but earth's unblameable heatless life,
hills peaking either side, huger frost forms
under which plates buckle. Japan's synapses
like hurled electric lift the demesne
of wilderness breaking in gas. The village,
the pony treading to the house's frozen
lamp's emissions. The moon
was parallel, and now this globe
of flour sprockets its soft mass,
hovers its winding bulk of menses
and light between me and the entrance.

In the city, charred fatty clothing
with merged globules of hair, the body's shade
fixed to a broken wall. I'm dust and light.
The dead in the bomb's brain, like burned
out midges, flit in a follicle of uprooted dust.
Ghosts offer their old-style
beery smiles like a twisted bottle-opener –
Japanese beer, a flowery taste: spills
over the flat Inn flotsams of dried liquid
its bulge dried in the bomb's hovering fist.

Here I'm dust and light, and wait.
No living flower, cat, or tonal insect hardy
with a fly's Aids, survives, Will you enter,
you, cold-veined hoverer? Famine, being hungry
even in a woman's breasts, pendulous without hope,
like a milking instrument, strewn against a door,
a smudge of milk corroding its hook. A rustle
of lightning, through snow. Behind the porch's legs
a door slides apart. The pony
tethered, rests like a bird.
My multiple conscious a fly's vision.

Poor limping insect.
I melt to floor and covering. The moon snows.
Fear's taken me in its arms. How many times
to fear the human, his initiative
of hay and gin.

I love this creature despite all

A frog, who bites screeching winged flies that vomit
and chew sugar, tears the pond to stir
on delicate elbows, the first model
of ours, unclasping the parents
who restrain its clammy person. A half-limbed adult
leaps before the unloving beneficent sun.
Freeing the self on little woman's elbows, his fixatives
of moisture, and cadaverous remedial
fingers, he stealths between dewy grasses
that fracture light. Eases in hiding past straws the boy
figures to insert in your anus, and blow,
for his amused human massage, pleasure, that's our nature.

Keep moving, delicate being, nature's
formed leap, it serves you.
You pass our deep-hanging cemetery, where souls flee ash
and heap for judgment, in a pit. Go by, rural
child, be free and know you eat winged cries
and the flies' heaped lisp of faeces and sugar, friend
of harmlessness. Now you spring in the body
of forgiveness. Who put you there? What will keep you
but your acts
got from the sac of mercies in you? Whose nature,
leaping possibilities,
is too much for you?

Aggression

Today I made a horse flinch. A woman
riding a sorrel, a white flense upon
its head, the creature backed from me.
Straight-lipped, upright, pretty, the woman, mounted
on her, said 'fuck-off'. I stood, angry.
And was afraid. The horse edging its body
before my car, like a simple widow.
I was travelling this metal carcase
to the ancient limits of England, where Cheviot
lifts herself, and the livid watery expanses
with crests of rough cast stars
from the wilderness.

Yet the horse, a hanging huge flower
of delicate patience. I shivered my fist
at the woman, but the horse thought that she
was the object of my anger.
She could have kicked me under her, but winced,
the flower-horse, delicate as a lemon
on a piece of twig,
growing in north England. So full with sour.

The sororities of Ponteland, its women of cash,
and her horse with thin clopping legs, and joints, bearing
the sexual blasphemer. The flower-horse flinched,
I, shaking my fist, like a clapper
to her head, a silent bell
strawberry tinted, with a mark. Like my white hand.
The creature carries my anger in her,
and her mistake forms like a hand.

Where will you find her?

A fly weeps on the ledge in her futures of victimisation.
Amidst human innocence
in suburbs, where the sun's falling-away
gives to the day huge distances
as a face in its depths stares into a silver dish,
the fly's peril neighbours the infant spider,
inert miniature, in her twanging web.
If there breeds innocence, what form
is it? what soft trumpet of proclamation,
                              what sound,
what snarling desisting from violence?

Distance me from it. No, I must face
this undesisting triple: honey, iron, gold.
This sleeping girl, innocence,
is passover light, the terror of life breathing through fog.
Yet passover drowns our tyrant. And we, his brutalised slaves
rejoice in Egyptian's suffocation.
Whose breath? Whose drowned light?

Innocence is what I wanted. A brumous bulb
glows behind a blanket, hung,
in poverty, dividing
two portions of sleep
renting one chamber.
She calls out, if you ask her.
Nourish her. The lady of feathers
in her scalps of beautification,
as if she were dressed in a cemetery
of creatures, is supplied.
So hold this other in your depth.

You'll find her, fair and poor,
her tingling hair of beauty and want,
she, a light my hand's flame shields
in lust, tenderness, responsibility.
I will never keep that out.
The alchemical transforming substance,

the phosphorus water flares.
But that's a change you'd hardly know about,
you, rough, unbitch-like beauty.
Tear darkness, tear silence, still
I come to you, the hand
in the tender excited garden.

'The soul is ghosted from its flesh'

The soul is ghosted from its flesh,
and the coat comforts the body as if
it were its soul sifting in cold, on lumpen beautiful stone,
you don't see this much nowadays.

The coat, the soul's earthly
substance and version. As he said, and she, his tacit wife,
it is *permitted* ('their Yid's word') to make blank
but not the body, the soul, each
trace of substantive Yiddity from
anyone's territory. So they took
these bodiless coats, fumigacious, and re-opened
the rusted-up but still viable chambers of Maidanek, near bulbous
Lublin, where the onionated unweeping dome of Russ
horizon-hover, and the roasters of Buchenwald,
the solid-working iron door-closures,
Buchenwald (Beech-walled) Beech-openness
the correct word gives the mind its grace
murmuring and mourning a forest of bees – for what
can trees mourn save life –
open them, he declared – like ovules, ovum
ovariated fire – and gas these coats.
Those who had children also did this task.

These rags were more docile than those
who wore them, less weeping, these twice-gassed,
in their nondescript beauty, in his beholding ragged eyes,

rack on rack of gassed-drab coats. But the lepine souls,
you would find them common over earth, dead souls,
akin to scurf, he said, –
we have taught you, he told us
a faded understanding. Disperse yourselves
back into your Adonai. And the oriole
at your aureate breast, Jew-woman, my immortal
sexual hatred has you at death's remove,
Queen of the Jews' God.
If we kill His humans, can this God remain?
David, angel-historian, he asks, bless my work.

Father, and the switch

My eyes vacant, I had meant to kill him,
gathered at the edge, a field, kiln, a chimney,
a heap of dilute whitening brick. He stood, irritable, plaintive
and injurious. Yet his life, an oak-like passion,
had structure, in rings, of xylem: leafless,
but a structure, refined past dying.
I, cotton thread slipping
from the bobbin, with 'best thread'
glued to bare wood stock. I was, might have been.
I was a cry, cleaned in a tin bath.

Between us, a rat-trap? A bamboo grill
to drain blood's muck and neither of us
to have blame. He waited, in lambswool coat,
so black it sucked in light, that his wife
had mothered on him, his whiter shoulders than marble,
gracious length of arm, cuffs worn with care.
The great-coat, unrenewable. So then, I cried, 'father.'
Light droops to the west, fruit of conciliation.
The gun's speedy kill, I cannot. 'Touch me, father.'
He, a melting Adam, dropped suspicious tears.
And I, scion, and thief of life

unfurled in the old arms of his traditional flesh
sacred as a head of leaf,
a bank, pillars of grey phlegm. On our society's troth.

Everything is unforeseen. He lay down in his white
clean body, like folded clothes his wife
stays by the bedside. No such place. He put
his ordered flesh by the switch that lit the watchful house,
and let the light touch all his achieved life,
and willed the light to search his achieved life,
that, by the way, is old and significant,
that's the burden of the oak
to branch and consolidate;
the trees, the tousled magnitude of leaves,
with, he denied, in that other place
their hissing magnitudes.

Sally sally

Moisture hangs to a lath; a flossy girl
steps up into a stone house,
Her body is finer than her words. Later, she sallies
into mother-being, and their child flown,
she makes herself new; he lowks
the soil for parsley, for the sake of berries.

Fools can make a child, also wildness may
in a religious moment, in fangs
of genetic flashes. Sally sally, in her.
This increase is part of what life brandishes
at evening, in the corner shop,
soap, tea, lemsip, also
stuffing for a slain goose at Christmas. We are fangs of light.
Sally never disremembers. David
watches a glistening worm re-enter soil. Two men,
he hears, showered
a woman in petrol. Fire.

Tarred laths give onto the room, and the stone structure.
We all wait, we hide.
Sally is ten.
As fat as a kangaroo's belly.
She stares at me, such ten years
like moisture, drop away. People say
evanescence, but I say death of a form,
her first dying. The essential irrecoverable child-sense passion,

re-woven.

She whistles up steps
and for her creation puts aside its laws.
She does what she likes. And what she likes is new.
The sun's hair springs from all of her.

'God said, "in this lifting rim of your life…"'

God said, 'in this lifting rim of your life, take
happiness, my holy candle's stump.' But I weep
for misery my security, sacrosanct
liquid, excrement of goodness.
Journeying to our Lord, 'include me,' I implored
the elders. At the chasm, where
from a wound in the rock water
dizzied into the cleft, below, 'here,' they said,
'fuck you, you're not the angel we thought you were.
Go.' 'Oh, thanks,' I said, 'Am I
disingenuous urine?'

In able gait, I canter
to my God. A non-arrival.

My artesian misery oozes, is a rescinded oil,
is water made joyful in misery. God giggles.
I work in misery, the crofter's reward, what
a manchild, who hacks the breathing stone beside
marram, these spiky suns,

scale of his life.
Yet the birds open up space. They open our door.
The travelling wheels all laugh.

You measure me for cloth, but I am in fear of joy.
Torn prisms of petrol in clayey
water, in urban fields – I stir this disorder
with a stick. And later: I see a man, split
in rags, hit by a bus onto a
pedestrian island, quite still. I am safe,
essence of my disorder,
horror nulling itself, some charge in me
betrayed and ceased, as this traffic
hubbed to its spidery riving of mercy
from its soul, motion, vanishes.

Into your palm, I put this fly of mercy
'please,' you say, 'what's this? I must measure you
from shoulder to shoulder.' Our train is sweet,
running in this unsafe night,
between earthquakes,
in which a lamp flowers
above the head of a girl reading in lovely
slovenly, solitary existence;
the locomotive, unfearful, trembles, this mountain horse
in mountainous energy. I touch the physique of happiness.
The sunflower, no light excepting its fine head gets it.

You giggle, eruptive, pulling
the completed shirt onto my shoulders.
Man enough? Our life is transacted
without measure, on reciprocal invoicing,
the hand-out water distilled to cloth.
'Thank you,' I must say. Your making
is modesty on the lips. We risky humans,
the angles in bland and blessed safety. Yeah
I kiss your distinct cheek, my curve
at your bone, this sculpted presence,
the floss, a touch
invisible in wholeness.

Relations

Now you're dead father isn't it time we ceased
speaking, alive silence also held,
    like a wall of wave over
us two ships, to disintegrate
                    its stone?
I was a cheerful small soul. In a jar of ash
now you are burned. In my dream you lay
on someone's bed, knees pointed up
making two vast equilateral triangles
in a side-room, off a party
with not much there to commend us, with a
large cancerous belly. I'm ok, you said.
How are you, father? Oh, I am alright.
Loving comminating smile filtering
death into life imprints your face hardly webbed.
Re-assurance, smiling. Barely

    touched me, though lately
I kiss your cheek, a field of severed wheat.

And now each night this confounding chat, your Yiddish
life, your other wife, first true
    scandalised backbitten Lilith,
          no screech-owl, profounder
Jewess than her you wedded, she,
               Jew to her parents' utmost,
though she who is a Jew is not a Jew born
she who is not a Jew, she is the Jew.

At night confiding in me – I never hear
    her during the day's equable rays –
but when you, father, go still, a radio station
shutting at 3.00 am, she waits, and speaks
who gave me the French novel *Adolphe*
in pure terse English and, dying, willed to me
the bonny two hundred and fifty.
                      Father, speak

to me as much as you're able, I am not
sure you loved me. But something
I am sure, like the wave
is stone to our ships

I am your son
only the one, the only kid

Ha'd ga'd yor
the one, and the only

blessings, father, upon your head
when I last saw your skull, the day before,
now way past the grave, what do I know, but still
air becomes the wind deposing its touch over the earth,
earth's fatuous kiss. God has not forsaken me.

A self-directing psalm

Like an aphid that cannot let itself be destroyed
the light in summer's night sky resists its extinction,
for either the sun holds up, or light struggles in fluid reflection,
luminous, unlike the burned prisoners in a camp, a journey to
ashes.
Theirs is an enfolded panel, like a crucifixion to no purpose,
like, and not like, the journey of Abraham with Isaac, to that
certain point
where the knife holds in the air, but then, the strong angel's hand
restrains Abraham. All is well, except
for Abraham's preparedness to kill his son.

Relief, servitude to fear, fear of life taking my life from me;
it's like two trees, their crowns roped to each other,
a man with each ankle bound to a crown, there he hangs,
the trees waiting release. But what release is this?
I will not anodyne my fear. And though you are dead,

if I ask you for money, do not release angry flies to swarm
at me who must feed my partner, and myself.
The scream of the vertical dive bombers is not like the whine of
a creature.
I could find the means to be aware of self other than mine.
Self, let me be conscious, O hell, outside myself.

The line

Grandfather backed a horse between his cart's shafts,
and tarpaulin keeping rain off wallpapers, it beaded her
easing forth her body stink. Intense flowering head,
muscular stem, the big flesh trots, it's kinds of gaiety,
dips into oats, her chest sashing, pulling
up her foot to rest the pastern
with feathery fetlock –
the huge pretty animal tilts her foot, she is
the heroine of this, drives a thickset
man out of the picture, and tumultuous from her
comes that body smell, not to be mistaken
for affection; it is her life, its odour.
She feeds the children he started, my mother alone
surviving, and taunted pain taints her heart.

A different life designs through her. Grandfather
and children, having no horse, haul a cart
and the flowering contents, its handbrake, against hills,
rasping Hebrew off ancient wheels. His stately wife
never separate from his loins, her body not
to be replaced, though ceasing its progeniture,
she takes the bridle. Rain moistens her cheeks.
The air to Briton Ferry, iron, coal, pebbly road
and little cakes of ordure. A valley focuses
protesting torches of miners into a large, gas-damp light,
wet cymbals of hatred, and the obligements of their children.
By these dear tokens I will see her different face
when I am born, and the new face of my father.

The basics of fire

If love is fire,
grainy systole and diastole
in liquefaction, consistent
to no form, silent.
Yet fire in the brazier-shape
tall, metal, webbed
and three-toed, one, prancing
two supportive: the lion-claws, stubbed
and simous, in which form
is fire, fluid slayer.

I intend to smother it, and do not want to,
I bring sulphurous coke
to the webbed metal tub,
sly resistant cone, pile it in
deliberate
handfuls, that smokes to extinction
bringing extinguishing coals.
It is love's pain, and you know that – fire
I can't extinguish, dare not
for fear I destroy that part of life I built
in respect of you,
your half-unwithdrawn hands –
in this brazier
the heart savagely not at rest.

Will this fire withdraw
to have our flesh mend, in mutual compassion?
Shall fire mend? Behind, quiver
our parents, in gas-like smiling tumbling
to smithereens of ash.
As the mothers will die, the wives do not.

How fire may find its gentleness

Blood inundates its fire, in coal
pulses a star-shape. Fire, be Daniel's
Daniel, since you harm no hair of yourself.
Just now you are energy unattached,
ungoverned by compunction. We douse you by lump
on lump of coal
dropped, on fire, molten Hebrew,
damaged promethean. Fire, be Daniel
and yield imagination, for the sake
of caring.

As the grin develops a stoic smiling
in the body's increase of pain, fire
may suffer imagination,
an uprush of empathy
that pairs the compassionate
with the anguished.
He that had such cat-thew
as to hook a claw in our blood, sucks
milk from the spoon you lift,
his hands holding your nourishing one.
Instruct me how, fire.

Fireball

These humans, heads of bent sorrowing drops,
and two firemen, water a cratered house. The pump
with its distributing ball inside the tank,
yet water hesitates, this life seizing
fire, its inanimate. Such water

in a flower's shape, bowing, is a man
having a stroke, the conscious self
fumbling a word, in its exact linkage.

'If only… help me, please.' Still one woman, smiling
asks, 'please, enter.' Her house
is a space, burned. In stocky, unquivering
steps, she grips my arm, and we trespass
the blessed interior
of creation

The sub-text of sadness

Water bursting onto the cone-form mountain
sprouts trees, much demure flowering, moistens
lava, on these hot flanks. They lift their faces.
Volcanic fire, this disturbed violent life,
will spurt death on the industrious growth;
the volcano's heart, its entrails specked
with fiery expansion, lithe as a snake its fertility nature –
burns and suffocates. Yet again,
the vegetation and sparkling insect life.
I cough near the winking crater, its eye,
this fragment of chaos.

You ceased, and for a year, sulked,
not speaking to me. For a mother, unseemly.
I spoke my truth, you gritted a shut mouth,
sick with my childish mewl.
In the event you, also, transgressed
the religious manifest through our interlocking
sleeps. But I was living.
You weren't much changed, same gracious stubbiness
and re-assuring Judaic aggression.
    I said, the house I now live in
where you lived, fills with girls, and their men.
    You said, 'take me to father's and my bedroom.'
in which brocade hung, colour of rezina.
    You leaned at the head of this motored hospital bed,
me at its foot, much befriending space between;

and thunderous small wheels hastened slackly
across beamy wood, past anxious
corners, empty made-up beds. The transgressed God
did not intervene
as we traced back to where my love
and others' uncounterfeited partnerships
grew. May you thrive, Ma'am
in this continent of heaven. These living transcripts
of our dreaming.

In this season between fruits and coming winter
the corn dolly alone in the cut field
as we break another husk, I drive the bus,
my livelihood of workers. Using their trust
and my headlights, we fan dusk into urban life,
its obligations of happiness. I carry
heads in many formats, the delicate
triangle, in papery orange, a rectangle
of mahogany, a white round smiling cranium,
a yellow visage, showering coppery hair.
      Quick past tram rails, through rubbery rain
greased in a quantum of 'go, go,' Sir,
I said in the cab in which no-one could overhear,
the two-speak radio switched to one-way,
when I'm dead, how may I speak with you?
Damn well you know I can't. But as I drive now,
can't I speak with you, I, who transgressed
speaking with my dead mother? Unblessed
silence. It makes me sick.
      Hating the familiar, yet staunch with family,
she, twelve Judaic tribes shouting,
screech owls, vibrant Liliths,
sexual power of Eden, to oust
the arsenical gradualist serpent's spit.
That's her. But God,
I am permitted to speak with you, who alive
am able to speak to you, who dead cannot.
As I am alive, won't
you speak with me? For which, thanks.

The red bus singes in orange mist.
You might speak with me, who have
a foundation, the rough basement
of charm, not messed with intellect.
Oh my gentle Maker, come on.

A red bus, Lilith rains her copper hair,
with others' shapely various skulls.
God, I am still after your word
to mix in with the throb of a bus idling
between Peckham and Brixton, beneath streaky electrics.
I travel in a metallic blessed safety –
swish under 14.7 urban pressures, almost
hit a mongrel, but did not, who once
saw a bus crash a child, screaming
over the kerb he crouched on, the bone splintered through.
At the 'request' stop shadows a man
where three whites knifed a single black. Justice held her breath.
My dainty clients, papery with paid-up fares.
Sir, your silence mixes with the trampling beams
of my lights pricking the uncertainties.

'Be men, not destroyers.'

I have one further shift, then I accept
I will switch my lights, these paying guests
their blessed onward tickets. Forgive me
for the faint-hearted religious patter.
Go on, buddy, speak a few words
won't you, spare a word, immensity wreathed in silence?

I pass my hand through You.

This is the kingdom

Bees dance from nectar the acid honey, flies rub their sorrowful
                                   limbs
to feast on muck or dissolve sugar cube, large as a bungalow.
Bees dance their day-labour before flowers, 'permit us these
                                 dainties.'
It is given, each instant, they dance
everything; after toil, in corbels they crouch, day's finish,
their dancing legs tucked up like folded thorns,
their cupola intricate as a bee's abdomen.

The day becomes slash and slash. Cavalry with sabres
dismember the hives, the intricacy of this regality.
Yet the diligent, loving their house, without
patriot amorousness, sting and die:
this hopeless envenoming of bees. With intent specialized juices
they pipetted their product, the future a vat,
a delicious fixed tumbler of substance, and they worked
ragged to age. This piteous killing was outside their world,
the death of their king, even, ordered, orderly, up a height.
Now they come with fulfilled honey-duty, on four limbs,
these winged dead, beside wounded humans
on whose palms are stings and nectar,
their mouths smeared victoriously, deliciously fed.
This unsaddled infantry anticipate their death
amidst the splayed hand-made dynasty of bees.

The life of tenderness

1

The words beg of meaning, their hermaphrodite
spirit, to 'give us flesh' –
'our joy (our joy!)
will be scandalous, as waking to fresh snow.'

These words, almost,
in rag-time.

2

We ask for life – embryo,
cell, or burst dead re-imagined
globule of life.

3

A camp-person's ashes
speak, 'give me back
my body's years' residue. You
the human, not God, or cancer, who stole
my life you couldn't add to yours.'

The shedding candle pleads,
also, for a new slug of fire.

4

The unborn's viscid effusions in s's
of fish. The penis gasps in its host.

5

I mean to buy a hat. Is this the ecstatic
shudder of ego? My dalliance, amidst dossed-in
spiritual clothes. Their smell of people
touches the mothy beams of this shop, from one of which
a lamp hooks its light
dripping in kinship
to earth's cyst of central fire, the locus
and binding-up of all mutual effort and filth.

This turbulent never-forming whole
confronts the blind greeny eye of paraffin.
Gentle, dangerous lamp. Human wordless lamp.
Local, general-store lamp.

6

In the shop
I try on a lightly-stained great-coat. Basic
Adamic fit, over first human nakedness,
this triumph that blesses the flesh
sly against the black sun.

7

Piteous beseeching words. Their humility
and commonness fleck the culpable self's snowy
hellish egoism. I'm to earn their use,
obduracy, persistence, the crazy-hand-fired bricks
of Babel, our unified human tribe.
Its persiflage grates the spirit.

8

Yet slenderness, your black hair considerate of the nape –
your compassionating intelligence, lotus-petalled
and lily-like pellucid covering
of praise, on the spirit's pang
that tears through space its widowed spark,
a heated metal's watery blasts
as she tempers. On you come.
You are the tender one.

A horse in the pasture

Bound in the sun's orbit, icy comet, your salmon-red
hair after you streams a million miles.
Your flight is structured, with a voluptuousness
of hair-like moisture. It means something,
that you are clung to, that the sun holds you
in blue pasture.

Seven more twilights – *tasogare*, the Japanese
say, meaning, *who is there in the evening?*
You are here, then you are not, as I will
melt away. As people like to melt each other.
The firmament showers your moisture from you
in a space, with parameters – tethered like a horse
grazing city fields our Town Fathers may dismember
disremembering this shared pasture. And I ask,
as if it matters, spare the grazer,
spare our circuit, our common fields.

Stay where you are

Feasible to offer
the quick flesh happiness; a cup
of chilled lemon; a kiss that drops
on the mouth, after sex.
A hand ferns the dying
forehead, and clasps the jewelled
tepid fingers. Goodbye.

The pain of your breast

I had the pain of your breast as you
lay down; this unfruiting and flowering red currant.
What are we making? 'Please, gently,' you asked me.

With your breast against mine, gentle
as I might be taught to be, out from
the mines of delicacy, not delicacy comes.

Choosing

The espalier of white roses, like flaked
pale pears, scents the stronger; the larger

rose, plum-red, is a visionary plasm
undenying, rejoicing. The sun has clothed you.

Rose crystal configures in its cluster. But you choose,
as the Cathars have, those imagining blossoms.

Their space is the burned mountains. You choose.

A wild cherry tree

Wild cherry by a village limits,
accessing fruits. Could it refuse,
it would not. Hands broke into
the untweeting pinnate leaves
and branch, no birds there, dangling
fruits, ripe
or immature, and trailed its limbs they broke.

That's a strange fruit, human needs various,
from burning the hissing flesh to juicing out
    this wildness of fruits: the 'I'll eat' to 'I'll tear.'
        A partly eaten cherry in spittle's
        foam, over smoky dust.

Dark

A sun, or lamp, its fuels
used, or
the sun
rinsed in hatred's petroleum –
that's dark.

Those Moors pleaded with the sun, 'don't you
burn us.' In apollonian
reason the light charitied, 'be dark, be the shade
I'm not.' Sun-treading Moors'
intelligence shared
with Europe the strategies
of trigonometry, and clothed
Aristotle in comprehension.
What's it
mean to Europe?

Christians envied
this intellection with
the sun, which
Blake, our equalizer of woes
but not our envy,
might not re-dress. Huh? Christians
burned Moors, with funky rose
of fire, voiding the Moors' pact
with the sun's genes, which
was a shame. 'Alas,'
some wrung their voices,
like birds.

On Spain's wintered
Atlantic flank, crucifixion
signs – incisions
in basalt, and gneiss, its generous flowing wrinkles.
Which this ocean
gnaws, shitting in globules
pink, blue, lifeless
delicate cinnamon shades
that life might be alert with,
as the fingers of a kangaroo
sensitize us.
The poet Bly said, earth
crouches on
all fours. God, come again
from your lovely consort's arms, weep the once
again, God-in-her-arms.

Cathars

for Maggie and John Comley

Like flowers, the church heaps in fire the Cathars.
Early Fathers burned the gnostic text
and, later, others lifted the cross
to put sisters and brothers in fire,
in a staked pit. Heretic flies winged
in diaphanous flame, and christian priests
wearing the jagged shape of Asmodeus' wings
darkened the air mixed with fatted smoke,
unconscious pollution of the Languedoc.

Ferrous-blood soil and cypress-green
are consubstantial with the dead. That is not true.
Their pain is substantiated, their death is substantiated
but not their flesh. No one comes again
after their burning. But fleshy erect flowers

with sultry acid-white moons of hatred
for the priests flying in smoke and whirled ash –
God's earth is inferno. Flowers curse, flowers hate them,
and when a priest flows into the shade
of his house, white lobe-like lilies stiffen;
and the routes and wild flowers of the Languedoc,
with hefty lorries, seating brick-red vine growers,
that screw the dust in wind-skids – they treat the priest
as if he had deranged the land, as if he had maddened creation
going about his God-thrashed work, as if he had forgotten,
as if he were Vichy, and his memory
had clotted with the acts it had concealed
in suffocated repudiation; and it is God's face
has turned aside for the stink of the ashen hair of the burned
that suffered their deaths, like children gripped in the passion
of paedophiles. The murdered, these different burned leaves.
In earlier belief, a dead leaf was a soul.

Female God

Are you hearing? Earth receives our boxes
of flesh, and grubs like starless drops,
not cyclical, unlinked to monthliness of light.

We become substanceless, turning through ourselves,
Female God, your gnosis says 'take life.'
Only gently, do it. Your wings beat crystal white.

High in the malls, huge on little flowers of rock
swished by waves, the browed depths, you wait;
the lighthouse, rough soldierly pulsar, beams and warns.

Break us to what we are; with your rucksack
of blessings – sideways in air, your wings
effortfully blossoming, open. Like light,

Goddess, you approach, strange in this element.
We seek warmth, food, and the lives of others.
I kiss this human. Chidelessly, let me live.

In fear of loss

    Tell me why a creature suffers
another's eyes; the heft turning
the prairie, and the sod with icy twinkling
blossoms reversed over. I remember

a chiropodist's touch, intelligence wiring it,
abrasive sweetness in my soul's changes.
The comet swarms its hair, the oak,
obdurate, flowers. Reluctance

may be indulgence. My loneliness,
in these city fields, where their unheard
energies nucleate my smaller,
receives succour. Windows go like water

at day's fall in the north's summer light.
You will not know what it means to not have
the spaces of the moors, until you do not have them,
and the dead, and the unborn, and grass flowering.

Innocent crime

On Town Hill, a rural ghost stares
in windows. Here my cousin hop-scotched
and stretched me to larger limbs, upon
her chest's pretty sail, as if I were
the Welsh wind scudding her, but my five years

prevented. Pain, a new and passionate
ingredient, filled me. We went in the house,
and I told myself 'nothing has happened:' it had.
By the large unfired kitchen range, like the bulbous head of a god,
you could open, I perceived its chill brain.

Without God, reason, or fulfilment came
a shaft of wind, fetching an old innocent crime,
such as love,
shaping the breath. I want you to know,
I said to myself – the shape of expectation
smiling in me. For how long must this be,
I asked? the question, fifty years later,
a cousin on my father's side asked of the god in me;
the ancestral crime of the unbeloved.

Against depression

When government is enraged, thugs
from a parliamentary meadow rise up, armed, but a torpid chamber,
and gangsters melt the commonweal
               to their commodity.

Wrongly our mercy fatigues. Is there a delicate witness,
one we mock and tease for his sensitivity,
one whom women touch, who comes with mild eyes,
watches for a new tentative earth, in equilibrium
gauges the rinsed fluttering petunias, of a peculiar
fragile watered silk?
Lets outdoors in freezing slush,
the mauve fury of winter's afternoon,
the deciduous buried creatures.

Motherland

You broke your hip, slipping across a mat.
Mother, this unloved love is us,
and your 'he should have died at birth', my child.
Only the head was wounded, not the mind.
The hermit crab, like loose eyes
among heathery pebble, he has his thirst.
Every creature adores its progeny.

                                   I understand
your muscular nature
not able to bear quicksilvery attention
detached from you. Your open face, beautiful,
as mine is not, forms with age. You smile
and move with a frame. A step, and then another,
as Hebrew multiplies its basic forms.

★

The angel born to avenge [—],[145] with fists and thighs
[—][146] down the thermals, the helix his eagerness
to murder back-sliding. He has his job. Who?
He electrifies me, this
sophisticated being, until that energy
flings me to burn, jams and fixes me,
in the grate's coal, agony's
unsavable from old, Durham blacklead range.
He has forced my willingness
for pain. Mother, upon this
last part, the watery shade
casts its unhappiness we have made.

★

Does the bird trill its adventure, which chevrons
his disguise, that feathers his death's arrowy flight?
His sound draws a hand upon him. The sound gravid
and mortal. Earth tugs this heavenly drop.

Like wedded buttocks, the underspace
of the bird's belly that droops shakes upwards,
and jerks its fantail in constant outrage: off off.
The bird's flesh is sound.

We listen, in walking to the bread-store.
Pay high, be bird-like, the till pings
its notes for you, and your pale-thighed foreigner-person.
Freedom.

★

Mother and motherland; I know
reconciliation builds with good graces
in her goodness. Everything
is maternal, or a warp of it. The machine of grief
the heart, heavy working creature.
Its curious valentine will come. Sure.
The marsupial insect weeps its chips of shit
like a diamond under a frog. Before
birth, dearly I loved my country.
How, and what did I form on? Memory breathes
and the subtle thief of youth grows its knowledge in me.

★

I wanted to leave, my motherland circumscribed
me with herself, true as a movement
in the shivered pond, of which my shaking
of its atoms – heavy
frantic yachts. Only away from this movement
can I have my maker, free
with meaning. That is not so.

★

Pell-mell large-eyed butterflies rest
open wings on petals. And moths, with stubby beating fliers,
sip fiery light, with an apocalyptic
intelligence. On the lake, suddenly

slant–wise in zig–zag quilled colours,
as the lake is dull, but in its mirroring extent
the butterflies rise, in flummoxed
awkward mating. I, in the dinghy,

irresponsible, love their scentless love, fire and transfiguration.
Mother, your girl's face moves her beauty,
you, pure lily of my failure,
and the bones of your face blossom with age.
It is the gods' gift they are transcendent with,
their numerous gifts, this one, giving.
And beware, the day of wings.

★

In the city's metro, thumb–like
mice, by the third rail
tear gum spat from tasteless mouths, and bear
silvery haphazard bits of human stuffs
they fasten, like a wasps' nest in a waxy lantern,
below the chassis of trains, sometimes burning.
They tear our mouths' incontinencies, newsprint,
to nestle a plump bird–like flesh. They are destructive,
devour electricity against the time
night switches its dark lamp, and the mammal's hubbub
with its sinful mind, despairs on the empty platform.
Mother, I am afraid we do
or do not love. Your languid
fanged visage – look,
mother, I'm on fire; what punitive
senior electrician
in celluloid insulating cuffs, is
she?

In collusion, courses our mutual dislike;
in my body, your gene, the
nuclei, the bashing
pathogens, tiding in both.
Yet above ground light breaking with leaves
is holy, and just.

Is the next world ashes? The stars, mother
laugh excitedly? Against grief's solid calm
is reconciliation,
like a little dancing movement
in a neutron bulb, possible where giant angels
fledge and practice wings
in the webs scabbed with our dead lives?
Earth's people install
the plucky angels to rule, and they
mouth-water on our bodies, crunching deaths,
only deaths, or we'd disband
their clapping philohuman wings, barbule
and hook. We'll have no tyrant goodness
purse its flashy wings on us. Look, you.
It's our bones they suck. So we absolve
us in their punishment, composing
hosannas, 'Lord, save us'
or 'Lord, we praise you.'
Either will do.

Dare we mother, in
this world's ash and filth
with kith in the blood,
in reconciliation mix with the angels, aspiring our
goodness, who like us
double-form a dark-and-white grace?
This is imagined and unnamed.

Their virtues are pleading with us. If
the madonna, the icon-pair,
of mothered child and son-cared-for frailhardy
mother initiate this, in earth's teeming
dissevering energies, some
may come to this
home-made bliss of care. But in the other case
these angels will crush the light,
for we made them
in wax and shimmering smoke,
human smoke, in death-form cypress-feeding,
with darkness shimmering.
If I can only steady my hand in our gentleness.

Smiling, you enter

A daisy in a daisy-cog of utmost
delicacy, retiring chairwoman, mother,
these kids make you a pot, 'I love
you' clayed on its belly, minds quick in their hands.
'Why not make this for her?' They make
this. Thread of lipstick on dark lips,
hair, like filaments of flowing water – you are short, unpaid.
Not dainty. Have the sharp wren's maternal strike.

Smiling, you enter this stanza. Quick,
for they're dabbing your name, 'Dora,
we love you,' wormed on its patted clay.
Later, a token entangled in esteem, a clock, 'Effrawater School
1979', a brass strip. These kinds of cognitions.

I spaded seams of clay onto your box,
you chose The Jews' Cemetery, that you might
lie by your sister, not your unbelieving husband
my father in ash miles distant.

Some of these children can't write, some are ceasing
to be kids, all create words
on a clay pot. So the cog-daisy in delicacy
becomes love, you, delicacy in caring.
Boys chalk 'fuk' under the Head's window,
and here the national front[147] doled out weapons,
the boys, clay, in creation's webbed feet.

Will

A translucent marble my cousin pushed
in your mouth to stop you biting off your tongue.
Dead death, I said, but even so, cousin told me
in death she will do it, and we must stop her,

the mouth, gums and uneven pearly teeth
staying comely. So I have listened
in a lingo of English mother and her father
gutturalized with the bronchial German of Yiddish.
We walked, I behind, on Westcliff's stumbling pier.

Hitler started what some English knew about.
The lousy Jews blown in ashy ovens.
It is to be dealt with in another world.

Your white skin was with blood swollen from drugs
applied to launder the roots of pain.
We folded your hands on each other, and we pulled
from fingers, rings with globules of diamonds.
'I desire to be by my sister, in Jewish ground.
I bequeath to my son half of his life.'
Among funerary pots the wind shatters
and flings up ash, like a Chagall soft-faced ruffian;
in this other place is my lonely father.
'By my sister, please,' insists my dead mother.
We found the Jewish plot, but mislaid my aunt's district,
where mother ached for the biology with her sister.

'This is Jewish land.' Though earth is just soil
a little heavy, mother, lifted on the shovel.
This poem is the crime. Touch me
I mean, as you never did, where the blame points at me.

'I see it coming'

I see it coming.
It will not be small.
Such a promise
as I cannot recall another, unbroken,
to raise these storms.

Still I do not recoil.
It is the same labour
inseparable from grief
that springs to life from winter.
I must give this birth.

Hushed, at the death
of you,
love will make it
much worse.

A room in the Moorish kingdom

You asked me, 'am I ok
in this dress?' 'Without your clothes
or with them,' I answered, 'you
are beautiful.' Smiling, you turned
to the burning centrifugal lamp shedding
light, and I became one who is
just one. The Hebrew lamp stands
in this passage, this quarter, steps rising
and falling away, huge walls with high
unreachable Jews' doors. In stone
contra solem the Hamite Moors
built, Jews and Moors dancing
together, in Spain, that mountain flower
soldiers of Christ burned,
though the sun did not. Our God
we Jews kept on a leash, candlelight
and alpine gentian, while you, the Moors,
made algebra, medicine, Averroes
clothing Aristotle in comprehension
again. You were our House, not
our home, and the pain is that you
are so familiar, yet not us, or our
home by the wide-wing cedar.
You are the West, and we, of

the east, flowered in the west
and died. You were the *Mensch*
of Hispania, and your deep-breasted
women, with maths, science
and dark skin, philosophy and sex –
'We'll house you,' you say.

So love, you tell me, by
the gazing lamp, where you're now unhappy,
and there is no-one here, is it
too much to turn back to you, love,
too intimate for the word 'love'?
And if it is, what word would be enough?

'To Jerusalem'

To Jerusalem
you came. Waiting outside its walls
these graves will lift, and their fortunate dead
unfasten Jerusalem's closed gate. But your slow
democracy is more virtuous. From the least tasselled
city, Newcastle, fringed
with Jews across the water, your house
upon you, that frailest part,
you reached Europe, from Marseilles
taking the sea-road which a friend
says Christ's wife and their fleeing
children never did pass over
to the community of Jews in France.
You crossed the Mediterranean
and entered
the Palestinian
and the Jewish cities
fortified
in each other, your breath's
horns of quiet,
silence your perseverance.

Intended endeavour
is a snail's faith.

Yet whose city? yet never
mind that. In its rocky folds, tear
the fleshy herbage into your body.
Embalmed
for the city's holiness in you, the end
of yearning, the eventual
honouring of you, all people
and all creatures.

Good opportunity

Fin of shark? a grey sail
tears water greeny
with melted stone, that bulk bruising
under its surface
with titanic liquidity.

From a trumpet's mouth silence ekes like mist.
My life is touching
her tensing instep and broad foot
flexible as a watery bird's,
the arm's hook and wrist's grace. Then lift the cloth

from the wicker basket of loaves
criss-crossing doughy fruit, a smell
yeast aches with,
the bub stiffening a nipple, the positioning
of organs unpacified until they make life
to mingle with pre-natal heads of existence.
On sand lilac bundles stack – such large neatness
of God's fingers: mana, the simple divine bread.
Collect and store for a long period.

Los Borrachos (the drinkers)
about 1628

Velasquez I'm truly sorry Englishing
your 'Los Borrachos',
drinkers' poorest flesh
                        their inchoate
wits distressing
                even their solvent. The man

holds the bowl a bit aslant
as Bacchus wilfully abandons him.

Is this the end of England's english
                    that beautiful lissom
tree, its long bow that once killed France?
Am I forfeit to England?
                            is that peasant
despised by the god? It seems
his spattered wits say this.

Look again. The smile
                    gleams idiot
like a priest rapt in his sure godliness
                but the eyes
are aware, and imagining,

like those of a man holding the arm of his lover,
not looking at her,
in a trinity, of her, his self, and
                    them both. So now

the deceiving god is in the teeth
        of his sly trap, not
able to gnaw his soul's limb from its caught flesh –
        you fool, you, god, dripping slyness
                        like an ichor
as undirected as the gum of a fir.
                    You too have your life.

Wales of the Welsh

This country station
              glistening, both sides of the main line,
oil-scent clings its quoins
from the locomotive in a fiery waiting.
Mother's brother, or was it us
stepped from a polite, tufted carriage,
his kiss the metal sting
adhering from Bull's Blood.
I still have it.

The station roof's glass
              of briny green
frees light
from brass receptacles, their brassy gleams
choking mother with joy;
They kiss in a brother's
            beams of solicitation.

This Jew born in Wales,
stocky genial musculature, hard to tell
       Jew, or Welsh person
the Welsh pod of dried potent seed.
You Celts of Britain, hauled to your feet, kingless in Wales,
in your country, you are the Jews,
coupling with brotherless linguistic Welsh women,
their heavy frames treading daintily,
whose pride is delicacy, a finger
hushing lips.

Appendix

Living

Two versions of the poem/sequence 'Living' are held in the Silkin Archive at Leeds University Library. The version in the main body of this collected edition of Silkin's poetry comprises only the first section of the sequence (see p. 153). The decision to include this 'single section' version rather than the full sequence in the main body of the book was based on Silkin's having signed his name at the end of the typescript from which it was transcribed (BC MS 20c Silkin/3/1/1). The typescript is clean other than the section number (1) having been scored through in ms. The presence of Silkin's signature suggests that he may have intended the single section for publication in a periodical, although no evidence of its having been published has been found.

The four-section sequence below is also transcribed from a clean typescript copy (BC MS 20c Silkin/3/1/4).

1

I melt into this room.
Mirror you have seen this flesh
Between the accretions of other
Feathery lives. Tell me
Through the lucid intervals
Bird-past skims into you,
As I stand in you, naked:
Have the thighs grown, or tough
Buttocks made sorts of progress:
The face: in what change
Of particulars might grace
Lurk in the hair; or under

A bit? But slightly more
In the colds of the ferocious mind
Stare, and evaluate,
On the air's whitish silences
As frost upon moist glass,
Since only I will hear:

A sense of largening
Of the big body yet
Of the heart perishing.
Which in this moral shrinkage
Man despairs of himself.

2

Life is growth although I
Seem with such hungering
I am meagrely the flesh
The thought a man turns over
Or, blithely, almighty God
Who making me a stinging
I torment myself with
Wrought for his creatures the torment
I am in all my sting
Of all their torment.

3

Some ways a man can die
Over and over. Thus life
In the blood-springs. And think:
It is not death that dies
Through persecution or
The body's shrinkage, or rotting.
It is the fleeing soul
Committed to as many of these roads
As it has thoughts. These are
The spirit's politics:
To know death, and be dead.

It shall not profit much
But the ways are many.

4

It seemed three times I drowned
I mean, three times sank
In earth's rimless pool.
Dying each falling through.
Then coming past, I walked
The airless world drowned
Seeing all, feeling all
A live man might feel
Yet distant purely from
The creatures nearby.
Thus me, committed in
The human act of death
To everliving death
Over God's sprawling earth.
Life has its teeth

A good farmer

In 1972, a limited edition of a poem titled 'A good farmer' was published by the Valley Press (Rochester, NY). Only 100 copies were printed, with the first 30 signed by Jon Silkin. The poem was later worked into the first of the 'Three Shetland Poems' published in the collection *The Principle of Water* (1974), and as such provides an interesting example of Silkin's working and reworking of his poems – and, in this case, the publishing and republishing of a poem in different forms. (See p. 407.)

A good farmer, his stone house in upraised hand, grew chill, and
numbed.
A monument to equity, in cared-for acreage.
He leant through his son, his words speaking of their release,
and gratitude.

These had for his son the legality of a will codified
and, with prescience, not to be altered.

The father begged his child to economize
with breath; again he begged him.

In the house: a diligence of objects. Ships in replica, coin;
layered sands in tubs.[148] And in one authoritative portrait, a dead
woman.

The hair darkened.

Your mother, and your two sisters.
The house. Promise you will keep
intact plaster and lathe. Let no maculation spore a room.
But, he said, in a smoky whisper, drawing off a little and
pulling aside his son as if to command secrets: promise me
the mortar surfacing the house be kept over its stone.

The hand clenched seriously.

The son smiled, abandoning inwardly his whole self to the shape.

He sifted the elation in Edinburgh's red stone; in Rose Street
the ruthless
abundance of waste, the patrimony trickling in silvered filth
along the
gutters of a street mantled with women's breath. He became his
father's whole life-time out-of-date. A tiny fish swimming in the
island's nearest voe, he watched himself agog for the silver hook
to pierce the large sacrificed worm.

Air that Pricks Earth with Life

The version of 'Air that Pricks Earth with Life' published in *Fuse*,
2 (November 1972) and reproduced here varies significantly from
that published in the long poem/verse play *The People* (Part III,

Testing) in *The Principle of Water* (1974). Drafts of *The People* up to its publication in *The Principle of Water* held in the Silkin Archive at Leeds University Library date from around 1968 to 1973, suggesting that by the time it was first published in its entirety, Silkin had been working on it for around five years. It was further revised prior to its publication in his *Selected Poems* (Routledge and Kegan Paul, 1980), resulting in a shorter work which Silkin suggested in his introduction was 'in some ways, a re-written one'.[149]

Air that pricks earth with life, and turns
with it, grows dark as with earth it thins
in chill distraction through the year's midnight.
    The sun in winter
drops a low arc through the horizon and
is absent. As we trudge the area where
our child lies, the soil is trodden on
by the mad, who, at the next spring, that is,
at the next world, may indeterminably
elide with its stark light the vacancies
in their maimed circuits. If no world exists
these dead may rise to; if the flower's concentric
flesh, missing the taxonomic nerve
the flower sees with, stays unmatched by a trace
of healing correspondence, this world
will have to do. One, in a group driftingly
involved, as if we beckoned, leaves, and is
behind us. Her back, stooping, slightly,
with large hands, her breasts hardly there,
some independent mildness touches the mouth,
branched over the cheekbones, brushing the eyes widening
in hunger.
She gazes, and slowly lifts my hand up to
her lips, and kisses it; then lets it go,
carefully, and leaves. Her gentleness
forming, without submission, as she kisses
my hand gravely – who shared the kiss –
in which instant sane or defective – shame
at my divisive question. Walk a bit

on to the ward. Out of its souring brick
birdlike, the mad alight, shake, and fold then
their movements to their bodies, gazing curiously,
or quiver in recognition, timid, but pressing
on us to touch us over our hands or faces,
or touch us with their eyes; and everywhere
their mild untrained gaze makes in certainty .
creaturely connections. And as I feel
her hand, earlier forms shed this flesh leaving
them bare. Twelve almost, to test
my sanity, I squatted on the pavement
and put a marble on my tongue, closing
my mouth on it. If I could swallow the thing
and die, I was insane. If I left
it balancing on my tongue, then I was mad
to do this. Days sank round their pivot healing
over the crux. Our child for them is mad.
We reach the twilit ward. Adam lies in
a bed, as if an adult. Through his face
his blood, making the skin chill, dampening it,
stirs. He breathes, yielding a changed breath.
We labour it, and press it, the lungs
that can't be relieved, letting it from them.
She rises, and slowly as she brings her mouth
to him, her lips widen. Lightly, and light,
as if she were withdrawing, as she sinks
beside his silence breathing, she kisses his eyes,
and then his mouth. She puts her finger, which
he holds, inside his palm, turning his head
to us. In the tidied, firm eyes breath
in a changing form enters; and a sharpening
form lights,
outlined, and with a flickering softness in
this shape. Over but not obscuring it
at all, moisture, of every place, gathers
into the eyes, swelling and widening them.
      And deliberately
impulses, but without force, of that which
connectingly formed him a creature grew,

grew and, as held this way, connected us,
holding us to him until
that moisture pressed with a thick
movement out of him.

Emmanuel

The imagery of a child holding a marble on his tongue and the association of this act with madness, which appears in the second paragraph of the first section of this previously unpublished prose piece, can also be found in the previously unpublished/uncollected poem 'Nearly' (see p. 199), and the section beginning 'Air that pricks earth with life…' in the long poem/verse play *The People* (Part III, Testing) (see pp. 383 and 842).

LORD, the little asp squats in my soul clipping his poison into me. His pincers are sharp, and I am polluted. Speaking to you like a child, I expected some reply, but I came to you with my fear, which, as, you will see, was the greatest, and most fitting, gift I could offer. I was received in silence, and I came away bearing a large space.

When I grew older the defection of madness in me grew. I carried marbles in my pocket. I sat down on the pavement and put one into my mouth. The slightly alkaline sweet that would not dissolve in my spit brought me nausea. If I did not swallow this then I was mad to try. If I did I was mad to kill myself.

If I could have been annihilated in sweetness, with the ravishing sweetness of an older love, I would have taken this; not as my due, but as a need. But sweetness, the gentle mouthings and careful teeth which love can have, and does use, are out of fashion. In my sex, I implored a wholeness I could not wholly desire, but you were away. You had many deaths and many sufferings to think about, and the boxed tears of a child were not to your taste. Besides, I could not come to you asking forgiveness for anything but the partial destruction of your being good.

Had I killed the labouring ant and the milky green fly, you

could have received and punished me. I did not kill them.

Consider, Lord, that there are many who produce a convolute, prolix evil. What is evil but the destruction of another? What had I to offer? What had I dared? In my goodness I was ineffective; in my evil there were, like the hairs in a barley field, many more sharp than I.

Was my language the fault? What language must I speak to you in?

I sweated in the bondage of my sex. I was trussed with it. I have come to it now. I am in earnest with myself. If there are things made and things destroyed; and if it is true that an omnipotent being such as yourself has created all, then it is evident you have propounded both these. Must you permit us to destroy what you already destroy? I am not your helper.

I hate your dual image. I abhor what is Satan in you and in calling you God I blaspheme against your identity. You shall hear me now, when before, when I asked merely, you would not.

The Reply

I have made you as a Man; what can you complain of? As you differ from another so he is not as you are. How have I offended you? You live longer than a beetle, and with more consciousness than the sweating frog. I have breathed life into your kind ancestors. If it does not please you, blame them.

Consider also that you have a merciful release in death. When you die nothing goes with you. While for me, a force making itself, there is no end of burdens. I am ceaseless. I am like a wheel of gold and like a bit of smashed glass. I persist whether in the shape of movement, or the shape of inert uselessness. Do not deny me this privilege.

The Reply Returned

In any case, it seems that the heaven you put me in mind of would have been tedious. Eternal rewards and punishments; small change minted and paid back. And you are no one man's property; you are protean. You lurk in a woman's womb like some gadfly that has found its way into a space that can give you nothing. You are the raised voice of the trumpet and you are the tilted brush. You are filed and you propagate. But what value shall I place on you? O should rather have what I have – a deficiency, and cultivate that. Then I shall become a moulded pillar. I shall reach up and support the roof on which your lives are depicted. If you should wish to see what is there you must come in under my spaces, which you have made.

A Further Reply

I suppose once is enough. How could I have expected you to reply again? It would not have been in character.

The spaces of the air are indignant with your silence. You provoke me so that I shall speak to you. Very well then, I shall list some of your attributes. But do not expect only the good things. All is entwined, compounded.

Creation, which is good: destruction, which I abhor.

Delight of the flesh, which I adore with my Being: pain of the flesh, which I hate, I think.

But pain is, at times, a pleasure. It is at least a preparation for pleasure. I must start again.

Desire, which is good; because it is pleasurable; because it can increase love and multiply the species.

But we desire those things also that wound, or crush.

Lord, is there nothing so sensible, but it is subtle; so clear but the very clearness is a fine solution of impurity; nothing that is inevitable, its own shape, substance, life; but one thing is alloyed with another?

You are all things; you are alloyed.

Nausea!

Poems published in *The Ship's Pasture*

Salome

Published in *The Ship's Pasture* as 'Salome's Self', the poem 'Salome' appeared in the *New Statesman* in 1980. There are quite significant differences between the two versions of the poem.

The rooted crystal lake
bleeds fish to the line. Tied at my ligament
to flutter
damselled,
a breastless haired puberty; what
thing am I?

Limb and eyelid flutter at the mothy tessellation
where ibex and fish preserve.
My hot self's plasm is pure space
but his heated eyes disparage me
to my darkness whose energy silences him
in me. I am freed
upon another world; the child's silence
is a halo of ash at the wall grief
loses her body at, relinquished and hale
to power's delirious fluctuations.
The soft pounding of pity throbs the pulse.
Tears of stone bulge the eyes.

Where is the mother to abort or save
me? 'I will,' he says
'be good to you.'
The soul, disparaged, dances eternity's strings.
Salome, undying in a moment.

Formations

'Formations' appeared in the *Times Literary Supplement* on 19 September 1980, and was published in *The Ship's Pasture* in 1986 with the title 'Envy of God', minus the dedication to the Gandelmans and the quotation attributed to Gregory of Tours. As with 'Salome', there are significant differences between the two versions of the poem.

for Claude and Tsili Gandelman

If you, priest of God, whoever you may be, are so learned…
that you find my style boorish, I yet implore you, do not destroy
what I have written.
– Gregory, Bishop of Tours (quoted by Auerbach, *Mimesis*, p. 93)

Fig, date, and balsam, they fringe
two pools: two shields resting
in Judah's desert, – gazelles hurtled
by fear, by fear checked.

Fig, gazelle, shield – words to do
with water whose desert the asp,
that minute king, grins with and flickers.
We wait for water to be at rest.

We are enough for Judah, the shields
would suffice us for ever. His psalm plucks
its sojourns of praise, and fills
my jealous mouth with His name.

He made the wild places, I, too, form songs.

The Jews in England

This version of 'The Jews in England' was published alongside 'The Jews of England' in *Poetry Kanto* no. 9 (1993). Both poems were collected in *Making a Republic*, and although there are few variations between the two versions of 'The Jews of England', the poem published as 'The Jews in England' in *Poetry Kanto* is substantially different to the collected version. Perhaps most significant is the long first stanza, which in the collected version comprises only three lines.

I force ice in me, for water with freezing
grows, where matter contracts. I have no voice,
borrowing to make your language harsh
in my struck larynx,
the Jews' plucking sounds, a hectic dissonance
out of Abraham's deceitful obedience, his son's life's derision.
Tender complex English,
like a grown child-person
fills earth's spaces.
It is your language. And I must find mine.

Here my speech, love, take notice of my self, and stay
within my acts. I am your tender Gentile.
And you have brought us this,
a poem that is one note, praise, the psalms
fresh as a changing glance, a fragrant look,
in an English we had not, but on our tongues
our lives' new dared fracture. She is she

who will not come again. Although I sit in grasses
and flowering, in their mutual forgiving allowance
of space, like feathery cats at a dish, the prairie,
its miles of sound, that adjusted to each new-comer,
has been cast up by the spade, its mattocked web.
I have no notion of how I shall die. I saw it die.
I see it, my brain, nails, digestion,
all to decay into new earth.

Revolving its cutting edges, a thresher:
and wheat, stalk, haulm and staff of floury seeds
stand, like torches, each eye broaching the same vision.
We face our God. And eat.

An Editorial Quandary

In selecting previously unpublished work from Jon Silkin's archive for inclusion in this book, we came across a number of poems where it was difficult, and on occasion impossible, to decide which version to include. Silkin worked on his poems over time, often extending a first draft, breaking it up, reassembling it, or cutting parts out to find a base for a new start. In some instances, sections were worked into other, new poems; in others, two, or sometimes more, seemingly 'complete' versions of the same poem exist.

The following poems – 'Black-eye bean', 'On glass'/'The originals' and 'The conduits'/'Policeman's holiday' – are examples of related versions of the same poem where we could not make a decision as to which to include. We have therefore chosen to reproduce two versions of what is essentially the same poem, each of which has its own merits. We hope that the reader will find the links and changes interesting as an illustration of Silkin's creative process.

Black-eye bean

BC MS 20c Silkin/3/1/7.

A dry bean, finger-nail's width,
its skin is tight, grained with crinkles
    tightly drawn towards its belly.
Round some of them, split slightly.
Its underside almost flat,
On it a black oval eye
Unites the skin's seam, its centre
White, a blind eyeball.
It is a complete object.
For the curious, it is curious; and for
    the hungry
Many must be boiled
To placate the angry, or diffident,
    human belly.

It remains dry, when cooked
Or ground up.

A feeder, not for itself only,
Some must be left
For the plant to go on. It is dry
With little taste.

BC MS 20c Silkin/3/1/8.

A dry bean, roughly
A finger nail's width, its skin is tight
With crinkles tightly drawn towards its
    belly;
And round some of them, split slightly.
Its underside is almost flat
And on this, a black oval eye
Unites the skin's seam. Its centre
Is a white, blind eyeball
Dry and ridged, like a tumour.
It is a complete object.
For the curious, curious; and for the
    hungry
Many must be boiled
To placate the angry, or diffident
    human belly.
Its strength strengthens.
It remains dry, even when cooked
Or ground up, and retains this.
A feeder, not for itself only,
Although some must be left
For the plant to continue its yield
Dry, and with little taste.

Drier than the burned flesh
Of mother, father, son
And also the bodies of their children.
A bomb has burned them. The body is
     ill.
It cannot moisten the bean.
The mouth and stomach
Cannot digest the bean's flesh.
The bean survives, as it is eaten
In the flesh. The dead survive
In the humus, strengthening a bean.

Dryer, much drier, and dried
Than the burned flesh of the family,
Their flesh dried by the bomb that
Burns the flesh severely
Which moistens the bean, in the mouth
And in the stomach;
Slowly, with passion,
Until it is too ill
To eat the bean's flesh.
Some survive. The bean survives
In the flesh. The dead
Strengthen the living tissue
Every way that can be thought of.

On glass

On glass, sheltered from rain by a lip of
     steel mullion,
probe and legs, in the blow to kill, waft
from the hand. Fizzing at glass's outer
     side,
I'll not let her in, though of God's
     forms also,
His goodness, whose lucid shafts twang
in our flesh. Affliction moves with the
     sun
carrying a blood-fed probe, that fine it
     pierces
adamant, and cold tough
as industrial diamond

    Yours God, yes, yours; yours, surely
     yours.

She flexes knees, to crouch on skin like
     one
voiding in a glazed bowl a cistern
     flushes.
The grief of pure evil frenzies in
     autumn rain:

    Yours, yes, yours; yours, surely yours.

God loans a hair, from his life; in her,
blood, captured and dying, swills
her capillaries with ciphoned jogging
     movements.
Fine as a spider's hair, she dangles
legs, and vulnerable defective gait
through vacant air. The point is,

The originals

She who takes blood, and gives poison,
shelters, at the lip of steel that mullions
     glass,
from the blow wafting off probe and leg,
Blood, captured and dying, swishes
in hydraulic capillaries, fine as wind
jingling a plateau of wheat. In Israel,
a wood board, for a loaf cut. That we
should live only by bread. On essence,
     she,
with frail foolish gait, unaware
of hands, that clap thunder, squats
like one who shits, and probes life
for blood, takes God's essence, created
not in the one day God had made –
     feature by feature
blood enters existence, as one watches,
     each day, ferns
slowly unlock from rhizome their
     wings' multitudes,
their jagged feathery barbs.
                Us, jabbed
In God's derision, our malarial body, He
regards sceptically. 'Did I make this?
They who have wrecked their home,
     this caulked, kelsoned ark,
shall have an unquiet grave. I promise.'

As in jambs of air she slow-steps, her
     shade
and another's tangle darknesses, though
     small
is hers to take on death, who perforates
her wings from a listless carcass – tear,

she shags blood. Smashed and delicate.
Jagged as pine. I am finished
with God's fragment, disdain.

The slot rushes for me. In non-visible
doorways of air hovers hers. Bland is
death detaching her wings. My mind's
    winged part I fed
as best I could, on fluttering vigorous
    pity
and a torn single voice

     yours, yes, yours; yours, surely yours.

Earth falling away, we flutter a tena-
    cious
diffident mobility. Meanwhile angels
    smash
on glass. We hang transparent,
for glass is melted sand, flowing
then held, the mosquito clinging, and
    jabbing
our transparency

     yours, yes, yours; yours, truly yours

mosquito, and human, the glass between,
        but the probe jabbing,
but the flesh jabbed, the creature my
    underside

     yours, yes yours; yours, truly yours

my foolish and dark and inchoate
    underside
jabbing and drinking another's blood,
the insect's and my life, registered,
poison and essence.
     We lose what we have –

     yours, yes yours; yours, truly yours

– not the glimmer we had
     the glow worm's winking green
reversed out of darkness

     yours, yes yours: yours, truly yours.

here,
as a butcher's knife frills a carcass, from
    the clad genitals
that frenzy the human appetite, where
    those parts
are precious to the creature.
'It forms the saddest act, to make, but hate
that which I made in love.' So He grins.

On flowing sand, halted as glass, we
hang, a diffident tenacious mobility,
where angels bash, and stun, pursuing acts
of obedient goodness. If this pains,
    think what comes,
the shadowy fiend, palpable as darkness.
    Who tears
the body an evil perforates, that like a
    leather-punch
thongs its cut-outs in us. I fear
this toothsome mind that totals human
    sin.
Our flesh is porous. He who fears light
has, like wool, the moth eat him,
    burning wings,
in the dust of which, genes make him
    stub
an anxiety of flesh in light. How, huge
    and blind,
should this respect my body? The moth's
a winged leviathan, softly its jaws crack
    us,
the murderous human ones, who cap
    knees
and spill the fluid brain. 'I can tell the
    sound
a knife makes as it enters the body.'

Yours yes yours, God, we are yours

this model, us, with no prototype,
    paralleling
the inchoate jabbing one who takes
    blood. She comes
for blood, with slow-dancing intent
    pulse.
Her apparatus, curves like a gas-hose.

Yet dying, our emerald is unhurt, in
    what we had,
emerald electrified,
a glow-fly green, that darkness surges,

to shine in black, or summer's medium
  darkness
we think is indigo, needs no re-fuel,
  glimmers
a luminous being, that flummoxes
the fiend's unwinking eye, pupil, élève
of madness, in darkness unlighthoused
in his cruelty. What's it for? The
  horror-human
model of this, turns, and tears
his fellow-artist, scooping
the flesh, with composite set of nails.
  Which is common.
The mosquito sips, and gulps. God
  licenses.
Now it's time to sleep. And time to wake
into created life, before the clap
of time's short noise ceases.

The conduits

That room for billiards, now, in aunt's
  house,
is table tennis, a gramophone winding
'Policeman's Holiday,' dementing our
  families
with my putting on, again, the music's
  step and spring
in the third phrase, mother's voice
  inside the walls, 'stop,
stop that.' The music's mocking jaunt
  ends.
Lifting the listening transmitting head,
  the needle
pricks me. Now the sun is strong,
hairs powdery bees. My cousin eight, I
  reach
for my sixth year, the daisy just a day,
its male-female head, of flexible milky
  spears.
I make a chain, of small consequence,
forms mine. The bay below watches
in mute adult survival.

At ten she makes Chopin, well, eyeing
the keys' teeth, and plays for her father.
He repairs watches and lets me try
intricacy's unmendable parts, abruptly
I'm fifteen, aunt with a cancer in her
  heart;

Policeman's holiday

A basement for billiards, now in aunt's
  regimen
is table-tennis, and a gramophone
winding again 'The Policeman's
  Holiday.'
I am increasing dementia in my family
because I re-play, and rejoice in the
  music's third phrase,
its stepping melodic spring, as the voice
of mother's 'stop, stop that,' comes in
  from the walls
through the music's mocking flaunting
  end. I lift up
the listening transmitting head, the
  needle pricks
my deaf finger. Music without end.

I go beneath a verandah, into sun that
  flowers
powdery bees. My six years, but my
  cousin's eight is like
the daisy's eye. The bay gradated below
has a heart, muted, adult, surviving,
and between sea and sky, light's mutual
  domicile. Oh,
would a child know that? A child did,
and knew the daisy's palpable head, a
  double-gendered

her good-looking mother grates horse-
   radish, and, weeping,
switches my male gene to life
in uncertain potency.

In aunt-like brilliance, dry elegant
   hands
your daughter splashed the keys with,
   you bare
your head's pendulous helplessness – I
   do not kiss
the moist forehead. And with untainted
   blood,
on what is there of early manhood in
   me
you sift a portion of your shade, as if
your daughter had become another's
   bride
and grief and mourning had become
   my life,
and giving me leave, you find early
   death,
sledge-hammers in London mending
   breached conduits.

crown of milky flexible spears. In the
   grass.
I am making a chain of no consequence,
   although
no consequence forms a chain. Alien
   night breathes
and adult eyes gauge my condition.

At ten, she plays Chopin. Not bad, not
   bad, eyeing
the keys' smoky buff teeth. She plays
for her bronchial father's 'I listen', that
   appreciative
infection of culture. His talent
to mend watches, I had the yen to
   make his broken
things work. His decency, to let me mess.

I'm fifteen. Aunt has a cancer, her
   mother
housed in the same road's leafage,
   stood, wept,
and, grating the garden's savage horse-
   radish,
switched my male gene to life.

You have a cancer, nothing to do
with your aunt-like brilliance, or the
   elegant dry hands
your daughter's hammered the keys with.
You bare the pendulous helplessness of
   your head –
I do not touch your moist forehead –
and with all your untainted blood,
staring at my manhood's early
   preparations,
upon whatever there is of that in me
you pour a portion of the shade you hold
from the generous gnostic-bearing tree –
which tells us to live. I will aunt, just that,
my mother's sister, but her sister,
   receding god,
and so you leave. And yet you have not.

Sources of Previously Unpublished and Uncollected Poems

All shelf references relate to the Silkin Archive held in the Special Collections department at Leeds University Library, BC MS 20c Silkin. For the most part, it has not been possible to date individual poems precisely. Their position within this collected edition of Silkin's poems is therefore approximate.

Title/first line	Source
My enemy weeps	BC MS 20c Silkin/3/4/5.

c. 1950–1954

'Gentile, Mohhamedan'	BC MS 20c Silkin/3/1/7. Typescript (ms revisions).
Sonnet: Inside	BC MS 20c Silkin/3/1/1. Typescript (clean).
'Once I put to that root'	BC MS 20c Silkin/3/1/1. Typescript (clean).
Lyric	*Poetry Manchester*, 4 (c. 1952).
Standing Still	*Poetry Manchester*, 5 (c. 1953).
Manley's Hands	BC MS 20c Silkin/3/1/1. Typescript (clean).
The Legend	*The Poet*, 'Poetry Survey' supplement (n.d.; c. 1952–1954).
Ballad of Bored Ships	*Chanticleer*, 1:2 (Spring 1953).
The Exiles	*Chanticleer*, 1:3 (Autumn 1953).
For a mad child among mad children	BC MS 20c Silkin/3/1/1. Typescript (ms revisions).

c. 1954–1958

To My Son	BC MS 20c Silkin/3/1/7. Typescript (ms revisions).
'And on the ground rests like'	BC MS 20c Silkin/3/1/7. Typescript (ms revisions).

'She is a milk-tender beauty'	BC MS 20c Silkin/3/1/7. Typescript (ms revisions).
White	BC MS 20c Silkin/3/1/7. Typescript (ms revisions).
The Link	BC MS 20c Silkin/3/1/1. Typescript (clean).
'A shirt, shirt or nightdress flaps on the line'	BC MS 20c Silkin/3/1/1. Typescript (ms revisions).
Relationship	BC MS 20c Silkin/3/1/1. Typescript (ms revisions).
Lives in Sand	BC MS 20c Silkin/3/1/1. Typescript (ms revisions).
'Do you see this park again'	BC MS 20c Silkin/3/1/1. Typescript (ms revisions).
The Confidence Trick	BC MS 20c Silkin/3/1/7. Typescript (ms revisions).
Easter Day: Victim	BC MS 20c Silkin/3/1/1. Typescript (ms revisions).
Speaking to the Conqueror	BC MS 20c Silkin/3/1/3. Typescript (clean).
Kierkegaard the cripple, addressing his God...	BC MS 20c Silkin/3/1/1. Manuscript (clean).
Rock	*Listen* (c. 1954).
The Forests	*African Affairs: Journal of the Royal African Society*, 55:218 (January 1956).
War Song to an Ocean Headland	BC MS 20c Silkin/3/1/1. Typescript (clean).
'By that house where we met'	BC MS 20c Silkin/3/1/7. Typescript (ms revisions).
'No tree spreads in this garden'	BC MS 20c Silkin/3/1/1. Typescript (ms revisions).
Park	BC MS 20c Silkin/3/1/7. Typescript (ms revisions).
Blossom	BC MS 20c Silkin/3/1/1. Typescript (clean).
Things	BC MS 20c Silkin/3/1/1. Typescript (ms revisions).

c. 1958–1961

A Walk in the Sun	BC MS 20c Silkin/3/1/5. Typescript (ms revisions).
'A handkerchief'	BC MS 20c Silkin/3/1/6. Typescript (clean).

Palinurus	BC MS 20c Silkin/3/1/3. Typescript (ms revisions).
The Making Act	BC MS 20c Silkin/3/1/5. Typescript (ms revisions).
For the disestablishing of Authority	BC MS 20c Silkin/3/1/3. Typescript (ms revisions).
For the Poor: Poem on the City of Leeds Rubbish Tip	*Poetry and Audience*, 6:7 (21 November 1958). Also BC MS 20c Silkin/ 3/1/7. Typescript (ms revisions).
Tip	*Poetry and Audience*, 7:2 (23 October 1959). Also BC MS 20c Silkin/ 3/1/5. Typescript (clean).
Conversion to Stone	BC MS 20c Silkin/3/1/2. Typescript (clean).
'The choked bird twitters in the organ pipe'	BC MS 20c Silkin/3/1/2. Typescript (ms revisions).
A Friend	BC MS 20c Silkin/3/1/6. Typescript (clean).
No civilized music here	BC MS 20c Silkin/3/1/7. Typescript (ms revisions).
Passing	BC MS 20c Silkin/3/1/1. Typescript (ms revisions).
Painting of a Woman	BC MS 20c Silkin/3/1/3. Typescript (clean).
'Walking, starved and avid'	BC MS 20c Silkin/3/1/3. Typescript (clean).
'I have not the purity'	BC MS 20c Silkin/3/1/3. Typescript (clean).
From the inside of the wilderness	BC MS 20c Silkin/3/1/3. Typescript (clean).
When First I Saw	BC MS 20c Silkin/3/1/3. Typescript (ms revisions).
Separation	BC MS 20c Silkin/3/1/3. Typescript (ms revisions).
Speech for a Politician	BC MS 20c Silkin/3/1/5. Typescript (clean).
Europe	BC MS 20c Silkin/3/1/7. Typescript (clean).
A New Country	BC MS 20c Silkin/3/1/6. Typescript (with revisions).
Going Away	BC MS 20c Silkin/3/1/2. Typescript (clean).
A Space Together	BC MS 20c Silkin/3/1/5. Typescript (clean).

'Listen to that sensual muse or paraclete'	BC MS 20c Silkin/3/1/3. Manuscript (with revisions).
'An image conceives in its meaning'	BC MS 20c Silkin/3/1/5. Manuscript (with revisions).
Living	BC MS 20c Silkin/3/1/1. Typescript (clean).

c. 1961–1965

Great!	BC MS 20c Silkin/3/1/8. Typescript (clean).
'Much did you think'	BC MS 20c Silkin/3/1/5. Typescript (ms revisions).
Nearly	BC MS 20c Silkin/3/1/6. Typescript (clean).
Why We Are All Socialists	BC MS 20c Silkin/3/1/6. Typescript (clean).
What Each Person Wants	BC MS 20c Silkin/3/1/6. Typescript (ms revisions).
Reality, and other places	BC MS 20c Silkin/3/1/4. Typescript (ms revisions).
'The poems of Clare's madness'	BC MS 20c Silkin/3/1/9. Typescript (ms revisions).
Some Changes	*Poetry and Audience* (March 1962).
'I am angry, which means little'	BC MS 20c Silkin/3/1/5. Manuscript (with revisions).
Circus	BC MS 20c Silkin/3/1/4. Typescript (ms revisions).
For the Dead Woman's Husband	BC MS 20c Silkin/3/1/7. Typescript (ms revisions).
'A girl danced, and she seemed'	BC MS 20c Silkin/3/1/1. Typescript (ms revisions).
The Landlord	BC MS 20c Silkin/3/1/6. Typescript (ms revisions).
The Bugs	BC MS 20c Silkin/3/1/9. Typescript (ms revision).
Choosing	BC MS 20c Silkin/3/1/6. Typescript (clean).
This Man in Pain	BC MS 20c Silkin/3/1/5. Typescript (clean).
At Durham	BC MS 20c Silkin/3/1/5. Typescript (ms revisions).
The Expulsion of Pain	BC MS 20c Silkin/3/1/5. Typescript (clean).

Lindisfarne	BC MS 20c Silkin/3/1/7. Typescript (ms revisions).
Which Kind do we Belong To?	BC MS 20c Silkin/3/1/5. Typescript (clean).
Going On	BC MS 20c Silkin/3/1/4. Typescript (clean).
An Age of Copper	BC MS 20c Silkin/3/1/5. Typescript (ms revisions).
The Island	BC MS 20c Silkin/3/1/4. Manuscript (with revisions).
Warriors	BC MS 20c Silkin/3/1/8. Typescript (ms revisions).
Ruthlessly	BC MS 20c Silkin/3/1/9. Typescript (ms revisions).
The Terms	BC MS 20c Silkin/3/1/9. Typescript (ms revisions).
'Was it, you say, because'	BC MS 20c Silkin/3/1/9. Typescript (ms revisions).
Two Women and a Man	BC MS 20c Silkin/3/1/9. Typescript (clean).
Hatred	BC MS 20c Silkin/3/1/4. Typescript (ms revisions).
Crocus	BC MS 20c Silkin/3/1/8. Typescript (ms revisions).
Sparrow	BC MS 20c Silkin/3/1/8. Typescript (clean).
Our Country	BC MS 20c Silkin/3/1/8. Typescript (clean).
The System, or what it said last	BC MS 20c Silkin/3/1/8. Typescript (ms revisions).

c. 1965–1971

Water Dispute	BC MS 20c Silkin/3/2/3. Typescript (ms revisions).
Seeds of Lead	BC MS 20c Silkin/3/2/9. Manuscript (with revisions).
A Forest Tale	BC MS 20c Silkin/3/2/9. Manuscript (with revisions).
'Concrete'	BC MS 20c Silkin/3/2/8. Typescript (ms revisions).
'Kevin, can you remember'	BC MS 20c Silkin/3/2/8. Typescript (clean).
Sea Anemone	BC MS 20c Silkin/3/2/3. Typescript (clean).

Snake	BC MS 20c Silkin/3/2/3. Typescript (clean).
Waste	BC MS 20c Silkin/3/2/6. Typescript (ms revisions).

c. 1971–1974

Lovers	BC MS 20c Silkin/3/2/6. Typescript (clean).
'My marriage day dressed'	BC MS 20c Silkin/3/2/1. Typescript (ms revision).
Wanting better	BC MS 20c Silkin/3/2/7. Typescript (clean).
The Clay Image	BC MS 20c Silkin/3/2/6. Typescript (clean).
'Beneath the hedgerows'	BC MS 20c Silkin/3/2/6. Typescript (ms revisions).
'The forehead rises a distance'	BC MS 20c Silkin/3/2/8. Typescript (ms revisions).
Life in the field	BC MS 20c Silkin/3/2/7. Typescript (ms revisions).
'All-eying moon, fury'	BC MS 20c Silkin/3/2/1. Typescript (ms revisions).

c. 1974–1976

'Where much grass drinks from its side'	BC MS 20c Silkin/3/2/3. Manuscript (with revisions).
'The map hovers open'	BC MS 20c Silkin/3/2/2. Typescript (ms revisions).

c. 1976–1980

In Mary's reign Justice Barton convicts…	BC MS 20c Silkin/3/2/2. Typescript (clean).
Samson's Hair	BC MS 20c Silkin/3/2/5. Typescript (ms revisions).
Six Poems from Metoula	BC MS 20c Silkin/3/2/5. Manuscript (with revisions).
Else Lasker-Schüler in Jerusalem	BC MS 20c Silkin/3/2/5. Typescript (ms revisions).
'A black sun streams its fresh medicinal'	*New Statesman*, 21 March 1980. Also BC MS 20c Silkin/3/4/16. Typescript (clean).
'A tram runs, and the soft flesh spills itself'	*New Statesman*, 18 April 1980. Also BC MS 20c Silkin/3/4/16. Typescript (clean).

'The back of the heart empties'	BC MS 20c Silkin/3/2/4. Typescript (ms revisions).
Condemned	BC MS 20c Silkin/3/2/5. Manuscript (with revisions).

c. 1980–1986

Filaments of the plain	BC MS 20c Silkin/3/3/26. Typescript (ms revisions).
'The broad Ohio'	BC MS 20c Silkin/3/3/29. Typescript (ms revisions).
Imprint	BC MS 20c Silkin/3/3/26. Typescript (ms revisions).
Opposed to death	BC MS 20c Silkin/3/3/26. Typescript (ms revisions).
The father	BC MS 20c Silkin/3/3/26. Typescript (ms revisions).
Tenderness	BC MS 20c Silkin/3/3/10. Typescript (ms revisions).

c. 1986–1992

Alpine	BC MS 20c Silkin/3/3/21. Typescript (clean).
A woman from Giannedes	*Lines Review*, 100 (March 1987).
Chrysalid	BC MS 20c Silkin/3/3/28. Typescript (clean).
A box of seeds	BC MS 20c Silkin/3/3/21. Typescript (clean).
Veining	BC MS 20c Silkin/3/3/13. Typescript (ms revisions).
The life that is marriage	BC MS 20c Silkin/3/3/28. Typescript (clean).
Words from below the level of speech	BC MS 20c Silkin/3/3/28. Typescript (clean).
'A leash rests its chain and clasp'	BC MS 20c Silkin/3/3/24. Typescript (ms revisions).
A tyrant changes the body	BC MS 20c Silkin/3/3/28. Typescript (clean).
A soldier visits home (L'étranger)	BC MS 20c Silkin/3/3/28. Typescript (clean).
My father's language was German	BC MS 20c Silkin/3/3/28. Typescript (ms revisions).
Hospital	BC MS 20c Silkin/3/3/21. Typescript (clean).

Duplicity	BC MS 20c Silkin/3/3/28. Typescript (ms revisions).
Daughter abandoned	BC MS 20c Silkin/3/3/28. Typescript (clean).
The Gallovidian martyrs…	BC MS 20c Silkin/3/4/16. Typescript (ms revisions).
Fathering	BC MS 20c Silkin/3/4/9. Typescript (clean).
Grass	BC MS 20c Silkin/3/4/9. Typescript (clean).

c. 1992–1997

Two women	BC MS 20c Silkin/3/4/16A. Typescript (ms revisions).
Jubilate	BC MS 20c Silkin/3/4/5. Typescript (clean).
Into the triangular yard	BC MS 20c Silkin/3/4/5. Typescript (clean).
Useful poem	BC MS 20c Silkin/3/4/5. Typescript (ms revisions).
Japan, exposure	BC MS 20c Silkin/3/4/7. Typescript (ms revisions).
Three poems	BC MS 20c Silkin/3/4/5. Typescript (clean).
I love this creature despite all	BC MS 20c Silkin/3/4/7. Typescript (ms revisions).
Aggression	BC MS 20c Silkin/3/4/16. Typescript (ms revisions).
Where will you find her?	BC MS 20c Silkin/3/4/17. Typescript (ms revisions).
'The soul is ghosted from its flesh'	BC MS 20c Silkin/3/4/12. Typescript (ms revisions).
Father, and the switch	BC MS 20c Silkin/3/4/7. Typescript (ms revisions).
Sally sally	BC MS 20c Silkin/3/4/13. Typescript (ms revisions).
'God said, "in this lifting rim of your life…"'	BC MS 20c Silkin/3/4/12. Typescript (ms revisions).
Relations	BC MS 20c Silkin/3/4/12. Typescript (ms revisions).
A self-directing psalm	BC MS 20c Silkin/3/4/14. Typescript (ms revisions).
The line	BC MS 20c Silkin/3/4/12. Typescript (clean).

'To Jerusalem'	BC MS 20c Silkin/3/4/19. Typescript (ms revisions).
Good opportunity	BC MS 20c Silkin/3/4/6. Typescript (ms revisions).
Los Borrachos (The drinkers)	BC MS 20c Silkin/3/4/18. Typescript (clean).
Wales of the Welsh	BC MS 20c Silkin/3/4/14. Typescript (ms revisions).

Appendix

Living	BC MS 20c Silkin/3/1/4. Typescript (clean).
A good farmer	Rochester, NY: The Valley Press, 1972.
Air that Pricks Earth with Life	*Fuse* (November 1972).
Emmanuel	BC MS 20c Silkin/3/1/1. Typescript (ms revisions).
Black-eye bean	BC MS 20c Silkin/3/1/7, Typescript (ms revisions); BC MS 20c Silkin/3/1/8, Typescript (clean).
On glass	BC MS 20c Silkin/3/4/12. Typescript (clean).
The originals	BC MS 20c Silkin/3/4/5. Typescript (ms revisions).
The conduits	BC MS 20c Silkin/3/4/18. Typescript (clean).
Policeman's holiday	BC MS 20c Silkin/3/4/17. Typescript (clean).

Select Bibliography

Poetry Collections

The Peaceable Kingdom (London: Chatto & Windus, 1954)

The Two Freedoms (London: Chatto & Windus, 1958)

The Re-ordering of the Stones (London: Chatto & Windus, 1961)

Nature with Man (London: Chatto & Windus, 1965)

Poems New and Selected (Middleton, CT: Wesleyan University Press/ London: Chatto & Windus, 1966)

Amana Grass (Middleton, CT: Wesleyan University Press/London: Chatto & Windus, 1971)

The Principle of Water (Cheadle: Carcanet Press, 1974)

The Peaceable Kingdom: Poems Newly Revised, with afterword by Merle Brown (Boston, MA: The Heron Press, 1975)

The Little Time-keeper (Ashington: Mid-Northumberland Arts Group/ Manchester: Carcanet/Sydney: Wild & Woolley/New York: Norton, 1976)

The Psalms with their Spoils (London: Routledge and Kegan Paul, 1980)

Selected Poems (London: Routledge and Kegan Paul, 1980)

The Ship's Pasture (London: Routledge and Kegan Paul, 1986)

The Lens-Breakers (London: Sinclair Stevenson, 1992)

Selected Poems (London: Sinclair-Stervenson, 1993)

Making a Republic (Manchester: Carcanet/Northern House, 2002)

Pamphlets

The Portrait and Other Poems (Ilfracombe: Stockwell, 1950)

Flower Poems (Leeds: Northern House, 1964)

Three Poems (Cambridge, MA: Pym Randall Press, 1969)

Killhope Wheel (Ashington: Mid-Northumberland Arts Group, 1971)

A good farmer (Rochester, NY: The Valley Press, 1972)

Air that pricks earth (Rushden: Sceptre Press, 1973)

A 'Jarapiri' Poem (Knotting: Sceptre Press, 1975)

Two Images of Continuing Trouble, with drawing by Alison Dalwood (Richmond: Keepsake Press, 1976)

Jerusalem (Knotting: Sceptre Press, 1977)

Flower Poems, 2nd edn (Newcastle: Northern House, 1978)

Into Praising, with photographs by Edward Easydorchik (Sunderland: Ceolfrith Press, 1978)

The Lapidary Poems (Knotting: Sceptre Press, 1979)

Autobiographical Stanzas (Durham: Taxus, 1983)

Footsteps on a Downcast Path (Bath: Mammon Press, 1984)

Watersmeet (Whitley Bay: The Bay Press, 1994)

Testament Without Breath (Cornwall: Cargo Press, 1997)

Snow Flies and other poems, with translations into Japanese by Toshiko Fujioka (Japan: n.p., n.d [c. 1998])

Anthologies and Selections

New Poets of England and America, ed. Donald Hall, Robert Pack and Louis Simpson, with an introduction by Robert Frost (New York: Meridian Books, 1957)

New Poets of England and America, ed. Donald Hall, Robert Pack and Louis Simpson. Second Selection (New York: Meridian Books, 1962)

Penguin Modern Poets 7: Jon Silkin, Richard Murphy, Nathaniel Tarn (Harmondsworth: Penguin, 1965)

Vernon Watkins and Jon Silkin: Poems (London: Longmans, Green, 1969)

The World's Contracted Thus, ed. J.A. and J.K. Thornton (Port Melbourne, Australia: Heinemann, 1975)

Anthology of Twentieth-Century British and Irish Poetry, ed. Keith Tuma (Oxford and New York: Oxford University Press, 2001)

Passionate Renewal: Jewish Poetry in Britain Since 1945, ed. Peter Lawson (Nottingham: Five Leaves Publications 2001)

Translations by Jon Silkin

Natan Zach, *Against Parting* (Newcastle: Northern House, 1967)

Translations of Jon Silkin

Anthologie bilingue de la poésie anglaise (Paris: Editions Gallimard, 2005)

Edited Works (selected and/or introduced by Jon Silkin)

The Town and Country School: An Anthology, with preface by Elizabeth Paul and Jon Silkin (London: The Town and Country School, 1956)

Living Voices, selected by Jon Silkin (London: Vista Books, 1960)

Flash Point: An Anthology of Modern Poetry, compiled by Robert Shaw with an introduction by Jon Silkin (Leeds: E.J. Arnold, 1960)

New Poems 1960: PEN Anthology, ed. Jon Silkin, Anthony Cronin and Terence Tiller (London: Hutchinson, 1960)

Pergamon Poets VIII, ed. Jon Silkin and Vernon Scannell (Oxford: Pergamon, 1969)

Poetry of the Committed Individual: A Stand Anthology of Poetry, ed. Jon Silkin (London: Gollancz/Harmondsworth: Penguin, 1973)

The Penguin Book of First World War Poetry, ed. Jon Silkin (London: Penguin, 1979)

New Poetry 5: An Arts Council Anthology, ed. Jon Silkin and Peter Redgrove (London: Hutchinson, 1979)

The Penguin Book of First World War Prose, ed. Jon Silkin and Jon Glover (London: Penguin, 1989)

Wilfred Owen: The War Poems, ed. Jon Silkin (London: Sinclair Stevenson, 1994)

An Anthology of Twentieth Century English Poetry, selected with commentary by Jon Silkin (Tokyo: Kenkyusha, 1994)

Drama

Gurney: A Play (Cullercoats, North Shields, Tyne & Wear: Iron Press Drama Editions, 1985)

Criticism by Jon Silkin

The list below covers as much of Jon Silkin's critical writing as we can find. The items are listed in date order of publication. We include the major critical books as well as short articles and reviews. It is an amazing achievement given that he was also writing poetry, and editing and selling *Stand*.

We have included much of his prose writing from *Stand*, though not every Editorial or Note. It is notable that he was making contacts in America from the mid-1950s, soon after the publication of *The Peaceable Kingdom*. The criticism also shows how far writing poetry, editing and publishing it, reflecting on it, and discussing it with others was an integral whole from Silkin's earliest days as a writer.

'The fields far and near', *Poetry* (Chicago), vol. 88 no. 6 (September 1956) [on Edwin Muir's *One Foot in Eden*]

'The Poetry of Isaac Rosenberg', in *Isaac Rosenberg*, exhibition catalogue (Leeds: University of Leeds, 1959)

'On his Flower Poems', *The Glasgow Review*, vol. 1 no. 4 (Winter 1964–65)

'The Forgotten Poet of Anglo-Jewry', *The Jewish Chronicle* (26 August 1960) [on Isaac Rosenberg]

'Rosenberg's Rat-God', *European Judaism*, vol. 4 no. 2 (Summer 1970)

Out of Battle: The Poetry of the Great War (London: Oxford University Press, 1972)

'The Poetry of Geoffrey Hill', *The Iowa Review*, no. 3 (1972)

'The Poetry of Geoffrey Hill', *British Poetry Since 1960*, ed. Grevel Lindop and Michael Schmidt (Oxford: Carcanet, 1972)

'The Identifiable Culture', *Southerly*, vol. 34 (1974)

'A New Cosmopolitanism?', *Southerly*, vol. 35 no. 2 (1975) [review of *New Poetry*, vol. 21 nos. 5 & 6, broadcast on *Books and Ideas* 1974, and printed with acknowledgment to ABC]

'The Identifiable Culture', *Southerly*, no. 3 (1975)

'For Rosenberg', *New York Review of Books* (19 February 1976)

Review of Paul Fussell's *The Great War and Modern Memory*, *The Review of English Studies*, vol. 28 no. 110 (May 1977)

'Polarities', *Poetry* (Chicago), vol. 130 no. 4 (July 1977) [review of books by R.S. Thomas, Edward Braithwaite, Peter Scupham, Michael Schmidt]

'Edward Hicks (1780–1849): The Peaceable Kingdom', *Stand*, vol. 19 no. 2 (1978)

'Which England Shall We Labor for? A Reply to Donald Davie's Conservative England', *Parnassus: Poetry in Review* (Fall/Winter 1978–79)

'Dead Man's Dump', *New Statesman* (20 April 1979) [on Isaac Rosenberg]

'The Silence Round All Poetry', *Poetry Review*, vol. 69 no. 1 (July 1979) [review of Tony Harrison's *From the School of Eloquence and other poems*]

'Ethics and Aesthetics', *The Tablet* (29 September 1979) [on Roy Fisher]

'Triumphant Silence: Some Aspects of Sidney Keyes, 1922–1943', *London Magazine* (April–May 1980)

'The Survival of Talent', *Stand*, vol. 21 no. 2 (1980) [on Michael Hurd's *The Ordeal of Ivor Gurney*]

'Keith Douglas', *Agenda*, vol. 19, nos. 2–3 (1981)

'David Gascoyne', *Agenda*, vol. 19 nos. 2–3 (1981)

'Working Someone Else's Poem', *Modern Poetry in Translation*, 41–42 (1981) [discusses translating Israeli poet Amir Gilboa]

'What kind of language is that?', *English in Education*, vol. 15 no. 1 (Spring 1981)

'A Double Burden', *Poetry Review*, vol. 70 no. 4 (March 1981) [review of Paul Celan, *Poems*, translated, selected and introduced by Michael Hamburger]

[Review of Patrick Galvin, *Man on the Porch: Selected Poems*], *Cyphers*, no. 14 (Spring 1981)

'The Unfolding Repetition', *Poetry Review*, vol. 71 no. 4 (1981) [review of *The Complete Poems of D.H. Lawrence*, ed. Vivian da Sola Pinto and Warren F. Roberts]

'Whitman's Canary', *The Poet's Voice* (1981)

'Quick Man: D.H. Lawrence's Poetry', *Stand*, vol. 23 no. 1 (1981–82)

'Stepney scarecrow', *The Times Literary Supplement* (16 April 1982) [on 'Rosenberg in the Trenches' broadcast on BBC radio]

'The Pity of War', Harrogate Festival Programme (27 July–10 August 1982) [introduction to a reading by Silkin and Frances Horovitz]

'Narrative Distances: An Element in Lawrence's Poetry', *Critical Quarterly*, vol. 27 no. 3 (1985) [also appeared in *Equivalencias* (Spring 1982)]

'Gene Baro: Obituary', *Stand*, vol. 24 no. 4 (1983)

'Whitman's Canary', *Equivalencias*, no. 7 (1983) [with substantial quotations and printed in Spanish and English on facing pages]

'Hebrew Visions of War', *Ariel*, 64 (1986)

'Sassoon, Owen, Rosenberg', in *English Literature of the Great War Revisited*, ed. Michael Roncoux (Presses de l'UFR Université Picardie, 1986) [proceedings of symposium]

'Critics and the Literature of the First World War', *British Book News* (November 1987)

'Feeling and morality: a survival from the Sixties', *Agenda*, vol. 30 no. 3 (Autumn 1992) [essay on John Bayley mentioning Silkin on Geoffrey Hill's 'September Song', with a reply from John Bayley and a further reply from Silkin]

'Living Through the Sixties', *Agenda*, vol. 31 no. 2 (Summer 1993)

'Jon Glover', *Contemporary Poets*, ed. Thomas Riggs, with a preface by Anthony Thwaite (Detroit: St James Press, 1996) [with comments from Jon Glover]

'Arthur Jacobs, Poet', in Arthur Jacobs, *Collected Poems and Selected Translations*, ed. John Rety and Anthony Rudolf, with foreword by Jon Silkin (London: The Menard Press/Hearing Eye in association with the European Jewish Publication Society, 1996)

'Look for It in the Pity: A Note on the Change in Hamburger's Poetry', *Agenda*, vol. 35 no. 3 (Autumn 1997)

The Life of Metrical and Free Verse in Twentieth Century Poetry (London and New York: Macmillan & St Martin's Press, 1997)

Journal discussions

'Poets on the Vietnam War', *The Review*, no. 18 (1968) [with contributions from Jon Silkin and others]

'Poetry 1970: A Questionnaire', *Tracks and Tamarisk* (Summer 1970) [with contributions from Jon Silkin and others]

'The State of Poetry: A Symposium', *The Review*, 10th Anniversary Issue, nos. 29–30 (Spring/Summer 1972) [with a contribution from Jon Silkin]

'Common Values? An Argument', including Michael Schmidt, '*Stand* Symposium on "Commitment"', and Jon Silkin, 'A reply to Michael Schmidt', *Stand*, vol. 20 no.1 (1979); Jon Silkin, 'The Rights of England', and Donald Davie, 'A Rejoinder to Jon Silkin', *Stand*, vol. 20 no. 2 (1979)

Dominic Hibbert, 'Silkin on Owen: Some Other War', followed by Jon Silkin, 'Owen: Elegist, Satirist, or Neither: a reply to Dominic Hibbert', *Stand*, vol. 21 no. 3 (1980)

Blake Morrison et al., 'Little Magazines', *Times Literary Supplement* (16 June 1978). Letters in response appeared weekly in following issues, including Jon Silkin's, *TLS* (30 June 1978 and 21 July 1978)

Jon Silkin, 'An editorial impasse', *Times Literary Supplement* (25 July 1986), followed by letters from Jon Stallworthy, *TLS* (15 August 1986), and Jon Silkin and John A.C. Griffin, *TLS* (29 August 1986) [on copyright and Wilfred Owen]

Jon Silkin, Douglas Kerr and Kenneth Muir: debate in four issues of *Connotations: A Journal for Critical Debate*. Muir, 'Connotations of "Strange Meeting"', *Connotations*, vol. 3 no. 1 (1993); Kerr, '"Strange Meeting" Again', *Connotations*, vol. 3 no. 2 (1994); Silkin, '"Strange Meeting" a Fragment? A Reply to Muir's "Owen"', *Connotations*, vol. 3 no. 2 (1993–94); Muir, '"Strange Meeting" Yet Again', *Connotations*, vol. 3 no. 3 (1993–94); Silkin, 'Owen's strange "Meeting": A Note for Professor Muir', *Connotations*, vol. 4 nos. 1–2 (1994–95)

Criticism on Jon Silkin

Listed here are articles, books and chapters in books which are concerned with Jon Silkin, his poetry and some of his major interests and contexts. Some are substantial and demanding; some of the references are brief or form part of a study on another matter but include Silkin as a point of comparison or background. In some cases the references, however short or occasional, suggest links and themes.

Silkin writes almost obsessively about Geoffrey Hill's poetry. Hill's allusions, for example, to Silkin on Ivor Gurney, hint at common interests. Silkin wrote about Gurney in articles and books. Christopher Ricks quoted Silkin at length on Hill's 'September Song', and that now appears on the web in many academics' reading lists as exemplary 'close reading'. We are not identifying a hidden conspiracy or intentions which are bound to be fallacious. The list also reveals that both have a commitment to the poetry of Isaac Rosenberg and D.H. Lawrence. We hope that the list will provide suggestions for reading and response to those great poets and that they will lead more deeply into Silkin's *Complete Poems*.

Bonamy Dobrée, 'English Poets Today: The Younger Generation', *The Sewanee Review*, vol. 62 no. 4 (Autumn 1954)

'News Notes', *Poetry* (Chicago), vol. 88 no. 4 (July 1956) [mentions *Stand*]

Geoffrey Hill, 'The Poetry of Jon Silkin', *Poetry and Audience*, vol. 9 no. 12 (1962)

'Jon Silkin', in *The Concise Encyclopedia of English and American Poets and Poetry*, ed. Stephen Spender and Donald Hall (London: Hutchinson, 1963)

Frederick Grubb, *A Vision of Reality: A Study of Liberalism in Twentieth Century Verse* (London: Chatto & Windus, 1965)

A.J. Gurr, 'Poetry in Pamphlets', *A Review of English Literature*, vol. 8 no. 1 (January 1967)

Michael Hamburger, Chapters 9 and 10 in *The Truth of Poetry: Tensions in Modern Poetry from Baudelaire to the 1960s* (London: Weidenfeld and Nicolson, 1969)

Anne Cluysenaar, 'Alone in a Mine of Reality: A Matrix in the Poetry of Jon Silkin', *British Poetry since 1960*, ed. Grevel Lindop and Michael Schmidt (Oxford: Carcanet, 1972)

W.E. Parkinson, 'Poetry in the North East', *British Poetry since 1960*, ed. Grevel Lindop and Michael Schmidt (Oxford: Carcanet, 1972)

Charles Tomlinson, 'Poetry Today', *The Pelican Guide to English Literature*, vol. 7, 3rd edn (Harmondsworth: Penguin, 1973)

John Berryman, 'Despondency and Madness: On Lowell's "Skunk Hour"', in John Berryman, *The Freedom of the Poet* (New York: Farrar, Straus & Giroux, 1976)

Merle Brown, 'Stress in Silkin's Poetry', *Contemporary Literature*, vol. 18 no. 3 (Summer 1977)

Mark Abley, 'The Hand that Erases', *Oxford Literary Journal* (Spring 1977)

Geoffrey Hill, 'Poetry as "Menace" and "Atonement"', *University of Leeds Review*, vol. 21 (1978) [Hill's inaugural lecture at the University of Leeds, 3 December 1977; also collected in his *Collected Critical Writings* (Oxford: Oxford University Press, 2008)]

William Baker, 'Reflections on Anglo-Jewish Poetry', *The Jewish Quarterly*, vol. 26 nos. 3–4 (1978–79)

Blake Morrison, 'Upper Grub Street', *Encounter*, vol. 53 no. 1 (July 1979)

Hugh Underhill, 'Kinds of Seriousness in Poems by Ben Jonson and Jon Silkin', *Ariel*, vol. 10 no. 4 (1979)

Michael Schmidt, *An Introduction to Fifty Modern British Poets* (London: Pan Books, 1979)

Voices Within the Ark: The Modern Jewish Poets, ed. Howard Schwartz and Anthony Rudolf (New York: Avon Books, 1980)

Merle E. Brown, *Double Lyric* (London: Routledge & Kegan Paul, 1980)

Jon Glover, 'Jon Silkin: The Voice in the Peaceable Kingdom', *Bananas*, no. 20 (April 1980)

Poetry Review, vol. 69 no. 4 (1980) – *Jon Silkin Special Issue*, ed. Roger Garfitt, with articles by Jeffrey Wainwright, Terry Eagleton, Lawrence Sail, Jon Glover, Anne Cluysenaar, Paul Mills

Christopher Ricks, *The Force of Poetry* (Oxford: Clarendon Press, 1984)

Jochen Achilles, 'Wirklichkeitsspaltung, Liebeswunsch und Todesnähe in der Dichtung Jon Silkin', in *Britische Lyrik der Gegenwart*, ed. Iain Galbraith (Mainz: E. Weiss Verlag, 1984)

Martin Booth, *British Poetry 1964 to 1984* (London: Routledge & Kegan Paul, 1985)

Geoffrey Hill, 'Gurney's "Hobby"', *Essays in Criticism*, vol. 34 (1984) [F.W. Bateson Annual Memorial Lecture; also collected in his *Collected Critical Writings* (Oxford: Oxford University Press, 2008)]

Holger Klein, 'Jon Silkin's "The Coldness"', *Stand*, vol. 27 no. 3 (1986)

'Jon Silkin', in *The Cambridge Guide to Literature in English*, ed. Ian Ousby (Cambridge: Cambridge University Press, 1988)

Roger K. Meiners, 'Mourning for ourselves and for poetry: the lyric after Auschwitz', *The Centennial Review*, vol. 35 no. 3 (Fall 1991)

Avril Pyman, 'Twentieth-Century Russian Poetry in *Stand*', in *Symbolism and After*, ed. Arnold McMillin (Bristol: Classical Press/London: Duckworth, 1992)

Eric Mottram, 'The British Poetry Revival', in *New British Poetries: The Scope of the Possible*, ed. Robert Hampson and Peter Barry (Manchester: Manchester University Press, 1993)

R.J. Ellis, 'Mapping the UK little magazine field', in *New British Poetries: The Scope of the Possible*, ed. Robert Hampson and Peter Barry (Manchester: Manchester University Press, 1993)

Edward Larrissy, 'Jon Silkin', in *The Oxford Companion to Twentieth-Century Poetry in English*, ed. Ian Hamilton (Oxford: Oxford University Press, 1994)

Jon Glover, 'Things Divided, Things Beyond: Jon Silkin's Recent Poem Sequences', *The Poet's Voice*, n.s. no. 2 (December 1995)

Romana Huk, 'Poetry of the Committed Individual: Jon Silkin, Tony Harrison and Geoffrey Hill, and the Poets of Postwar Leeds', in *Contemporary British Poetry: Essays in Theory and Criticism*, ed. James Acheson and Romana Huk (Albany: State University of New York Press, 1996)

Ian Gregson, *Contemporary Poetry and Postmodernism: Dialogue and Estrangement* (Basingstoke: Macmillan, 1996)

Peter Childs, *The Twentieth Century in Poetry: A Critical Survey* (London: Routlege, 1999)

Jill Sharp, *Written in Stone: England's Literary Heritage* (London: English Heritage, 2005)

Antony Rowland, *Holocaust Poetry* (Edinburgh: Edinburgh University Press, 2005)

Peter Lawson, *Anglo-Jewish Poetry from Isaac Rosenberg to Elaine Feinstein*, with a foreword by Anthony Rudolf (Edgeware, Middlesex and Portland, OR: Vallentine Mitchell, 2006)

Jon Glover, 'Editorial', *Stand*, vol. 11 no. 3 (2013) [on Silkin, *Stand* and the founding of Northern House]

John Greening, 'Something Else… Jon Silkin and the Music of Division', *Stand*, vol. 11 no. 3 (2013)

Ag Jones, 'The Selling Fields', *Stand*, vol. 11 no. 3 (2013)

Hannah Copley, 'Committed Rootlessness: The Anglo-Jewish Perspective and Rhetoric of Jon Silkin', *Stand*, vol. 11 no. 4 (2013)

Hannah Copley and Emma Trott, 'A Joint Editorial', *Stand*, vol. 11 no. 4 (2013) [on Silkin's legacy as an editor to new editors]

Jon Glover, 'The 1959 Isaac Rosenberg Exhibition in Leeds: Annie Wynick and Isaac Rosenberg's Work Amongst the Living', *Stand*, vol. 11 no. 4 (2013)

Anthony Rudolf, *Silent Conversations* (Chicago: Seagull Press, 2013)

Interviews, biographies, memoirs and obituaries

'No politics, no poetry', *Stand*, vol. 6 no. 2 (1963) [discussion between Jon Silkin and Anthony Thwaite]

Raymond Gardner, 'Silkin Purse', *The Guardian* (26 March 1971) [interview]

'Attend to the Unnecessary Beasts', *Vanderbilt Poetry Review*, vol. 1 no. 2 (Summer 1973) [conversation between Jon Silkin, Peter Marchant and Michael Waters in the Writers Forum series at State University of New York, Brockport, 4 November 1971]

'The Small Magazine since 1960', in *British Poetry since 1960*, ed. Grevel Lindop and Michael Schmidt (Oxford: Carcanet, 1972) [recorded conversation with Jon Silkin]

Mike Duggan, 'From the soul of Silkin', *The Journal Newcastle* (1 September 1979); *Northern Echo* (1 September 1979) [interview]

Peter Lawson, 'Interview: Jon Silkin', *Sphagnum*, no. 11 [1982?][interview conducted at the University of York, 19 November 1981]

Roger Garfitt, 'Jon Silkin', in *Poets of Great Britain and Ireland 1945–1960*, ed. V.B. Sherry Jr., *Dictionary of Literary Biography*, vol. 27 (Columbia: Bruccoli Clark, 1984)

45 Contemporary Poems: The Creative Process, ed. Alberta Turner (New York and London: Longman, 1985) [with Jon Silkin's answers to the editor's questions on composing 'The Child']

Jon Silkin, 'The First Twenty-Four Years', *Contemporary Authors: Autobiography Series* (Michigan: Gale, 1987)

Lloyd Parry, 'Interview with the Committed Individual', *Isis*, no. 1 (1989)

Stephen Forster, 'Interview with Jon Silkin', *Printed Matter*, vol. 15 no. 2 (Summer 1991)

Lyuben Lyubenov [interview on translating poetry], *English for Everyone* (May 1992)

Antonio Casella, 'Interview with Jon Silkin, Editor of *Stand*', *Ulitarra* (1996) [interview conducted in Newcastle upon Tyne, February 1996]

Carol Simpson Stern, 'Jon Silkin', in *Contemporary Poets*, ed. Thomas Riggs, with a preface by Anthony Thwaite (Detroit: St James Press, 1996) [with comments from Jon Silkin]

Rodney Pybus, 'Jon Silkin', *The Independent* (1 December 1997) [obituary]

Peter Forbes, 'Standing up for poetry', *The Guardian* (1 December 1997) [obituary with an additional column by Lawrence Sail]

Anon., 'Jon Silkin', *The Times* (1 December 1997) [obituary]

Jon Glover, 'Poetry powered by personal tensions', *The Guardian* (4 December 1997) [an appreciation]

Anon., 'Jon Silkin: bleak poet and magazine editor with the looks of a teddy bear and the temper of a grizzly, who idealised a working class that no longer existed', *Daily Telegraph* (11 December 1997) [obituary]

Anthony Rudolf, 'Tribute to Jon Silkin', *Jewish Chronicle* (12 December 1997)

Michael Glover, 'Memories of a poet's passion', *Eye on Wednesday* (4 February 1998) [remembering Jon Silkin at the Troubadour Café]

Rodney Pybus, 'Jon Silkin (1930–1997)', *Stand*, vol. 39 no. 2 (Spring 1998) [obituary]

Jon Glover, Obituary, *PN Review*, no. 120 (March–April 1998)

Tribute, *Poetry Review*, vol. 88 no. 1 (1998)

Jon Glover, 'Jon Silkin', *The New Oxford Dictionary of National Biography* (Oxford: Oxford University Press, 2002)

Reviews of Jon Silkin's poetry

The Peaceable Kingdom
Anthony Thwaite, *The Isis* (24 November 1954)

Hugh Creighton Hill, *Zebra*, no. 11 (December 1954)

[Gordon Wharton?], 'Themes for Poetry', *Times Literary Supplement* (11 February 1955)

The Two Freedoms
'Poetry in Observations', *Times Literary Supplement* (18 July 1958)

The Re-ordering of the Stones
Terry Eagleton, *Poetry Review* (1961)

'Poets in the Middle', *Times Literary Supplement* (14 December 1962)
Ronald Gaskell, *London Magazine*, vol. 1 no. 11 (February 1962)

Flower Poems
James Dickie, *The Glasgow Review*, vol. 1 no. 4 (Winter 1964–65)
'The Craft and the Cause' (25 August 1966) [also including review of
    Poems New and Selected]

Nature with Man
'Catching the Audience', *Times Literary Supplement* (29 July 1965)

Poems New and Selected
Anthony Hecht, *Hudson Review* (July 1966)
'The Craft and the Cause' (25 August 1966) [also including review of
    Flower Poems]
Joseph Bennett, *New York Times* (4 September 1966)
Ralph J. Mills Jr., *Poetry* (November 1966)
Louis L. Martz, *Review* (March 1967)
Adrianne Marcus, *Shenandoah* (Spring 1967)
Robert L. Stilwell, *Sewanee Review* (September 1968)

Amana Grass
Jonathan Raban, *The Review*, no. 26 (Summer 1971)
Raymond Gardner, *The Guardian* (26 March 1971)
Ian Hamilton, *The Observer* (5 April 1971)
Alan Brownjohn, *New Statesman* (7 May 1971)
Tom Lowenstein, *European Judaism* (Summer 1971)
Martin Seymour-Smith, *The Scotsman* (12 June 1971)
Peter Mortimer, *Journal* (12 June 1971)
Jewish Chronicle (25 June 1971)
'News from underground', *Times Literary Supplement* (30 July 1971)
David Harsent, *Agenda*, vol. 9 nos. 2–3 (Winter 1971)
Louis L. Martz, *Yale Review* (Spring 1972)
Michael Schmidt, *Poetry* (June 1972)
Ian Wedde, 'Poetry: City People, Country People', *London Magazine*,
    vol. 11 no. 8 (December 1971–January 1972)

Killhope Wheel
Newcastle Evening Chronicle (2 January 1971)
Robert Garioch, *Lines Review*, no. 36 (March 1971)

The Principle of Water
John Fuller, 'Personal Columns', *New Statesman* (5 July 1974)

Elizabeth Jennings, *The Scotsman* (13 July 1974)

Michael Schmidt, *Times Literary Supplement* (19 July 1974)

'Feeling for the physical', *Times Literary Supplement* (19 July 1974)

Martin Dodsworth, 'Taking things seriously', *The Guardian* (8 August 1974)

Thomas Blackburn, *The Tablet* (10 August 1974)

Les Murray, *Sydney Morning Herald* (10 August 1974)

Clive Sansom, *Nation Review* (10 August 1974)

Roger Garfitt, *London Magazine* (August/September 1974)

Lyman Andrews, 'Personal Visions', *Sunday Times* (15 September 1974)

Norman Nicholson, *Church Times* (8 November 1974)

Kevin Hart, *Canberra Poetry*, vol. 2 no. 4 (Winter 1974)

Douglas Hill, *Tribune* (17 January 1975)

Douglas Dunn, 'Redundant Elegance', *Encounter*, vol. 44 no. 3 (March 1975)

S.R. Lavin, 'Jon Silkin: an overview', *Margins*, no. 19 (April 1975)

Michael Mott, *Poetry*, vol. 117 no. 3 (December 1975)

The Little Time-keeper

Peter Mortimer, *The Journal* (12 August 1976)

Jewish Chronicle (13 August 1976)

Martin Booth, *Tribune* (20 August 1976)

Peter Porter, *Observer* (22 August 1976)

D.M. Thomas, 'Sorrows and Sparrows', *Times Literary Supplement* (24 September 1976)

The Tablet (30 October 1976)

Norman Nicholson, *Church Times* (24 December 1976)

Arthur C. Jacobs, 'Recent Poetry', *The Jewish Quarterly*, vol. 24 no. 4 (Winter 1976–77)

Mark Abley, *Oxford Literary Journal* (Spring 1977)

Rosemary O'Grady, *24 Hours* (March 1977)

Tim Thorne, *The Australian* (25 June 1977)

Ben Howard, 'British Wells', *Poetry* (Chicago), vol. 131 no. 5 (February 1978)

The Psalms with their Spoils

Jewish Quarterly, vol. 28 no. 3 (1980)

Brian Merrikin Hill, *Pennine Platform*, no. 2 (1980)

John Horder, *Times Educational Supplement* (9 May 1980)

Simon North, 'In Praise', *The New Statesman* (23 June 1980)

James Campbell, 'To asyntactical extremes', *Times Literary Supplement* (4 July 1980)

Martin Booth, *Tribune* (11 July 1980)

Thomas McCarthy, *Irish Times* (9 August 1980)

Gavin Eward, *British Book News* (August 1980)

Peter Bland, 'Exile and late Vuillard', *London Magazine* (August/September 1980)

Rodney Pybus, *Arts North* (September 1980)

Joseph Leftwich, 'Poetic Sensibilities', *The Jewish Quarterly*, vol. 28 nos. 2–3 (Summer/Autumn 1980)

Howard Sergeant, *South East Arts Review* (Autumn 1980)

Edna Longley, 'Terse Cock', *Quarto* (June 1980)

James J. McAuley, 'Three Transatlantic Poets', *The Slackwater Review*, vol. 4 no. 2 (1981)

Efraim Sicher, *Argo* (Summer 1981)

Selected Poems (1980)

Ian Hamilton, 'Origins of the poetic species', *Sunday Times* (28 September 1980)

Martin Booth, *Tribune* (24 October 1980)

James Liddy, *Irish Times* (3 January 1981)

Edward Larrissy, 'Holding in affection', *Times Literary Supplement* (16 January 1981)

Simon North, *New Statesman* (23 January 1981)

Roger Garfitt and Bill Scammell, *Arts North* (February 1981)

Alan Hollinghurst, *Encounter* (February/March 1981)

Sharon L. Drache, *Canadian Jewish News* (5 March 1981)

Alan Wall, *Literary Review* (May 1981)

Mary Kinzie, *The American Poetry Review* (November/December 1981)

Dick Allen, *The American Book Review* (January/February 1982)

Ronald Blythe, *Eastern Arts*, vol. 12 no. 11 (November 1983)

Into Praising

John Cassidy, 'Energy and Shape', *Poetry Review*, vol. 69 no. 1 (1979) [on *Flower Poems* and *Into Praising*]

Autobiographical Stanzas

Anne Stevenson, 'Thinning Out', *Poetry Review*, vol. 74 no. 2 (June 1984)

John Lees, 'Review', *Iron*, 43 (1984)

John Barnie, 'Five from Taxus', *Poetry Wales*, vol. 19 no. 4 (1984)

The Ship's Pasture

Martin Booth, *Tribune* (29 August 1986)

Roger Garfitt, 'Ungentlemanly behaviour', *Arts North* (September 1986)

Adam Thorpe, *The Literary Review* (September 1986)

John Forth, 'Moving Houses', *London Magazine* (October 1986)

Frank J. Lepkowski, *Library Journal* (USA) (1 November 1986)

Alan Bold, 'The mechanics of successful poetry', *The Scotsman* (15 November 1986)

David Heal, 'Gabriel blows the Old Devils away', *Daily Post* (Liverpool) (4 December 1986)

Slightly Soiled, issue 3–4 (December 1986)

Emanuel Litvinoff, *Jewish Quarterly*, vol. 34 no. 4 (1987)

Ian Crichton Smith, *Iron Magazine*, no. 53 (1987)

Martin Green, *The Anglo-Welsh Review*, no. 87 (1987)

Fred Beake, *Acumen* (1987)

Tim Dooley, *Times Literary Supplement* (6 March 1987)

David Craig, *North West Arts Review* (March 1987)

B. Gordon, 'Silkin's poetry focuses on "real world"', *The Daily Iowan* (8 April 1987) [on *The Ship's Pasture*, *The Penguin Book of First World War Poetry*, *The Penguin Book of First World War Prose*, *The War Poems of Wilfred Owen*]

Aloma Halter, 'Poetry and Poezak', *Jerusalem Post* (15 May 1987)

David Hart, 'War and peace', *New Socialist* (USA) (May 1987)

Brian Morton, *Jewish Chronicle* (24 July 1987)

Mario Relich, 'The Struggle against Brutality', *Lines Review*, no.106 (September 1988)

Selected Poems (new edition, 1988)

Sunday Times (24 April 1988)

Michael Standen, *Iron*, 56 (October 1988)

Hayden Murphy, *Lines Review*, no. 107 (December 1988)

Lawrence Norfolk, *Times Literary Supplement* (30 December 1988)

Douglas Houston, 'Voices of Experience', *Poetry Review*, vol. 79 no. 2 (Summer 1989)

The Lens-Breakers

Anthony Rudolf, *Jewish Chronicle* (28 February 1992)

David Kennedy, *Poetry Review*, vol. 82 no. 2 (Summer 1992)

Elizabeth Jennings, *The Daily Telegraph* (29 June 1992)

Bernard O'Donoghue, 'Death of a Moth', *Times Literary Supplement* (4 August 1992)

Peter Forbes, *The Guardian* (6 August 1992)

Carol Rumens, *Jewish Chronicle* (14 August 1992)

Adam Thorpe, *The Observer* (16 August 1992)

Michael Standen, 'The Bounding Line: Poetry Now', *Reportback* [WEA magazine], vol. 4 no. 2 (Autumn 1992)

Stephen Forster, 'Next Waves', *Printed Matter*, vol. 16 no. 4 (Winter 1992)

Michael Standen, *Iron*, 68 (November 1992–February 1993)
Keith Silver, *Poetry Nation Review* (January/February 1993)
Fred Beake, *Acumen* (April 1993)

Watersmeet
David Whetstone, *The Journal* (6 October 1994)
Richard Kell, *Iron*, 79 (1995)
Fred Beake, *Long Poem Group Newsletter*, no. 4 (September 1997)

Selected Poems (1993)
Herbert Lomas, *Ambit*, 138 (1994)
M. Wynn Thomas, *Acumen*, 20 (October 1994)
Simon Carnell, *London Magazine*, vol. 34 nos. 9 & 10 (December 1994/January 1995)
David Kuhrt, *Agenda*, vol. 35 no. 1 (1995)

Audio-visual
The Poet Speaks, Record 8, recorded in association with the British Council and the Poetry Room, Lamont Library, Harvard University, ed. Peter Orr (London: The Argo Record Company Ltd, 1967) [Jon Silkin and others read and discuss their poems; Silkin recorded in Newcastle, 15 September 1966]
Artists of the North: Jon Silkin, directed by Roy Thompson, produced by Rodney Pybus (Carlisle: Aidanvision, 1981) [Jon Silkin is interviewed, and reads and discusses his poems]
Silkin on Silkin: Jon Silkin talks about his life and reads a selection of his poems, recorded by Adrian Mitchell (Sheffield, 1992)

Electronic resources
Stand magazine: http://www.standmagazine.org
Leeds Poetry 1950–1980, University of Leeds: http://library.leeds.ac.uk/special-collections/collection/12/leeds_poetry_1950-1980
The Leeds Poetry 1950–1980 website provides information about poets connected with the University of Leeds as Gregory Fellows, staff and students during the 30-year period when the Gregory Fellowship scheme operated. Includes a page dedicated to Jon Silkin, discussing his activities at Leeds (http://library.leeds.ac.uk/special-collections/collection/13/poets_at_the_university_of_leeds/29/jon_silkin), and an online search facility for the Silkin and *Stand* archives.
'Jon Silkin', Carcanet: http://www.carcanet.co.uk/cgi-bin/indexer?owner_id=696

Notes

1 Spelled thus on Silkin's typescript.

2 The words 'We'll see' are italicised in the poem as published in *Poetry and Poverty*, 4 (c. 1952–1953).

3 Albert Schweitzer (1875–1965), the German theologian, philosopher, physician and medical missionary. Schweitzer was awarded the Nobel Peace Prize in 1952 for his 'Reverence for Life' ('Ehrfurcht vor dem Leben') philosophy. He founded the Albert Schweitzer Hospital in the French colony of Lambaréné, now Gabon, in 1913. Medical research at the hospital has been key in seeking to combat malaria.

4 George Sutherland Fraser (1915–1980), poet and critic.

5 The second section was published in *The Poetry Review*, 46:4 (October–December 1955) with the title 'From "The Animal Dark"'. There are variations to the collected version (listed in notes 6–7).

6 'I place your word'.

7 'Closely beside it'.

8 Cynthia Redpath.

9 Another version of this poem, in four parts, is held in the Silkin Archive at Leeds University Library. See Appendix, pp. 839–41.

10 Published in *New Left Review*, 8 (March–April 1961) with variations (see notes 11–12).

11 An additional line is inserted, followed by variation in subsequent lines: 'He found no position save in / The copiously inflamed / Multiplications of lust / Which overcame him'.

12 This line runs on from the previous, with no space.

13 'But touching this' in the poem as published in *New Left Review*, 8 (March–April 1961).

14 Anthony Thwaite. See Introduction, p. lxxix–lxxx.

15 Elements of this poem are worked into (or worked from) a prose piece written by Silkin (estimated date range 1954–1962), titled 'Emmanuel'. See Appendix, pp. 845–47.

16 'As was their customs, still' in the version published in *Poetry and Audience* (March 1962) – it has been assumed that this is a typographic error.

17 'our homes' ('our' not capitalised) in the version published in *Poetry and Audience* (March 1962) – most probably a typographic error.

18 Published in *Poetry and Audience*, 9.2 (1961), pp. 6–7, with variations (see notes 19–24).

19 Becomes no cleaner.

20 And on

21 Then the blood, / Mixed with partly digested / Carrion, flowed out / With

faeces pressed through / The body's hollows, the infernal pump / Urging through the slime / Beyond the ends of veins; / While the severed head

22 Over it. Net on net / And how it binds itself / With pride that cannot nurse it / And thought which cannot pity / Cutting the agonised / Features, which exude / A sweat of pain; the mouth, / A fine mesh of oaths / And screams; the unshaven cheeks / Swollen with bellowing. / There is not much else left. (There is no line space before the next line, '"O pity, pity, pity"?'.)

23 The whole of / Nature

24 The entire function

25 'So women who crochet' in the poem as published in *The Sewanee Review*, 70:2 (Spring 1962).

26 Published in *Marxist*, 1:4 (1963), with variations (see notes 27–30).

27 There would have been more folk

28 Humus, the living muck

29 Although since you were not honoured

30 Four additional lines appear: 'Or anything casual, / I think that now it would / not be dishonouring you, / or letting you down, if I / Wept. Without your knowing.'

31 Published in *The Poetry Review* (Autumn 1964) with variations (see notes 32–36).

32 Pervades like grass

33 It is a composure grass gives

34 This stanza is omitted.

35 a set of fibres

36 It is corded, thickly braided

37 The variations noted for poems 1, 2 and 3 (notes 38–57) refer to the poems as published in *Three Poems* (Cambridge, MA: Pym-Randall Press, 1969). Poems 2–6 were published in *Lines Review*, 33 (1970) as 'Five Cemetery Poems'.

38 flowers, the neckline of headstones

39 as the record plays does your hand open once more my lips?

40 their territorial bitterness lapsed

41 the roots strain under with orderly presence

42 the bones shaped into their form

43 The tree

44 by the untearful pool,

45 the one for the other?

46 Or between even you and me;

47 your tear tugging like a metal-like / leaf, – at the eye of the one who would weep, toward the one weeping herself.

48 Spelled thus (rather than 'contributory') in original; Silkin probably intended a pun on 'tributary'.

49 'Tree' was later included in the 'Killhope Wheel' sequence, which appeared as a pamphlet published by the Mid-Northumberland Arts Group in 1981, and was also included in Silkin's next collection, *The Principle of Water*.

50 'Tree', the first poem in the 'Killhope Wheel' sequence, was also published in Silkin's previous collection, *Amana Grass*.

51 Silkin revised *The People*, making it shorter, prior to its republication in *Selected*

Poems (London: Routledge and Kegan Paul, 1980). For the purposes of the current edition, the version published in *The Principle of Water* has been retained. Prior to its publication in *The Principle of Water*, *The People* was broadcast in July 1974 as a radio play on the BBC's Third Programme, produced by John Scotney and read by Miriam Margolyes, Nigel Anthony and John Rowe. It was also performed at the Joy of Living Festival at Darling Downs Institute of Education, Queensland in September 1974 during Silkin's three-month Australian Arts Council-sponsored lecture tour.

52 This section of *The People* was published with significant variations in *Fuse*, 2 (November 1972) as 'Air that Pricks Earth with Life'. See Appendix, pp. 842–45.

53 A poem titled 'A good farmer' was published by the Valley Press (Rochester, New York) in 1972 in a limited edition of 100, with the first 30 signed by Silkin. This poem was subsequently worked into the first of the 'Three Shetland Poems', published in *The Principle of Water* in 1974. See Appendix, pp. 841–842.

54 Published in *Poet*, 2 (Summer 1974) with variations (see notes 55–65). The introduction to the version published in *Poet* reads: 'The poet was asked to fix the location of this poem. He wrote: As a matter of fact it's not specifically about the northeast coast line etc; the poem began, if it can be said to have begun at any specific date, with a now abandoned poem about Scotland; the jelly fish were seen and written about off Portobello (near Edinburgh) about 1965. The rest of the poem came from writing a poem about MacDiarmid, using him as a figure, more or less; this too had been abandoned, or rather, developed and de-restricted. Thus the country is Scottish lowlands border country round Biggar, and what isn't is, of course, the North (of England), Yorkshire and a bit of Northumberland. The poem first appeared in *Responses*, published by the National Book League in 1971 for the Book Bang.'

55 crouched pipes sulphur

56 opening and closing themselves jellyfish squeeze day

57 its mind's cells

58 His mind, seeing this, / suffers a feeling recension.

59 it did over;

60 flashing dispersions of creatures, braiding / them in work together.

61 This shape, their work taking it in.

62 Feels the stained clay skin rankling

63 from us is lifted.

64 brutally squats in me:

65 it hits,

66 Word illegible – 'accoursing' suggested by the editors.

67 Also published under the title *A 'Jarapiri' Poem* (Knotting: The Sceptre Press, 1975).

68 'the abutment of God's fleet' in *Two Images of Continuing Trouble*, Keepsake Poem 28 (Richmond: The Keepsake Press, 1976).

69 'Laundress's' in clean typescript BC MS 20c Silkin/3/4/16.

70 'the Sabbath's candle' in *Jerusalem* (Knotting: The Sceptre Press, 1977); also in 'Jerusalem', *Poetry Review*, 68:3 (1978).

71 The version of 'Water' published in the *Times Literary Supplement*, 1 February 1980, is laid out in two-line stanzas.

72 This poem may work towards 'Crossing a River', published in *The Ship's Pasture* (1986).

73 A poem with this title was published in *The Lens-Breakers*, but appears to be unrelated.

74 The variations in notes 75–115 relate to versions of the poems in the sequence *Autobiographical Stanzas* published by the Taxus Press (Durham) in 1983.

75 across their limp flow, igniting

76 sifts its juice through the ragged sweetness of / the ferns, although a coarse mummering / lifts flame curved round that first discourse / of gentleness, light.

77 its stony lyrical.

78 enriching in small

79 in branches

80 even the house

81 on its flags

82 splitting a Jew in Christian doubleness. [The following line is not present.]

83 nature forms gold

84 I sniff gas,

85 in it a carbuncle, adamant;

86 the Welshman's English – inauthentic metal.

87 between them both:

88 father solemnly;

89 each forbidden lamp

90 'My microscope-set, quick', I said

91 pebble, their hands huge

92 Walking the knobbed woods

93 [There is no space between this line and the next.]

94 with silvery tongue.

95 me, I hung

96 reappraisal of the sons,

97 return, in need,

98 peters to nothing. Presented

99 but it cost me

100 in livid strips – a train

101 like eyes, the insides; rather, the insides of / a bird's crop, with its spurt of muscle portioning / a mash of half-stored seed, and grit, onto / a sinewy gulf effort concentrates.

102 Effort of winter.

103 frightened me; charge

104 with boredom, made a threat

105 cartage of light

106 straight tread, precipices,

107 to negotiate imbedded

108 at night, the same village; but night

109   glowing curiously; viridian forms

110   erect, oblongs

111   that strip of road hung livid in, with lakes

112   gashed indifferently to

113   [There is no space between this and the following line.]

114   This poem has the title 'The hand'.

115   The bus piped drops

116   Published in *The Jerusalem Post Magazine* with the title 'Salome'. The poem was evidently revised between its appearance in *The Jerusalem Post Magazine* and its publication in *The Ship's Pasture*. See Appendix, p. 848.

117   Published in the *Times Literary Supplement*, 19 September 1980, with the title 'Formations', and dedicated to Claude and Tsili Gandelman. The poem was evidently revised between its appearance in the *TLS* and its publication in *The Ship's Pasture*. See Appendix, p. 849.

118   This poem was published in pamphlet form as *Footsteps on a downcast path* by the Mammon Press (Bath) in 1984. The variation in note 119 relates to this version. The pamphlet version of the poem is prefaced by an 'Argument' as follows:

> As if it had tunnel vision, the poem narrates events crucial to the Jewish calendar, beginning with the destruction by the Romans of the Jerusalem Temple in 70 C.E., and finishing with the struggles of the Jewish Ghetto in Warsaw in 1943.
>
> The narrator however has a dogged interlocutor who is demonic, less jovial than Mephistopheles, with a colourless lethal vitality. In a mental sense, at least, this figure is bent on destroying the narrator, but this good liberal indignant Jew is to profit from his interlocutor – he who asks a few of the right questions, if for the wrong reasons.

119   the salt is the same, as water

120   'Prayers with rifles mingle' in version published in *Iron*, 40 (1980).

121   Silkin's own footnote to the poem. There is no explanation of where the 'library' was or who might have done the underlining.

122   Possibly Mick Standen, poet and novelist.

123   This poem works towards 'Psalmists', published in *The Lens-Breakers*.

124   Word illegible.

125   A poem concerning two martyrs drowned in Galloway for not renouncing their faith was published in *The Lens-Breakers* ('Galloway's religious killings, and the lonely language of Gaelic'). Although based on the same subject matter, this poem differs significantly.

126   Published in *Lines Review*, 100 (March 1987) with variations (see notes 127–30).

127   its existence

128   in which no car can pass

129   cracks are lizards.

130   its pargetting / flaky

131   Published in *Poetry Kanto*, no. 9 (1993) with variations (see notes 132–35).

132   cast over, and where then forsaken she is / I have no inkling

133 'kill them.' What is the question which she / has no need to ask what the answer is?

134 English and English Jews

135 We cram the earth, and are poor

136 The variations in the version of 'The Jews in England' published in *Poetry Kanto*, no. 9 (1993) are substantial. See Appendix, pp. 849–50.

137 The variations in notes 138–44 relate to the version of 'Watersmeet' published in pamphlet form by the Bay Press (Whitley Bay, 1994).

138 until this year dies.

139 God's child, entering

140 but moss

141 (some dress in Chryslers).

142 This section continues as part of section 4.

143 This line is not indented or italicised.

144 Section 4 ends at this point, and the following, from 'Water sinks through stones…', is numbered as section 5.

145 Word illegible.

146 Word illegible.

147 Lower case ('national front') in Silkin's typescript.

148 In the copy no. 29 of the poem, 'tubs' is corrected in ms in Silkin's hand to 'tubes'. It is unclear whether or not this was done to rectify a printing error.

149 See Jon Silkin, 'Note', in his *Selected Poems* (London: Routledge and Kegan Paul, 1980), pp. ix–x.

Index of Titles

INDEX OF TITLES   893

INDEX OF TITLES   895

INDEX OF TITLES 899

Index of First Lines

INDEX OF FIRST LINES

INDEX OF FIRST LINES